# More praise for
# MICHAEL JACKSON:
# The Magic and the Madness

"A cool and surprisingly interesting corporate history of Jackson and his family ... Jackson's story is that of an absurdly gifted prodigy who, bit by bit—with a considerable expense of energy, and through an impressive display of stubbornness and determination—took control of his own career, began to write his own material, practically invented a new genre of mass entertainment, and made himself into the most popular performer in the history of American music.... Taraborrelli is convincing on the situation at Motown in the early seventies—a time when its golden Detroit period was just behind it."
*The New Yorker*

"An indictment of the entertainment business."
*The Cincinnati Post*

"Tells you everything you ever wanted to know ... about the 32-year-old moonwalking superstar and his fractious family. The sex scandals, the plastic surgeries, the backstabbing. (The Brady Bunch they're not.)"
*The Orlando Sentinel*

"Taraborrelli has a good ear for dialogue and brings a cinematic eye to certain events."
*The Seattle Times*

# MICHAEL JACKSON

*The Magic and the Madness*

## J. Randy Taraborrelli

BALLANTINE BOOKS • NEW YORK

Copyright © 1991 by J. Randy Taraborrelli

All rights reserved under International and Pan-American Copyright Conventions. Published in the United States of America by Ballantine Books, a division of Random House, Inc., New York, and simultaneously in Canada by Random House of Canada Limited, Toronto.

No part of this book may be reproduced in any form, except by a newspaper or magazine reviewer who wishes to quote brief passages in connection with a review.

Queries regarding rights and permissions should be addressed to Carol Publishing Group, 120 Enterprise Avenue, Secaucus, N.J. 07094

Library of Congress Catalog Card Number: 91-2792

ISBN 0-345-37532-7

This edition published by arrangement with Carol Publishing Group

Manufactured in the United States of America

First Ballantine Books Edition: June 1992

For Lena Roth

*Everybody* has deep, dark secrets . . .
　　　　　　—Michael Jackson
　　　　　　in an interview with
　　　　　　J. Randy Taraborrelli
　　　　　　August 22, 1978

# ✿ Preface ✿

MARCH 25, 1983. Twenty-four-year-old Michael Jackson is on-stage at the Pasadena Civic Center as the star attraction on Motown's twenty-fifth anniversary special. He has just finished performing a nostalgic medley of songs with his brothers—Jackie, Tito, Jermaine, Marlon, and Randy—in a reunion performance of The Jackson 5. Now he is alone.

It has been years since his last television performance, and he looks different: slimmer, almost fragile. His nose is now stream-lined and sculptured, a tribute to a twentieth-century Michelan-gelo—his plastic surgeon. The new face has been skillfully enhanced: almond-shaped eyes outlined in black and lightly shadowed, high cheekbones emphasized by the merest hint of rouge, lips glossed to a subtle sheen. His former Afro hairstyle has been replaced by soft curls which frame his face; two wisps adorn his brow.

Spotlights have ignited his dazzling black jacket, his strobo-scopic silver shirt, and his left-handed cotton glove with twelve hundred hand-sewn rhinestones. His black shoes and twinkly white socks sparkle.

As the music starts to pulsate, Michael Jackson jams a black fedora over his eyes and strikes a pose—his right hand on his hat, his left leg bent and poised for action. The stance may be a tribute to Bob Fosse or Sammy Davis, Jr., but Michael has imprinted it with his own magic. Though the audience goes wild, he is oblivious to them. While most entertainers perform for their audiences, Michael performs for himself. It's his catharsis, his way of dealing with his personal pain, his way of exorcising the demons in his life.

He throws the hat aside. He moves constantly. Even when he is standing still, he seems to be moving.

Words, music, motion, emotion.

"Billie Jean is not my lover," Michael sings with a pained expression. "She's just a girl who says that I am the one. But the kid is not my son." It's a deeply personal song Michael wrote about fathers and sons, about denial, entrapment, and hypocrisy, about coming close to the outer edges of madness.

The whole of Michael's performance is spellbinding, but during "Billie Jean"'s brief instrumental interlude, Michael executes a combination of moves that will seal his reputation as a dance legend. He commences with a series of split-second locking moves and poses before gliding across the stage via his now-famous sleek and graceful moonwalk—a reversed syncopated glide, heading forward and sliding backward all at the time same. The moonwalk gives way to that equally renowned spin—now refined, after years of practice, to tornado speed—and then, immediately, he is up on his toes. Nobody but Michael Jackson dances quite like this, and the auditorium erupts into applause.

The place is in chaos now, with patrons dancing in the aisles, men loosening their bow ties and women in evening finery standing on chairs in their stocking feet.

Since he was a child and lead singer of his family's singing group, The Jackson 5, Michael Jackson has had a magical ability to move an audience with his singing and dancing. But somehow, tonight, something is different. Tonight, his audience is just as exhilarated by the force of his personality as they are by his voice and fancy footwork. To be sure, videotapes of Michael Jackson's performance this evening will not begin to capture the pandemonium his act has generated. These minutes Michael Jackson has spent onstage alone at the Pasadena Civic Center add up to the performance of his career. After this evening, his life—both personally and professionally—will never be the same again.

When it is over, Michael appears surprised and even does half a step more before he realizes that the music has stopped. Or maybe it is just his own momentum carrying him on. A standing ovation rocks the hall. Michael bows, then straightens and raises his arm. His doe eyes look straight ahead. His body is motionless. He doesn't smile or acknowledge the magic moment.

Backstage, his brothers await him. All five—Jackie, thirty-two; Tito, thirty; Jermaine, twenty-nine; Marlon, twenty-five; and Randy, twenty-one—embrace him as he exits the stage.

"What a job, Mike," Jackie exclaims.

"I've never seen anything like it," Jermaine adds.

They're all talking at once. They had no idea what Michael was going to do during his solo spot; he had decided not to tell them. He no longer wanted to share his career, the secrets of his success.

For over fifteen years, Michael Jackson has been a part of a high-profile family perceived by the public as being ideal. Keeping up this charade has not been easy for any of them. In truth, The Jacksons' family is far from exemplary. All of the siblings, as well as their parents, have experienced as much heartache and misery—and, quite often, at the hands of each other—as they have success and status.

In the years following his performance this evening, Michael Jackson would go on to become one of the most celebrated men in the world. His album *Thriller* would sell more copies than any other in the history of popular music. He would be listed in the *Guinness Book of World Records* as the most successful artist ever.

Even though Michael Jackson's story is, in some ways, a triumphant one of great success and accomplishment, it is ultimately a sad one of betrayal and exploitation. In the end—despite the millions for whom he has performed—Michael's story is one of abject loneliness and great despair. It is also a story that has never been told . . . until now.

# MICHAEL JACKSON

*The Magic and the Madness*

# Chapter

## 🌿 1 🌿

THE TOWN OF Los Olivos in Santa Barbara County is little more than a hundred years old. Mattei's Tavern, opened in 1886 as a stagecoach stop, later became a station for the narrow-gauge Pacific Coast Railroad; what is now Los Alamos County Park was once a hideout for bandits. In the early 1900s, a major rail line was built thirty miles closer to the coast. Los Olivos was bypassed, and the population of the once-thriving town dwindled.

It has since been rediscovered. The original tavern is now a charming restaurant. Art galleries, antique stores, and gift shops flourish in restored buildings, thanks to a recent influx of tourists.

Three hundred and fifty people call Los Olivos home. One of them is Michael Jackson.

In the Santa Ynez Valley of Los Olivos, Figueroa Mountain Road winds upward through green rolling hills dotted with oaks and maples. A half mile back from the road, behind an imposing oak gate, lies a Danish-style farmhouse, its brick and masonry walls crisscrossed with wooden beams. There are seventeen rooms on the first floor, sixteen on the second. The house features a formal dining room, a wine cellar, and a fireplace in the master bedroom. A barbecue area outside the kitchen seats two hundred. Several new guest wings have been built onto the main split-level home. The property was once called Sycamore Ranch, but when Michael bought it, he renamed it Neverland Valley.

Michael is in the process of building his own amusement park on the property, including a merry-go-round, a giant sliding board, and a Ferris wheel.

The twenty-seven-hundred-acre estate was originally a ranch for farming dry oats and running cattle. Thousands of oak trees now shade the beautifully landscaped grounds, which include a five-acre man-made lake with a five-foot waterfall and a stone bridge. The property came on the market listed at $35 million. Michael purchased it on May 2, 1988, for $17 million.

Two thousand miles east, in the grimy industrial city of Gary, Indiana, a small, two-bedroom, brick and aluminum-sided home sits on a corner lot at 2300 Jackson Street. The property is about a hundred feet deep and fifty feet wide. There is no garage, no landscaping, and little grass. The neighborhood is nicely kept but obviously disadvantaged. Behind the house is the Roosevelt High School football field and an asphalt playground with basketball hoops.

This is where Michael Jackson first lived as a child, with his father, Joseph; mother, Katherine; brothers, Jackie, Tito, Jermaine, Marlon, and Randy; and sisters, Maureen, LaToya, and Janet.

Joe and Katherine Jackson were like most parents. They wanted their children to have the best lives possible. In the early fifties that meant living in a house with more than two bedrooms and one bath for eleven people. It meant clothes and shoes bought at Sears and not in secondhand stores. It meant an almost-new van and eating at a fast-food restaurant once a week. And it meant that when the kids graduated from high school, they would find steady work—but not in the mills.

When Joe and Katherine discovered that their children had musical talent, their dreams grew. The children would win contests. They would be discovered.

After the boys cut their first records, Joe and Katherine's dreams grew more grandiose: a big house in Hollywood with a swimming pool and servants; a car for everyone, the fancier the better; three-piece suits and a diamond pinkie ring for Joe; a mink coat for Katherine. They dreamed of turning on the television and seeing their kids. The family would be recognized and asked for autographs. They would meet famous people—maybe even the President of the United States or the Queen of England.

Joe and Katherine Jackson wanted their children to have the best lives possible, and they wanted this for themselves as well. So they wished for fame and fortune. But as proverbial wisdom has it, Be careful what you wish for. You just might get it.

Joseph Walter Jackson was born on July 26, 1929, to Samuel and Chrystal Jackson in Fountain Hill, Arkansas. Samuel was a high school teacher, and Chrystal had been one of his students. Joe was the eldest of five children; a sister, Verna, died when she was seven. Samuel was a strict, unyielding man who raised his children with an iron fist. They were not allowed to socialize with friends outside the home. "The Bible says that bad associations spoil youthful habits," Joe's mother once explained.

"Samuel Jackson loved his family, but he was distant and hard to reach," remembered a relative. "He wasn't a warm person. He rarely showed his family any affection, so he was misunderstood. People thought he had no feelings, but he did. He was sensitive but didn't know what to do with his sensitivities. Joseph would take after his father in so many ways."

Samuel and Chrystal divorced when Joe was a teenager. Sam moved to Oakland, taking Joe with him, while Chrystal took Joe's brother and sisters to East Chicago. When Samuel married a third time, Joe decided to join his mother and siblings in Indiana. He dropped out of school in the eleventh grade and became a boxer in the Golden Gloves. Shortly thereafter, he met Katherine Esther Scruse at a neighborhood party. She was a pretty and petite woman, and Joe was attracted by her affable personality and warm smile.

Katherine was born on May 4, 1930, and christened Kattie B. Scruse, after an aunt on her father's side.* (She was called Kate as a child, and those closest to her today still call her that.) Kattie was born to Prince Albert Screws and Martha Upshaw in Barbour County, a few miles from Russell County, Alabama, a rural farming area that had been home to her family for generations. Her parents had been married for a year. They would have another child, Hattie, in 1931.

Prince Scruse worked for the Seminole Railroad and also as a tenant cotton farmer, as did Katherine's grandfather† and great-grandfather, Kendall Brown. Brown, who sang every Sunday in a Russell County church and was renowned for his voice, had once

---

*On January 26, 1949, when Martha Upshaw signed "An Affidavit to Amend a Record of Birth" to reflect her name change by second marriage from Martha Upshaw to Martha Bridgett (later, she would be known as Martha Bridges), Kattie B. Scruse took the opportunity to change her name to Katherine Esther Scruse, which is how it appears on the affidavit. At this time, the Scruses resided at 806 East 155th Street in East Chicago, Indiana.

According to census records, the family had always previously spelled their name *Screws*, which is how it was generally spelled by anyone in Alabama at that time. The new spelling appears for the first time on Kattie B. Scruse's (Katherine's) birth certificate.

†In 1910, Prince Albert Screws's family, Katherine's grandparents, were listed in the census as mulatto.

been a slave for an Alabama family named Scruse, whose name he eventually adopted as his own.

"People told me that when the church windows were opened, you could hear my great-grandfather's voice ringing out all over the valley," Katherine would recall. "It would just ring out over everybody else's. And when I heard this, I said to myself, 'Well, maybe it is in the blood.' "

At the age of eighteen months, Katherine was stricken with polio, at the time often called infantile paralysis because it struck so many children. There was no vaccine in those days, and many children—like Joe's sister Verna—either died from it or were severely crippled.

In 1934 Prince Scruse moved his family to East Chicago, Indiana, in search of a steady job. He was employed in the steel mills before finding work as a Pullman porter with the Illinois Central Railroad. In less than a year, Prince and Martha divorced, and Martha remained in East Chicago with her young daughters.

Because of her polio, Katherine became a shy, introverted child who was taunted by her schoolmates. She was always in and out of hospitals. Unable to graduate from high school, she would take high school equivalency courses as an adult and get her diploma. Until she was sixteen, she wore a brace or used crutches. Today, she still walks with a limp.

Her positive childhood memories are of music. Katherine and her sister, Hattie, grew up listening to country-western radio programs and admiring such stars as Hank Williams and Ernest Tubbs. She and Hattie were members of the high school orchestra, the church junior band, and the school choir. Katherine, who also sang in the local Baptist church, dreamed of a career in show business, first as an actress and then as a singer.

When Katherine met Joe, she fell for him immediately. He married someone else, but the marriage lasted only a year. After his divorce, Joe and Katherine began dating and soon became engaged. Both of them were musical: he was a bluesman who played guitar; she was a country-western fan who played clarinet and piano. When they were courting, the two would snuggle up together on cold winter nights and sing Christmas carols. Sometimes they would harmonize, and the blend was a good one, thanks to Katherine's beautiful soprano voice. Michael Jackson feels he inherited his singing ability from his mother. He has recalled that in his earliest memory of Katherine, she is holding him in her arms and singing songs like "You Are My Sunshine" and "Cotton Fields."

Joseph Jackson, twenty, and Katherine Scruse, nineteen, were married by a justice of the peace on November 5, 1949, in Crown Point, Indiana, after a six-month engagement. Katherine has said that she was so affected by her parents' divorce and the fact that she was raised in a broken home that she promised herself that the same would never happen to her own children. She vowed that once she found a husband, she would stay married to him—no matter what.

"Katherine loved Joseph desperately," recalled Ina Brown, a distant cousin of Joe's. "He wasn't an easy man to love because he would only get so close before he'd pull away from you. But I heard that Katherine felt she could reach him. It was said that from the beginning of their romance, Katherine suspected that Joe was unfaithful from time to time, but that didn't matter to her."

"He was a wild boy," Joe's mother, Chrystal, would say of him. "He liked to be with many girls. I was glad to see him settle down with a lovely woman like Katherine. I was sure she would be a good, quieting influence on him."

The newlyweds settled in Gary, Indiana, a grim, dark industrial town where the skyline was made up mostly of smokestacks that spewed waste into the air. Their first child, Maureen, nicknamed Rebbie (pronounced Reebie), was born on May 29, 1950. The rest of the brood followed in quick succession. On May 4, 1951, Katherine's twenty-first birthday, she gave birth to Sigmund Esco, nicknamed Jackie. Two years later, on October 15, 1953, Tariano Adaryl* was born; he was called Tito. Jermaine LaJuane followed on December 11, 1954; LaToya Yvonne on May 29, 1956; Marlon David on March 12, 1957 (one of a set of premature twins; the other, Brandon, died within twenty-four hours of birth); Michael Joseph on August 29, 1958 ("with a funny-looking head, big brown eyes, and long hands," said his mother); Steven Randall on October 29, 1961, and then Janet Dameta on May 16, 1966.

All eleven members of the family lived in a small, two-bedroom clapboard house at 2300 Jackson Street in an all-black neighborhood. The home had one bathroom, a living room, a kitchen, and a small basement. Katherine and Joe had purchased the $8,500 house with a $500 down payment in 1950. Their monthly mortgage payment was $60. "You could take five steps from the front door and you'd be out the back," Michael said of the house. "It was really no bigger than a garage."

Katherine and Joe shared one bedroom with a double bed for

---

*Tariano's name has also been spelled "Toriano." However, on legal documents, it is Tariano.

themselves. The boys slept in the other bedroom in a triple bunk bed: Tito and Jermaine sharing a bed on top, Marlon and Michael in the middle, and Jackie alone on the bottom. The three girls slept on a convertible sofa in the living room; when Randy was born, he slept on a second couch. In the bitter-cold winter months, the family would huddle together in the kitchen in front of the open oven.

"We all had chores," Jermaine remembered. "There was always something to do—scrubbing the floors, washing the windows, doing whatever gardening there was to do, which wasn't much," he said with a smile. "Tito did the dishes after dinner. I'd dry them. The four oldest did the ironing—Rebbie, Jackie, Tito, and me—and we weren't allowed out of the house until we finished. My parents believed in work values. We learned early the rewards of feeling good about work."

Joe worked a four o'clock-to-midnight shift as a crane operator at Inland Steel in East Chicago. In Michael's earliest memory of his father, he is coming home from work with a big bag of glazed doughnuts for everyone. "The work was hard but steady, and for that I couldn't complain," Joe said. There was never enough money—Joe seldom made more than sixty-five dollars a week in the early sixties, even though he often put in extra hours as a welder—so the family learned to do without. There are few school pictures of the Jackson children, because they could not afford to buy them after posing for them. For the first five years that they lived on Jackson Street, the family had no telephone. When Jermaine contracted nephritis, a kidney disease, at the age of four and had to be hospitalized for three weeks, it hit the family hard—emotionally and financially. Katherine would make the children's clothes herself or shop at the Salvation Army store.

They ate simple foods: bacon and eggs for breakfast, egg-and-bologna sandwiches and sometimes tomato soup for lunch, fish and rice for dinner, and potatoes practically every night. Katherine enjoyed baking peach cobblers and apple pies for dessert. Whenever Joseph was laid off, he found work harvesting potatoes, and during these periods the family would fill up on potatoes, boiled, fried, or baked.

"I was really dissatisfied," Joe remembered. "Something inside of me told me there was more to life than this. What I really wanted more than anything was to find a way into the music business. I wanted to perform, so me and my brother started a group."

Joe and his brother Luther and three other men formed a rhythm-and-blues band they called The Falcons, which provided extra income for the family. The group performed in small clubs and bars.

Joe's three oldest sons—Jackie, Tito, and Jermaine—were fascinated with their father's music and would sit in on rehearsals at home. (Michael has no recollection of The Falcons.)

In the end, the group was not successful. When The Falcons disbanded, Joe stashed his guitar in the bedroom closet. The instrument was his one vestige of a dream deferred, and he didn't want any of the children to get their hands on it. Michael referred to the closet as "a sacred place." Often Katherine would take the guitar down from the shelf and play it for the children. They would all gather around in the living room and sing together, country songs like "Wabash Cannonball" and "The Great Speckled Bird."

Gary was a tough city, and the Jacksons' neighborhood proved to be rough and often dangerous. Katherine and Joseph lived in constant fear that one of their children would be hurt in the streets. "We were always protected by our parents," Jackie recalled. "We were never really allowed to have fun in the streets like other kids. We had a strict curfew. The only time we could actually play with people our own age was in school. We liked the social aspect of school."

From the beginning, Joe was as strict a disciplinarian as his father had been. He would not hesitate to strike his children if he felt they deserved to be punished. Joe says he doesn't remember any beatings as being especially violent, but his children seem to. If they weren't physically scarred, they were most certainly emotionally injured by the way they were disciplined. Jermaine, who seemed particularly affected by his upbringing, stuttered as a child and teenager.

Katherine Jackson was a strong force in Michael Jackson's early life, and religion was a strong force in hers. She had been a Baptist and then a Lutheran but gave up both religions for the same reason: she discovered that both ministers were having extramarital affairs. When Michael was five years old, Katherine became a Jehovah's Witness, converted by a door-to-door worker. She was baptized in 1963 in the swimming pool at Roosevelt High in Gary. From then on, Katherine expected the rest of the family to get dressed in their best clothes every Sunday and walk with her to Kingdom Hall, their place of worship. Joe, who had been raised a Lutheran, went a couple of times for Katherine's sake but dropped out when the children were still young "because it was so boring," Marlon recalled. Michael, LaToya, and Rebbie would eventually become the most serious about their religion.

Had that religion been any but the Jehovah's Witnesses, Michael Jackson would have probably grown up to be a far different adult than he is now. The Jehovah's Witnesses are so removed from mainstream Protestantism that sometimes they are considered a cult.

The International Bible Students—they would not be known as Jehovah's Witnesses until 1931—were organized in 1872 by Charles Taze Russell. By 1976 there were Jehovah's Witnesses in over two hundred countries. No matter where they live, no Jehovah's Witness will salute a flag (they believe it is idolatrous to do so) or serve in any armed forces (each Witness is considered an ordained minister and therefore exempt). They consider both Christmas and Easter to be pagan holidays. They will not contribute money to any group outside their own church because they consider preaching the gospel the only worthwhile charitable deed. Jehovah's Witnesses periodically make news because they refuse to receive blood transfusions for themselves or their children, no matter how gravely ill the patient may be.

"I don't ever remember their religion as being an issue that was discussed outside the immediate family," recalls Ina Brown. "I know that Joe wasn't interested. But Katherine was so fiercely protective of her religion that Joe could never dissuade her from it. She wanted the children all to be Jehovah's Witnesses, and that was fine with Joe. He didn't care one way or the other as long as she didn't try to force it upon him. Joe liked the religion because it was so strict. He liked it more for its laws than for its spiritualism."

Jehovah's Witnesses take great pains to separate themselves from everyone but other Jehovah's Witnesses. They even change the church terminology from time to time, so that only those who are faithful know the right words; an apostate is spotted immediately. Indeed, says Ina Brown, "Katherine had no real friends that I know of except the few she knew from her church. She didn't want the children to socialize much either. Joe was antisocial by nature. They were not a social family by any stretch of the imagination."

Another distant cousin, Johnny Jackson (not the Johnny Jackson who would perform in The Jackson Five's band), remembered, "Most people in the neighborhood thought of them as being a little odd. There were some who thought they were snooty, that they thought they were better than everyone else. When people found out that they were Witnesses, some were scared. It was as if they belonged to some strange coven or something. No one in the neighborhood had the slightest idea what a Jehovah's Witness was. Katherine had been through the whole neighborhood witnessing to all her neighbors. I heard that she would bring some of her kids with her, door to door. But still, no one I knew had a clue as to what the hell she was talking about. It went right over everyone's head.

The ones who did understand were scared to death. It's a scary religion.''

Jehovah's Witnesses consider themselves the sheep; everybody else is a goat. When the great battle of Armageddon is fought—it was expected in 1972 and then in 1975—all the goats will be destroyed at once and the sheep will be spared. The sheep will then be resurrected to a life on earth as subjects of the Kingdom of God. They will be ruled by Christ and a select group of 144,000 Witnesses who will reside in heaven by Christ's side. At the end of a thousand years, Satan will come forth to tempt those on earth. Those who succumb to his wiles will be immediately destroyed. The rest will live idyllically.

''They didn't force their religion on anyone,'' said Gladys Johnson, the principal of Garnett Elementary School where the Jackson children were educated. ''At Christmas, Easter, or a party of some kind, they didn't make a big point of it. They simply absented themselves from school. Of course, the boys never stood for the pledge of allegiance to the flag, but they were so quiet about it, they were almost unnoticed.''

At first glance it may seem surprising that the Jehovah's Witnesses, with its hierarchy of white males (it was the last religious group to be desegregated in the South) and its demands for total conformity, should have such a large black following. Estimates are that 20 to 30 percent of its members are black. However, when people who are stuck in dead-end jobs with little hope for advancement because of the color of their skin are asked, ''Do you want to live in peace and happiness? Do you desire good health and long life for yourself and your loved ones? Why is the world so filled with trouble?'' they sometimes pay attention. And once they do, they learn that the Witnesses are judged solely by their good deeds— their witnessing, or door-to-door proselytizing—and not on new cars, large homes, expensive clothes, and other status symbols. Because of her adherence to the Jehovah's Witnesses, Katherine became satisfied with what she had in Gary, Indiana.

But Joe, now working the swing shift at Inland Steel and the day shift at American Foundries, wanted much more for himself and his family. It was the early sixties and ''everybody we knew was in a singing group,'' Jackie recalled. ''That was the thing to do, go join a group. There were gangs, and there were singing groups. I wanted to be in a singing group, but we weren't allowed to hang out with the other kids. So we started singing together 'round the house. Our TV broke down and Mother starting having us sing together. And then what happened was that our father would go to work, and we would sneak into his bedroom and get that guitar down.''

"And I would play it," Tito continued. "It would be me, Jackie, and Jermaine, and we'd sing, learn new songs, and I would play. Our mother came in one day and we all froze, like 'Uh-oh, we're busted,' but she didn't say anything. She just let us play.''

"I didn't want to stop it because I saw a lot of talent there," Katherine would explain later.

This went on for a few months until one day Tito broke a string on the guitar. "I knew I was in trouble," Tito recalled. "We were *all* in trouble. Our father was strict and we were scared of him. So I put the guitar back in the closet and hoped he wouldn't figure out what had happened. But he did, and he whipped me. He tore me up, even though my mother lied and said she had given me permission to play the guitar. She just didn't want to see me get whipped. Afterwards, when he cooled off, he came into the room. I was still crying on the bed. As I was crying, I said to him, 'You know, I can play that thing. I really can.' He looked at me and he said, 'Okay, lemme see what you can do, smart guy.' So I played it. And Jermaine and Jackie sang a little. He was amazed. He had no idea, because this was the big secret we had been keeping from him because we were so scared.''

When Joe discovered his children's talent, he must have felt a surge of excitement. "I decided I would leave the music to my sons," he said. "I had a dream for them. I envisioned these kids making audiences happy by sharing their talent, talent that they'd maybe inherited from me. I wanted them to make something of themselves.''

He went to work the next day and returned holding something behind his back. He called Tito and handed him the package. Tito opened it. It was a red electric guitar. "Now let's rehearse, boys," Joe said. He gathered his three sons together—Jackie, nine, Tito, seven, and Jermaine, six—and they practiced. "We'd never been so close," Tito would recall. "It was as if we had finally found something in common. Marlon and Mike, they would sit in the corner and watch. Our mother would give us some tips. I noticed our mother and father were happy. We were all happy. We had found something. Something special.''

Joe began teaching his children rhythm-and-blues songs that were very different from the country numbers Katherine had already taught them. Every day, for at least three hours, they would rehearse. "When I found out that my kids were interested in becoming entertainers, I really went to work with them," Joe Jackson would tell *Time* magazine. "When the other kids would be out on the street playing games, my boys were in the house working—trying to learn how to be something in life."

"The house on Jackson Street was just bursting with music," Michael would remember.

The Jacksons' music brought them closer together as a family but further alienated them from everyone else. "Already, people thought we were a little strange," Jackie would remember. "Now they were sure of it. They'd say, 'Yeah, look at those Jacksons. They think they're somethin' special.' See, 'cause everyone else used to hang out on the corners and sing with their groups. But we weren't allowed to. We had to practice at home. So the other kids thought we thought we were too good to sing on the corner."

By 1962, five-year-old Marlon had joined the group, playing bongos and singing, mostly off-key. (Marlon couldn't sing or dance, but he was allowed in the group anyway because Katherine would not have it any other way.) One day when the boys were practicing while Joe was at work, Katherine watched as Michael, who was four years old, began imitating Jermaine as he sang a James Brown song. When Michael sang, his voice was so strong and pure, Katherine was surprised. As soon as Joe got home, she met him at the door with the news. "I think we have another lead singer."

Little Michael was a fascinating child. "Ever since Michael was very young, he seemed different to me from the rest of the children," Katherine said. "I don't believe in reincarnation, but you know how babies move so uncoordinated? Michael never moved that way. When he danced, it was as if he were an older person."

Michael was always precocious. His mother has recalled that at the age of a year and a half he would hold his bottle and dance to the rhythm of the washing machine. His grandmother, Chrystal Johnson (her later married name), has recalled that he began singing when he was about three. "And what a beautiful voice he had," she enthused. "Even back then, he was a joy to listen to. But he was a bad boy, sometimes."

Tito remembered that Michael was "so quick that if my mother or father used to swing at him, he'd be out of their way. They'd be swinging at air."

Michael was particularly sensitive to being disciplined. Once, when Michael was three, Joseph spanked him for something he had done. Michael took off one of his shoes and hurled it at his father. Joe ducked and the shoe missed him. Infuriated, Joe grabbed Michael and, according to Marlon, held him upside down by one leg and "gave him a whoopin' Michael probably never forgot. But he deserved it.'' Michael screamed bloody murder every time his father hit him.

"He didn't like it at all when Joe put his hands on him,'' said one family friend. "Of course, what kid does? But while the other children in the family put up with it, Michael never wanted to. Katherine was not above smacking her children across the face as well. She too had a temper. But she knew how to balance that anger with love. Joe didn't. At first, Michael was scared of his father. But after years of abuse, he began to hate the man. This was the root of Michael's hatred for this father, the way Joseph treated him when Michael was a child.''

Michael recalled that his father "was always a mystery to me, and he knows it. One of the things I regret most is never being able to have a real closeness with him.'' None of the Jackson children ever developed a closeness with Joe, who was never very affectionate. Sometimes he took his boys camping and fishing on weekends or taught them how to box to defend themselves, but he never paid much attention to the girls. As a toddler, Janet liked to crawl into bed with her mother and father, but she had to wait until Joseph was asleep. Joseph would scare the young boys half to death by hoisting himself over the window ledge of their bedroom and then climbing in, all the while wearing a fright mask. He said he was trying to demonstrate why they should not leave the windows open at night, but he did this more than once.

Michael slowly began pulling away from his father and clinging to his mother, whom he adored. "Even with nine children, she treated each of us like an only child,'' he would remember. "Because of Katherine's gentleness, warmth, and attention, I can't imagine what it must be like to grow up without a mother's love. The lessons she taught us were invaluable. Kindness, love, and consideration for other people headed her list.''

Michael began attending Garnett Elementary School at the age of five in 1963. His mother has said that Michael was generous to a fault. He used to take jewelry from her dresser and give it away to the teachers as gifts. A stubborn child, he continued to do so even after his mother chastised him for giving away her possessions. One of Michael's first memories concerns performing at the age of five, when he sang "Climb Ev'ry Mountain'' from *The Sound of Music* a cappella for his class. The other children were impressed as much by his self-confidence as by his talent; he received a standing ovation. The teacher started to cry. Katherine attended the performance with Joe's father, Samuel, who was not a sentimental man. Even he cried.

"I don't know where he got it from," Katherine would say. "He was just so good, so young. Some kids are special. Michael was special."

Five-year-old Michael had so much energy and charisma that Jackie, who was twelve, decided his younger brother would become "the lead guy." That was perfectly fine with Michael; he enjoyed being the center of attention. Jermaine's feelings were hurt, however. He had been the lead singer of the group, and now suddenly he wasn't good enough. Some family members have theorized that one of the reasons he stuttered as a child was a lack of confidence. Still, Jermaine would support the family's decision because Michael was so obviously a natural entertainer.

"He became this great little imitator," Jermaine would remember. "He'd see something—another kid dance, or maybe James Brown on TV—and next thing you knew, Michael had it memorized and knew just what to do with it. He loved to dance too. Marlon was a good dancer, maybe better than Mike. But Mike loved it more. He was always dancin' 'round the house. You'd always catch him dancin' for himself in the mirror. He'd go off alone and practice and then come back and show us this new step. We'd incorporate it into the act. Michael began choreographing our show."

"Finally it was time for us to enter a talent contest," Michael recalled. "This is something I remember like it was just yesterday. Everyone on the block wanted to be in the talent show and win the trophy. I was about six years old but I had figured out then that nobody gives you nothin'. You got to win it. Or, like Smokey Robinson said in one of his songs, 'You got to earn it.' We did this talent contest at Roosevelt High School in Gary. We sang The Temptations' 'My Girl'—Jermaine did the lead—and won first prize."

The boys also performed their rendition of the Robert Parker hit song, "Barefootin'." During a musical break in the middle of the song, little Michael kicked off his shoes and started doing the barefoot dance all over the stage, much to the crowd's enjoyment.

"After that, we started winning every talent show we entered," Michael said. "The whole house was full of trophies, and my father was so proud. So proud, I can't tell you. Probably, the happiest I ever saw my mother and father was back there in Gary when we were winnin' those talent shows. That's when we were closest. Back in the beginning when we didn't have anything but our talent."

The group played its first noncontest show at a Big Top supermarket in 1964 where, as Michael remembered it, "people would

come and buy somethin'—maybe some baby powder or somethin'.'' Sometimes, the group called itself The Ripples and Waves
Plus Michael. In 1965, The Ripples and Waves won Gary's first
City-Wide Talent Show. ''That's when our father knew we were
going all the way,'' Michael remembered. ''And that's when I knew
that nothing was going to stop us.''

By 1965, Joe was making only about eight thousand dollars a
year working full-time at the mill. Katherine worked part-time as
a saleswoman at Sears. When Joe wanted to start spending more
money on the group—musical equipment, amplifiers, microphones—Katherine became concerned.

''I was afraid we were getting in over our heads,'' she would
recall. ''But Joseph convinced me that the boys were worth it. No
one ever believed in his sons more than my husband believed in
those boys. He used to tell me, 'I'd spend my last dime on those
boys if that's what it took.' ''

''You have to understand that I saw this great potential in my
sons,'' Joe said. ''So yes, I did go overboard. I invested a lot of
money in instruments, and this was money we did not have. My
wife and I would have heated arguments about this 'waste of
money,' as she would call it. She'd yell at me that the money should
have been put into food, not into guitars and drums. But I was the
head of the household and what I said was the final word. I overran
her opinion.

''Black people were used to struggling and making ends meet.
This was nothing new for me or any of us. I came up struggling.
So my kids knew how to economize. They had no choice. We made
a penny stretch by eating foods like chitterlings and collard greens.
I used to tell them we were eating soul food in order to be able to
play soul.''

Soon Joe was driving his children to Chicago to compete in talent
contests there. Chicago was a city bustling with sensational sixties
soul music and teeming with talent like Curtis Mayfield, The Impressions, Jerry Butler, and Major Lance. Joe may not have been
a showman, but he certainly knew about performing. He taught his
boys everything he knew—by experience, observation, and instinct—about how to handle and win over an audience. ''It's incredible how he could have been so right about things. He was the
best teacher we ever had,'' Michael would say.

''He wouldn't make it fun, though,'' Michael added in another
interview, with entertainment writer Gerri Hirshey. '' 'You're doing it wrong; you gotta do it like *this*,' he'd say. Singing was fun,
but he didn't do it in a way like, 'Oh, that's nice,' jolly and happy-

go-lucky. He was more like, 'You gotta do it right.' But we loved doing it. He told me how to work the stage and work the mike and make gestures and everything.''

"I became a great spy," Joe Jackson recalled. "I'd go out and check out all the other musical groups that would come through Gary. I'd take a notebook and jot down everything they did that I thought was interesting. Those other soul acts always looked the same, always looked good. One singer did the lead. He had the place of prominence. Three or so other singers would stand off to one side and do perfectly timed choreography as they sang the background music. Their voices blended well, especially if they were all members of the same family. So I took some of those elements and added some of my own ideas to come up with a formula for the boys.''

When the group played its first paying performance at a Gary nightclub called Mr. Lucky's, Joe changed the name from The Ripples and Waves Plus Michael to The Jackson Brothers. They made roughly seven dollars for the engagement. When the boys began playing in other clubs, the patrons would throw coins and bills onto the stage. "My pockets would just be bustin' with money," Michael would remember. "My pants couldn't even stay up. Then I would go and buy candy, loads and loads of candy for me and for everyone.''

Many neighborhood boys would accompany the Jacksons as musicians from time to time, and by 1966, Johnny Porter Jackson (no relation) was added to the group as a permanent drummer. Johnny's family was friendly with the Jacksons, who, in time, would consider Johnny a "cousin." Ronny Rancifer, a keyboardist, was also added. The boys played clubs in Gary and as far away as Chicago. Michael was eight years old and singing lead. Tito was on guitar, Jermaine on bass guitar; Jackie played shakers and Johnny Jackson was on drums. Marlon sang harmony and danced.

"We're gonna make a lot of money, boys," Joe told them. Joe rehearsed them every morning before school; then as soon as they got home from school, there was more rehearsal. "Nobody wanted to work that hard, but we had no choice," Marlon has said, pointing to his father's dogged determination.

Katherine was just as excited about her boys' success as her husband. History has painted a picture of a woman just standing by and watching as her husband coaxed, tutored, and bullied his sons on to stardom. But Katherine was just as eager to see that the boys became famous. She enjoyed making costumes for them, driving them to engagements, and doing her part to support them.

Sometimes, though, she became uneasy. The family's priorities were shifting. Suddenly, the emphasis in their making music was no longer on familial fun but on finances. It appeared that earning money made it all right to want more money. But if the Jehovah's Witnesses emphasized good works over money, then why was the money so important? She was worried at how happy the children seemed to be when they'd come home with their pockets full of dollars. "That's not the important thing," she would tell them. But what kid would believe her? Especially when she herself was encouraging them to win more talent shows—and more money. She would carefully clip out the notice of their winning in the newspaper and paste it into a scrapbook she had begun. She fretted constantly that the boys wouldn't be "discovered" in time, and she pushed Joe to make it happen.

The Jacksons' Volkswagen bus would pull up to 2300 Jackson Street at five in the morning on Monday, after a weekend of performing. Then the boys would sleep for a couple hours while Katherine cooked breakfast. They would gobble it down and then go off to school like all the other children in the neighborhood.

"We have got to get them a recording contract before they get too old," Katherine said. Joe sent a tape of songs to Motown Records, but there was no response. "Then try another label," she insisted.

In a shopping mall in Gary, the group got a new name. "I got to talking with a lady named Evelyn Leahy," Joe recalled. "She was a beautiful woman who used to model all over the state. The boys were performing in a department store, and she said to me after the show, 'Joe, I think The Jackson Brothers sounds a little old-fashioned. To me, it sounds like The Mills Brothers. Why don't you just call them The Jackson Five?' Well, that sounded like a good name to me, Jackson Five. So that's what we called them from then on." (In her own interviews, Katherine claims to be the one who had that conversation. She says that she and Evelyn were instrumental in naming the group and that Joe wasn't even involved.)

The group soon found themselves doing more club dates out of town on weekends. Joe put a luggage rack on top of the family's Volkswagen bus for their equipment before hitting the so-called chitlin circuit, two- to three-thousand-seat theaters in downtown, inner-city areas of cities such as Cleveland and Washington, D.C. There would always be many other acts on the bill, all vying for the audience's favor. Sometimes these would be established artists, but often they would be unknowns, like The Jackson Five. This arrangement gave the upstarts an opportunity to learn from the experienced players. After their act, Michael's brothers would go off on their own, but Michael would stay behind and watch the other performers on the bill. Whenever anyone wanted to find eight-year-old Michael, they always knew where to look: in the wings, watching, as he remembered, "every step, every move, every twist, every turn, every grind, every emotion."

This was a valuable time of instruction for Michael Jackson. Soon he began to appropriate routines and shtick from the best of the acts on the same bill, like James Brown, whom Michael says he would watch over and over again. Michael would leave the backstage and go to the back of the theater. He would take mental notes and try to incorporate Brown's routines into The Jackson Five's show.

"James Brown taught me a few things he does on stage," Michael would remember in 1970. "It was a couple years ago. He taught me how to drop the mike and then catch it before it hits the stage floor. It only took me about thirty minutes to learn it. It looks hard, but it's easy. All I wanted at that time was a pair of patent leather shoes like James Brown's. But they didn't make them in kids' sizes."

The Jackson Five won the amateur talent show at the Regal, a theater in Chicago, for three consecutive weeks, a major coup for the family since the Regal's audience was just as critical as the one at the Apollo Theatre in Harlem. The Jackson boys were becoming more experienced and polished, their lead singer, Michael, more poised and professional. They played St. Louis, Kansas City, Boston, Milwaukee, and Philadelphia. Not only did they open for The Temptations, The Emotions, The O'Jays, Jackie Wilson, Sam and Dave, and Bobby Taylor and the Vancouvers, but they formed friendships with these artists and learned firsthand from many of them what to expect of the entertainment world.

Before one talent show, one performer remarked to another that they'd better watch out for The Jackson Five, " 'cause they got this midget they're using as a lead singer." Jackie overheard and couldn't stop laughing. He shared the remark with Joe, who also thought it was very funny.

When Michael heard about it, he was hurt. "I can't help it if I'm the smallest," Michael said, crying.

Joe pulled his young son aside and explained to him that he should be proud that he was being talked about by the competition. "That means you're on your way," he told him.

"I still didn't like it," Michael would remember years later. "Even back then, I didn't like people talking bad about me."

In August 1967, The Jackson Five performed at the famed Apollo, located in Harlem at 125th Street, in that theater's amateur show. Joe and Jack Richardson, a close friend of the family's, drove the boys to New York in the family's Volkswagen. At this time, Jackie was sixteen; Tito, thirteen; Jermaine, twelve; Marlon, ten; and Michael had just turned nine. They entered the "Superdog" contest, the most prestigious category.

The Apollo was famous the world over. Working the Apollo was the dream of most young black entertainers at the time. In his book *Showtime at the Apollo*, writer Ted Fox observed, "[The Apollo was] not just the greatest black theatre but a special place to come of age emotionally, professionally, socially, and politically."

Michael remembered, "That was the toughest place of all to play, the Apollo Theatre. If they liked you there, they really *liked* you. And if they hated you, they'd throw things at you, food and stuff. But we weren't scared. We knew we were good. At the other gigs we'd played, we had 'em in the palms of our hands, you know? I'd be on stage singing and I'd look over at Jermaine and we'd wink at one another. We always knew we had it."

Backstage at the Apollo, The Jackson Five found a small log that had been mounted on a pedestal. That log came from the fabled Tree of Hope. According to legend, the tree from which the log was cut stood across the street from a rib restaurant in Harlem called The Barbecue. Over the restaurant were rehearsal halls used by the bands of such black entertainment stalwarts as Louis Armstrong, Count Basie, and Cab Calloway. The tree stood in front of Connie's Inn, where Louis Armstrong performed in the Harlem version of Fats Waller's *Hot Chocolates*. Standing under that tree, one could hear Satchmo's work, listen as he made his own dreams come true through music, his personal contribution to African-American show business. Over the years, hundreds of performers stood under that tree and touched it for luck. It became tradition.

When the city widened Seventh Avenue, the tree was to be uprooted. But Bojangles Robinson arranged for the Tree of Hope—which he named—to be moved to a street island at Seventh Avenue south of 132nd Street. Eventually, the tree was cut down; no one remembers why. A plaque is all that remains at this final location. At the Apollo, however, a small log from the Tree of Hope was mounted on a pedestal. Tradition had it that the first-timer who touched the tree would be destined for good luck: he would join the ranks of those black performers who had struggled to make their dreams a reality, who had fought for respect, who had paid their dues and eventually triumphed, shaping American popular culture in the image of their race and heritage.

The pedestal was placed off to the side of the stage, in the wings but also in the audience's view so that the crowd could watch as the performers touched it. It was a Wednesday night and The Jackson Five were on the bill with a group called The Impressions. One of the members, Fred Cash, went over to Michael before the show and told him about the tree.

"Hey, guys, did you know 'bout this?" Michael asked his brothers. "Touch this tree and we'll have good luck."

"Nah. I don't believe in luck," Tito said.

"Well, I do," nine-year-old Michael countered. "Wish I could take that log home with me. Then I'd *always* have good luck."

"Ladies and gentlemen," the announcer said. "Here they are, The Jackson Five."

Showtime. The lights went up. It was time for The Jackson Five to take their rightful place in history. Joe watched proudly as each of his sons touched the log. First Jackie, then Tito, Jermaine, Marlon, Michael, and then "cousin" Johnny. The group then ran out onto the stage as the audience offered polite applause. Michael, though, was the last to come on.

He had to run back to touch the Tree of Hope one more time, just to be on the safe side.

# Chapter

## 2

AFTER THE JACKSON Five won the amateur contest at the Apollo Theatre, the boys had a small taste of stardom, and nine-year-old Michael found some of the perks of celebrity fascinating. "At the Apollo, girls bought stuff for us," Michael said in 1970. "You know, watches and rings and things. And we didn't even tell them to do it. We didn't even know they were coming. I mean, we didn't even know them and they were giving us watches."

Joe and the boys were ecstatic over their success. "I'm so damn happy, I could fly back to Gary without an airplane," Joe said with a big grin. Elated and proud of his sons, he was determined to do whatever he had to do to ensure their fortune in a tough, competitive business. He decided to work only part-time at Inland Steel so that he could devote more time to his sons' careers. In 1968, Joe earned only fifty-one hundred dollars rather than his usual eight to ten thousand. He gave up relative financial security in order to gamble on his kids. But the boys were now making six hundred dollars per engagement, so the hard work had obviously begun to pay off. With the new influx of money, Katherine and Joe were able to redecorate their home and buy their first color television.

Rehearsals were still held twice a day, before school and afterwards. Neighborhood children thought the Jackson boys were wasting their time. During practice, voices from outside would taunt, "You ain't *nothin'*, you Jacksons!" Rocks would be hurled into the living room through open windows.

Undaunted and by now accustomed to being considered different, the Jackson boys and their father continued to work. Once, Joe tried to convince Michael to execute a dance step a certain way. Michael refused to listen. According to Johnny Jackson, Joe smacked Michael across the face. Michael fell backward and hit the floor with a thud.

"Now, you do it the way I told you to! You hear me?" Joe hollered at the nine-year-old.

Michael began to cry. His right cheek turned red and sore. "I ain't doin' it that way," he said.

Joe glared at him and took one step forward, his hand raised to strike again.

Michael scrambled up off the floor and backed away. "Hey, don't you hit me," he told his father. " 'Cause if you *ever* hit me again, it'll be the last time I ever sing. And I mean it." Michael must have said the magic words. Joe turned and walked away.

Michael recalled that as Joe got older, he became more violent. "If you messed up during rehearsal, you got hit," Michael would remember. "Sometimes with a belt. Sometimes with a switch. But I'd get beaten for things that happened mostly outside of rehearsal."

Michael would say that the more his father beat him, the angrier he became. The angrier he became, the more he antagonized his father, and the more his father would beat him. Katherine tried desperately to break this vicious cycle by not telling her husband when Michael had been disobedient. However, the brothers—and Rebbie as well—have said that Joe beat Michael because he had a bad attitude at rehearsals. Michael realized that he was becoming an indispensable part of the group and would act like a spoiled brat. But whatever the reason for the beatings, they were apparently fierce and recurring.

"I'd try to fight back," Michael would recall, "just swinging my fists. That's why I got it more than all my brothers combined. I would fight back and my father would kill me, just tear me up."

Michael has admitted that he never understood his father and was scared of him for as long as he could remember. "Michael understood that Joe wanted the best for them, but he couldn't understand why Joe used to hit them," said one family friend. "To a nine-year-old, the back of a father's hand is a very scary weapon. Joe used it more than he should have. Katherine would talk to him about it, but mostly she felt it was wise to stay out of it. I once heard that Michael was late coming to rehearsal, and when he walked in, Joe came up behind him and shoved him into some musical instruments. Michael fell into the drums and got banged up pretty bad. Maybe Joe didn't mean to shove him so hard, I don't know. But Michael was affected. I know for a fact that Michael began to dislike his father at a very early age. Whereas the other boys could take their father's temper more or less with a grain of salt, Michael was especially sensitive to it.''

Another problem troubled Michael's relationship with his father: as a ten-year-old, he could not understand Joe's refusal to accept religion. Michael was being raised a Jehovah's Witness and could not understand why his own father did not want to be saved like the rest of the family. Joe always spoke about the importance of being a family when it came to performing. But if being a family was so important, Michael reasoned, then Joe should be in Kingdom Hall on Sundays with the rest of them. Michael began to distance himself from his father and bond closer with his mother.

At about this time, 1968, when Michael was almost ten, the Jacksons faced a family crisis. Eighteen-year-old Maureen had fallen in love with Nathaniel Brown, a devout Jehovah's Witness. She announced that she wanted to marry Brown and move to Kentucky with him. Katherine, happy and excited for her daughter, encouraged the marriage. It was Katherine who adhered to family values and the importance of finding someone to settle down with for life.

But Joe was against the marriage. "It was all cooked up by Maureen and her mother," he would say. "I wasn't happy about it at all." This would be just the first of such crises in the family as the children chose to marry against their father's wishes.

Maureen—Rebbie—had a powerful voice, and her father wanted her to consider show business as a career. He realized that if she married and raised a family, she would never be able to devote her attention to the entertainment field. But although Maureen had taken dance and piano lessons as a child, she never became serious about a music career. She preferred the comfort and security of a happy home life to the instability of show business.

The real problem here, however, wasn't Maureen's lack of interest in becoming a professional singer. It was her insistence on marrying despite her father's opposition. Joe wasn't used to that kind of defiance from his children. The arguments went on for weeks until finally Joe gave in. Maureen could get married, if she insisted, but Joe would have the last word. He would not give her away.

After winning another talent contest, this one at Beckman Junior High in Gary, Indiana, the boys were brought to the attention of Gordon Keith, who owned a small local label, Steeltown Records. Keith signed the brothers to a limited deal. One Saturday morning, Joe took his brood to Steeltown's recording studio. The boys were led into a small glass booth. Michael was given a large set of metal headphones; when he put them on, they came halfway down his neck. His brothers plugged their instruments into amplifiers. There were backup singers and a horn section. This was show business—at last! The Jackson youngsters were excited and Joe was too, though he tried to appear nonchalant. It took a few hours to record the first song. After that, they would return every Saturday for the next few weeks and record more. One was an instrumental; Michael sang lead vocals on the other six. It was obvious that Michael was to be the centerpiece of the group.

A number of songs were eventually recorded, and two singles were released on Steeltown in 1968: "Big Boy" backed with "You've Changed" and "We Don't Have to Be Over 21" backed with "Jam Session." Both were mediocre and didn't even hint at Michael's talents as a vocalist, but the boys were thrilled with them just the same. The entire family gathered around the radio to hear station WWCA premier their first recording. When the record was played, they listened, stunned to hear The Jackson Five on the radio for the first time. Then, when it was over, they laughed and embraced one another. They felt they had arrived.*

Ben Brown, a former high-level executive at Steeltown, remembered a day the Jackson boys were taking publicity photos in March 1968. "After the photographer positioned the boys, Michael left the lineup and stood off to the side, pouting," Brown said. " 'This isn't gonna look like a publicity picture,' Michael complained. 'It's gonna look like a family portrait.' 'Well, fix it,' Joe said. Then Michael went and rearranged the whole group, put himself in front on one knee, and said, 'Go ahead, take the picture now.' We took it, and you know what? That was a great shot."

In May 1968, the group was invited back to the Apollo to perform and this time be paid for their appearance. They were on a bill with Etta James, Joe Simon, and another family group, The Five Stairsteps and Cubie—who was only two years old.

"Michael was a hard worker," rhythm-and-blues singer Joe Simon said in an interview, echoing the memories of practically everyone who ever worked on the same stage as the young Jackson

* When the Jackson Five became successful at Motown, "We Don't Have to Be Over 21" backed by "Some Girls Want Me for Their Lover" was issued on the Dynamo label under the name The Jackson Five. Also rereleased was "Let Me Carry Your Schoolbooks" backed by "I Never Had a Girl," with the label copy reading "Ripples and Waves Plus Michael."

star. "There was a part of me that thought he was a midget. His father was a slick businessman, I had heard. (It would've been just like him to pass a midget off as a child.) I remember going up to Michael and looking at him real close, thinking, Okay now, is this kid a midget or not? 'Hey man, stop starin' at me, okay?' he told me."

"I remember him being talented, yes," Etta James said, "but polite and very interested too. I was working my show, doing my thing on stage, and as I'm singing 'Tell Mama,' I see this little black kid watching me from the wings. And I'm thinking, 'Who is this kid? He's distracting me.' So I go over to him in between songs, while the people are clapping, and I whisper, 'Scat, kid, get lost. You're buggin' me. Go watch from the audience.' I scared the hell out of him. He had these big ol' brown eyes, and he opened them real wide and ran away. About ten minutes later, there's this kid again. Now he's standing in front of the stage, off to the side. And he's watching me as I work."

Etta remembered being in her dressing room taking off her makeup after the show when there was a knock on her door.

"Who is it?" she asked.

"It's me."

"Who's me?"

"Michael," the young voice said. "Michael Jackson."

"I don't know no Michael Jackson," Etta said.

"Yes, you do. I'm that little kid you told to scat."

Etta, a robust black woman with dyed blond hair and a big, booming voice, cracked the door open and looked down to find the nine-year-old gazing up at her with large, wondering eyes. "Whatcha want, boy?" she asked.

In a manner that wasn't the least bit timid, Michael said, "Miss James, my father told me to come on back here and 'pologize to you. I'm sorry, ma'am, but I was just watchin' you 'cause you're so good. I mean, you're just so *good*: How do you do that? How do you make them want more? I never seen people clap like that."

Etta, now flattered, smiled and patted the boy on the head. "Come on in here and sit with me," she kindly offered. "Let's talk. I can teach you a few tricks."

"Really?" he asked.

"Yeah, really."

"I don't remember what I told him," Etta recalled, "but I remember thinking as he was leaving, Now, there's a boy who wants to learn from the best, so one day he's gonna *be* the best."

When Joe was at the American Federation of Musicians' hall in

New York filling out forms for the Apollo engagement, he met a young white lawyer by the name of Richard Arons. After talking to him for just a few moments, Joe asked Arons to help him manage the group. Even back then, Joe relished the idea of having white help in managing his sons—a preference that would cause a problem for him in years to come. After seeing the boys in action, Arons began working in an unofficial capacity as a comanager.

Joe and Richard Arons continued booking the group for stage appearances while Joe tried to interest the record industry. He tried to contact Berry Gordy but had no luck. He sent an audiotape of some of the Jacksons' songs to Motown; there was no reaction from anyone.

When The Jackson Five played The Regal in Chicago in 1968, Motown recording artist Gladys Knight arranged for some of Motown's executives—but not Berry—to attend the show. There was some interest then, and perhaps word got back to Berry that the Jacksons were talented. No one can be certain. Even Berry doesn't remember.

In July 1968—when Jackie was seventeen; Tito, fourteen; Jermaine, thirteen; Marlon, ten; and Michael, nine—the group was performing at Chicago's High Chaparral Club as an opening act for Bobby Taylor and the Vancouvers (including Tommy Chong, later of Cheech and Chong fame). Bobby Taylor and the Vancouvers were popular at that time with their hit record about interracial romance, "Does Your Mamma Know About Me?"

Bobby Taylor telephoned Ralph Seltzer, head of Motown's creative department and also head of the company's legal division, to suggest that the Jacksons be allowed to audition for Motown. Seltzer consulted with one of Motown's producers, Raynard Miner, who told him that he was aware of The Jackson Five and that he agreed with Bobby's evaluation of them.

"But I still had some serious doubts about this group of youngsters," Ralph Seltzer would recall. "Creative considerations aside, I had some concerns about their age and the way they would change when they grew older, in terms of their appearance and their voices. But there was some excitement about them. So I told Bobby Taylor to bring them to Detroit."

Just a few hours before the Jacksons were to leave Chicago for New York, Bobby Taylor convinced Joe to take the boys to Detroit instead. He would arrange to film the audition. If the boys passed the Motown audition, Ralph Seltzer would forward the tape to Berry Gordy in Los Angeles.

Katherine called the High Chaparral Club to talk to her husband

and was told that they had gone to the Motor City. "Detroit?" she said, puzzled. "You mean to tell me they gave up that television show to go to Detroit? What in the world for?"

"Motown," said the voice on the other end. "They've gone to Motown."

By 1968, Berry Gordy had made an indelible impression on the entertainment world with his Detroit-based record company, Motown, housed in a cluster of small bungalows at 2648 West Grand Boulevard. After the Detroit riots of July 1967, the offices were moved to a ten-story high-rise at 2457 Woodward Avenue in the heart of the city. (Some of the offices and recording studios remained on West Grand. Today, a Motown museum is housed there.)

The legendary Berry Gordy, Jr., is actually the third to bear the name. His great-grandfather was Jim Gordy, a white slave owner whose union with Esther Johnson, a black slave, resulted in a son born around 1854 and named Berry. Berry married Lucy Hellum, a woman of black and Indian heritage, when he was in his teens. They had nine children, including a son named Berry born in July 1888.

The first Berry—an ambitious and enterprising man who farmed for himself on 268 acres in Oconee County, Georgia—influenced his son to be a shrewd businessman. The son took over the family business when his father was struck by lightning and killed. The younger Berry married a schoolteacher, Bertha Ida Fuller, in 1918. They had three children—Esther, Fuller, and George—before moving to Detroit, where Berry Gordy, Jr., was born on November 28, 1929. There were three more daughters and another son born in Detroit as well—Gwen, Anna, Louyce, and Robert.

Bertha Gordy, an industrious, hard-working woman, was a graduate of the Detroit Institute of Commerce; she also studied business at Wayne State University. Her husband, an astute businessman, owned plastering, printing, and carpentry businesses. Ambition and family solidarity had been the hallmark of the Gordy clan for decades, and Pops Gordy (as he was called) and Bertha continued to instill those same values in their own children.

Their son Berry Gordy, Jr., quit Northwestern High School in the eleventh grade, at the age of sixteen, to become a professional featherweight boxer. He was drafted into the army in 1951, where he obtained his high school equivalency diploma. Months after his discharge at the age of twenty-four, he married nineteen-year-old Thelma Louise Coleman; they would have three children: Hazel Joy, Berry IV, and Terry. After starting his own retail record store, which went out of business, Gordy began working on the Ford assembly line in 1955. He earned $86.40 a week. A year later, his marriage to Thelma ended acrimoniously.

Berry Gordy became interested in songwriting, and in 1957 he wrote "Reet Petite" for Jackie Wilson, which became a hit on the rhythm-and-blues charts. More successes for Wilson followed. Berry Gordy had seemingly found his niche as an impressive, instinctive songwriter.

In 1958, Gordy met Raynoma Liles. The two became business partners and formed the Ray-Ber Music Company, which specialized in cheaply recorded demonstration records. Liles remembered Berry as a sloppy dresser "with a vague, musty aroma" and a bad haircut. According to Liles, Gordy was down on his luck when she met him. She says he needed some direction in his life, and she was there to offer it.*

On January 12, 1959, Gordy and Liles started Tamla Records with an eight-hundred-dollar loan from his family.† Gordy still insists that Raynoma had nothing to do with the founding of Tamla or Motown. "That's very interesting that she would claim that," he said when asked about Raynoma's charge that she has not been recognized for her contribution, "because she was not there."

The company, known as Hitsville U.S.A., was soon housed in a $25,000 bungalow Liles found on 2648 West Grand Boulevard. Gordy put down $3,000 on the property and would have a $140-a-month mortgage payment. This was the first home occupied by Motown; soon other houses on the block would be taken over by the company and used for offices and recording studios. By working in different capacities at the company, all of the Gordy family members contributed to Tamla's success. Tamla would eventually evolve into a subsidiary record label of the dominant label, called Motown (after Motor Town).

Berry Gordy's parents may have instilled strong familial values in their children—and certainly where the immediate Gordy family is concerned, they were always devoted to each other—but Berry was never much of a conventional family man. In the spring of

---

*Liles's book, *Berry, Me, and Motown*, published in 1990 by Contemporary Books, provides a most fascinating account of the early history of Berry Gordy and Motown Records.

†Though Raynoma Liles is seldom mentioned in connection with these early days, she is acknowledged (along with Berry and his sister Esther) as a member of the company's original board of directors, according to the Motown Record Corporation's articles of incorporation, dated March 25, 1960.

1960, Gordy, thirty, married Raynoma Liles, twenty-three. They already had a one-year-old son, Kerry. According to Liles, while she waited for Gordy on their wedding night, he left her to have sex with a seventeen-year-old girl, Margaret Norton. After Gordy and Liles were granted a Mexican divorce a year later, Gordy and Norton had a child. Though it has been reported over the years that Gordy and Norton were wed, Liles has said that Norton once confessed to her that they never were.

Berry Gordy would sire two more children without benefit of marriage. In 1971, he would father Diana Ross's first-born daughter, Rhonda Suzanne. (Since Ross married another man, the paternity of this child would remain a closely guarded secret for almost twenty years). In 1976, Gordy and Nancy Leiviska, an attractive blonde and former Motown employee, would have a son.

By the end of 1960, Gordy had begun to establish a solid reputation in the music business with successful records by The Marvelettes ("Please Mr. Postman"), The Miracles ("Shop Around"), and Mary Wells ("Bye Bye Baby"). The hits would continue to flow for years.

Berry Gordy was a born leader whose enthusiasm for his business proved contagious. His success was largely the result of his brilliance at surrounding himself with the most talented writers, producers, and artists that Detroit had to offer. "They were young kids who had to have three things: talent, the desire to be a superstar, and character," Berry's sister Esther Edwards recalled in October 1990. "And most of the early ones were from single-parent or no-parent families. Stevie Wonder was ten and a half years old when he first came [to Motown]. His mother used to cry because she thought when he grew up he'd have to sell pencils and apples to make a living."

The Supremes, The Temptations, Mary Wells, Smokey Robinson and the Miracles, Stevie Wonder, Martha and the Vandellas, and The Marvelettes were all young, black hopefuls—some with only a modicum of talent—plucked from urban street corners by Gordy and transformed into international stars.

By 1968, after nine years' work, Gordy and his staff of writers and producers—Smokey Robinson, Brian Holland, Lamont Dozier and Eddie Holland, Norman Whitfield, and Barrett Strong, to name just a few of many—had formulated an original, contagious style of music that sold millions of records. It was called the Motown Sound.

Smokey Robinson explained in a 1990 interview, "Berry had a formula. He wanted to put good songs on good tracks that had good funk on the bottom and good beats—but mainly to have really good songs with good stories. All we were doing was putting good songs on good tracks, songs that anybody could relate to.''

A muscular rhythm section, engaging hook lines and choruses, and witty lyrics were all standard elements of songs like ''Where Did Our Love Go?'', ''I Can't Help Myself,'' ''Dancing in the Streets,'' ''Please Mr. Postman,'' ''Stop! In the Name of Love,'' ''The Tracks of My Tears,'' and countless others which became not only anthems of an entire generation but also emblems of the period in American history in which they were recorded.

A major factor in the success of so many of Gordy's artists—and one that has been written about incessantly by music historians over the years—was the Artist Development division of Motown. For this department, started in 1965, Gordy hired professional etiquette, dance, and music instructors to train his young stars (most of whom were in their early twenties) so that they would be able to perform not only in theaters on the so-called chitlin circuit, but also in swanky—white—nightclubs like the Copacabana in New York. When The Supremes played the Copa in July 1965, it was a turning point for the entire company. That group's success opened the doors for similar triumphs by other company acts. Soon the Motown stars were performing their hit records—as well as demonstrating their versatility with Broadway standards and show tunes—not only for a teenage following, but for that audience's parents as well.*

As a result of a plethora of books written in recent years about him and his Motown stars, Berry Gordy—and his mercurial personality—is no longer much of a mystery. Indeed, as often reported, Gordy was a tough taskmaster who encouraged intense competition among his groups, writers, and producers. Paradoxically, he also encouraged his staffers and artists to feel that Motown was their family.

Accounts have also revealed, though, that this idea of ''family'' was Berry's clever way of keeping all of the youngsters and employees in line. He even had Smokey Robinson write a company anthem, which was sung at all creative meetings. As long as they believed that the company's spirit was all for one and one for all, the workers behaved themselves and were productive for the com-

---

*The Artist Development division of Motown was history by 1969 when The Jackson 5 moved to Los Angeles to begin perfecting their new Motown stage show. Suzanne dePasse and other Motown employees (including her cousin, Tony Jones) would be largely responsible for grooming the group.

pany. Berry Gordy was a lot of things, but he was not idealistic or sentimental.

The biggest criticism leveled at Berry Gordy—by outsiders at first and then, later, by the artists themselves—was aimed at the complete control he exercised over his dominion. Practically none of the artists had any idea how much money they generated for the company, and they were always discouraged from asking questions. Books written by founding members of The Temptations and The Supremes have underscored the fact that most of the artists who recorded for Gordy in the sixties made very little—if any—money for themselves.

"I never saw a tax return until 1979," Diana Ross, who signed with Gordy in 1960, has said. "Berry was such a mentor and strong personality, you found yourself relying on that. You didn't grow."

Today, when Motown produces a company anniversary special for network television, Suzanne dePasse, president of Motown Productions, has to beg and cajole former Motown stars to appear on the show. And convincing current Motown attractions who have long histories with the company to make appearances is just as difficult and even more frustrating for her. "It doesn't matter anymore," one Motown official has said. "No one believes the Motown family bullshit. Let's face it."

Most of the artists have long since forgotten what Berry did *for* them and can only remember what he did *to* them. As the late Florence Ballard once said, "You hope you can leave it all behind you and start over. But you can't. You just can't forget what should have been when your own family has done you wrong."

Joe Jackson, who in 1968 was about to link his own troubled but talented bloodline to Motown's, probably said it best: "Nobody— no best friend, no business associate, no person on the planet— nobody at all can hurt you, truly hurt you, the way a member of your own family can."

# Chapter

## 3

IT WAS QUARTER to ten in the morning on July 23, 1968, when the Jackson family's Volkswagen minibus eased into a parking space in Detroit in front of the small white bungalow at Hitsville U.S.A. Joe Jackson and Jack Richardson, the close family friend who traveled with them, were in the front seats, and crammed in the back were the excited boys and the instruments, amplifiers, and microphones that would not fit on top. The bus also carried thermoses and sandwiches that Katherine had packed for the boys before they left Gary. "There's no point in your being hungry," she told her sons.

"Get out and in line for inspection," Joe ordered. The boys stowed the remains of their breakfast and clambered out onto the already-warm Detroit street, where they lined up according to age: seventeen-year-old Jackie; fourteen-year-old Tito; thirteen-year-old Jermaine; ten-year-old Marlon; and nine-year-old Michael. Seventeen-year-old Johnny Jackson joined the group. Though they were not related, Joe treated him just like he treated his own sons, and Johnny obeyed just as quickly. "All right," Joe growled. "Ten o'clock. Let's go. Remember everything I taught you, and except when you're singing or spoke to, keep your mouths shut."

They walked up the sidewalk and into the main building. The first person to greet them was a sharply dressed black man. When he asked how he could assist them, Joe explained that they were the Jackson family from Gary and that they had an appointment for an audition. The man said that he'd been expecting them. "You must be Michael," he said and then, pointing to the boys in turn, correctly called each one by his name. "And you, sir, you must be Joseph," he announced as he and the Jackson patriarch shook hands. The boys looked at each other, amazed.

31

The boys were led into a small studio. As they walked in, they noticed someone setting up a film camera on a tripod. There were ten folding chairs in front of the small, elevated wooden platform which would serve as a stage. Suzanne dePasse, creative assistant to president Berry Gordy, entered the studio wearing a blue mini-skirt and a yellow blouse with ruffles. Her high heels clicked as she approached the group to introduce herself. She was an attractive young black woman with shoulder-length, soft hair and a bright, friendly smile. The boys would remember that they liked her immediately. Ralph Seltzer was the next person to appear. He served as Gordy's chief attorney and head of Motown's creative division. Seltzer, a tall white man wearing a dark suit and conservative tie, seemed much more intimidating. He shook the hand of each boy, and then Joe's and Jack's.

After all of the boys' equipment was lugged in from the van and set up, eight more staffers who did not introduce themselves filed into the studio, each carrying a notepad. Michael was ready to speak into the microphone when he heard someone in the corner snicker and say, "Yeah, the Jackson Jive." (*The Jackson Jive* is an old slang expression.) It sounded like an insult. Ralph Seltzer cleared his throat, then glared at the person who made the remark.

"First song we'd like to do is James Brown's 'I Got the Feeling,' " Michael announced. "Okay? Here we go." He counted off—"A-one, a-two, a-three"—and then Tito on guitar, Jermaine on bass, and Johnny Jackson on drums began to play.

"Baby, baby, baa-ba. Baby, baby, baa-ba. Baby, baby, baa-ba," Michael sang. He grimaced and grunted, imitating James Brown. "I got the fe-e-e-lin' now. Good *Gawwd* almighty!" Michael skated sideways across the floor, like Brown does. "I feel *goooood*," he screamed into the microphone with a wicked expression on his little face.

Suzanne dePasse and Ralph Seltzer smiled at each other and nodded their heads. The other Motown executives kept time to the music. Joe, standing in a corner with his arms folded across his chest, looked on approvingly.

After the boys finished, no one in the audience applauded. Instead, everyone began feverishly writing on their notepads.

Confused, the youngsters looked at each other and then at Joe for some hint as to what they should do. Joe motioned with his hand that they should continue with the next number.

"Thank you. Thank you very much," Michael said, as though acknowledging an ovation. "We 'preciate it."

Michael then introduced the group, as he did in their live show.

Then they sang the bluesy "Tobacco Road." Again, no applause, just note taking.

"Next song we'd like to do is a Motown song," Michael announced. He paused, waiting for some smiles of acknowledgement. There were none. "It's Smokey Robinson's 'Who's Loving You.' Okay? Here we go. A-one, a-two, a-three . . .'"

They closed the song with a big finish and waited for a reaction from the Motown staffers.

Again, everyone was writing.

"Well, hey, how was *that*?" Michael blurted out.

"Shh," Jermaine hissed.

"Jackson Jive, huh?" someone in the room said. "These boys ain't jivin'. I think they're great."

Michael beamed.

Ralph Seltzer cleared his throat and stood up.

"I'd like to thank you boys for coming," he said. His voice gave no hint of how he felt the audition had gone. He shook each of their hands before walking over to Joe and explaining that the company would be putting them all up at the nearby Gotham Hotel. "I'll be in touch with you," Seltzer concluded, "in two days—"

"When Mr. Gordy renders a decision," Joe said, finishing Seltzer's sentence. He didn't sound happy.

The boys were clearly disappointed. As they filed out, no one said a word.

The brothers packed up their equipment, got into their van, and drove off. They spent the day driving around Detroit seeing the sights. After dinner in a coffee shop, they went to bed early. Joe locked the door to the boys' rooms before he and Jack Richardson went out on the town.

Two days later, Berry made a quick decision. "Yes, absolutely, sign these kids up," he told Ralph Seltzer.

On July 26, Seltzer arranged a meeting with Joe Jackson and Jack Richardson in his office at Motown. The boys all waited out in the lobby during the two-hour meeting. Seltzer explained that Berry Gordy was interested in signing The Jackson Five to the label and outlined the kind of relationship he hoped the company would develop with the Jackson youngsters. He spoke of "the genius of Berry Gordy" and Gordy's hopes that The Jackson Five would become major recording stars. "These kids are gonna be big, big, *big*," Seltzer enthused, his manner much more cordial than it had been on their first visit. "Believe me, if Mr. Gordy says they're gonna be big, they're gonna be big." Joe must have felt like he was dreaming.

Then Seltzer presented Joe with the Motown contract. As Jackson and Richardson listened, Seltzer explained the nine-page document, Motown's standard, boilerplate agreement.

Ralph Seltzer quickly explained the contract to Joe and Jack. They nodded their heads as if they understood the legalese. Then Joe called his boys into the office.

"We got it, boys," he announced.

"Oh, man, that's too much!"

"We're on Motown!"

"We got us a contract!"

They all began jumping up and down and hugging one another.

Ralph Seltzer gave each boy a contract. "Just sign right there on that line, fellas."

They looked at Joe.

"Go ahead. It's okay. Sign it."

Though Joe had not even read the contract, and neither had any of his sons, each boy signed.

"And here's an agreement for you, Mr. Jackson," Ralph Seltzer said, handing Joe a paper. "This is a parental approval agreement and it says, quite simply, that you will make certain that the boys comply with the terms of the contract they just signed."*

Joe signed the agreement.

"Well, congratulations," Ralph Seltzer said with a smile and a firm handshake for Joe. "And let me be the first to welcome you to Motown."

Joe turned to his sons, smiling broadly, and congratulated them all. There were handshakes and pats on the back all around. It was a happy moment.

Joe would later recall, "I did not read these agreements nor did my sons read these agreements because they were presented to us on a take-it-or-leave-it basis. Since my sons were just starting out in the entertainment field, we accepted these contracts based on the representations of Ralph Seltzer that they were good contracts."

Ralph Seltzer would, however, later claim, "I have no recollection of ever saying to Joseph Jackson or The Jackson Five that the agreement being offered by Motown was a good agreement."

---

*Katherine Jackson would also sign a similar parental approval agreement on October 17, 1969. It appears that she did not actually read the agreement, for in it she and Joe are referred to as the parents of John Porter Jackson. "Neither my wife nor I read this document," Joe Jackson would say in a deposition in February 1976, when his family and Motown were suing each other.

Later, after leaving Seltzer's office, Joe telephoned Richard Arons, whom he had hired as his lawyer and the group's unofficial comanager. Arons would recall, "Joe called me up and said he had signed with Motown. There wasn't much I could offer at that point."†

Furthermore, the third clause stated that Motown was under no obligation to record the group or promote its music for five years, even though this was purportedly a one-year contract! Some other contractual stipulations that Joe might have questioned had he fully understood what Ralph Seltzer had read: Motown would choose all of the songs that the group would record, and the group would record each song until "they have been recorded to our [Motown's] satisfaction." However, Motown "shall not be obligated to release any recording," meaning that just because a song was recorded, it would not necessarily be issued to the public. The group was paid $12.50 per "master," which is a completed recording of a song. But in order for the recording to be considered a master, the song had to be released. Otherwise, they were paid nothing.

It's been written that the Jacksons received a 2.7 percent royalty rate, based on wholesale price, a standard Motown royalty of the 1960s. Actually, according to their contract, the boys would receive 6 percent of 90 percent of the wholesale price (less all taxes and packaging) of any single or album released. This amount had to be split five ways among the Jackson brothers. In other words, Michael would receive one-fifth of 6 percent of 90 percent of the wholesale price—or a little under one-half of a penny for any single and $.0216, about two cents, per album released.*

As per the terms of the contract, Motown was obligated to pay the cost of arrangements, copying, and accompaniment and all other costs related to each recording session, whether the song was released or not—but these expenses and others would have to be recouped by Motown from the royalties generated by sales of the records that were released. This arrangement led to many complaints by Motown artists, and it would be a big problem for The Jackson Five, one that Joe could have foreseen if he had understood the contract. But he never imagined that the group would record so many songs that would not be issued.

Some of the contract clauses were downright laughable. For in-

---

†Richard Arons would sign an official comanagement agreement in 1970, entitling him to 5 percent of the group's income.

*These figures are based on an assumed wholesale price of $.375 a single and $2.00 an album.

stance, Motown had the right to respond to the Jacksons' fan mail "with any answers the company deems necessary" and was allowed to "affix to such answer and photographs what purports to be your signature." On the other hand, the company wasn't obligated to answer *any* mail or forge any signatures, if it didn't want to.

Also, if Michael or any of the brothers were to leave the group, he would have no right ever to say that he was a member of The Jackson Five, "and shall have no further right to use the group name for any purpose whatsoever." And Motown could, at any time, replace any member of the group with any person the company chose. An even more limiting clause—number sixteen—stated that "Motown owns all rights, title, and interest in the name 'Jackson Five.' "

In tiny, barely legible handwriting, Michael signed the contract "Michael Joe Jackson." Of course, Michael's signature meant nothing since, at nine years of age, he was a minor. Having him and his brothers sign contracts was only intended to make them feel part of the Motown family. Underneath Michael's signature, Joseph W. Jackson signed as guardian.

Immediately, the Jacksons began to record at the Motown studios under the direction of Bobby Taylor. For the next few months, they would spend their weeks in Gary attending school and their weekends—and many of their weeks as well—in Detroit, sleeping on the floor of Bobby Taylor's apartment. Motown convinced Taylor's wife to leave her job and spend her time cooking and cleaning for The Jackson Five when they were in town. She was never paid.

While in Detroit, the boys recorded fifteen songs, most of which would surface later on their albums. Taylor would say later that he was not paid for those sessions. "I would have liked the recognition for having discovered The Jackson Five," he said. "But recognition don't pay the bills."

One day, Berry Gordy and Bobby Taylor were talking about the boys, and Bobby was saying how thrilled he was to be in on the ground floor of something as exciting as The Jackson Five.

"Taylor, let me tell you something," Gordy said. "As soon as they get rich, they're gonna forget who you are."

On September 27, 1968, Motown booked The Jackson Five in a benefit concert at Gilroy Stadium in Gary, Indiana, the purpose of which was to defray the costs of Richard Hatcher's mayoral campaign. On the bill were Motown recording artists Gladys Knight and the Pips, Shorty Long, and Bobby Taylor and the Vancouvers.

The Jackson Five opened the show. In years to come, the Motown story for public consumption would be that *this* was where Diana Ross saw the boys for the first time, "discovered" them, and brought them to Gordy's attention. In truth, The Jackson Five were already signed to the label. Moreover, Diana Ross was nowhere near Gary at the time. She was in Los Angeles, rehearsing for The Supremes' opening October 1 at the Coconut Grove.

Around Christmastime, Berry Gordy hosted a party at the Detroit estate he had purchased in 1967 for a million dollars. (Though he had moved to the West Coast, he still maintained this residence.) The Jackson Five were asked to perform for the Motown artists and other friends of Gordy's. The three-story house boasted a ballroom with marble floors and columns, an Olympic-sized swimming pool, a billiard room, a two-lane bowling alley, a private theater linked to the main house by a tunnel, and an authentic pub whose furnishings were imported from England. All of the rooms were decorated with gold leaf, frescoed ceilings, and elaborate crystal chandeliers. Expensive oil portraits of Gordy's friends and family decorated the entryway. Most of the guests were dressed in lavish outfits. With her hair pulled back in a chignon, Diana Ross looked regal in a white, draped silk gown. Host Berry Gordy wore a tuxedo, as did some of the other Motown executives.

If the Jacksons had ever seen a home like this before, it was only in movies where the occupants usually were royalty—white royalty. "Black people actually live like this?" Joe asked himself as he wandered throughout the mansion, shaking his head. "I just can't believe that this kind of thing is possible." When Gordy happened to overhear the comment, he put his hand on Joe's shoulder and whispered something in his ear that made Joe smile. The two men shook hands in agreement and Gordy led Joseph into the living room. "So tell me, man, what do you think about this?" Gordy asked, halting before an enormous painting of Gordy dressed as Napoleon Bonaparte. It had been commissioned by his sister Esther.

"Jesus. What can I say?" Joe asked. "That's *you*? Man, it's too much to believe."

"Well, do you like it?" Gordy pressed.

"I, uh . . . You, uh . . ." All Joe could do was stammer. Just at that moment, his son Michael came running up to him. "Hey, who's that silly lookin' guy in the picture?" he asked.

Joe cringed and then shot his son a look. Gordy smiled benevolently.

"I'll never forget that night," Michael would say. "There were maids and butlers, and everyone was real polite. There were Motown stars everywhere. Smokey Robinson was there. That's when I met him for the first time. The Temptations were there, and we were singing some of their songs, so we were real nervous. And I looked out into the audience, and there was Diana Ross. That's when I almost lost it.''

After the boys' performance, Berry Gordy introduced them to Diana Ross for the first time.

"I just want to tell you how much I enjoyed you guys," Diana said as she shook their hands. "Mr. Gordy tells me that we're going to be working together."

"We are?" Michael asked, his eyes wide as saucers.

"Yes, we are," Diana said. Her smile was almost as overwhelming as the diamonds she wore at her ears and around her neck. "I just can't wait. Whatever I can do to assist you, that's what I'm going to do."

"Well, Miss Ross, we really appreciate it," Joe Jackson managed to say. Usually a smooth talker, Joe was not having an easy time that night.

"Oh, that's quite all right," Diana told him. Her smile was warm and sincere. She turned to Michael. "And you, you're just so cute." When she pinched his cheek, Michael blushed.

The boys were speechless.

The next eight months were difficult. Berry Gordy did not feel The Jackson Five were ready to have a release yet; he wasn't satisfied with any of the songs they had thus far recorded. Everyone in the Jackson clan was becoming impatient, especially since conditions in Gary were getting worse. More street gangs were terrorizing the neighborhood: Joe had been mugged, and a street tough had pulled a knife on young Tito. Katherine was anxious for the family to leave Gary once and for all. She told Joe that she thought he should try to get out of the Motown contract and find another label. "I'm tired of waiting for Motown to put out a single," she complained. "We have to get out of Gary, and *now*." Every day, the family would wait for that call from someone—*anyone*—at Motown, telling them what the next step in their lives would be.

On March 11, 1969, the Motown contract was finally signed. The delay was caused when Ralph Seltzer discovered that The Jackson Five were still committed to Steeltown Records, despite Richard Arons's previous efforts to extricate them from that deal. Motown had to make a settlement with Steeltown, much to Gordy's chagrin. By this time, according to Ralph Seltzer, Motown had spent in excess of thirty thousand dollars on The Jackson Five's accommodations and recording sessions, and this sum did not include any settlement made to Steeltown. Gordy was anxious to begin recouping his investment.

The call from Motown finally came in August 1969. Gordy wanted Joe, his five sons, Johnny Jackson, and Ronny Rancifer to move to Los Angeles. They would attend school on the West Coast while recording at Motown's new Hollywood facilities. In time, the whole company would be relocated to California.

Though Gordy wasn't enthused by any of the Jacksons' songs, he was certainly impressed with young Michael Jackson. "Michael was a born star," he would say in a 1990 interview. "He was a classic example of understanding everything. I recognized that he had a depth that was so vast, it was just incredible. The first time I saw him, I saw this little kid as something real special."

Joe, Tito, Jack Richardson, drummer Johnny Jackson, and keyboardist Ronny Rancifer drove to Los Angeles in the family's new Dodge maxivan. Motown paid for Jackie, Jermaine, Marlon, and Michael to fly out a few days later. It was Joe Jackson's decision not to move the entire family from Gary to Los Angeles until he was fairly certain that their future in Hollywood would be secure. It was possible, after all, that Berry Gordy could be wrong, that the group would be a failure, and that they would have to start all over again. So Janet, Randy, and LaToya would stay behind with Katherine in the house in Gary.

"Janet will probably be a singer one day," Joe said at this time. "She tries to sing now, but she's a little young at four. Randy is eight and thinking of joining the group, but he's still getting his thing together with the conga drums. As soon as he gets a little tighter, he'll be in the group. LaToya, who is fourteen, likes show business, but she really doesn't want to perform. She takes care of the fan mail. She'll probably get involved in the business end of the group soon."

Michael, almost eleven at the time of the move, would be the most affected by the living arrangements because he would be apart from his mother, to whom he was extremely close. "The separation was most painful for Michael," Katherine has said. "He was so sensitive as a boy."

Despite Gordy's enthusiasm for the Jackson family as potential Motown money-makers, he was cautious. He would spend as little as possible on them at this point. Jackie and Tito each had an upper front tooth missing, which was very conspicuous. Gordy decided to forego visits to the dentist for the time being. In publicity photos, the missing teeth would be touched up. Jermaine had a scar over one eye, the result of a collision with another boy on a baseball field. There was talk of plastic surgery. "It's too early for that," Berry Gordy said. "No one will notice." (The scar was never treated.)

Gordy registered them at one of the seediest motels in Hollywood, the Tropicana, on Santa Monica Boulevard. Michael, Marlon, and Jermaine shared one room while Tito and Jackie were in another. Joe was by himself down the hall. The family saw little of their rooms. Since it was still school vacation, they spent most of their waking hours at Motown's Hollywood studios recording test records and rehearsing new songs.

Eventually, Gordy pulled them out of the Tropicana and moved them closer to Motown headquarters. The Hollywood Motel, across the street from Hollywood High, was a dreadful residence for young boys; prostitutes and pimps used it as a place to conduct business.

None of that mattered to the Jackson brood. They were living in California. Even if they did not see a movie star on every corner as they might have dreamed, Los Angeles was heaven compared to Gary. Michael had never seen a real palm tree before. "And here were whole streets lined with them," he once recalled. And fancy cars. Everybody seemed to wear sunglasses, even on those overcast mornings when the sun didn't emerge until noon. The young Jacksons were surprised to find that many people wore them at night, long after the sun had gone down.

When the boys went to the beach, they saw surfers clustered offshore waiting for the right wave so they could "hang ten." Sidewalk surfers—on skateboards—were almost as much fun to watch as they wove recklessly in and out among pedestrians. At Grauman's Chinese Theatre on Hollywood Boulevard, they compared their hand- and footprints with those of movie stars they'd admired for years, as well as those they'd never heard of. Sometimes they'd have to wonder if all of this was a dream. "Sometimes we'd feel real sorry for anybody who wasn't living in Los Angeles," Jermaine remembered.

On those rare off days, Joe rented a car and took the boys to Disneyland or Knott's Berry Farm and other theme parks. They bought a "Map of the Stars" and tried to track down the homes of their favorite celebrities. "Those were heady days," Michael has recalled.

Right after they arrived, Gordy called a meeting at Diana Ross's home. This was the first time the boys had seen her since the show they gave at Gordy's home in Detroit the previous winter. Diana

Ross's house may not have been spectacular by Hollywood standards—she was a single woman living in a three-bedroom temporary residence in the Hollywood Hills while in the process of purchasing a new, much more opulent home in Beverly Hills—but when the five Jackson boys and their father compared it to their garage-sized house in Gary, it was hard for them to act cool.

Michael has recalled that Gordy sat the boys down in Diana's living room and had a talk with them. "I'm gonna make you kids the biggest thing in the world," he told them. "You're gonna have three number one hits in a row. They're gonna write about you kids in history books. So get ready, 'cause it's coming."

That was what the boys—and especially their father—wanted to hear. Joe sought nothing more for his sons than success. He instructed them to do whatever Mr. Gordy wanted them to do. (The boys called him Mr. Gordy, as did Joe and Katherine.) Joe was in awe of Berry but at the same time intimidated by him. "Here's a black man who has made millions of dollars in show business," Joe had said. "If I can just learn a few things from this guy, then I'll have it made too."

Just as the meeting ended, Diana came sweeping into the room looking magnificent in a black satin hot pants outfit, huge natural hairstyle and gold hoop earrings. "She always looked like a goddess," Jermaine recalled. "I remember that when she walked into the living room that day, all of our mouths dropped open." Although the boys had met her before, they were still awed by her presence. Joe fell all over himself to make an impression.

"I just want to tell you boys once again that I'm here for you," she said. "If there's anything I can do for you, I hope you'll let me know."

She seemed quite sincere, Jermaine would remember. "It was hard to believe that she was saying those words to us," he said. "I mean, what did we do to deserve her assistance? Talk about luck."

What Jermaine remembers most about that day is the telegram that Diana showed them. "This is from me to lots and lots of people," she explained, taking it out of the envelope and handing it to Michael. It read, "Please join me in welcoming a brilliant musical group, The Jackson Five, on Monday, August 11, 6:30 to 9:30 P.M. at the Daisy, North Rodeo Drive, Beverly Hills. The Jackson Five, featuring sensational eight-year-old Michael Jackson, will perform live at the party. [signed] Diana Ross."

"I told her, 'I think you made a real mistake,' " Michael would recall many years later. " 'I'm not eight years old. I'm ten.' "

Berry patiently explained to the youngster that what they were dealing with at this meeting was not a lie but rather a matter of public relations. Then there was some discussion with the boy about the art of public relations; he was reminded that, as far as the media were concerned, Diana Ross was the one who had brought him and his brothers to Motown. He should always remember that because, as Diana explained to him, "It's all for your image."

Michael would later recall, "I figured out at an early age that if someone said something about me that wasn't true, it was a lie. But if someone said something about my *image* that wasn't true, then it was okay. Because then it wasn't a lie, it was public relations."

Michael was a quick learner.

Diana Ross introduced her new protégés with the kind of pomp and pageantry often accorded major Hollywood debuts. Three hundred of Gordy's and Diana's "closest" friends and business associates crammed into the chic Beverly Hills private club, the Daisy, all having been personally invited via Diana Ross's telegram. They stood and cheered as Michael Jackson and The Jackson Five—as they were introduced by Diana—performed old Motown songs like Smokey Robinson's "Who's Loving You," and even Disney classics like "Zip-a-dee-do-dah" for the crowd. The fellows wore identical green vest suits with pale gold shirts and matching green boots. Every move had been carefully choreographed and rehearsed in the Motown tradition. A Motown press release was distributed to everyone present. Incredibly, two years had been shaved off the age of each boy.

"They stole the hearts of every hardened, jaded old newshound there," remembered Judy Spiegleman, at that time a writer for *Soul* magazine, the publication that first gave national attention to the group. "I fell in love at that moment with Michael Jackson—an eight-year-old kid who became a man when a microphone was in his hand. So did everyone else."*

Beaming with pride at their reception, Gordy announced that The Jackson Five would appear in concert with Diana Ross and the Supremes at the Forum just five days later, on August 16, and then later in October when Diana would play hostess on "The Hollywood Palace" television show.

---

*The show at the Daisy proved a complete success, so much so that Berry decided to have Diana record a couple of songs with The Jackson Five: "For the Rest of My Life" and "Baby, It's Love." The recordings were never completed.

Each Jackson boy met the press in a receiving line, with Diana Ross making the introductions: "This one's Michael. Isn't he adorable? And that one's Jermaine. Isn't he cute? And over there's Jackie. Look how tall he is," and so forth.

*Soul* reporter Judy Spiegelman recalled, "I remember being impressed with the courteous, outgoing attitude of the youngsters. After all, they were just kids and certainly not at all affected by the attention."

Pauline Dunn, a reporter from the *Sentinel*, a Los Angeles black newspaper, approached Michael.

"How's it feel to be a star, Michael?" she wanted to know.

"Well, to tell you the truth, I had just about given up hope," Michael said with a grin. He was wearing a black British bowler over his Afro-style hair. "I thought I was gonna be an old man before being discovered." Then, in a hushed, dramatic tone he concluded, "But then along came Miss Diana Ross to save my career. She *discovered* me."

"And just how old are you, Michael?" she asked.

Michael looked up at Diana, who was standing proudly behind him, her hand on his shoulder. Berry Gordy stood nearby.

"Eight," Michael said quickly.

"But I thought you were older. Going on eleven, maybe," the suspicious journalist pressed.

"Well, I'm not," Michael insisted. "I'm eight."

"But I heard—"

"Look, the kid's eight, all right?" Gordy broke in. "Next question."

"Next question, *please*," Michael corrected. He smiled and winked at Pauline Dunn as if to say, This is how we play the game.

Her story in the *Sentinel* said that he was eight.

# Chapter

## 4

WITHOUT QUESTION, THE early 1970s were the most significant transitional years Motown Records had undergone since firming itself up as major musical force. By the end of the 1960s, although the company was still producing some superb pop and rhythm-and-blues music, the formula by which it had built its greatest success was beginning to block the musical progress of some of its artists.

For example, some of the label's biggest stars were quietly grumbling about Motown's conveyer-belt method of creating hit records. The late sixties were, indeed, a period of change, both socially and politically, and the production of pop music—how it was created—did not go unaffected. To keep pace with the times, many labels eventually dismantled their songwriting/production staffs and signed prolific singer-songwriters and self-contained bands that wrote and performed their own music, much of it reflective of the new freedom the era brought with it.

Some Motown acts now craved artistic freedom. Stevie Wonder and Marvin Gaye were the chief complainers. Both felt that they'd outgrown manufacturing music the Motown way—singing songs supplied to them by staff writers and producers. They must have finally realized that staff producers and writers like Smokey Robinson and Norman Whitfield were earning large sums from songwriting royalties without having to sweat through grueling forty-city tours and public appearances. They wanted to get in on some of that action too.

The fact is, music wasn't at the forefront of founder Berry Gordy's reasoning when he decided to relocate Motown from Detroit to Los Angeles. Gordy picked up and moved two decades' worth of Michigan roots for the same reason optimistic high school graduates and pretty young runaways swarm to the City of Angels every day from all over the world: the silver screen. Berry Gordy wanted to get into films, and his protégée Diana Ross was to be his ticket. In masterminding the westward move, Gordy was his usual methodical self. He used the occasion to clean house. Employees and artists considered deadweight would be left behind in the Motor City, while desired staffers could keep their jobs, but only if they were willing to relocate to Los Angeles.

To many of the company officials and artists, moving to Los Angeles seemed tantamount to visiting the moon. Certainly, Detroit and Los Angeles had their differences. Detroit was then, as it is today, a working-class town. No matter what glamour Motown injected, Detroit musicians were, for the most part, musicians for music's sake, not for fame and a babe on the arm. In Detroit, success was a two-story brick home with two top-of-the-line Detroit-built cars in the driveway. In Los Angeles, a house hanging off the side of the Hollywood Hills or on beachfront property and a leased Mercedes were generally considered the ultimate goal.

Still, even though the lure of movies took Gordy to the West Coast, the nagging issue of his company's musical expansion could not be denied. While Motown's might in the 1960s was enough to thrust the label into the new decade with honor, the 1970s presented Berry Gordy and company with an enormous challenge. Sly Stone's exciting new sound was a major influence on black music, and even The Temptations had begun adapting to this new black pop. They were also getting older. They were no longer contemporary. How would a company built largely on, according to some critics of the day, the concept of the bourgeois Negro lifestyle, suddenly get hip? The business was in disarray. Diana Ross busily prepared herself for a solo career, which would not bode well for The Supremes. The Temptations' various personnel changes and other eternal woes overshadowed their continued success. Smokey Robinson was playing out his last years with The Miracles. Martha and the Vandellas, The Marvelettes, and many other company stalwarts would be abandoned in Detroit. Indeed, now more than ever, Motown needed some new blood, an act that would be as hip as the times, yet politically harmless in the great Motown tradition.

When Berry Gordy saw the film of The Jackson Five's Detroit audition, he must have realized that these youngsters were just what Doctor Feelgood had ordered. Not only would this group usher in a new musical era for Motown, but they would do so with a hit single supplied by Motown's own production staff. These kids didn't want to write and produce their own songs, they just wanted to be stars. For Gordy, this was déjà vu. How he longed for a time not so long ago when Stevie Wonder and Marvin Gaye cared only about singing and not about publishing. Signing a group that would be exclusively reliant on Motown for its material would validate the tried-and-true Gordy process for at least a few more years. Even Gordy couldn't have predicted, though, how much Jobete would prosper as a result of his signing The Jackson Five.

By 1969, Motown's West Coast Division operated under the direction of one of the company's top staff writer-producers, Deke Richards. Part of Richards's job as Creative Director of Talent for Motown's West Coast Division was to search for promising new writers and artists to help bolster the company's roster. That year, he was introduced by an associate of Berry Gordy's to two talented young writers, Freddie Perren* and Fonce Mizell.

"At that time I was thinking to myself about the dues I had paid at Motown," Richards said. He had written and produced some of Motown's best material for Diana Ross and the Supremes, The Temptations, and Martha and the Vandellas. "I wasn't the only white person at the company—there were two others—but I was the only one who was producing for myself, as opposed to working for someone else. Just as at any record company, there were always little political things going on. I had been through a lot of changes between the black faction and the white faction. Looking back on it, I thought it would have been interesting if I could have been allowed to just do my work to the best of my ability and then have it judged on its own merit without all of the interfering politics."

Richards continued, "Wouldn't it be fascinating, I thought, if somebody who had no track record at all could come into Motown and get a hit without having to pay any dues or deal with the politics? I could run interference for this person and cut through all the red tape. So Freddie and Fonce were like my guinea pigs, so to speak, to see if such a thing were possible. I wanted to get them a writer's contract and money advance from Berry, which I managed to do. Then it was time to get them that hit, something right off the bat."

Deke Richards had heard through the Motown grapevine that Bobby Taylor had discovered a group of youngsters from Gary and was recording material with them in Detroit. Taylor was producing good songs, but there wasn't a hit record in the bunch. "We were trying a lot of cover records," Bobby remembered. "We didn't

---

*Perren went on to become a mainstay of seventies disco music when he produced songs like "I Will Survive" for Gloria Gaynor and "Shake Your Groove Thing" for Peaches and Herb.

have a direction yet. I cut a couple of Temptations tunes on them ["Born to Love You" and "(I Know) I'm Losing You"], a Four Tops song ["Standing in the Shadows of Love"], a Stevie Wonder ["My Cherie Amour"], and material like that. The songs were good. The boys were talented. I agreed, though, there weren't any solid hits in there."

Deke Richards and Berry Gordy had enjoyed a close relationship for the previous few years. In fact, Richards had a phone line exclusively for Gordy's use. Gordy would call him at all hours of the early morning, always brimming with enthusiastic ideas.

Richards had been an integral part of a writing-producing team at Motown called the Clan,* responsible for some of Motown's biggest hits, including "Love Child." As much as Gordy respected the work that had been done by the Clan, he was weary of the ego conflicts that often seemed to result whenever talented writers and producers collaborated. When Richards suggested that he, Fonce Mizell, and Freddie Perren unite as a team on a par with Holland, Dozier, and Holland, Berry wasn't keen about the idea. H-D-H and Motown were embroiled in an expensive lawsuit at the time. The writing-producing team felt they should have been awarded stock in the company because they had written and produced many of Motown's biggest hit records, but there were other writers and producers at the company who had also helped to shape Motown. None of them had stock in the company either. "Gordy didn't want to encourage any more backroom superstars," Freddie Perren concluded.

Finally Gordy relented, and for the next three months, Richards, Perren, and Mizell collaborated on a song entitled "I Want to Be Free," intended for Gladys Knight and the Pips. Richards had been the first producer to record Knight and the Pips—her brother Merald "Bubba" Knight and cousins Edward Patton and William Guest—in 1967 when they signed with Motown; however, those songs were never released.

According to Freddie Perren, "Deke said that one way to get the spotlight on you right away at Motown is to find someone who was cold and write a hit for them. So that's what we set out to do. Gladys hadn't had a hit in a while. We were determined to rectify that."

The Richards team went into the Motown studio with a talented

---

*The Clan consisted of Deke Richards, Frank Wilson, R. Dean Taylor, and Hank Cosby. Berry Gordy also had a hand in many of the songs written and produced by the Clan.

corps of musicians and cut the track for "I Want to Be Free," remembered fondly by Perren as "one of Motown's greatest instrumental performances."

Meanwhile, Berry invited Deke to the show The Jackson Five gave at the Daisy. Deke was duly impressed. Fate had begun to intervene. When Deke played the track of "I Want to Be Free" for Berry, he liked it so much he thought it might be ideal for "those kids from Gary." Berry would recall for *Rolling Stone* magazine that he told Richards: "Give the song a Frankie Lymon treatment, and we'll see what happens."

Deke recalled, "Berry lived with the track for a while and had a couple of ideas which were good. He was starting to get excited now. I *wanted* Berry to get involved for two reasons. Number one, the man's an excellent songwriter, and number two," Deke said with a chuckle, "he had some clout at that company. The creative process in him was happening. Finally I said, 'Look, Berry, why don't you *really* get involved in this thing?' He said, 'Okay, I'll do it, but just at the top end. In other words, I'll listen to stuff and give you regular critiques.' Well, that was perfect, because Berry had this wealth of experience and now we had it at our disposal. This was starting to become a very exciting proposition for all of us."

Deke decided to call the team of Mizell, Perren, himself, and Gordy the Corporation, which would reinforce the democratic premise that there would be no overblown egos involved in the work and that everyone would be treated fairly. The profits were split: Richards would get 50 percent, since it was his concept and he was producing as well as writing, Freddie and Fonce would split 40 percent equally as writers, and Berry would get 10 percent of the writing profits for his participation as "sounding board." Unfortunately, in years to come, some of Deke Richards's better compositions would be released under the Corporation banner, meaning that he would not be personally recognized for some of his most superb work.

Richards remembered, "After the basic instrumental track was more or less finished, it was time to begin rehearsing the kids' vocals to record over the track. The boys came over to Berry's house, and that's when we started talking about the song with them and developing a rapport. I then started having the boys rehearse at my apartment in West Hollywood. The kids worked a tremendous number of hours on this song, a minimum of six hours a day to a maximum of twelve. I'd either pick them up or take them home at the end of the day. It was hard work."

Michael has recalled that when he was eleven years old he would sometimes sit and watch children playing in a park across the street from the Motown studio. "I'd just stare at them in wonder—I couldn't imagine such freedom, such a carefree life—and wish more than anything that I had that kind of freedom, that I could walk away and be like them. When you're young and you're working, the world can seem awfully unfair."

Work did not stop him from having fun in the studio when he could. Freddie Perren recalled that Michael "was a lot like other kids. He used to get a piece of paper, scribble on it, put some tape on the back of it, and then come up to you and say, 'Hey man, how ya doin', while slapping you on the back. On the paper would be printed 'Kick me.' "

Deke Richards continued, "After taking the kids home, I'd run the tape of that day's work back to Berry and he would add some ideas and critique it. Then we'd take it back and work on it some more. It got down to the difference between flat and sharp notes on the chorus, that's how precise this production was. Eventually it was retitled 'I Want You Back.'

"The biggest problem with The Jackson Five was not the willingness to work. That was there, and the excitement to work was always there as well. The problem was that you not only had to be a producer, you had to be a phonetics and English teacher. It was draining. The pronunciation of words. We had to go over and over words one at a time, which was tough. If Michael had any problems other than phonetics, they had to do with attacking and sustaining words and notes. Like any kid, he tended to throw away words, or he would slur a note rather than hold on to it. He'd be thinking about dancing or whatever and not concentrate on getting the lyrics out. I'd have to tell him, 'I need those notes, Michael, every last one of them.' As a singer, though, he was great. As far as tone and all, he was terrific. We'd put a lot of pressure on him, because whenever you find a little kid who can sing like that, the feeling is 'Yeah, he's so great I want him to be even greater.' I felt that if he could be that good in the raw, imagine how amazing he could be if you really polished him up."

"I remember that Deke Richards was one of my first teachers," Michael Jackson said. "God, we spent so much time on that song. He was really patient with me, all of us. Over and over and over, I think I must have recorded that thing two dozen times. That was hard work. I had no idea that recording could be such work. I remember falling asleep at the mike. I wondered if it would ever be finished. Just when I thought we were through, we'd have to go back and do it again."

Jermaine Jackson added, "This is when I began to understand the Motown philosophy of recording a song until it's perfect. We were all sayin' to each other, 'Okay, enough already. The song's good enough.' But at Motown, it wasn't a done deal until it was a perfect record. By the time we finished with 'I Want You Back,' it was more than perfect. It was *unbelievable*."

The final recording session for "I Want You Back" lasted until two in the morning. "This had to be the most expensive single in Motown history up to that point," Deke Richards added. "It had cost somewhere in the vicinity of ten thousand dollars. At that time the cost of a Motown single was averaging between two and three thousand. We kept adding and subtracting to the very end. In fact, my original intro to the song started off with just the guitar, but at the last minute I wanted a piano glissando at the top. I had Freddie and Fonce go in there and run their fingers down the piano to really kick the song off."

Finally the Corporation was done with the session, and then with mixing and mastering the recording. On October 2, 1969, after the final mixing of "I Want You Back," Berry asked Deke how he thought the group's name should appear on the record's label. Jackson Five? *The* Jackson Five? Jackson Five featuring Michael Jackson? Deke said he thought the group should be called simply The Jackson 5, with the numeral 5. Berry agreed, and that's how they would be known from that time on. At this time Jackie was eighteen; Tito, fifteen; Jermaine, fourteen; Marlon, twelve; and Michael was eleven.

"I was really excited about the song, about its presence and excitement," Deke said of "I Want You Back." "I'll never forget that the first person I played it for was Stevie [Wonder], because this was a guy I really respected. We were friends. Everyone else was too influenced by Berry to give me an objective opinion. He listened to it carefully, and he said, 'Naw, man. I don't like the drums.' I had to laugh. Can't please everyone, you know?"

While his father and brothers were shuffled from one hotel to another, Michael moved in with Diana Ross in October 1969. "It was a calculated thing. I wanted him to be around her," Berry Gordy once explained. "People think it was an accident that he stayed there. It wasn't. I wanted Diane to teach him whatever she could. 'Course, I didn't expect her to take a lot of time with the kid. She was quite busy at this time, touring with The Supremes a lot. Diane's a very influential person. I knew that Michael would pick up *something* just by being around her when she was home. And

Diane had said that he sort of reminded her of herself at age eleven. Michael was anxious and interested, as well as talented. Like Diane was when I first met her. She was sixteen then. I asked her if she minded and she didn't. She wanted him around. It was good for her to have someone else besides herself to think about.''

As Joe was being influenced by Berry, Joe's son, Michael, was learning from Diana Ross. As much as she may have wanted to help, Diana Ross was so wrapped up in her own career, she was not ready for the role of surrogate mother. Michael's lifestyle in the Ross household must have seemed to be everything he had been brought up by his mother, a devout Jehovah's Witness, to shun as wicked. Nothing else really mattered in these surroundings but show business. "You are going to be a great, great star," Diana kept reminding the little boy. Diana meant well; she liked Michael very much. But being a star, *the* star, had been the focus of her life for so long, she wasn't the ideal person to instill values in a growing boy.

Though Diana Ross remained at home during the month of October, she was an extremely busy woman. She may have tolerated Michael around the house only because Berry asked her to. After all, this was a chaotic time for her. She was about to leave The Supremes and embark on a solo career. She'd been working toward this goal for many years and was anxious to make her own mark in show business. Meanwhile, she and Berry were having a tumultuous romance. Michael, no doubt, heard many arguments between the couple, and then probably watched as they smiled and cooed at one another for the sake of reporters. He was learning a lot about show biz—about public relations—but only time would tell how he would be affected by it.

Michael attended school during the day and recorded in the studio until late at night, but he insists today that during the time he lived with Diana Ross, she taught him about art. In truth, it was Katherine who inspired him to draw. As a young girl she had taught herself to sketch while undergoing a long convalescence from polio.

"We'd go out almost every day, just the two of us, and buy pencils and paint," Michael wrote about Diana in his autobiography, *Moonwalk*, though that doesn't seem likely. "When we weren't drawing or painting, we'd go to museums."

Michael says that Diana Ross introduced him to the works of Michelangelo and Degas, and that this was the start of his great interest in art and the masters.

"Diana Ross didn't know the first thing about Michelangelo until she married me [in 1971]," Bob Silberstein, Ross's ex-husband, once stated. Could it be that Michael misread indifference ("Here are some paints, kid. Now go paint and don't bother me.") for real interest?

"Michael probably really thinks Diana Ross taught him how to paint," said Virginia Harris, a close friend of the Jackson family who once knew Diana very well. "But, believe me, Diana Ross does not know how to paint. This is not to take anything away from Miss Ross. It was very gracious of her to allow Michael to stay at her home. Marlon spent about a week there as well. But even today, years later, Michael still wants to believe that he and Diana were great friends. He idolized her so much when he was young. He likes to hold on to his fantasy memories, no matter how empty they are."

Michael's fascination with Diana Ross—some saw it as an obsession—would last for many years. She was a star and he studied her constantly.

"I remember I used to just sit in the corner and watch the way she moved," he recalled. "She was art in motion. Have you ever seen the way she works her hands? I was," he struggled for the right word, "*enthralled* by her. All day long when I wasn't rehearsing my songs, I'd be listening to hers. I watched her rehearse one day in the mirror. She didn't know I was watching. I studied her, the way she moved, the way she sang, just the way she was. Afterwards, I told her, 'I want to be just like you, Diane.' And she said, 'You just be yourself and you'll be a great star.' "

Michael, at age eleven, was terribly lonely living in the Ross home for the month he stayed there; he missed his mother a great deal and talked to her on the telephone incessantly, running up Diana's phone bill.

Katherine was troubled by Michael's life in the Ross household, according to one family friend, a woman who asked for anonymity because she is someone in whom Katherine still confides. "Katie truly was concerned about Diana Ross's lifestyle and how it might influence her son," said the friend. "She didn't want her son to be corrupted by Ross or her show-business circle of friends. Also, she knew very little about Diana. She knew her as a star who had a bad reputation for being egotistical. The whole time Michael was away from her, Katie could only imagine what was going on in the Ross household and how Michael was coping with it. She would have had to be a saint not to wonder what kinds of values Diana was passing on to her son."

Moreover, Diana seemed reluctant to talk to Katherine directly. When Katherine would telephone to check in on her eleven-year-old son, she would have to talk to one of the household staff if Michael wasn't available. Diana would usually not come to the phone to talk to Katherine. Of course, Diana did not yet have any children of her own, so she could not relate to a mother's concern.

If Katherine was distressed about the possibilities of wild parties at the Ross residence, she need not have been. Diana was not very sociable in those days. She would go to bed early in order to be up on time for her appointments. She may have neglected Michael when he lived there, but it's doubtful that she corrupted him in any way.

Stardom for Michael and his brothers was just around the corner. "I Want You Back" was released in October 1969. It wasn't an immediate hit. The song entered *Billboard*'s Top 100 at number 90. Motown's promotion and sales department really had to work with the song, encouraging disc jockeys to play it, stores to stock it. Finally, ten weeks later, on January 31, it went to number one, displacing B. J. Thomas's "Raindrops Keep Falling on My Head."

With "I Want You Back," Berry Gordy, Deke Richards, Fonce Mizell, and Freddie Perren launched Motown's latest find with a blast, and the record label into a new and exciting decade. A precocious yet completely adorable and endearing Michael led his older brothers into the hearts, homes, and stereos of middle-class white America. The rousing single also found success on the black or rhythm-and-blues charts.

As with the successful Supremes formula of the sixties, The Jackson 5 sound presented a wholesome, nonthreatening soul music, easily digested and readily accepted by all races of record buyers. Without their necessarily realizing it, the general audience of Motown was accepting the lighthearted sound started by The Supremes. The record was only number one for a week, but it went on to sell 2,060,711 copies in the United States and another 4 million abroad.

" 'I Want You Back' is probably the best pop record ever made," wrote Motown historian Don Waller in his book *The Motown Story*. "And when I say 'pop' I mean the way the record just explodes off your turntable. The arrangement is faultless—the bass playing alone is enough to turn your hair into snakes—and a ten-year-old Michael sings as if his lungs are about to burst into flames any second."

"The pros have told us that no group has ever had a better start than we did," Michael Jackson has remembered. "Ever."

Once "I Want You Back" was released, The Jackson 5 had an image makeover. Suzanne dePasse—now president of Motown Productions—was responsible for repackaging the youngsters. Stylists with Colorform models worked with them to come up with the best haircuts and stage outfits for each group member. Motown's famous charm school—the artist development classes held in Detroit to turn street kids like The Temptations into savvy showpeople—was no longer in business now that the company had relocated to Los Angeles. All of the image-changing work was done by whomever Gordy could coax into helping.

October 18, 1969, marked a major milestone—The Jackson 5's first appearance on national television, on "The Hollywood Palace," hosted by Diana Ross.

Backstage, Joe Jackson kept peppering his boys with last-minute advice, the way he always did before they performed. Michael once recalled that it was usually easy to tune Joe out; he'd said the same things a hundred times before. This evening, Joe was even more intense, according to Jack Lewis, a set designer on the ABC program.

"Joe paced back and forth backstage like a lion," he remembered. "There's no doubt in my mind he was more nervous than his kids. The boys were excited about the break. Diana Ross kept going backstage and having private conversations with Michael. She patted him on the head a lot, which I noticed annoyed him. Gordy was backstage also. Right before they went on, Gordy pulled all of them together in a huddle and had an impromptu conference. Then when he finished, Joe did the same thing. These boys were coached within an inch of their lives."

The fellows were dressed alike in the costumes they had worn for their debut appearance at the Daisy: pale lime green double-breasted, wide-lapeled, sleeveless jackets with matching bell-bottom slacks and suede boots in exactly the same shade. Their shirts with the full-gathered sleeves were pale gold. While many observers assumed that these outfits were paid for by Motown, actually they were purchased off the rack by Joe and Katherine back in Gary.

From behind the curtain, they heard Diana's introduction: "Tonight, I have the pleasure of introducing a young star who has been in the business all of his life. He's worked with his family, and when he sings and dances, he lights up the stage."

At that moment, Sammy Davis, Jr., came bounding out onto the stage. He supposedly thought Diana was introducing him. But Diana explained that she was referring to "Michael Jackson and the Jackson 5."

At that, the curtain opened and The Jackson 5 were on, singing "Sing a Simple Song."

Meanwhile, according to set designer Jack Lewis, Joe Jackson and Berry Gordy were having a heated conference backstage. "What's this 'Michael Jackson and the Jackson 5' stuff?" Joe demanded to know. "No one told me about that. No one cleared that with me."

Berry shrugged his shoulders. "It wasn't written that way on the cue card," he explained. "Diane, she just blurted it out."

"Well, I don't like it," Joe fumed. "All the boys are equal. We're not singling Michael out. It'll cause problems."

"But he's obviously the star." Berry tried to reason.

"They're *all* stars," Joe countered.

"Too late now," Berry said, shrugging his shoulders again. Then the two of them watched the rest of the performance. When the brothers finished their two songs—"Can You Remember?" and "I Want You Back"—the applause, led by Diana, was generous. She wore a white midriff-baring halter and white slacks which emphasized her reed-thin figure. Her hair was pulled into an elaborate topknot; her shoulder-length silver earrings flew to and fro when she started to dance with Michael.

"Are you sure Sammy Davis got started like this?" Michael asked during the routine.

At his name, Davis appeared and joined the dance briefly. Then he pulled Diana away for an "angry" exchange, acting as if he were upset that Michael had upstaged him. Unconcerned, Michael danced on until Sammy grabbed him. "I'm gonna put you in a sack, you eighty-one-year-old midget," Sammy growled, dragging him off the stage.

The words were said in jest, but the sentiment would be repeated time and time again. Michael Jackson was already a scene stealer. Any performer who shared a stage with him would have to watch out for him- or herself.

After the show, there was pandemonium backstage, with the boys whooping and hollering, slapping one another on the back, hugging each other. Joe was in the middle of it all, enjoying this sweet moment of victory with his sons.

Diana walked into the backstage area and went right to Michael. "I am so proud of you," she enthused. She hugged him tightly. "You are the best! Just the greatest. You're gonna be a big, *big* star."

Then she turned from Michael. "Will someone please get me a towel?" she asked. She raised her voice. "There should have been a towel back here waiting for me."

"I'll get you a towel," Michael offered. He disappeared for a moment and came back with a fluffy white towel. "Here, Miss Ross. Here's a towel," he said eagerly.

Diana smiled and took the towel. "Thanks, Michael." She patted him on the head. "Call me Diane. Okay?"

He beamed and ran off.

Berry walked over to Diana and as Jack Lewis listened, he asked her, "What was with that introduction, 'Michael Jackson and the Jackson 5?' "

Diana looked at him with a proud expression. "I threw that in myself."

"I know. But the father was really pissed off about it," Berry said.

Diana looked at Berry as if he were daft for caring what Joe thought. "So what?" she wanted to know. "Here, take this." She handed him the towel.

"Yeah," Berry agreed. He threw the towel over his shoulder. "So what?"

Not since Sammy Davis, Jr., had the world seen a child performer with such an innate command of himself on stage. Both as a singer and dancer, young Michael Jackson exuded a presence that was simply uncanny. After this youngster was heard recording Smokey Robinson's plaintive, bluesy "Who's Loving You," the question among Motown's staffers was "Where did he learn that kind of emotion?" The answer is that he didn't learn it anywhere, it just seemed to be there for him.

"I'll tell you the honest-to-God truth. I never knew what I was doing in the early days," Michael has confessed. "I just did it. I never knew how to sing, really. I didn't control it. It just formed itself."

Producers were always astonished at how Michael would play all the games that preteen children enjoy—cards, hide-and-seek—between recording sessions, and then step behind a microphone and belt a song with the emotional agility and presence of an old soul who's seen his share of heartache. Equally amazing was the fact that, aside from listening to demonstration tapes of the songs sung by a session singer to give him direction on the lead melody and Richards's constant prodding to clean up his diction, Michael was pretty much left to his own devices in the studio.

When he was told to sound like a rejected suitor, no one in the studio actually expected him to do it, to understand the emotion involved in heartbreak. How could they? After all, this was an eleven-year-old too small to sing up into the suspended boom microphone.

Producer Deke Richards used to have to sit Michael on top of a trash can in order for him to sing into that mike. Jermaine and Jackie would stand on either side of Michael—Marlon and Tito rarely recorded backing vocals since neither had a knack for harmony—and sheet music would be positioned in front of Michael's face on a music stand. From the control booth, all Richards could see in the studio were Jermaine and Jackie standing on either side of two sneakers dangling at the sides of a trash can. And he was to expect emotion from *that*?

Michael Jackson certainly wasn't the first black youngster America had heard sing so well for his age. Black teen-star Frankie Lymon, who fronted the group The Teenagers in the fifties, also had a vocal manner that belied his years. However, Michael's roots as a vocalist seemed more steeped in traditional black gospel—even though he never sang in a choir—and he was much more inventive and agile as a dancer than Frankie.

When Michael and his brothers became professional performers, there were probably a million youngsters with as much raw dancing talent. What set Michael apart from the schoolyard hoofers was his execution, undoubtedly gleaned from years of observing headliners in the rhythm-and-blues revues in which he and his brothers used to appear. The kid had an eye for what worked.

From legendary soul singer Jackie Wilson, Michael mastered the importance of onstage drama. He learned early on that dropping dramatically to one knee, an old Wilson tactic, usually made an audience whoop and holler. However, for the most part, watching young Michael at work was like observing an honor student of "James Brown 101." Michael appropriated everything he could from the self-proclaimed "hardest-working man in show business." Not only did he employ Brown's splits and the one-foot slides, he worked a microphone bold-soul style just like Brown—passionately jerking the stand around like a drunk might handle his girlfriend at the corner pool hall on a Saturday night.

Michael also pilfered James Brown's famous spin. However, back then, the spin didn't go over nearly as well with a crowd as Michael's version of another dance of the day that Brown popularized, the Camel Walk. When Michael strode across the floor of "American Bandstand" during The Jackson 5's first appearance on that program, even the audience of preppy white teenagers got caught up in the frenzy of excitement.

Young Michael wasn't influenced only by men. From Diana Ross, Michael got not only a sense of style, but an appreciation of power. Diana had a *quiet* authority, the power of presence. He'd observed how people reacted to her when she walked into a room. She was revered. Catered to. A special power. He liked that.

There was one other thing Michael got from Diana: his early *ooohs*. Michael's early vocal ad-libs were almost always punctuated with an *oooh* here or there; not a long-drawn-out *oooh*, but rather a stab, an exclamation mark. Diana used this effect on many of The Supremes recordings. Michael delighted in it, adopted it, and put it in his grab bag of influences. Every little *oooh* helped.

"He was driven, determined, intense, the biggest talent we'd seen since Diana," Smokey Robinson told writer David Ritz (who co-wrote Robinson's 1989 autobiography, *Smokey—Inside My Life*). "And the accompaniment of his brothers, bad-ass singers and dancers themselves, only added to the appeal."

On October 29, 1969, Ralph Seltzer petitioned Superior Court in California to review the Motown contract in order to be certain it satisfied California labor laws, since the Jacksons would now be residing in that state. This was a safeguard that Seltzer, a smart attorney, sought in order to avoid a potential problem. He did not want the Jackson family ever to be able to claim in a court of law that the contract should be considered invalid for not satisfying child labor laws. Seltzer, who was in Detroit, did not attend the hearing. Suzanne dePasse did, representing Motown. The Jackson boys and their father also appeared.

A deputy clerk asked each member of the group and Joseph Jackson if they were happy and satisfied with the contract and if it had been fully explained to them. All said they were and it had. Did they have any questions regarding the contract? No, they did not. "I think this is a good contract," eleven-year-old Michael, who hadn't read the agreement, stated. "I really do. I got no problem with it."

Judge Lester E. Olson then reviewed the agreement and seemed skeptical about the justness of some of the provisions. However, it was not his responsibility to make a decision about the contract's fairness. His purpose was to make certain that the contract satisfied child labor laws. The court decided that 25 percent of any money Michael Jackson and his brothers made, since all were legally minors, would be deposited into a savings account with Joseph Jackson as trustee—a routine arrangement since the Coogan Act of 1939. Seventy-five percent could be spent by the boys' parents without any culpability. Also, the judge decided that any brother who went on to record a solo single or album would not have to split his royalties with his siblings.

In court records filed six years later when the Jacksons were suing Motown, Suzanne dePasse recalled, "No member of The Jackson 5, or Joseph Jackson, ever expressed any opposition to the contracts. On the contrary, they were very enthusiastic about the contracts when they were in court."

Finally, at the beginning of November 1969, Berry Gordy leased a house for the Jackson family at 1601 Queens Road in Los Angeles. Michael moved in with his father and brothers. By this time the older boys had enrolled in Fairfax High School. According to Susie Jackson (maiden name, Smith), a classmate who would go on to marry Johnny Jackson, "My twin sister, me, and a friend were introduced to Jackie, Tito, and Johnny. We were told that these guys were with Motown. I thought, 'Big deal. They're probably from Detroit. Everybody in Detroit says they're with Motown.' I remember they had a bodyguard even back then, named Jack Richardson. Jack was an extremely close friend of the family's and Joe's right-hand man. Everyone called him Uncle Jack. Uncle Jack would pick them up after school every day in a van that had 'Jackson 5' written on the side of it. Finally, the boys told him to park near my house so they could walk us girls home and then drive on from there. Jackie started liking my sister, Tito liked a friend of mine, and Johnny liked me.

"One Saturday, we three girls snuck out and went up to the boys' big pink house on Queens Road. Oh, we were so nervous and scared to be up there because no visitors were allowed. Joe was very, very strict. They were up there rehearsing 'I Want You Back' for a performance. We had never heard it before. We listened as Michael sang. You knew he was a star, even then. He just had it, whatever it is. We were saying, 'My, my, if only he was a little older, like his brothers.' We said to each other, 'Wow, these guys are really good. They may go somewhere, sometime.'

"Afterwards," Susie Jackson continued, "they took us for a walk in the hills, showing us the homes of all the celebrities up there. As I was walking these hills, I got a sharp pain in my side. Five days later, I had an appendicitis attack and had to have my appendix removed. The next day I got a delivery, three dozen red roses from Johnny. My mother wanted to know, 'Who is this Johnny Jackson?' When I told her, well, what a scene! I'm Jewish and he was black.

"So while I was in intensive care, Joseph called the hospital to see how I was. My mother got on the phone with Joseph and he proceeded to tell her how we girls had snuck up to the house and, he said, 'They looked like they were gettin' ready to get into something.' Joe played watchdog the whole time we were up there, so we weren't about to get into *anything*. I mean, we were just fifteen years old and scared to death.''

In December 1969, Katherine, Janet, LaToya, and Randy joined the rest of the family in Los Angeles. Motown paid for their flight. It was their first plane ride.

Katherine was so relieved now that her family had left Gary. For years she had been waiting for this move. Her husband and Jack Richardson met her and the children at the Los Angeles airport. If Katherine was disappointed that the boys weren't there to meet them too, she didn't show it. After waiting this long to see them, another half hour or so wouldn't mean that much. Joe tried to hug his wife but found it difficult as Katherine tried to keep the three very excited youngsters firmly in check. When Joe roared, ''Whoa, calm down,'' they stopped jumping, but only momentarily.

''Welcome to California, Kate,'' he said. ''Sure took you a long time to get here.''

As the car drove up to the house, the boys were waiting on the front lawn. Michael was the first to throw himself into Katherine's arms. ''My, my, but you got so big,'' she said, tears streaming down her face, as she hugged each of her boys in turn. Jackie, ever the tease, lifted Marlon up and tossed him in the air. ''Me next, me next,'' three-year-old Janet squealed.

Katherine would recall that, once inside, she took a long look around the living room. It was so large—twice the size of the entire house in Gary—that she was dumbstruck. ''It ain't Gary, that's for sure,'' Joe told her with a proud smile. Then Joe had Katherine close her eyes. He led his wife, her eyes firmly shut, out to the backyard patio. ''Okay, you can open them now,'' he told her.

Stretched below their hillside home lay the panorama of nighttime Los Angeles. Thousands—*millions*—of lights twinkled like earth-bound stars. ''This must be what heaven looks like,'' Katherine said when she could speak. ''I've never seen anything so beautiful.''

''Well, it's here for you every night,'' Joe told her.

Katherine asked that she be left alone for just a moment. She would recall shaking her head in wonderment at the view and hoping that all of this wasn't a dream, that she would never wake up back in bed in Gary.

''It's lovely, isn't it?''

Katherine whirled around at the sound of the woman's unfamiliar voice, but before either of them could say anything, Michael was at Katherine's side.

"Momma, this is *her*. This is Diana Ross. Isn't she beautiful? Isn't she just beautiful?"

Later, telling a friend about the incident, Katherine would remember that, although it was too dark to see Diana clearly, she could tell that she was as slim, young, and attractive as she appeared on the television screen. Katherine became painfully aware of how she herself must have looked to the glamorous Diana. But much to her surprise, Diana seemed warm and friendly. She took Katherine's hand. "Mrs. Jackson, I am so happy to meet you. Your kids have talked about you so much. They are just the best."

As pleased as she was to hear her children praised this way, Katherine would recall that she could not help wondering why Diana was there and when she had come. Diana must have sensed her unspoken questions. "Oh, I was just visiting," she said by way of explanation. She hugged Katherine warmly and kissed her on the cheek.

Katherine told her that she was grateful for all Diana had done for her boys, especially Michael, and that she was happy to be able now to raise him herself. At this point, Diana seemed to become uncomfortable; her attitude suddenly changed.

"I'm thrilled for you, I really am," Diana said. "I'd love to chat about the whole thing, but I can't because I'm very busy."

"Can't you at least stay for a cup of coffee?" Katherine offered.

"No, not really. I must run now. I'm sure you understand."

"Oh . . . sure," Katherine said, "sure I do."

Without another word, Diana turned and walked into the night.

"Bye," Michael called, but Diana didn't answer.

Katherine hugged Michael. Then, without a backward glance at the incredible view, mother and son walked hand in hand into the house to begin their new life.

# Chapter

## 5

By the end of 1969, Michael Jackson, now eleven years old and finally reunited with his mother, was a bubbly, energetic, and happy youngster. "All I want now is to see how far we can go as a family," he told *Soul* magazine reporter Judy Spiegelman. "I like show business, Hollywood, and all that stuff, the things people like Berry Gordy do to make you look good. I'm real excited about things."

In December, Motown Records released The Jackson 5's first album, *Diana Ross Presents The Jackson 5*. It would go on to sell 629,363 copies, amazing for a debut album.

"Honesty has always been a very special word for me—a special idea," Diana Ross wrote in the liner notes. "But when I think of my own personal idea of honesty, I think of something being straight out, all there, on the table—the way it is . . . That's how I feel about The Jackson 5—five brothers by the name of Jackson whom I discovered in Gary, Indiana. They've got great talent," Diana Ross concluded. "And above all, they're honest."

Michael read an advance proof of the album jacket in one of the Motown offices as his brothers and a promotion man looked on.

"Wouldn't even let us play our own instruments on the album," Tito grumbled. "But here we are in the picture holdin' 'em like we played 'em. Don't seem right to me."

Tito and Jermaine were not permitted to play their bass and guitar in the Motown sessions. All of the instrumental music was recorded before they even got to the studio. Yet they would have to learn to duplicate the sound when they performed live.

"I think we should be playin' on this record album here," Tito decided.

Michael rolled his eyes. "So?" he asked.

"So, it's not true," Tito said.

"And what about this part?" Jermaine asked, still looking over Michael's shoulder. He pointed to Diana's line about discovering the group.

Michael shrugged his shoulders. "It's called *public relations*," he said, matter-of-factly. "C'mon, guys. Get with it."

"He was really into this image thing at a pretty early age," said Stan Sherman, the independent promotion man who witnessed the above exchange. "The other boys were sort of befuddled about all the lies. But not Michael. Once you explained it to him, he not only agreed with it but, I think, he even started to believe it. That was, to me, just a bit frightening. He seemed a little too eager to adjust to the fantasy of it all."

Later in the month, on December 14, 1969, The Jackson 5 appeared on "The Ed Sullivan Show." Although they had already made one national television appearance ("The Hollywood Palace" in October), being asked to perform on "The Ed Sullivan Show" was an important milestone in their career. The prestigious program, which had made its debut in June 1948 as "Toast of the Town," had become "The Ed Sullivan Show" in 1955 and would continue weekly—and live—until June 1971. The CBS Sunday 8:00-9:00 P.M. time slot became the TV mecca for entertainers.

The program couldn't credit its success to its host. Stiff and unsmiling, Sullivan, a columnist for the *New York Daily News*, did little more than introduce his guests, whose names he routinely mispronounced or forgot. The audience could not have cared less. The lure of the show was its roster of guests. Newcomers knew they had the brass ring in reach when they were asked to perform; those already established were assured they were still on top. Ed Sullivan never bothered with has-beens or wanna-be's.

Before the group's performance, Sullivan encountered Michael wandering around backstage. He had watched the boys in dress rehearsal and been impressed. He went up to the eleven-year-old, shook his hand, and said, "Never forget where your talent came from, that your talent is a gift from God." As soon as Sullivan introduced this "sensational group," Marlon, Jackie, and Michael, flanked by Tito and Jermaine on guitar, started their set with their rendition of the Sly Stone song, "Stand." They were dressed in a variety of mod clothes purchased off the rack in Greenwich Village by Suzanne dePasse.

In some respects, this was an awkward appearance. Tito looked as though he'd rather be somewhere else; Jermaine sounded loud and slightly off-key, and Jackie had the misfortune of being bracketed by two brothers who didn't even reach his shoulders. Although he was not a dreadful dancer, Jackie was longer on energy than finesse, and being part of such a trio made him look like an uncoordinated giant counting "one-two-three-turn-stomp-step-stomp."

Michael, again, was clearly the star. When he sang, his eyes sparkled. He looked adorable in his magenta cowboy hat. Anyone who saw the performance would remember how impossibly cute this little kid was. No diamond in the rough, this one. He was already a polished, seasoned performer, an odd but fascinating combination of James Brown theatrics and Diana Ross charisma. When he sang "Can You Remember?" his voice had a purity and range of tone that belied his years. By the time The Jackson 5 finished the set with a rousing "I Want You Back," the audience had been completely won over.

As was his tradition, Sullivan engaged in some minimal banter with his guests, but he soon turned his attention to a member of the audience, "the person who discovered The Jackson 5, Diana Ross." Diana, clad in what can only be described as a grown-up version of a little girl's pink organdy party dress, stood and modestly took a bow. After a round of handshaking, complicated by Sullivan's having too many hands to shake, Sullivan waved the Jacksons offstage. Just to appear with Ed Sullivan was an accomplishment. To receive such rousing applause seemed a clear prophecy for success.

At this particular time, Joe and Katherine began to question the wisdom of having Berry Gordy's and Diana Ross's names so absolutely linked to the success of their children. As the boys' parents, they felt they were ultimately responsible for the group's success. They began to feel slighted when Motown played up Berry's and Diana's contributions and played down theirs—especially in press interviews.

Soon Joe began arranging interviews for himself and his wife, which did not sit well with some of the Motown bigwigs, especially Gordy, who felt that the parents were not sophisticated enough to handle the media with Motownlike aplomb. Not much could be done about it, however, since Gordy wasn't able to keep the parents quiet when they felt the need to publicly pat themselves on the back. "Let 'em say whatever they want to say," Gordy decided in one high-level meeting. "But keep me posted on what they end up saying." Ever the company watchdog, Gordy wanted to protect his corporate assets, and didn't want anyone to interfere—and that included the Jackson parents.

Now the difficult task at hand was to follow The Jackson 5's first number one record with another chart-topper. Berry Gordy gave the chore to Deke Richards and the Corporation, as it was his policy to allow the writers and producers of any hit song the opportunity to come up with another one just as successful.

"One night I was at Fonce's [Mizell] and Freddie's [Perren] apartment and we were fooling around on their electric piano," recalled Deke Richards, "and I started thinking about Holland, Dozier, and Holland and how they often did the same types of records over and over again, using the same progressions. Theirs was a proven hit formula. So I took a section of 'I Want You Back'—the part where the group sings the chorus—and decided to make those exact same chords the foundation of their next single.

"I was sitting at the piano and playing these chords and I came up with the lyric 'A, B, C.' The guys looked at me like I was crazy. So then what? 'I know,' I said. 'How about, "One, two, three." ' By now they thought I was nuts. And then I came up with the next line, 'Do, re, mi.' And I finished with a big bang, 'You and me.'

"That's it," Deke told them. "That's a hit. Now, you guys work on it and get back to me." After Deke came up with the premise of the song, it was just a matter of writing appropriate lyrics. In a short time, Deke, Fonce, and Freddie were in the studio recording the song "ABC" with Michael and his brothers.

"ABC," when finished, would turn out to be the only Jackson 5 record ever done with no instrumental overdubs. In other words, the instrumentation heard on the record is exactly what was played in the studio the first time it was recorded, with nothing added later.

"I loved 'ABC' from the first moment I heard it," Michael said. "I had more enthusiasm for that than I did for 'I Want You Back.' It was just such a hot song, such a great idea with a great track. I couldn't wait to record it. I remember when Deke Richards and the other guys were making up the middle of the song right there on the spot, the 'Siddown girl, I think I love you . . .' Then it was 'Shake it, shake it, baby,' you know, like The Contours and old groups like that. I didn't know you could do that in the studio, just come up with parts like that at the last minute. I always wondered how much it cost to record 'ABC.' I'll bet it was a fortune, because we spent a lot of time on it."

When the song was finally recorded, Deke played the tape for

Berry. "Oh, no. Man, you've blown it," Berry told him. "You have really blown it."

"What do you mean?" Deke asked.

"Your lyric is 'A, B, C, easy as one, two, three.' But that's all wrong. It *should* be 'One, two, three, easy as A, B, C.' Start the song off with one, two, three. In fact, you oughta call it that: 'One, Two, Three.' "

" 'One, Two, Three'? No way, man. No way!" Deke argued.

In retrospect, this certainly sounds like a comical disagreement, but when one considers the money invested in The Jackson 5's career and the fact that much of Berry's success over the years had been the result of sheer instinct, it was an argument Deke had to take seriously.

Berry was unrelenting, so Deke went back into the studio and recorded The Jackson 5 singing the lyrics Gordy's way. After they were done, he played the tape for Berry. Berry shook his head and laughed. "You were right, man," he said. "It definitely should be the other way. 'ABC,' not 'One, Two, Three.' Sorry. Now, you'll have to rerecord it."

"No, I won't," Deke said with a sly grin. "I never erased the other one. I had a feeling you'd see it my way, eventually." Berry had to laugh.

In February 1970, Motown released "ABC," the second Jackson 5 single. As Deke Richards predicted, Gordy's Corporation had developed a successful hit formula for The Jackson 5 in much the same way that Holland-Dozier-Holland had done for The Supremes. Buzzing basses, sprightly keyboards, and a charmingly enthusiastic Michael took their second Motown single straight to the top of the *Billboard* charts only six weeks after its release, supplanting "Let It Be" by The Beatles. The song, which sold 2,214,790 copies—even more copies than "I Want You Back"—seemed to poke fun at, and also make acceptable, a new and growing trend in popular music, the predominantly white "bubble gum" style. The Jackson 5 were on a roll.

"They just wanted to entertain," Joe Jackson said of his boys as they hit number one. "I don't think they expected all of this to happen to them so fast. I wanted them to go straight to the top. It's what I've always wanted, what I've been pushing for. And that's where they're going. They're going to be superstars, mark my words."

Freddie Perren recalled, "After those two hit singles, Berry Gordy kept saying, 'What about the follow-up? What about the follow-up?' He wasn't worried, but he really wanted to bring that third one home. We were cutting the track at the Sound Factory in Hollywood; Berry never came to a tracking session, but he came to this one. We hadn't finished it yet. He stayed and listened for about fifteen minutes, then said, 'It's okay. You guys got a hit. I'm not worried.' And he left. That's when we knew we had it.''

That song was "The Love You Save," released in May 1970, another terrific teenybopper song with a breathless lead by Michael and many of the same chords from "I Want You Back" and "ABC." Cute verses and a bit of clever pleading in the chorus was the bait. The infectious combination of guitars and percussion was the hook. At 1,948,761 sold copies, this one came up a little short in comparison to the sales of the preceding two singles but was still considered a huge hit. Gordy wanted three number one songs for the group, and, as usual, he got what he wanted. "The Love You Save" also gave The Jackson 5 the distinction of being the first group of the rock era to have their first three songs go to the top. Again, they knocked The Beatles ("The Long and Winding Road") out of the number one spot.

The Jackson 5 made their first concert appearance as a Motown attraction at the Philadelphia Convention Center on Saturday evening, May 2. Despite their terrific record sales, no one could have guessed how popular they had become in barely five months. In an incident recalling The Beatles' reception when that group first stepped foot on U.S. shores in 1964, more than thirty-five hundred screaming fans mobbed Philadelphia International Airport hoping to catch a glimpse of the young brothers. Only a huge force of Philadelphia's finest and airport security officers protected the Jacksons from being completely overwhelmed. Hysterical fans broke through barriers at the airport to mob the group. The scene was repeated the following evening at the concert, with one hundred police officers forcing the audience back from the stage time and time again. Three motorcycle-escorted limousines managed to get The Jackson 5 back to their hotel after the concert. Once Michael got into his room, he broke down and started crying.

"Michael [who was eleven years old] was scared to death," Jermaine said. "The rest of us were more amazed than scared, but Mike was genuinely frightened. 'I don't know if I can do this forever,' he said. 'Maybe for a little while, but not forever.' ''

The pandemonium served as a warning to Motown that the next time the brothers made a concert, the company should be better prepared.

That same month, The Jackson 5's second album, *ABC*, was

released. It would go on to be even more successful than the debut album, selling 867,756 copies. While the group took pictures for the jacket at Santa Monica beach, one of Berry Gordy's former girlfriends, Chris Clark, found a snake in the bushes. Michael was thrilled by the discovery. He caught the snake with a paper bag just before it crawled into a hole and then took it home with him as a pet. It was the beginning of Michael's fascination with snakes.

Berry Gordy arranged for the family to move from the home on Queens Road to a bigger one on Bowmont Drive above Trousdal Estates. Liberace lived nearby, as did Davy Jones of The Monkees. "They [the Jacksons] were kicked out of several houses," Berry Gordy explained to Michael Goldberg in a rare interview in *Rolling Stone*. "You see, they would make too much noise. They had their band, and we would put them in a house, and then they would get kicked out. We'd lease another place, and they would make too much noise, and they would get kicked out."

The Bowmont Drive home was a modern structure built on stilts; it looked like a motel. In fact, one reporter referred to it as "The Jackson Motel" in his feature for *Crawdaddy* magazine. "You can drive right under the house and stop, get out and check in at the desk," he wrote, "then drive around and park in a lot that would hold fifteen cars, easy." He described the stucco home as "massive, blank and square," with "wall-to-wall shag, plastic furniture and trophies." A female German shepherd named Lobo patrolled the premises. The family's friends would wait outside in their cars in the parking lot and call up to the check-in window, "Where's Lobo?" and then wait for an answer before venturing onto the property.

"That dog," Michael noted at the time, "you turn your back on her and she jump right *on* your back. Jumped on Tony Jones [a Motown executive] last week. We pulled her off just in time."

Soon after they moved into their new home, the family discovered—much to their amazement—that their address was included in the "Map to the Stars," sold to tourists in novelty shops and on street corners. As a result, fans often visited the family. Young girls would show up unexpectedly in the parking lot.

"I hear ya'll are havin' a party up there," one of them once shouted up to the house. Lobo sat in the corner, slobbering menacingly. After no reaction, her older friend, who had driven them there, shouted, "Hey, ya'll! We need to use the *bathroom* up there and we scared of dogs." Katherine decided that the fans were cute, and, as she often did, she put Lobo in a walk-in closet and invited the girls to dinner. Katherine may have lived in a fine house on a hill, but she still had a down-home heart. She made everyone feel welcome.

"Livin' up on this big hill is weird," Jermaine observed to writer Tim Tyler for *Creem* magazine. "The nearest store is five miles away."

Michael mentioned later, "We have to make our own beds. We don't have no maid here."

In July 1970, The Jackson 5 broke attendance records at the Los Angeles Forum, raking up 18,675 paid admissions. The concert grossed $105,000. "I was at that concert at the Forum with Berry and Diana," said the group's producer Deke Richards. "We almost got trampled to death. Before they started 'The Love You Save,' Michael said something like 'Here it is, the tune that knocked The Beatles out of number one,' and that caused sheer pandemonium. We were in the third row, and in the middle of the concert we heard this tumultuous sound and the rows were folding one at a time, people falling all over themselves. Someone ran onto the stage and got the kids off. They didn't even finish the song. Berry, Diana, and I got out of our row just in time before it was toppled over by kids trying to get to the stage."

A month later, the company issued The Jackson 5's first ballad, "I'll Be There." Switching gears to a ballad seemed to Gordy to be the obvious next step, yet it would have to be the right song in order to be accepted by fans accustomed to an upbeat sound.

"It was time for a change," Deke Richards says. "I didn't mind that I hadn't worked on that one. That was just a solid hit. It had to be done. The Corporation moved too slow, I guess. I was such a stickler for detail, we couldn't come up with the change record fast enough. So Berry had them cut 'I'll Be There.' "

"I'll Be There" was a tender blend of soulful pleading and sweetly delivered inspiration. To the strains of harpsichords and keyboards, Michael's performance was flawless. The song is considered to be the one record that solidified The Jackson 5's success as versatile recording stars. It was number one for five weeks.

Recalled its writer, Willie Hutch, "Berry and I put that together for the boys and Hal Davis produced it. We cut him [Michael] in a higher key than usual, which gave his voice a really angelic sound. I remember that Michael's performance was so flawless, it made us both want to cry. And Berry and I were tough guys; we didn't cry easily. The kid had such amazing interpretive power.

"Berry used to have a girl at the company [Suzy Ikeeda] stand next to Michael in the studio and coach him, trying to get the performance out of him. Each and every word was the product of a great deal of thought in terms of how it was delivered. It wasn't impromptu or ad-lib by any means. Just like Motown, it was all well planned and executed. A lot of people predicted that 'I'll Be There' would go nowhere, but Berry believed in the record. As always, Berry was right. In three days, the record sold over two and a half million copies.''

"I'll Be There" pushed Neil Diamond's "Crackling Rosie" out of the number one position on *Billboard*'s pop charts and became Motown's biggest-selling record; the company claimed that over 4 million copies sold, but actually the figure totaled some 800,000 copies less, 3,178,523 copies. The Jackson 5 became the first act in pop music history whose first four singles each became number one hits on the *Billboard* chart. Or, as Michael put it, "It just kept gettin' better and better.''

In October 1970, the group took their act on the road again for additional dates on the East Coast. Motown executives discovered that even the most careful planning could be thwarted by any number of unexpected events, especially the enthusiasm of overzealous fans and the unpredictability of Mother Nature. Motown's Bob Jones (who is Michael Jackson's publicist today) remembered the tour's kickoff at the Boston Garden on October 9.

"Before they were able to finish their last number, we had to get them out of there real fast. Even with the security force and twelve-foot-high stage, the group was rushed by overly enthusiastic fans.''

Meanwhile at Cincinnati Gardens Stadium where they would play the next day, officials prepared for the worst. Jones recalled, "Workmen constructed not only the fourteen-foot-high stage that had originally been ordered, but a barricade of risers to ring the stage as further precaution. A double force of security police mapped our security strategy, which included a cordon of officers around the barricade to protect the boys from any attempt at mobbing by the audience. Tickets to the concert were sold out and thousands of kids had to be turned away. During the show, fourteen girls fainted and had to be carried out as Jermaine sang a song called 'I Found That Girl.' The aisles were mobbed throughout the performance and local disc jockeys had to beg for quiet and order.''

After that brief, five-city tour, Jones reported, "When the total tour figures were computed, everyone at Motown was amazed. The boys had entertained one hundred thousand people and grossed $580,000. Home again in Los Angeles, the guys nursed sore throats and road-weary bodies for one day before it was back to private school . . . and worrying how they were going to dress up for Halloween.''

In November 1970, three dates in Texas were placed in jeopardy when the concerts were opposed by members of the Southern Christian Leadership Council's Operation Breadbasket. Dick Clark was promoting the tour and Breadbasket representatives felt that someone black should have been hired by Motown.

''That's absolutely ridiculous,'' Berry Gordy said. ''Black, white. What the hell's the difference as long as we all make money.''

Still, the protestors had leaflets printed up and were preparing to picket at the concert sites. The press was waiting for a scandal. ''Just what we need,'' Berry told a Motown promoter working with Dick Clark. ''Cancel. Tell Clark to cancel the whole goddamn state. They'll see The Jackson 5 when they get some sense.'' The dates were canceled.

# Chapter

## 6

IT'S NOT GOING to be all fun and games," Diana Ross had told Michael Jackson. "There's going to be a lot of hard work too."

By January 1971, twelve-year-old Michael Jackson understood that entertainment was a difficult business—he had seen it firsthand for the last couple of years—but still managed to take in stride all the pressures of recording, touring, and making television appearances. His success was still too new to be anything but a constant thrill. "This is the best thing that ever happened to us," Michael said of his family's accomplishments. "Diana Ross has told me that people in show business can get hurt. I don't see how, to tell you the truth. Maybe one day I will, but I kinda doubt it."

Nineteen seventy-one started out on a sentimental note when, on January 31, The Jackson 5 returned to Gary, Indiana, their hometown. At this time, Jackie was nineteen; Tito, seventeen; Jermaine, sixteen; Marlon, thirteen; and Michael, twelve. On behalf of Mayor Richard Gordon Hatcher's reelection campaign, the group was asked to perform two concerts at Westside High School. The distance between Gary and Los Angeles can be measured in miles, but the distance between Gary and stardom can only be measured in light years. The Jackson 5 were coming back as stars. They arrived in style, in a helicopter that landed in Westside High's parking lot, where two thousand students gathered in subzero weather to cheer.

Both concerts were a sellout. Fifteen thousand lucky ticket holders—most of them with their own (largely imaginary) personal recollections—came to pay homage to five homeboys. Two years ago, neighborhood kids had thrown stones at the Jackson house to taunt the group as they rehearsed; now these very same people were touting themselves as former best friends. As the spotlights revealed the Jacksons in their rainbow-hued regalia, the group's fans started screaming. The gym was packed to the rafters with what was probably the noisiest audience the Jackson boys had ever encountered. There were so many flashbulbs popping at once, it looked as though flocks of fireflies had come to swarm.

The group put on a high-energy performance in spite of obstacles that could have thrown more experienced performers. With a loud band behind them and constant cheering out front, they often couldn't hear their own voices, yet they carried on with thorough professionalism. Gary was justly proud of them and it showed.

After the first concert, Mayor Hatcher escorted the Jackson family back to their former residence on Jackson Street, which had, for the day, been renamed Jackson 5 Boulevard in their honor. A sign was placed on the lawn in front of the old homestead at 2300 Jackson Street: WELCOME HOME JACKSON FIVE. KEEPERS OF THE DREAM. Fans hurled themselves at the tightly closed windows of the limo as it pulled away. Their next stop was city hall, where the group was presented individual keys to the city while their new single, "Mama's Pearl," played in the background.

The Jackson 5 had returned home as heroes and symbols of hope. Mayor Hatcher said he was honored that "The Jackson 5 has carried the name of Gary throughout the country and the world, and made it a name to be proud of."

"We're glad to be home," Tito said during the presentation. "There's no place like home."

During their brief stay in Gary, a cousin hosted a party for them in the basement of his home, and the Jackson boys met relatives they didn't even know they had. Everybody brought cakes and fried chicken and treated each boy as if he were a prince. Their reign as royalty was only temporary. Their return to Los Angeles meant school and work.

On a stylistic par with their previous upbeat singles, January 1971's "Mama's Pearl" featured Michael in the lead again, surrounded by his brothers offering an occasional lead line through the verses, buzzing guitars on the choruses, and the Corporation's swirling production throughout. It was another first for The Jackson 5, for the single ascended the charts within the usual monthly span but failed to reach the top position. "Mama's Pearl" was halted at number two.

From the beginning, there was some hesitation about "Mama's Pearl." Deke Richards decided to have Fonce Mizell and Freddie Perren work on a Jackson 5 single without him. What they came up with was a song called "Guess Who's Making Whoopie (With Your Girlfriend)."

Deke Richards walked into the studio to find Michael sitting on his trashcan and singing into the boom mike a line that went, "He said what's mine is his and his is all mine . . ." The song was about girl swapping, certainly not the right image for the young Jacksons. Richards had Perren and Mizell rework the lyrics, and eventually they came up with "Mama's Pearl"—same track as the original composition, just new lyrics.

Even though the record "only" went to the number two on *Billboard*'s chart, it was number one on *Cash Box*'s, so Berry was satisfied.

Motown's merchandising campaign for The Jackson 5 was in full swing by this time. In his book *Trapped: Michael Jackson and the Crossover Dream*, writer Dave Marsh noted, "Gordy understood that the increasing assimilation of the black middle class into American consumer culture and the new affluence of the highest level of black workers [the kind of guys who had union jobs in the steel mills of Gary and the auto factories of Detroit] had created a black teen-age market with amounts of surplus spending money similar to those of white teens. But nobody was marketing to the black kids—there was no category of teen idols to appeal especially to *them*."

There had never been soul idols for young blacks before. The Temptations, Miracles, Four Tops—none of their members was considered a teen idol in Motown's heyday. They were all much too old. Berry Gordy found a need, and he was anxious to fill it.

Gordy hired Fred Rice, an entertainment marketing specialist, to orchestrate the sales of Jackson 5 novelty items like posters and buttons with their pictures on them. Rice had done similar work successfully for The Beatles and Monkees.

"This is the first time in my twenty-four years in the business that we've had anything like this," he said at the time. "I call 'em the black Beatles. They're heroes, it's unbelievable. Of course, we tested the market with paper first. Poster and decal stickers with pictures of the kids, and if they go, then you do the toys, clothes, buttons, the hard stuff. We're just now getting out the clothes, and we're negotiating for a Jackson 5 hairspray and for a Jackson 5 watch."

Berry Gordy had never seen pandemonium like this before. The closest he had ever gotten to such a phenomenon occurred when The Supremes endorsed Coca-Cola and lent their name to a brand of white bread in Detroit. "We're gonna make a mint," he was telling all of his Motown associates. "We're gonna make a fuckin' mint on these kids."

Fred Rice's enthusiasm could not be contained. He told a reporter for *Creem* magazine, "All their stuff has their logo on it, a J-5 with a heart growing out of the bottom of it, and some of 'em have a heart in a circle, that means soul . . . and I'm putting out the Jackson 5 magazine, we call it *TCB*, that'll come out quarterly with all of their vital statistics, color pictures, song lyrics. We're doing everything. The kids just grab this subteen market. The twelve-to-thirteen-year-old girl, she just flips over Jermaine, and now that Michael's coming along, it's a whole new subteen adoration . . . that used to come in the movies. Now it's in records, because movies are too expensive a way to develop new young talent, music is the economical way to do it . . ."

Rice also issued a record release with Motown called *Jackson 5 Rapping*. No music. Just the five Jacksons talking about themselves.

From the beginning, Motown executives were always concerned with public relations. Berry Gordy and his artistic staff trained their top Motown stars, like Diana Ross and the Supremes and The Temptations, to participate in interviews, be amiable, and reveal nothing of consequence. They were encouraged to be suspicious of reporters and to protect their public images.

While it may be good business from time to time to withhold information that could actually harm a career and an artist's reputation—one member of The Temptations was a drug addict, and it certainly wouldn't have been a good idea for him to make this information public—Motown artists were encouraged to lie about the most mundane things, making these issues much more important than they actually were. For example, Diana Ross would insist that the neighborhood in which she grew up was a ghetto slum when in truth it was lower-middle-class and respectable. Her version made her look like a modern-day Cinderella.

From the time Michael Jackson was ten—and was told to shave two years off his age—he knew he had an "image" to cherish and guard. Michael was taught to believe that the press was out to get him and that in this media war it was every man—or boy—for himself. Motown publicists would bombard the group with sample questions and have them memorize pat answers. Michael repeated the Diana Ross discovery story so many times with such sincerity it seemed that even *he* believed it after a while.

Although the fellows wore the large Afros that were in style at the time, they weren't allowed to discuss the relevance of the look or how it related to their African ancestry.

Once, an *Ingenue* interviewer asked if their hairstyle "had something to do with Black Power," and a Motown press agent almost had a fit. "These are children, not adults. Let's not get into that," he bristled. Jackie was humiliated. He was twenty at the time and eligible to vote. Michael—a media master at the age of thirteen—understood that his lack of social consciousness would not look good when the writer's story appeared. Before he left, he gave the writer a soul handshake and a big wink. After that, Motown's press department insisted that anyone who wanted to interview the Jacksons agree not to ask any questions about politics or drugs. The more the press was forbidden to ask, the more curious it became.

Although Michael Jackson rarely grants interviews, he is considered by most reporters to be "poor copy" when he does deem to spend time with a writer. It is the rare journalist who can squeeze in-depth responses out of Michael or any of his brothers.

In the beginning, Motown was so concerned with protecting the Jackson's precious wholesomeness that the fellows were taught rote answers to stock questions, but they were never taught how to analyze their careers or their music. It was as if none of them—especially the older ones—had even a clue as to how their sound was developed at Motown, what their influences were, and what importance they were beginning to have in the world of pop music. When they were asked probing questions, they often mistook these queries for criticism and reacted by being defensive. Tired of being "picked on," they would revert to saying as little as possible in any necessary interview.

If they appeared dull, that was fine with Joe Jackson. He had ruled the family with an iron fist, giving the boys very little freedom, and was proud of the way they had turned out. "You see, my sons were never allowed to run the streets like a lot of other kids did," he said. "They were never out all times of the night. They always had to be in just when it would start to get dark, and we knew where they were at all times.

"They never went riding around in different cars with different kids, and they never got into any kind of trouble. Their record is clean and we hope to keep it clean. As a father, you have to stand behind your kids and talk to them and help them learn what is right and what isn't. We're a strong family. My kids are well behaved. It's been that way ever since they could walk. And I intend to make certain it stays that way."

Joe thought he was doing the right thing by making their decisions for them. But in the end, he harmed his sons. For too many years, every aspect of their lives was controlled—by Motown and by Joe. Someone was always telling them what to wear, what to say, what to sing, and what to think. Because they were rarely allowed to experiment with new ideas, either personally or professionally, as adults they would find it difficult to cope with relationships and finances.

Joe was once asked how he disciplined the youngsters. "Holding back their allowances is the one thing I find that really gets to them," he said. "I manage their money, of course, and a lot of it is held in trust. But we have a strict allowance system too. I take away their allowance when something comes up wrong."

"I don't know what Joe was like as a parent, but I do remember Michael as being the most well-behaved, cute kid," said Eddie Carroll, who—for fifteen dollars a haircut, which Motown paid for—cut Michael's hair regularly when the Jacksons first became successful. "When he would come into the shop [in West Hollywood], the whole place would go nuts and everyone wanted to watch as I cut his hair. If someone wanted an autograph, Michael would get up out of the chair while I was trying to cut his hair and go over and sign his name for someone. He wasn't at all shy or introverted. I found him to be outgoing and friendly. A limousine would bring him to the shop and then take him back home after the haircut."

Meanwhile, the Jackson's success began encouraging other family acts to get into the business. None made as much of an impact as The Osmonds. Formed in 1959 as a barbershop quartet, the sons of George and Olive Osmond first sang at their Mormon Church's family night in their hometown of Ogden, Utah. In December 1962, the group first appeared on "The Andy Williams Show," and they remained regulars throughout its five-year run. Donny joined the act when he was six years old.

In 1971, The Osmonds' lineup consisted of Alan, twenty-two; Wayne, twenty; Merrill, seventeen; Jay, sixteen; and Donny, fourteen. Writer George Jackson had submitted a song to Berry Gordy for The Jackson 5 in 1970. Gordy didn't like the song because he thought it was too juvenile, and he rejected it. A year later, The Osmonds were signed by Mike Curb to MGM Records. Curb saw The Osmonds as his answer to The Jackson 5. He sent them to Fame Studios in Muscle Shoals, Alabama, where producer Rick Hall recorded them singing the song Gordy had rejected. The group managed to do a fascinating impersonation of The Jackson 5 with

Donny affecting a Michael-like shrill counterlead to Merrill's "soulful" Jermaine-sounding lead vocal. That record, "One Bad Apple," went on to be a million-selling number one song. It stayed at the top of the charts for five weeks.

"When 'One Bad Apple' became a hit, Berry just slapped his forehead and said, 'Jesus, who would've guessed?'" according to longtime associate Nancy Leiviska.

Joe Jackson was a little less composed. This was the first time he questioned Berry's judgment. "He handed those white boys a song we should have recorded," Joe told a reporter in an off-the-record interview. "To me, that's fuckin' unbelievable. And Mormons too. They don't even let blacks in their religion! Every time I hear those white boys imitating my sons, I cringe."

Michael may have been only twelve, but even he could see that sometimes imitation is not the sincerest form of flattery. "They could have been a little more original," Michael said. "I mean, that record sounds exactly like us. Exactly!" Michael would recall that "our own relatives thought 'One Bad Apple' was us."

The Osmonds—with nine siblings in the family, just like the Jacksons—would continue to have Jackson 5 soundalike records ("Double Lovin'," "Yo-Yo"). Their first album for MGM would include a medley of Temptations songs they called "Motown Special."

Deke Richards observed, "The problem, of course, was that the Osmonds were white and the Jacksons were black, and if middle America had its choice at that time, and parents saw their kids watching these two groups that they loved and had a feeling for on television, I think in a second they would rather have them watching five young white kids than five black kids."

Motown's official statement about The Osmonds, from the company's vice-president, Ewart Abner: "This is an older white group. They have been out there for a long time and finally hit on something that is commercially successful. We here at Motown are not mad at anybody. We wish them luck, while we go on doing our thing, and they go on doing—our thing."

The Jackson 5's next single, "Never Can Say Good-bye," was released in March 1971 and peaked at number two a month later.

The song's writer, actor Clifton Davis, recalled, "This was an emotional song that meant a lot to me when I wrote it. I wanted to sing it myself, really. But how could I resist letting Michael Jackson have it. His was one of the great voices of the time, and Motown was one of the great powers. But I was worried that Michael might not understand the lyrics of pain and heartbreak. I recall him asking about one of the lines. 'What's this word mean? *Anguish,*' he asked me. I explained it. He shrugged his shoulders and just sang the line. "There's that anguish, there's that doubt," he sang. And I believed him.''*

It wasn't enough that The Jackson 5 was phenomenally successful; the company still felt it had to exaggerate sales figures. The official Motown word was that "Never Can Say Good-bye" netted sales of 1,213,000 copies in just five days. That doesn't seem likely considering that, when all was said and done, the record sold "only" 1,605,016 copies. Still, the song sold over a million, closer to 2 million, and The Jackson Five was on a commercial roll.

That month, March, the group embarked on another major tour. Besides Joe, Johnny Jackson, and Ronny Rancifer (who played drums and organ respectively), also in the entourage were a Motown road manager, a company still photographer, a magazine photographer, a five-man cinema crew hired by Gordy, the Jacksons' chauffeur, the Motown publicist, and the tutor who accompanied the boys on all of their road tours. There was also a truckload of instruments, amplifiers, and other electronic equipment. The Jacksons played Shreveport and New Orleans, Louisiana; Tampa, Florida; and Jackson, Mississippi; the tour ended in Memphis, Tennessee, on April 1.

Suzanne dePasse, now president of Motown Productions, was road manager on this tour. "I was only five years older than the eldest, Jackie [who was twenty-one at the time]. I was responsible for nineteen people on that tour, and I couldn't even get backstage because the security people at the concert halls thought I was a groupie. We hadn't gotten sophisticated about credentialing yet. We had a lot of fun. We had pillow fights and 'hide her purse' and 'hide her shoes.' Real mature games like that. Michael was the master of practical jokes."

On April 18, The Jackson 5 appeared with Diana Ross on her first solo television special, "Diana!" It was always difficult for the boys to have to appear in comedy sketches; Michael used to cringe at the thought. On "Diana!," after The Jackson 5 finished their musical set, twelve-year-old Michael came out crooning while impeccably dressed in a double-breasted tuxedo, coat slung over one shoulder, gray fedora at a rakish angle. Although the Sinatra-like

---

*Clifton Davis was brought to Motown by Supremes lead singer Jean Terrell—who replaced Diana Ross in the act—in the hopes that her group would have "Never Can Say Good-bye" as a single. No such luck. Though they did record it, the song was not released by The Supremes.

mannerisms and the words to the parody of "It Was a Very Good Year" brought laughter, Michael's clear-as-a-bell voice gave the ballad an unexpected poignancy.

He sauntered over to where twenty-seven-year-old Diana was seated at a table, stunning in a silver lamé gown covered by a full-length gray chinchilla coat and holding a cigarette holder half as long as her arm.

"Darling, I got your note," she said. "You print nicely."

"I always did," Michael replied, sneaking a look at the cue cards. As long as he is singing, he's a marvel. Once it comes to dialogue, he's on shakier ground.

The "comedy" continues. Michael tells her their affair is over. Diana is distraught. "When will I find somebody with your charm, your wit, your lips?" she cries.

"You won't, but hang in there," Michael says. He gives her a playful punch in the arm.

As the sketch progresses, Michael looks more and more ill at ease. Finally, Diana accuses him, "You men are all alike—cruel, heartless, and egocentric."

"Flattery will get you nowhere," Michael replies. From the laughter, he can tell that the audience thinks it's funny, but from the expression on his face, it's plain that he doesn't understand the joke at all. He has the look of someone who wishes he were someplace—anyplace—else.

A month later, the Jacksons moved into a large estate at 4641 Hayvenhurst in Encino, California. Joe and Katherine purchased the property on February 25, 1971, from Earle and Elouise Hagen for $250,000; they moved in on May 5, 1971, the day after Katherine's forty-first birthday. Katherine asked her husband not to sell the two-bedroom home in Gary—just in case the family fortunes took a turn for the worse and they had to move back to Indiana. Although Joe didn't think that such a thing could ever happen, he decided to lease out rather than sell the house at 2300 Jackson Street. (The property is worth roughly $50,000 today. Twenty years ago, it was probably worth less than half that much.)

The couple had never made as large a purchase as the Encino estate and, according to Motown sources, didn't have a clue as to how to go about it. At first, Joe Jackson wanted to pay cash for the house, but didn't have that much money. Berry Gordy convinced him that the family needed as much of a tax write-off on the property as they could get, since their income was increasing monthly. Gordy offered to lend Joe and Katherine the down payment on the home, but Joe Jackson declined. "If we're going to live in that house, it's gotta be ours," he told Gordy. Berry Gordy already had too much control over his kids; Joe didn't want him to have a vested interest in the family home as well.

Although Joe decided to put down as little as possible on the Encino property, his credit profile was not good and he had to raise nearly 40 percent in order to qualify for a mortgage from Great Western Bank. Joe did manage to get the hundred thousand, but he had to secure a large advance on his sons' future earnings. The advance came from Berry Gordy.

Encino, which is a thirty-five-minute drive from downtown Los Angeles, is one of the wealthiest communities in Southern California and home to many celebrities. The two-acre estate, resplendent with eighteen citrus trees and countless exotic plants, was guarded by an electronic gate and flanked by a guest house, playhouse, and servants' quarters. "The house had five bathrooms and six bedrooms," recalled Susie Jackson. "Jackie and Ronny shared a room. Tito was with Johnny, Jermaine with Marlon, Michael with Randy, and LaToya with Janet. And then there was one left for Joe and Katherine, so there were a lot of people living there."

The grounds contained an Olympic-size swimming pool, a basketball half-court, a badminton court, and an archery range. Immediately, plans were made to add a hundred-thousand-dollar recording studio and a twenty-five-thousand-dollar darkroom. The boys' friends called this place the Big House because it would become as much a prison to the family as a home.

Jackie Jackson's Datsun 240 Z was usually parked in the driveway, along with Katherine's new Audi, Joe's gold Mercedes 300 SE convertible, and the family's huge van.

The family room had a recessed floor surrounded by a wraparound couch, and the walls were lined with numerous plaques, gold and platinum records signifying million-selling singles and albums. One reporter said the room resembled "a cross between a motel lobby and the foyer of a Sunset Boulevard record company."

Johnny Jackson and Ronny Rancifer, The Jackson 5's drummer and organist, moved into the household with the rest of the family. This arrangement occurred because Joe and Katherine were concerned about the influence both boys—but particularly Johnny—were having on their sons. Both youngsters liked to spend whatever little money they were given, rather than save it. They were smoking cigarettes and drinking liquor. Joe considered letting them both go but decided that that wouldn't be fair since the boys had been a part of the band since the early days in Gary.

Johnny Jackson once shared equal billing with the group when they were known for a short time back in Gary as The Jackson Five Plus Johnny. Although he was introduced by Motown as a cousin, Jackson really was not related to the brothers. However, he was extremely close to the family. Joe was even made his legal guardian. When The Jackson 5 became famous, Johnny was relegated to the background with the other musicians. Fokay Jackson, the grandfather who raised him, would say in an interview that Johnny often called home and asked for money, indicating to his grandparents that he was not being treated fairly and not making the money he deserved. When Johnny's grandmother looked into the matter, she was told in no uncertain terms by a Motown attorney that if she did not stop her investigation, Johnny would be booted out of the group.

Johnny had signed a Motown contract, along with the Jackson boys. But Joe claimed that this had been a "mistake" and sent Richard Arons, his business partner and lawyer, to Gary, Indiana, to convince Fokay Jackson to talk his grandson into nullifying the deal. Fokay was upset by this request, but eventually Johnny agreed to have his contract nullified as long as he would still be a member of the band. In desperation, he begged his grandparents to leave him alone and allow him to continue with his career. It certainly seemed to most observers that the Jackson family was interested in keeping all the money generated by the group in the immediate family and not sharing with "relatives."

In 1972, when Johnny's grandmother died, Johnny, according to Fokay Jackson, cut off all ties with his family. Fokay was crippled from a stroke and suffered from a heart ailment and high blood pressure. He lived on a pension and Social Security in a slum basement apartment—a health hazard and a target for thieves—for which he paid $125 a month. He said that his grandson could not give him any money because he barely made ends meet himself, despite The Jackson 5's fame. Even though rats lived in the walls, Fokay said he refused to move because he was afraid his grandson would not be able to contact him.

Johnny Jackson loved the Jackson family as if it were his own, and the Jacksons said they thought of him as a member of the family. However, his former wife, Susie, insists that Johnny was never fairly compensated.

"But we did have fun up at the Big House," said Susie Jackson. "It wasn't all drama and backstabbing. There were parties and, in the beginning, I felt that we had a special closeness. I remember a lot of fun times when they first moved in. They were always roasting peanuts in that house. Every time you were in that house, they were roasting peanuts."

Katherine enjoyed the new house, but ironically (considering how desperately she wanted to leave), she missed Gary, Indiana. Now that she had finally left Gary, she was not as happy as she had thought she would be. Mostly she was lonely for old friends and relatives. When any could come to visit, Katherine was overjoyed to have them.

If Southern California had to be her new home, Katherine would not allow the opulent surroundings to make her or her family act in a pretentious manner. She was determined to maintain a sense of normality around the household. "I have always told the boys to never let all the success they have make them feel superior towards people," she told The Jackson 5's fan club president, Steve Manning. "The same people you meet on your way up to the top, you will surely meet on the way down, so treat everyone with respect. As far as the house goes, we don't have a maid and I do have a housekeeper who helps me around the house, cleaning and washing clothes. In the evenings, I always have dinner ready for the family. Of course, I cook it myself. LaToya [fifteen-years-old] sometimes helps. The boys love soul food, so that's usually what I prepare. Occasionally, they like to eat chile, which I make myself. But you know what? I find myself making plenty of tacos at least once a week."

As Katherine talked to the fan club president, thirteen-year-old Michael entered the room and announced that he was going shopping. "If you overspend today, you'll have to wait until your next week's allowance," Katherine told her son. "So be careful what you buy."

The Jacksons' phone number would be routinely changed by the phone company every month to guard against outsiders having it. Nevertheless, the number always got out. Once, a girl from Newark called to talk to Michael at two in the morning—just one day after the new number was assigned. As always, Joe limited phone calls to five minutes and would not hesitate to use a strap on any family member—with the exception of Katherine—who broke that rule, pop star or not. To say the least, the children were well disciplined. The boys were known in Hollywood circles as the best-behaved youngsters in show business. "You sometimes thought they were too nice," said one reporter. "It was as if something was wrong somewhere. They were sort of spooky."

Jermaine has recalled that when the family moved into the Encino home their closeness began to dissipate. "We were real close when we had the other homes—before Encino," he remembered. "In Gary, we had two bedrooms—one for our parents and one for all of us. You *had* to be close. You felt that closeness as a family. But in Encino, the place was so big we had to make plans in advance to see each other. I think that Michael, in particular, was unhappy there. He felt, as I did, that we were all losing touch with each other."

"The place is almost totally impersonal," wrote *Time* magazine correspondent Tim Tyler of the Jackson's new mansion.

In June 1971, The Jackson 5 released another single. Deke Richards recalled, "Sammy Davis had just been signed to the label, and Berry wanted me to handle him. I ended up spending a lot of time with him, liked him, and wanted to write a great song for him. I was after a song structure like something the old group The Delphonics would have done, yet I wanted to be contemporary at the same time. I came up with a song and called Berry at five in the morning and said, 'I got a smash for Sammy. It's a hit.' He said, 'C'mon over right away,' which I did. I got there, he came down in his robe, and I went to the piano. As the sun was coming up, I started singing the lyrics in my best Sammy Davis Broadway voice: 'I don't know how many stars there are, up in the heavenly sky. . .' And Berry was just groovin' on this."

"Man, that is a smash," Berry said after Deke finished the ballad. "But we can't give it to Sam. That's gotta go to Michael and The Jackson 5."

"Oh, Berry, you're blowing my mind," Deke said. "The song is Sammy Davis all the way."

"No way," he said. "That's Michael. Trust me."

Deke went into the studio with The Jackson 5 and cut the song, "Maybe Tomorrow." It went on to sell 830,794 copies, not as many as previous efforts but still a respectable number.

On July 9 and 10, the group taped its first television special, "Goin' Back to Indiana," for ABC-TV. (It aired on September 19.) The special highlighted the group's return to their home and included footage filmed in Indianapolis on Memorial Day.

Between July and September, the group performed fifty shows on tour, the longest series of one-nighter performances the act had ever attempted, beginning at the Coliseum in Charlotte, North Carolina, on July 20 and ending September 12 at the H.I.C. Arena in Honolulu.

"I wish for once we could finish a show and not have to leave before the end because of the crowds rushing the stage," Michael complained. "We have a real good ending, but we never get a chance to do it." The Commodores (with Lionel Richie in the lead) were The Jackson 5's opening act on this tour.

At Madison Square Garden in August, the show had to be stopped after only two minutes when the audience stormed the stage. "Return to your seats, please!" Michael begged. Ultimately, though, the group had to be extracted from the crowd and rushed away from the premises. The show resumed after the audience calmed down. Sixty minutes later, when the concert was over, the Jacksons sprinted to waiting limousines—without finishing their last number—in order to get away as quickly as possible. The audience went berserk. Once the fans realized that the group was gone, they surged onto the stage like an angry flood, sweeping away police and security men, and into the dressing rooms looking for their idols.

Lionel Richie recalled, "The only thing I can say I remember about that tour was the screaming crowds, and how amazing Michael was as a performer. For someone as young as he was, he had an amazing ability to entertain and make it seem so effortless. Also, he was fearless. The other guys were a little afraid of the crowds, but Michael wasn't. He would want to go out among them and sing, but of course he wasn't allowed to. They'd have killed him. Sadly, I learned later that he would develop a real fear of that kind of thing, but in the beginning he loved it.

"The other thing I remember about young Michael is his Sidney Poitier impression. He used to do a great impression of Sidney in *Blackboard Jungle*. Had the lines memorized and was pretty good for a little guy. Used to crack us all up. I also recall that he used to do a mean Johnny Mathis singing 'Stormy Weather.' I used to look at this kid and, I swear, I thought he was a midget. An adult midget. No kid could be that talented, I used to think."

The tour proved profitable. When asked what the group was doing with its money, fourteen-year-old Marlon told a reporter for the *Los Angeles Herald-Examiner*, "We're makin' money for the future. But later we'll have to spend it in order to make more. That's what you have to do. We'll probably buy a Howard Johnson's or some other kind of hotel where there's money coming in after you spend yours."

This was a heady time for the boys from Gary, and they were never again to be as close as they were during these early days. They certainly were not able to make friends while on the road. Protected from outsiders by the Motown representatives and their father, they had only each other for company. They occupied their free time by dropping water balloons and paper bags filled with water from hotel room windows, having pillow fights with one another, and playing Scrabble, Monopoly, and card games. The boys gave Jermaine the nickname "Las Vegas" because he was such a good card player. Michael has fond memories of tag-team wrestling matches and shaving cream wars with his brothers while they were holed up in hotels. Or fast-walk races down hotel hallways once their Motown security chaperon was asleep. Michael, who was twelve, liked to phone room service, order huge meals, and then have them sent to strangers staying in the hotel. Michael was quite a prankster. He especially enjoyed setting up a bucket of water as a booby trap above his and Jermaine's hotel room door (they always shared a room), drenching whoever happened to walk in.

"Mike always blamed me," Jermaine recalled with a grin. "He loved practical jokes, locking us out of our rooms in our underwear, squirting us with water pistols. They were almost always his idea."

Michael also spent a lot of his spare time drawing pictures of his brothers and throwing them out to fans who congregated to meet the boys at airports.

The Motown organization ran a tight ship where The Jackson 5's tours were concerned; every detail was worked out in advance so that there would be no glitches. The boys were constantly being rushed from one place to the other—always having to be smuggled in and out of auditoriums and hotels because of the unruly crowds they attracted. "In Detroit, we had to jump off the plane without waiting for the ladder, they was comin' so fast," Jackie remembered with a touch of exaggeration.

"Security was the primary concern throughout the tour," recalled Bob Jones, Motown's top press agent, who accompanied the group on the road. "For that reason, the flight times and hotel accommodations were kept secret. Before we left on the tour, stage escape routes were planned from schematic drawings of the various arenas, so that in the event the group was mobbed on the stage, everybody would know how to get out."

The boys were constantly amazed by the manic enthusiasm of their young fans. Michael says he'll never forget the little girl in Dayton, Ohio, who got to meet him and Marlon in their hotel room because she won what they called "The Mama's Pearl Contest." Once she was faced with the boys, she couldn't say a single word. She just sat there shivering.

"I had The Jackson 5 on my show when Michael was nine or ten," recalled Larry King about an interview he conducted when Michael was actually twelve. "I mean, we had all five of them on— they were doing some kind of benefit in Miami—and he stole the show. We were in a restaurant, and all the people were going, 'Oh, there's a cute little kid.' Not shy at all, running around eating rolls—

they had rolls on the table—and the minute we'd take a break for a commercial, he'd run out and grab one, and everyone was shouting, 'Michael, you stop that!' But once he got on the air, he was like the showman of the group.''

Indeed, success was sweet and innocent for The Jackson 5. "We don't have no gold records,'' Michael would say to a surprised reporter with a sad expression on his face. And then, after a beat, he'd explain, "They're all *platinum*! Ha-ha!'' and everyone would laugh. This became a favorite joke, just as rehearsed as any part of the group's stage act. It was all good, wholesome fun.

Inevitably, there was always a bevy of young female fans—groupies—that followed the boys wherever they went. Mostly, at this time, the fellows simply ignored the girls; all the brothers were much too shy to do anything but smile and blush. They simply were not used to so much attention. Yet.

Occasionally one of the Jacksons would show some interest in the opposite sex. Backstage at the Hollywood Bowl, where the group performed on August 26, Berry Gordy's only daughter, Hazel, sixteen, had her arm around Jermaine, also sixteen, and seemed to be nibbling on his ear. Joe watched with great interest and pulled Jermaine aside.

"What's the deal with her?'' he wanted to know.

"I don't know,'' Jermaine said, shrugging his shoulders. "She likes me, I guess.''

Joe seemed interested. He squinted as though in thought and then nodded his approval. "Berry's kid,'' he muttered to himself. "Hmmm. Not bad. Not bad at all.''

During the concert, Jermaine decided to dedicate his solo of "Bridge Over Troubled Water'' to "Hazel, for her birthday.'' The audience's reaction was lukewarm. Whereas he usually got a standing ovation for the number, this evening it seemed that the female fans in the crowd did not appreciate Jermaine's honesty about his friendship with Hazel.

Jermaine recalled, "My father pulled me aside, I remember, and he said, 'You'd better not do that again.' And I said, 'You know, you're right. I'd better not.' And I didn't.''

The group's popularity continued when "The Jackson 5 Show,'' a weekly animated series, began airing on Saturday mornings September 11. The Jacksons' actual voices were heard in musical numbers, but their dialogue was provided by young black actors. Motown made an agreement with Videocraft, a production company, to produce the series. Joe Jackson and The Jackson 5 had no idea how much Motown was paid for the concept. They knew *they* were only paid $3,500 per episode by Motown, an amount which had to be split among the group members, minus Joe's percentage. This was the minimum amount the group could be paid under Screen Actors Guild regulations.

Janet Jackson, who was five years old at the time, remembers watching the series. "They [her brothers] were out of town; they were on the road. It was Saturday morning, and I had on my pajamas. I was sitting in my mother's bedroom on the floor, waiting for that cartoon to come on. And when they finally came on, I remember screaming and jumping up and down and dancing."

After the cartoons aired, Michael was talking to a reporter backstage after a concert when he blurted out, "We'd like to do all kinds of things in the future. Dad says maybe we'll even form a corporation of our own. Maybe even be our own managers." Realizing immediately what he'd said, Michael covered his hand with his mouth. *That* certainly wasn't a part of their rehearsed interview speech. A Motown official overheard the remark and made a quick note in a stenopad.

In June 1971, MGM Records released a single, "Sweet and Innocent," with Donny Osmond as a solo act. It would be the first of a string of major hit records by Osmond without the group. That record's success guaranteed Donny Osmond teen-star status in the predominantly white teenybopper magazines. Most observers agreed that because of their color, The Jackson 5 could never be perceived as teen idols in those magazines, despite all of their success and good looks. Though the Jacksons would make occasional appearances in magazines like *16* and *Fave*, the Osmonds and other white stars always dominated those magazines. Were it not for *Soul*, a black-oriented entertainment publication which went out of business in 1983, and *Right On!* magazine, a black teen publication still in existence, The Jackson 5 might not have attained the status of teen idols among the black youth.

After Donny Osmond's first single, Joe decided that Michael should also record on his own. He and Gordy had a meeting in July and decided to release "Got to Be There," as Michael's first solo, instead of as a group effort as originally planned. Michael would still be a part of the group, just as Donny Osmond was a part of The Osmonds. "But we can all make more money," Joe reasoned.

"Got to Be There" was issued in October. Although it would not reach the top of the charts, it had to be a reality check of sorts for the Jacksons when brother Michael cracked the Top Five as a solo artist. This lushly produced and orchestrated, mid-tempo love song was the perfect vehicle for launching Michael's solo career, for it's surely one of the most beautiful songs in Motown's publishing catalog. At the time, it was the envy of many artists whose flagging careers could have been salvaged by such a versatile, well-tailored number. It could easily have salvaged the careers of The Supremes and The Temptations. Instead, it served to bolster the enormously popular lead singer of The Jackson 5 who, with his brothers, had just hit the Top 20 with the summertime ballad "Maybe Tomorrow." "Got to Be There" sold 1,583,850 copies.

The Jackson 5 garnered good will with local appearances. Early in December they performed at the Los Angeles chapter for the Junior Blind. On December 23, instead of giving the usual Motown Christmas party, Berry Gordy hosted seven hundred underprivileged children. It was a nice gesture. One of The Supremes led the youngsters in singing carols and playing games until The Jackson 5, each dressed in a Santa Claus outfit and beard, arrived to distribute gifts and records.

In the joyous spirit of the season, Motown announced that Michael's recording of "Got to Be There" had become a number one record on the *Cash Box* charts just six weeks after its release. Immediately after Christmas, the group embarked on a concert tour of the South. In Dallas on December 28, a reporter arranged an interview in their hotel room. Fans quickly congregated outside the door, chanting "Michael! Michael! Michael!" Tito went out in the hallway hoping to quiet them down. When he opened the door, a group of girls burst into the room and began kissing and hugging the youngest brother, totally ignoring the other fellows.

Michael's brothers did not appear to be jealous and treated the incident as a chance to tease Michael. "Just wait till I get my solo released," Jermaine said. "Then I'll be the ladies' man 'round here."

"Well, right now Michael's the real ladies' man," Jackie said after the girls were escorted out of the room by security guards.

"Aw, c'mon, you guys," Michael responded bashfully.

"You *are*, Mike," Jermaine agreed. "But not for long . . ."

Then all four brothers suddenly jumped on Michael, tickling him good-naturedly and wrestling him to the ground.

You could hear the laughter all the way down the hall.

# Chapter

# 7

As THE JACKSON 5 became more popular, so their lives became more stressful. And as the boys became older, real trouble began brewing. It is the rare child performer who can make the transition from youth to teen to adult without difficulty.

Adult entertainers are there by choice. But young stars, like the Jackson boys, are usually thrust into the limelight by well-meaning parents before they know what's happening to them. Many such parents—either performers themselves or, as in Joe Jackson's case, frustrated ones—use their children as their main source of income once the child becomes successful, again, just as Joe and Katherine did. It's an enormous burden for children to feel responsible for their family's financial well-being. Chances are they cannot balance a checkbook, but they are constantly reminded that if they don't work, the family will not eat or, worse, their parents will not love them anymore. Parental pressure to perform at times can be tantamount to child abuse.

The stereotype of the overbearing stage mother is well known, but today more fathers are assuming responsibility for their children's theatrical careers. According to Andrea Darvi, author of *An Insider's Look at the World of the Hollywood Child Star*, "Stage fathers tend to develop intense insecurities that lead to a compensatory overassertiveness and ruthlessness. Fathers are more dominant and possessive of the child."

Joe Jackson was that kind of parent.

When he recognized that his sons had talent, he insisted they practice every afternoon, without fail. Although they could hear other children playing games outside, they were not allowed to join them. "The other kids on the block, they'd laugh at us," Michael recalled. "We wanted to play, but we couldn't. We had to rehearse.

They'd say, 'Oh, those Jacksons won't amount to much.' I wanted to perform, but I wanted friends too. We couldn't have both.''

At least the older brothers had had a few years to act like kids. Michael never did; he was barely five years old when thrust into the limelight.

It is not only the vast sums of money child stars earn which set them apart. Most child performers are shortchanged on their education. Few have ever attended public school regularly. In the film industry, they are tutored on the set. MGM even had a school for the youngsters who worked in their movies. Although the children were supposed to study a certain number of hours each day, filming often took precedence over education.

Besides not getting enough book learning, child performers are often cheated out of learning social skills—the art of getting along with people. The other children they associate with daily are usually working children like themselves. Some of Judy Garland's happiest memories were of the short time during her teens when her career seemed to be going nowhere. She left the studio school, enrolled in Hollywood High—hiding her background from her fellow students—and enjoyed herself immensely. (That happy period came to an abrupt end when a vice-principal told her she shouldn't be enrolled in school with ''normal people.'')

The couple of years the younger Jackson boys spent in public schools are fondly remembered by Michael and Marlon as high points of their lives. Michael attended sixth grade in room eight at Gardner Street Elementary in Los Angeles—not consistently because of his work schedule, but as much as he possibly could.

His sixth-grade teacher, Laura Gerson, remembered, ''Once I was teaching the kids a song with a three-part harmony, and I hit a flat note that made my hair stand on end. Michael's eyes popped wide open. Nobody but him noticed. He never talked about himself. He just settled down and was one of the kids. Occasionally, he would disappear and turn up on television . . .''*

In the seventh grade, Michael joined Marlon at Emerson Junior High. But by this time, the group's accomplishments at Motown robbed them of their privacy, and they had only two weeks at Emerson before they were forced to leave. ''There were mobs of people standing in the hallways just looking into the classrooms,''

---

*On October 11, 1989, school officials at Gardner Street Elementary School dedicated the ''Michael Jackson Auditorium'' in Jackson's honor. Michael Jackson attended the ceremony. ''This is the happiest day of my life,'' Michael said in his brief speech. ''I love you all.''

Marlon recalled. "It was pretty embarrassing." And frightening, as well.

During their last week at Emerson, the school received a death threat against Michael. Joe and Katherine were upset enough to pull both boys out of public school entirely.

The two were then enrolled in private schools. California law requires that minors have a minimum of three hours of schooling a day when they are working. So Mrs. Rose Fine, accredited by the state as a "children's welfare supervisor," became the tutor for all of the younger Jacksons. Much of their traveling time was spent studying for tests that they would take as soon as they checked into their hotel rooms. Between their studies, rehearsals, sound checks, and concerts, and the usual goofing off, the Jacksons were kept busy.

Michael disliked private school, was bored by his studies, refused to do his homework, and was fairly miserable. During class, he would draw pictures of animals and monsters when he should have been paying attention to the teacher. When called upon for an answer, Michael didn't have a clue and didn't care.

Jackie and Tito attended Fairfax High School, a public school in Los Angeles, at the time when the Jacksons were just becoming famous. They have bitter memories of that time. Because the demands of their careers made normal routines almost impossible, they couldn't be on any of the sports teams—a special disappointment for Jackie, who loved baseball. As they became more well known, they received a lot of attention from classmates who had previously ignored them, and the brothers became suspicious of who their friends really were. Jackie and Tito could at least look back on a time when they were exposed to people who weren't in show business. Michael, Marlon, and Jermaine could not.

Jackie and Tito would graduate from Fairfax when they were eighteen. Jermaine, Marlon, and Michael were granted high school equivalency diplomas by Rose Fine, who was empowered to award them. However, the Jacksons did not obtain a good grounding in basic subjects. To this day, they have problems with penmanship, grammar, and (Michael in particular) spelling. They lack a sense of history.

One wonders if Michael is even aware of the similarities between his life and that of Jackie Coogan, the child actor who achieved prominence at the age of six in 1920 for his role in *The Kid* with Charlie Chaplin. So great was Coogan's appeal that in 1923 he was given a $500,000 bonus plus a contract for four pictures over two years for a total of $1 million plus a percentage of the profits to leave First National for Metro. Although his mother claimed Jackie led a "normal life"—just as Katherine Jackson insists—his childhood was anything but normal. At the height of Coogan's career, his mother took him shopping downtown, where they were mobbed by three thousand people and had to be rescued by the police. Jackie Coogan, who found the experience terrifying, became very careful about going out in public. He stayed home, surrounded by a ten-foot fence, frightened of the world around him.*

Michael would one day withdraw in much the same way. In fact, as early as 1972, when he was barely fourteen, Michael began exhibiting behavior unlike that of his other brothers. While they took the pressures of success in stride, Michael had been affected by it. "He's just more sensitive than the others," Katherine explained.

By the time Michael was fourteen, Bill Bray (The Jackson 5's security man, who still works for Michael) would often arrange for him to have access to freight elevators in hotels, rather than take public lifts along with "normal people," as Michael called them.

Just a year earlier Michael had told Judy Spiegelman of *Soul* magazine, "I'm just like other kids." Now he realized he was not. The other group members didn't seem to mind "normal people"— as long as they weren't in the form of a pack of rioting fans. But Michael was always the boy who garnered the most attention. If he entered a room with any of the other brothers, he was the one to whom the fans would flock.

When the others would go out sightseeing, Michael preferred to stay in his room. "He was an introvert," Bob Jones, former head of Motown's publicity department, remembered. "Once he came off the stage, he would come back to the hotel, put on his robe, and relax in his room. He carried a big easel with a big pad of paper on it. He spent his time drawing and reading. While the rest of the guys were out sightseeing, playing ball, or whatever, Michael was very much into doing something more creative. Something by himself, alone. Needless to say, he was the star. And everything cen-

---

*Jackie Coogan's father, who invested his son's money wisely, died in an accident when Jackie was twenty. When his mother remarried, his stepfather lived so lavishly that Coogan eventually sued them, in 1938, to get control of the money he had earned as a child. It turned out there was little left to recover. A year later, Congress passed the Child Actor's Bill, better known as the Coogan Act, which required that 25 percent of the money child actors earn be held in trust.

tered around that. He was the key to the J-5, and everyone just sort of overprotected him.''

Michael's brother Tito, a brooding, quiet eighteen-year-old, was the first member of the group to marry. His bride was seventeen-year-old Delores (Dee Dee) Martes; they were wed on June 17, 1972, after a secret, seven-month engagement. Dee Dee, personable and attractive, was raised in New York's Harlem. In 1968, her family moved to a small house in Watts. After moving to Hollywood, she attended Fairfax High School, where she met Tito three months before the group became famous in 1969.

Joe and Katherine were against the union. But they realized that if they did not allow Tito to marry, he would probably elope, which wouldn't bode well for the family image. So they reluctantly consented.

''Tito wanted out of the house,'' recalled Susie Jackson, Johnny Jackson's former wife. ''When he fell in love with Dee Dee, he was determined that they would marry, even though Joe and Katherine felt he was making a big mistake. Joe and Katherine didn't like Dee Dee at all because she was of Mexican extraction from the Dominican Republic, and from the ghetto. It's sad, but true. They were afraid she would turn out to be a gold digger.''

Joe made it clear to one reporter that what he called ''special protections'' had been set up ''for the boys when they get married. As long as the boys' wives stay with them and help them and enjoy some of the good living they can share, that's fine. We're only interested in seeing to it that the boys are happy.''

''They made Dee Dee sign a prenuptial agreement,'' Susie Jackson said. ''She didn't have much choice, if she wanted to marry Tito. Tito wanted the prenuptial as much as his parents did. Dee Dee is a sweet girl. She loved Tito and would do anything he asked.''

Pauline Powell, a family friend, recalled, ''Tito's was a small wedding at a place called the Joy House Wedding Gardens, a chapel in Inglewood [California], nothing like what one would expect from the Jacksons at this time. That was because the bride's mother handled all of the arrangements. Jermaine was the best man, and I think Dee Dee's brother-in-law [her sister's husband] gave her away. All of the brothers were there, and the rest of the groom's family, grandparents . . . The reception was at the Inglewood Women's Club, not the fanciest place on the planet. The only celebrity there was Dick Clark. They didn't have a honeymoon, at least not to my knowledge. Their first baby, a son named after Tito, was born about a year later [August 1973]. Tito was on tour, so LaToya acted as

Dee Dee's Lamaze labor coach. Dee Dee is a lovely lady. They're still married today, in fact. Maybe that's because they had marriage counseling before they were even married. They were young but also sensible.''

Tito did not mind the small, unpretentious wedding. ''I'm not the type of guy who thinks he's anything special or wants to drive a Caddy just because I can afford it,'' he told *Soul* magazine writer Walter Burrell at the time. ''And I don't care about having high-class friends who are rich and famous. I don't forget where I came from and how it was down there.''

Still, there was a bit of Joe in Tito. ''Dee Dee gets bossy sometimes,'' he said later. ''But I'm the man of the house. Got to be. Or else I'll be walking down the street in a dress.''

Tito was out of circulation now, but it was open season for his brothers. The Jackson's fame brought female groupies to their doorsteps. Young fans would stop at nothing to have sex with the handsome brothers and Jermaine and Jackie began acting irresponsibly. With women—even young girls—thrown at their feet, the brothers saw no reason not to take advantage of the situation.

''Every groupie would have sex with Jackie first,'' said a friend of the family's. ''And then with Joe, who would also fool around, and then with Jermaine if the girl had anything left to give. That was the standard lineup. No one knows how it started.''

Reporter Greg Shaw quizzed Michael, then thirteen, about his personal life for a story in *Crawdaddy* magazine at this time. It went like this:

''Do you smoke?''

''Naaah.''

''Do you drink?''

''Naaah.''

''Has being a superstar changed your sex life?''

(Michael giggled and shrugged off the question.)

''Do you have a girlfriend?''

''No.''

''Would you like one?''

''I'm not old enough.''

''If you had one, what would you like her to be like?''

''Nice . . . and quiet.''

Michael admitted that his household chores included dusting the living room and keeping his bedroom tidy (Katherine put up a sign in his room: ''Keep America Beautiful—Clean Up Your Room''). He was a typical thirteen-year-old who spent his seven-dollar-a-week allowance on bubble gum and art supplies, who loved his

German shepherd, Lobo, and who would wave good-naturedly at the girls who congregated outside his home's front gate. Michael may have been saving himself for someone "nice and quiet," but by 1972, his older brothers were leaving a long trail of broken hearts as they toured city after city.

Thirty-six-year-old divorcée Rhonda Phillips lives in Long Beach, California, in a modest two-bedroom home with her three children. She was eighteen when she met her idol, Jackie Jackson, who was twenty-one at the time. For one night, Phillips became a part of Jackson's "world." She remembers the circumstances vividly.

"It was late August 1972, and The Jackson 5 were doing a concert at the Forum in Inglewood [California]. My fifteen-year-old sister and I were their biggest fans. I had all of their records and played them every day, constantly. I couldn't get enough. We used to collect all of the posters in the teen magazines and thought they were so cute, so adorable. Jackie was my favorite, Jermaine was my sister's.

"They were so good and generous," she went on. "I recall that they had made hundreds of concert tickets available free to kids in poor areas who could not afford to see the show otherwise. That was just like them. For instance, in Philadelphia they had visited two children's hospitals handing out copies of their latest album and signing them for the patients. That's the kind of generosity that made me want to know these guys better.

"When the tickets went on sale, I borrowed money from my parents to buy a set for me and my boyfriend and my sister and her fellow. Somehow I ended up with seats in the very first row, which was exciting."

The night of the concert, Rhonda had her hair braided and wore high-waisted red slacks with a tight matching tube top. "I had a good figure at that time," she recalled wistfully. She had pinned Jackson 5 buttons with their pictures on them all over her top. She even wore earrings with the J-5 logo. Rhonda's sister brought along binoculars—as if they weren't seated close enough—and she also managed to smuggle in a camera.

"The show was sensational," Rhonda remembered, "even though you couldn't hear their voices because of all the screaming. I remember that Randy was making one of his first appearances with the group, playing congas. Michael, who had just turned fourteen, was so amazing as a performer. He was obviously the star of the show, the real center of attention."

During the concert, Rhonda noticed that Jackie seemed to be

looking at her, staring. She thought that it must have been her imagination. But her sister kept nudging her as if to say, "He's looking at you! He's looking at you!"

"After the show, we were getting ready to file out of the auditorium and this black guy comes running up to me," Rhonda remembered. " 'Jackie Jackson would like to meet you, miss,' he told me. You could have knocked me over with a feather. 'Who me?' I asked. I mean, there were eighteen thousand people in that place. Why me? By this time, my boyfriend was pissed off. 'Go on and meet Jackie Jackson, see if I care,' he told me. So my sister and her friend and my boyfriend went on without me. How I was going to get home never crossed my mind. I just wanted to meet Jackie Jackson."

Rhonda was escorted backstage by the Jacksons' representative. "I was nervous. I looked around me and they were all there. Jermaine, Marlon, Michael, Tito. It was like a dream. I remember they were perspiring heavily since they had just gotten off stage; they had white towels around their shoulders. I felt a tap on my back and turned around. It was Jackie. He was so handsome, just gorgeous, with the most perfect face. He had features that looked as if they had been sculpted from marble, a work of art. His eyes were deep and dark, his teeth were bright. He had a strong jaw line. His natural [hair] was perfectly combed. I remember shaking his hand and noticing that it was so big and warm and soft. What struck me was that he had a high speaking voice, which was such a contrast to his masculine features. He told me he wanted to get to know me better, and I didn't know what he meant by that but didn't care. I felt as if I was about to pass out, that's how nervous and awed I was by this gorgeous man. I couldn't believe that he was standing there."

Jackie gave Rhonda a slip of paper with an address on it and told her to meet him at that location in one hour.

Rhonda said she was standing in the hallway alone trying to decide whether to meet Jackie when she sensed someone behind her. She turned around. It was Michael. He introduced himself. They shook hands. "He was just a cute little guy," she said. "He had big teeth, a flat, wide nose, a perfectly combed natural; he looked like any pretty fourteen-year-old black boy you'd find in the neighborhood somewhere. He noticed the slip of paper in my hand."

"Did Jermaine give you that?" he asked.

"No, Jackie."

According to Rhonda, Michael seemed to know what was written on the paper. "He wants you to meet him, doesn't he?" Michael asked.

"Yes," Rhonda said. "I don't know if I should . . ."

Michael cut her off. "Don't," he said. It sounded like a warning. "I don't think you should meet him."

"But he's only fourteen," Rhonda remembered thinking. "What can he possibly know?"

Rhonda asked Michael why she shouldn't go. She remembered his answer: "My brothers, sometimes they don't treat girls too good. They can be mean. I don't know why they do these things, but they do. Please, don't go."

Rhonda changed the subject and asked Michael for his autograph. She thrust the piece of paper Jackie had given her at him, and he wrote something on it and handed it back to her. "Don't forget what I said," he told her. "Just go home, okay?" Someone called Michael's name, and he turned around. It was Jermaine alerting him that the limousine was ready to take them back to Encino. Jermaine walked over and introduced himself to Rhonda.

"Say, are you busy later tonight?" he asked her.

Michael rolled his eyes as if he was disgusted with his brother. "C'mon, Jermaine, let's go," he said impatiently as he pulled on Jermaine's elbow.

"But wait, Mike . . .," Jermaine protested.

As they were walking away, Jermaine looked back over his shoulder. "Maybe I'll see you later, good-lookin', " he said with a wink.

The group's representative had arranged cab fare for Rhonda to meet Jackie. "I was too excited to consider what I was doing," she remembers. "I thought we were going to have a wonderful, romantic dinner. I wished I had memorized the list of dos and don'ts that had been published in one of those fan magazine articles about "How to Be Jackie's Girl." ["The girl most likely to get close to Jackie must be happy and willing to be a good friend. If her appearance is neat, she has a very good chance of being the girlfriend of Jackie Jackson."]

"All the way, in the cab, I dreamed of being engaged to Jackie Jackson and then marrying him, having his children. I kept repeating to myself, 'Rhonda Jackson. Rhonda Jackson. The most perfect name in the world. Mrs. Rhonda Jackson—of The Jackson 5.' "

Rhonda Phillips discovered that the address she was given was for an apartment building in Encino, a good hour away from Inglewood. As the car pulled up to the curb, she happened to turn the slip of paper in her hand over and realized that Michael had written more than just his name on the back of it. There was a message. "I hope you don't go," it said. And it was signed "Michael Jackson."

When she stepped out of the cab, a man who claimed to be from Motown was waiting for her at the curb. He brought her up to an apartment.

"Jackie's gonna like you," he told her.

"I certainly hope so," she said.

She knocked on the door. It was open a crack, so she walked in.

"It was dark inside," she remembered. "There was only a candle lit on a table. I smelled incense burning. I thought I detected the scent of marijuana but couldn't be sure. I walked inside, more curious than afraid. Suddenly, I heard a voice from the darkness. 'Glad you could make it.' It was Jackie. He came out from the shadows wearing nothing but his underwear—white briefs—and white gym socks. I immediately got dizzy. His muscular, brown body in the candlelight was almost more than I could bear.

" 'You're a big fan, aren't you?' he asked me.

"I told him I was. I could barely speak.

" 'Thanks for buying my records,' he said.

"I told him he was more than welcome.

"He walked over to me, wrapped his arms around me, and hugged me tightly. His body was so warm. I felt comfortable being with him.

" 'We could never make it without fans like you,' he said. 'I mean it, I really appreciate it. I love your J-5 earrings. They're the best.' He reached around and put the palms of his hands on my buttocks. He squeezed.

"Then he kissed me, and my knees got weak. I felt his tongue in my mouth and I just, I don't know, swooned, I guess. I melted in his mouth like honey. We continued kissing, and before I knew it he was taking off my clothes, piece by piece by piece. 'Your breasts are the perfect size and shape,' he told me as he removed my bra.

" 'Is it okay if I take these off?' he asked, referring to my panties. He was so polite. Eventually, I was standing naked before him. I felt awkward.

" 'You can take mine off,' he told me. He motioned to his briefs.

" 'No, I don't think I can.'

" 'Go ahead,' he urged. 'Sure you can.'

"My hands were trembling as I ran my fingers over his chest and down his stomach," Rhonda remembered. "Finally, I slipped my hands into the sides of his shorts and pushed them down his legs. He moaned, then he stepped out of them.

"I was a virgin. I had never even seen a man naked before. But all I could think of, I swear to God, wasn't that this was my first experience. And it wasn't whether I was right or wrong in doing it, but rather it was 'I am standing here looking at Jackie Jackson, and the man is nude.'

" 'I won't hurt you, I promise,' he said.

"He took my hand and walked me into a bedroom. Then we had sex. I was a willing partner, believe me. But I can't even remember what we did or how, it was such a dizzying experience. All I remember is begging him for more. I do recall that he was extremely gentle with me. He wasn't rough. He was very patient, even loving. I thought he was the most wonderful man.

" 'You know, I won't be able to see you after this,' Jackie told me when we were finished. I knew that, though I don't know how or why. I began to cry. Suddenly I was ashamed. I was very confused. He held me for a little while and then told me that the guy from Motown would be waiting outside to take me home. He kissed me passionately and I left. The whole thing took less than half an hour."

As Rhonda was walking down to the street, a white Rolls-Royce pulled up. The driver was the man who had claimed to be from Motown. Michael and Marlon were sitting in the back seat. The car pulled up to the curb. The boys got out and Marlon ran past Rhonda up to the apartment. Michael came over to her.

"What are you doing here?" he asked. "Were you up there with Jackie?"

"Yeah, I was," she answered.

"Well, what did you guys do?"

"We had a date."

"What's that mean, you had a date?" Michael pushed. He looked at Rhonda suspiciously. "Did you just have sex with my brother?"

Rhonda began to cry. Michael shook his head sadly. "He looked at me with the saddest, most understanding eyes," Rhonda remembered. " 'I'm sorry,' he said. 'Did he make you do it?'

" 'No, I wanted to.'

" 'You *wanted* to?' he asked me. He seemed astonished. 'But why would you *want* to do that?' "

Rhonda got into the car. The driver never once turned to look at her. She rolled down the window. Michael was still standing at the curb.

"Don't ever do that again, okay?" he said to her. "Are you gonna be all right?"

"Yeah, I will be," she answered.

"By now, I was really sobbing," Rhonda recalled. "Then I noticed that Michael had tears in his eyes too. I rolled up the window and the car pulled off. I looked out the back window and the last thing I saw was Michael Jackson standing there waving goodbye to me.

"I never saw him again. Or his brother."

# Chapter

## 8

THE MOST IMPORTANT thing of all is that we don't betray our fans, or take advantage of them," Michael Jackson said when he turned fourteen in August 1972. "I hate that, when entertainers don't do their fans right. That makes me sick to my stomach. I once saw a big star, I won't say who it was, make a girl go out on a date with him just 'cause he was who he was. How can people do that? I think my whole family should be grateful for all this success. I think we are, or I hope so anyway."

"The thing about Mike is that he lets things get to him," sixteen-year-old Jermaine said to Walter Burrell of *Soul* magazine. "He's real serious and sensitive that way. We appreciate our success, yeah. I think we show it when we can."

Indeed, the Jackson family did not hesitate to show their appreciation to people who had helped them in their careers. Instead of small, intimate gatherings, they preferred large, ostentatious affairs where quantity was the most important consideration. Katherine looked at these parties as come-on-overs. Only instead of root beer and pretzels on the back porch, she put out a lavish spread at the family estate. Always a gracious hostess, she made everyone feel welcome. Joe's pride in the house was obvious. He would give tours to anyone who seemed remotely interested. In September 1972, after The Jackson 5 finished their engagement at the Forum in Los Angeles, Katherine and Joe held just such a party at the family home for about fifty press and show business friends.

Katherine and Joe did not disappoint their guests. The twelve-foot-long buffet offered hamburgers, roast beef, chile, shish kabob, fresh chilled fruit, and seafood. Pastries were heaped on a cart decorated with red and yellow roses. In the middle of the family's oval swimming pool, Joe floated a huge J-5 logo made of roses and tinted carnations. For entertainment, The Jackson 5 challenged The Temptations to a basketball game (Jacksons won).

By this time, Motown had released two more solo singles by Michael Jackson. Considered by many as a nonsensical waste of time, the silly "Rockin' Robin" scored big for Michael. While he twitters through the song, the session player bangs out the easy ditty on the piano. This was a terribly "white bread," bubble gum kind of song back in 1958 when it was recorded by the late Bobby Day, so it was a surprise to see Motown feed this music and lyric to their budding young star during the racially aware early seventies.

Surprisingly enough, "Rockin' Robin" was a bigger hit than "Got to Be There." The song peaked in the same position for Michael as the original did fourteen years earlier for Day, at number two on the pop charts.

Another title that brought snickers was "Ben." The words of the song extol friendship. There is no clue anywhere that the song is about a rodent. (In the film, a young boy befriends a rat named Ben.) Michael's voice complements the delicately orchestrated piece, with its solo guitar accompaniment; the recording is layered at all the emotional peaks with a precise string arrangement. The song obviously stood on its own apart from the film. It sold 1,701,475 copies but, said its producer, Deke Richards, "It wasn't played in Los Angeles until it was a major hit everywhere else in the country. The main L.A. radio station program directors were so turned off by the song's subject matter, they just didn't want to play it."

"Ben" not only became Michael's Jackson's first number one solo, but was nominated for an Oscar.

Michael saw the movie *Ben* countless times, sitting in the back of the theater just waiting to hear his song and then see his credit on the screen: " 'Ben' sung by Michael Jackson." As a child, Michael loved rats. At one point, Katherine was horrified to find that Michael had thirty rats in a cage in his bedroom. He was passionate about the rodents until the day he discovered that they were eating each other—as rats will do. Sickened by the sight, Michael put the rat cage outdoors.

In addition to his solo records, Michael started recording the group's songs separately from his brothers, putting the lead vocal on tape alone in the studio. Later, the brothers would come in and record their background vocals. Often, additional—anonymous—singers would be added to the mix. (By 1967, Diana Ross usually recorded this way as well, leaving the other Supremes—or whoever happened to be in the studio—to lay down background vocals at a later date.)

Michael was unhappy with the way he was being recorded at this time, tired of having to sing the songs exactly the way the Motown producers told him to. He felt he deserved more respect. After all, he could memorize three songs in less than a half hour. "I know what I'm doing," he would insist.

At one point, during the recording of "Lookin' Through the Windows," he telephoned Berry Gordy, complaining, "They won't let me sing the song the way I want to." Berry rushed down to the studio and insisted that producer Hal Davis give Michael more freedom in the studio. But this restriction of his creativity would continue to be a problem for Michael, even at this young age (fourteen). He recalled, "I always knew what I wanted to give to a song, but at Motown I was seldom allowed to do it."

In November, The Jackson 5 embarked on a whirlwind twelve-day European tour, which would begin with a royal command performance before Queen Elizabeth. British teenagers swarmed London's Heathrow Airport to welcome The Jackson 5. The ensuing mob scene was reminiscent of the uproar that accompanied The Beatles everywhere during their heyday. Beatlemania, it was called.

"Large plugs of hair were jerked from the scalp underneath Jermaine's giant Afro by souvenir hunters," read Motown's November 22 press release. "Noise so intense that it drowned out the whine of jet engines drove tears to Michael's and Marlon's eyes. Tito was bruised and shaken by the stampede of the thundering herd. Randy nearly panicked when frenzied females devoured him with bear hugs and wet kisses. Jackie was cool but more than a little bit worried. It was sheer pandemonium. It was near chaos. It was frightening. It was JACKSONMANIA."

For once, Motown wasn't exaggerating. The mob of fans that met the group at the airport became so uncontrollable, the brothers scrambled madly in different directions trying to find their limousine. Besides losing a shoe, Michael was almost choked. "He should have been really frightened," recalled Jermaine. "They were pulling on both ends of his scarf, actually choking him. He had to put his hand up under his scarf and start screaming so that it wouldn't tighten up on his neck."

Michael had come to despise these mob scenes. He claims that he still has scars on his body from these days, and that he can associate each mark with a particular city and frightening encounter. He had to run through crowds of screaming girls with his eyes covered by his hands for fear that their nails would scratch him. He has hidden in closets, hoping they would rush by and not look for him. "They grab your hair and pull hard and it hurts like fire," he recalled. "You feel as if you're going to suffocate or be dismembered."

Fans barricaded the entrance to the Churchill Hotel where the group stayed in London, preventing them from leaving for their royal variety performance. Joe called the police, who arrived on the scene with water hoses which they unleashed on the fans, "encouraging" them to disperse. The next day, a nine-year-old girl threatened to use a knife on a burly hotel doorman unless he allowed her access to Michael's room. She was detained by the police. A Rolls-Royce limousine carrying the group sustained twelve thousand dollars' worth of damage when it was dented and scratched by young girls clawing to get to their idols. While the Jacksons were inside performing at the Talk of the Town nightclub, souvenir hunters stripped the limousine, leaving a heap of junk.

Complicating matters, someone in the competing Osmonds' camp got the unfortunate idea to book that group into the same hotel as the Jacksons. This double-booking attracted hundreds more fans, some armed with knives, one with a sledgehammer. The fans in the streets became so rowdy at one point, officials asked The Jackson 5 to perform an impromptu concert on the hotel roof in order to calm the screaming, shoving crowd. In Amsterdam, Dutch fans rioted in the streets when the Jacksons would perform only a one-nighter. The group also visited Brussels, Munich, Frankfurt, and Paris.

When the group returned to the United States, they starred in their second special for CBS. Recalled Gil Askey, musical director of the special, "By this time the boys were different. They had lost some of their enthusiasm for the work and were more interested in other stuff—girls, whatever. Except for Michael. Michael was only interested in the work. He tried to keep his eye on that more than anything else."

On April 17, 1973, Joe got some bad news. Tito had been arrested. According to the Los Angeles Police Department, Tito and The Jackson 5's drummer, John Jackson (no relation), had been involved in buying stolen television sets and stereos. A friend of theirs, Sanders (Bubba) Bryant had allegedly used a passkey to enter and burglarize fifty apartments in the San Fernando Valley area of Los Angeles in February and March. An unidentified seventeen-year-old girl was also involved. Johnny Jackson was charged with one count, Tito with two.

Tito was freed on two thousand dollars' bail, as was Johnny.

What really happened is still a mystery, but it would appear both became mixed up with a criminal element. "They just bought some stuff from somebody not knowing that it was hot," recalled Susie Jackson. "The next thing I knew, they were arrested."

Joe was extremely upset by this turn of events. It was bad enough that Tito was caught. Worse, it was such a petty act. Joe knew how the public would react upon hearing that one of the rich and famous Jackson boys was buying hot stereo sets. If Tito was hooked on drugs, people might be sympathetic. But this looked like nothing but greed and stupidity. That would be hard for the public to accept.

Walter Jackson (no relation), a former friend of Tito's, recalled, "Joe's whole thing was 'How could Tito allow himself to get involved with something like this that could ruin the group's reputation?' The family kept very secretive the details of what Tito had or had not done. Michael told me that what happened wasn't Tito's fault and they were just hoping it would all go away. I also heard that Gordy was on the phone with Joe Jackson as soon as Tito was arrested, trying to figure out how to handle it. This was a serious image problem. It was decided that the arrest would be kept a secret, and Motown somehow managed to hush the whole thing up. There were no reports of his arrest at all."

"It was swept under the rug," Susie Jackson concluded, "just like everything else."

Tito was arraigned on October 3, 1973. There was no way to keep his appearance a secret. The press came to the courthouse as soon as word got out that Tito Jackson was inside. "I don't have no comment," was all Tito would say to the media. "Yeah, he don't have no comment," Joe repeated.

All charges against Tito Jackson were dismissed in February 1974, four months later, after Johnny Jackson pleaded guilty. There were rumors that Johnny took the rap for Tito, but he has never discussed the matter.

In the summer of 1973, The Jackson 5 toured Japan. Katherine went along with her sons and husband on this trip. Bob Jones, of the Motown press department, accompanied the group, along with an awesome entourage of security people, musicians, and technicians. While in Japan, the family visited Buddhist temples, art museums, tea gardens, and the Oriental Gardens of the Takanawa Prince Hotel where the group was headquartered. They took a 150-miles-an-hour train from Osaka to Tokyo, during which they saw the Japanese countryside, including rice paddies and workers.

"It was all better than school," Michael said later. "I think I have had the most amazing education anyone could ask for. We saw things most kids our age never saw." Michael, Jermaine, Marlon, and Randy all earned educational credit every time they toured overseas.

In Tokyo, they took in Sammy Davis, Jr.'s show. "He's the most amazing entertainer on the planet," Michael said. "I learned so much just watching him relate to his audience." After the show, Michael, Jermaine, and Marlon went back to Jermaine's room where they watched pornographic movies, which were shown after eleven P.M. on closed-circuit television.

"Jackie apparently found the Japanese girls very attractive," recalled an editor of *Soul* magazine, "because in the photo of the group getting off the plane in Japan, which we ran on our cover in June [1973], he is obviously sexually aroused. I noticed this at the last minute while we were at the printer. I had to quickly scratch out the offending protrusion from the photo with the side of a pencil. You can see my handiwork on the magazine cover."

Since they were in a country whose culture is based so much on courtesy, Joe made sure his sons learned some Japanese phrases, which they used during their performances. It helped make the Japanese leg of the tour a smashing success.

After Japan, the boys toured Australia, doing concerts in Brisbane, Melbourne, Perth, Adelaide, and Sydney. In Perth, the performance took place outdoors, on a frigid night. The audience was seated in two groups in front of and behind the stage. Separating both contingents from the stage were two swimming pools. When the lights went down while Michael was singing "Ben," he heard the sound of loud splashes heading in his direction. The stage lights were quickly brightened, and it was discovered that female fans had jumped into the freezing water and were swimming toward him from both sides. He had to be rushed off the stage.

Despite the group's popularity, there was trouble brewing behind the scenes where their record sales were concerned. Whether from overexposure or lack of promotion, The Jackson 5 hadn't scored a hit record in some time. Actually, the down trend started in April 1972 with "Little Bitty Pretty One," a rhythm-and-blues number first recorded by Bobby Day in 1958 and later by Thurston Harris. Except for a seasonal release of "Santa Claus Is Coming to Town," this was the poorest-selling Jackson 5 single to date, netting only 590,629 copies. Its followup, "Lookin' Through the Windows" did worse: 581,426 copies. And then "Corner of the Sky," from the Broadway musical *Pippin* (which Gordy had financed), fared even poorer: 381,426 copies sold.*

"What the hell is going on?" Joe fumed. He began showing up at Motown, harassing the sales staff, badgering the promotion executives—all of whom were completely powerless because they took their orders from Ewart Abner. Abner had been put in charge by Berry Gordy because Gordy was devoting most of his time to Diana Ross's blossoming film career. Although he was still the company's chairman of the board, he seemed interested only in Hollywood wheeling and dealing and filmmaking. A movie titled *Mahogany* starring Diana was in the works, and this venture monopolized his time.

Motown was on a roll with a newer, more socially conscious sound, and perhaps the Jackson 5's audience had become hungry for a hipper sound than they got with "Hallelujah Day," a simple little bounce number issued in February 1973. A huge flop, it sold fewer than a quarter of a million discs. The more Joe complained to Abner, or to Berry Gordy when he could reach him, the worse things got.

Ewart Abner cared for nothing but the bottom line. If sales figures were low and The Jackson 5 was losing its audience, it was the group's fault, not Motown's. Perhaps, Abner reasoned, the group's success had run its course. "They already had their own cartoon, for Christ's sake," he argued. "Why spend any more money on them?" Ewart and Joe became fast enemies.

A single called "The Boogie Man" was planned but did not get released. An album, *Skywriter*, was released in March and sold only 115,045 copies, the group's poorest-selling album to date.

Joe firmly believed that all of the records which had been failures could have been successful if Motown had simply promoted them—expressed interest in the product to radio station program directors, thereby encouraging them to add the tunes to their playlists; purchased full-page advertisements in trade publications like *Billboard* and *Cash Box* so that the group would have a "presence" in the industry; and booked the group on more television programs so that they could sing their songs and thereby generate sales.

A major issue concerned the group's main songwriting-producing team. The Corporation (Deke Richards, Fonce Mizell, Freddie

---

*According to Deke Richards, "Corner of the Sky" was originally intended for the new Motown acquisition, The Four Seasons. When lead singer Frankie Valli continually made himself unavailable for the recording session, the song was given to The Jackson 5.

Perren, and Berry Gordy) had disbanded over a disagreement having to do with Richards's producing "Corner of the Sky" without Mizell and Perren. Suzanne dePasse had assigned the project to Richards independently and told him she would clear it with the other two, which she never did. That broke up the team. Just as The Supremes and The Four Tops had suffered in the sixties when Holland-Dozier-Holland stopped working with them, so would The Jackson 5 suffer when the Corporation dissolved.

"That was the beginning of the end of The Jackson 5 at Motown," said Deke Richards. "Nothing was held together anymore as a concept for them. After five years with the company, there was no direction anymore. I was hoping to build separate acts, continue with Michael's, Jermaine's, and Jackie's careers, but also do a solo guitar album on Tito and a vocal album on Marlon. Marlon was weak, but I felt I could do something with him anyway. But it was too late for any of this. Jackie, Marlon, and Tito were not great talents and, to be honest, no one would care about them as individual artists except for the fact that they were a part of The Jackson 5. If The Jackson 5 were not hot, then we were limited with what we could do with Jackie, Marlon, and Tito. In other words, the dream was dying."

Just when Joe was becoming obstreperous about the group's sagging sales figures, producer Hal Davis put together a terrific track for the group called "Get It Together," a cohesive, well-balanced work. The production was tight; the music, background vocals, and Michael's maturing lead sound blended nicely on this departure from the sweeter, pop music styles associated with the group up to this point. The Jackson boys used to complain to their producers that when they went to parties they never heard their records played. Their friends, they complained, wouldn't dance to their songs because they didn't think the music was rhythmic enough. If, indeed, that was true, "Get It Together" remedied the situation. Released in August 1973, it sold over 700,000 copies. Though not a million-seller, it encouraged Joe in his belief in his sons. To his way of thinking, The Jackson 5 was not finished. If anything, he was finished with Motown. As far as Joe Jackson was concerned, the party was over. Now the riot was about to start.

# Chapter
## 9

MOST WEDDINGS ARE bittersweet. Except for the bride and groom, who are usually oblivious of everything but each other, guests arrive with a full range of emotions. Memories of past loves and what might have been contrast with the realities of today and hopes for tomorrow. Tears of joy and tears of sorrow often intermingle. The marriage of Berry Gordy's only daughter Hazel to Jermaine Jackson was no exception.

Hazel Gordy and Jermaine Jackson were married on December 15, 1973, in an expensive, ostentatious wedding. "If my kid is going to get married," Berry had said, "she's going to marry in style." He ordered that Michael Roshkind, one of Motown's top executives, and Bob Jones, the company's publicity chief, organize the event. "Sky's the limit," he insisted. In all, the wedding would cost him $234,000. (Perhaps to offset criticism from the black community, Gordy contributed a check to the Avalon Carver Community Settlement House in Los Angeles to enable "twelve hundred needy black families to enjoy Christmas." The amount of the contribution was not made public.)

It was a striking statement on America: the coming together of the handsome son of a former construction worker turned record industry mogul and the pretty daughter of a former assembly line employee who now ran a show business empire. The fact that the prime characters in the drama were young—Jermaine had turned nineteen four days before and Hazel was just nineteen years old herself—and black made the festivities even more exciting especially for the black media. *Ebony* magazine called it "the wedding of the century." Guests were overheard comparing it to the royal wedding in London when Princess Anne, daughter of Queen Elizabeth II, had married Captain Mark Phillips a little more than a month earlier. Abe Lastfogel, a William Morris founder, called it "the most lavish merger I've ever seen." To ensure that the media would report the details correctly, Motown handed out publicity releases to the invited reporters.

Sixteen-year-old Marlon was the best man. Fifteen-year-old Michael, along with brothers Jackie (twenty-two), Tito (twenty), and Randy (eleven), were ushers. Michael's duties that day were not complicated: escort guests to seats before the ceremony and escort one of the bridesmaids out after it. However, people close to the Jackson family have indicated that Michael felt preoccupied on this day. Jermaine, who had always been his favorite big brother, was getting married. It was going to make a difference.

"At first Michael had thought it wouldn't matter," said one close family friend. "Tito was married and The Jackson 5 had continued as before. His wife was a sweet, naive type who really had nothing to do with group business or politics. But Jermaine was marrying Hazel, the boss's daughter, a lady who had strong opinions and got her own way. As the wedding day got closer and closer, Michael could not help but notice that Jermaine started to look at things differently—through Hazel's eyes." Jermaine was becoming less Michael's best friend and more Hazel's man. Michael would feel the loss keenly.

At a group rehearsal shortly before the wedding, the brothers tried to work out a problem in choreography with Suzanne dePasse, the Motown employee who supervised the Jacksons' rehearsals. A decision had been made on how best to handle the situation, and the brothers were all in agreement. But then Hazel, who had begun attending all rehearsals, pulled Jermaine aside and whispered something in his ear. Jermaine listened, nodded his head, and walked back to his brothers. "I think we oughta change this step," he announced.

"But why?" Michael protested. "It's perfect as it is."

" 'Cause Hazel had a great idea. Look, Mike [sometimes the family calls Michael, "Mike"], you stand here. And Tito here, Marlon there, and Jackie over there." Jermaine then demonstrated to his brothers Hazel's "great idea" which, when executed, made Jermaine much more prominent in the routine than he had previously been.

Suzanne dePasse watched the new steps and then looked over to Hazel, who was smiling innocently. Since Hazel was Berry Gordy's daughter, Suzanne really had no choice but to agree with her suggestion. "Looks fine, guys. Let's keep it."

"Well, I hate it," Michael announced, looking at Jermaine. "C'mon, Jermaine," he said. "I thought we agreed."

Jermaine looked away.

The other brothers tried to ignore what had happened. "It ain't that important," Tito decided.

"Well, I think it *is* important," Michael concluded, defeated. "But you guys can do whatever you want." He then looked over to Jermaine—who was in another conference with Hazel—shook his head and rolled his eyes.

December 15, 1973, started out overcast, but by noon the temperature was sixty degrees and the sun was shining. No matter what the weather was like outside, for the one hundred guests invited to the ceremony and the other five hundred–plus invited to the reception and luncheon, it was a winter wonderland at the exclusive Beverly Hills Hotel. Artificial snow-covered pine trees, 175 white doves in white cages, and thousands of white camellias, chrysanthemums, and carnations decorated the rooms in which the wedding, reception, and luncheon took place. In keeping with the winter decor, the bride wore a princess-style white satin dress trimmed with white mink at the neckline, wrists, and hem. The dress and its twelve-foot, white-mink-trimmed train were decorated with seventy-five hundred hand-sewn pearls. Her short veil cascaded from a white mink-trimmed headdress. It was the kind of costume that made guests sigh "Oooh" as Hazel walked down the aisle on the arm of her beaming father. When they reached the altar, Berry Gordy lifted Hazel's veil, kissed her lightly on the cheek, and the ceremony began.

The groom was equally resplendent all in white. His suit with a cutaway jacket had bugle beads trimming the lapels and trouser stripes; he wore a white velvet bow tie. Marlon, his best man, and all the ushers, including Jackie, Tito, Michael, and Randy, wore gray cutaways with velvet lapels and gray satin piping. The father of the groom wore a lilac shirt with his gray cutaway. His mother wore sapphire blue chiffon.

After the ceremony, a reception was held in the Lanai Room, followed by luncheon in the Crystal Room. Show business celebrities, including Smokey Robinson, Diana Ross, Lola Falana, Diahann Carroll, and Billy Dee Williams, mingled with other notables such as Coretta Scott King, Mayor Tom Bradley and Mrs. Bradley, and superagent Sue Mengers. As the guests sipped 1966 *Moët & Chandon* champagne cocktails and sampled Iranian caviar, an all-string orchestra played excerpts from Chopin and Tchaikovsky, as well as the theme songs from *Love Story, Doctor Zhivago*, and *Gigi*. Considering that this was a marriage between Hazel Gordy, whose father set musical standards for an entire generation, and Jermaine Jackson, whose name was now synonymous with contemporary musical fare, the choice of background music was ironic.

It was not the only irony. Hazel had asked Smokey Robinson to write a song for the occasion because "he and his wife, Claudette, have been married for so many years, and they are so happy, they're inspirational to all show business couples." The song was "From This Time and Place," and as Smokey began crooning "We're going to write the book on happiness," tears started streaming down his face. Claudette, his wife of fifteen years, holding their six-year-old son Berry in her lap, was crying as well.

The bride and groom seemed to glow as Smokey sang about undying love. "Tears were in my eyes," Smokey would recall of his performance. "For young love, old love, love lost, and love refound." Later, friends would learn that at this time Smokey was having an affair with an eighteen-year-old "Soul Train" dancer who swore she was twenty-one and only interested in starting a fan club for him. "That's man's nature," Smokey would explain to Claudette. Although Smokey claimed he felt genuine affection for his wife, he was still reeling from a previous affair-gone-bad with a Playboy bunny named Kandi. In an effort to sort out his feelings, Smokey had recently moved out of the Robinson home.

"It's not easy for a woman to be married to someone in show business," Berry Gordy said of his daughter. "I just pray it works out better for her than it has for some of my friends."

Smokey and Claudette were not the only ones there who had separated. Katherine and Joe were having marital difficulties at this time. Katherine had discovered that Joe was being unfaithful to her—a "friend" had telephoned Katherine to give her the news—and, her long-time suspicions confirmed, she decided to take action. "I didn't believe he'd risk all that we'd worked for as a couple," she said. Oldest daughter Rebbie, who was twenty-three, couldn't even stand to be in the same room with her father after she heard of the affair, and tried to convince her mother to leave Joe. Katherine would say later that she could not bring herself to file for divorce, even though she was "devastated" by Joe's actions. In fact, she did file for divorce on March 9, 1973, in Los Angeles.

Katherine Jackson was faced with a dilemma, however, when she and the Beverly Hills law firm she had hired to represent her, Newson and Wolfberg, began filling out the required forms. She didn't have a clue as to the value or extent of her community property with Joe. She had no idea how much her husband—or children—earned. She didn't even know Joe's social security number. So she had to leave two pages of questions regarding this personal information unanswered. Her lawyer, Neil C. Newson, typed on the form, "The information required in this declaration is currently being compiled. A separate amended financial declaration will be filed." Katherine paid him $150 and then tried to figure out how to discover the answers to so many questions she'd never even thought of before. She did not move out of the house, and neither did Joe.

"When Motown learned that Katherine had filed for a divorce, all hell broke loose," remembered one family friend. "This could ruin everything. All of those stories about how close they were, what a loving family they were . . . It had the potential to be a public relations disaster. No one was to know that Katherine and Joe were splitting up. It was a closely guarded secret. Katherine was badgered constantly by company officials who said they were friends and who tried to convince her to reconcile with Joe for the sake of her family's image. That pressure, combined with the fact that she was disgusted with trying to fill out the forms, eventually encouraged her simply to drop the whole matter of divorce, much to Motown's relief."

But then, shortly before Jermaine's wedding, Katherine Jackson suddenly left town. "The children were devastated by what was happening, Michael in particular because he was so close to his mother," recalled Joyce Jillson (not the syndicated astrologer), a former friend of Katherine's. "He said he wanted to go with her, but she refused. 'If you're leaving, so am I,' he told her. 'I'm not going to let you go without me.' " Michael didn't want to find himself living in the Jackson home with his brothers and sisters and father, unless Katherine was present. To Michael, she was his only link to sanity. But now even she had become unpredictable. Katherine had never done anything like this before. She certainly must have had good reason, because it was very unlike her to disrupt the family.

"I think she just couldn't take it another second," Jillson concluded.

The timing was wrong. Katherine loved Jermaine and wanted to be at his wedding. Besides, she knew the wedding was bound to garner national attention, and had she not been there—for any reason—her absence would have kindled a bonfire of gossip which would be bound to hurt her children. Already, a reporter from *Soul* magazine had received an anonymous telephone tip that Katherine had moved out of the Jackson home because of problems with Joe. According to the source, Katherine had actually confronted the other woman, and a loud argument ensued.

Although the reporter had started to follow up on the lead, he let it drop rather than jeopardize a relationship with Gordy that promised advertising revenue in the future. When Katherine heard through friends that this reporter knew about her leaving home, she must have been concerned. There was no way of telling how many other writers, who were not as friendly with Motown, were also privy to what had transpired.

So Katherine made the best of a bad situation and forgave Joe. She returned home after a few days; it's not known where she went but it hardly mattered. Susie Jackson, Johnny Jackson's former wife, observed, "She loved Joseph and just hoped he would stop screwing around."

At Jermaine and Hazel's wedding, Katherine would force herself to act as if nothing was wrong in her own marriage, even though she was desperately unhappy. No matter how hard she tried to conceal it, some of the sadness was apparent. As soon as the photographers finished taking pictures of her and Joe, she would pull away from him. She seemed preoccupied. At one point Michael, concerned, asked his mother if she would like a glass of punch. Katherine shook her head absentmindedly as she gazed over her son's head at Joe. "I don't feel like dancing, honey," Katherine said. Michael watched with reddened eyes as his mother turned from him and walked into the crowd. To even the most casual observer, she seemed very alone.

However, the reporters there had more than enough newsworthy people to talk to. One of them asked Gordy, "Why would you allow your nineteen-year-old, Pepperdine College–educated daughter to marry a man with only a high school education?"

Gordy just glared at the writer. But when he realized that other members of the press had begun gathering to hear his answer, he regained his composure.

"At first thought, you think about a doctor, a lawyer, a professional person for your daughter to marry," he began, very diplomatically. "But when it all comes down to human values and what life is all about—happiness, contentment, desire to achieve—I think that's what really counts. Jermaine is a fine human being. Of all the men she could have fallen in love with, she found one whom I like very much and who is a great moral person and a great human being." (Hazel Gordy, a Beverly Hills High School alumna, attended Pepperdine for a brief time; she did not graduate.)

Joe Jackson, standing behind Gordy, listened intently. When Gordy finished, Joe muttered, "What a bunch of crap," to the person standing at his side, not realizing that she also was a journalist because she was not holding the required notepad. "This man is the biggest bullshit artist of all time," he said before walking away.

According to many guests at the wedding, Berry appeared to care about his new son-in-law. One of them said, "The last time I saw him look that way at anyone was Diana Ross. And look what happened to her."

Joe should have been delighted. He had worked hard behind the scenes to make this wedding come about. Jermaine had liked Hazel when they first met, but not nearly as much as she liked him. After a short time, Hazel told Jermaine she was in love with him, even though he made it clear that he was not sure he could return her affection. He was a teenage idol, a star, and could have his pick of dozens of willing young women any time he wanted. This idolatry was pretty heady stuff; it made the idea of settling down with one woman seem confining, no matter who she might be.

"Jermaine likes girls too much to get married," Michael had said. "I think he'll be in his thirties before he does anything like that."

However, Hazel was a young, idealistic girl who wanted more than anything to marry and have a family. Not only had her father been divorced three times, but she had witnessed Berry and Diana Ross's tumultuous, heart-wrenching affair, one that lasted for many years and never resulted in marriage because Berry would not commit himself. Hazel must have realized that true love was elusive, yet she, a true romantic, once said, "I can truthfully say that since I fell in love with Jermaine I have never even thought about any other man." Jermaine, a playboy in the tradition of his own father, observed, "I guess every young man who gets married at twenty [*sic*] has wondered if he might have missed out on something real special just around the corner."

Observed one family friend, "Berry Gordy had been lavishing his only daughter with gifts for as long as she could remember. She told him that she was in love with one of The Jackson 5 and she wanted him for her own. Her feelings for Jermaine were so strong, she was afraid to let him slip through her fingers for fear that no one like him would ever come along again. She was jealous when she would see Jermaine with female fans. 'Michael can have fans, but you can't,' she used to tell him, which was ludicrous. Berry made sure she usually got what she wanted. Now she wanted Jermaine.''

Even The Jackson 5's own fan club president, Steve Manning, had to admit, "One reason that no other girl ever had a chance with the dude [Jermaine] is that Hazel was always around him. She is rich, and whatever Hazel wants, Hazel gets—in this case, Jermaine.''

Susie Jackson recalled, "From what I heard from Johnny [Jackson], Berry gave Hazel as much money as Jermaine was worth at that time so that they could start out on equal footing. This way she wouldn't have to decide whether or not to sign a prenuptial agreement. It wouldn't have been necessary.''

But Hazel had an unexpected ally in Joe Jackson, who might not have insisted on a prenuptial agreement anyway. He was certain that marriage between the two would ensure job security for the Jackson clan at Motown. He did all he could do to help. He encouraged Jermaine to marry Hazel, and soon Jermaine was calling her "my Hazel" and saying that he loved her.

Had Joe given the matter more thought, he might not have been so sure of the wisdom of his plan. Berry Gordy's sister Anna was married to Motown singer Marvin Gaye, and that alliance never gave Marvin any special privileges at the company. In fact, according to Marvin, his marriage only served to complicate his life and his career because Anna sometimes acted as a spy for her brother when Marvin was trying to protect his own interests. Marvin Gaye was rarely able to make a move that Berry didn't know about in advance. Also, Marvin said that he always felt a strong conflict of interest whenever he and Berry Gordy battled, which was often.

Marvin boycotted the wedding. "I refused to go," he would say in a later interview. "It was obvious to me what was happening. I was being replaced. Jermaine Jackson was marrying into the Gordy family as I had. Berry no longer cared about me. He wanted a newer, younger Marvin Gaye, and that's what he was priming Jermaine to do, to be the next Prince of Motown. No way was I going to watch the crowning ceremony.''

Many of the guests apparently felt as Marvin did that Jermaine was about to be groomed by Berry to become a major Motown artist. While it's true that Jermaine's two solo releases for the company—"That's How Love Goes" and "Daddy's Home"—were successful, Jermaine just did not have his brother Michael's range or vocal control. Some critics cited strong similarities between Jermaine's vocal style and Marvin Gaye's, but that seems unfair to Marvin in retrospect.*

Steve Manning, in a letter he wrote to *Ebony* magazine after the wedding, observed, "Jermaine doesn't have to worry about his future now. He's got it made. Whenever The Jackson 5 go on their own, Jermaine won't have to worry about a thing. He's married to the boss's daughter."

But Joe wasn't thinking of breaking up the act as much as he was hoping that the Jermaine-Hazel union would allow the Jacksons to have special perks at Motown. Berry Gordy wouldn't intrude in family matters, Joe must have reasoned. The Jacksons were a family first, and as head of that family, Joe was certain that everybody would listen to him. That's the way it had always been, and it's unlikely that he saw any reason that things would change, even though Jermaine had a new and powerful father-in-law. In time, Joe Jackson would wish he had thought all of this through more carefully.

Joe Jackson always did his best to make it appear that he was a man to be reckoned with. Berry Gordy had dispersed his body-guards throughout the crowd to keep a watchful eye on the proceedings. Not to be outdone, Joe arranged for his own coterie of security. Whenever one of Gordy's men crossed paths with one of Jackson's, the two would glower at one another.

"Have you noticed all of the bodyguards around here?" Walter Burrell, from *Soul* magazine, asked Michael Jackson.

Michael looked around. "Oh, you mean those guys? Gee, I thought they were guests," he said. Then he smiled and winked.

The security guards were probably so busy looking at each other that none of them noticed the fire. "In the midst of all of this, the whole place almost burned down," Walter Burrell remembered. "At the dinner table where I was sitting, a frightening and sudden burst of smoke and flames erupted when an electrical circuit over-loaded on a hot plate. Incredibly, when we at the table called, choking, to the waiters for assistance, they ignored us totally and continued to serve prime rib without batting an eye or missing a plate, as though the smelly electrical fire was of no consequence whatsoever. An elderly waiter finally smothered and beat the flames

---

*The reason Jermaine started singing leads in the first place was that the group's producer, Deke Richards, was hospitalized with a slipped disk. He didn't want his partners, Fonce Mizell and Freddie Perren, to work with Michael without him, so he told them to write something for Jermaine. That song was "I Found That Girl," the flip side of "The Love You Save."

down at no small risk, and after a few minutes we were able to reseat ourselves. Despite that, I was, quite frankly, awed by the entire production. Especially the amount of money that was obviously spent.''

The incident was mostly overlooked, possibly because the reporters were so busy interviewing the guests. Diana Ross, in her light green silk outfit, was the center of attention.

"Miss Ross, how about a shot of you and Claudette together?" asked a photographer.

"Oh, of course," Diana said eagerly.

"No, I don't think so," Claudette demurred. "How about a shot of me and this little guy here?" She grabbed Michael, who had been standing on the sidelines watching. Michael put his arm around Claudette and smiled obediently as flashcubes popped all around them. Diana stood nearby glaring at the two of them. After the photographers finished, she ran over and pulled Michael away.

"*I* brought him to Mr. Gordy's attention, and now look where he is today. *Everybody* wants to have their picture taken with this cutie. It's just so amazing." Diana squeezed fifteen-year-old Michael tightly as if he were a trophy. Then she smiled for the photographers. "Isn't he cute? Just look at his little suit." Michael winced at that remark.

"You're awfully grateful to Miss Ross, aren't you, kid?" a reporter asked Michael.

"Uh . . . yeah," Michael agreed. He must have wondered just how long he was going to have to live with this lie that Diana Ross had "discovered" him. "Real grateful," he repeated.

"Isn't he sweet?" Diana cooed.

Michael slipped away as quickly as he could.

It would be understandable if he felt he had to get away by himself and sort out his thoughts. It probably seemed to him that everywhere he turned, he was surrounded by hypocrisy, just as he had been for as long as he could remember. Michael was sensitive enough to know that it was business as much as love that motivated this marriage. The political ramifications of the Gordy-Jackson union didn't escape him. "People were winking at us now, saying that we'd always be looked after," he recalled.

Fifteen-year-old youngsters know a lot of things. Michael Jackson knew less than some of his peers, a lot more than others. He may not have known as much about basketball, baseball, or other sports as some boys, but he knew how to mesmerize an audience with his voice and stage presence; he knew how to record a song that could sell millions of copies; he knew how to dodge aggressive fans, how to strike a pose for a pinup poster, how to be a teen idol.

But standing there at his brother Jermaine's wedding reception, he certainly didn't know how to fix what was going wrong. He would admit later that he had to question whether his brother really loved Hazel or was simply going along with the marriage to appease his father. He must have known that the lavish display was more a promotion for Motown than a religious ceremony. That some guests, many of whom didn't even know the young couple, looked on the event as a chance to get their names or pictures in the paper. That his own parents, who had once promised to love, honor, and obey until death do them part, were in discord. Worst of all, he knew that there was very little he himself could do to change any of it.

So Michael Jackson rejoined the guests and smiled as he watched the bride and groom cut the eight-tiered, seven-foot-high wedding cake. And he joined as everyone toasted the newlyweds in the engraved silver goblets which Berry intended each guest to keep as a memento of the day. And he probably shrugged his shoulders when Diahann Carroll, who had just signed a recording contract with Berry, was stopped by a Motown official for walking out the door with four of them. Her explanation as she kept on walking: "But Berry and I are friends, and I'm sure he won't mind."

After all, wasn't *everybody* friends?

# Chapter

# 🌸 10 🌸

IN FEBRUARY 1974, shortly after Jermaine Jackson returned from his honeymoon in Switzerland, The Jackson 5 embarked on a ten-day tour of the Republic of Senegal, Africa, on the heels of Stevie Wonder's much-publicized announcement that he was going to leave the United States to live there. (Later, Wonder decided not to move.) "Before Stevie told the public about moving there, he told me," Michael Jackson recalled. "I asked why and he said he would feel safe there because that was his home. I could live there."

When the group arrived in Senegal at dawn, a long line of Africans dancing in native costumes with drums and shakers greeted their plane. They performed a tribal dance to welcome The Jackson 5 to their country. "The people are warm and kind," Michael said of the Africans. "I always thought that blacks, as far as artistry, were the most talented race on earth. But when I went to Africa, I was even more convinced. They do incredible things there. They've got the beats and rhythm . . . I really see where drums come from. I don't want the blacks to ever forget that this is where we come from and where our music comes from. I want us to remember."

The boys, and Michael in particular, were struck by the impoverished conditions of the cities they played in Africa. "There are a lot of people there who don't have food and who can't afford it," Michael said later. "Before people here throw away food, they should stop and think. The hunger hurts me."

The conditions for the Jacksons were terrible. There was no running water for bathing, the accommodations were filthy, and the boys were anxious to get back home.

The Republic of Senegal, the Nebraska-sized country on the westernmost bulge of Africa, is a nation with a long history of contact with the outside world. As early as the tenth century, Arab caravans crossed the Sahara from North Africa to trade and to convert the natives to Islam. The earliest European traders, the Portuguese in the 1400s, were followed by the Dutch, French, and British, all of whom dealt in gold, ivory—and slaves. Through most of the eighteenth and nineteenth centuries, Senegal was a center of the slave trade. Until Senegal became independent in 1960, it was the hub of France's West African holdings. In spite of so many foreign influences, and although Dakar boasts one of the busiest ports in all of Africa, Senegal retains its West African cultural heritage through its language and lifestyle.

Barren Gorée Island is a two-mile ferry ride from Dakar. Although it is small—only eighty-eight acres in all—and it only takes an hour for a visitor to walk the narrow streets to see its sights, the island still attracts many tourists. The Maison des Esclaves (House of Slaves) is preserved much as it was when it was built around 1776. From then until 1848—when France abolished slavery—men, women, and children were crammed into windowless holding rooms in the basement to await shipment to North and South America. This first step of their captivity so weakened many of them that they fell ill and died in the miserable ships carrying them to their destinations.

Since the younger members of The Jackson 5 could not attend regular school because of their work—and they could only learn so much from the tutors that traveled with them on the road—tours of this nature were the best kind of education for the Jackson boys.

"Michael and Marlon learned a lot," recalled Jackie. "I studied Gorée in high school and college, but I never did know exactly what it was like until I went there and saw. I never did know the places were that small, or how they captured them [slaves] and chained them up like that."

In contrast to the somber trip to Gorée Island, an exciting event occurred in Dakar when, after the boys' performance there, Joe was awarded a silver medal of commendation for what was called "his contribution to the arts." The nation's tourism director said the medal symbolized "both the resurgence of black culture and the civilization of the black man." The last American recipient of the award was Duke Ellington in 1966. Jackson made a brief acceptance speech calling for "black Americans and Africans to strengthen the ties between us."

Their tour of Africa was an unforgettable experience for all of them, reminding them of their heritage and inspiring in the Jackson family a renewed respect for and pride in their race.

When interviewed about the tour, Jermaine said, "If black

Americans would go to Africa and build it like we should, there is no reason Africa couldn't be the number one power in the world. These people here in America are going around hollering 'Black Power' when they should be putting their heads to trying to build a unit, trying to get things together, so when they go to Africa they can feel proud. It's really a shame to see all those white people walking around there, when they're the ones who did all the dirty work, treating the slaves as they did. It makes me upset. I don't like what happened and never will. There is a poem I'm writing about Africa, and it's about a little African boy calling out to this little black American boy, 'Black boy, come home, so we can be strong.' ''

"In the books, they hide a lot of things about black Americans," Marlon said after the group returned from Africa. "For instance, the books say the first guy to go to the North Pole was a white guy, but that isn't true. The first guy was a black guy. They hide a lot of things from us. We've been told we weren't good for anything but slaves. But we know now that's untrue. In Africa, you're around your family, your brothers and sisters. You all are one."

To the press, the boys were outspoken about black pride and unity, which was unusual for a Motown act. Gordy tolerated it, hoping they would eventually get off the subject; they did.

Privately, though, the Jacksons were disgusted with the impoverished conditions of their accommodations at every step along the way. They were used to living in luxury and couldn't wait to get back to Encino. Toward the end of the tour, Jermaine turned to Richard Arons and said, "Richard, I'm sure glad you white people brought us to America."

Once back in the United States, The Jackson 5 would have their own problems with unity. Jermaine's marriage to Hazel was causing dissension. Granted that all newlyweds want to be together as much as possible, it still appeared to friends that she was trying to drive a wedge between Jermaine and his family by her possessiveness. One friend remembered, "Hazel wanted nothing to do with the Jackson family, really. Her main interest was Jermaine, whom she was madly in love with. She seemed to resent LaToya quite a bit. LaToya was very pretty, and Hazel was always self-conscious about her looks, even though she was not bad looking. She and LaToya did not hit it off at all. Hazel got along well enough with Katherine but kept her distance from Joe. To her, Jermaine was a prize. A trophy. She didn't really want to share him, even with his own family."

Although there were rumors, any cracks in the family unity were plastered over whenever the media came to call. To hear the Jackson family tell it, "Wedding Bells Are Breaking Up That Old Gang of Mine" was not going to be part of their repertoire—certainly not the repertoire for public consumption.

When the group returned, Motown issued "Dancing Machine," a fine rhythmic production by Hal Davis. As the onslaught of disco began to homogenize the pop-R&B scene, The Jackson 5 managed with this single to maintain their originality while capitalizing on the new disco trend. A high-spirited Michael bantered the lyrics above the strong choral chants of his brothers, and all to a very infectious beat. In the pop music world, the Jackson brothers were clearly holding their own alongside the likes of The Temptations, The Spinners, and The Four Tops, who were no longer idols, but peers. The Jackson 5 were many years ahead of their time and on to the electric sound of the eighties; the style of "Dancing Machine" is similar to a sound that, a dozen years later, would be known as "techno-pop." The song would eventually hit number two on the *Billboard* charts and sell 2,170,327 copies, the most singles sales for the group since "Never Can Say Good-bye."

At this time, the group appeared with Cher on her television series. From their ruffled white shirts and black cutaway jackets with the silver-beaded lapels and cuffs, to their trousers with the waist-to-hem silver-beaded stripe on the outer legs, right down to their white dancing shoes, The Jackson 5 looked mighty classy. Like a column of silver in a slinky halter-top pantsuit, Cher was her outrageous self. Her hairstyle was remarkable—sprinkled with silver paillettes, her short, pyramid-shaped bob was almost as wide as her shoulders. Guests and hostess were perfectly costume-coordinated.

They performed on a large red initial "C" placed on its side, which served as a ministage and ramp, marking the area as Cher's territory. During a medley of The Jackson 5's hits, Cher hung in like a good sport, singing and dancing up a storm. Anything Michael could do, she could do—sort of. By the time they got to the last number, "Dancing Machine"—during which she and Michael mimicked robots in a choreographed routine—it looked as though Cher was winding down. All except her hair. No matter what Cher did, her hair never moved a strand during the whole routine.

After the medley, Cher and the Jacksons graciously accepted the audience's applause. Once backstage, Cher collapsed in a chair. "Jesus Christ," she said, out of breath. "You guys work so goddamn hard. How do you do this every goddamn night? That's what I'd like to know.''

Somebody handed her a cigarette. She took a long drag. ''Shit,'' she exclaimed, turning to her assistant. ''Is this a menthol, or what? It just about burned my goddamn lungs.''

Michael's eyes widened like saucers. It wasn't often he heard language like this. And from a lady, no less.

''Uh, you were real good, Cher,'' Michael offered, hesitantly. He started to blush. ''I mean, you know, the dancing and all.''

Cher studied Michael's embarrassed reaction for a moment. After gulping down a glass of water, she answered, ''Next time you're on my show, I'm not dancing with you, Michael Jackson. You can forget *that*. Damn.'' Cher obviously knew her language was getting to Michael.

''Well, I, uh . . . ,'' he stammered. ''It's been nice seein' you again,'' he concluded. ''Gotta go now. Oh, Jermaine, wait up.''

When Michael rushed away as quickly as he possibly could, Cher burst out laughing.

Joe Jackson, always a competitive man, seemed even more so after the wedding, as though Jermaine's alliance with Berry made Joe consider himself a David determined to slug it out with the Motown Goliath. To make more of an impression on the entertainment industry, Joe formed his own record company, Ivory Tower International Records, and signed a female quartet from Ashtabula, Ohio, called M.D.L.T. Willis. The company and group would not go far, which only served to reaffirm Berry Gordy's feeling that Joe was well-meaning but inept.

But one thing Joe wanted to do that Berry wasn't interested in was to break his sons out of the teen-idol mold and into a more secure niche. He realized that the careers of most teen idols last about two years before newer stars come along to replace them. Joe Jackson wanted to change his sons' public images.

In the winter of 1974 during a family meeting, Joe made the announcement. ''Boys, we're gonna play Las Vegas.''

''White folks play Vegas, don't they?'' Jackie wanted to know. ''It's the thing you do when you don't have no hits, when you don't have no choice.''

''The brothers thought hangin' out in the hotels with white people would be no fun,'' Michael recalled later. ''But I wanted to play Las Vegas immediately. To me, Las Vegas was part of show business tradition. At that meeting, our father told us two things: First, he said he was trying to show the world that we were every bit as good as The Osmonds; then he told us about Sammy Davis and what he went through so that guys like us could play Las Vegas.''

It was 1945 when Sammy Davis, Jr., his father, Sammy, and his uncle, Will Mastin, were booked into the El Rancho Vegas hotel in Las Vegas for five hundred dollars a week. Las Vegas was the new show business mecca, with the El Rancho and Last Frontier being the first luxury hotels. But though invited to appear as an opening act in the showroom, Sammy and his relatives were not permitted to stay in a room there because of the color of their skin. They had to live in a boardinghouse with the black porters and dishwashers who worked at the hotels. Their accommodations consisted of a shack made of wooden crates and cardboard outside of town—at twice the price of accommodations at the El Rancho. This was not unusual. Even a headliner like Billy Eckstine, who was also working in Vegas at the same time, could not stay at the hotel at which he appeared. The showrooms and casinos were also off-limits to black patrons; blacks could entertain but not gamble or socialize with whites.

In years to come, Sammy Davis, Jr., would break through these barriers by sheer virtue of his talent and persistence. He went from being a member of the Will Mastin Trio to being a solo star paid over $175,000 a week in Vegas by the 1970s. By using his celebrity power and refusing to take no for an answer, ''Mr. Show Business'' was instrumental in desegregating the town so that blacks could not only appear but also vacation and have fun there. By attending city hotel board meetings and working *within* the political system instead of against it, Davis also made it possible in the late fifties for more blacks to be hired at the Sands, where he performed. When Davis died in May 1990, the Las Vegas strip went dark for ten minutes in his memory.

''I wanted that more than anything, to be a part of the tradition,'' Michael would say six years later. He had been a Sammy Davis admirer since the age of ten. ''To me, it was important. A giant step.''

Berry Gordy was not enthusiastic over the April 1974 Vegas booking, even though Joe managed to strike a deal with Bernie Rothkopf, entertainment director at the MGM Grand, the newest and most prestigious hotel in the city. The group would be coheadlining with popular impressionist Frank Gorshin. (The Osmonds used impersonator Rich Little as an opening act.)

''If you decide to do this thing, you'll be doing it on your own,''

Ewart Abner, a high-ranking Motown official, told Joe. "Motown won't be involved. These kids aren't ready for Las Vegas."

Berry telephoned Joe when he heard about the upcoming engagement. "You're makin' the biggest mistake of their career," he told Joe. "What, are you crazy? These boys shouldn't be doing Vegas yet."

"Butt out!" was Joe's response. "These are *my* kids. Vegas has a good tradition, and I want them to know about it. It's time for them to grow."

It has been said that when Berry reminded Joe that he was dealing with "my son-in-law's career," Joe hung up on him.

Certainly Berry Gordy understood the value and prestige of having The Jackson 5 appear in Las Vegas because he had championed the Vegas breakthrough with The Supremes in 1966. But that was only after years of careful honing of their act. A year prior to the Vegas engagement, The Supremes had played the Copacabana nightclub in New York in order to appeal to a white, adult audience and open the doors into that marketplace for the rest of the Motown artists. Berry wanted his acts to appeal to adults, especially white adults, but he didn't think it was time yet for The Jackson 5 to make this transition.

Success in Las Vegas was the guarantee that an act could always work, regardless of its status on the charts. But failure in Vegas could help end a performer's career. Berry was certain that because of their lack of experience with the kind of material necessary to please a middle-of-the-road, predominantly white audience, the boys would fail miserably. In the end, he apparently decided, this failure would be fine with him.

"Let 'em go into Las Vegas if they want," Berry reasoned to one of his aides. He was still stung by Joe's reaction. "They'll fall flat on their faces, and it'll teach Joe a good lesson. Too bad the boys gotta suffer, especially Jermaine, but that's just the way it is. This will be such a major disaster they'll come back to me crawlin' on their knees."

Joe was anxious to teach Berry a lesson of his own. At his urging, the entire family rallied together to prove Berry mistaken.

"We knew that Motown didn't believe in what we were doing," Jermaine recalled. "My father was out to prove them wrong, and the brothers were behind him one hundred percent. I was torn by it. I had a suspicion that maybe Berry was right."

The Jackson 5's act might be strong enough to interest the touristy Vegas crowd, but for added ammunition Joe decided to follow the way of The Osmonds and recruit other family members for the act. Whereas The Osmonds brought in younger brother Jimmy and sister Marie for their Caesars' engagement, Joe recruited LaToya, seventeen, as well as Randy, twelve, and Janet, seven. (Maureen—who told Joe she would like to give show business a try herself now—was also expected to perform, but when she sprained her ankle, her debut was postponed a few months until June in Chicago.)

"My dad asked me if I wanted to sing in the Vegas act. I was so shy at the time, I can't believe he asked me," Janet recalled in a 1990 interview. "Being in front of this huge audience for the first time, I could easily have gotten stage fright, but thank God I didn't. It would have ruined the whole show."

None of the new additions to The Jackson 5 show was breathtakingly talented, but their marginal ability did help gloss up the overall show. It was Katherine's idea to have Randy and Janet do impressions of Sonny and Cher, rhythm-and-blues stars Mickey and Sylvia, and even Jeanette MacDonald and Nelson Eddy. Janet also did a cute Mae West in a backless, pink satin gown and feather boa, which *Variety* would call "hilarious."

LaToya Jackson joined the tap dancing routine to "Forty-second Street." There was a bit of a problem with LaToya, who desperately wanted to sing a solo in the act but had no vocal talent whatsoever.

"She wanted the spotlight," remembered a friend of hers. "And she wanted it bad. She would rant and rave, cry and throw fits. Joe told her that all she would be allowed to do was mouth the words of songs on stage in group numbers, acting as if she were singing but not really singing at all. She didn't like that, but she had no choice."

On stage, the MGM Grand orchestra loomed behind the Jacksons. It was the kind of orchestra that would not fit on most stages. A small group of musicians—Motown's rhythm section—was added to the mix to help recreate the sound of those famous Jackson 5 hits. Bright and colorful fireworks patterns burst across a pale blue backdrop as the Jacksons appeared on stage, much to the excitement of their audience.

Reed-thin Michael was, of course, the act's centerpiece with his solo star turns and impressions (he did a fairly adept impersonation of Diana Ross). As the *Hollywood Reporter* noted, "[he is] the Diana Ross of the Jacksons and an obvious choice for the next solo star status."

"When we started out, I used to be little, cute, and charming," Michael said in the act. "Now I'm big, cute, and charming."

Spinning like a human top in a sparkling white suit in front of the large symphony orchestra and flanked by his siblings, Michael effortlessly churned through each number, changing pace again and again but always maintaining that mesmerizing grip on an audience's eyes that is so essential for a performer. After each song, Michael would walk down to the footlights and accept the plaudits of his fans.

Most reviewers, and even Jackson 5 fans, were perplexed by the group's new nightclub act—with their impressions of groups like the Four Freshmen and the Andrews Sisters—fearing that the family had abandoned its black core audience in favor of a new, white "money crowd." Michael was as mystified by their concern as they were by his and his brothers' performance. "They just don't understand," he said at the time. "There's nothing wrong with trying new things. There's nothing wrong with expanding."

"Like Frank Sinatra," Jackie told Vince Aletti for the *Village Voice.* "He don't have to put out a hit record; he can still go to Las Vegas and pack 'em in."

On opening night, April 9, 1974, the family was presented with a key to the city by the mayor of Las Vegas. It was a proud moment. "We ain't what we should be, but thank God we ain't what we were," Joe Jackson said. Jackson was paraphrasing Martin Luther King, Jr.'s prophetic words, "We ain't what we oughta be, we ain't what we wanna be, we ain't what we gonna be, but thank God we ain't what we was."

For this first Las Vegas stint, the Jackson family had worked their hearts out. They didn't need Joe to remind them that this was it, that their whole future in show business could well depend on this night. Sure, there had been applause after each number. Katherine, in the audience with a group of friends and relatives, had done her best to ensure that. But when the Jackson sons brought out the sisters for those final bows, it wasn't only family and friends who stood up to cheer. As all of them—Jackie, Tito, Jermaine, Marlon, Michael, LaToya, Randy, and Janet—joined hands and raised their arms into the air triumphantly, the entire audience erupted into enthusiastic applause and then a rousing standing ovation.

In the wings, stage right, Joe rocked back and forth on this heels, hands jammed in his tux pockets, a grin from ear to ear spread across his face. With the exception of the absent Maureen, this was the realization of Joe's greatest dream: all of his children on stage and performing together. "They did it," he said to no one in particular. "They did it."

In the wings, stage left, directly across from Joe, three Motown officials slapped each other on the back. "They did it," said one. "We got ourselves some Vegas stars."

When Berry Gordy learned that The Jackson 5 was a Vegas smash on opening night, he sent a contingent of Motown executives to the hotel to present an image of corporate support. "We were always certain that the boys had what it took," he told the press in a prepared statement published in the local newspaper. "This is just the tip of the iceberg where The Jackson 5's talent is concerned . . ."

Joe Jackson read the article to his sons backstage after the fourth performance. This triumph was his to claim, not Gordy's. The family felt betrayed. After finishing the feature, Joe crunched the newspaper up in his hands and hurled it into a nearby trash can.

Though stars by night, the young performers were still expected to keep up with their studies during the day. Janet, seven; Randy, twelve; Michael, sixteen; Marlon, seventeen; and LaToya, seventeen; were being tutored by Mrs. Rose Fine. During the day, because of labor laws, the five of them had to accumulate three hours of schooling as well as have time for recreation. "We always got the school time but rarely the rest of it," Michael recalled.

As puberty set in, Michael's voice began taking on new dimensions. Gone was the pubescent shrill popularized on "I Want You Back," "ABC," and "The Love You Save." It was replaced by a clearer, more refined tone. "These are days for sober reflections and quick rearrangements of old [musical] charts," observed writer Ben Fong-Torres in his review of Michael's 1974 performance for the *Village Voice*. He noted that "Michael copes with his [vocal] slippage by switching registers in the middle of phrases and by changing the keys of most of those hit songs."

"Change is just change," Michael would reply with a bored shrug, publicly. Privately, he was concerned. "Michael doesn't want to let go of his voice," LaToya observed to her mother. "He doesn't want it to change. I think he's scared of what will happen."

The group continued making television appearances, now adding Randy to the lineup but retaining the name The Jackson 5. Unofficially, they were known as The Jackson Five Plus One. From the beginning, the group was popular not only because of Michael's talent, but also because he was so cute. As the boys—especially Michael—matured, the group risked losing their general audience appeal and being relegated to a teenybopper attraction. To counter this possibility, Randy became the Designated Cute One. The strategy apparently worked, for the group appeared on the quintessential mainstream-American show of this time, a Bob Hope special, with Ann-Margret and John Denver. For this performance, The Jackson 5 took their costuming cue from what their host wore. In line with Hope's light gray, superbly tailored suit, the Jacksons wore pale colors, simple lines, and a minimum of glitter.

After their performance, there was the obligatory repartee with Hope, who started off complimenting them on their performance by calling it "a six point two on the Richter scale." When one of the boys asked what that meant, Bob replied, "That means beautiful downtown Burbank is now in Fresno." It was the kind of joke Hope's audience always enjoyed, but some of the Jacksons looked as though they didn't get its meaning. (Maybe they had never been to Fresno.)

When Bob Hope remarked on how young they were, they reminded him that Jackie was twenty-one, "old enough to be an Osmond." (Actually Jackie was twenty-three. Someone from Motown must have had script approval.)

Hope countered about having trouble with these kids who come up too fast.

"Fast!" Marlon exclaimed. "We worked *weeks* to get where we are."

"That long, huh?" Bob said, joining the audience's laughter. "What held you back?"

"Too much homework," Randy said. His smile was tentative, as though he wasn't sure he got it exactly right. He was cute. But he wasn't as charming as Michael at twelve.

After the Las Vegas engagement, Joe announced that his sons would star in the motion picture *Isoman Cross and Sons*, with an original screenplay written, directed, and produced by Raymond St. Jacques. The script, set in the mid-nineteenth century, dealt with a slave family struggling for freedom. St. Jacques would also portray the boys' father.

"I have good memories about that experience," he said regarding his time with Joe Jackson and sons. "Joseph Jackson was, as far as I could tell, the consummate father. He cared about nothing but the welfare of his sons. He was very protective, especially, I thought, of Michael. Michael was particularly excited about the opportunity to act, and Joe wanted to make sure that whatever vehicle was chosen would be the right one. Joe also was a risk-taker in the sense that he would take a career gamble if he thought it would pay off. I respected that about him. After all, that's how the boys got to California in the first place, isn't it?

"I thought they were a good, solid, upstanding family. I was proud of what they'd achieved. Michael was an eager little kid, anxious to please his father. Wouldn't make a move without looking at Joe first to make sure it was okay. The other boys were sometimes misdirected, their thoughts nearly always on girls, cars, whatever young boys think of. But my impression of Michael was that he was single-minded—show business all the way."

Gordy was not enthusiastic about *Isoman Cross and Sons*. He didn't feel the Jacksons could act, and he was right. None of them displayed any ability at all in comedic sketches. Moreover, he was not about to allow The Jackson 5 to appear as slaves. "Tell Joe to forget it," he said. "I won't even consider it."

"Who asked him?" was Joe's reaction. "The important thing here is to get the boys into films. It's time to take the next step. It's the best thing for the boys."

"In the end, though, Gordy apparently prevailed, because the film was never made," St. Jacques recalled.

To Joe, it seemed that Gordy was working against him and his family. Sometimes Joe would win, as he did in Vegas. But then Berry would land a punch to even the score, as he did with this film.

Then, in the summer of 1974, Joe made a critical mistake. Motown was forced to cancel the group's tour of Britain when Joe, in an effort to generate publicity, apparently divulged to a British newspaper the arrival time of the Jacksons' flight into Heathrow Airport on June 9. After hundreds of young girls had been injured—one died—at a David Cassidy concert at London's White City Stadium, the British promoter worked with Motown to ensure that security for the Jacksons' concert be beefed up. Joe's publicity stunt did nothing to help matters, and apparently when Gordy learned of the danger, he ordered that the entire tour be canceled, much to Joe's chagrin. "Again, he was trying to show Joe who was boss," said one Gordy employee.

Album releases were becoming less frequent. Whereas The Jackson 5 formerly had at least three a year, in 1974 there was only one, the *Dancing Machine* album. Two singles released at the end of the year, "Whatever You Got I Want" and "I Am Love," were not successful, and Motown then canceled the release of a Michael Jackson single, "Doggin' Around." It's always been interesting to Motown aficionados that the company would spend large sums of money to mix, master, and even distribute songs recorded by rebellious artists, only to sabotage the records by either refusing to release them or failing to promote them. At around this same time, The Supremes were battling with Gordy over promotion and rights to the group's name, and the women actually suspected that some-one at Motown was paying disc jockeys *not* to play their records. This was indeed an odd form of payola. Whether or not anyone at Motown was ever guilty of such a thing is an open question, but a string of unsuccessful records did usually put disgruntled artists in their places, and the Jackson family was having quite a losing streak on the charts.

In August 1974, The Jackson 5 was booked into the MGM Grand in Las Vegas again, but it was difficult for Michael and his brothers to concentrate on their performances because of serious problems mounting at home between Joe and Katherine. While the brothers worked Vegas, Katherine discovered that her husband was having an affair with a Jackson 5 fan from Kansas, a twenty-six-year-old black woman. She had apparently been attracted to Jackie at first, but when he expressed no interest, she became involved with Joe.

It was rumored that the woman was pregnant. The issue was not discussed openly; the boys whispered about it among themselves. The question was obvious: was Joe the father? The thought that Joe was having a child with another woman must have been upsetting to Michael. This act would be the ultimate betrayal of his mother.

After one of the shows in Las Vegas, Joe called a group meeting to discuss glitches he saw in the fellows' performance. Where he was concerned, the show had to go on, despite any personal prob-lems the family might be experiencing. But Michael decided to boycott the meeting.

Later, Joe caught up with him as Michael was wandering aim-lessly through the casino of the MGM Grand. He tapped Michael on the shoulder. Michael glanced back, saw who it was, and con-tinued walking, faster this time. Joe roared, "What the hell," and shouldered aside patrons in an effort to reach his son.

"I remember it like it was yesterday," recalled Steven Huck, a Jackson 5 fan who had gone to Las Vegas to see the show. "Michael was dodging his father all over the casino, hopping around like a jackrabbit, trying to outrun Joe. 'You listen to me,' Joe demanded. Then he grabbed Michael by the arm. I had no idea what was happening, what the problem was, but I couldn't help but watch."

Huck recalled that Joe spoke softly, rapidly into Michael's ear. Michael listened, his face a blank. Then, in mid-sentence, it seemed, he shook himself free of Joe and pushed him away. "Don't you ever touch me again. Just don't. Do you hear me?" Michael's voice could be heard above the din of the slot machines. People in the vicinity turned to stare, recognized him, started to whisper among themselves. No one came forward.

"I never dreamed that Michael Jackson could raise his voice to his father, or to anyone else," Huck said. "I was shocked. He sounded hurt. When he shouted, it was an odd sound. Like a wounded animal."

Joe seemed shaken. Father and son glared at each other for a moment before Joe raised his right hand as if he were about to strike his son. It wouldn't have been the first time, but the expression on Michael's face clearly indicated that it would have been the last. Michael didn't flinch. Then Joe backed up two steps. He didn't know what to say.

With tears in his eyes, Michael ran off into the bustling casino.

It would be years before he would learn the truth about his father's affair—and about his half-sister.

Whatever Katherine Jackson felt at this time, she masked her emotions and continued granting interviews and posing for happy family portraits. The entire Jackson family appeared on the cover of *Ebony* in December 1974. Inside, photographs depicted the clan together at the breakfast table, but without Joe. Katherine looked decidedly unhappy; there were no photos of her and her husband together. The article noted that "Mother Katherine Jackson travels almost everywhere with the group since her husband has other interests which take up part of his time." She told the reporter, "The family is close, very close."

"A family *has* to be close," Joe Jackson told the writer.

At this time, Michael's twenty-three-year-old brother, Jackie, made newspaper headlines when he suddenly married the former Enid Spann, a lovely girl who is part Korean and part black. Jackie had met her at a birthday party for Hazel Gordy five years earlier. Enid attended Beverly Hills High (as did Hazel) and was just fifteen when she and Jackie, three years her senior, started their romance.

"The first time Jackie was to come over to my house, he called me and said his attorney, Richard Arons, was with him," Enid recalled. " 'Is it okay if he comes with me?' he asked. So I said, 'Sure.' They came over and Richard checked me out and then looked over the house. 'Nice home,' he said. I thanked him. He asked me what school I went to. I told him. He asked to meet my mother. I introduced him to her. You would have thought me and Richard were the ones who were going out on a date," she laughed.

Afterwards, Jackie, Enid, and Richard went to the Hayvenhurst house. The boys were rehearsing, and Richard pulled the girl aside and said to her, "You know, Enid, any girl who marries a Jackson has to sign a prenuptial agreement."

Enid said she looked at him for a moment to see if he was serious. He was. "So?" she asked. "Why are you telling me this? Jackie and I haven't even started dating yet."

Arons answered, "Just in case you do, and just in case you think you're going to marry him, you ought to know."

"Let me tell you something," the teenager said to the lawyer. "If and when I marry Jackie Jackson—which, now, I doubt will ever happen—if signing that marriage license isn't good enough for him, then I don't need him and I don't want him."

Arons was speechless.

"And another thing," Enid said. "I wouldn't talk, if I were you, because *you're* the one who's living off of their gravy."

Arons ended that conversation and left the room as quickly as he could. Then he reported the whole scene back to Joe, which didn't bode well for Enid.

Enid recalled that she was "totally turned off" to the Jackson family after that incident. "And when I told my mother what had happened, she was very upset. It was a mean thing to do to a fifteen-year-old, let's face it. After that, me and Jackie didn't hit it off too good. I thought he had something to do with the conversation. But when I finally told him what Richard had said to me, he got so mad at Richard and told him 'How dare you say that to her!' "

Enid and Jackie finally began their romance and five years later were married. Their wedding was the antithesis of the grand Jackson-Gordy affair. Jackie and twenty-year-old Enid were married in a small private ceremony in Jackie's room at the MGM Grand in Las Vegas during another family engagement there. Joe was said to have been opposed to the marriage because he felt that Enid had ulterior motives for marrying his son, especially since, unlike Tito's wife, Dee Dee, she would not sign a prenuptial agreement.

Joe felt that Enid was too outspoken and independent, and he tried to convince Jackie that she might be a problem. But, looking back, Enid said that she and Jackie were deeply in love; she didn't care about his growing wealth.

"Even though I came from a middle-class family," she said, "there was nothing I ever needed or wanted. My father always got me the best of everything. If I shopped at a cheap store for clothes, he was the type who would go and throw them away and buy me better. I mean, I had a brand new Cougar when I was fifteen. There was nothing I was ever denied. So marrying Jackie was not some kind of culture shock.''

Joe and his eldest son had been having serious problems ever since Jackie decided, at the age of twenty-one, to move out of the Encino home. The relationship between Jackie and Joe came to a head over a car. Jackie had purchased his first, a Datsun 240 Z, and took a great deal of pride in it. In February 1972, Jackie and a friend were joyriding when they crashed at fifty miles per hour into a parked car. Jackie's head smashed into the windshield; he could have been scarred for life but, luckily, he and his friend suffered only minor injuries. The car was written off by the insurance company as a total loss.

The entire family was shaken by the accident, and Joe was infuriated at his son for his carelessness. He refused to permit Jackie to buy another car, which resulted in an acrimonious argument between father and son over Jackie's independence. Jackie, anxious to extricate himself from Joe's tight grip, moved out of the house. But as long as Joe was his manager, he would never truly be independent—and neither would any of his brothers or sisters.

People accuse Joe Jackson of being demanding, unreasonable, stubborn, impatient, and arrogant. And it's true. He has all of those characteristics. Yet, if he had been a different man, The Jackson 5 probably would not have existed. A frustrated performer himself, he probably started off by wanting to live his own dreams through his children—to have them succeed where he had failed. Joe may not have had much talent, but he had ambition, and that ambition led to The Jackson 5's success.

However, he was making a mistake with his children by holding on too tightly, and it was a mistake he would pay dearly for in the future. In a way, it's the same mistake Berry Gordy made with many of his Motown performers—some left the fold claiming that Berry refused to allow them personal and artistic freedoms—but Joe was a parent as well as a manager. Most of the time, he seemed unable to tell where one role began and the other ended. He would treat his business associates in the same way that he would treat his children. Joe was a man who negotiated by pounding his fist on the table and yelling louder than anyone else in the room. Among his family, Joe was considered a bully who tried to control all their lives. His behavior was frightening to his wife and daughters, emasculating to this sons. Michael dealt with it by distancing himself from his father—by openly siding with Katherine. The other boys dealt with it by marrying early, as though saying "I do" would confer manhood upon them and make them capable of dealing with Joe Jackson.

That Joe forbade Jackie to marry Enid Spann only served to motivate his eldest son toward the altar. For Jackie, the fact that he was uniting himself with a woman with whom he presumably would spend the rest of his life seemed less important than the fact that he was defying his father. The transcript of an interview conducted with Jackie Jackson for *Soul* magazine on December 6, 1974, plainly indicates a lackadaisical attitude toward his new marriage. His demeanor seemed so odd, the periodical killed the story.

*Soul*: When did you get married?

Jackson: About six days ago?

*Soul*: You mean you don't know the exact date?

Jackson: Nope.

*Soul*: Well, was it Saturday or Sunday?

Jackson: Saturday, I think.

*Soul*: Who was best man?

Jackson: A friend.

*Soul*: Who was the maid of honor?

Jackson: I didn't have all that. There weren't a lot of people. I got married in my gym shoes and jeans.

*Soul*: What did your wife wear?

Jackson: Same thing. She got our wedding bands at K Mart.

During that November-December 1974 Las Vegas engagement, Theresa Gonsalves, a devoted fifteen-year-old fan from Boston, Massachusetts, met Michael Jackson for the first time.

Gonsalves had been writing fan letters to Michael for a couple of years and had also struck up a pen-pal relationship with eighteen-year-old LaToya, who told her, "Michael and I like your letters because you write about things we don't know about. Drugs, street life, partying, and being a teenager. We don't know much about that."

Theresa had said in one letter to Michael that she planned to fly to Las Vegas for her sixteenth birthday and meet him. When she got to Las Vegas, Theresa and sixteen-year-old Michael struck up a friendship that would last for the next four years. It got off to a rocky start, however. Theresa met Michael on an elevator after his second show at the MGM Grand. "I did not like him at all," she recalled. "My first impression of him was 'What a snob.' Bill Bray had said to him, 'Well, Michael, two down and fourteen more to go,' meaning they had finished two shows and had fourteen more performances to do. And Michael said, in a real curt tone, 'Look, don't knock it, Bill. Just don't knock it.' He had a real attitude and was the most stuck-up little kid I had ever met. Then, in a belligerent tone, he said to Bill, 'I'd like to see you in my room, *please*.' When they left, I said to myself, 'After all these years of being a fan, I don't even like this kid. I'm ready to go home now.' "

The family, however, welcomed Theresa with open arms, mostly because they were awed by her nerve, the fact that she had flown all the way from Boston to Las Vegas on her own. It was difficult for her to cut her trip short. Katherine Jackson asked her for her mother's phone number and said she was going to telephone Rosetta to tell her that she would personally keep an eye on Theresa.

"They were all very nice," Theresa recalled. "Janet, in particular, was sweet. She was only eight at that time, and performing two shows a night. I never for a moment got the impression that she was spoiled. Eighteen-year-old LaToya, on the other hand, was prissy. For some reason, Joe was not there. I don't know where he was, but it was said that had he been there, the family would not have been so open to me.

"The Jacksons, at that time, were upset with Tito's wife, Dee Dee, because they felt she was spending too much of his money. Jackie and Enid had just gotten married. Enid was fun to be with and excited about being a newlywed but, I think, a little confused about the attention Jackie got. For instance, one night while Katherine, Enid, and I were sitting at a table watching the boys' show, Enid pointed out two girls in the audience. 'See those two over there?' she said. 'They follow my husband everywhere. No matter where in the country he is, there they are. It's really unnerving, and I don't get it. I think it could lead to trouble.' "

Theresa stayed for a week and attended every show, courtesy of the family. During that time, Michael warmed up to her—and she to him. He began teasing her during performances, making faces at her from the stage. One night, backstage after a show, Jackie grabbed Michael and pushed him toward Theresa, trying to force him to kiss her. "He was scared to kiss me, and I was frightened as well. We were just sixteen. The brothers liked to tease him about me."

The family treated her to many meals—she still has a number of photographs of herself with all of them—but as much as she enjoyed being with them, she still longed for some time alone with Michael. She got her wish on her last night in Las Vegas, when Michael decided he didn't want to go out to dinner with the rest of the family in between shows. "That was my chance," she said.

But after everyone left for the restaurant, Michael went into his dressing room, started reading the Jehovah's Witness Bible, and then closed the door. "Finally, he came out and invited me in," Theresa recalled. "On a wall in his dressing room was a picture of the moon. On another wall were photos of the solar system. Motioning to a picture of some stars, he asked me, 'When you look at that picture, what do you think of?' I shrugged. He said, 'Doesn't that make you think of God?' "

After a few minutes of awkward silence between the two teenagers, Theresa asked him what he was reading. He handed her the Bible and pointed to a scripture by Matthew. "Then he explained to me that the world would be coming to an end soon, and he started telling me what signs to look for when this was about to happen. I was thinking to myself, 'Why is he telling me this?' and I started getting scared."

"Do you believe in the devil?" Michael asked her.

Theresa refused to answer. "Mostly, I was afraid to answer. Nobody had ever asked me a question like that," she said.

Finally, she was able to change the subject. "It wasn't easy because the only part of his life he wanted to talk about was God. Finally we started talking about our studies. He was sweet then, and we chatted for about two hours. He was shy, as I knew he would be. I was surprised at his devotion to his religion. That was not played up in the press at all, so I didn't know about it. He wasn't a normal kid, that's for certain. But I enjoyed being with him. I liked his innocence and was influenced by him. In fact, I stayed away from boys because of the way Michael had influenced me that night. I didn't believe in sex before marriage for a long time, because of talking to Michael about it. He was firm that premarital sex was wrong and was very convincing about it."

In January 1975, Motown released a fourth solo album on Michael, *Forever Michael*. It would not be a success, peaking at only 101 on the charts, eight notches lower than the poorly selling *Music and Me* album of 1973. "That's it!" Joe decided. "He's not recording any more solo albums for Gordy. That man's gonna ruin Michael!"

Joe had become increasingly agitated by Motown's lack of promotion and Berry's attitude that the group had no writing and producing ability. He shrewdly realized that his sons would never make big money unless they owned the publishing rights to their own songs. If an artist writes his own material, he makes not only an artist's royalty, but an additional royalty as writer, since songwriters are also paid a royalty on every record that is sold. At this time, the rate was an additional two cents per copy sold, split fifty-fifty with the song's publisher. So the flip side of a million-selling song—the side that rarely if ever gets radio airplay—could be worth up to twenty thousand dollars. At least, Joe reasoned, the boys should be able to write their own flip sides.

Most of Gordy's songwriters were signed to Jobete, Gordy's publishing company. So these writers had to split their two cents with Berry. Joe wanted his boys to establish their own publishing company so that they could keep the money in the family. The more he pressed for this opportunity, the more Berry balked.

Berry had always been notoriously reluctant to share money generated from publishing rights to Motown songs. At this same time, Smokey Robinson, Berry's closest friend, was trying to convince Berry to allow him to publish his own songs. Jobete owned all of Smokey's songs, and Smokey, like Joe Jackson, wanted a bigger piece of the pie. But, according to Smokey, Berry decided that his friend's legitimate concern over publishing was "piddly shit" and told him to "leave me alone." Then Berry stormed out of the meeting. "I was stung, disappointed, and pissed," Smokey recalled. "Berry was my best friend, and here he was treating me like dirt. Fuck the motherfucker, I thought, walking out the door."

Eventually, Berry did allow Smokey to begin sharing publishing money, and Berry apologized. But this acrimonious encounter occurred between best friends. What could Joe Jackson—certainly no friend—expect from Berry Gordy? He and his sons stood little chance of controlling publishing rights to any material as long as the group was signed to Berry's company.

By this time, Berry was spending less and less time on Motown record business and more on the film division of the company.

"Now instead of Berry being president of Motown Records, he was chairman of the board of the whole company," Deke Richards said. "Berry was moving himself further away from things. The problem, as he saw it, was that everyone could get to him on a first-name basis, and this was one thing he wanted to stop. He told me, 'I want this to change so I can devote more time to movies.' A lot of people didn't like it, though."

Ewart Abner now practically ran Motown, and he was a man Joe Jackson disliked. There were other things at stake. Joe's mind was made up: The Jackson 5 would have to leave Motown. Katherine was ambivalent. "If you leave Motown, the boys won't work and neither will you," she warned Joe. The group hadn't voted on the decision yet, but Michael said later that he knew the brothers would agree with Joe. Michael was as unhappy as the rest of the family, but he felt loyal to Berry Gordy and perhaps even a bit guilty about the fact that regardless of Gordy's stubborn business practices, it was largely due to his confidence in the group's talent that the family was now in a position to pick and choose among record companies. This was a major decision for Michael, and he didn't want his father—a man he no longer trusted because of the way he had betrayed his mother—making it for him.

It was time for sixteen-year-old Michael Jackson to grow up and take matters into his own hands. He picked up the phone in his bedroom and dialed.

"Mr. Gordy, I think you and I need to talk. Alone."

# Chapter

## 11

By May 1975, Michael Jackson was sixteen years old and, in so many ways, misunderstood by his own family. The other Jacksons thought of him as being bashful and reserved, which he most certainly was in most cases. But there was another dimension to Michael, a side he did not often show but which was there just the same: his resolve.

"If there was a problem, Michael was the brother with suggestions as to how to clear it up," recalled Gil Askey, the musical conductor of many Motown acts. "I don't think anyone really knew that about Michael, mostly because his father was pretty shrewd and usually found a way to solve the problems. The other kids relied on Joe, but I know for a fact that sometimes Michael would do things on his own."

Askey concluded, "When I think of the one thing people don't know about Michael Jackson, I come up with that: his nerve. He was never the wimp people thought he was."

None of the Jackson sons had ever had a private meeting with Berry Gordy. Until now, there had never been a reason for one. It's unlikely that Berry would have consented to meet with Jackie, Marlon, Randy, or Tito at this juncture. But curiosity alone would have encouraged Berry to see Michael. Because of Michael, The Jackson 5 had real value at Motown—none of the others possessed his commercial voice or magical showmanship—so perhaps Berry felt he owed it to the teenager to hear him out.

Michael didn't care how his father felt about his decision to meet privately with Berry. In fact, he didn't even discuss his idea with Joe. Still angry at his father for what he had done to Katherine, Michael made up his own mind. Moreover, he would never have told his brothers of his secret plan because he must have known that they would try to talk him out of it. In a group that prided itself on one vote each, his siblings would most certainly have thought that their sixteen-year-old brother was seizing more power than he was entitled to.

Michael called Berry and arranged a meeting at Gordy Manor in Bel Air on May 14, 1975. "It was one of the most difficult things I've ever done," he would recall. Mustering up his courage, he quickly made his position clear.

"We're all unhappy, Mr. Gordy," he recalled having said. "Do you really want us to leave Motown, or what?"

After years of meetings like this with disgruntled artists, Berry was probably so used to trying to determine his opponent's ulterior motive, it never occurred to him that Michael had no hidden agenda. Besides, even though he liked Michael, he considered him shy and meek—hardly the person to be blunt and forthright. Michael's question wasn't meant to confuse. He wasn't attempting to be cunning. He just wanted an answer, but he wouldn't get a direct one from Berry.

Michael remembered Berry's response: "Someone as smart as you should know that without Motown, The Jackson 5 would still be in Gary, Indiana, today."

"That doesn't exactly answer my question, Mr. Gordy."

Michael would later recall that he complained about the fact that Motown would not allow the brothers to write or produce their own music or control publishing rights. Their 2.7 percent royalty rate was far too low. He was unhappy because he hadn't been allowed to contribute to The Jackson 5's most recent album, *Dancing Machine*, despite the fact that he thought he had some strong songs he could have added to the package. If he could have had just one song on the album, Michael said, it would have shown that Gordy had confidence in him as a songwriter.

At this point, Gordy became irritated. "I've been hearing this from my artists for years," Michael recalled him saying. "But we can work it out. I worked it out with Stevie [Wonder], with Diane [Ross]. I don't want you fellows to leave Motown. How can you do that? After all we've done for you. If you think you can get a better deal somewhere else, then you have to go somewhere else. But it just won't be right, or fair."

To Michael, Berry Gordy was a hero. He respected him and admired the tenacity with which he had transformed The Jackson 5 of Gary, Indiana, from homeboys to superstars. He considered him to be one of the smartest men he had ever met and was awed by the manner in which Gordy had built Motown into an international success. Gordy was an inspiration to the young Michael, and to hear him say that the Jackson family was being unfair to Motown—after Motown had brought the group to Los Angeles, arranged homes for them to live in, paid for their education, and made them stars—was a bitter pill for Michael to swallow.

"The Jackson 5 wouldn't have gotten the treatment they got at Motown anywhere else," Tom Noonan, a former Motown employee observed. "If they had signed anywhere else, someone would have cut a record on them and left them right there in Gary, Indiana, to fend for themselves."

Michael would say later that his gut instinct told him this difficult situation with Motown could be worked out if only his own father weren't so ill-tempered and possessive.

"Joe never got used to Berry being the one to tell his kids what to do," Smokey Robinson concurred. "He believed that since he was their father, he was their boss, and that was the end of that. But Joe Jackson was not a businessman and never has been. He kept screwing things up and pissing people off. No one wanted to do business with him, and all of this was a poor reflection not only on the Jacksons but also on Berry and Motown. Without Joe's involvement, Berry would have worked things out with the Jacksons the way he did with me, Stevie Wonder, and anyone else who was unhappy at Motown but ultimately stayed on."

"Let me ask you a question," Michael would recall Berry having said to him during that meeting. "What makes you think you can write or produce your own hit?"

"I just know it," was Michael's answer.

Berry looked at him doubtfully. "I don't know that that's good enough," he countered.

Michael thought about Berry's comment for a moment, then retaliated. "What made *you* think you could build Motown into such a giant company?"

Gordy didn't answer.

"You just *knew* it, right?" Michael challenged.

Gordy flashed a tolerant grin. "He nodded at me as if to say, 'You're going places, kid,' " Michael recalled. The meeting ended with Gordy emphasizing that he thought of himself as a father-figure to Michael, yet stressing that it was important for the teenager to honor his natural father. "He said he believed I would do what was best," Michael concluded. Michael would add that he "felt a little sick about the whole thing," especially when Gordy hugged him as he was leaving. "I promise you this," Gordy said to Michael. "I won't do anything to hurt you or your family."

Michael's meeting with Berry Gordy showed great initiative, not to mention courage. This was the first indication that Michael Jackson was more than just the cute lead singer of a family group. At sixteen, he was a businessman in the making. He understood the value of communication and negotiation, even better than his father. In his naïveté, Michael was able to cut through the back-stabbing politics so rife in the record industry.

Joe had heard from a friend at Motown that Michael had made an appointment to see Berry. When Michael got back to Encino, his father was waiting for him at the house. Michael has not discussed details of the argument that ensued between him and his father, but it isn't difficult to imagine that Joe felt Michael was out of his league in trying to negotiate with someone of Berry Gordy's stature. Yet once he calmed down, he certainly had to admire his son's nerve, regardless of the outcome.

"Michael had no right to meet with Berry Gordy," one of the brothers said later. "It was unfair of him to go behind our backs. We were all mad at him. And really, what did he accomplish?"

Perhaps Michael didn't accomplish much in terms of The Jackson 5's future at Motown, but this meeting with Berry Gordy was an important personal milestone for many reasons. He had obtained Berry's full attention, which was something even his father had not been able to do. Acting on his own initiative, Michael had stood up to Berry and was probably surprised to find that the world didn't end. The meeting filled Michael with an exciting sense of self-confidence, and even though he would not have an opportunity to demonstrate this newfound maturity for some time, the seed was planted.

After meeting with Berry Gordy, Michael Jackson did not want to leave Motown. But because he had such a strong allegiance to his brothers, he felt he had no choice but to stick with them. Without Michael, no record company would be interested in the Jacksons. His brothers would never have admitted this, but Michael surely must have known in his heart that without him, The Jackson 5 would probably not have been as popular.

Despite his belief that the group could be making a serious mistake—and that his father should at least try to renegotiate with Berry if only for sentimental reasons—Michael was just one member, albeit the most important one, in a group.

"Michael always had his own idea of how things should be done," Marlon Jackson once said, indicating that the brothers resented Michael's obvious preeminence in the quintet. "But The

Jackson 5 was a group, not his special project, and his was just one vote.''

That night in Encino, Joe called a meeting. All of the brothers were invited, except for Randy and Jermaine. Even if Jermaine had not been on holiday with Hazel, he probably still would have been excluded from the family's talk. Said Jermaine in retrospect, ''Because of me being married to Hazel, they thought they couldn't trust me so they kept me in the dark.'' The four brothers—Jackie, Tito, Marlon, and Michael—took a vote on whether the group should leave Motown, and it was unanimous that they should, even though Michael was still clearly ambivalent. ''I just want it to be done fairly, and something about this whole thing doesn't seem fair,'' Michael told his brothers. They ignored his concern.

''Berry's a jive-ass,'' one of the brothers told Michael. ''It's time for us to be making the big bucks.''

Joseph and his associate Richard Arons quietly began scouting for a new record deal, meeting first with Atlantic Records, which had a long experience with rhythm-and-blues music. However, Atlantic's chairman, Ahmet Ertegun, was not enthusiastic about signing The Jackson 5 because of their spotty record sales at Motown in recent years. Joe was not interested in trying to convince anyone of his sons' capabilities. He had had enough of that at Motown. ''If Ahmet's not ready for us, fine,'' he said. ''We'll go somewhere else.''

As it turned out, Joe was more interested in the CBS Records Group anyway, at which most of the black acts were contracted to the Epic subsidiary. CBS was renowned for its excellent record distribution and promotion network. ''They make Motown look sick,'' is how Joe put it.

Ron Alexenberg, president of Epic, and, ironically enough, a former protégé of Motown's Ewart Abner, was very interested in The Jackson 5. Joe Jackson respected Alexenberg. Under Alexenberg's guidance, Epic had increased its annual billing from less than $10 million to over $100 million. He was a competitive company leader with his finger on the pulse of the record industry. He felt certain that Berry Gordy had only tapped a small percentage of The Jackson 5's full potential. He wanted to find out what else was there.

At this time, Epic's roster included guitarist Jeff Beck, rock star Ted Nugent, rhythm-and-blues and pop artist Minnie Ripperton, and the singing trio LaBelle—headed by Patti LaBelle—who had recently charted with a number one hit, ''Lady Marmalade.'' LaBelle—previously known as Patti LaBelle and the Bluebelles—

was considered passé before signing with Epic. They had peaked years before with the minor success of "I Sold My Heart to the Junkman." But Alexenberg orchestrated a resounding resurgence for that group, a feat which greatly impressed Joe Jackson. If Alexenberg could transform LaBelle from has-beens to a number one attraction, imagine what he could do for The Jackson 5, who were just lying dormant.

Epic also had a strong lineup of country stars including Charlie Rich, Tammy Wynette, and Johnny Paycheck. Joe was enthusiastic about the label's versatility, but what really attracted him to the CBS Records Group was the company's profitable relationship with Kenny Gamble and Leon Huff, producers of the so-called Philly Sound, which had generated millions with hit records by black groups like The O'Jays and Three Degrees. Gamble and Huff had their own label at CBS, which they called Philadelphia International.

Though Joe felt that Philadelphia International was too small a subsidiary for The Jackson 5, he admired CBS's commitment to black music and hoped that one day the company would award him his own label as well.

Ron Alexenberg was eager to begin negotiating with Joe for The Jackson 5's services at Epic, and he informed Walter Yetnikoff, president of CBS Records, to whom he reported, that he wished to sign the group immediately. Yetnikoff was skeptical. "They haven't been hot in a long time," he said. "Now they're into this Vegas trip."

"Trust me," Ron Alexenberg told him. "This group isn't finished. It hasn't even begun yet."

The negotiations were quick, and a deal was struck. The group would receive an advance—known in the record industry as "a signing bonus"—of $750,000. They would also receive an additional $500,000 from a "recording fund"—money meant specifically to produce the group's albums. They were guaranteed to be paid $350,000 per album, far more than they ever received at Motown for anything they had ever recorded (but many millions less than Michael Jackson would be paid for his services a scant five years from then).

All of the advance money from CBS was to be recouped from royalties, but the royalty rate the new label offered was 27 percent of the wholesale price for records released in the United States. At Motown The Jackson 5 had been paid a mere 2.7 percent, which was practically nothing, especially considering that standard Motown practice was to subtract the group's expenses—including studio time, over which the act had no control—from royalties.

At this time, 1975, an album retailed for approximately $6.98, $3.50 wholesale. So at Epic the Jacksons would make approximately 94.5 cents per album sold in the United States, and 84 cents abroad. At Motown, they made roughly 11 cents per album sold in the United States, with no difference in the European rate.

As outlined in the Epic deal, after each Jackson 5 album topped $500,000 in sales, the group's royalty rate would jump to 30 percent, about $1.05 a disc. In terms of income, this new deal was worth about five hundred times more than the one the group had at Motown. Though this was a better record deal than anything Berry Gordy had ever offered, and Joe was ecstatic, this arrangement didn't really mean much money for the individual group members since all of the finances had to be split among them. Their big bucks would still have to be generated from concert revenues.

A problem in negotiations arose when Walter Yetnikoff refused to allow the Jacksons to write and produce—or even choose—all of their own material. He simply did not have confidence in any of the fellows' abilities as writers or producers, since none of them had track records at Motown to indicate that they had potential in this area. Ron Alexenberg assured Yetnikoff that the "demos"— roughly recorded samples—of songs penned and produced by the Jacksons were excellent. Still, Yetnikoff was not moved. The best Joe could negotiate was that his sons could choose at least three songs on each album. There was an unwritten understanding with Ron Alexenberg that if the fellows came up with three good songs they had written, the songs would get fair consideration for use in their recordings. This, too, was more than they had ever been guaranteed at Motown.

Michael was simply amazed by this new deal. He had no idea that the group was worth so much, that this was the kind of contract other superstar acts—except those at Motown—were accustomed to. He had to admire his father's tenacity. After all, had it not been for Joe, The Jackson 5 might have slid into obscurity at Motown. "I have to admit it," Michael noted. "This is one incredible record deal. My father has done an amazing job for us."

The realization served to confuse Michael even more. He was torn between his feelings of loyalty to Motown and his good business sense, so he decided to try to talk to Diana Ross, his much-publicized mentor. It was difficult to reach her because of her hectic schedule, but when he finally did, her reaction was predictable. She said that she really had no influence over Berry where business matters were concerned—and she wasn't lying, she really didn't—and that Michael should just listen to Berry because, as always, he knew what was best for all of his artists.

"I just believed that the boys should stay at Motown," she recalled in a 1981 interview. "I was loyal to Berry at that time, and I felt that they should be as well. I told Michael that loyalty is the most important thing, not money."

In just a couple of days, the CBS contracts were drawn up, and each of the four brothers eagerly signed.

The problem now was how to break the news to Jermaine. The conflict of interest was obvious. Jermaine's father-in-law was the enemy, and Joe realized that Berry had a powerful influence on his son. Berry had promised Jermaine an exciting and lucrative future at Motown. He trusted him enough to give him his only daughter's hand in marriage. Now it would be Joe's challenge to convince his son that the wishes of the Jackson family should prevail over Gordy's. He waited three days before calling his son, trying to determine a strategy. He then apparently decided that there was no easy way to coax Jermaine away from Berry. After all, Joe reasoned, he himself was Jermaine's blood father. He was certain that Jermaine would make the "right" decision, and if not for family obligations, certainly for monetary considerations. "After all," he reasoned, "Jermaine's not stupid. I hope."

"Come to the house tonight," Jermaine recalled his father telling him on the phone. "And come alone. Don't bring your wife."

"That's when I knew something was wrong," Jermaine said. "Hazel is a very strong person and asks a lot of questions. I'm sure my father thought he could get me to do anything if Hazel wasn't there. I was afraid to go. Afraid of what I'd find."

When Jermaine arrived, Joe escorted him into his master bedroom and closed the door. The contracts were spread out on a bureau, signatures on four of them. A fifth contract was still unsigned. "They saved me for last because they knew I'd be trouble," Jermaine recalled.

Joe picked up Jermaine's contract and handed it to him. "Sign it," he ordered.

Jermaine refused.

"I said, sign it."

Again, Jermaine refused.

"You sign this damn contract, Jermaine."

"I ain't signin'." Jermaine crossed his arms and shook his head, frowning.

"Think about the money," Joe shouted. "Real money. You think Motown's gonna come close to this deal?"

"I don't care."

"Don't care! You gotta be crazy! That's what you are. Crazy!" Jermaine recalled his father's shaking his fist at him. "You sign this contract, Jermaine, or you'll be sorry. CBS has promised that The Jackson 5 would be the next Beatles, and you know that's what we've been working for."

"Hell no. I don't want to be no damn Beatle," was Jermaine's reaction. "I'm not signing. You can just forget it." Jermaine wouldn't even take a look at the sweet deal CBS had offered him. "Not interested," he told his father.

With that, Jermaine remembered, he ran from the bedroom, down the stairs, and out of the house. Once in his red 450 SL Mercedes-Benz, he knew that he had to tell his father-in-law what had happened and that the news couldn't wait until he got home. He pulled over to a pay phone and called Berry.

"The brothers, they signed with CBS," he blurted out as soon as Berry answered the phone.

"He was very quiet at first," Jermaine later recalled. "He didn't say anything, like he was mulling it over."

Finally, Berry spoke. "Are you absolutely sure, Jermaine?"

"They already signed the contracts. I saw them with my own eyes."

"Well, what about you? Did you sign?" Berry asked.

"The brothers are leaving because there are problems at Motown," Jermaine said, "but I want to stay, Berry. I want to help work out the problems."

Jermaine recalled, "I told him I didn't sign and that I wasn't going to. He told me to come by his house, which I did. We talked it out. He became like a second father to me. A sensible father. 'You're on your way to the top,' he would tell me. 'You could be running Motown one day.' And that's what I wanted. I wanted to be the president of Motown. I knew I could do that. I knew I had it in me, even if my father never believed I did. Berry gave me the confidence to know that I could go places if I stayed with him and the company. I believed him. I didn't believe anything my father had to say. I believed in Berry, not in Joe."

The next few weeks were difficult ones. Joe had booked a concert date in Washington, D.C. The promoters, apparently novices, did not arrange ample security. A near riot broke out among the overzealous fans, and the group had to cut their show short and escape. Because of that incident, Mayor Joseph Bradway refused to permit the group to perform in Atlantic City, the next stop, on July 5, 1975, on a bill with James Brown. The show was expected to draw twenty thousand fans; it was canceled.

"My father just wasn't taught for managing," Jermaine complained. "Booking us here and there, just taking a shot at it."

For audiences, a concert just happens. Most ticket buyers are unaware of all that is involved in organizing an event the magnitude of a Jackson 5 performance at this time. Besides the obvious—sound and lighting—there was always a myriad of other concerns, from dealing with concert promoters, both scrupulous and unscrupulous, whose job it was to put up "front money" for the show and then be reimbursed through a percentage of ticket sales, to organizing a strong security network that would protect the artists from frenetic fans and gate-crashers, to arranging for adequate publicity and promotion.

Joe Jackson's job as the group's manager was a complex and never-ending one, but he always worked tirelessly for what he perceived to be his sons' best interests. To many observers, it seemed that Joe Jackson would do anything for his offspring, and, indeed, many of the tasks he undertook as their manager were thankless jobs the fellows didn't even know about. But Joe had the courage to take chances. Often he was successful; sometimes he failed. Though he was humiliated by his failures, he remained undaunted. "I'll do it all for my boys," Joe would say proudly, "because we're family. They need me."

But the "boys" were growing up; the act had been together now for over seven years. When there were problems on the road, they would secretly blame Joe. Jermaine wasn't the only group member who felt that his father didn't have the expertise to be a personal manager. However, he was the only one who dared to voice his opinion.

The next stop was the Westbury Music Fair on New York's Long Island and they still had to perform together as if there was harmony offstage as well as on. Michael tried to act as referee between Jermaine and Jackie, who argued incessantly about the merits of CBS versus Motown. In the end, the brothers—with the exception of Michael—turned against Jermaine. "They couldn't understand how I could go one way and they the other," Jermaine remembered.

Michael took a more even-handed position. "I thought he would see things our way," Michael remembered. "I never had a doubt things would work out."

The pressure was manifesting itself in many ways. Hazel—who

almost always traveled with the group—had become extremely protective of her husband, not allowing him out of her sight for a second. Recalled one family friend, ''We were all down in the hotel lobby having fun, the other brothers and their friends, but Hazel said [sarcastically] that Jermaine couldn't come out and play. I went up to their suite and knocked on the door and asked her why Jermaine couldn't come out. She said, 'He needs his rest.' But Jermaine didn't have another performance until the next evening. Why did he need more rest than the others? Hazel began shouting at me, 'I said he can't come out and so he can't come out. And that's final.' I wanted to hit that girl, I really did. Her whole thing at that time seemed to be to separate Jermaine from his family.''

Jermaine has said that Berry Gordy sat down with him and Hazel ''and told us that the first loyalty of a husband and wife must be to *themselves*, not to *anyone* else, not to anything else in the world.''

According to Jermaine, Berry said to the couple, ''Whether it's me or Motown or the Jackson family or whatever, *everything* comes second to yourselves as man and wife, because you are the two people who are going to have to live with each other and with whatever decisions you make.''

Berry's diplomacy aside, it seems almost unthinkable that Jermaine would feel free to choose another record label and still hold on to his marriage to Hazel. Whether he really loved Hazel at this point or was just a trapped possession of hers is difficult to say. He insisted he did love his wife, saying that ''as time passed, I've realized that love and marriage and family are far more important than trying to get next to every lady I meet.'' But in the same breath he also said, ''Both my parents and Hazel's parents taught us that it takes love and morality and principles and respect for each other to make a marriage. And it takes trust too, because if you don't trust somebody, how can you love them?''

When he tried to discuss the matter with his mother, she was just as angry at him as his father. Jermaine reminded her that Berry was the one ''who put steaks on our table and teeth in our mouths.'' Katherine would remember that she couldn't believe her ears. ''We were *already* eating steaks in Gary,'' she told her son. ''And as for the teeth he put in Jackie's and Tito's mouths, he's recouped that money hundreds of times over.'' (It doesn't seem likely that the Jacksons were ''eating steaks in Gary'' despite what Katherine said to her son.)

Gordy sent Motown president Ewart Abner to Westbury to keep a corporate eye on Joe Jackson and his sons. Mostly, he had to make certain that no one in the Jacksons' camp said anything controversial to the media about the problems with Motown. But once there, Abner started his own controversy when he complained to *Soul* magazine reporter Cynthia Kirk that Gordy had only agreed that Joe could scout out a deal with another label in order to determine the group's current market value. Then Motown was to have been allowed to match any offer. "But they signed with CBS and never gave us an opportunity to match the offer. Joseph never even attempted to renegotiate a deal with Gordy."

When Jackson heard that Abner had made him sound duplicitous to a reporter—even though the story had not yet run—he called Bob Mazza, a writer at the *Hollywood Reporter*. "I have a scoop for you," he said. He then divulged to the media for the first time that his sons were definitely leaving Motown and glad of it. The next day the *Reporter*—read by thousands of record industry executives—ran the front-page headline "Jackson Five Moves to Epic from Motown."

"We're not stopping for anything," Jackson declared.

The *Hollywood Reporter* story further humiliated Berry Gordy. The morning it ran, Diana Ross was on the phone with him. One Gordy assistant recalled, "She seemed to be screaming at him on the other end, and he kept saying, 'I'm doing everything I can to keep them here. What do you want from me? This isn't any of your business anyway.' "

It is curious that Diana Ross would trouble herself with the turmoil at Motown involving The Jackson 5. Perhaps she felt the situation was potentially embarrassing to her, since, according to the story she and Berry had concocted years ago, it was she who had brought the group to the label in the first place. She supposedly promised them that Motown would always be home and that Berry would take care of them "like a father."

The first show at the Westbury Music Fair went beautifully. Although The Jackson 5 had, for the most part, built their reputation on rhythmic music they had recently started to showcase a variety of song styles, as typified by the new medley they introduced at this time. Even though some of their fans were not in favor of these experiments, the brothers enjoyed doing them because it gave each a chance to sing a solo part.

Even the presentation was different. Instead of dancing, they sat quietly on tall stools side by side with mikes in front of them. Their outfits this evening could best be described as "mariachi-band mod." The waist-length jackets worn over ruffled, white, open-neck shirts were reminiscent of those that draped strolling Mexican musicians, but the resemblance ended there. These costumes had sequin-scrolled lapels and were in untraditional colors: olive, green, pumpkin, pink, purple, and gold. The bell-bottom trousers were light olive green, pale orange, maroon, lavender, and brown. White patent shoes had clunky two-inch heels.

The medley began with Tito strumming on guitar—he played his solo instead of singing—followed by Michael's sultry rendition of Roberta Flack's "Killing Me Softly." On the last line, when Michael sang, "And this is his song," he turned to Jermaine, who started a gentle version of Glen Campbell's "By the Time I Get to Phoenix." Midway through the number, Michael and Jermaine began to harmonize. It seemed so effortless, their voices blending together to create a sound so natural, so right. Without pause, the music segued into "Danny Boy," an excellent choice for Jackie's falsetto voice. As Marlon joined in, the two sang as one. There was none of the vocal interplay shared by Michael and Jermaine a moment before; still, the two voices—sounding like one—created a full-bodied, clear-as-a-bell tone. The set ended with all three songs being interwoven—a line here, a line there, each one joining the other. It was obvious the fellows had worked hard on perfecting this intricate, beautiful arrangement. The audience could feel the closeness among them. More than fellow performers—brothers.

The standing ovation was loud and long.

After the show, during a break before the next performance, the phone rang in the Jacksons' dressing room. It was for Jermaine. Berry calling.

As his family watched Jermaine's face for a hint as to what the conversation was about, Jermaine listened carefully but didn't say much, other than good-bye before hanging up.

"I'm leaving," Jermaine announced.

"Now? We go on in thirty minutes!"

"But you can't go!"

"How're we gonna work around you?"

"I can't believe you're doing this to us."

Everybody was talking at once. Joe's voice was the loudest. "Are you crazy?" he stormed. "*We're* your family. Not Gordy."

It's the ultimate show business sin to walk out on a group just before a performance—all the more so when the other performers are your brothers.

It was not a simple choice. No matter which side Jermaine chose, the other side would hate him. Whether Jermaine acted on impulse or understood the ramifications of what he was about to do, he rushed out of the dressing quarters with tears in his eyes, and went up to his hotel room, where he packed his suitcase. "I'm outta here,'' he said. A black Motown stretch limousine was waiting to whisk him to the airport and back to Los Angeles, where he and Berry Gordy would outline his future as part of the Gordy family.

"We were surprised, really in shock," Marlon remembered. "But we had a show to do. We really didn't talk about it. We knew what we had to do."

Michael would say later that he felt betrayed by Berry Gordy because of the way he seemingly persuaded Jermaine to abandon his family. Michael apparently thought that he had developed a heart-to-heart line of communication with Berry the afternoon the two of them met at Gordy's Bel Air home. He had been so proud of himself after that meeting, but in retrospect, what did it all mean?

"Why didn't he tell me he might talk Jermaine into leaving the act?" Michael wondered to a Motown employee years later. "He should have done that. He should have warned me."

Michael must have questioned his own instincts. Had he been suckered? "I won't do anything to hurt you or your family," Berry Gordy had promised him that afternoon in Bel Air. "I trusted him," Michael said, sadly. "I really trusted him." This was one hurt Michael Jackson would never forget.

That night, Michael Jackson and his brothers exploded onto the theater-in-the-round stage of the Westbury Music Fair with such elation that no one in the audience could ever have guessed at the backstage drama that had just unfolded. As always, Michael's only responsibility at this time was to his audience. He was just sixteen, but he already seemed to know all the tricks of the trade. During "Dancing Machine," for instance, Michael whiplashed the mike stand into a wobble, did a motorized shuffle across the stage as if he were a robot, and then executed a split just as the mike stand came crashing down on his shoulder. He looked at the instrument with a disdain that implied mortal insult. The crowd roared its approval.

Then, during an ironic tribute to the Motown Sound, Michael prowled the stage like a fierce, balletic wolf—"I Want You Back," "ABC," "The Love You Save," "Never Can Say Good-bye," all the Motown hits and more with graceful and often demanding choreography. Whatever it took to please his fans, that's what Michael would do. It was as if he had transformed his personal frustrations and insecurities into sheer energy for this performance. As Michael accepted his audience's absolute approval, he seemed purged of all anxiety. His smile was as bright as stage lights. Finally, he was with the only people he knew he could trust completely—his audience.

The plaintive riff from the Jackson 5 hit "I'll Be There" rang even more bittersweet as Michael Jackson performed it this evening. "Let me fill your heart with joy and laughter," he sang to his fans in a strong, expressive, yet sad voice. "Togetherness, well it's all I'm after." Marlon took Jermaine's solo part in the song.

There were three standing ovations. It had been a dizzying performance and by the time it was over, the audience was bouncing in their seats. Jermaine had been missed only by his brothers.

Afterwards, backstage, there was no music, no partying, no laughing as there usually was after a good performance. Everyone returned to his dark mood. "Why does the show have to end?" Michael asked his brother Jackie. "Why can't it just go on forever?"

Joe Jackson sat in a corner silently. Tears were in his eyes. The act—his family—was breaking up, and it seemed that there was nothing he could do about it. Berry Gordy had won a critical victory in what was turning out to be a bitter war between families. In Joe's eyes, Berry had convinced his own son to stab him in the back. If, indeed, this was what Berry had intended, it was a cunning masterstroke. What better way to choreograph a battle against a man obsessed with family unity than to turn one of his children against him.

Michael went over to his father and studied him a moment. Joe must have seemed uncharacteristically vulnerable now, as he sat slumped over in a chair, exhausted and emotionally spent, shaking his head over and over as if to say, "I just don't understand it. How in the world could this have happened to us?"

"It's my blood that flows through Jermaine's veins," he bellowed, standing up and storming out of the dressing room. "Not Berry Gordy's."

# Chapter

## ❧ 12 ❧

MICHAEL JACKSON, WHO was about to turn seventeen in August 1975, had begun to have some serious doubts about his father's ability as an entertainment manager. To his way of thinking, Joe had begun to make mistakes. "Maybe he understands show business, but I don't think he understands people," Michael said then, "and you gotta understand people in order to get ahead."

In Michael's view, the group—indeed, the family—lost Jermaine to Berry Gordy because Joe lacked any talent for diplomacy. Michael said that he felt that his brother would have stayed if their father had not attempted to browbeat him into the decision.

Indeed, Joe Jackson had made some serious mistakes along the way, and Michael was savvy enough to see and understand them for what they were. Nevertheless, despite his vision and maturity, Michael did not seem able to comprehend that, were it not for his father, his career could very well have been nearly over.

If it weren't for Joe's decision to extricate his sons from Motown's stranglehold, Michael Jackson and his brothers might very well be an obscure show biz act now. There's no doubt in the minds of most music historians that The Jackson 5 would have stagnated at Motown much the same way many other groups who were forced to stay did, acts like the post–Diana Ross Supremes.

What happened to The Temptations at Motown is illustrative. Because The Temptations were never allowed to cultivate any writing and producing ability they may have had—even though Berry Gordy did permit a couple of halfhearted attempts at song writing and producing—they have had to rely on Motown's dwindling staff of in-house writers and producers. As a result, The Temptations haven't had a number one record in almost twenty years, since "Poppa Was a Rolling Stone" in 1972. In fact, the last record they had that even cracked the pop Top Ten was "Masterpiece," in 1973. Sadly, for the last eighteen years the group—still with Motown today*—has been putting out records that most people seem not to care about. They've turned into a nostalgia act.

Of course, some nostalgia acts make a decent living on the concert circuit. For instance, The Four Tops haven't had a number one record in almost twenty-five years, since October 1966, with "Reach Out (I'll Be There)," and they haven't stopped working since. At Motown, though, that group was never permitted to nurture any of its writing ability, even though Obie Benson, a member of The Four Tops, proved he had some talent by cowriting Marvin Gaye's classic "What's Going On?" without Berry's knowledge. That group has left Gordy's stable a number of times only to return just as often, but no matter what happens to The Four Tops—short of a vinyl miracle—they will forever be considered a nostalgia act.

There is a very good chance that Michael Jackson and The Jackson 5 would also be a nostalgia act today, a group making a living performing former successes for fans eager to recapture the past for just one night. Twenty years later, Michael and his brothers could be performing on "oldies-but-goodies" revue shows with The Temptations and Four Tops. Michael Jackson could have gone into his thirties still singing "I Want You Back" and "ABC" to make a living. This is what would probably have happened if the Jackson boys had never had the freedom to write and publish their own songs, choose their own producers, express themselves their own way—if Joe Jackson hadn't had the foresight to get them away from Motown when the time had obviously come.

No matter what some industry observers may think of Joe Jackson as a personal manager, in the final analysis, the man saved his sons' careers. He may not have been perfect, but at least he was there, and he cared.

Joe Jackson may have been a man with vision, but in 1975 he felt not only betrayed by his son, Jermaine, but also outfoxed by Berry Gordy. His friends say he didn't know whom to blame for what had happened. How dare Berry steal his son away from him? And what part did Hazel have in all of this? Had she encouraged her husband to abandon his family in favor of hers? To Joe, it all must have seemed like a retelling of the biblical Adam and Eve fable, with Jermaine as Adam trying to make a choice, Hazel as Eve tempting him with the Motown apple, and Berry the snake.

*The Temptations signed with Atlantic Records in 1977 and stayed for two years before returning to Motown in 1980.

One can imagine Joe ranting about the damn viper that stole his son from the Garden of Eden and into the hell of Motown.

In the weeks to come, the company would prepare a new Jackson 5 album release, entitled *Moving Violation.* Although the album was promoted, as promised, there were no major hits. The album, produced by Holland-Dozier-Holland, featured a bombastic reworking of The Supremes' "Forever Came Today" as its strongest track. The chanting and dancing to the disco beat that the group started with "Dancing Machine" continued with "Forever Came Today," but the charting did not.

During the summer of 1975, when Motown released this cover of Diana Ross and the Supremes' Top 30 hit from 1968, The Jackson 5 was left in the dust of such number one successes as The Captain & Tennille's "Love Will Keep Us Together," Van McCoy's "The Hustle" and KC and the Sunshine Band's "Get Down Tonight." It's difficult to assess the failure of "Forever Came Today" to make the Top 40 charts for The Jackson 5, because it had all the key elements to follow successfully on the heels of "Dancing Machine." It was obvious that Motown did not have any interest in promoting the song to the top of the charts.

The group's success—or lack of it—at Motown was of no concern to Joe at this point. He was busy meeting with the CBS executives, mapping out plans for The Jackson 5's future and helping to decide who would produce their first album for the label.

Leaving Motown would be easier than Joe thought. Up until this point, Gordy did nothing to prevent their departure. He was much too preoccupied with Motown's film business. Because Gordy did not want to deal with Joe at all, Motown Records president Ewart Abner handled most matters that concerned Motown and The Jackson 5. Joe Jackson considered this delegation of authority to be a sign of disrespect.

It was always Motown's company "policy" that no act leave the label without some difficulty. Berry, who had always considered defection from Motown the ultimate act of treason, never allowed any of his artists to leave without a fight. Motown employees still remember the time former Temptations' lead singer David Ruffin demanded a release from his contract. When Gordy adamantly refused, Ruffin threatened to sit in a Motown lawyer's office until Gordy gave in to his demands for freedom. Finally, hours later, the lawyer called the police. Ruffin took a swing at a cop and was arrested and jailed. The next day, his brother, Jimmy, also a Motown artist, had to apologize and ask the attorney for five hundred dollars for David's bail. Gordy authorized the loan. It was easier to get out of jail than it was to get out of a Motown contract.

Motown still held the trump card where Joe was concerned. After a conference with Motown attorneys, a search was conducted to locate some important paperwork that had been filed away and forgotten. Once those documents were found, Ewart Abner played his hand. The last week in June 1975, he had Michael Roshkind, Gordy's vice-chairman of Motown Industries, make a phone call.

At Abner's behest, Michael Roshkind laid a bombshell on Joe Jackson. He informed the Jackson patriarch that the company—not the family—owned the name "Jackson Five." So, if the group left Motown, they would have to leave the name behind.

Joe was livid and called Roshkind a "son of a bitch." After all, Jackson was his family name. How dare Gordy claim it?

"Look, there are forty thousand Jacksons running around this world. We made five of them stars. We can make five more stars," Roshkind said. He threatened to take five other kids named Jackson and turn them into stars even bigger than the original Jackson Five.

How could this be?

Clause sixteen of the Motown recording contract—which Joe never read but signed back in 1968—stated, "It is agreed that we [Motown] own all rights, title and interest to the name 'The Jackson Five.'"

Furthermore, just to be on the safe side, on March 30, 1972—right after The Jackson 5's first string of hit records—Berry Gordy applied to the United States Patent Office to register the logo "Jackson 5ive" as well as the name "Jackson Five" as being exclusively owned by Motown Record Corporation. Joe and his sons would say later that they knew nothing about this.*

It had been common practice for Motown to register the name of its acts whenever possible. Often, when an act attempted to leave the company, the members would be informed at the last minute—just before signing a new label deal—that they would not be able legally to use the name that had made them famous.

Usually, Berry was adamant about his acquisitions and would not give them up. Sometimes, he could be otherwise persuaded. When The Temptations decided to sign with Atlantic Records in 1978, they discovered that Esther Edwards—Berry's sister—had registered the name "Temptations," "behind our backs," as Temptations founding member Otis Williams put it.

---

*On August 7, 1973, the U.S. Patent Office accepted Berry Gordy's request; he now owned the logo and the name.

It was only when his friend Smokey Robinson reasoned with him that The Temptations were allowed to take the name to a new label.

But there was no one to reason with Berry on the matter of The Jackson 5's name. Over the years, Joe had alienated everyone in any position of power at Motown. The group's departure from Motown had turned into an embarrassing situation, and anything Berry could do to demonstrate his power to the scrutinizing industry he would do, even if that meant preventing the fellows from using their name. "That was hardball, of course," Michael said.

Michael was intrigued by Gordy's tactic. "I never even *thought* of that," he told Jermaine. He was awed. It was as if Michael Jackson was as much a student of Berry Gordy's as he was an adversary. The other brothers just watched and waited, but Michael learned. "I want to know how he did it," Michael said of Berry's having registered the name. "I'll have to remember all of this," he added. It was as if he was stockpiling information for future use.

"If Berry owns the name, he owns the name. We don't have to be The Jackson 5, do we?" Michael reasoned to his father. "Can't we just be The Jacksons?"

"We might not have a choice," Joe told his son.

For the next three years there would be legal wrangling over the name, but, in the end, Gordy would prevail as he usually did in these matters.

Meanwhile, without Jermaine, it would have to be business as usual for the family. The group appeared on Carol Burnett's CBS variety show at this time. The Jacksons rarely dressed alike when performing. However, on "The Carol Burnett Show," they all wore three-piece vest outfits of light denim patchworked with darker denim and silver. Their Afro hairstyles were cut to exactly the same length. Each one had a self-portrait painted on the back of his vest—except on the television screen, it looked as though all the pictures were the same. Intentional or not, the implication was that since there were five Jacksons here, the audience was seeing The Jackson Five. The fact that Jermaine was absent wasn't mentioned at all. When they performed "Forever Came Today," Randy and Marlon lip-synched Jermaine's lines.

On Monday, June 30, 1975, Joe arranged a press conference to announce the family's new affiliation with CBS. With over eight months still to run on the Motown contracts, Joe Jackson seemed more eager than ever to leave Motown and would stop at nothing to embarrass Gordy in the bargain. Even though he was extremely busy at this time dealing with Diana Ross and postproduction on her film *Mahogany*, Gordy fought back. On the morning of Joe's announcement, Michael Roshkind told the press that if CBS expected to get all of the members of The Jackson 5, they wouldn't be getting them—meaning that Jermaine would never leave Gordy's side. Furthermore, Roshkind said, "There is no way the group will ever sing under that name for anyone else. They'll never get all five members of the group, and they won't be getting The Jackson Five."

Earlier that morning, Gordy had one of his lawyers, Frank Rothman, send a telegram to Arthur Taylor, president of CBS Records, warning him that his company had better not host a press conference relating to The Jackson 5 since Gordy had exclusive rights to "issue authorized publicity." When a desperate Gordy learned that Taylor planned to ignore the warning, he sent him another telegram warning him not to refer to the group as The Jackson 5 at the media summit since Motown owned exclusive rights to that name.

The press conference took place at the Rainbow Grill atop Rockefeller Center in Manhattan. As a room full of reporters and photographers recorded the event, eleven members of the Jackson family were solemnly ushered into the room single-file by a CBS publicist. There were no smiles. Each Jackson took his seat on the dais, where ten high-backed black chairs were arranged behind a long, narrow table. All of the family members—with Jermaine conspicuously absent—put forth a united front to announce the group's signing with CBS, effective March 10, 1976, the day their Motown contracts expired. Katherine, Maureen (Rebbie) and her young daughter, Stacy Brown, LaToya, Janet, and Randy were told by Joe to participate in order to demonstrate family solidarity.

The atmosphere was somber, such as one might find at a meeting at the United Nations. Joe—stage right, at the end of the dais—in a dark pin-striped suit, announced that the Jacksons had signed with CBS Records; he then turned the floor over to members of the family.

Jackie explained that the group—referred to this afternoon as "The Jackson Family"—was signing with Columbia, "because Columbia is an album-selling company, and albums is what really make you known." When asked if the group had tried to renegotiate with Motown, he answered, "Yes, but the figures, they was just Mickey Mouse."

Michael, in a black velvet jacket and matching vest, didn't have much to say. "I think the promotion will probably be stronger," he meekly observed. He seemed awkward and uncomfortable, especially when contrasted with his confident brothers. It was painfully obvious that Michael wished he were somewhere else.

"How will all of this affect your relationship with Berry Gordy?" asked one writer.

Everyone on the dais looked to Joe for an answer. He shrugged his shoulders and forced a thin smile. "You take it as it comes," he said. "Next question."

"Will Jermaine be joining the group?"

Again, Joe answered. "Yes. But it'll take a while. Next question."

"Why isn't Jermaine here?"

"Next question."

A woman sitting behind a reporter for *The New Yorker* magazine and Susan Blond, a publicist for CBS, nudged them both and observed, "Do you know that show 'The Jeffersons'? Well, Mr. Jackson is Mr. Jefferson, and the children are his dry-cleaning stores." The writer made a note in his pad. The publicist squirmed uncomfortably.

That same day, Gordy had been on the phone with Jesse Jackson. For the past several years, Gordy had sent The Jackson 5 to perform for Jesse's PUSH Black Expo, a nonprofit, black self-help organization. According to one source, Jesse Jackson was asked to stop CBS from stealing a black act from a black record label. Although he did eventually meet with the CBS executives, he got nowhere.

"Jesse Jackson is up at CBS trying to start a lot of trouble," Joe Jackson complained to one black newspaper. "I just hope black people will realize that the Jacksons didn't leave Motown for nothing. There are many reasons, and I hope no one plays on that black stuff. We left because we couldn't get what we wanted at Motown and were able to get it somewhere else."

Gordy filed a lawsuit against Joe Jackson, The Jackson 5, and CBS, seeking $5 million in damages for signing with CBS before the Motown contract had expired. Joe countersued, claiming Motown owed the family royalties, unpaid advances, and especially expenses. By the terms of their contract, The Jackson 5 were liable for the costs of all of the songs they recorded for Motown, *including the ones that were not released.*

To say that Motown had kept the boys busy would be an understatement. Michael Jackson and The Jackson 5 recorded 469 songs for Motown in the six years from 1969 to 1975. That's about 75 songs a year, which is astonishing considering that this isn't *all* the boys did for a living. Besides having to learn those songs before they could record them, they also constantly rehearsed their ever-changing stage show, toured the world with their act, appeared on many television programs—including their own specials—sat through countless interviews, posed for innumerable photos (there are thousands of photos of the boys the public has never seen), and also tried to have a semblance of a personal life outside of show business.

Of those 469 songs recorded by The Jackson 5, only 174 were actually released, or 37 percent. The other 295, Gordy had decided, were not up to Motown's standards. So, much to the group's chagrin, the Jacksons owed Motown over $500,000—and it's difficult to believe that that figure was not somehow inflated, considering other artists' experiences with the label—for songs that the public never even heard, many of which the fellows probably didn't want to record in the first place, if the tunes really were not up to Motown's ''standards.''

After the press conference, Berry Gordy was infuriated with the entire Jackson family and considered them all traitors. In turn, some of the family members and group representatives began to fear for their lives. One of the biggest misconceptions about Gordy is that he is a dangerous, violent man. He is not. He just seems like he is because he wields such great power and is an intimidating and sometimes bullying personality. Indeed, the Gordy legend is so overwhelming, many artists have been afraid to ''cross'' him over the years.

What really distressed the artists, though, was an incident at Gordy's Los Angeles home in the early 1970s when one of his bodyguards was murdered during a party. According to rumor, the occurrence was somehow related to the Mafia, but there were no witnesses to the shooting and no charges were filed. Diana Ross's photographer Harry Langdon said that the bodyguard ''got into a shoot-out at the house. Next thing I knew, he was off to that big Motown studio in the sky.'' This incident made an indelible impression on all of Berry's artists, some of whom thought that Berry was responsible.

After the press conference, Joe and Richard Arons were certain that Berry was going to have them killed. They began looking under the hoods of their automobiles for bombs before starting the ignitions. They plotted ways to avoid Gordy's assassins.

Berry was angry, but the man wasn't crazy. He allowed the matter to be settled in lawsuits that would jump about in the court system for the next four years.

On July 31, 1975, Motown executive Tony Jones sent a memo to Joe Jackson requesting that a month's period of time be blocked out in order to record new Jackson 5 and Michael Jackson albums.

Joe's reaction: "No way. We're not recording another note for Motown." If Motown wanted to release product on the group, Joe reasoned, then the company should dip into the vaults and release any of the hundreds of songs already recorded but unissued. Joe didn't want to have to pay for *more* Motown sessions from which songs might or might not be released.

This decision was a mistake on Joe's part because the group was *obligated* to record for Motown at the company's request whenever the company asked them to. Now Joe was breaching the recording contract.

The other brothers did not care. But Joe and Michael argued because Michael felt that the brothers did owe Berry the recordings and that they should live up to their agreement. Joe was adamant, however, that his sons were not going to record any more songs. "Then we're going to be sorry," Michael warned. "This is wrong."

As a result of Joe's decision, Motown placed his sons on "suspension," which would not bode well for the family when a final court decision would be rendered.

It would be eight months before the Jacksons would be able to record for CBS. Even though they signed with the new label before their Motown agreement had expired, they would have to wait until their Motown contract ran out before they could go into the studio. To fill the lag-time, Joe signed them to CBS-TV for a summer variety series to begin airing in June 1976.

At this time, Michael was often asked about Jermaine in interviews, and he tried to stress that "business is business and family is family. He still comes over," Michael said of his brother. "We talk to one another. We go different places together. That's very important, because that's the basis of our whole organization: good friendship and a strong family. The show business part is important, but even more important is that the family stick together at all times."

Wishful thinking. The family was not close, even though Michael yearned for it to be. Jermaine did visit now and then, but only when Joe was not around.

"My father made some crazy statement about it's his blood that flows through me, not Berry's," Jermaine said. "He said it privately at first, then liked the sound of it so much he started saying it to the press. I read it in *Sepia* magazine! I just couldn't stand to be around him anymore. He had hurt me so deeply. My own mother was asking me what was wrong with me and how could I betray the family as I did. It was tearing me apart."

The other brothers still harbored resentment against Jermaine for his decision. "I was open to talk to them, but I have my pride," Jermaine remembered. "Why should I keep calling these guys if they refuse to talk to me? They were hanging up on me, man. One of them told me I was no longer a brother. How could they hurt me like that? No matter what, I thought we were family. After all, that's what we were always preaching. But when it came time to act on it, I didn't see that happening. I was an outsider."

Hazel Gordy Jackson observed later, "No matter what people said and thought about my husband's decision to stay with Motown, it never really affected the relationship the two of us have. What helped us was how we've always felt about each other, and when we looked at each other it wasn't as if he was a Jackson and I was a Gordy, it was as if we were one, it was us. I think that's how a marriage has to be if it's going to last."

"In the end, in the final analysis, Hazel was blamed for everything that had happened," said Susie Jackson, wife of Jackson 5 drummer Johnny Jackson. "But that was her husband. What could she do? She wanted what was best for her husband, and she felt that Berry was best. Jermaine really missed his brothers, but he had Hazel."

Jermaine and Hazel may have been finding shelter in each other's company, but other members of the Jackson family seemed to be growing more antisocial, shunning exposure to people outside the gated Jackson estate (by Joe's orders) and burying themselves in their Jehovah's Witness faith (by Katherine's suggestion). None of the siblings who were still living at home—LaToya, nineteen; Marlon, eighteen; Michael, sixteen; Janet, nine; and Randy, twelve—seemed to have any relationships outside of their own family.

"I don't date," LaToya told a reporter firmly. "I don't trust people. To be honest with you, I have no friends outside of my family. It doesn't bother me. When I get lonely, I read the Bible."

She said that she rarely went out in public unless she was with other family members. She expressed no interest in marriage or raising a family of her own. "I would never bring a child into a society like this one."

It was as if the Jackson siblings were being raised to mistrust all outsiders, and Joe was quick to point out the breakup of Jackie's marriage, an unhappy union from the start, as evidence that people can't be trusted.

In September 1975, nine months after Jackie and Enid married, Enid filed for divorce and demanded five thousand dollars a month alimony, plus Jackie's forty-eight-thousand-dollar Rolls-Royce convertible, which he had hidden from her. She said Jackie could keep his eighteen-thousand-dollar Porsche. Enid's attorney estimated Jackie's financial worth at more than $10 million (which, according to Motown royalty figures up until this point, was not possible). She was asking for half.

"You see that?" Joe told his son. "After just nine months, look at the problem you got on your hands."

It had been said by people close to the Jackson inner circle that Enid was pregnant when she and Jackie married. Indeed, *Soul* magazine reported in its October 13, 1975, issue that Mrs. Jackson "recently suffered a miscarriage." According to Enid, however, she had not been pregnant.

When Enid arrived at Los Angeles Superior Court with her petition for divorce, she discovered that Jackie had beaten her to it and had already quietly filed his own petition, asking that he not have to divide his property with his estranged wife. In November, a judge ruled that Enid get only fifteen hundred dollars a month in temporary support until final settlement of their divorce case was made.

In January 1976, the couple reconciled. "Jackie figured out that it was cheaper to keep her," one friend said. They would remain married for eleven more years, but an impression had been made on Michael. His parents had opposed Tito's marriage and insisted that his wife sign a prenuptial agreement. Jermaine and Hazel's marriage seemed more a corporate merger than a true love story. And Jackie's marriage proved to be unstable.

In January, after Jackie and Enid reconciled, Michael's eighteen-year-old brother, Marlon, made an announcement that rocked the family. He had apparently been secretly married for the last four months, without telling his brothers or sisters. Or Joe and Katherine.

While the group appeared in Las Vegas in August 1975, Marlon filed for a marriage license at the Clark County courthouse in Las Vegas and then married an eighteen-year-old fan from New Orleans, Carol Parker. The ceremony took place on August 16.

"Marlon did not want to trust any of his brothers with the news because he was sure they would tell Joseph," said a friend. "He didn't want to go through what Maureen, Tito, and Jackie had gone through with their marriages, the way Joe had tried to interfere. And he didn't want Joseph to know, especially since Carol did not sign the prenuptial agreement. Whatever it took to avoid Joe's wrath, that's what his sons would do, even if it meant betraying their trust in one another."

"He could be married and I wouldn't know about it," Joe told a reporter in January 1976. He was obviously feeling hurt and betrayed. "These kids, they just slip off and get married. Marlon did not tell me a thing," he said. "I've been hearing about it from other sources, but not my own son. I wasn't even invited to the wedding. What can I say? I hear a lot of things," Joe concluded, when asked if any member of his family knew of Marlon's decision, "and if I start to investigate this whole thing, I may find the type of answers that I'm not ready to accept."

"The whole family didn't like Carol at all," Susie Jackson said. "I admired her myself. But the other sisters-in-law didn't like her because they thought she was uppity. Enid and Dee Dee were always up at the Big House getting into everyone's business, but not Carol. She didn't want anything to do with any of them, just Marlon."

Marlon's secret marriage became a problem on many levels. Not only did it raise serious questions of trust within the family, it also presented a public relations dilemma. Marlon and his brothers were still considered teen idols; their fans spent millions of dollars annually supporting the group. By keeping such an important secret from them, it appeared that Marlon had betrayed their young fans. "You betray your fans, you're finished," Joe warned his sons.

*Right On!*, a popular magazine geared to black teens, confirmed Joe's worst fears when they published letters criticizing Marlon's decision in the April 1976 issue. One such letter read:

Dear Marlon,
    Tell me something. How come all of you stars lie so much? If a fan asks you if you are going with anybody, you always say "No!" Then, before you know it, you're getting married. You stars lie because you think your fans will be mad if you get married. But let me say this, Marlon, fans don't get mad just because their favorite stars get married, but they do get real mad when they find out their idols lie to them. Please learn to be honest, that's all.
    Marlene Thomas
    Baltimore, Maryland

"You boys are going to ruin yourselves!" Joe stormed. "Go ahead. Do yourselves in. See if I care."

Michael was deeply hurt by Marlon's secret wedding, because he thought he and his brother were close. "We share all the bad times, but never the good ones," Michael complained. "I don't understand my family at all. And I don't like some of the things my brothers do to their wives. I'm never going to marry," Michael said then. "I just can't take it. It's awful, marriage. I don't trust anyone enough for that."

"What did he know about trust?" asked a former associate of Michael's in an interview. "He despised Joseph. His brothers obviously didn't trust each other. Jermaine's loyalty was to Berry Gordy. At this point, Michael began envying the fact that Jermaine got out of this mess while he could," recalled the associate. " 'I don't know who to believe in. What kind of family is this, anyway?' he asked me. Then he put his hand over his mouth and looked around nervously to make sure no one else heard his remark."

At a time when he should have had genuine enthusiasm for life and all that it had to offer a seventeen-year-old with a future as promising as his, Michael Jackson seemed on the verge of hopelessness and despair. "People hurt each other over and over and over again," he said bleakly. "I spend a lot of time being sad. I'm just sad a lot."

Now that four of The Jackson 5 were married—Jackie, Tito, Jermaine, and Marlon—there were even more key players in the family's many dramas. "Everybody wanted what they thought Tito and Dee Dee had, the perfect marriage, the perfect little house, the perfect kids . . . But even Tito and Dee Dee had problems," said Susie Jackson. "The women all got gifts, jewelry, Mercedes-Benzes, diamonds. If one got a diamond, they all had to get one. It was all very competitive among the sisters-in-law. Of course, as far as they were concerned I was far, far beneath them because I wasn't married to one of the brothers, just the drummer, even though he was supposed to be part of the family. Johnny didn't make the money they made, so I'm afraid I was looked down upon. I was usually invited to things—though I wasn't invited to Hazel and Jermaine's wedding—but I never felt a real part of the family."

"One thing that is very true about the Jacksons," observed Joyce McCrae who in a few years would work for Joe Jackson, "they don't like you to talk about them. They may talk about each other; they feel that's their right. But they resent it when outsiders do. And everyone who is not a Jackson is considered an outsider, including the wives. The wives were an intrusion. In fact, that's what Katherine used to call them, 'the wives.' "

Often, a couple of the sisters-in-law tried to inject themselves into group business. "One of them, and I won't say who, got in the middle of it all when Joseph was considering firing Johnny and Ronny Rancifer, both of whom had been with the family since

Gary,'' recalled Susie Jackson. ''It was a delicate issue. Johnny had a bad drinking problem. He would get very violent and indignant. Joe finally said, 'Enough is enough.' But they never examined *why* Johnny drank. He was miserable and unhappy because he wasn't getting paid anything. He was considered a part of the family—Joe had been his legal guardian—but not when it came to splitting the money. He was so upset and he had no way to vent it, so he took it out on me and was very violent.

''Somehow, one of the wives got wind of Joseph's intention,'' Susie Jackson continued. ''She telephoned Ronny on the road—I believe they were playing a theater in Santa Maria, California—and told him, 'Joe's getting ready to fire you and Johnny.' Ronny got mad and said that he was gonna quit before Joe had the chance to fire him, which is what he did. Ronny told Johnny to get out while he could, and Johnny said, 'No, I can't. That's my family. I can't do it to them.' He loved Katherine with all his heart. Ronny told him, 'Man, they don't care about you.' Johnny came home and said, 'I'll bet he's right, but I just can't quit. They're my family.' Of course, he *was* right and Joe *did* fire Johnny.

''At one point, Joe banned the wives from going on the road. They did a concert in San Diego, and Dee Dee and Enid drove down to meet the boys. After the concert, Jackie and Enid were in bed in a hotel room and Joe walked in on them. Enid was embarrassed and ran into the bathroom crying. Joe did not like the wives on the road because it caused too many conflicts.''

In early 1976, the Jackson brothers gave their depositions regarding the lawsuit against Motown. When Michael gave his on January 15, it became clear how little he knew about the group's recording career. He was questioned by attorneys Richard H. Floum (representing The Jacksons) and Patricia L. Glaser (for Motown).

Q: Do you recall when you first recorded for Motown?
A: No, I don't. I don't know.
Q: Do you recall what you recorded in Detroit in 1968?
A: Oh. I guess that was *Diana Ross Presents The Jackson 5* album. Part of that, I guess. I mean, that was the first one. I don't really know . . . I know we did ''I Want You Back'' in Los Angeles and the other stuff I guess was done in Detroit. Yeah, that's right.
Q: How did you meet Diana Ross?
A: Who?
Q: Diana Ross.

A: You mean how do people think we met her?

Q: No. How did you meet her?

A: Oh. Uh, well. I, uh. Well, through Berry Gordy. We were at his house in Detroit and she was there.

Q: Why was the album called *Diana Ross Presents The Jackson 5*?

A: I, uh, well, okay, it's like this. See, she didn't discover us, okay? We wanted people to think she did, but she didn't. See, she presented us to the public. It wasn't a lie, really. I mean, she did present us.

Q: Do you know how many tunes you recorded?

A: No. I don't know the numbers. But it was a lot of tunes. That I do know. Lots of them. I never worked so hard. Day and night. They really worked us.

Q: More than ten?

A: I don't know for sure.

Q: Can you specify how long the recording sessions were?

A: No, I don't know.

Q: Do you know how many albums that album sold?

A: No, I don't know.

Q: Do you know if it was over two hundred thousand?

A: Yes, because it was a million-seller. It sold millions and millions.

Q: Well, how do you know that it was a million-seller?

A: Because we got a gold record for it from Motown so of course it was a million seller.

What Michael apparently did not realize is that Berry Gordy would not allow the Recording Industry Association of America (R.I.A.A.), which officially certifies million-sellers, access to the company's record sales, and with good reason. He did not want to pay to the R.I.A.A. the escalating charge the firm demanded, a fee that was based on the number of records sold. He also didn't want the R.I.A.A.—or anyone else, for that matter—to know how many records the company was selling. Motown customarily boosted its sales figures for public consumption. So when Motown artists were presented with the kind of gold record Michael referred to in his testimony, it was often just an ordinary Motown disc spray-painted gold and then framed. It hardly represented the official recognition of the industry.

Michael also indicated in his testimony that he did not understand why the group was not recording songs for Motown during the remaining term of their contract with the company. "To be right, we should be recording for Motown,'' Michael said. ''Joe telling us not to record while we're under contract is a giant mistake, and we're all going to end up regretting it. I'm not stupid. One thing I'm not is stupid. I know we have to at least honor our commitment to Berry or we're gonna lose the whole lawsuit. It's not right. You can't win when you're not right.'' But as noted earlier, Michael was powerless.

Q: Was there ever a joint decision among your brothers not to record for Motown?

A: No, there was not.

Q: So you have no idea why you are not now recording for Motown.

A: No. I don't know why. That's the question I want to know the answer to.

Q: You do not know?

A: Correct. My father instructed us not to. Other than that, I do not know why we are not recording for Motown.

Joseph was so completely bored by the depositions that when it came time for his own, he kept falling asleep until, finally, opposing counsel asked him if he was on narcotics. After Joe was briefed by Richard Arons on how better to deal with the depositions, he began answering his questions by saying, ''To the best of my recollection, I don't remember.''

While the legal wrangling continued, an announcement was made that the Jacksons would star in their own television series. Since Jermaine was obviously not a part of the proceedings and would not have any Motown solo product in the market until November 1976, Motown was anxious to keep the prodigal son in the public eye. The company's press department arranged a number of interviews for Jermaine in order to maintain his celebrity profile. He gave a fascinating interview to writer Cynthia Kirk in April 1976 while his brothers toured Manila.

The interview was conducted at Jermaine's hillside home in Los Angeles. Motown press agent Bob Jones, wearing a plastic hairdryer cap, greeted Kirk at the door explaining that Hazel Gordy had just cut and washed his hair. Actually, the hair dryer was a ploy. Whenever Kirk hit upon an area that Jones felt was not safe, ''he would turn on the hair dryer, effectively obscuring any tentative original thought from Jermaine and at the same time reminding him to keep silent,'' Kirk said.

As the Motown artists became more mature, management found it difficult to prevent them from saying what they really felt. Jermaine was too old and experienced at twenty-one to be completely controlled by the Motown machinery, but that didn't mean Gordy's staff wouldn't try. The company executives now relied on cheap tricks to control and to censor Jermaine's interviews. Kirk recalled, "After Jones positioned himself in such a way as to be able to flash signals to Jermaine without being seen, the interview began."

At one point, Jermaine began to discuss the problems of mixing a personal life with his career. "[Our fans feel] that all we're supposed to do is sing on stage and entertain them. But that's a job . . . that's our career. But they feel that's all we're supposed to do."

At this point, Jones turned on his hair dryer full blast, wiping out the rest of Jermaine's words.

"Bob!" Jermaine exclaimed, obviously irritated.

"I just didn't want that investigated," Jones said calmly.

Later, during the interview, Jermaine got a phone call. Jones turned the hair dryer on loud so that the reporter would not hear Jermaine's conversation. When he returned to the interview, Jermaine asked the reporter about some unfatherly remarks made by Joe and reported in the media. "I guess you all had to print it, 'cause he said it. But the public thinks . . .''

Again Bob Jones turned on the hair dryer. Now Jermaine was becoming angry. "Meathead!" he muttered softly enough for the reporter to hear but not loud enough for Jones's ears.

In two months, Michael Jackson would turn eighteen. "I'm old enough to have an opinion," he said in one deposition relating to the Motown case. "It bothers me that no one listens to what I have to say."

Indeed, Michael's vote was just one of five when it came to group decisions. There was always a sense among the brothers and Joe that Michael was special, indeed, the most important group member. But they were loath to allow his opinion special consideration. They feared that if they did, Michael would one day have the confidence to separate himself from the family—which was the last thing they wanted. Michael recognized this fear. "They don't listen to me because they're afraid to," he said to one associate. "I guess I can understand that. They don't want to lose me. They don't want me to have too much power. But it makes me mad."

Michael Jackson had made it clear to his father and brothers that he did not want to do what he now calls "that stupid summer replacement TV series. It was a dumb move to agree to do that show," he says, "and I hated every minute of it." He was outvoted, as he often was, and forced to appear on the show. Michael believed then what Donny and Marie Osmond, Helen Reddy, Tony Orlando and Dawn, Sonny and Cher, and so many other pop recording stars now know: a TV series kills record sales. People become so accustomed to seeing the performers every week as preposterous characters in silly sketches, they no longer take them seriously as entertainers, let alone recording stars. It took Donny Osmond over ten years to recover from the damaging effects of the "Donny & Marie" show.

"The Jacksons" was a thirty-minute program that ran for four weeks. The first episode, aired June 16, 1976, featured guest Sonny Bono. Mackenzie Phillips, Ed McMahon, and Joey Bishop were guests on subsequent shows. As in the family's Las Vegas act, LaToya, Janet, and Maureen participated. It was the first time a black family had ever starred in a television series, and if the show received decent ratings, there was a good chance CBS might pick it up in January as a mid-season replacement.

Michael appeared to be miserable while he taped the four programs. The schedule proved grueling, and there was no time for the boys to polish any of the routines to the kind of perfection Michael demands of himself. He hoped that the show would not be renewed.

On television, the family's appeal was immense. Each week, the announcer's voice boomed out "The Jacksons—starring Michael [seventeen], Marlon [nineteen], Tito [twenty-two], Jackie [twenty-five], Randy [fourteen]," then, almost as an afterthought, "and the Jackson sisters [Rebbie, twenty-six; LaToya, twenty; and Janet, ten]. The fellows would perform a raucous opening number while, behind them, flashing bulbs spelled out "Jacksons" with enough wattage to light up an entire town.

People in the audience were standing and applauding from the outset. Those in front would reach out their hands, hoping to touch one of the brothers, who never paid them any heed.

On one show, they were clad in understated glitz: blue-gray tuxedos with just a sprinkling of matching beads on the sleeves. Their silver lamé vests were cut conservatively and had no additional adornment. They looked polished as they danced in unison.

"We're the Jacksons," Michael announced. "All of you who were expecting the Osmonds, do not adjust the color of your set." The line got a good laugh, a smattering of applause. The Jackson sisters were then introduced. Rebbie and LaToya were dressed in suits made from the same material as their brothers', but without a sparkle; they looked like they were going on job interviews to be lady executives.

"Okay, let's go," Michael yelled out as the family prepared to reprise their opening number.

"Hold it!"

Janet stomped on stage, her boots giving her outfit a paramilitary look. "Nothing goes till *I* say it goes," she boomed.

One of the highlights of the series was the family's dance routine to "Steppin' Out with My Baby." For those viewers who grew up enjoying the Busby Berkeley routines of yesteryear, this was pure nostalgia. Dressed in white top hats and tails and carrying silver canes, the brothers escorted their sisters onto the stage for a razzle-dazzle tap-dance routine. The girls looked elegant in long satin gowns with feather aigrettes in their hair.

The Jacksons' series became the launching pad for young Janet Jackson's acting career. The format of the television show interspersed musical numbers with comedy sketches, so the youngsters had to learn lines as well as music. Some were quicker studies than others, but it's doubtful anyone could have topped Janet.

On one episode, she premiered her incredible Mae West impersonation. Dressed in a pink satin hourglass-shaped creation trimmed in tulle with a matching parasol and picture hat covering her platinum blond wig, Janet sashayed onto a bar set where Ed McMahon as W. C. Fields poured himself a generous libation of "medicine" (scotch). One of the most difficult tasks for an actor is to learn the art of timing (some professionals claim it can't be learned), but Janet seemed to have a natural instinct for it.

"Hi, big fella," she said. "I'm Mae West."

"My goodness!" McMahon exclaimed.

Janet fixed him with a long, baleful look and patted her blond curls. "Goodness had nothin' to do with it," she purred in her Mae West voice. It brought the house down.

When she strolled out on Cab Calloway's (Randy's) arm, Janet rolled her eyes and drawled, "When I'm good, I'm very good. But when I'm bad, I'm better." At ten, she probably didn't even know what the lines meant, but she made them sound believable—and funny. Even back then, it was obvious who the next big star in the family would be.*

---

*For Janet Jackson, the television series proved a worthwhile career move. Her performance caught the eye of producer Norman Lear, who sought to cast the role of Penny Gordon, an abused child, on the sitcom "Good Times." Janet auditioned, and after doing a series of her impressions, she won the part. She stayed with "Good Times" for two seasons (1977-79) before moving on to roles in "A New Kind of Family," "Diff'rent Strokes," and "Fame."

Unfortunately for Michael, the ratings were solid enough for CBS to order more episodes to begin airing in January 1977. Badgered by his brothers to agree to another contract with CBS-TV, Michael cringed . . . and signed.

"I never knew Michael hated the show," Biff Manard, who was a writer for the series, once observed. "With the family, he was always alone. Michael would wander around the CBS hallways by himself. Or if he was with the brothers, he always stayed in the background. Even in the wings, he was downcast and shy. I'd say, 'Gee, you really look good tonight,' and he'd barely say 'Thank you.' But then, on stage, forget it, the pot boiled over."

In his autobiography, *Moonwalk,* Michael recalls that the Jacksons' TV series did not continue because "I was the one who refused to renew our contract with the network for another season." Actually, the show was canceled because of poor ratings when it returned in January 1977. It is very difficult for Michael to accept the fact that all of the hard work he devoted to that series went unappreciated by the television viewing audience. The show plummeted to the bottom of the ratings—seventieth for its last showing in April 1977.

The era of variety shows was winding down; family sitcoms were now the popular fare, with "Happy Days" and "Laverne and Shirley," "One Day at a Time" and "Three's Company" leading the bunch. Along with the cancellation of "The Jacksons" went the variety series starring Sonny and Cher, Tony Orlando and Dawn, and The Captain and Tennille, all in one fell swoop.

As good as they were in the musical segments, the siblings were, with the exception of Janet, sorely lacking in the comedy sketches. "I'm not a comedian," Michael said in retrospect. "Is it really entertaining for me to get up there and crack a few weak jokes and force people to laugh because I'm Michael Jackson, when I know in my heart I'm not funny?"

"The Jacksons" proved to be more trouble than it was worth, especially when Motown used the program as an opportunity to amend its original lawsuit against the group, raising the damages sought from $5 million to $20 million. Apparently, someone at CBS-TV, probably a hapless assistant in the art department, accidentally used a picture of the old Jackson 5 with Jermaine in a *TV Guide* advertisement for "The Jacksons" series. As soon as Joe Jackson alerted CBS to the innocent mistake, the network pulled the ad and sent a letter to Motown apologizing profusely and promising that it would never happen again. Gordy decided to sue anyway.

Michael Roshkind maintained that the mistake "had a severely damaging effect on our credibility" and "caused us real dollar damage," which was ludicrous since the ad was just one half page and the art work so blurry no one could even recognize Jermaine in the picture. It was obvious that Joe was not the only one holding a grudge.

In the end, Berry Gordy would not be awarded the millions he demanded, but rather $600,000 in damages—including unrepaid advances and compensation for the group's signing with CBS before the Motown contract had officially expired, as well as compensation to Motown for damages suffered when Joe would not allow the group to record new songs at Motown's request in July 1975. This judgment is exactly what Michael had predicted.

Joe Jackson tried everything he could to prove in a court of law that he had been treated unfairly by Motown, even admitting in his deposition that on the day in Detroit (July 26, 1968) when he sat with Gordy's attorney Ralph Seltzer and was presented with the contract, he didn't read it before allowing his children to sign it. Gordy's lawyer, Ralph Seltzer, concurred, admitting in his deposition, "I do not recall that any of them [The Jackson 5 or Joe Jackson] read it through in its entirety prior to signing it."

Why not? "Because the extent of my formal education is through the eleventh year of high school," explained Joe. "The nineteen sixty-eight contract with Motown was the first recording contract that I was ever presented with or ever looked at." This didn't seem likely, especially since Joe's sons were signed to Steeltown Records before they were signed to Motown. And besides that, the court ruled, Joe should never have signed the parental guarantee agreement if he hadn't read the Motown recording contract, because by signing that agreement—which said that he would make certain his sons abided by the provisions of the recording contract—Joe had implied that he had at least read the contract. But Joe didn't even read the parental agreement before he signed *it*. Joe hadn't read anything. He'd just affixed his signature where Ralph Seltzer told him to sign.

"This is a gratifying day—not because of our winning, but because it was a matter of principle," Motown vice-president Michael Roshkind said. In the end, the Jackson family had very little—if any—capital when they left Motown Records. Motown also retained ownership of and full rights to the name "Jackson 5."

* * *

The first Jacksons album for CBS, *The Jacksons*, was released in spring 1977 on the Epic label. The executive producers, Kenny

Gamble and Leon Huff, managed to work a deal whereby their company, Philadelphia International Records, was also recognized on the album's disc label copy. "Blues Away," one of the first songs Michael had ever written, and "Style of Life," written by the brothers, were both included. Those two songs were coproduced by The Jacksons. For the rest of the album, Gamble and Huff recruited their staff producers—including Dexter Wansel, Gene McFadden, and John Whitehead—to assist them in compiling a strong, if not innovative, collection of songs. Michael says he learned a great deal from working with Gamble and Huff and company, in terms of structuring a melody and what he calls "the anatomy of a song."

*The Jacksons* spawned one major hit for the group, "Enjoy Yourself," their first single for Epic. This was a rollicking dance number which would go on to become their most successful record since "Dancing Machine" three years earlier. The single went to number six on the pop charts. Because it was the only hit side from the album, *The Jacksons* peaked at only number thirty-six. The public seemed confused, because Gordy issued his own Jacksons album, called *Joyful Jukebox Music*, made up of previously unreleased music, in an obvious attempt to cash in on CBS's promotion of the group. The Motown album was not successful; still it served Gordy's purpose by diluting the impact of the CBS product. As Michael would put it, Gordy was playing "hardball, of course."

*The Jacksons'* showing on the pop charts proved disappointing, but not as upsetting as Jermaine's first Motown release. After all the public and private angst, *My Name Is Jermaine*, Jermaine's first album after leaving the group and coming under Berry's individual tutelage, peaked at 164 on the Top 200. The single, "Let's Be Young Tonight," only went to number 55.

Without Jermaine the Jacksons continued to tour. They performed in Memphis, Tennessee, in May 1977. During that engagement, Michael had to escape to the roof of a Woolco department store when ten thousand people caused a near riot as they waited in line for hours hoping to jam into the store's record department, where Michael had promised to autograph copies of *The Jacksons*.

That same night, backstage before the show, John Seaver, who worked for the firm that promoted the Memphis engagement, later recalled, "I showed a *Billboard* article to Michael that said Jermaine's Motown album was a big bomb. It made the comparison to The Jacksons' album, saying that that one was a smash. Michael read it and didn't say anything at first. Then he said, 'He'll bounce back. I know it. Jermaine won't let this get to him.' He seemed genuinely sad, sorry for Jermaine.

''The article was passed along to the other brothers, who scanned it. Marlon said something about 'too bad.' Tito said that the album wasn't any good but that Jermaine would probably come up with something stronger next time out. I remember he said, 'No matter what, he's our brother and I don't like to see him do anything that's not a success.' They all agreed with Tito.''

Then Joe came into the dressing room.

''What are you boys reading?''

Jackie handed him the article. ''Read this, about Jermaine.'' Joe read it quickly while everyone in the room waited for a reaction.

''Serves him right,'' Joe said, his voice full of triumph. His sons looked at each other with raised eyebrows, but no one spoke except Michael.

Looking at his father, Michael shook his head in disgust. ''Some father,'' he muttered.

# Chapter
# 13

By the time Michael turned nineteen years old in August 1977, he was not only one of the best-known entertainers of recent years, but also the idol of many girls and young women who would purchase color pinups of him, proudly hang them in their bedrooms, and even dream about what he might be like as a lover. His brothers, particularly Jackie and Jermaine, often took advantage of the female opportunities that presented themselves while on tour, even after they were married. Though much of Michael's music was sensual, and his dancing was often suggestive, he was not a sexual young man.

"I think it's fun that girls think I'm sexy," Michael said. "But I don't think that about myself. It's all just fantasy, really. I like to make my fans happy so I might pose or dance in a way that makes them think I'm romantic. But really I guess I'm not that way."

For years, the public has speculated wildly about Michael Jackson's personal life. Is he straight or homosexual? Or neither? It is fascinating that the sexual identity of a performer with as much on-stage sexual allure as Michael Jackson has always seemed so clouded.

Certainly from the beginning, messages Michael Jackson received about sex were mixed. The message from Katherine was loud and clear. With her strong faith in the Jehovah's Witnesses, lust—in thought or in deed—was sinful. According to 1 Corinthians 6:9, none of the unrighteous—"neither fornicators, nor idolaters, nor adulterers, nor effeminate men, nor abusers of themselves with mankind"—would inherit the Kingdom of God. Sex was reserved for marriage, and even then, sexual choices were limited. Oral and anal sex were forbidden, not because they were wrong in them-

180

selves, but because they were activities in which homosexuals often engaged.

However, from their father, Joe, who shunned the religion that their mother embraced, the boys received a different message, one that came more from his actions than from his words. In the group's very early days, Joe would book his boys into dives and strip joints. Nine-year-old Michael knew those were wicked places. Ordinarily strict, Joe apparently gave the boys free rein at those times, allowing Michael to stand in the wings and watch as men in packed, smelly clubs whistled at voluptuous women who took off their clothes lasciviously, piece by piece, until they were naked. They would throw their panties into the audience, and the men would sniff them. "That, to me, was the most horrible, disgusting thing," Michael would say later.

Beverly Hills psychiatrist Dr. Carole Lieberman observed, "Michael's experiences when he was a little boy would affect him for the rest of his life. For instance, at nine years old, Michael would have been psychologically unequipped to fully understand what was happening on stage with the various strip teases he saw. I'm sure that these performances were sexually arousing to him because, even though many people think children cannot be sexually aroused, they can be and practically always are.

"Michael would not necessarily have recognized he was sexually aroused, rather it would have been just a very confusing array of stimulation. From an early age, there was a confusion. On one hand, he had an overly rigid view of the world from his mother. On the other hand, he was having an overly promiscuous view of the world from his father."

Once, at the Apollo, nine-year-old Michael watched fascinated as a well-endowed, obviously experienced stripper took off everything but her underwear. At that point, she pulled two large oranges from her bra and took off her wig to reveal that she was a he. Michael was shocked.

Joe wasn't. He knew what would capture an audience's attention. One of The Jackson 5's numbers was Joe Tex's raucous "Skinny Legs and All." As part of the act, Joe encouraged young Michael to go out into the audience, crawl under tables, lift up women's skirts, and look under. No matter how embarrassed Michael may have been, he embellished his performance by rolling his eyes and smiling wickedly because the crowds loved it enough to throw money onto the stage. The boys would scramble for the loose change, running for the halves and quarters first. "I had so much money in my pockets, I couldn't even walk," Michael recalled.

After the show, the boys went home to Katherine, who would remind them of the virtues of being a good Jehovah's Witness. When The Jackson 5 finally became stars and were on the road for extended periods of time, Katherine remained at home with the younger children. Joe, who toured with the group, would openly date other women, attracting them by bragging that he was the father of the famous Jackson brothers. All of the boys were aware that he was exploiting their success for the purposes of sex.

Marlon has recalled his father's coming into the boys' hotel rooms with a bevy of shapely beauties on both arms, all giggling. "G'night, fellows," Joe would say. The boys, in bed in their pajamas, would watch as their father and his lady friends closed the door. They could hear the laughter from Joe's room next door. It was as if he wanted to be certain that the boys knew what was going on.

Joe Jackson was an insecure man with his own problems. He never felt fully appreciated by his family, and his life was filled with immense sadness. No matter how successful and popular Joe Jackson made his sons, no matter how much he gave to his wife and daughters, he sensed a lack of gratefulness and respect. They rarely showed him any affection. There was rarely a tender moment. Perhaps it was because he himself was never an affectionate person, and his family did not know how to relate to him. So Joe tended to wander outside his household for appreciation and validation.

Dr. Carole Lieberman also observed, "One has to wonder if one of the reasons the father was having extramarital affairs was because the mother was not a very sexual person. Perhaps she felt that there were all of these dos and don'ts as a result of her strict religion. Or, maybe, that's why she even became a Jehovah's Witness. Many people will latch onto a religion because they are afraid of their sexuality. If they join a religion which has a lot of sexual taboos, they have an excuse for their fears. I'm not trying to pardon the father, but it takes two people to have a bad relationship. The wife must have contributed to their poor sexual relationship in some way."

"He used to do the meanest things to us," Michael recalled. Michael has said he was disgusted by the very thought of what was happening in the next room between Joe and his dates.

"Joe thought it was funny, but we were very upset by it," Marlon recalls. The Jackson boys were all deeply hurt by their father's blatant display of infidelity. They wondered how he could betray

Katherine in this manner time and time again and apparently not be at all ashamed of his actions.

To make matters worse, none of the boys ever hurt Katherine by telling her. Having to lie to their mother was an additional burden on all of them. "The kids saw what their father was doing out on the road with the other women," Susie Jackson recalled. "They did not like it one bit. It made them feel badly for their mother, who was sitting at home. Katherine, of course, has never had a lover. She's always been faithful to Joseph. This only made them love their mother even more."

Dr. Lieberman speculated, "The father's infidelity would certainly have hit the youngest child exposed to it the hardest. [In this case, that would have been Michael, since he was the youngest member of the group privy to Joe's indiscretions. It would be years before his younger brother and sister, Randy and Janet, would know about their father's philandering.] He would have thought that by not telling the mother he had betrayed her the most.

"Michael was, at eight, just at the end of his Oedipal stage, a time when it's most important for boys to be getting love and attention from their mother as it is for little girls from their father. He would be wanting to be the favorite loved figure of his mother at that time. To now be put in a situation where his mother is being betrayed by her husband, the person who would be his rival for her love and attention, must have made it seem all the more unfair.

"In a normal Oedipal case," the doctor concluded, "the youngster would never have the power to dethrone the other parent. But in this case, Michael had the ammunition—his rival for his mother's attention was actually abusing his privileges—but he couldn't use it for fear of hurting her. This would have been a particularly difficult time for young Michael."

At eight years of age Michael was old enough to understand what was going on and sensitive enough to be aware that hypocrisy played a large role in his life, even in his own actions.

Michael was not such a goody-goody, however, that he never yielded to temptations, albeit relatively minor ones. When they played the Peppermint Lounge in Chicago, there was a peephole in the boys' dressing room through which they had a view into the ladies' bathroom. They would take turns watching. "We learned everything there was to know about ladies," Marlon recalled.

Years later, the group was performing in London when Michael, thirteen, and Marlon, fourteen, discovered another peephole in their dressing room that looked directly into an adjoining room occupied by theater star Carol Channing.

"Look, she's naked!" Marlon said excitedly as he peered through the hole.

"I can't look," Michael protested.

"But she's naked. Carol Channing is *naked*."

Michael took a quick look. "Ugh," he groaned. "She *is* naked."

As their popularity grew, so did the number of groupies eager to have sex with The Jackson 5. LaToya once discovered a girl in Michael's bathtub. Michael dreaded such behavior, but the older boys took advantage of it—just as their father did. When Marlon was fifteen and Michael fourteen, they would share a hotel room with Jermaine, seventeen, who would wait for their security man, Bill Bray, to go to sleep before sneaking down to the lobby to pick up girls. Often, he would bring them back to the room and instruct Michael and Marlon to, as Marlon recalled it, "play sleep."

Yolanda Lewis is thirty-four, married, and living in St. Louis today. In an interview, she recalled an experience she had with Jermaine Jackson in 1972 when she was sixteen and Jermaine was a year older. "I was a real groupie," she remembered, "and the boys did a concert in Cleveland, where I was living at the time. Afterwards, a group of us girls went to the hotel where we knew they were staying. We had our J-5 buttons and posters, just wanting autographs, hoping to see the guys, maybe get a picture with them. Jermaine came down and struck up a conversation with a few of us. He was so sweet, acting as if he was shy when he obviously wasn't. He pulled me off to the side and asked me very directly if I would like to come up to his room. Of course, I said yes. I was all tongue-tied and cross-eyed, that's how excited I was. He was so handsome, with his big natural and pearly white teeth.

"We got up to the room, and I walked in behind Jermaine. It was pitch-black in there, with just a night light on in a corner.

" 'Michael and Marlon are sleeping,' he whispered to me. 'So we have to be quiet. Take off your clothes. Quick.' He wasn't exactly what you'd call romantic.

"The next thing I knew, I could see in the dim light that Jermaine was sitting on the bed in a lotus position, naked and frantically rubbing some kind of lotion—baby oil, I believe—between his legs, all the while moaning to himself. He had the smoothest body I'd ever seen on a young man, and I remember being a bit disappointed because I hoped he would be muscular and cute like his brother, Jackie, who I had slept with the last time the group was in Cleveland. Even in the dim light, you could see Jermaine's ribs poking out from under his skin. I began taking off my clothes slowly, but

Jermaine's whole thing was, 'Strip, baby, and let's get to it now 'fore I come without you.' So I jumped into bed with him and he quickly climbed on top of me. We made love. *That* was not disappointing. Jermaine was very experienced. He knew positions I still don't know how to get into. It was like he was double-jointed or something. As we climaxed, he shuddered so loudly I was afraid he would wake up Michael and Marlon, who were sleeping three feet away together in the next bed.

"Or at least I thought they were sleeping. As I was slipping out of the room, I heard Michael say to Jermaine, 'Nice job. Now will you please go to sleep?' "

Even though it certainly seems unlikely, Marlon says that Michael was just as promiscuous as Jermaine. "I remember back in the early days, Michael was something to keep up with where the girls were concerned. Believe me, Michael ain't a virgin. No way."

It seems odd that Marlon would go to such lengths to declare his brother's manhood, when to most people who know Michael it was obvious that sex seemed frightening to him. He probably exhibited a natural curiosity about sex as he went through puberty and may have felt some sexual arousal himself. But to succumb to such feelings would have meant going against his deep religious convictions and risking alienating the one person in the world he loved most—his mother. After years of traumatizing overexposure, the very idea of sex had become disgusting to him.

One associate, who had known Michael since 1974, recalled, "Once I was having a conversation with Rebbie, and she happened to say to me, 'Michael just doesn't have time for girls.' I asked her, 'What kind of guy doesn't have time for girls?' She said that there were special circumstances with Michael. When I asked her what she was talking about, she told me a truly horrible story.

"She said that when Michael was fifteen years old, a certain member of his family, someone he trusted—I won't say who, even though Rebbie did—decided he was old enough to have sex. The time had come. So this person arranged the services of two hookers for Michael, told them to work him over, and then locked Michael up in a room with them. Rebbie said that this incident absolutely traumatized her brother. I don't know whether or not Michael actually had sex with the hookers. Rebbie didn't say."

Certainly, if this story is true, such a setup must have had a great psychological impact on Michael Jackson, as it would on any youngster going through puberty. After that happened, it's been said, Michael turned to prostitutes, but not for sex.

It was as if Michael were retaliating against his brothers' actions by trying to reassure himself that women were good for more than just good times in bed. Recalled James McField, the group's former pianist and band director, "I know that sometimes—maybe once, maybe twice—Michael just needed to have someone to talk to and—maybe once, maybe twice—a woman would be introduced to him as someone very nice that he could be with, to have the company of a female. But he wouldn't have sex with her, to my knowledge. As far as I know, nothing intimate would ever happen. He liked nice girls, very pure girls, who would appear to have no street background."

"I remember that his brothers used to tell us these wild stories about how they used to go out and get girls and bring them back to the hotel room for Michael," Susie Jackson said. "Then Michael would supposedly have sex with these girls. But I feel these stories were just not totally true. To me, the brothers were just trying to protect Michael's image.

One such "date" remembered her meeting with Michael after a concert in New York. "I was hanging around backstage, working Madison Square Garden's dressing area," the source said, "when someone who introduced himself as an employee of the Jacksons came over to me and asked me if I wanted to spend an evening with Michael. 'Hell, yeah,' I said. He asked me how much, and I told him I would do it for free. I wanted to have sex with Michael Jackson. Who wouldn't?

"So he brought me back to the dressing room, and Michael was sitting in there, alone. I walked in, and Michael told me to close the door. The first thing out of his mouth was, 'Why are you a prostitute?' Immediately, I was insulted—I don't know why—but I answered, 'because I need the money.' He said to me, 'Would you like to have sex with me?' and I said, 'Yes, of course I would.' He asked me how much. I told him, 'No charge.' He seemed interested. So I undid my blouse and showed him my breasts. Immediately, he turned his head, as if my tits were the worst thing he'd ever seen. 'Stop. I can't have sex with you. Please put them back,' he said.

"When I asked him why, he told me, 'Because I just can't.' I thought he meant he couldn't get an erection, he looked so sad. Then he said, 'Can we just talk about you and your life?' I didn't want to talk, that's not why I went there. So I gave him my telephone number.

" 'Any time you want to get off, you call me,' I said. Michael looked at me and asked, 'What does that mean, to *get off*?' I swear he was totally sincere. 'It means *fuck*, Michael,' I told him. 'Anytime you want to fuck, you call me. Get it?'

"He said, 'Oh, okay. Maybe I'll call you someday. I doubt it, though.' And then I left.

"He struck me as so pitifully lonely and naive," she concluded. "Just a nice, mixed-up, good-looking guy who wanted some female companionship. No way was he about to have sex that night, though. He seemed scared to death. I wondered if he would ever call. He never did."

"No one really knows if Michael has had relationships or not," said his first cousin Tim Whitehead. "He is just the opposite of his brothers in that he keeps his personal life a real secret—even from his family. Lots of people can guess, but Michael makes sure no one knows."

Most people who were close to Michael Jackson by the time he was nineteen—or at least as close as he would allow anyone to get—agree that he probably never had a serious romantic life. Michael did not seem to be able to trust anyone enough to allow that person to penetrate the shell he had built around himself. Perhaps he felt he had been betrayed too often by people he loved or admired—his father, his brothers, Berry Gordy—to permit himself the vulnerability a relationship demands. Still, Michael understood the value of public relations and show business hype. So, for public consumption, he paraded a few "relationships."

Michael has said that actress Tatum O'Neal, who was thirteen in the summer of 1977, was the first girl in whom he, at nineteen, became romantically interested. O'Neal, daughter of actor Ryan O'Neal, won an Oscar at the age of nine for her role as the chain-smoking, swearing companion to a Bible-belt swindler (played by her father) in the film *Paper Moon*. At five feet six inches, she was tall for her years, with long, slender legs she liked to emphasize with skintight, thigh-high boots. She was an excellent actress; when Richard Burton worked with her in *Circle of Two* (1980), he said, "She is one of the five or six really first-rate actresses I've worked with in films."

But Tatum O'Neal had had a difficult childhood, and when she told Michael about her life, he said he had never heard a story so tragic.

Born to actress Joanna Moore and Ryan O'Neal, Tatum saw her parents split up when she was three. For a while, Tatum lived on a ramshackle ranch with a dying horse, some dead chickens, and her mother, who was addicted to drugs. At seven, Tatum grew flowers in a wrecked car in the yard and cooked breakfast and lunch for herself and her younger brother, Griffin. Her father was permitted to visit on weekends.

"When she was living with her mother, I could always tell what shape Tatum was in by the look of her hair," Ryan said. "I knew if it was healthy, she was at peace with herself. If things were bad, there were clumps missing from her hair. She'd sometimes take a scissors to herself."

Joanna, anguished and on the verge of defeat by 1972, decided to seek help from her ex-husband Ryan, who had been giving her thirty thousand dollars a year in alimony. He paid for her rehabilitation and she, in turn, agreed to surrender eight-year-old Tatum to him. Tatum hated Joanna. When the little girl went to visit her in the hospital, Tatum became so disgusted with her mother that she spat in her face.

"It was the most painful experience of my life—like having a child die," said Joanna. "It was the most undisguised, outrageous hate I have ever known."

"My mother is like a saint," Michael once said. "When I hear about Tatum's mother and what she went through with her, it makes me thank God for Katherine Jackson. People think I have had a hard life. But look at Tatum's. That's why I like her, because she's a survivor."

Ryan was enthralled by his daughter's precocity. When she was five, she still sucked her thumb compulsively. One day he said to her, "Tatum, if you stop sucking your thumb, I'll give you a dollar."

"In advance?" she asked.

"Yes, in advance."

She never sucked her thumb again.

Unlike Michael, whose goal it was to be an entertainer, Tatum became an actress quite by accident. Ryan helped her get her first role mostly as a way to keep an eye on her while he worked on *Paper Moon*. He was the consummate concerned parent, always trying his best with the girl, even though she was often too much for him to handle. He never wanted her to be an actress because, as he put it, "An actor's life is filled with anxiety and disappointment." After *Paper Moon*, Tatum decided that she wanted to buy a ranch and raise horses with her sixty-thousand-dollar fee for the film. "What sixty thousand dollars?" Ryan wanted to know. "*I* got sixty thousand dollars. *You* got six thousand."

Tatum was shocked. "I can't believe that," she exclaimed. "I won an Oscar for that movie."

"Sell it," Ryan told her. "And then you'll have six thousand sixty."

When Tatum became a working actress, Ryan O'Neal took over her career much the same way Joe Jackson commandeered Michael's. "I chose *International Velvet* for her," Ryan said. "She didn't even read the script. I just said, 'This is the one you're doing,' because I knew it was good."

Tatum would complain about the way her father ruled her life, and Michael would empathize. "I know exactly what you're talking about," he told her.

But Tatum did make some of her own decisions. She once told Michael the story of how she turned down the role of the young hooker in *Taxi Driver*, a part that eventually went to Jodie Foster. Coproducer Julia Phillips was explaining the movie to Tatum, who said she wanted to play the part of the taxi driver. Tatum was twelve.

Julia ignored Tatum's suggestion and kept talking up the role of the hooker until finally Tatum said, "Frankly, I think the part's too small. I did win an Academy Award, you know."

"I can't believe you said that. I don't think I would ever have the nerve," Michael told her. "I want to be like that. I want people to think of me as having a lot of nerve."

By the time she was thirteen, Tatum's persona seemed much older than her years. Not only was she renowned for her youthful, budding talent, she was known in Hollywood for her rebellious childhood and for dancing the nights away in discos with Bianca Jagger, Margaux Hemingway, and Cher, who told her that she'd better clean up her language if she expected to socialize with her daughter, Chastity. Michael found Tatum fascinating. O'Neal was a youngster who, at least so it seemed to Michael, got away with anything. She was even driving her father around at the age of fourteen; Michael was deathly afraid to drive. "And anyway, you're not supposed to drive until you're sixteen," Michael told her.

"So?" was her response. "Jeez, Michael. Live a little."

Michael and Tatum first met in 1975 at a party Paul McCartney hosted aboard the *Queen Mary* in Long Beach, California. At that time, he was seventeen and she was twelve. They had no contact with each other again until the spring of 1977, when Michael spotted Tatum with her father at the On the Rox club in Los Angeles. Michael was socializing with two publicists from Epic, Susan Blond and Steve Manning. Michael recalled that he was sitting at a table with some friends when "all of a sudden I felt this soft hand reach over and grab mine. It was Tatum." The fact that Tatum had deigned to hold Michael's hand was, for him, a colossal event. "It was serious stuff to me. *She touched me*," he said.

The next day, thirteen-year-old Tatum invited Michael to a dinner party at *Playboy* publisher Hugh Hefner's rambling Holmby Hills estate, long a playpen for the chic Beverly Hills jet set. There they watched *Roots*, the highly rated Alex Haley television miniseries, on videotape. When Tatum became bored, she asked Michael to go into the hot tub with her.

"But I don't have a bathing suit," he said.

"Who needs bathing suits?" Tatum responded.

When Michael began to blush, Tatum asked one of Hefner's assistants for two swimsuits, then handed one to Michael.

Tatum's hair at this time was soft blond and flowed just below her shoulders. Her skin was baby pink and her figure quite ample for a girl who wouldn't turn fourteen until close to the end of the year. She was almost plump. "She's like a sacred doll," Michael said of her to a friend. He said that while soaking in the water and watching for shooting stars, the two shared secrets with one another. Eventually, rumor has it, they were nude together in the hot tub. The idea was tantalizing to the public, and the rumor persisted for months, fed by Tatum's fast-life reputation.

"We weren't naked," Michael firmly pointed out in an interview, "as people have said. We both had on bathing suits, just enjoying ourselves. And that's it. Why do people have to always find something dirty in everything?"

"He doesn't believe in presents or birthdays or Christmas or Halloween or any of those things," Tatum said of Michael. "It's so strange, because I'd like to send him a Christmas card and he says I mustn't do it. Strange, no presents. I think that's so weird. I love presents more than anything and I thrive on them."

"I fell in love with her (and she with me) and we were very close for a long time," Michael wrote in his autobiography. He says that O'Neal was his first love "after Diana." Tatum O'Neal has indicated, however, that her relationship with Michael was strictly platonic. And Ryan O'Neal characterized the relationship as "no big thing." It's very telling of the fantasy world in which Michael often seems to live that the women he claims to have had romances with— including Diana Ross and Brooke Shields ("We were romantically serious for a while," he wrote of Shields in his book)—have all denied ever having sex with him.

Says actress Sarah Jackson (no relation to Michael), who was a friend of Tatum's at this time, "Tatum told me that Michael was a nice guy, but so shy, how can any girl have a relationship with him?

When we're together, he hardly says two words. I know he's a virgin. Someone needs to have a talk with him about it. I wonder if he's afraid to have sex. He doesn't seem very interested.''

Michael's ''romance'' with Tatum lasted a couple of years and, apparently, ended the night of a Hollywood party at the guest house at Rod Stewart's Beverly Hills home in 1979. The occasion was a rock concert Michael had attended with Tatum and some of her friends.

A lawsuit has been filed regarding reported events that allegedly took place at that party. According to one published report in *Star* magazine, Tatum persuaded Michael to go with her and a few friends, including model-novelist Carole Mallory, to a small party at Rod Stewart's. Stewart was not home.

According to the assertions of the complaint filed by Carole Mallory in her lawsuit, Alasdair Buchan reported that Tatum tried to convince Michael to have sex with her and Carole Mallory. Mallory and O'Neal were supposed to have made a pact that this evening would be ''let's bed Jackson night.'' Mallory reportedly told O'Neal, ''Well, if you don't want him, I'll have him, darling.'' To which Tatum said, ''Even better, why don't we let *him* decide.''

The two starlets then supposedly climbed into a bed with actor Leif Garrett.

''Come to bed with Carole and me,'' Buchan reported Tatum O'Neal as having told Michael Jackson.

As the others at the party cheered him on, the shy Michael stood up and headed for the bedroom with Tatum and a scantily dressed Mallory. But Buchanan reported that, in the end, Michael refused their offer of sex. As a result, he was taunted and embarrassed in front of the other party-goers.

According to ''Starfucking as Research,'' a *Playboy* magazine article about Carole Mallory, the ''ex model was inspired by her nights under the stars—some forty celebs, she says,'' to write a sexy Hollywood novel, *Flash*, published in 1988. The dust jacket of *Flash* describes the book as portraying ''the wild fantasies, the perverse desires, the amorous delights the way a woman really experiences them. And what the boys didn't know, Carole Mallory tells.''

Even though Carole Mallory is popular for living a rather sensational lifestyle, when asked to clarify the accuracy of the report that she and Tatum O'Neal tried to seduce Michael Jackson, she became outraged and indignant. ''How dare you? How dare you ask me such a question?'' she said. ''If you so much as use my name in your book, I will sue you. I swear it!''

The next day, Mallory's attorney, Elliot Livingston, reiterated her threat. Finally, Mallory would insist that the story was not true, and that she was suing the tabloids that published it. Indeed, she did file suit against *The Star* and *News of the World* (which also reported the story) for $50 million, in September 1988, claiming that "as a result of the extraordinary personal effort, struggle and hardship, [I] for at least approximately eight years [have] been and [continue] to be a reformed and rehabilitated alcohol, cocaine and sex addict."

Whatever really happened that night remains a mystery. Michael Jackson has never commented on the matter.

Michael and Tatum would be seen in public together a few times after that, but he always appeared ill at ease. Tatum would do most of the talking, and Michael would answer only in monosyllables. Tatum was quoted as having said, "Sex was something Michael neither knew nor cared about."

After that Hollywood party, two rumors began spreading about Michael Jackson, rumors that he apparently allowed to hurt him deeply. It's not known if these stories were invented by someone at that gathering, but most Jackson confidants agree that they probably were. According to the popular gossip, Michael Jackson was gay. Moreover, he was going to have a sex-change operation and marry television actor Clifton Davis (most recently seen as one of the stars of the series "Amen"). Davis wrote the Jackson 5 hit "Never Can Say Good-bye."

This story spread like wildfire around the world. Numerous publications cashed in on it and rushed to the presses with headlines pairing the two entertainers.

Michael was buying records in a Sears department store down South while on tour when he first heard about the rumor. "This one girl came up to me, and she said, 'Please tell me it isn't true! Please tell me!' And she was crying hysterically," Michael recalled. "I said, 'What? What isn't true?' And she said, 'Tell me you're not going to become a girl.' "

"Where in the world did you read that?" Michael asked the fan.

"*Jet* magazine," she responded. "It was in *Jet* that you were going to have a sex change."

"I felt I didn't know who I was at that moment," Michael said. "I told her to tell all her friends that it was just a stupid rumor."

It seemed that everywhere Michael went, he heard this rumor. "It's disgusting to me that people think I'm gay," he said. "And having a sex change! How awful."

After the rumor had been circulating for months, Michael was at Caesars Palace to see Diana Ross perform when he ran into Clifton Davis. Davis was backstage with Leslie Uggams. "I was with Diana, holding her hand," Michael remembered. "Clifton was standing next to me, and he was holding Leslie's hand. As I was standing there posing for the photographers, I thought, 'Oh no, this is a perfect setup for some magazine to doctor up this picture so that it looks like Clifton and I are holding hands.' That's how paranoid I was getting about that story," Michael confessed.

After the photographers departed, Clifton went over to Michael and joked, "Hey, look at you. You're not a girl after all, are you?"

"I was really upset about that rumor," Clifton Davis would recall. "Angry enough to put my lawyers on the case to try to track it down. Not only did it imply that Michael was gay, it said I was too. Michael Jackson is a very sensitive person. The story upset him a great deal."

Michael has never gotten used to the stories that he leads a secret gay life, and he is always very upset whenever confronted with a question about his sexuality.

"Are you or are you not gay?" one reporter asked him point-blank in 1979.

"No, I am not gay," Michael snapped. "I am not homo. Not at all. People make up stories about me being gay because they have nothing else to do. I'm not going to let it get to me," he continued. "I'm not going to have a nervous breakdown because people think I like having sex with men. I don't and that's that. If I let this get to me, it will only show how cheap I am. I'm sure I must have a lot of fans who are gay, and I don't mind that. That's their life and this is mine. You can print that," he told the writer. "What is it about me that makes people think I'm gay?"

The journalist shrugged his shoulders.

Michael continued. "Is it my voice? Is it because I have this soft voice? All of us in the family have soft voices. Or is it because I don't have a lot of girlfriends? I just don't understand it."

Michael Jackson would never allow himself to have homosexual relationships, even if he did have feelings for other men. He is much too puritanical, a result of his religious background. The Jehovah's Witnesses firmly believe that world destruction is imminent and that only a few of God's servants will survive the horrible holocaust. This threat hung over young Michael's head for his whole life, and he must have wondered if he and his family would win salvation or burn in hellfire. If Michael wanted to be saved—if he wanted to be with his mother through all eternity—he would have to live up to all of the church's rigid teachings.

Indulgence is not a feature of the Jehovah's Witnesses' creed. Any congregant who does not adhere to the rules and dogma is shunned—disfellowshipped. By the time Michael was a teenager, he had been trained to live his life a certain way. He would not be able to break that conformity.

He was too fearful as well. Michael knew that in any relationship he had, he ran the risk of the other person's reporting to a newspaper or magazine that would pay astronomical sums for such a story—especially if it were a sensational one. Although there are more public figures who are homosexual coming out of the closet today than when Michael was in his teens, many entertainers still hide their true sexual identities from their fans because they fear rejection. Ever practical where his work is concerned, Michael must have been aware that such rumors could eventually damage his career—and his relationships with his family. How would his brothers react if he were to announce that he is, as he put it, "a homo"? (Marlon, for one, would probably continue to disbelieve it. "Michael is definitely not gay," he once said in an interview. "I would know if he was, wouldn't I?")

One could assume that Joe's reaction to such an announcement from Michael would be a violent one. And his mother? "When I first heard the rumors that he was gay, I thought I'd go crazy," Katherine Jackson once said. "He's my son and I know the truth. He knows the truth too. We both talked about it and cried about it. Michael was very hurt by the rumors. He is not gay. It's against our religion."

When it comes to child raising, Jehovah's Witnesses are encouraged to withhold affection from any child who disobeys the rules of the church or parent. Even as a teenager, Michael didn't want Joe's affection anymore. But he needed Katherine's and would probably have done anything to keep it, even bury his true identity and feelings.

Indeed, the late seventies were traumatic years for Michael Jackson. Most people have difficult times in adolescence, but Michael's teen years often seemed overpoweringly sad. Sexual issues aside, he was much more sensitive than most people his age about the common pitfalls of puberty, perhaps because he was always the subject of such intense public scrutiny. His face had broken out severely with acne in the mid-seventies, and he was so ashamed of the way he looked that it was almost impossible for him to go out into public. "I seemed to have a pimple for every oil gland," he recalled. Onstage, this condition was difficult to notice because of carefully applied makeup and pastel lighting. But offstage it was obvious. Reporters would comment to each other about Michael's skin. Fans would be shocked at his appearance. Michael could barely stand the humiliation.

"I became subconsciously scarred by this," he has confessed. "I got very shy and became embarrassed to meet people. The effect on me was so bad that it messed up my whole personality."

Michael couldn't look at people when he talked to them. He would look down or away. He wouldn't even look at his mother when he spoke to her. "He didn't even want to leave the house," Katherine would recall. "When he did, he kept his head down." He would never really recover from the psychological effects of the acne. "The changes that it wrought in him became permanent," Katherine said. "He was no longer a carefree, outgoing, devilish boy. He was quieter, more serious and more of a loner."

Complicating matters was his certainty that, acne aside, he was not a good-looking young man. He felt that his skin was too dark and his nose too wide.

Even though his family was aware of Michael's sensitivity, the brothers did not afford him any special treatment. The Jackson sons were a rowdy bunch offstage and always teased each other playfully.

At this time, Michael was nineteen and very grown-up in some ways, yet strikingly immature in others. He was afraid to drive. Whereas most youngsters are eager to get behind the wheel of a car by the age of sixteen, Michael was petrified. "I just don't want to," he said, when pushed. "I just don't have the desire. Whenever you do something, you have to want to do it. And even though there are some things you just have to do, I don't have to drive. And I simply don't want to. There's nothing special about it for me." Michael would usually have a limousine take him wherever he wanted to go, though often one of his brothers would drive him.

Besides the fact that he was scared of driving, Michael didn't want to go to the Department of Motor Vehicles to take the driver's test. He was afraid he'd be recognized and then be humiliated because he didn't drive. So he tried to get special consideration so that he wouldn't have to go to the D.M.V. for the testing, but the Encino division is accustomed to dealing with celebrities and doesn't consider any of them special. It was all just another roadblock, and Michael didn't want to be bothered. It didn't matter enough to him. Michael would be twenty-three before he'd get his driver's license, at his mother and father's insistence. "But suppose you're someplace and your chauffeur gets sick,'' Katherine argued with him. ''You need to be able to drive.''

Michael's teenage misery intensified when The Jacksons' second album for CBS, *Goin' Places*, released in the winter of 1977, was a major disappointment. Despite the fact that the first album for the new label had received mixed reviews and had only gone gold when everyone was hoping for platinum sales, CBS sent the group back to Philadelphia to work once again with Kenny Gamble and Leon Huff. The title track only went to number 52 on *Billboard's* Top 100; the album peaked at 63 on the Top 200. However, The Jacksons at Epic were still faring better than Jermaine was at Motown. His *Feel the Fire* album, released at the same time, peaked at number 174, encouraging most industry observers in their belief that Gordy was somehow intent on wasting Jermaine Jackson's career even if he was married to his daughter.

On *Goin' Places*, Michael wrote an itchy rhythm number called ''Different Kind of Lady,'' which became a successful club hit— played in discotheques but seldom on the radio—even though it was not issued as a single. Another song penned by the group, ''Do What You Wanna,'' also went unreleased as a single. By this time, The Jacksons hadn't had a number one record since ''Mama's Pearl'' in 1971. Joe was becoming concerned. The new relationship with CBS wasn't working out as they had hoped it would.

Joe Jackson decided to meet with Ron Alexenberg, the man who originally signed The Jacksons to Epic, to try to convince him once and for all that the group should be able to write and produce its own material. Perhaps Joe remembered the way Michael used his own initiative to meet with Berry Gordy when the chips were down, because he asked his son, now nineteen, to accompany him.

Michael was astonished that his father would ask for his assistance and couldn't help but be suspicious of his motives. He agreed to go along. Michael considered the family so important that he was willing to overcome—at least temporarily—his aversion to his father and cooperate with him on this matter. Just as Joe put on his public facade as father, so Michael put on his public facade as son.

It is not difficult to imagine that his brothers would have resented the fact that Michael had been put into this powerful position. During the meeting in a CBS boardroom, Michael and Joe explained that they were unhappy with the way the Jacksons' careers were going at CBS and that the time had come for the company to allow them control over an album. If CBS was not willing to allow the group more control over its music, then it was time to end the relationship before more money was wasted on unsuccessful product. Ironically, unbeknownst to Joe and Michael, new CBS Records president Walter Yetnikoff had already decided to drop The Jacksons from the label.

It seemed to Yetnikoff, and most industry observers, that The Jacksons were no longer commercially viable. The two CBS albums were not successful enough to warrant a third. Recalled Bobby Colomby, then head of Epic's West Coast artist relations, "The people I was working with at CBS really wanted me to get out of the deal. They wanted me to try to buy them [The Jacksons] out. But I felt so bad for these guys—and I liked them, they were so sweet and innocent—I said to myself, 'My God, if I give these people a hundred thousand dollars to go away, they're going to pay their bills and be out of the business forever.' "

Imagine the utter humiliation Joe and his sons would have suffered if, after all they had gone through to sever their ties with Berry Gordy, the new label's president were to drop them from the roster. The setback probably would have finished The Jacksons for good, and Joseph would surely have been blamed, whether or not it was his fault. Luckily for all concerned, Bobby Colomby managed to convince his bosses to give The Jacksons one more chance at Epic. This time, the fellows would have more involvement in their work. If they failed, they would have no one else to blame but themselves.

"That went pretty well, didn't it, son?" Joe said to Michael in the elevator after the meeting. He emphasized the word "son." They were descending in a car full of CBS executives and employees during lunch hour. Michael was observed smiling bitterly at his father. He himself has recalled that the subsequent ride back to the hotel was "a silent one."

Joe and Michael were two businessmen aligned in their mission to free The Jacksons from the choke hold of outside writers and producers. The rest of the family depended on them; hundreds of thousands of dollars were involved in the outcome of their dealings. Michael wisely realized that he could learn a great deal about the record business and entertainment management just by observing his father. After all, Joe Jackson was nothing if not shrewd and determined. Just as Michael considered Berry a great teacher— despite all that had happened—he knew there was something he could learn from Joseph, which is precisely what Michael called his father from the time he was nineteen. "Joseph." Never "Dad." Never again.

# Chapter

## 14

By 1977, NINETEEN-YEAR-OLD Michael Jackson seriously questioned the wisdom of the people responsible for his career. Berry Gordy, though a brilliant show business strategist, had proven to be a great personal disappointment to Michael Jackson when he refused to grant the family either financial or artistic independence. Michael, like the rest of the family, felt that Berry had somehow convinced Jermaine to abandon his siblings, and he would never be able to forget that. Michael also felt alienated from this father on a personal level and had doubts about his ability as their business manager.

However, Michael was often outvoted in decisions that would ultimately affect him, even though he was the most important member of the group. He was still unhappy over his family's insistence that the group star in their ill-fated variety series. He was beginning to distance himself emotionally from his family, a process that would take years to complete. It seemed that his brothers and Joe realized what was happening.

"He was still the soft, tender Michael Jackson everyone thought he was, but something was definitely different," said James McField, the Jacksons' pianist and band director at this time. "Everyone who dealt with him closely, family included, began to tread softly when dealing with Michael. The quiet power he was gaining was amazing to me. I'd never seen anyone have that much influence over people without having a stern attitude. I noticed that when he spoke, people were starting to listen. He was still outvoted on things, but now it was more reluctantly. Joe and the brothers were beginning to give him space. I began to notice that if they saw one iota of displeasure in his face, they began to get worried. For sure, things were changing as Michael was growing up."

Now Michael Jackson wanted to make a few of his own decisions regarding his career, just as his much-publicized so-called mentor, Diana Ross, was doing at this time.

Diana Ross, who had been completely dominated by Berry Gordy for seventeen years, was beginning to break his hold on her by 1977. Determined to be a film actress, she was anxious to find a property in which to star, and one she could claim responsibility for finding—unlike her previous two opuses, *Lady Sings the Blues* and *Mahogany*, both Motown discoveries.

At the same time, through a production deal with Universal, Berry Gordy's Motown Productions had acquired *The Wiz*, a musical based on L. Frank Baum's classic, *The Wonderful World of Oz*. *The Wiz*, an all-black production, had opened on Broadway in January 1975 and gone on to win seven Tony awards. Michael Jackson wrote in his autobiography, "Motown bought *The Wiz* for one reason, and as far as I was concerned, it was the best possible reason: Diana Ross." Nothing could be further from the truth.

Rob Cohen, a twenty-four-year-old white wunderkind who headed Motown Productions, had been trying to launch *The Wiz* for some time and recalled that the project was intended to be a low-budget film "possibly featuring Stephanie Mills, who starred in the Broadway play and was heavily campaigning for the role." Mills, a native New Yorker, had been a Motown artist for a short time, signed to the label at the behest of Jermaine Jackson, who had seen her on Broadway. Her experience at Motown was not a happy one; her one album for the label, *For the First Time* (produced by Burt Bacharach and Hal Davis), flopped in 1975. Appearing in the motion picture version of *The Wiz* would have been a real coup for Stephanie Mills, but Diana Ross decided that she wanted to play Dorothy. "I absolutely believed in Dorothy and in her search to find who she is," recalled Diana. "It seemed so very parallel to who I am."

To Diana Ross, here was an opportunity to show Berry Gordy that she had not only talent but creative vision as well. The fact that he thought casting her in *The Wiz* was a dreadful idea only encouraged Diana to want it even more. A tug-of-war ensued between Svengali and protégé. Eventually Diana prevailed, though practically everybody involved agreed that, at thirty-three, she was too old to, as Berry put it, "play anybody's damn Dorothy." Gordy and Cohen secured a million-dollar contract with Universal for her. "I wanted to do this project, and I honestly didn't care what I was going to be paid," Diana said at the time. "I was very happy, though, to be paid what, at this point in my life, I *should* be getting paid.''

After the Ross casting, Berry washed his hands of the entire project rather than have to make another movie with Diana Ross. Their last film together, *Mahogany*, had ended with star Ross slapping producer-director Gordy in front of an Italian film crew and then storming off the set, thereby ending production prematurely. Gordy needed a break, so he decided to give full responsibility for her new vehicle to Rob Cohen. Cohen recruited Sidney Lumet—who had recently completed work with Richard Burton on *Equus*—as director. Lumet, whose film credits included *Serpico* and *Dog Day Afternoon*, had never directed a musical before.

It was Lumet's decision to make the film a modern-day Manhattan fantasy using actual New York locations. Diana Ross would play a twenty-four-year-old schoolteacher—Dorothy—who is whisked into Oz by a blizzard. Ted Ross was hired to play the Lion and Nipsey Russell the Tin Man. Richard Pryor and Lena Horne were also featured players. Lumet wanted to cast comic Jimmie Walker as the Scarecrow. Walker is best remembered for his overblown portrayal of the loud-mouthed J.J. on CBS-TV's black sit-com ''Good Times.''

''I thought that was a horrible idea,'' Rob Cohen recalled. ''All I could think of was Walker as the Scarecrow in this surreal fantasy screaming out *'Dy-no-mite!'* in that irritating way he used to do it on that series. I felt that the role of the Scarecrow needed youth, innocence, and purity.

''I was always impressed by Michael Jackson,'' recalled Cohen. ''He struck me as being so polished, yet still pure. Plus he could sing—which Walker could not—and this *was* a musical.''

Rob Cohen suggested to Diana Ross that Michael would be right for the part. She thought it was, as she put it, ''the most perfect idea of all.'' Diana suggested to Michael—who had seen the Broadway show seven times—that he audition for the movie, but he was reluctant to do so. He felt that Gordy would probably use his influence to have him rejected because of the bad blood between the Jacksons and Motown. When Diana reassured him that she would see to it that he would be given a fair chance, Michael tried out for the part. A few days later, Sidney Lumet telephoned him at the Encino estate and told him that he had won the role.

Joe Jackson was not happy about Michael's good fortune. Quite simply, Joe did not want Michael to have the attention that starring in a movie would afford him. Since family prosperity had always been Joe Jackson's goal, he never stressed individuality. He had always resisted the temptation to single Michael out from the rest of the group, and even when Michael recorded solo albums at Motown, it was with the understanding that Jermaine and Jackie have the same opportunity. (Tito and Marlon also worked on solo album projects for Motown, though the records were never released.)

Joe realized that without Michael's voice, personality, and charisma, The Jacksons were much less commercial. The group could continue to make money as a popular record-selling and concert attraction only if Michael remained in the forefront. If The Jacksons made money, so did Joe and so did the rest of the family. Joe's philosophy had not been a problem for Michael in the past because he had always been group-minded. But now that he was older, he was feeling constricted by the group's democratic mentality.

Joe had been trying unsuccessfully for years to find a property that would star all of the Jackson sons together. Michael was tired of waiting for such a project to materialize. Moreover, making a film was a dream his brothers did not share with him. "I just watch movies constantly and envision how it would have been if I could have been the star," he recalled. "I wanted nothing more than to be a movie star." As much as he wanted the role, taking it could not have been an easy decision. He had to defy his father openly and risk the disapproval of his entire family. And he was going to perform in an unknown medium. A weekly TV variety show was insufficient preparation for a major movie role. Michael, always the perfectionist, must have wondered whether he would be up to the challenge.

Michael agonized over what to do, and in the end, he decided to follow his heart. "I'm doing the movie, and that's the end of it," he told Joe.

Michael received little family support. Although his mother, LaToya, and Janet encouraged him in his dream, his father and brothers continually played on his insecurities. "You won't be very good," he was told. "You'd better reconsider. You're not ready for this."

"It's not a good time for you," Joe told him. "This is a big mistake."

"We thought he was biting off more than he could chew," recalled one of his brothers. "We didn't think it was right for him, or good for the group."

"It was jealousy, basically," a family friend said. "Jackie had been up for the role of the disc jockey in Motown's *Thank God It's Friday* movie but didn't get it. [The part went to late actor Ray Vitte.] He didn't care about movies anyway; none of them did but

Michael. Yet they didn't want to encourage anything in Michael
that could complicate his relationship with the group. Also, Joe
was worried that if the movie bombed, any bad reviews for Michael
might affect the group in a negative way. Since he and his sons
couldn't stop him, they made him feel guilty about the time he
would be taking away from the group while filming in New York.
They kept whining and complaining that they would all be sitting
around wasting time while Mike was out on a lark making a movie.
His feelings were hurt, but still he couldn't wait to leave.''

 " 'I have to make this film for personal reasons,' he told me,''
Rob Cohen recalled. " 'There are some things I have to prove. To
myself and to others.' ''

*The Wiz* offered Michael a temporary avenue of escape from his
family. When he moved to New York in July 1977 to begin prepro-
duction on the film, he asked LaToya to accompany him. The two
resided in an exclusive two-thousand-dollars-per-month, thirty-
seventh-floor apartment located in Manhattan's expensive Sutton
Place. These few months would be the first time the two Jacksons
had been away from the rest of the family.

LaToya was nervous about being away from home and turned to
chocolate for comfort. "She ate chocolate the whole time she was
in New York," Susie Jackson said. "She became absolutely addicted. She told me that it got so bad, she had such chocolate fits,
that she would take Hershey's cocoa and just mix water with it and
drink it. That's how addicted she was. By the time she came back,
she had gained twenty pounds. That girl was in full bloom.''

LaToya may have had some apprehension about being away from
home, but Michael basked in his new independence. "He was
nothing like the odd Michael Jackson you hear about nowadays,''
Rob Cohen remembered. "I really don't know what he's like today,
but back then, God, he was such great fun. We had the best of
times. He, LaToya, me, and some of the others involved with the
project would go to clubs every night to dance. For some reason
he was not fearful of going out in public. He never had any kind of
special security. He was excited about being away from home, like
a little kid in the Manhattan playground. The only thing on his
mind was work during the day—and I've seldom seen anyone work
as hard, other than perhaps Diana Ross—and play at night.

"Manhattan was full of excitement for Michael," Rob Cohen
recalled. "He met Jacqueline Onassis at the Rainbow Grill one
night and was absolutely awed by her. Talked about her for days
afterwards, how glamorous and sophisticated she was, how he
hoped one day to know her better. He met Caroline and John Ken-

nedy at some tennis tournament [the Robert Kennedy Tennis Tournament]. This was a good, growing time for him. He did much more socializing then in public than he does today, except with Diana Ross. I don't think I ever saw them together except on the set, even though Michael would insist that they were the closest of friends. I don't remember seeing that closeness.''

Whatever closeness was there seemed to come under considerable strain from the beginning. In July, the cast started to rehearse their musical numbers at the St. George Hotel in Brooklyn. Michael is a natural, accomplished dancer; Diana is not. She can execute any kind of choreography after hours of intense work—from which she has never shied. But Michael can usually remember a choreographer's direction immediately and execute the step with precision and elegance.

During one particularly trying session where Diana performed badly, missing even the most elementary steps over and over, she pulled Michael aside. ''You're embarrassing me,'' she hissed.

''What do you mean?'' Michael asked. His surprise was genuine.

''You're learning the dances too quickly.''

Much later, Michael would relate the incident with a smile, but it was different at the time. ''I was sort of shocked,'' he recalled. ''I didn't mean to embarrass her, that's for sure. So I tried to act like I didn't always know what I was doing, so I could make her feel better.''

At this time, Michael's friend Theresa Gonsalves, whom he first met in November 1974 when she went to Las Vegas for her sixteenth birthday, telephoned him to say that she was going to New York for a visit. She would turn nineteen in November; Michael had turned nineteen in August.

''We made plans to see each other,'' Gonsalves recalled. ''When I got to the apartment building, he told the doorman to send me up. 'Toya answered the door, and she was sort of irritated. 'Michael didn't tell *me* that the two of you made plans,' she said. It was as if he was supposed to check with her in advance before he made plans, and he hadn't.

''So I asked 'Toya where he was, and she said that he was in the kitchen baking chocolate chip cookies. After Michael and I talked and ate the cookies, I took a look around. The suite had a balcony. Michael used to like to hang over it like he was going to jump. He loved acting like a fool to upset his sister. 'Toya had the most wonderful room, a real showplace with a huge bed with a mirror above it. It was a penthouse bedroom befitting a real star. On the other hand, Michael had a small, simple bedroom with a twin-sized bed in it and a desk. I asked myself, 'Why does she have such a great room and he's stuck with *this*?' ''

Michael told Theresa, ''There are these two girls who keep coming here to the building every day bugging me. They follow me everywhere. I don't know what to do. They even showed up on the set. Diane [Diana Ross] was so upset with them for bothering me that she went over to them and said, 'Why don't you just leave Michael alone? Just stop botherin' him, do you hear me?' Diane doesn't take stuff from people. I love that about her. But I can't be that way, and so I don't know what to do about these girls. What should I do?''

''Tell the doorman to let them come up here and meet you,'' Theresa suggested. ''Then after they meet you and get it out of their system, they'll leave you alone.''

Just then the phone rang, and it was the two girls in question. Michael put his hand over the mouthpiece of the receiver and whispered to Theresa, ''Should I?'' When she nodded her head yes, he invited them up.

''Then we all sat around and talked about child abuse,'' Theresa recalled. ''Michael was fascinated with child abuse. He wanted to know everything we girls had ever heard or read about it. He said he liked to read about child abuse as much as he possibly could.

''It turned out that one of those girls later went crazy, became obsessed with Michael, and then broke into his house in Encino. Eventually, she killed herself over him.''

Theresa went back to Boston and then returned to New York a few weeks later. Since Michael was busy with his work on *The Wiz*, she spent most of her time with LaToya. ''We constantly talked about girl things,'' she said. ''LaToya was so naive. For instance, Bobby DeBarge of the DeBarge singing group was in love with her, writing songs about her at this time. Jermaine was partly responsible for bringing DeBarge to Motown, and he wanted 'Toya to go out with Bobby. She told me that she didn't know what to do, because she didn't really like Bobby. She was twenty-one at this time but not very sophisticated about dating or even the simplest relationship problems.''

Michael came home from the studio very excited about a new set that had been built for him. ''Follow me,'' he told Theresa. She followed him into his modest bedroom. As the two of them stood at his desk, he started showing her a scrapbook of photographs of the movie set.

"So what do you think? Great, huh?" Michael asked.

"Yes, you're so lucky," Theresa enthused.

Michael closed the book and looked into Theresa's eyes thoughtfully. He tilted his head and leaned over to her. He was about to kiss her.

But then LaToya walked in. Michael pulled back nervously.

"So, anyway, I uh . . . ," he stammered.

Theresa said, "I wanted him to kiss me so badly. And I know he would have if 'Toya hadn't surprised us.

"While we were in New York, I learned that Stephanie Mills [the young actress who originated the role of Dorothy in *The Wiz*] was in love with Michael Jackson. Stephanie and LaToya were friendly. I was in a room with 'Toya when Stephanie telephoned one afternoon. The two of them started having a conversation about Michael. I gleaned that Stephanie wanted to know what she could buy Michael to interest him in her. 'Buy him a book about show business,' 'Toya suggested. But in the end, Michael really was not interested in Stephanie. There was no magic there for him."

In September 1977, Universal held a press conference at Astoria Studios in Queens in New York City to announce the making of *The Wiz*. The conference was conducted on the cavernous set that was being utilized as the sweatshop of Evilene, the Wicked Witch of the West (played by Theresa Merritt). Although cast members—Ross, Jackson, Nipsey Russell, and Ted Ross (who was recreating his Tony Award-winning Broadway role as the Lion)—were present to answer questions, all eyes were supposed to be on the star. Diana was dressed in a pinstripe suit, looking every inch the ultimate lady executive until she opened her jacket to reveal a string of marble-sized pearls that came down to her waist and a blouse whose vee neck did the same. After the announcement, there was an informal gathering for the cast and press.

Although Diana continued to answer a few of the reporter's questions as she sauntered about, for the most part she appeared haughty and unapproachable, in sharp contrast to Michael, who wore a striped shirt and jeans and acted as casually as he was dressed. Gregarious and talkative, he had already endeared himself to the media during the earlier part of the conference. Now, although he was not the star of the film, he quickly became the star of the press conference. Or as reporter Timothy White of *Crawdaddy* magazine put it, "Cuteness conquered calculation."

Michael has only had kind remembrances to share with the press where Diana Ross and *The Wiz* are concerned. "She would come into my dressing room every day and ask what she could do to make things more comfortable," he said. "She was like a mother to me. I love her very much."

Whether or not Diana was maternal on the set, Diana as "Dorothy" was like a mother to Michael as "Scarecrow," especially when she told him to "believe in yourself as I believe in you." The fact that he did not receive a similar vote of confidence from his family had hurt him deeply, but he refused to let the ambition inside of him die just because few family members shared his vision. Michael Jackson is a born gambler, though few thought of him in that way at this time. Exhilarated by ideas and dreams, he wanted to take chances. But his family worried that anything he might do would imperil *their* lives and careers. So they did everything they could to discourage him. After the film was finished, Michael admitted, "No one, not my father, my brothers, thought I could handle doing *The Wiz.*"

Scarecrow's first number in the show was "You Can't Win." Hanging awkwardly from a pole, surrounded by jeering crows, Michael sang about people telling him that things were going to change, but no matter what they said, things kept staying the same. Michael recognized how close it was to his own situation.

He recalled, "It's about the feeling you get when you know there are people out there who don't want to believe in you. They don't really hold you back, but they don't push you ahead either. Instead, they prey on your mind and work on your insecurities so that you hold yourself back. I could relate to that in many ways."

When Scarecrow sang, "You only have yourself to blame," Michael may well have heard it as a message to take charge of his own life, an action he had already begun by playing this role. He was beginning to see himself more clearly in relationship to his family: he was their meal ticket, and they feared his independence.

Tin Man was looking for a heart—which Michael already possessed. Lion was looking for courage—which Michael had demonstrated in dealing with Berry Gordy in the past and also in accepting this role. But Scarecrow was looking for brains, and Michael had always felt self-conscious about his lack of formal education. One day he rehearsed a scene in which he pulled a slip of paper from his stuffing and read a quote by Socrates. He attributed the statement to *Soh-crates,* as if it rhymed with "no rates." "That's the way I had always assumed it was pronounced," Michael said later.

When he heard the crew giggling, Michael winced.

"*Sock-ra-tease*," someone whispered in his ear. "It's *Sock-ra-tease.*"

He turned and saw Quincy Jones, the film's musical director.*

The older man extended his hand. "I'm Quincy Jones," he said with a warm smile. "Anything I can do to help . . ."

Michael would remember the offer.

Filming the $24 million movie—at the time one of the most expensive films ever made—took place from October 3 through December 30, 1977, at Astoria Studios. It was hard work. Each day—six days a week—Michael would awake at four in the morning in order to leave for the studio by 5:30. Following her mother's instructions, LaToya would prepare an early breakfast for her brother, usually consisting of orange juice, bacon, buttered toast, herb tea, and oatmeal. Michael Jackson's makeup for his role as Scarecrow took cosmetologist Stan Wilson (best known at the time for his aging makeup on Cicely Tyson for *The Autobiography of Miss Jane Pittman*) five hours to apply.

"I loved it more than I can tell you," Michael said after the film was done. "I was the Scarecrow from the time the makeup was put on until the time it came off, which I hated." Sometimes he would even go home at night with his makeup on.

The makeup was a welcome cover for the bad case of acne that had erupted all over his face. Once it was applied, and his phony nose and fright wig of steel-wool pads were in place, Michael could escape to the land of Oz—a place where his father and brothers could not go, a fantasy world where people helped each other achieve their goals by believing in each other. No wonder he never wanted it to end.

Out of costume, he was the same odd Michael. One of Sidney Lumet's teenage daughters asked Michael to sing for her and a couple of her friends. Though he is so obviously comfortable performing for a crowd of thousands, Michael loathes singing in front of a small group. "Okay, I'll sing for you," he told the teenagers. "But cover your eyes."

After the movie was filmed and prior to its release, it was back to business as usual for The Jacksons, except that now Michael felt different about his family and his career. Feeling good about what he was doing—and being praised by people whose work he re-

---

*The Socrates quote was ultimately edited from the final cut of *The Wiz*. Michael had actually met Quincy Jones when he was twelve, at Sammy Davis, Jr.'s home. Michael doesn't remember the meeting, though Quincy does.

spected—filled Michael with a new confidence in himself as an individual artist. He wanted to begin work on that solo album he had been promised by Epic as soon as possible, even though the rest of the family wanted to concentrate on the third Jacksons group album for the label. The family won again.

The group went into the studio to record *Destiny*, the first Jacksons album said to be written and produced by the group itself. Although the Jacksons did, indeed, write all but one of the songs, and although they were pictured on the inside jacket posing proudly behind a recording control board, executive producer Bobby Colomby and Mike Atkinson did most of the real production work. When there was some disagreement as to what credit they should receive, Michael was the only one of the brothers who felt that Colomby and Atkinson should be credited as executive producers. Ultimately, Colomby and Atkinson had to obtain affidavits from engineers and musicians involved in the project to prove their input and get the credit—and money—they deserved as executive producers when the album was released in mid-December 1978.

*Destiny* was, by far, the most exciting Jacksons album to date, including all of those recorded at Motown. For the first time, the group released a cohesively structured album. There were no filler songs. At Motown, and even on the first two Epic albums, there were always a few standout numbers padded with material that would never have been considered for single release. On *Destiny*, all eight songs were worthy of being issued as singles.

Michael Jackson had never sounded better than he did on this album. His performance on the dreamy ballad "Push Me Away"— with its orchestral sweep and rapturous melody—seems so carefree and effortless. Yet upon closer inspection, it becomes obvious that Michael's delivery is both tightly measured and precise. He knows exactly how to settle his mind on the heart and story of a song in order to create the proper mood. As a result of years in the studio and in front of audiences—and a genuine love for singing—he had become an intuitively brilliant stylist.

Though off to a bad start with the high-flash pop of "Blame It on the Boogie," a single which didn't even make the Top 40, *Destiny* would fare much better than *Goin' Places*. The real showcase here was the mesmerizing "Shake Your Body (Down to the Ground)," written by Michael and Randy. When released (in February 1979) it would become the biggest hit of the album, peaking at number seven on the pop charts and selling two million copies. "Shake Your Body," with its crackling lead vocal by Michael, whip-snapping chorus from the brothers, and insistent, persistent backbeat, personified the contemporary disco trend. It is still regarded by many music critics as the perfect dance record and certainly one of the strongest Jacksons efforts.

The Jacksons did many interviews with the press to discuss their new album, always emphasizing that although they had been writing songs for years, this was the first time they'd been able to dominate an album with their own compositions. The Jacksons could not be criticized in terms of their ability to write songs; they proved themselves with *Destiny*. However, what is striking about the fellows at this time is how really uninteresting they were as interview subjects. They were not able to discuss their music with any kind of depth or authority. Mostly, the brothers—Jackie, twenty-seven, Tito, twenty-five, Marlon, twenty-one, Michael, twenty, and Randy, sixteen—were ambiguous in their comments, serving up heaps of platitudes about how wonderful it was to write and produce and how they hoped to continue doing so, "forever and ever," as Marlon put it. Because of their early training at Motown to say to the press only what they were told to say, now that the Jacksons could express themselves freely, they really didn't know how to.

I was one of the reporters the Jacksons spoke to when they were promoting their *Destiny* album, but I decided to stay clear of any in-depth musical discussions, since I knew from past experiences with the Jacksons that I would get few observations of interest from them. The interview took place on August 22, 1978, and the memory of that bizarre summer afternoon at the family's Encino home will always remain with me.

When John Whyman, the photographer, and I pulled up to the ominous black wrought-iron gate at 4641 Hayvenhurst, the Jacksons' estate, it stood open, but Whyman pressed the buzzer on the squawk box anyway. We had heard about the vicious guard dogs and did not want to take any chances. An electronic camera, conspicuously mounted on a fifteen-foot-high pole, seemed to zoom in for closer inspection. Our images, we later learned, were being projected on a closed-circuit television screen in the Jackson kitchen. "You may come in," said a disembodied male voice.

We pulled into the circular driveway, a cache of Cadillacs, Rolls-Royces, Mercedes-Benzes, Datsun 240 Zs, and a Pantara. Three angry sentry dogs, penned up at the end of the drive, hurled themselves against the chain-link fence. Their ferocious barks were in contrast to the raucous cries of three large peacocks—one pure white—caged nearby. The sound from the peacocks was something akin to a baby's wail and a cat's howl. We decided to wait in the car.

Looking around, I noticed a custom-made street sign, JACK-SON 5 BOULEVARD, nailed to a nearby tree trunk. To the left stood a basketball court. I glanced up at the two-story house and noticed four expressionless faces staring down at us from as many windows. Michael, LaToya, Randy, and their mother, Katherine, had their countenances pressed against the panes as if they were prisoners in a compound.

It seemed that nobody would rescue us, so we took our chances, got out of the car, and approached the front door. I rang the doorbell. Twenty-two-year-old LaToya, in a white tennis outfit, answered. When Michael approached seconds later, she excused herself, walked out into the driveway, got into a sporty red Mercedes convertible, and sped off.

"Glad you could make it," Michael said as we shook hands.

He was wearing a yellow *Jaws* T-shirt, black jeans, and a safari hat, around which his Afro seemed to billow. His feet were bare and, to me, he looked painfully thin. He spoke in an odd, falsetto whisper, which seemed even softer than it had the last time we talked. In exactly a week, he would turn twenty.

Michael led us through the house toward the living room. A huge yellow and green parrot sat perched on a ledge outside the window, shucking peanuts. A red, blue, and yellow cockatoo eyed us warily through another window. It let out an ear-piercing screech as we sat down. I suddenly felt like I was at a zoo.

"How come you're not getting your guests lemonade?" Katherine asked her son when she came into the room. I could not help noticing that Michael's mother walked with a slight limp, the result of a bout with polio she had as a child. At some times the handicap was more pronounced than at others.

"Oh, sorry," Michael murmured. He dashed off to the kitchen, giving me an opportunity to talk alone with his forty-nine-year-old mother while the photographer set up his equipment.

The house, which they had lived in since 1971, was a combination pale yellow, soft green, and white, a reflection of Katherine's warm personality. She was gregarious, friendly, and she had a benevolent glow about her. She told me that she had decorated the house herself—as an assignment for a home-decorating class. She mentioned that Michael's favorite foods were hot apple turnovers and sweet-potato pies.

"Only now I can't get him to eat *anything*. I try and try," she said, shrugging her shoulders. "I keep thinking he'll eat when he gets hungry, but the boy never gets hungry. Have you noticed how skinny he is? It worries me."

I looked around at the opulent furnishings. "These last few years have certainly been good ones," I said to Katherine. "Maybe the best of your life?"

"Not really," she answered thoughtfully. "The best years were back when Michael was about three and I used to sing folk songs with him. You see, I'd always wanted to be a country star, but who'd ever heard of a black country star back then? Those restrictions, again. Anyway, we had one bedroom for the boys and they all slept together in triple bunk beds. Before going to sleep, we'd all sing. We were so happy then. I'd switch my life now and give up all that we have for just one of those days back in Gary when it was so much simpler. When we first came to California, I don't know how many times I said, 'I wish things were the way they used to be in Gary.' But things have never been the same," she added sadly. "It's all changed now."

Michael came back into the room juggling two glasses of lemonade. He handed one to me and the other to the photographer and then sat in a chair, lotus position. Katherine excused herself.

During our two-hour interview, Michael shared his thoughts on a wide range of topics. "I don't know much about politics," Michael admitted. "Nothing, I guess. Someone told me recently that Gerald Ford was president."

He laughed a silvery peal, as he did often; he was in good spirits this afternoon, not at all the shy, reclusive superstar he would become in a few years. I laughed with him because I was certain we were sharing a joke, but we weren't. He was serious.

"I remember when he was vice-president," Michael continued thoughtfully. "*That* I remember. But president?" He shrugged his shoulders helplessly. "That I missed."

In just a few years, Michael would become an avid reader and exchange ideas about politics with Jane Fonda. But at this time, Michael was quite naive about current events. Astounded at the extreme isolation of this twenty-year-old's world, I began to probe deeper. "How do you keep up with current events? Do you read newspapers? Watch TV?"

"I watch cartoons," he told me. "I *love* cartoons." His eyes lit up. "I love Disney so much. The Magic Kingdom. Disneyland. It's such a magical place. Walt Disney was a dreamer, like me. And he made his dreams come true, like me. I hope."

"What about current events?"

Michael looked at me blankly. "Current events?"

"Do you read the paper?" I repeated.

He shook his head no. "See, I like show business. I listen to music all the time. I watch old movies. Fred Astaire movies. Gene Kelly, I love. And Sammy [Davis]. I can watch these guys all day, twenty-four hours a day. That's what I love the most. Show business, you know?''

We talked about old movies for a while, and about his involvement in *The Wiz*, the film he had just finished shooting in which he plays the Scarecrow. I asked what he saw as his biggest professional challenge.

"To live up to what Joseph expects of me."

"Joseph? Who's Joseph?" I wondered.

"My father. Joseph."

"You call your father by his first name?" I asked.

"Uh-huh.''

"And living up to what he expects of you is a *professional* challenge?''

Michael mulled over my question. "Yes. A professional challenge.''

"What about the personal challenges?''

"My professional challenges and personal challenges are the same thing," he said uneasily. "I just want to entertain. See, when I was in the second grade, the teacher asked me what I wished for. I asked for a mansion, peace in the world, and to be able to entertain . . . Can we talk about something else?''

"Do you have any friends that you can really confide in?''

Michael squirmed. "No, not really. I guess I'm pretty lonely.''

"How about Tatum O'Neal?" I wondered.

Michael shrugged his shoulders. "She's nice. She was really happy for me when I got the part in *The Wiz*. She and Ryan were on my side, helping me with my lines, and I owe them a lot. Tatum understands me, I guess. She's gonna teach me to drive a car. She introduces me to people, famous, *famous* people. But my real dates, they're the girls who stand outside the gate out there. I go out and sign autographs for them when I can. They like that. They stay on one side of the gate, and I stay on the other.''

"You mean you keep the gate closed?" I asked.

"Oh, yeah. Of course.''

"Any other friends?''

"Well, I do have one friend," he said. "A very dear, close friend that I can tell my deepest, darkest secrets to because I know she won't tell anyone, not another living soul. Her name is . . .'' He paused dramatically. "Miss Diana Ross.''

"You have deep, dark secrets, Michael?''

He laughed. "*Everybody* has deep, dark secrets.''

At this point, Michael was joined by his brothers Jackie, Tito, Marlon, and Randy.

Michael talked about the group's success at Motown and about the fanatical hysteria generated by their fame, which Motown tagged "Jacksonmania."

"Once at a record store in San Francisco, over a thousand kids showed up," he said in a hushed tone. "They all pushed forward and broke a window. A big piece of glass fell on top of this girl. And the girl's throat . . .," he paused for effect, "was *slit*." Michael swiftly ran his index finger across his neck.

"Michael, don't do that. That's gross," his youngest brother, Randy, said.

Michael ignored Randy and continued with his story. "She just got *slit*. And I remember there was blood everywhere. Oh God, so much blood. And she grabbed her throat and was bleeding and everyone just ignored her. Why? Because *I* was there and they wanted to grab at *me* and get *my* autograph." Michael sighed. "I wonder whatever happened to that girl."

"Probably dead," Tito muttered. Jackie tried to stifle a laugh.

Fans were as much a curse as a blessing. "We got these three guard dogs. One is named Heavy, one is Black Girl, and the other one don't got no name," Michael said. "We *have* to have them," he insisted. "See, once a lady jumped over the gate and into the house and sat down in the den. We came home, and she looked at us and what did she say?" He turned to Marlon for help. "What'd that lady say?"

"She said, 'I'm here 'cause God sent me,' " Marlon replied.

"Yeah, God sent her," Michael repeated.

Jackie laughed again. "Yeah, God sent her to sit in The Jackson 5's den and wait for them to get home so she can get their autograph, and maybe her picture with 'em too. She was on a divine mission. Man, that's funny."

"And then once, a whole family managed to get into the estate somehow, and they toured the whole house," Michael continued. "Lookin' all in our stuff. Findin' all our most *private* things. And Janet was here all by herself. It was scary. And sometimes, fans ask weird questions. They don't think you're real. Once a fan asked me the most embarrassing question and in front of everyone. She said, 'Do you go to the bathroom?' I was *so* embarrassed."

In the middle of the interview, the good-natured ribbing among the brothers turned nasty when someone brought up the subject of nicknames.

"Mike has a nickname," Jackie mentioned. "It's a real good one."

Michael's smiling face suddenly turned dead serious. "Don't, Jackie," he warned. He looked away.

"We call him—"

"Please, you guys!" Michael pleaded.

"Big Nose," Jackie continued, oblivious to Michael's embarrassment.

The brothers laughed among themselves. Michael's face became flushed.

"Yeah, Big Nose," Marlon repeated, grinning. "We call him Big Nose. Marlon reached over and punched Michael in the arm playfully. "What's happenin', Big Nose?"

But Michael was not laughing. He seemed to curl up inside himself.

The others ignored him, continuing their game until Michael seemed close to tears. He would hardly say anything the rest of the afternoon. "That ain't funny, guys," Tito said in his monotone.

After the interview, we walked outside to take photographs in the warm California sunlight. Father Joseph Jackson, a hulking six-footer with a mole on his face, a pencil-thin mustache, and a pinky ring with a diamond the size of a marble, came swaggering into the yard. "The boys aren't taking any pictures," he said to photographer Whyman.

"But the publicist from Epic said for us to come dressed for pictures," Marlon protested.

"Maybe we can get a couple of shots with you in them," Whyman offered, hoping to charm Joseph.

Joe considered the offer. He took in a deep breath and puffed up his chest. "Let's take us some pictures, boys."

After the picture session, the photographer and Michael went off to the aviaries nearby, which were stocked with large, colorful birds. Joseph Jackson approached me.

"You see, I have a philosophy about raising children," he suddenly said, although I hadn't asked him a question. "My father was very strict. He was a schoolteacher, and he treated me like I was one of his students, not like I was his son. I never got any special treatment from him. And I'm glad that happened. I got a strict raising when I was young, and I've been able to accomplish a lot because of that. And my kids have gotten a strict raising, and look at what *they've* accomplished. I think children should fear their parents more. It's good when they fear you a little. It's good for them, and it's good for the parents too. I did my best with those boys, the best I could do.''

"Have they ever disappointed you?" I asked.

Joe pondered the question. "Lots of times," he said. "Look at the thing with Jermaine. Jermaine's over there with Berry at Motown instead of with us. Chose Berry over me. Do you know how that makes me feel? It hurts deep. It hurts right here.'' Joe thumped the left side of his chest with a clenched fist.

"I've been disappointed lots of other times too," he continued. "But I don't think I have ever once let my boys down. If I did, too bad for them. You do the best you can do, raising kids. It helped that they had something to look forward to.

"My boys, they always had entertainment, and me to rehearse them. And they also play character-building sports like football and baseball," he said proudly. "Did they tell you that? Jackie coulda been a baseball player if he wanted to. In the majors. Chicago White Sox. They're all good at sports. Except for Michael. Never picked up a bat in his whole life." Joe smiled. "Wouldn't know what to do with a baseball bat. We tease him about it, but he don't like that too much. Michael has always been very, very sensitive.

"Another thing you should know about Michael," Joe said, "is that ever since he was four, he wanted to be an entertainer. And he always wanted to be number one. That's why sports upset him so much, 'cause his brothers can whip him and outdo him at sports and he can't be number one. But in music, Michael *knows* he's number one. Number one," Joe repeated, nodding his head. "That's what Michael has always wanted to be. Number one.

"And speakin' of Michael, Marlon told me about what happened. You're not gonna write that part about Michael's nickname, are you?" he asked.

I told him I wasn't certain how I would handle it.

"He doesn't like that nickname they gave him. Liver Lips.''

"Liver Lips? They told me his nickname is Big Nose.''

"Oh, yeah," Joe said. "That boy's so sensitive about his nose. Do you see anything wrong with his nose?"

I shook my head. "No, not at all.''

"Me neither," Joe said. "But that's all he ever talks about. His damn nose. Threatened to have it fixed. What can he do with it?" Joe looked perplexed. "I told him I'd break his face if he ever had it fixed." He laughed. "You don't fix something that ain't broke. He's got a great nose. It looks like mine.''

Afterwards, Michael returned to the living room for some final thoughts about his life and career. As the photographer and I watched, he crossed his left leg over his right knee and began absentmindedly picking at his toenails.

"When I'm not onstage, I'm not the same. I'm different," he observed. "I think I'm some kinda stage addict. When I can't get onto a stage for a long time, I have fits and get real crazy. I start crying, and I act weird and all freaked out. No kiddin', I do. I start to dancin' 'round the house."

He began to talk rapidly. "It's like a part of me is missin' and I gotta get it back, 'cause if I don't, I won't be complete. So I gotta dance and I gotta sing, you know? I have this craving. Onstage is the only place I'm comfortable. I'm not comfortable around . . .," he paused, searching for the right word, "*normal* people. But when I get out onstage, I really open up and I have no problems. Whatever is happening in my life don't matter no more. I'm up there and cuttin' loose and I say to myself, 'This is it. This is home. This is exactly where I'm supposed to be, where God meant for me to be.' I am *unlimited* when I'm onstage. I'm number one. But when I'm off the stage," he shrugged his shoulders, "I'm not really . . ." Again, he paused, trying to find the right word. "Happy."

Earlier in the day, I had conducted an interview with Sidney Lumet, director of *The Wiz*. "Michael Jackson is the most gifted entertainer to come down the pike since, I guess, James Dean," Lumet told me. "He's a brilliant actor and dancer, probably one of the rarest entertainers I have ever worked with. His talent is awesome."

I shared Lumet's observation with Michael. He seemed embarrassed for a moment. "Who's James Dean?" he asked.

Later, he began talking about his role as the Scarecrow in *The Wiz*. "What I like about my character," he observed, "is his, I guess you could call it, his confusion. He knows that he has these, uh, these problems, I guess you could call them. But he doesn't exactly know why he has them or how he got that way. And he understands that he see things differently from the way everyone else does, but he can't put his finger on why. He's not like other people. No one understands him. So he goes through his whole life with this, uh . . .," he paused, "confusion."

Michael Jackson looked away from his toenails for a split second. "Everybody thinks he's very special," he concluded thoughtfully. "But, really, he's very sad. He's so, so sad. Do you understand?" He asked urgently. "Do you understand his sadness?"

At this time, Joe Jackson severed his ties with lawyer Richard Arons, who had been working as unofficial comanager of the group.

In Arons's wake, Joe decided to recruit Ron Weisner and Freddy DeMann as official comanagers. His sons were in agreement with this decision. Both were experienced in the entertainment field, Weisner as a business manager and DeMann as a promoter. Joe Jackson said later that he felt that he needed the assistance of these two white men in order to guarantee that CBS would promote The Jacksons as they did their many white artists. Jackson felt that the company considered his sons a black act and was therefore restricting the way it promoted and marketed the group.

This is a common—and quite often justified—complaint of many black acts signed to record companies, like CBS, that are manned predominantly by white executives. Like Joe Jackson, many black managers feel that white executives don't know how to market black entertainment ''across the board''—to white record buyers as well as black. Joe Jackson argued that he did not want *Destiny* or any of The Jacksons' records to be successful only with black radio stations and black audiences. Perhaps this desire really was the reason he hired Weisner and DeMann. However, since Richard Arons is also white, one might speculate that Joe had some other motive.

Apparently, Joe's strategy, whatever its motive, worked. *Destiny* sold over a million copies and reached number eleven on *Billboard's* album chart, not bad for a group that hadn't scored with a major record in some time.

But Michael was unhappy just the same. Despite what his brothers said, he knew in his heart that The Jacksons were not fully responsible for the success of *Destiny*. Epic had whipped up quite a frenzy about how terrific the brothers were as producers; Michael hated living this lie. The group was about to embark on a concert tour to promote the album, and he dreaded the thought of it. He no longer had much in common with his brothers; Michael felt that none of them understood him or his ambitions. Also, he realized that if anything went wrong on the road—which was inevitable— he would probably be outvoted on how best to handle it. To make matters even worse, he detested having to answer to his father or even having to be around him.

Many people thought, based on the success of *Destiny*, that Joe Jackson was becoming a brilliant career manager, but Michael would admit later that he was not one of them. He would say that it seemed to him that Joe favored the shotgun approach: ''If you shoot enough bullets, one will hit the target eventually,'' he explained. That strategy sometimes worked, as it was doing for The Jacksons at this time. ''But you can waste a lot of ammunition and maybe hit some target you would rather not,'' Michael told one

CBS executive. "I mean, look at the way Joseph alienated Berry and everyone else at Motown." Some people, on the other hand, determine the target, stalk it as long as necessary, and then get it cleanly with one shot. "That's the way to go," Michael reasoned. Indeed, he was continuing to learn his lessons by example.

*The Wiz*, when it was finally released in October 1978, became a major disappointment, a box-office disaster. Most of the reviews, if not raves, were at least respectable, especially the critiques of Michael's performance. What killed the movie was not the critical response but the word of mouth. Word got around that the movie was so bad, ticket sales dropped dramatically from week to week. The film was an overblown spectacle that most people who were involved with it would just as soon forget. Even the single release of "Ease On Down the Road," which teamed Michael with Diana Ross—a union that seemed destined for the Top 10 in theory—didn't crack the Top 40. Berry Gordy—who had nothing to do with the movie at all—to this day won't even discuss *The Wiz*.

"It was a big dream that got away," said producer Rob Cohen in retrospect. "A brilliant idea gone very wrong. The knowledge that two years of my life, $23 million of Universal's money, thousands of man-hours of labor, and all the love, hopes, and dreams of everyone involved had gone into this movie that didn't stand a chance absolutely made me sick."

Michael disguised his unhappiness, and does to this day, by parroting for public consumption nothing but praise for *The Wiz*. "I think it was a wonderful, wonderful movie," he has said publicly. "The messages in our version were much deeper and more meaningful than those in the original. I don't think it could have been any better, I really don't."

On one level, he really believed it. Being the Scarecrow had been an overwhelming personal achievement. Identifying himself with his role gave Michael a chance to look deep into his own psyche and find strength and self-confidence. "Working in the movie showed me what makes kings of the world," he said, "what makes giants. It showed me how I can believe in myself in a way I could never before."

He had also expanded his professional horizons and won the respect of his fellow workers and critics alike. Still, he could not ignore the fact that *The Wiz* was a failure at the box office. That made him feel shattered. He had never before been involved with such a failure.

"Did I make a mistake?" he asked Rob Cohen. "Maybe I

shouldn't have done this. Maybe I should have listened to my family. What will it mean to my career?''

"You followed your instincts," Cohen told him. "We all did. Don't second-guess yourself now. We have nothing to be ashamed of. We did the best job we could.''

"But—''

"But nothing," Rob recalled telling him. "Go on with your life and career. Be a star. You've only just begun.''

# Chapter

# 15

MICHAEL JACKSON HAD never been as discouraged about his life and career as he was when he finally finished the 1979 Destiny tour. He had lost his voice while on the road. Marlon would sing Michael's higher-register parts while he would just stand on stage moving his mouth as if he were singing. He found the lip-synching humiliating. Doctors made Michael cancel two weeks of performances because of his throat problems. He was constantly tired and discouraged and didn't have that unlimited supply of energy on which he had always relied. As enthusiastic as the audiences were, Michael felt that something was missing. Barely twenty-one, he'd stopped growing professionally.

"It was the same thing over and over," he would recall in an interview. "It was all for one and one for all, but I was starting to think that maybe I should be doing some things on my own. I was getting antsy."

There had been a couple of film offers as a result of Michael's work in *The Wiz*. Michael said that he had been offered the part of a transvestite in the movie version of *A Chorus Line*. Michael was baffled, even hurt, that he came to mind when the part was cast.

"Why me?" he asked. "If I do it, people will link me with the part. Because of my voice, some people already think I'm that way, homo. Though I'm actually not at all. It's just a lot of gossip."

"He anguished over whether he should play a homosexual on the screen," said one associate. " 'Why can't I?' he told me at one point. 'If I'm a good actor, I should be able to play any role.' But he was kidding himself. Michael is too fanatical about his image to seriously consider such a thing."

Michael decided that if a film wasn't in the offing, then he wanted to record a solo album. He spent day after day alone in his bedroom pondering, as Marlon would say, "who knows what, he's very secretive." Perhaps Michael felt that a solo album would ease the overwhelming feeling of restlessness that had plagued him ever since the Destiny tour ended.

"Michael didn't feel that the group had really made an impact after leaving Motown," said the associate. "Even though they had a hit with 'Shake Your Body,' Michael was tremendously depressed. He was tired of The Jackson 5 image, really. He told me, 'I feel it's time for me to move on, but how do I do that without hurting my family?' He felt trapped."

The brothers realized that something was wrong. "Mike was acting strangely," Tito would remember. "It was as if something had snapped in him. He stopped showing up at family meetings, and when we discussed our future plans, he had nothing to offer. Maybe he was plotting to go out on his own. I don't know. He never did say much. You never really knew what he was thinking."

Michael had become frustrated. Sometimes he would take it out on his family. Once, he came down from his room and saw Katherine, Janet, and LaToya watching television. "Don't you know that you're just wasting precious time?" he scolded them. "Get up and do something. Write a song." He would later say, "I feel guilty just sitting around when I know I can be doing something."

"I didn't think it was fair that I had stopped recording solo albums," Michael would say. "Part of our contract with CBS was that I would get to record on my own. When that wasn't happening because we hadn't been able to find the time, I started getting nervous and upset."

The Jacksons were successful, but their success was no longer personally fulfilling to Michael. CBS did release a single of Michael singing "You Can't Win" from the soundtrack of *The Wiz*. While not a major hit, this tune captured the essence of the disco era in a gaudy, overblown Quincy Jones production that packed the dance floors for a while. Unbeknownst to the record-buying audience, this song may have marked the beginning of Michael's own fixation with success. "You can't win, / You can't break even, / You can't get out of the game." The record only reached eighty-one on the *Billboard* pop charts.

"I don't care about that," Michael said of the song's failure. "I hear an ideal record in my mind," he told a reporter. "Maybe with Quincy again. We'll see."

Michael told his father that he wanted to record a solo album. "Why not?" was Joe's lackadaisical reaction. "Go ahead, do what you want as long as it doesn't interfere with group business."

"What does that mean?" Michael wanted to know.

"You know what it means," his father warned him. "Family is the most important thing."

Joe couldn't get enthusiastic about Michael doing a solo album because, realistically speaking, Michael's albums never amounted to much. His first two for Motown, *Got to Be There* and *Ben* (1971 and 1972 respectively), each sold a little over 350,000 copies, which wasn't bad at all. But then his third album, *Music and Me* (1973), sold only 80,286 copies, a dismal showing. His last solo album for the company, *Forever Michael* (1975), did a little better (99,311 copies).

Albums featuring all of the Jackson boys always sold better than solo albums, and Joe had always felt it was in everybody's best interest to keep the act together. He had made it clear that he did not want special treatment for Michael as far back as 1969, when Diana Ross introduced the group as "Michael Jackson and the Jackson 5" to the Hollywood Palace studio and television audience.

"He's not the star," Joe insisted to Berry Gordy. "They're *all* stars."

So if Michael needed to record a solo album in order to "get it out of his system," that was fine with Joe—as long as he remembered that his first allegiance was to his family and to the group, not to himself.

When Michael Jackson set out to make the record that would become *Off the Wall*, he really didn't know what he wanted. He knew what he *didn't* want, and that was another record that sounded like a Jacksons album. From the start of his professional career, someone had always decided the direction of the music Michael made. First it was Motown's production staff, and later the artist and repertoire executives at Epic, who urged The Jacksons to use the then-hot production team of Kenny Gamble and Leon Huff for *The Jacksons* and *Goin' Places*.

Though the family was given the freedom to write and produce the *Destiny* album, Epic insisted that the record include a song they didn't write, "Blame It on the Boogie." Other concessions and compromises were made along the way with the three albums, and Michael never felt much in control of the results. While *Destiny*'s hit single, "Shake Your Body" reestablished The Jacksons in the marketplace, many people in the music business felt the brothers had left their magic at Motown.

Now Michael wanted more creative freedom. He wanted to do his next album totally outside the family, even though the brothers tried desperately to make his solo album a group production as soon as they heard about it. They were hurt that Michael was excluding them from the project, but Michael stood firm. "I'm doing this on my own," he said. "They're just going to have to understand. For once."

"Going on your own opens up many avenues for you," Sammy Davis observed. Davis had worked with his father and an adopted uncle as a trio in the early days of his career. "I think that's probably what Michael was thinking. It comes from being in this business as a child, and you see another horizon over there, and you know that the best way to get over that peak is to do it alone."

Uncertain how to proceed, Michael called Quincy Jones, who he remembered had offered a helping hand during production of *The Wiz*. Michael asked Quincy to suggest some possible producers. Quincy suggested himself.

Quincy Jones* seemed a rather unlikely choice for Michael to work with. Jones had found success in the pop-R&B arena with his own albums, which were virtual music workshops of musicians, writers, and arrangers with Jones overseeing. Quincy had also found mainstream success with the Brothers Johnson, a sibling duo out of Los Angeles whose platinum albums he produced. Still, most industry observers privately felt that Jones was too musically stiff to make a great rhythm-and-blues record; many of these people believed that Jones's records with the Brothers Johnson, for instance, though successful, sounded much too homogenized.

Jones had already had a long and varied show business career, starting as a fifteen-year-old trumpet player and arranger for Lionel Hampton. Over the years, he immersed himself in studio work, arranging, composing, and producing for Dinah Washington, Duke Ellington, Big Maybelle, Tommy Dorsey, and Count Basie. In the early sixties, he was a vice-president of Mercury Records—the first black executive at a major label. In 1963, he began a second career in Hollywood, where he became the first black to reach the top rank of film composers, with thirty-eight pictures to his credit, including *The Wiz*.

"I didn't even want to do *The Wiz*," Quincy has said. "I thought, 'There's no way the public is going to accept a black version of *The Wizard of Oz*.' I kept telling Sidney Lumet I didn't want to do it, but because he's a great director and because he hired me to do my first movie soundtrack [*The Pawnbroker*, 1965], I did it. Out of that mess came my association with Michael Jackson."

*By 1991, Quincy Jones had been nominated for seventy-six Grammy Awards and had won twenty-five.

When Jackson and Jones came together in a recording facility in Los Angeles to start laying rhythm tracks in 1979, the artist and producer turned out to be a perfect match. Jones's in-studio work method was to surround the artist with superior songs and fine musicians and then let that artist have free reign. Michael had been so accustomed to being on an artistic leash that he was ecstatic when Quincy began taking his musical ideas seriously. Quincy recalled that, at first, he found Michael "very, very introverted, shy, and nonassertive. He wasn't at all sure that he could make a name for himself on his own. Neither was I."

Quincy, on the other hand, hadn't worked with unharnessed brilliance like Michael's since his days with some of the jazz greats. In Michael, he'd finally found what he'd been looking for in a talent—a hard worker who would rise to the occasion with every take of a song.

At a press conference, Quincy would say, "Michael is the essence of what a performer and an artist are all about. He's got all you need emotionally, and he backs it up with discipline and pacing. He'll never burn himself out. Now I'm a pretty strong drill sergeant when it comes to steering a project, but in Michael's case it's hardly necessary."

If anyone can get a performance out of an artist, Quincy Jones can. He's not intimidated by superstars; when a recording artist isn't delivering, Quincy finds out why. Once, when he was producing Donna Summer, she was giving a halfhearted performance in the studio. "If you think you can sing as good as Chaka Khan," he taunted her, "you're gonna have to prove it."

Quincy was amazed at Michael's versatility. "He can come to a session and put down two lead vocals and three background parts in one day," he said at the time. "He does his homework, rehearses and works hard at home. Most singers want to do everything in the studio—write words and music, figure out harmonies, try different approaches to a song. That makes me crazy. All I can see is dollar signs going up. Studio time is enormously expensive, and that's why someone like Michael Jackson is a producer's dream artist. He walks in prepared. We accomplish so much in a single session, it stuns me. In my opinion, Michael Jackson is going to be *the* star of the eighties and nineties."

The two developed a close rapport outside the studio as well, and over the years, Michael would think of Quincy as a hip father figure. Michael would confide in Quincy and take direction from him in a way that reminded many observers of the kind of relationship the public always *thought* Michael had with his father. Indeed, to Michael, Quincy Jones must have seemed the absolute antithesis of his own father.

"When I'm in the studio, I don't believe in creating an atmosphere of tension or hostility," Quincy once told Oprah Winfrey in an interview. "That serves no purpose. I believe in creating an atmosphere of love."

Quincy invited Michael to a party at his Bel Air home. When Michael drove up to the house, he saw so many cars parked, he got nervous and drove away. "That's just the way he is," Quincy said with a smile. "I would expect that from him."

Quincy Jones's nickname for Michael Jackson is "Smelly." Why? "Because he's so polite and proper, I can't even get him to say the word 'funky.' Honest to God," Quincy explained to *Rolling Stone* magazine. "He's the purest product in America today. He was up at the house the other day with my old pal Marlon Brando. Brando was talking trash, telling raunchy street stories while Smelly was covering his ears."

From Quincy, Michael Jackson learned the true meaning of quality control. The producer was constantly on the prowl for the best songs. And if he found some that were better, he would use those instead. It was a frustrating process—especially when some of Michael's own compositions came under fire—but Michael came to appreciate this methodology and would embrace it himself on future projects.

Finally, after listening to hundreds of songs, Michael and Quincy decided on a batch to record. Among them were three Michael Jackson compositions—the funky "Don't Stop 'Til You Get Enough," the dance-floor scorcher "Working Day and Night," and the prowling, urgent "Get on the Floor" (cowritten with Louis Johnson, bassist of the Brothers Johnson).

Quincy sought to balance the funk with melodic pop ballads like the emotional and symphonic "She's Out of My Life," contributed by songwriter-arranger Tom Bahler; the bright, melancholy "It's the Falling in Love," written by David Foster and Carole Bayer Sager; the cute, sugary Paul McCartney song "Girlfriend"; and most significantly, the romantic, mid-tempoed "Rock with You," the driving "Burn This Disco Out," and the mighty title track, all written by Rod Temperton, chief songwriter and keyboardist for the Britain-based pop-R&B band Heatwave.

With the songs selected, Jones then summoned a handful of crack session players—keyboardists Greg Phillinganes, George Duke, and Michael Boddicker; guitarists David Williams and Larry Carlton; bassist Louis Johnson; percussionist Paulinho DaCosta;

and the Seawind Horns, led by Jerry Hey—and they all went to work.

During "Don't Stop 'Til You Get Enough" (which would become *Off the Wall's* first single), Michael unveiled a playful, sexy falsetto no one had ever heard from him before. All of the right elements were in place on this song—an unstoppable beat, a meticulous, well-balanced delivery of lyrics and melody, and a driving energy. Michael explained that he couldn't shake the song's melody when it came to him one day. He walked throughout the house humming and singing it to himself. Finally, he went into the family's twenty-four-track studio and had Randy put the melody down on the piano (Michael can't play). When Michael played a tape of the song for Katherine, she had some questions about the meaning of the title.

"Well, if you think it means something dirty, then that's what it'll mean," he told her. "But that's not how I intended it."

"Don't Stop" was released on July 28, 1979. In less than three months, it was number one, Michael's first solo chart-topper in seven years. It also was to be his first solo video. When compared to the kind of musical video Michael Jackson would do just three years later, "Don't Stop 'Til You Get Enough" comes across as primitive. In the only attempt at innovation Michael appears briefly dancing in triplicate.

The album *Off the Wall* was released in August 1979. Almost as much attention had been lavished on the jacket as on the contents. The cover photograph showed Michael smiling broadly and wearing a natty tuxedo—and glittering white socks. "The tuxedo was the overall game plan for the *Off the Wall* album and package," said Michael's manager at the time, Ron Weisner. "Michael had an image before that as a young kid, and all of a sudden, here was a hot album and somebody very clean-looking. The tuxedo was our idea as managers," Weisner concluded. "The socks were Michael's."

Fans and industry peers alike were left with their mouths agape when *Off the Wall* was issued to the public. Engineer Bruce Swedien had made sure Quincy Jones's tracks and Michael Jackson's voice showed to the best advantage. Michael's fans proclaimed that they hadn't heard him sing with such joy and abandon since the early Jackson 5 days. The album showcased an adult Michael Jackson, for the first time a real artist, not just someone's vocal stylist.

Indeed, Michael Jackson had officially arrived. The performances revealed sides of him that most record buyers hadn't heard before. No one knew Michael could be as smooth and sophisticated as he was on the album's outstanding track, Stevie Wonder's "I Can't Help It." The song was important to the project because its luscious chord changes were the closest Michael had ever come to singing jazz on record.

Even more revealing was an emotional Michael crying real tears on the tail end of "She's Out of My Life." (Jones would later comment that Michael cried every time they cut the vocals. After several attempts with the same results, the decision was made to leave the tears on the track.) The understated arrangement of this song—a crowd pleaser in concert—with its sparse keyboard accompaniment, allowed Michael to soulfully plead his regret of lost love in a touching, sometimes searing, delivery.

When "Rock with You" also made number one, and then "Off the Wall" and "She's Out of My Life" both went to number ten, Michael became the first solo artist to have four Top Ten singles from one album. Although *Off the Wall* would sell six million copies, it never went beyond number three. Michael was excited but cautious. "It's a start," he would say.

It was a fine start, so when *Off the Wall* won only one Grammy (in an R&B category), Michael was crushed. "It bothered me," he said. "I cried a lot. My family thought I was going crazy, because I was weeping so much about it."

"He was so disappointed," Janet concurred. "I felt bad for him. But he finally said, 'You watch. The next album I do, you watch . . . I'll show them.' "

On August 29, 1979, Michael Jackson turned twenty-one. It was a turning point for him in many ways. He had often said, "When I become twenty-one, things will be different. I really feel that being a man is doing exactly what you want to do in this life and to do it successfully and to conquer a goal. That's the whole thing in life, I guess, to do what you want to do. And if it's great, to share it. To me, Walt Disney is a real man. Charlie Chaplin, a real man. Fred Astaire, a real man. Bill Robinson, a real man. Because not only have they conquered goals, but look at how much joy they have given to other people, how many they have influenced. Other people looked up to them. They made paths."

After his birthday, Michael and Joe had a bitter argument. Michael had told Joe that he wanted to have more control over his own career. Although Joe humored him by saying, "Sure, if that's what you want," he probably doubted that Michael would ever really try to follow through.

Michael had arranged to meet a new attorney, someone to look over all of his business affairs to determine exactly where the money was going. Joe was truly hurt by his son's decision. Prior to this time, Michael used Joe's attorneys and accountants. Now that Michael wanted his own, Joe felt as if his son didn't trust him. Of course, Michael didn't trust him, but this was a rude awakening for Joe Jackson.

Michael Jackson was a millionaire now—worth a little over one million dollars—though he loathed discussing the matter. "Talking about how rich you are and standing next to fancy cars and things is tacky and tired," he said at this time. "Just say that we've been out there working a long time, and we've been financially successful." When pressed, he added, "Well, sure, we're all millionaires . . . at least that, but why talk about it?"

Michael's accountant at that time, Michael Mesnick—who also represented the Beach Boys—arranged for Michael to meet with three entertainment lawyers. The first was John Branca, a thirty-one-year-old native New Yorker with a background in corporate tax law and music industry negotiations for the Beach Boys, Neil Diamond, and Bob Dylan. He had once represented the Howard Hughes heirs. Branca was bright, young, aggressive, and determined. He was eager to make a name for himself in the entertainment industry.

John Branca was not familiar with Michael's music—he was more of a rock-and-roll fan—but when checking with some of his show business colleagues he was told the Michael Jackson was perceived by the music industry as having the potential to be a superstar. Branca figured that Jackson was an artist with whom he could establish his own career as an attorney, and in a big way.

The meeting was an odd one. Michael took his sunglasses off only at the beginning when he eyed Branca and asked if the two had ever met before. When they established that they hadn't, Michael smiled and put his sunglasses back on. Mesnick asked all of the questions, and Michael listened. He seemed shy and uncomfortable. Later, Branca must have realized that Jackson and Mesnick had carefully discussed the line of questioning in advance.

In that meeting Michael said—through Mesnick—that he wanted independence from his family, and especially from Joe. At that time, the Jacksons had a group contract with Epic; Michael now wanted one for himself as a solo artist as well as a group member. He wanted all of his business affairs reviewed, including his publishing and his record sales.

After meeting John Branca, Michael realized he had found his man. He canceled the other two interviews and hired Branca.

Early in their relationship, Michael Jackson told John Branca that he had two goals: First of all, he wanted to be the biggest star in show business. Secondly, he wanted to be the wealthiest. He told Branca that he was furious that *Off the Wall* had only garnered one Grammy nomination. "I sold five million in the U.S., six million foreign. That's a big record. It was totally unfair and it can't ever happen again," Michael said.

John Branca was impressed with Michael's total belief in himself. It was infectious, and Branca could not wait to get started working for him.

For nearly the next eleven years, John Branca would unarguably be the single most important figure in Michael Jackson's career. He would negotiate every business deal for him, become a trusted friend and adviser, and see to it that this talented kid from Gary realized both of his goals. Most of Michael Jackson's associates agree today that were it not for Branca, Jackson's story would have been a very different one.

The first thing Branca did was to renegotiate Michael's CBS contract with Walter Yetnikoff. As a result, Michael's contract would be different from the one the Jacksons had with the label. Branca got Michael the highest royalty rate in the business at that time— thirty-seven percent of a hundred percent of wholesale, which was the same rate Neil Diamond and Bob Dylan were getting. Branca also made a deal with Yetnikoff and—begrudgingly, with the Jacksons' legal representation, John Mason—that Michael could leave the Jacksons any time he wanted to, and with no penalty to the group (in other words, the label would still be obligated to the brothers, even without Michael). From this point on, legally, Michael Jackson never had to record another song with his brothers if he didn't want to. The brothers didn't like this new setup at all, but the full ramifications of the deal would not hit them for a while. They were accustomed to Michael's doing solo albums, and still felt secure that he would remain with the group.

After the new deal was struck, Randy Jackson tried to hire John Branca. Jackson had aspirations for his own solo career at Epic. But Michael insisted that Branca turn Randy down. He did not want his attorney representing anyone else in the Jackson family. Now Michael was staking out his own territory.

John Branca followed Michael's direction and did not take Randy on as a client.

At this time, Michael was also interested in boosting his image in the media. He yearned to be on the cover of *Rolling Stone* and asked his publicist Norman Winter to try to arrange it. "We would very much like to do a major piece on Michael Jackson but feel it is not a cover story,'' was publisher Jann Wenner's response in a letter to Winter dated November 27, 1979.

Michael was angry. ''I've been told over and over again that black people on the covers of magazines don't sell copies,'' he complained. ''Just wait. Someday those magazines are going to be *begging* me for an interview. Maybe I'll give them one. And maybe I won't.''

# Chapter

## 16

MANY OF JOE Jackson's associates would say that he always seemed like a man who was trying to hide something. Because of clandestine meetings and hushed telephone calls, it was obvious to Joe's office employees that they did not know everything there was to know about their boss. This secretiveness was apparent to his family. "Sometimes, I think he leads a double life," Michael once said of his father. "He is a very mysterious person."

In early 1980, one employee, Gina Sprague, had become particularly close to Joe. Though many Jackson intimates do not believe her, she insists that she and Joe were not having an affair. They were, she says, close friends who trusted one another. "He needed a friend," she said. "He was so estranged from his family. He's a needy person, just like everyone else. Sometimes he would need to talk. I was there for him. But not sexually, and I'd like to make that clear. I knew he had this reputation of being a womanizer. But that is not what our relationship was about. He's a handsome man. He reminded me of a lion. And a good-hearted man, and generous too. He gave me a gold necklace, a lion, because we are both Leos. He bought me a car as a bonus because of some work I had done on LaToya's first album.

"If he believed in you, he gave you enough strength and courage to try and attain your goal, even if you didn't think you could. Once I knew him, I could understand why the family and especially Michael had become the megasuperstars they are. What I always had to remind Joseph of is that he should be pretty proud of himself. I used to tell him, 'Sure, Michael and the rest get all of the attention, but look at where they came from.' Everything Joseph ever did, he did for that family. Then he felt abandoned by them."

One day Gina, concerned about Joe's moods and mercurial behavior, asked him point-blank, "What are these secret meetings you're always going to? What's happening with you, Joseph? If I can help you, please confide in me."

"Well, I'm not gonna tell you," he said, hesitantly. "Instead, I'll show you."

He drove her to an apartment building in a neighborhood in suburban Los Angeles. They knocked on the door, and a pretty, light-skinned black woman answered. Joe introduced her to Gina. Then a small black child, about six years old, came bounding into the living room.

"Daddy! Daddy!" she exclaimed.

"There's my little girl," Joe said to her with a big smile. He scooped the child up in his arms and hugged her tightly.

"His whole face lit up," Gina Sprague remembered. "It was so obvious how much he cared about this child, this adorable girl. I'd never seen this kind of transformation in Joseph before. And I said to myself, '_Now_ I know what those secret meetings were all about.'" Joseph and a woman by the name of Cheryl Terrell had had an affair back in 1973. The result of that relationship was a daughter, Joh' Vonnie.

Joe had kept the baby a secret for all of these years. Finally, in 1980, he apparently decided that he wanted to become more involved in the child's rearing. Because he loved her and wanted her to be recognized as a member of the family, he planned to establish in her name a trust corporation (which would be finalized on February 23, 1981, when she was six and a half years old).

It is not known when he told Katherine and the rest of the family about Joh' Vonnie, but Katherine's friends have indicated that it was around 1980.

"Katherine must have been devastated," said a friend of hers who would only discuss the matter anonymously. "For years, she feared this kind of thing would happen. Now it had."

Certainly Joe's infidelity had been a part of their marriage for years. Katherine had tried to live with his indiscretions as best she could. She had confided to friends that it was difficult for her to pose happily with her husband for magazine features that acclaimed the stability of the family. She must have realized that her marriage had become a publicity sham. But for the sake of her children and their public image, she dutifully went along with the program. It's no wonder she is so revered by her children.

"I have never known a more beautiful, caring, loving, understanding, and intelligent woman than you," Janet wrote in the dedication to her mother for liner notes of her 1990 album, *Rhythm Nation.* "Someday I hope to be exactly like you."

Joh' Vonnie had been born on August 30, 1974—the day after Michael's sixteenth birthday—at Centinela Valley Community Hospital in Los Angeles County. Joseph Walter Jackson's name appears on the birth certificate. His occupation was listed as "entertainment manager." His age was recorded as forty-six at the time of the baby's birth. The mother's age was twenty-six.

Cheryl Terrell, the child's mother, had purchased a five-unit, twenty-three-year-old apartment building in Gardena, California, on March 19, 1973, apparently while she was dating Joe. She bought the complex for $59,000. However, she mortgaged $44,200 of the value of the home. It is suspected by family friends that Joe gave her the $15,000 down payment. It is a well-kept building and grounds, still owned by the woman today. Tenants appear to be lower middle class.

Cheryl and her daughter lived in apartment A of the building. Joe would visit quite often, according to neighbors. "He'd pull up in a black Mercedes or a white Rolls, and once he was in a black stretch limousine," one neighbor recalled. "You don't see a lot of cars like that around here. In fact, the cops pulled him over one time wanting to know what he was doing in the neighborhood. They probably thought he was a pimp."

No doubt Katherine was upset. But as a practical woman committed to family values, she agreed with Joe that he had a responsibility to Joh' Vonnie and her mother. "Who knows why Katherine stayed with Joe," observed Joyce McCrae, one of Joe Jackson's employees at this time. "Only Katherine knows. I guess she loved him. What else could it be?"

Katherine and Joseph purchased a three-bedroom home in Van Nuys, a suburb of Los Angeles, for $169,000 with the intention that Katherine would eventually endorse an individual quitclaim deed, thereby effectively signing the property over to Joe. As a trustee of his daughter's estate, Joe signed the property over to the child. Joe and Katherine Jackson bought the home on March 25, 1981. Katherine signed the grant deed on March 29, 1984.

Mother and child moved into the home once the paperwork was completed. They still live there. A locked wrought-iron gate bars the front door of the home. "Beware of Dog" signs are posted on the gate. There is no name on the mailbox.

None of the family could be certain how Katherine really felt about Joe's child because she simply would not discuss the matter. "This is between your father and me," she would insist.

"Let's just say it's not a subject she's fond of discussing," said her nephew, Hattie's son Tim Whitehead. "Joseph wanted the child to be accepted into the family, but there was no way. It was too painful for my aunt. This was a difficult—sort of heartbreaking, I guess you might say—period."

According to Jerome Howard (who would manage Joe and Katherine's money in 1988), "Katherine told me she went into the grocery store one day and saw Joe's girlfriend and the daughter. She said she just stood there, frozen. 'Jerome, the girl looked exactly like Joseph,' she said."

Though Katherine was acting logically and sensibly, she was not unfazed by the news. Michael would indicate later that he sensed an emotional transformation in his mother. She rarely smiled any more and seemed angry. Her temper would flare over unimportant matters.

Even though Katherine Jackson had become a changed woman and the family was being torn apart, the Jacksons tried to avoid confronting their personal problems. Publicly, it was business as usual as they continued to proclaim strong family unity. But now Michael Jackson had a six-year-old half-sister who looked exactly like his father. He, more than any member of his family other than his mother, was desolated by the news. Even though Joe would do everything to try to make up to his family for this mistake—and that's what his infidelity was always referred to as, "a mistake"— Michael would never recover from the hurt.

"Michael felt that Kate, the one person in his life he loved more than any other, had been betrayed in a very serious manner," Marcus Phillips, a family friend, said. "This deception is something I'm sure he has never gotten over. He cried a lot. He said he felt powerless and he was tired of feeling that way. He had no control over any of it, and it was making him crazy. His heart was broken. I can honestly say, he has never been the same. Never. The way he feels about Kate seemed to most people to be stronger than the way most sons feel about their mothers. To him, Kate was a goddess. He believed in her and trusted her more than any other person on earth. When she hurt, he hurt."

As tempting as it may be to say that Katherine's misery may be a primary reason Michael Jackson shies away from personal relationships as an adult, marriage and family counselor Carol L. Kerster, who practices in Redondo Beach, California, believes it is misguided to "hang behavior on a single experience. It is always an accumulation of things." Certainly in this case, there was a long history of infidelity on Joe's part well before the discovery of the child. But Michael's attachment to Kate has its own long history.

Freud coined the term Oedipus complex to describe a boy's undue attachment to his mother. (Oedipus unwittingly killed his father and married his mother.) Feeling attached to the opposite-sex parent is a normal stage in child development; five-year-old boys often proclaim they will marry their mothers when they grow up. However, by the time a boy is six, he usually starts to put the mother-son relationship in its proper perspective and begins to identify with his father. If his mother remains overwhelming, however, the young son finds it difficult to detach from her. If the father is equally domineering or more so, the child may still remain emotionally close to his mother because she's safer. Most psychologists agree that if such a child doesn't complete the separation process from his mother and start identifying with his father by the onset of adolescence, it's unlikely that he will develop a happy relationship with any woman and may well continue to view his father as a rival for his mother's attention.

An adult with an unresolved Oedipal complex can place his mother on such a high pedestal that no other woman can approach her perfection. Many of Michael's associates feel this is the case where Michael and Kate are concerned. There are those who will say that one of the reasons Michael remained a Jehovah's Witness was to please his mother. And he not only continually professed that he loved his mother, he identified with her. So when Joe hurt Katherine, he hurt Michael as well.

On March 4, 1980, Michael's eighteen-year-old brother Randy was in a terrible car accident. He suffered severe injuries to both legs when the Mercedes Benz he was driving—which belonged to his girlfriend—skidded into a light pole, trapping him inside. "It had been raining and he was driving too fast," Gina Sprague recalled. "He hydroplaned into the pole. They had to use the 'Jaws of Life' to get him out of the car. It was horrible. The doctors thought his legs would have to be amputated." Randy had just obtained his driver's license three months earlier.

Katherine and Joe heard about the accident when a friend of theirs, who happened by the awful scene, telephoned them with the news at four in the morning. Joe, Katherine, Michael, Janet, and LaToya went into a panic, telephoning all of the local hospitals, searching for the one to which Randy had been admitted. Finally they found him at St. Joseph's Medical Center in Burbank. When they arrived at the hospital, Randy was in a state of shock. Shards of glass were in his hair, he was covered with a blood-smeared sheet, both of his legs were shattered from the thigh down and bone was visible. All of his toes were broken, every bone in his left foot was fractured, as were his knees, his ankles, his shins. He had a cracked pelvis. He nearly died in the emergency room when a nurse accidently gave him a dose of methadone intended for a heroin addict in the next room.

"The morning after the accident happened was a terrible scene at the office," Gina continued. "The media wanted to know what was happening, a press conference was being scheduled at the St. Joseph's hospital, and it was all just too much to take because we were so concerned about Randy. He was so young and his life was just beginning. Joe just put his head down on the desk and cried. It was the first time I had ever seen him cry. He couldn't talk to the press. All he knew was that his baby son was hurt."

Finally, doctors decided that Randy's legs would not have to be amputated, but there was nerve damage and serious doubt that Randy would ever walk again. The Jacksons had been planning a national tour for the summer, but those plans were now scrapped.

Michael was inconsolable about Randy's accident. It seemed so senseless, and he would say, "What kind of fate is that? One minute you're healthy and the next you can be paralyzed." Michael was not willing to accept the reality that tragedies happen every day to all kinds of people. "Where Michael was concerned, this was just another example of something over which he had no authority," Marcus Phillips said. "It may seem odd, but Randy's accident only served to frustrate Michael even more. He was going through his life feeling that he and everyone in his family were completely out of control. It upset him that there were so many things over which he had no power."

"Katherine was also in bad shape after the accident," said another family friend. "This was truly a nightmare for her. She prayed and prayed. She asked Michael and LaToya to join her in prayer, and they did. I remember she told me at the hospital, 'If my boy would just walk again, I will bear witness forever.' She said that and I believed her."

The family was with Randy when the doctors told him he probably would never walk again. Katherine began to cry. Michael and his brothers started weeping. Joe kept a stoic demeanor, as he usually did in front of people, even his family.

"Get out!" Randy shouted at them. "Go away if that's the way you're going to act. I *will* walk again. I *will*!"

Katherine ran to her son and cradled him in her arms. "I know you will," she said. "I believe it. I do."

After six months of intense, excruciating therapy, Randy Jackson would not only walk again but dance on stage with his brothers as if nothing had ever happened. "It was a miracle," said Katherine's friend, "and some of the family referred to it as 'Katherine's miracle.' They believed that this was a phenomenon brought about by Katherine's devotion to her religion. It truly was astonishing, because I saw Randy in the hospital with his legs all torn up, and I never thought that boy would walk again. But he did."

"All the time I knew I was going to be okay," Randy said. "I really didn't pay that much attention to the talk that I would be paralyzed. There were too many people—my family, my friends, and my fans—pulling for me."

By this time, twenty-one-year-old Michael Jackson was making show business history with *Off the Wall*. But it was difficult for those closest to him to be jubilant about his success, because of the terrible tensions in the family.

Katherine was clearly angry, but she was torn by her rage. She was a religious woman who desperately wanted to be a forgiving Jehovah's Witness. Her son was recovering from his accident, so she could be thankful for that. But still, the fact that her husband had an illegitimate child was something her friends say she could not accept. She couldn't extinguish the flames of bitterness that seemed to be consuming her. "I'm worried about Kate," Michael told one of his sisters at this time. "I think there's something terribly wrong with her."

Katherine apparently would not confide in anyone about her anger; she would not discuss her hurt over what had happened with Joe and his daughter. She was a proud woman who did not easily share her family's indiscretions. It simply wasn't polite. It was just a matter of time before her rage would erupt, especially when she heard more rumors in the summer of 1980 that Joe was having an affair with Gina Sprague. Some of her friends felt that Katherine Jackson was like a time bomb, ticking, ticking, ticking . . . just waiting to go off.

Gina Sprague met Joe Jackson in 1979. A former "American Bandstand" dance contest winner, she had just finished touring with the Jeff Kutash dance troupe. Joe was impressed with her and offered to manage her career. However, she began working at Joe Jackson Productions as a receptionist. "If you start at the bottom and work your way up, there's no telling what you can do," Joe told her.

"Joseph saw how aggressive I was, and he let me move on up just as fast as I could," she said. "He was a great boss. He knew that if he asked me to do something, he wouldn't have to ask a second time. And the fact that I was a self-starter, that he didn't have to explain every little step to me, helped tremendously." Soon she was promoted to be Joe's administrative assistant.

"I did everything from planning tours to promotion to publicity. At that time, we were working on LaToya's first album. I also took phone calls, of course. One thing that struck me very strange is that Michael and his brothers and sisters called their father Joseph. The first time Janet came into my office she was about thirteen, and she walked in and said, 'Hi, where's Joseph.' I almost died. Or Michael would call. 'Hello, Gina, this is Michael. Is Joseph there?' And I would say, 'Your *father* is in a meeting at the moment.' I mean, if it hadn't been for Joseph, Michael wouldn't have been the star that he was. Perhaps it wasn't my place to remind him of that, but I just felt that all of them should have had more respect for their father.

"I remember walking into Joseph's office one day [in 1980] and he was so upset with Michael, just absolutely livid. It turned out that Michael had put on a disguise—a beard, an old hat, old clothes, like a bum. Then he somehow got to one of the seediest, most dangerous, worst parts of downtown Los Angeles so that he could mingle with the winos. Michael wanted to see what it was like to be a bum, what it was like to be homeless. To him, being homeless was something he couldn't relate to, and he wanted to understand it. So that's what he did. I mean, what kind of person does that? Someone very sensitive, someone who really wants to know about other people. Someone who must really care about people, I thought.

" 'That is just like Michael,' Joe said. 'He has always had this natural curiosity that drives me crazy. That kid is going to get hurt,' he said. 'If someone doesn't watch out for him, something's gonna happen to Michael.' Joseph was always concerned about his children, all of them, but I felt that he was particularly concerned about Michael, because Michael had this certain unusual sensitivity."

Gina's story calls to mind another about Michael that happened a year later, in 1981, in Atlanta at an antique store. The owner recalled that a black man in tattered clothing came in and hid in an antique armoire. He appeared quite disoriented, as if he were drunk. "I made a lot of noise, shouting that we were closing and that he had to come out," said the store owner. "After ten seconds, he appeared. He looked so weird. He refused to move. It was then that I called the police."

When Michael put his hand in his pocket, the store proprietor thought he had a gun. He smacked Michael in the face. Michael went down. "Hey! What are you doing?" Michael screamed. "Don't you know who I am?"

As Michael got up, the owner grabbed him in a headlock. By now, Michael must have been scared. The police were called. Arresting officer Jeff Greene said, "Jackson looked like a bum. I didn't know who he was, and when he told me he was Michael Jackson, I didn't believe him."

According to a deputy in the Atlanta Police Department, "Michael Jackson was in the antique store dressed so that he would not be recognized. We did consider charging both men, Jackson with criminal trespass and Nolan [the proprietor] with assault, but the charges were never written up."

Only Michael knows what he was doing—what role in his theater of life he was playing that day—but as Gina Sprague says, "That's exactly like Michael to do that, and why Joseph was concerned about him.

"I remember that when LaToya's first album came out, it was a huge bomb. Really, let's face it, LaToya tries very hard; she's a very nice girl, but she is not much of a singer," Gina said. "Joseph knew that. We all did. 'What in the world can I do with this girl?' he wondered. 'She can't sing, what do we do?' I had this idea that she should concentrate on her looks, on makeup, because she is an extremely beautiful woman. Max Factor did not have anyone black representing them at the time, and I came up with an idea. If LaToya can't sing, make her a model. Joseph and I worked up a terrific proposal, and Max Factor loved the idea. They wanted to do it, make LaToya a cover girl, but then we presented the concept to LaToya, who said, 'No. I must sing.' Joe tried and tried to convince her. Years later, of course, she would get smart, pose for *Playboy*, and make a name for herself. But back then, she wanted to be the female Michael Jackson, and there was just no way."

Gina Sprague is of Mexican-English-Irish descent. She was nineteen years old in 1980. At five feet five, one hundred pounds, with shoulder-length brown hair, she was—and still is—a gorgeous woman. Sprague, who is vivacious, intelligent, and ambitious, is working today in different capacities in the entertainment business.

Gina and Joe developed a special relationship. He found her to be an intuitive, understanding young woman, far more mature than her years. With her, Joe could confide about his daughter, Joh' Vonnie, how much he cared for her, his plans to make her a model or possibly an actress in television commercials. He had Gina track down photographers who might be able to take publicity photos of Joh' Vonnie. Joe could share his private thoughts and fears with her and not feel as if he were being judged.

"He is the biggest softy," Gina said of Joe. "He's just a puppy dog."

She confided in him as well. He helped her move into an apartment closer to the office. They had dinners together. They were not, according to Gina Sprague, having an affair, even though many people thought they were, including Cheryl Terrell, mother of Joseph's illegitimate child.

"He had Cheryl and his new daughter and Katherine," Gina said. "The man had his hands full. He needed, more than anything, a confidant. He had no one like that in his life. He would come to my apartment and not want to leave because he didn't want to go home. I had this illusion that the Jacksons were this happy, devout family. I was shocked to find that wasn't true. Since I liked Katherine so very much, I asked Joseph one day, 'How could you do this to Katherine? How could you have this other child?'

"He said he had been hurt by his family. That he turned to Cheryl because when his family got to a certain point, he felt he wasn't needed anymore. And whatever his relationship was like with Cheryl, he had emotional needs as well, just like everyone else. 'Why does my family hate me so much?' he would ask me. 'What did I ever do to hurt them?' Maybe he hurt himself with his family, I don't know. But there was a remoteness, a detachment, from his children. He had sacrificed a lot to make them what they were, and now they didn't seem to care at all about him. That's why his new daughter was so important to him.

"Joh' Vonnie loved him unconditionally, and he definitely wasn't getting that kind of love from his other kids. Joh' Vonnie was his little girl. There were pictures of The Jackson 5 and LaToya and Janet in Cheryl's house on the stereo, and Joh' Vonnie would say, 'These are my brothers and sisters.' She was very proud of them. However, the Jackson kids had no relationship with this child, their half-sister."

Joyce McCrae, another of Joe's employees at that time, said, "Joseph lavished all kinds of presents on that child, that beautiful baby girl. He gave her all of the love and fatherly attention he never gave his other nine children. I think Joseph was very confused. He came across like a bulldog, or like if you came near him, he'd blow your brains out. But, and I may be wrong, I think there was a soft heart under all of that anger.''

"I was happy to be there for him," Gina Sprague said of Joe. "I am not ashamed of my friendship with Joseph Jackson. I think I was a very good friend to him. I continued to cover for Joseph every time he wanted to see the child or spend time with her. Even though the family knew about the girl, he didn't want to flaunt her. It wasn't that I was being disloyal to the family, but my first loyalty had to be to Joseph. He was my employer. I never had a problem with Katherine, though she looked at me kind of funny at times.''

Whenever Joe would call Gina into his office for a meeting, and the door to his office would close, people on the other side would whisper about "the affair." One woman who worked in the office was apparently a spy for Katherine. Gina said that she allowed this woman to spend a night in her home, and the next day she discovered that some of her possessions were missing. She told Joe about it. According to Gina, that's when this woman began feeding misinformation back to Katherine, who was already suspicious of all of Joseph's female friends and still reeling from the shock of the illegitimate child.

One day, the phone rang. Gina picked it up. "Good afternoon, Joe Jackson Productions.''

"You quit your job. Do you hear me? Or we're gonna come and get you.'' It was a female voice.

"What? Who is this?" Gina asked, panicked.

The anonymous caller hung up.

Gina was understandably upset. She went into Joe's office and told him what had happened. She didn't want to quit her job, she said. She enjoyed working for him and for his family. What should she do? Would someone actually come and "get" her? Would she be hurt?

"That's nonsense," Joe told her. "No one is gonna come after you. I promise you. You'll be fine.''

According to the Los Angeles Police Department Preliminary Investigation report, this is how Gina Sprague described what happened the next day to police:

On October 16, 1980, at about three o'clock in the afternoon, Gina was sitting behind her desk in the reception area of Joe Jackson Productions, 6255 Sunset Boulevard, Suite 1001 [the same building in which Motown Records is housed] when Randy Jackson, eighteen years old, entered. Randy asked two other employees to leave the office so that he and Gina could be alone.

The two employees left the office. Randy then left and returned with his sister Janet, fourteen, and Katherine. An argument ensued.

Janet grabbed Gina's right wrist and began to twist it while Katherine began pulling on Gina's hair, screaming at her, "Bitch, I told you we were gonna get you."

As Gina began to scream, Janet placed her hand over Gina's mouth. Randy then pulled Gina out of her chair and knocked her to the ground. Katherine and her children then grabbed Gina and dragged her across the carpet and out of the office. All the while, Katherine was hitting Gina on the face with a closed right fist and yelling, "Bitch, you better leave my husband alone." At that point, Katherine removed a blunt object from her purse and struck Gina numerous times on her back with the object. Gina was then dragged to the stairway.

Jim Krieg, an office employee, heard the screams and ran to aid Gina. He observed Randy holding Gina against the wall while Katherine was hitting her with her purse. Upon seeing the guard, Janet said, "Leave, mister. This is a family affair."

Randy then opened the stairway door and attempted to pull Gina into the stairwell. Other office employees began to gather when they heard Gina's screams, at which point Katherine grabbed a gold medallion from Gina's neck. "Bitch, this belongs to me," she said. "Not you."

Then Katherine, Randy, and Janet fled the building.*

Later, more details would surface. There had been other witnesses. One of Diana Ross's brothers had called Gina that morning and happened by later, during the incident. "Mother, what are you doing?" he asked Katherine. "Stop. You're hurting her, Mother." (Many friends called Katherine "Mother.")

"Go about your business, this is a family matter," she allegedly told him. Diana's brother ran.

*The details of the incident are taken directly from the police report filed by Gina Sprague on October 16, 1980. Other than the substitution of Katherine Jackson's, Randy Jackson's, and Janet Jackson's names for the terms "Suspect One," "Suspect Two," and "Suspect Three," respectively, and the addition of the ages of Randy and Janet, there have been no embellishments. When Jim Krieg, named on the police report as a witness to the incident, was contacted for this book, he refused to discuss what he saw. "I don't want to talk about something that happened ten years ago," he said. "I just don't want to be involved in any way." When asked if he was afraid of repercussions from the Jackson family, he said, "No."

One witness reported that Sprague, apparently delirious and concerned about the family's public image, kept saying to Katherine, "Get out of here while you can, before someone recognizes you."

Joe was in a meeting with his door closed while the violent incident took place. When Gina came back into the office, she was crying hysterically. She closed the door to the suite. On the other side, people were gathered, wondering what was going on and why. Joe came running out of his private office while Gina was attempting to dial a telephone, trying to contact her sister.

"My God, what happened to you?" Joe asked.

Gina was too upset to speak. An ambulance, summoned by the building's security guard and police officers, arrived quickly. Medics lifted Gina to put her on a gurney. She let out a piercing scream from the pain. As they tended to her, Joe leaned over and whispered in Gina's ear, "Tell me, who did this to you? Was it some crazy fan? Who was it?"

Gina recalled that, through her tears, she managed to say, "It was Katherine."

Joe's eyes widened in horror.

"And Janet."

"Oh, no. My God, no."

"And Randy."

"It can't be," Joe said. "It just can't be true."

"It is, Joseph. You said they wouldn't hurt me," Gina cried. "You promised me. You promised."

Gina recalled that Joe ran to a telephone and called home. There was no answer. He came back to Gina's side and, she said, whispered in her ear. "Please, *please*, don't hurt my family. We've come too far. Please."

Gina looked up at Joe and shook her head. All she wanted to hear from him was that he was sorry for what had happened. He never said that. Tears ran down her face. Her lip was bleeding. She began to black out.

"We've got to get her to a hospital, *now*," one of the medics said. "She has a head injury."

"Don't let her drift off," someone else said.

"Gina. Gina. Wake up!" Someone slapped her on the face lightly.

Joe leaned over her. "I'll see you at the hospital," he told her.

"Joseph, don't leave me. Please."

Joe backed away from her.

"Wait," Gina said as a paramedic opened the office door. Even in her delirious state, she noticed all of the people crowded in the hallway.

"Cover my face with a towel," she told one of the medics. "Please, don't let them see me. No one must know."

"Yes," Joe agreed. "No one must ever know."

Gina Sprague was taken to Hollywood Presbyterian Medical Center, where she was treated for multiple cuts, bruises, and a head injury. Joe did not visit her there.

She was released the next day. When she got home, neighbors gathered, asking what had happened to her. "It was a car accident," her sister told them. "A terrible car accident."

Gina went to bed. While she dozed off, she heard an argument. It was a friend, who had been watching over her, arguing with Joe in the doorway. He had come to visit, and Gina's friend would not let him in.

"You get out of here, you sonofabitch, you stupid nigger!" Gina's friend screamed at Joe. "How dare you come here? How could you allow this to happen?"

"I just don't know," Joe said, shaking his head, helplessly. "I don't know how it could have happened."

Gina went to the door. "Let him in," she said to her friend.

Joe walked into the living room and sat down. Gina sat opposite him. With some hesitation, her friend left them alone.

"Why, Joseph?" Gina remembered asking. "I told you that they were going to hurt me. Why didn't you believe me?"

"I didn't know that she would do that," Joe said.

"You're a liar, Joseph. You *did* know. And why did you abandon me?" Gina pressed on. "Why didn't you come to the hospital with me?"

Joe began to cry. Gina recalled that he couldn't answer. He was too upset.

"Answer me!" she demanded. Now she was crying as well. "Why did you abandon me?"

"Because you're going to hurt my family," Joe said. "And you know how much I love my family. My family is everything to me. Everything. You know that."

Gina said that she looked at Joe, shaking her head in disbelief. "I was trying to cover up for you, and this is what happened to me because of it," she said. "Don't you even care about that?"

"I care about my family," Joe insisted. "And I know you're going to hurt us."

At this, Gina was flabbergasted. "I'm going to hurt your family?

Joseph, *they* hurt *me*. Look at me. Just look at what they did to me. And you can't even say you're sorry. You don't care about me at all, do you?''

"You already talked to the police. Now everybody's going to know," Joe said. He wiped his eyes with the back of his hand. He looked exhausted, as if he hadn't gotten any sleep since the incident happened. He seemed like a desperate man. He reached into the breast pocket of his jacket, pulled out an envelope, and handed it to Gina. She opened it. Inside, Gina recalled, there was a check for a large sum of money.

"Take it," Joe instructed.

She looked at him incredulously.

"I don't want your money, Joseph," she said. Now she was getting angry. She crumpled the check and threw it at him. "You can take your money, and shove it! You leave my house," she said, sobbing. "How dare you? *How dare you?*"

Gina said that when Joe left, she slammed the door behind him. Then she broke down, sobbing.

Michael Jackson was completely stunned by what his mother, sister, and brother had "allegedly" done to Gina Sprague. He especially could not reconcile this violent act with his image of his beloved mother, a woman he said many times he considered to be one of the most gentle people he knows, and his sister Janet, the family member to whom he was closest. He refused to believe it, and insists to this day that it never happened.

"He was blind to even the thought of it," said Marcus Phillips, a family friend. "He wanted nothing to do with it. He insisted that it wasn't true, and as far as he was concerned, it wasn't. 'The way that girl said it happened, that's not the truth at all. Not at all,' he said. 'That's not Kate, and anyone who knows her knows that she could never, ever, do anything like that. Anyone who believes that story is crazy. It's not true.' Then after that, he never discussed it again, ever.''

Michael was not the only one who didn't believe the incident happened. Joyce McCrae, who was in her office with the door closed while the incident was taking place in the hallway, also insists that Katherine was innocent. "That police report is a complete fabrication. Whatever it says, it says, but I'm telling you that the police report is full of shit. An incident did take place at the office, but it was not as Gina Sprague reported it." Joyce McCrae refused to elaborate her version of the story.

Joyce McCrae was fired shortly after the incident. "There was simply too much hostility between Joe, Katherine, and the kids over whatever really happened with Gina and whatever else was going on. I saw a lot of things go down during the Gina Sprague experience. So I went up to Joe one day and said, 'Joe, when family is your business and business is your family, you don't fuck over your family while doing business.' He didn't appreciate that, and I got fired.''

One of Katherine's former employees said that when she was hired, in 1983, Katherine told her very specifically what had happened with Gina Sprague. "Katherine told me this, and I think it's the honest-to-goodness truth," she said. "She told me that there was this girl named Gina screwing around with Joseph up at the office. Katherine called her up one day and told her to leave, to quit her job. But the girl wouldn't leave. And Katherine told me she went up there with Janet and Randy. She said, 'I beat the *dang* daylights out of that girl.' She'd never say 'damn' because she doesn't swear.''

"Basically, Joe was in love with that girl [Gina]," recalled Tim Whitehead, Katherine's nephew, "and my aunt didn't like it and wanted it to stop. Then Joyce McCrae gave some information to my aunt about Gina and my aunt became extremely upset, and went to the office to see Gina. Everything happened because of what Joyce said to my aunt. Katherine had just reached her breaking point. You can only push a person so far.''

"If Katherine did what they say she did, she was like a wild lioness protecting her cubs, her family," Marcus Phillips said. "She was a desperate woman trying to hang on to her marriage, her household. But Michael didn't believe it. If you brought it up in his presence, he would leave the room.''

Gina Sprague filed a $21 million lawsuit against Joe, Katherine, Janet, and Randy, even though a lawyer told her, "You have to understand, these people are not going to jail. Rich people just don't go." Sprague had trouble serving Joe and Katherine with the legal papers; she had to ambush them at a celebrity baseball game. Gina began receiving anonymous, threatening phone calls. "No, I am not going to shut up," she decided. "They'll have to kill me before I do.''

Details of what had happened went whipping through the entertainment industry. Gina Sprague was effectively blackballed from working in show business. "It was obvious to me at that point that my career was over," Gina Sprague said. "I never asked Joseph for anything. He never said he was sorry, not once. All I wanted now was to clear my name so that I could work in the industry again. Nobody would hire me. I hit rock bottom. I finally got a job working for an executive at Motown, and everything was fine. I was so relieved. I went to work and was the perfect employee for almost a week. Then he called me into his office. I knew what was up. I said, 'What took you so long?' He said my working there was a 'conflict of interest,' even though the Jacksons were not with Motown anymore. He fired me.

"I just could not find a job. Nobody cared about my side of the story. Not once did anyone ever come to me and ask me what really happened. All I wanted to do was get on with my life and work, but you have to understand that I was blacklisted. Nobody would hire me for fear of upsetting the Jackson family." (It would be five years before Gina Sprague, who never gave up, would be able to work in the entertainment business again.)

"This was bad publicity," according to Susie Jackson, who had befriended Gina Sprague at this time. "This could hurt the family, and this could especially hurt Michael. Michael was hot and getting hotter. This was a terrible scandal that would reflect on Michael Jackson more than on anyone else. This was his mother, his family. Everyone knew the ramifications. Many people in the entertainment industry thought it was very brave of Gina to stand up to that family, even though no one would help."

Gina Sprague would say in court papers that it was obvious to her that Katherine had orchestrated this attack to intimidate her and force her to quit her job. She was angry at Joe, she said, because "he had knowledge of the dangerous propensities of Katherine Jackson based on previous incidents involving other employees working for Joe Jackson who had also been subjected to physical injury by Katherine Jackson, and for similar reasons [Sprague did not elaborate]." She said that if Joe had warned her about his wife, she might have taken some kind of precautions, maybe even quit her job. But he didn't want to lose her, so he didn't take any such action.

Gina Sprague showed up in court with her close friend Susie Jackson. The family was shocked that Susie had taken Gina's side. "I was so nervous that day in court," Susie Jackson said. "I hadn't seen the family in a while, only once in two years and that was when I went to visit Randy in the hospital after his accident. I liked Joseph because, of all the family, he was the only one who seemed to care about me after Johnny and I were divorced in 1979. To the rest of them, me and my three children no longer existed. It hurt me, because I knew all those Jackson kids when their hair was nappy and their noses were out to here, Michael and the rest. I

mean, I used to see Michael with rollers in his hair sitting in his
pajamas watching cartoons. I remember that Michael used to get
very upset when Johnny would drink too much and violently abuse
me. He was a little kid, but so sensitive. However, after the divorce,
none of them would have anything to do with me. I ceased to exist.
So I felt I had to support my friend, Gina, which is what I did.''

Susie bravely walked over to Katherine Jackson and greeted her
by casually saying, ''Hello, Mother.'' ''Janet and Randy just stared
at me,'' she said. ''Katherine was stunned.''

''I cannot explain Katherine's expression,'' Gina Sprague recalled. ''It was like 'How dare you? Why, you traitor, you. How
dare you be on the side of the enemy?' Immediately, I was scared
for Susie, because I felt I was setting her up for something potentially dangerous for her. But she didn't care. She insisted on
standing by me because she believed in me.''

Katherine Jackson, Randy Jackson, and Janet Jackson categori-
cally denied that the incident ever happened. They claimed in court
papers that Sprague would never have been injured if she had exercised ''ordinary care in her behalf.''

''Randy and Janet would have done anything for their mother,''
Susie Jackson says. ''They worshipped this woman, just as the rest
of the family did. I'm sure she didn't ask them to go with her the
day of the incident. I'm sure they volunteered, because that family
would stand by their mother to the very end. They were mad at Joe
for pushing their mother over the edge. They were mad at the victim. But never at Mother. Never. She knew that her kids were
behind her one hundred percent.''

''I did not sue them for money,'' Gina Sprague said. ''It was a
matter of basic principle. This kind of thing just cannot be allowed
to happen to a person. I just don't feel that anybody has the right
to put their hands on another person. No one had the right to do
this to me, and especially the way they did it. It was so unfair. For
years, I was humiliated by it. It is an ugly spot on my life, and I'm
very embarrassed by it, still.''

Gina Sprague was represented by a number of attorneys, all of
whom quit or were fired from the case, either because they were
anxious to make a name for themselves as a result of it or because
they were intimidated by the Jacksons' power and celebrity. No one
really wanted to go up against the powerful Jackson family. Finally,
Gina and Joe made an out-of-court settlement, the details of which
she is not at liberty to discuss. Gina Sprague filed for dismissal of
the action on July 21, 1983.

Gina Sprague says that, despite what happened, she does not

harbor any animosity toward the Jackson family. "Of course I don't hate them," she has said. "I feel sorry for them. I loved that family. I know now that I was the proverbial straw that broke the camel's back. But like I told Katherine in court, next time, kick *his* ass. Not mine."

At this time, the autumn of 1980, Michael supervised a music video of the Jacksons' song "Can You Feel It?" The song, written by Michael and Randy, is an anthem to loving human relations. In the video, the brothers, appearing as superhuman behemoths, hoist a colorful rainbow that lights the heavens. They sprinkle stardust upon the earth. This causes small children of all races and colors to beam with appreciation. Bathed in rainbow hues, they gaze up in wonder at Michael and his brothers. The Jacksons smile down upon the children benevolently; Michael has the biggest smile of all.

"It's a nice place Michael comes from," Steven Spielberg has observed. "I wish we could all spend some time in his world."

Meanwhile, in the real world, a CBS Records executive telephoned Michael to ask him how he should handle the matter should the press begin to ask questions about the incident involving his mother and Gina. The conversation, according to the executive who tape-recorded it, went like this:

Q: What do you want us to say about the matter regarding your mother?
A: What do you mean?
Q: The Gina Sprague incident.
A: Who's Gina Sprague?
Q: (a pause) The woman who got into the, uh, disagreement with your mother, Randy, and Janet.
A: Tell the press it never happened.
Q: But . . .
A: I'm sorry, but I have to go now.

With that final comment, Michael Jackson hung up the phone.

# Chapter

# ❧17❧

By 1981, MICHAEL Jackson felt totally out of control of his own life. When he was onstage, performing, he could transform himself into the desirable person of his dreams: a sexy, outgoing, confident person who exerted total control over himself and his audience. But offstage was another story. When he looked in the mirror, he saw a person he didn't like very much, a person who allowed himself to be controlled by other people, whose talent was respected but whose opinions didn't matter. He couldn't do much about any of that. He focused his anxiety on the way he looked. *That* was something he might be able to control.

Michael considered a nose job, but before he could decide, he tripped during a dance routine and fell onstage in 1979. When his face hit the stage floor, he broke his nose. Michael had always had a fixation about the size of his nose anyway, and his brothers had made matters worse when they nicknamed him Big Nose. Wide, flat noses were a Jackson family trait, inherited from Joe. Michael had been threatening to have a nose job for years, but he was too afraid actually to go through with it. Now he had no choice. He flew back to Los Angeles and had his first rhinoplasty surgery in the spring of 1979.

"Joseph told me that it was all a result of the accident on stage," Gina Sprague recalled. "He doubted that Michael would ever have had the nose job if he didn't have to. That was the first. No one ever dreamed what that nose job would lead to. After the bandages came off, Michael liked what he saw."

The result of that first rhinoplasty is the nose on the cover of Michael's *Off the Wall* album—a nose just a little smaller than the one with which he was born. Michael's face had been surgically transformed, confirming his idea that his appearance was one thing over which he could exert control.

However, the doctor who performed the nose job did not do it properly. There were some breathing problems. Michael was referred to Dr. Steven Hoefflin, who would suggest a second nose job in the not-too-distant future. Hoefflin would perform this surgery, and all of the others Michael would eventually have.

By 1980, Michael had his new nose, but his face was still broken out. He had read that the kinds of greasy food he liked best only contributed to his acne problem. Jermaine, hoping to clear up his own acne, was a vegetarian by this time, and Michael decided that he would become one as well. Michael was not obese, not by any stretch of the imagination, but he still had baby fat around his waist and his face was full. He longed to be slimmer, to have what he called "a dancer's body."

In time, Michael's figure would become more streamlined and the roundness in his face would disappear, all as a result of diet. His acne would also clear up. Many people would think that Michael had surgery on his cheeks in 1980, but the new, clearly defined lines of his face were brought about by the gradual weight loss he experienced after becoming a vegetarian, and also by maturity.

He may have had a new nose, but Michael Jackson was still clearly unhappy. "Even at home, I'm lonely," he said. "I sit in my room sometimes and cry. It's so hard to make friends, and there are some things you can't talk to your parents or family about. I sometimes walk around the neighborhood at night, just hoping to find someone to talk to. But I just end up coming home."

The picture of Michael Jackson—world-renowned superstar—walking around his Encino neighborhood looking for someone to talk to is indeed an astonishing one. No one could have imagined the depth of Michael's despair and loneliness.

On February 20, 1981, Michael bought a three-bedroom, three-bathroom condominium, unit nine at 5420 Lindley Avenue in Encino, for $210,000. He paid $175,000 in cash. The rest of the money—$35,000—came from Katherine, who was given equity in the condominium as sole and separate property, meaning she did not have to share it with Joe as community property. The family home was being remodeled, and Michael, thinking ahead, realized that some family members would need a place to stay.

But more than that, this purchase was another attempt to control his own life; Randy had already moved into an apartment in Van Nuys, and Michael was astonished at his brother's courage. The

Jackson siblings didn't move out of the house unless they married first. Since Randy paved the way, Michael wanted to follow his lead. In the end, he could not go through with it.

"I just don't feel it's time for me to move away from home yet," he said. "If I moved out now, I'd die of loneliness. Most people who move out go to discos every night. They party every night. They invite friends over, and I don't do any of those things." (Michael would eventually move into the condominium temporarily—along with other family members—when the Encino home was remodeled. He still owns the condominium, and it is used as a haven for his brothers when they are having marital difficulties.)

By April of 1981, there were plans for the group to embark on a thirty-nine-city concert tour of the United States to support their new *Triumph* album. Michael didn't want to go. One problem he had with touring concerned the enormous amount of preparation and work involved. Then when it was over, it was over—unlike a movie or a video, which is timeless and lasting.

"What's so sad about the whole thing is that you don't capture the moment," he said of live performances. "Look at how many great actors or entertainers have been lost to the world because they did a performance one night and that was it. With film, you capture that, it's shown all over the world, and it's there forever. Spencer Tracy will always be young in *Captains Courageous*, and I can learn and be stimulated by his performance.

"So much is lost in live theater. Or vaudeville. Do you know how much I could have learned by watching all of those entertainers? It would be unreal. When I perform, I'm starting to feel like I'm giving a whole lot for nothing. I like to capture things and hold them there and share them with the world."

But he really had no choice. He threatened that this would be his last tour. "I sometimes feel like I should be seventy by now," the twenty-three-year-old singer would tell *Los Angeles Times* writer Robert Hillburn. "We've been around the world twice, performed before kings and ambassadors. It's time to move on."

But the tour would gross $5 million for the family, and Michael felt a responsibility to go through with it. Perhaps he figured that the tour would in some way unite the family during this difficult time. He was frustrated and upset, but he would force himself to look at the good side of the tour.

"It's beautiful at the shows when people join together. It's our own little world," he would say. "For that hour and a half, we try to show there is some hope and goodness in this world. It's only when you step outside the concert hall that you see all the craziness.''

Before embarking on the Triumph tour, Michael would have the second rhinoplasty Dr. Steven Hoefflin had recommended. "He didn't tell his family he was doing it," said Marcus Phillips, a family friend. "He just did it. He came home all black and blue and bandaged, and Katherine said, 'Michael, what in the world happened to you?' She must have thought he'd been beaten up. When he told her he had had another nose job, she was truly baffled. 'Did you break your nose again?' she asked. He told her he hadn't, that his doctor recommended a second operation because the first had been botched. Then he went to his bedroom and stayed there for a week, coming down to the kitchen every now and then for some vegetables.

"One thing I know to be true is that Michael was elated about the fact that with the second nose job he looked less like his father," Marcus Phillips said. "That appealed to him very much. If he couldn't erase Joe from his life, at least he could erase him from the reflection in the mirror. Already, he was talking about having a third nose job."

There was so much confusion and turmoil in the family at this time—as well as preparation for the upcoming tour—nobody seemed to care about Michael's nose. At most, they considered it another of Michael's eccentricities. These nose surgeries seemed insignificant compared to all the other drama. Even though Michael never discussed his surgery with anyone, he was crying out for help. He was becoming obsessed with the man in the mirror, and a dangerous pattern was beginning.

The Triumph tour would commence in Memphis, Tennessee, on July 9, 1981, and end with a record-breaking, sold-out, four-night engagement at the Los Angeles Forum. It was a grueling schedule. Being out on the road together made the Jackson brothers realize how far Michael had distanced himself from them. He started talking to the press about the possibility of a solo career.

"I think that will happen gracefully in the future," he told Paul Grein of *Billboard*. "I think the public will ask for it. That's definitely going to happen."

It was not what his brothers wanted to hear. It didn't make them feel any more secure when Michael began involving himself more in the business end of the show. At one point he was scheduled to go into a full dress rehearsal with the group when someone handed him a copy of the contract for the trucks that were to carry the equipment for the tour. Michael glanced at it and said, "Wait, I need to check something with my lawyer."

"That can wait, Mike. This rehearsal is more important," Jackie said.

Michael ignored him and left the stage area. He found a telephone and called John Branca. "He wanted me to explain a paragraph that dealt with what happened if the truck broke down, if it had a flat tire, or the road washed out," Branca recalled. "I explained the paragraph. He asked a couple of questions and said, 'Okay, I understand.' " Michael went back out to the stage, signed the contract, and went back to work.

Being out on the road and forced to mingle with fans whenever he ventured out into the world—which wasn't often—was also difficult for Michael. "Sometimes you get the real mean ones," he said of his fans. "Those who'll come up to you and say 'Siddown! Sign this for my baby.' I say, 'I don't have a pen.' 'What! You don't have a pen? Go hunt for one.' I say, 'Oh my God, how can they be so bold and cruel?'

"And also, it hurts to be mobbed," he complained. "Not mentally, but physically. Your body feels like a noodle, being pulled by ten different people. They don't realize it. They love you so much they just want a part of you. They say, 'I gotta get a piece of this guy, if it's his shirt, his hair, his face, anything.' There are fans who actually have pieces of my hair.

"I could go to England right now, and they'd show me and say, 'This is your hair from three years ago. I'd say, 'Oh my gosh.' And it's sitting in their wallet. They collect *hair*. There are fans who know the back of your head, the way your body's shaped. I have walked across fans with my head totally down, and I will puff my face out so they don't know who I am—and they stop you anyway. It's amazing. I don't know how they know."

The biggest numbers of The Jacksons' show were always Michael's solo songs from the *Off the Wall* album. There were special effects arranged by magician Doug Henning: Michael seemed to disappear into a puff of smoke after performing "Don't Stop 'Til You Get Enough." Offstage, Michael also seemed to disappear. He stayed to himself, rarely socializing with his brothers or the rest of the entourage. "This is my last tour," Michael Jackson said. "I will *never* do this again. Ever."

By September 1981, despite CBS Records' best efforts to keep what had happened a secret, most industry insiders were well aware of what had happened between Katherine Jackson and Gina

Sprague. Michael had made it clear that he did not want to have to face any reporters, because he was afraid that he might be asked to comment. However, the press grind would continue, Michael's wishes notwithstanding.

I was scheduled to interview Michael on October 3, 1981. My interview had been arranged by CBS Records, Michael's label. I had been warned against mentioning the name Gina Sprague or asking about what was referred to by the record company as "the incident." I was compiling a list of questions when the phone rang. It was Michael.

He got to the point immediately. "There's a certain way I want to do this interview."

"Which is?"

"Well, I want Janet to help."

"Help do what?" I asked.

There was a pause.

"Janet is going to sit in on our interview," he told me. "You'll direct your questions to her, and then she'll pass them on to me. Then I'll give her the answers, and she'll pass them on to you. It's the only way I'll do the interview. I hope you understand."

It took a moment for me to digest his directions. He made it all sound so logical, I thought I had misunderstood. I asked him to repeat himself, which he did.

"Michael, I don't get it," I said. "You're giving me an interview, but you're not talking to me? What kind of madness is that?"

"It might seem like madness to you," he said. "But there are reasons for the things I do. You just have to try to understand."

"But—" I began.

"If you're willing to do it my way, I'll see you tomorrow. Goodbye."

He hung up the phone. The discussion had ended.

The next day, I arrived at the Encino home on time for the interview. "Glad you could make it," Michael said as we shook hands. He was wearing a black T-shirt and matching jeans. His feet were bare, as they had been the last time I interviewed him two years earlier. I noticed that his nose was different, thinner and more defined since our last interview. He spoke in an odd, falsetto whisper, which seemed even softer than it had the last time we talked. He was now twenty-three.

After Michael and I exchanged a few pleasantries in the living room, Janet, age fifteen, walked in wearing a red leather miniskirt, black boots, and a plaid sweater. She did not say hello. She simply sat at Michael's side.

Michael introduced me to her. We shook hands, but she never made eye contact with me. I sat opposite them.

"Now, you'll do the interview the way you promised, won't you?" he asked me.

"I didn't promise anything, Michael," I reminded him.

He rose from his chair. "Then we can't do the interview," he said.

"Wait," I told him. "Okay, let's try it. Let's start with the Jacksons album, *Triumph*. How do you feel about it?"

Michael glared at me and nodded toward his sister. I redirected my question.

"Janet, please ask him how he feels about the album."

"He wants to know how you feel about the album," Janet said to her brother.

"Tell him I'm very happy with it," Michael said. "Working with my brothers again was an incredible experience for me. It was magical."

Janet nodded her head and turned to me. "He told me to tell you that he's very happy with the album," she said. "And that working with his brothers was an incredible experience for him."

There was a pause.

"You forgot the part about it being magical," Michael said to her. He seemed irritated.

"Oh, yeah, he said it was magical."

"Magical?" I repeated.

"Yes," she said. "Magical."

Michael and I stared at each other for a moment as I tried to think of another question for Janet to ask her brother. Everything I had planned to ask suddenly seemed too complicated.

The interview did not last long. Occasionally, young Janet would interject a comment. "Remember when that girl got upset because she had heard you had a sex change?" she asked Michael. "You remember what happened to her? She got so upset, she jumped out of a window. I think she died." Michael just stared ahead, not saying anything.

After five more questions—and five answers from Michael by way of his sister—I said that I'd rather not continue. "Why not?" Michael wanted to know. "Janet will tell you what happened when I visited Katharine Hepburn last month," he offered.

"I'd rather *you* tell me, Michael," I pressed.

Janet let out a sigh of relief.

"Well, I can't . . ."

"Then, look, just forget it. Let's just forget this whole thing."

"Okay, if that's how you feel," he told me as he got up. He smiled, shook my hand, and disappeared. Janet followed.

What was happening to Michael Jackson, I wondered. He used to be such an adorable, happy little kid, totally unaffected by show business—or at least that was how he had seemed when he and his brothers first became famous as The Jackson 5 in the 1970s. On the day of this interview, however, he seemed unhappy and mistrustful. He had told his record company that he no longer sought direct contact with the media for fear of questions about Gina Sprague. He apparently preferred to withdraw. But when the label's executives, and Michael's own father, insisted that he continue courting the press, he rebelled. To please them, he would make himself available to the media, but to please himself, he would not have direct contact with the reporter. This tactic might seem ludicrous to some people, but desperate people sometimes take desperate measures just to make a point, especially when nobody will listen.

Beverly Hills psychiatrist Carole Lieberman observed, "In Michael's pretend world, he no doubt reasoned that if there was a problem with the story, he never really said anything to the writer at all; Janet did. Also, his actions were his way of distancing himself from the question as to whether or not his mother really did assault that lady. This is the kind of behavior that, in the extreme, makes people schizophrenic."

Upon leaving, I met Michael's father, Joe, in the driveway. I told him what had happened. He smiled, shrugged his shoulders and said, "That's Michael."

As I pulled out of the driveway and through the front gate, I felt a grudging admiration for the way Michael had gotten what he wanted. He had manipulated the situation and made a mockery of the promised interview. I never wrote about that episode. Instead, I canceled the feature altogether. Michael got what he really wanted: no story.

I was not the only reporter subjected to Michael's odd interviewing style. Reporter Judy Spiegelman also witnessed such a scene, and writer Steve Demorest had a somewhat similar experience. Even though Demorest was asked to direct his questions to Janet, who then redirected them to Michael, Michael gave Demorest his answers directly.

In his interview, for *Melody Maker* magazine, Demorest asked Michael about the possibility of his having children in the near future. Michael shook his head no. He'd like to raise a child, but if he did, it would be one whom he would adopt, "in the far future."

He would not procreate. "I don't have to bring my own into the world," he said uneasily.

Michael continued, "One of my favorite pastimes is being with children—talking to them, playing with them in the grass. They're one of the main reasons I do what I do. They know everything that people are trying to find out—they know so many secrets—but it's hard for them to get it out. I can recognize that and learn from it. They say some things that just astound you. They go through a brilliant, genius stage. But then, when they become a certain age . . ." Michael paused. His face looked sad. "When they get to a certain age, they lose it."

Michael was obviously withdrawing deeper into a fantasy world, perhaps because the real one in which he lived was so turbulent and painful. The Jacksons were supposed to be a positive example to millions of young people as to what could be accomplished with hard work and family unity. Michael sincerely wanted his family to be outstanding role models. "Everybody has somebody to look up to," he said. "The Jacksons give them strong role models. People look up to us. We have a responsibility to them to lead our lives right. And we do."

# Chapter

## 18

MICHAEL JACKSON, WHO would turn twenty-four years old in August of 1982, was nothing if not a study in contrasts. He was a decisive young man, as he proved many times over the years, but he was also extremely vulnerable and often acted confused and naive. By this time, he was beginning to seize control of his career, but he was also reluctant to sever completely his professional ties with his family. "I'd die if I were alone," he said. He was unable to leave the womb, to move out of the house. Instead of growing up, he seemed in many ways to be regressing—playing childlike games, buying toys, withdrawing into his fantasy world.

Michael had ambivalent feelings about his father—indeed, he was beginning truly to resent him—but he loved his mother deeply. To Michael, Katherine Jackson could do no wrong. Katherine had been an unhappy woman for years, and Michael was aware of this. It broke his heart to watch his mother endure an insufferable marriage. "Do something about it," he told her. "Don't take it anymore."

"I never thought I wanted to marry," Michael said at this time. "But I especially feel that way now, after seeing what happened to Kat [Michael often called his mother 'Kat']."

Most of the rest of the Jackson children agreed that Katherine should rectify her problems with Joe. Rebbie, in particular, was very distrustful of her father and felt that Katherine should divorce him. Some of the boys weren't so sure there was a problem. They could relate to their father's lust for women, but not Michael.

In what was probably one of the quietest divorce actions in recent music industry history, Katherine Jackson filed for divorce from Joe on August 19, 1982. Her action got little press coverage. She

259

was discreet, not wanting to jeopardize the family's image with a public divorce. In her petition, she said:

"Approximately one year ago, Joseph told me that we were running short of money. I asked him questions about the business and he told me to 'stay out of the business.' From time to time thereafter he would talk about losing money. I would ask him if he would like me to help him in his business office and he would reply once again that I should stay out of the business. Joseph has always had control of all of the money and would only give me the monies that I needed from time to time. I am informed and believe that within the last year, Joseph has spent in excess of $50,000 on a young woman and has purchased for her parcels of real property from our community funds. I am fearful that unless restrained by an order of this court, Joseph will continue to dissipate community funds and transfer community funds in jeopardy of my community property rights."

Though Katherine had only a vague idea of exactly how much community property existed, she wanted to keep Joe from transferring or otherwise disposing of any of it. The property she was aware of included her interest in the Encino home, furniture, furnishings, and other personal property, and her interest in Joe Jackson Productions and in various bank accounts. She made a list of the rest of the community assets: a 1979 Mercedes-Benz (color not indicated in legal documents), a 1971 blue-gray Mercedes-Benz, a 1971 white Rolls-Royce, a 1978 brown Mercedes-Benz, a 1971 blue Rolls-Royce, a 1974 G.M.C. motor home, a 1981 Toyota truck; a 1980 white Cadillac limousine, a 1978 Ford van, two boats (day cruisers) with trailers, and a Keogh financial plan.

There was only one snag in Katherine's declaration of independence. Jerome Howard, who would become Katherine's business manager in 1988, recalled, "She told me that after she filed for divorce, she expected Joe to move out. But he refused to leave the house. So what could she do? She didn't want to make a big legal scene, so she let him live there while the proceedings were going on."

"My parents are divorcing, and yet Joseph still lives at the house," Michael lamented to one associate. "Have you ever heard of anything like this before? I have a feeling Kate is trapped. She'll never be able to get out of that marriage."

"I think Joe has been misunderstood in many ways," Jackie's wife, Enid Jackson, said. "I don't know about his problems with Katherine; that was none of my business. But he's a pussycat, really. He has people thinking he's tough, but he has a soft heart. Coming from Gary, Indiana, and not having any experience in the music industry, and being a father, and being black? It has not been easy. He has been through a lot, and yes, it has affected his personal relationships. There have been a lot of people along the way who have tried to make him feel like less than he is, never giving him the credit he deserved for what he did for the Jacksons. There have been people who've downgraded him unfairly, tried to make him look bad in front of his kids. He might not have made all the wisest business decisions, but not purposely. It has been tough on Joe, and maybe it affected his marriage. He's been hurt, Katherine's been hurt. There have been joys, but sadnesses too.''

At the same time, Michael's older brother Marlon filed for divorce from his wife of seven years, Carol. The couple had three children, including a year-old boy, Marlon, Jr. Marlon hadn't done as well financially as his brothers. The couple only had two cars, a 1980 Rolls-Royce and a 1982 Jeep wagon. Besides their home in Encino, they owned another property in New Orleans. In court records, Marlon listed his monthly income as only $3,218, yet his monthly expenses totaled $16,664. They had $5,000 in one savings account, $61,000 in another, and $10,000 in stocks.

The family was stunned by Marlon's divorce action, which he filed in October 1982. He claimed that although Carol had been a good mother, her behavior became erratic after he informed her of his divorce plans. He said that his wife threatened to take their children from the home. Marlon claimed that Carol had told the children that their father didn't love them and that he would never see them again. ''The children have become extremely emotionally upset, as have I,'' Marlon said.

Marlon said that since the separation, Carol had not been herself. He felt that she was temporarily distraught and would eventually come to her senses. Still, he loved his children and wanted to be certain they would be there for him. One reason Marlon had less money, as he explained, was that he had limited his career and work schedule so that he could be with his children as much as possible. He was very family-oriented. He was able to get temporary custody of his three youngsters.

Carol said that she ''loved Marlon desperately'' and did not want a divorce. ''My sadness and my fear of losing my husband has possibly made me more anxious than I have ever been,'' she said. ''I dearly love my husband and wish to restore the joy and love we have had and known together.'' She said she never threatened to take the children from Marlon, but begged that she be allowed to take them to Louisiana to visit their maternal grandparents for the

Christmas holidays. She was on an allowance from Marlon's accountant, which she found entirely acceptable.

Though they were still separated, Carol's reasonable attitude delighted Michael. "She wants to go to a marriage counselor," Michael enthused. "And Marlon has agreed. That's the way it should be in a marriage. That's how I think couples should be."

Through all of this domestic turmoil, Michael tried to be as independent of his family as possible, though sometimes it was difficult for him. Singer Mickey Free (formerly of the group Shalamar) remembered his first meeting with Michael in the winter of 1982. "I was signed to Diana Ross's management company at that time. She was staying at the Beverly Hills Hotel and asked me if I wanted to come down to her bungalow and meet Michael Jackson. Well, who wouldn't?" he recalled. "So I had dinner with Michael, Diana, and Gene [Simmons, Ross's boyfriend then]. I was freaking out because I always wanted to meet Michael, and he was so nice. So it came time for me to go home. Diana's car had brought me there, and she said, 'Okay, I'll call the driver to come and get you.' Michael very softly said, 'Oh, that's okay, I'll take Mickey home.' "

Diana and Gene were astonished. "Are you sure you want to do this, Michael?" Diana asked, concerned. "I mean, are you sure you can handle it? Driving him home and all?"

"Yeah, I can do it, Diane," Michael said, confidently.

Mickey got into Michael's Silver Shadow Rolls-Royce, and the two sped off down the driveway in front of the Beverly Hills Hotel. "Be careful," Diana hollered after them. "Don't drive too fast, Michael."

"This was really a big deal for him," Mickey said. "Driving me home and all."

When they got to Mickey's apartment building about fifteen minutes later, Michael drove around the block a few times before he sheepishly confessed, "You know what? I can drive this thing, but I don't know how to parallel park it. Can you park this for me?"

"Heck, yeah, I can," Mickey replied.

"I rode around the block ten times trying to find a parking place so people could see me driving Michael Jackson around in this fabulous car," Mickey Free recalled. "Michael was nice. We went up to my apartment, looked at pictures. He stayed about fifteen minutes, and I walked him back down to his car. He drove off. Didn't crash into anybody or anything."

As Michael began to feel an increasing distance growing between him and his family, he began to socialize more with Jane

Fonda and hers. He had known Jane for two years and had visited her on the set of *On Golden Pond* in 1980; he stayed with her in a private cabin.

"A lot of people thought that was very strange," said Sarah Holiday, who worked on the film as a publicist. "But Jane just thought Michael was a fascinating person. She made it clear that if anyone were to ever gossip about her and Michael, that person would be in serious trouble. 'He's too delicate to handle gossip,' she would say. She had been in the business for so long, she said it was nice to talk to someone who seemed so unjaded by it all."

"We were all alone there on the water," Michael said of his night with Jane Fonda, "and we just talked, talked, talked about everything. It was the greatest education for me: she'd learn, and I'd learn, and we'd just play off of each other. We talked about all kinds of things, you name it—politics, philosophy, racism, Vietnam, acting, all kinds of things. It was magic."

Michael was intimidated, at first, by Henry Fonda, but soon the two of them struck up a friendship. Henry baited fishhooks for Michael, then took him out on a jetty where the two of them spent hours together fishing and talking about theater. "Yes, he's strange," Henry said of Michael. "So what?"

"We just sat and talked for a long time," Michael would recall. "He was such a wise man. He gave me a lot of tips about acting, and about stardom. How he handled it, and all."

Jane Fonda wasn't surprised that her father and Michael got along. She told *Rolling Stone* writer Gerri Hirshey, "Dad was also painfully self-conscious and shy in life. He really only felt comfortable when he was behind the mask of a character. He could liberate himself when he was being someone else. That's a lot like Michael. Michael reminds me of the walking wounded. He's an extremely fragile person. I think that just getting on with life, making contact with people, is hard enough for him, much less having to be worried about whither goest the world."

On August 11, 1982, Henry Fonda succumbed to a long bout with heart disease. Afterwards, Jane went to the family home to be with her stepmother, Shirlee, and brother Peter. Michael telephoned to see if he could come by.

"The night Henry died, I went over there and I was with the family," Michael would recall in an interview with Bob Colacello for *Interview* magazine. "They were talking and watching all the different newspieces. Although her father had just died, Jane was still able to show an interest in my career, asking me had I gotten the right film yet, and I thought that was very sweet. Months and months before he died, she was talking as though it was going to be any day. It happened and there were tears sometimes and laughter sometimes, and they ate a little.''

On the set of *On Golden Pond*, Michael also met Katharine Hepburn. Their first meeting did not go well. She thought he was odd, didn't understand him, and was suspicious of him. She shook his hand, curtly told him it was nice to meet him, then walked away quickly. Michael was crushed. "She doesn't like me," he complained to Jane. "And she's like an idol of mine. I hate it when my idols don't like me.''

"What is it with him?'' Katharine asked someone on the set. "First of all, why is he here? That's what I don't understand. And why does he talk like that, with that whisper? What is he trying to pull?''

"There are a lot of people she doesn't like,'' Michael said of Hepburn. "She'll tell you right away if she doesn't like you. When I first met her, it was a little shaky because you hear things about her. Jane filled me in. I was kind of scared.''

Jane had a talk with Katharine about Michael and tried to explain what she knew about Michael to the older actress. That afternoon, Michael sat alone in a corner watching a rehearsal. Katharine Hepburn came up behind him and tapped him on the shoulder.

"You and I are having dinner tonight, young man,'' she said.

"We are?'' Michael gasped.

That night, Michael and Katharine had dinner and became great friends. "We call each other on the phone, and she sends me letters,'' he would say of her. "She's just wonderful. I went to her house in New York and she showed me Spencer Tracy's favorite chair and his private things in his closet, his little knickknacks.''

In June 1982, Michael and Quincy Jones began work on a storytelling record book of Steven Spielberg's film, *E.T.* Michael would also be featured as vocalist on one song, "Someone in the Dark,'' written by Alan and Marilyn Bergman. Michael was so enchanted by the story of *E.T.* that he couldn't wait to meet the extraterrestrial robot when a publicity photo session was arranged. "He grabbed me, he put his arms around me,'' Michael said of the robot. "He was so real that I was talking to him. I kissed him before I left. The next day, I missed him.''

Later in the month, Michael went into the studio with Diana Ross to produce a song for her called "Muscles''—named after his pet snake. Michael was ecstatic about the opportunity to produce his idol. There were many people—public and critics—who had said that Michael had had his plastic surgery in order to look more like Miss Ross. But as one Jackson confidant put it, "If Michael Jackson wanted to look like Diana Ross, believe me, he has the millions to look *exactly* like her. That was never his intention. Ever. But that's not to say that he wasn't tickled by the fact that people thought he resembled her. I mean, he *idolized* this woman."

At this time, Diana had left Motown and was recording her second album for RCA, *Silk Electric*. The album was shaping up to be a disaster and she needed something outstanding on the collection, which is why she contacted Michael. "I was coming back from England, working on Paul McCartney's album, zooming along on the Concorde, and this song popped into my head," Michael recalled. "I said, 'Hey, that's perfect for Diana.' I didn't have a tape recorder or anything, so I had to suffer for like three hours. Soon as I got home, I whipped that baby on tape."

Diana has said that Michael seemed intimidated by her while the two of them worked together in the studio. He couldn't bring himself to direct her, tell her what to do and how to do it.

"You're the man," Diana insisted. "You're the boss on this one." Diana wanted Michael to show some of his own "muscle" and control the recording session, but it was difficult for him. "In the end, the song just sort of produced itself," said a friend of Diana's. The kinky lyrics of "Muscles" extol the joys of a man's muscles "all over your body."

"I don't know whether it's supposed to be Michael's fantasy or mine," Diana said when it was released. Either way, it was a hit and a Top Ten record for Diana Ross.

In August 1982, Michael and Quincy Jones began work on a new album at Westlake Studios in Los Angeles. The album would be entitled *Thriller* and consist of nine songs that the two had pared down from three hundred selections. The album would cost $750,000 to produce.

On December 1, 1982, *Thriller* was released to a holiday market of seasonal shoppers. The album was dedicated to Michael's mother, Katherine. Quincy Jones predicted it was going to be a hit. As he told Alex Haley for a *Playboy* magazine interview, "I knew from the first time I heard it in the studio, because the hair stood straight up on my arms. That's a sure sign, and it's never once been wrong. All the brilliance that had been building inside Michael Jackson for twenty-four years just erupted. I was electrified, and so was everyone else involved in the project.

"That energy was contagious, and we had it cranked so high

one night that the speakers in the studio actually overloaded and burst into flames. First time I ever saw anything like that in forty years in the business.''

It might have sounded terrific in the studio, but once they played the master pressing of the record, it didn't sound as good. In fact, it sounded terrible. The mix was wrong, and Michael was crushed. He ran out of the room, crying. As Berry Gordy would say, solving the problem would prove simple but not easy. It was a matter of remixing each song—bringing up the level of some orchestration and voices and toning down others. Time-consuming, tedious work at the rate of two songs a week, but in the end it proved to be well worth the effort. When Michael heard the finished product, he was delighted.

Quincy Jones, Ron Weisner, and John Branca sat with Michael in the studio as he listened to a playback of the album. To Michael, the music sounded terrific. He was extremely optimistic and smiled broadly as each cut played.

"Mike, you know, the record market is off right now," Ron Weisner told him as the title track blared from the speakers. He had to almost shout to be heard above the music.

"Yeah, Mike," Quincy agreed. "You can't expect to do with this one what you did with *Off the Wall*."

"These days, two million is a hot album," Weisner added.

"Yeah, it's a tough market. Nobody's having hits," Quincy added.

"Turn it down," Michael instructed the engineer. Michael's smile was now gone.

"What's the matter with you guys?" Michael wanted to know. "How can you say that to me? You're wrong. You are dead wrong."

"But, Smelly—" Quincy began.

"Look, don't talk to me," Michael said, turning away from Jones. "I've had it with you. I'm really mad. Don't ever tell me anything like that again. What kind of attitude is *that* to have?"

John Branca sat in a corner and watched the scene. He probably knew better than to say anything.

"I'm outta here," Michael said as he stormed out of the studio.

By the next day, Michael had worked himself into a fury. He telephoned John Branca and told him how angry he was at Weisner and Jones for predicting that *Thriller* would "only" sell two million copies. "There is no way," Michael said. "*There is no way*. This is a *big* album."

Michael was so incensed that he decided that he wasn't going to submit the album to CBS Records. He told Branca to telephone

Walter Yetnikoff and cancel the *Thriller* project. "If Quincy and Ron don't have faith in me," Michael decided, "then let's just forget it. I'm not even going to let the album come out. *Thriller* is gonna be shelved forever."

After hanging up with Branca, Michael decided to telephone Walter Yetnikoff himself. When he told Yetnikoff what had happened at the studio, the CBS record president tried to calm him down. "What the hell do they know?" he said of Jones and Weisner. "*You're* the superstar, not them."

Whereas most of the CBS artists were intimidated by Walter Yetnikoff, Michael was not. "Listen, Walter, this album is the biggest album of all time. I just feel it," Michael told him. "The music is that strong. So it had better be a success, and you'd better make sure of it."

Yetnikoff had probably heard that evaluation of a record before— at least a hundred times, in fact—but from the artist's representative and rarely from the artist himself. Bemused, he told Michael he would make certain the record was promoted properly.

"I hope so," Michael told him, "because if not, then there's no point in putting it out."

After Yetnikoff reassured him, Michael was satisfied.

It's ironic, considering the eventual impact *Thriller* would have on the record industry, that when CBS released the album's first single (in October 1982, a little over a month before issuing the album to the marketplace), most observers thought the *Thriller* album would be a huge disappointment. The auspicious pairing of Michael Jackson with Paul McCartney for the mid-tempo "The Girl Is Mine" (which the singers cowrote while watching cartoons together) appeared to be of greater interest than the song itself, which was more cute than good, and lacking in substance. Many in both the black and white music communities felt that Michael and producer Quincy Jones had gone too far in consciously tailoring a record for a white, pop audience, and if this first single was any indication of what *Thriller* was to be like, then Michael Jackson seemed to be in big trouble.

And then came "Billie Jean."

Dark and sparse by Quincy Jones production standards, "Billie Jean" prowled in rhythm like a predatory animal. It's a disturbing song Michael wrote about a girl accusing him of fathering her child. No doubt, Joe Jackson's extramarital affairs and illegitimate child must have come to mind when Michael wrote the lyrics. But there was another experience Michael had that became the catalyst for "Billie Jean."

In 1981 a female fan wrote Michael a letter claiming that he was the father of her baby. She enclosed photographs of herself—a young, attractive, black woman in her late teens whom he had never met—and of the infant. Michael, who receives letters of this nature often, ignored this one as he does the others.

This teenager, however, was more persistent than the rest. She loved Michael desperately, she claimed, and longed to be with him. She wrote about how she could not stop thinking about Michael and waxed rhapsodic about how happy she and Michael would be as they raised their love child together. She seem obsessed.

In months to come, Michael would receive dozens of letters from this woman. In one, she claimed that the baby and Michael had similar eyes and wondered how Michael could ignore his own flesh and blood.

Michael began having nightmares about this woman. "Why won't she stop?" he asked. "Why won't she leave me alone? Is she crazy?"

He could not get her out of his mind and constantly wondered where she was, when she would show up, what he would do if she did. It seemed that he had become as obsessed with her as she was with him.

Finally, she sent Michael a package. When Michael opened it, he discovered another photograph of her: it looked like a high school graduation picture. She was smiling with girlish innocence. Lying next to the picture was a weapon. In an accompanying note, the fan asked that Michael kill himself on a particular day and at a certain time. She wrote that she, too, would do the same—right after she murdered the baby. She had decided if the three of them could not be together in this life, perhaps they would in the next.

Michael was aghast at her proposed suicide pact. He took the photograph, framed it, and put it in the dining room on a coffee table.

"God, what if she shows up?" he fretted. "What will I do? I have to remember this face. Just in case . . . I can never forget this face."

She never showed up. In fact, that disturbed young woman was eventually sent to an insane asylum.

After "Billie Jean" came out, Michael would say that he wrote the song with her in mind. He would never say, however, what kind of weapon she had sent to him. Michael told many people this frightening story in 1981, but he decided not to include it in his *Moonwalk* memoirs for fear that it might encourage similar incidents.

Ironically, Quincy Jones did not want to include "Billie Jean" on the *Thriller* album because he did not think it was a strong enough song. Michael was extremely angry about this and still has not forgiven Quincy for questioning his judgment.

The relationship between Michael and Quincy had rapidly deteriorated during the recording of the *Thriller* album, especially when Quincy would not give Michael co-producing credit on "Billie Jean" and "Beat It." Since the demonstration tapes Michael had recorded of both songs—before Quincy worked on them— sounded almost exactly like the final product released on the album, Michael felt it was only fair that he be given co-producing credit, and additional royalties as well. Quincy disagreed, much to Michael's chagrin.

Closer inspection of *Thriller* as a whole revealed a most ambitiously crafted work that moved in a variety of directions. The suburban, middle-of-the-road calm of "The Girl Is Mine" was the antithesis of the rambunctious "Beat It," another highly charged Jackson composition. In this one, Michael augmented his crossover rhythm-and-blues style by employing a harder-edged rock-and-roll sound. Some observers felt "Beat It" was a shameless quest to attract hard rock fans; the track featured rock guitar hero Eddie Van Halen (whose band Van Halen was the preeminent rock group of the moment) on searing guitar bridges. While the tune was obviously a marketing concoction—in the past, Michael had never shown any particular fondness for straight-out rock and roll—"Beat It" would still find acceptance among rock fans.

On the other hand, if the funky "Wanna Be Startin' Somethin' " sounds like a distant relative of *Off the Wall*'s songs "Don't Stop 'Til You Get Enough" and "Working Day and Night," the similarity occurred because Michael wrote them all during the same period. In "Startin' Somethin', " surprisingly one heard Michael pointedly reveal his feelings on gossips and unwanted babies, and all to a bulleting bass and shuffling percussion. The tune's centerpiece—a climaxing Swahili-like chant—gave the song an international flavor. It was difficult to listen to Michael spit out angry lyrics about hate and about feeling like a vegetable and not question his state of mind.

There were other standouts: the moody and introspective "Human Nature," written by Steve Porcaro and John Bettis, was an expansive pop ballad whose sheer musicality kept it from being mushy. The funky "PYT," credited to James Ingram and Quincy Jones, and Rod Temperton's sultry ballad "Lady in My life" were both clearly efforts to beef up *Thriller*'s R&B direction. The former

is a gleaming mélange of pop-funk music guaranteed to fill a dance
floor every time. Even though the slang in the lyrics—like *tenderoni*
and *PYT* (code for "pretty young thing")—had played out among
the street crowd by the time Michael decided to exploit it, no lis-
tener could deny the tune's infectious groove. Frank DiLeo, Epic's
promotion director, however, liked the song better than Michael
did. "Lady in My Life," on the other hand, was as close as Michael
had come to crooning a sexy, soulful ballad since his Motown years.
Maybe that's why it required so many takes before he got the lead
vocal to Quincy Jones's liking.

The title track, "Thriller," was its own animal. The song said
much about Michael's fascination with the supernatural and the
lurid. "Thriller" is a typical Rod Temperton song—melodic, with
a fluid bass line and a big, mind-imprinting hook. The lyrics had
excitement and intrigue, and the song concluded with a rap by the
master of the macabre, Vincent Price. "Thriller" would have been
even more compelling as the title track of a concept album, but
*Thriller*, the album, had no focus. Even the album's cover art—a
photograph of a casually posed Michael uncharacteristically dressed
in white jacket and pants—seemed incongruous.

*Thriller*'s pop music diversity would be its major appeal. Michael and Quincy had successfully engineered glossy, authentic
versions of pop, soul, and funk that appealed to everyone. However, no one in the music business expected the public to take that
appeal so literally. At some point, *Thriller* stopped selling like a
leisure item—like a magazine, a toy, tickets to a hit movie—and
started selling like a household staple. At its sales peak, CBS would
report that the album was selling an astounding 500,000 copies a
week.

The more *Thriller* was heard—and it was possibly the most
played record of all time, both privately and on the radio—the better
it sounded. Michael and Quincy had achieved their goal: to many
listeners—whites, blacks, highbrows, heavy metal fans, teenyboppers, parents—*Thriller* was the perfect album, every song an exercise in pop music production, every arrangement, every note in
the perfect place. This achievement made Michael Jackson more
than a hero; the music industry promoted him to higher ground,
almost sainthood. Indeed, in entertainment circles, even the most
untalented artist who sells huge amounts of product becomes a
"visionary." But Michael's phenomenal sales, along with his
astounding talent, established a precedent of excellence with
*Thriller*—and one that he would, very likely, secretly attempt to
surpass for the rest of his career.

# Chapter
## 19

JOE JACKSON IS known among his friends and business associates as a man given to overextending himself by investing in unsteady business ventures outside of the careers of his sons. Some of the investments have been profitable. For instance, a limousine company he owned did manage to turn a profit. Often, though, Joe would lose his investment and then some. He started his own record company at one point, which cost him a small fortune. He had invested a great deal of money in producing and managing singing groups, perhaps to prove that he could do for others what he did for his sons. But none of his acts ever amounted to much.

By the beginning of 1981, Joe Jackson was apparently having financial problems serious enough to warrant his wanting to sell the Encino estate. He found the perfect buyer. His own son, Michael Jackson. It's unknown how closely Joe examined the ramifications of his offer to Michael. Once he changed roles from owner to tenant, his relationship with Michael would have to change as well.

Barring unusual circumstances, in most families whoever heads the family provides the lodgings; when the children become adults, they move on to their own homes. Changing roles in a basic way can contribute to family dysfunction. Joe had always held the theory that a father should be able to control his children—no matter what their ages, their desires, their expertise. Being so determined to be in charge, Joe would probably feel threatened by having to live in his son's house—especially when it had once been his own.

Perhaps he didn't foresee what might happen. Perhaps he was in such desperate need of money he didn't care. One friend of Joe's has said that Joe felt he was doing Michael a favor, providing him "a solid investment," by selling him 50 percent of the house.

Even Michael had to admit, "I'd say we were among a fortunate few artists who walked away from a childhood in the business with anything substantial—money, real estate, other investments. My father set all these up for us. To this day I'm thankful he didn't try to take all our money for himself, the way so many parents of child stars have. Imagine stealing from your own children. My father never did anything like that."

Michael paid about $500,000 for his equity in the house. Katherine and Joe owned the other half. Eventually Joe would sell his quarter to Michael, leaving 25 percent to Katherine.

Michael completely demolished and rebuilt the house once he became part-owner. The address may have remained the same, but the new house—Michael's house, which took two years to finish—became palatial. While on tour in England a few years earlier, Michael had become enchanted by the Tudor-style mansions he saw in the countryside there. He wanted to recreate that look in Encino because, as he put it, "I think Kate would like that best."

The estate is, indeed, special. The brick-laid drive opens to an ornate three-tiered white fountain in front of a Tudor-style home. All of the windows of the house are made of leaded stained glass with beveled panes. When Michael was in residence, the Rolls-Royce that Tatum O'Neal helped him pick out always sat parked in front of the four-car Tudor-style garage opposite the home. Michael was still uneasy about driving; he would much rather take an hour-long detour than drive on the freeway in Los Angeles. "I can't get on 'em," he complained, "and I can't get off 'em, either."

A large "Welcome" sign appears above the garage doors. In the center of the garage structure stands an oversized clock with Roman numerals. Upstairs, on the second floor of the garage, a visitor enters a three-room picture gallery with many hundreds of photographs of the Jackson family on the walls and even the ceilings. At the head of the stairs, leading to the gallery, Michael placed a plaque that reads, in part:

> To take a picture
> Is to capture a moment,
> To stop time.
> To preserve the way we were
> The way we are.

One room is devoted to early Jackson family memorabilia, including a reproduction of Joe and Katherine's marriage certificate. The second room is dedicated to Jackson 5 history, and the third concentrates on Michael as an adult. It contains photos of him with celebrities like Jacqueline Onassis and Jane Fonda.

Outside, graceful black and white swans could be found in back-yard ponds. A pair of peacocks (Michael's favorite bird) named Winter and Spring, two llamas named Louis and Lola ("Lola Falana the Llama," after the singer), two deer named Prince and Princess, a giraffe Michael called Jabar, and an animal some have said is a ram (though others aren't certain) named Mr. Tibbs were Michael's favorite pets. The animals, kept in stables at night, were allowed to roam freely during the day. When Michael lived at the estate, he kept the well-tended cages of a dozen or so animals—rabbits, expensive birds, rats—on the kitchen counters of the guest house because he felt they were too fragile to be outdoors. He would stop at each cage every day to chat with the animals.

Michael also owned an eight-foot boa constrictor named Muscles which, he joked, was "trained to eat interviewers." In fact, Michael would feed the snake a big, healthy rat once a week. Once Katherine was straightening out the living room when she discovered Michael's boa constrictor under one of the couch cushions. "She let out a scream that you could hear all over Encino," Susie Jackson said with a laugh.

Neighbors constantly complained about the animals. Howard Davine, an attorney whose backyard adjoins the Jacksons', said, "During the hot summer months, it became very difficult for us to enjoy our property. Those animals, by their nature, emit a certain odor."

Next to the garage, Michael had a miniversion of Disneyland's Main Street U.S.A. constructed, including the candy store. Michael's antique collection was housed on this "street." There was a replica of the robotic Abraham Lincoln, which spoke, just as the Lincoln attraction did at Disneyland. Whenever Michael would go to Disneyland, his favorite place on earth, there would be total chaos because of his fans. He always liked it best when the Disney employees would lead him through the back doors and tunnels of the attractions. Now he was building his own little world of Disney at home. Other puppet characters were added to the private amusement park. "These will be like real people," Michael had explained. "Except they won't grab at you or ask you for favors. I feel comfortable with these figures. They are my personal friends."

Beyond, winding brick paths decorated with exotic flowers and neatly cut shrubs lead to secluded corners of the large estate where Michael would often wander alone to think. The swimming pool is huge and inviting. Water spouts from four fountainheads carved

like bearded Neptunes on a wall behind the pool. A waterfall spills
in front of two lovebirds, a ceramic fashioned by elaborate, colorful
tilework. The water cascades down into the main pool and then
flows into a bubbling Jacuzzi.

The main kitchen is located on the ground floor of the home.
Always spotless, the kitchen contains white tile floors and chrome-
and-black ovens, stove, and appliances. The game room near the
kitchen is lined with arcade video games like Space Invaders and
Pac Man.

The foyer of the home is lit by a huge and dazzling chandelier,
which hangs from the ceiling two floors above. A grandfather clock
ornamented with gold filigree stands in a corner. A vase full of
freshly cut flowers sits on a square, gold-leaf table. There are graceful Greco-Roman-style bronze statues standing in the corners. The
dining room is always filled with flowers. Peacock-printed chairs
are placed around a mahogany table.

In the den, beneath a leaded stained glass window (depicting a
knight in armor looking up at a black castle on a hill) stands a
mahogany bar. The bar is really an old-fashioned soda fountain,
which Michael kept stocked with a variety of ice creams for milk
shakes and sodas. A couch faces a fireplace and a built-in television
set. A large clock with Roman numerals hangs above the mantel-
piece. In the living room, all of the furniture and rugs are covered
with floral prints.

Also on the ground floor is a thirty-two-seat theater with plush
red velvet seats; it is equipped with a 16-millimeter and a 35-
millimeter projector, operated by union projectionist Lee Tucker.
The walls and the curtain in front of the screen are teal blue. Michael spent countless hours in this theater, where he would watch
*Fantasia* about once every two weeks. There were always Fred
Astaire movies ready to be screened, as well as Three Stooges
films. "I put all this stuff in," he said, "so I will never have to go
out *there*."

There is also a wood-paneled trophy room downstairs, off the
foyer. Many of Michael's trophies are displayed in mahogany cases.
All of the Jacksons' gold and platinum albums cover the walls. The
family jokes that if LaToya ever manages to get a gold album, there
will be no place to hang it. So far, that has not been a problem.

Amid the magazine covers and other memorabilia, there is a six-
foot-long diorama of Snow White and the Seven Dwarfs. "One day
I got a call from Mike," Steve Howell, who was employed by
Michael Jackson as a video historian, remembered. " 'Come by
with the video equipment, you'll never guess who's comin' over.'

'Who?' I asked. 'Snow White and the Seven Dwarfs!' I said, 'Oh, okay. That should be interesting.' Nothing was really unusual when you worked for Michael."

Howell's video of that day shows a childlike Michael, twenty-six years old at the time, playing with the dwarfs in the trophy room and being serenaded by Snow White. He looks like this is one of the happiest days of his life.

A circular white marble staircase, partially carpeted in green, leads to the upstairs quarters.

Upstairs are the bedroom suites, each with its own bathroom, and a gym. Michael's bedroom was large and cluttered. "I just want room to dance and have my books," he said when he was supervising the building of it. Steve Howell recalled, "He had no bed. He slept next to the fireplace on the floor, which was covered with a plush green rug. Some of the walls were covered with a fabric material. Pictures of Peter Pan were on other walls. There were wooden shutters over the windows, which he usually kept closed. A winding stairway led from the bedroom up to a private balcony on which Michael had an outdoor Jacuzzi for his own use. The room was always a mess, not slobbish, just messy—books and records everywhere, posters on the floor that he intended to hang but never got around to, videotapes and music tapes stacked high. Fan mail everywhere, which was eventually forwarded to a fan club. His bathroom was impressive, all black marble and gold. The sinks had brass swans for faucets."

Howell remembered a strange addition to the bedroom's decor. "There were five female mannequins of different ethnic groups— Caucasian, black, Oriental—posed in different parts of the room. They were well dressed, life-sized, and looked like high-fashion models, wearing expensive clothing. Michael had someone design them for him, I don't know why. I walked in one day, they were there, and I just acted like they weren't. He never said why he had these mannequins in his room."

Michael said that he originally planned to have one room in the house specifically for the mannequins, but he changed his mind and decided to keep his plastic friends in his room. Katherine must have been relieved.

"I guess I want to bring them to life," he said. "I like to imagine talking to them. You know what I think it is? Yeah, I think I'll say it. I think I'm accompanying myself with friends I never had. I probably have two friends. And I just got them. Being an entertainer, you just can't tell who is your friend. So I surround myself with people I want to be my friends. And I can do that with mannequins. I'll talk to them."

The mannequins—all of whom had names given to them by Michael—would neither grab at Michael nor ask him for personal favors. Knowing Michael's gift for self-delusion, having such a racial mix probably reinforced his opinion that he was color-blind. He may have also reasoned that all races could live in harmony if they just kept their mouths shut, like his mannequins. And perhaps the female mannequins represented to Michael that women are so much less threatening if seen but not heard. By surrounding himself with mannequins, Michael Jackson had, in a sense, created a small, perfect world in which he was God.

Dr. Paul Gabriel, a professor of clinical psychiatry at New York University Medical Center, observed of Michael's keeping company with mannequins: "That's a special eccentricity. It's what we put in the category of narcissism. We like to think we're beautiful. We make images of ourselves. Kids are very narcissistic. After age five or six, they begin to give some of that up."

Later, there would be a crib in the corner of the bedroom. This is where Michael's chimpanzee, Bubbles—who became a celebrity himself—slept. Bubbles lives part-time with Michael and the rest of the time with his trainer, Bob Dunne.

LaToya's bedroom was down the hall from Michael's. "Thank God," she said in an interview. "He makes so much noise. You hear music in his room when he's trying to create. Or you hear the Three Stooges on TV, and he's up all night laughing real loud. The light is always on. Michael is forever reading books. You can't get in his room for the books and junk. I feel sorry for the housekeeper." Michael liked to hide bugs and spiders under LaToya's sheets so that she would find them, scream, and wake up the whole household. He would constantly run down the hallway and burst into her bedroom—which was always spic-and-span clean and perfectly tidy—with questions for his sister. One day he asked her what she thought of the title "Billie Jean."

"You don't think people will believe I'm talking about that tennis player, do you?" he asked. She didn't think so. (Quincy Jones thought so, however, and wanted to change the title of the song to "Not My Lover." Michael vetoed that.)

Michael has always been very snoopy and wouldn't think twice about going into anybody's bedroom, opening drawers, and looking inside. He frequently exasperated his family members by poking his nose into their personal business, but he would become very upset if anyone ever did it to him.

Hayvenhurst—unofficially named after the Encino street on which it was located—was the perfect retreat for Michael Jackson from the outside world. It was certainly a far cry from the modest home in which he had been raised as a small child. From the roof of the house, he would watch the sunset and the lighting of the twinkly white lights that decorated all of the property's trees and outlined the framework of the house.

He spoke to some employees about "the magic of Hayvenhurst" at night. At one time, Michael considered making a videotape of his home. Steve Howell has a six-page video concept he says he and Michael worked on together. In his barely legible handwriting, Michael wrote of waking up and saying "hello to the most gorgeous day ever." He waxed rhapsodic about "the inspiration of it all" and the "beuty [*sic*] of grass" and wrote that he wanted his home movie to show him "moved by the beauty of the sunset." He noted "the film must be too good to be true, like a fairytale."

"I went to see him about some music," said one songwriter, "and while I was sitting in the living room waiting for him, I had this sensation that he was in the room somewhere, watching me. Then he came in, we talked, and he just disappeared. I looked out in the yard and he was darting in and out among these bushes and trees, chasing these little animals. He was like one of them."

Once Michael and Jane Fonda were driving together in a car (Jane was behind the wheel) while Jane tried to figure out what kind of film property would be best for Michael. "God, Michael, I wish I could find a movie I could produce for you," she said. Suddenly, it occurred to her. "I know what you've got to do. It's *Peter Pan*," she enthused. "That's it!"

Tears began to well in Michael's eyes. He wanted to know why she suggested that character. She told him that, in her mind's eye, he really *was* Peter Pan, the symbol of youth, joy, and freedom.

Michael started to cry. "You know, all over the walls of my room are pictures of Peter Pan. I totally identify with Peter Pan," he said, wiping his eyes, "the lost boy of Never-Never Land."

Indeed, all children, except one, grow up . . .

On March 12, 1983, the comanagement contract Michael Jackson and his brothers had with their father, Joe, and with Weisner-DeMann expired. It was expected that Michael would renegotiate and sign a new deal. However, he was not eager to do so. "Let's just wait and see what happens," he kept saying when the subject was broached. Michael, who was now twenty-four years old, had experienced great solo success and, as a result, had become more confident in his own decisions. He no longer felt compelled to follow the leads of his brothers, who had said they wanted to continue with Joe. From this point on, Weisner and DeMann and Joe Jackson would continue working, without a contract.

Certainly, if Joe Jackson wanted to continue managing Michael Jackson, he was not scoring any points with his son by mistreating Michael's beloved mother. Michael Jackson had witnessed a great deal of domestic heartbreak in recent years and could not separate the man he held responsible for a good deal of it from the man who comanaged his career. He was now beginning to think about his options. Why did Joe have to be in the picture at all, he wondered. "Just because he's my father? That's not good enough," he decided.

Perhaps Michael was still troubled by the angry letter his father had written to Weisner-DeMann back in 1980 in which he assailed the managers for spending too much time on Michael's career and not enough on the other brothers. Joe probably did not expect the letter to get into Michael's hands, and it was a number of months before it did. But once Michael saw that letter, he had to wonder what it really meant. After all, it was not in the interest of the family, Joe must have realized, for Michael to become any more enchanted with his own solo success. Certainly, Joe's future with Michael was shaky. It served him well that Michael had the other Jacksons as an anchor. On his own, Michael would become too unpredictable, especially since he had just been presented with a double-platinum award for *Thriller* at a press conference held at CBS's West Coast offices. Michael was starting to realize just how powerful he was.

In March 1983, Michael hit number one again with "Billie Jean." It would stay in the number one position for seven weeks. "When his people approached us about doing the video for 'Billie Jean,' they didn't have any ideas at all," recalled Simon Fields, who produced the "Billie Jean" video for his Limelight Productions. He said that the concept came from the video's director, Steve Barron. "Basically, Michael was just following our direction," Fields recalled. "But the guy is a genius, so you can count on him to do wonderful things."

"Billie Jean," the first video from the *Thriller* album—and Michael's first major music clip—is ultimately too arty for its own good.

In the video, the viewer is intrigued watching Michael Jackson play high-tech hide-and-seek with a stalking, probing photographer—the only other major character—especially since the concept clearly suggests Michael's paranoia about the press. But "Billie Jean" the song—about a girl who haunts Michael, insisting that he is the father of her son—boasts too strong and visual a storyline to be overlooked. It seems a waste that Michael and company did not attempt to follow the song's lyrical content but chose rather to work with a series of abstract shots that look good on their own but don't always connect as a whole. In the end, the video is largely a series of odd scenes strung together.

Michael Jackson's biggest advance with this video—considering that it is such a letdown—was in showing viewers a new side of himself. (Indeed, the element of surprise seems to underlie many of Michael's successes. There is something to be said for his practice of cloaking all of his projects in secrecy until their formal presentation.) Here Michael was cool, mysterious, and evasive. The most compelling moment in "Billie Jean" comes, as usual with Jackson, when he dances. With each step he takes, the sidewalk underneath his feet lights up like, as Michael would say, "magic." Aside from his trademark spin, Michael doesn't do a lot; nevertheless, the action of mostly poses and gestures is still pure passion.

Suzanne dePasse was an old friend of Michael Jackson's and instrumental in his early Motown career. In March 1983, she attempted to mount an NBC special that would celebrate Motown's twenty-fifth anniversary, "Motown 25—Yesterday, Today, and Forever." DePasse was now the president of Motown Productions and had established herself as Berry Gordy's respected right-hand woman. DePasse and Gordy expected all former Motown stars—most of whom had left the company acrimoniously—to reunite for this one night. It was time to pay tribute to fifty-four-year-old Berry Gordy, the man who started it all, who gave so many young but talented upstarts a chance at stardom.

All the brothers agreed that it would be an excellent idea to have a reunion for "Motown 25"—all, that is, except Michael.

Michael did not want to appear on television. He enjoyed making music videos because he could control the product. Every aspect of his performance could be perfected—either by multiple takes or in the editing process. Performing "live" for a studio audience on a show taped for television broadcast was a risky proposition for Michael. He would not have as much control as he felt he needed to duplicate the magic of his work on video.

Also, working with the brothers again for a national, prime-time audience wasn't as appealing to Michael as it was for the rest of the family. For years he had depended on his family for love and professional status. But recently he had begun breaking away—emotionally, by distancing himself from them, and professionally, by outscaling his brothers' success with his own as a solo star. He never actually made an announcement that he was leaving the group, but he no longer wanted to be perceived as one of The Jackson 5.

Beyond that, Michael still had ambivalent feelings about Berry Gordy. He hadn't forgotten the meeting they had had back in 1975 at Berry's home. Berry had promised that he would do nothing to hurt Michael's family. But soon after, he pulled Michael's favorite brother, Jermaine, out of the group. It was a bit more complicated than that, but that's the way Michael chose to remember it. He felt that Berry had betrayed him. He also felt that Motown had exploited the young Jacksons by not paying fair royalties on their hits and worse, by preventing them from using the name "Jackson 5" at CBS. So Michael still had unfinished business with Berry Gordy, and he was not eager to participate in a tribute to him.

Michael's father, Joe, thought the idea of a reunion was a good one. He no longer harbored any animosity for Berry Gordy: he didn't care about him one way or the other. Not only did Joe relish the idea of a reunion appearance, he immediately began thinking of ways he could parlay this broadcast into a reunion tour, an idea that would make Michael shudder. However, Michael Jackson is no pushover, despite popular opinion about him. He disregarded Joe's opinion and discussed the matter with his other managers, Ron Weisner and Freddy DeMann, and decided that he wasn't going to appear.

One night soon after, Michael Jackson was editing a special mix of "Billie Jean" in a Motown recording studio he had rented for the session. Berry ambushed him there. At first, Michael was completely flabbergasted but quickly regained his composure.

Sitting at the control board, Berry asked Michael very directly why he would not appear on the program. Michael explained how much he disliked performing on television. However, he did not offer the reservations he had regarding his brothers or even Berry. Finally, Berry began badgering him by recalling "old times" and "how big I made The Jackson 5" until Michael decided that perhaps he would appease Berry, provided he got something out of the deal for himself. In other words, if he was going to be exploited by Motown once again—this time for television ratings—he should benefit as well.

"Listen, if I do this thing, I want to have a solo spot," he warned Berry.

"Hey, man, that's cool," Berry said eagerly. "I *want* you to have one too."

Naturally, Berry assumed that Michael was talking about singing one of his Motown solo recordings, such as "Got to Be There" or "Ben." Berry began rattling off a list of the songs. He even mentioned "Never Can Say Good-bye," which, of course, was not a solo recording. To Berry—who was never much for Motown history—they were all the same.

Michael shook his head. "I want to do 'Billie Jean,' " he said very firmly.

Berry started chewing on his tongue, as he always does when he's deep in thought. He gently tried to explain that the special was a celebration of Motown and that since Michael now recorded for CBS, "Billie Jean" would be out of place.

Michael told Berry that if he couldn't do "Billie Jean," he would not appear on the show. He wasn't being petulant or acting spoiled, he was simply trying to negotiate a fair deal: Motown's former wunderkind was going up against Motown's legendary boss.

"I don't know about 'Billie Jean,' " Berry said, stalling. "It doesn't seem right to me."

"Well, then, Berry, I'm sorry. . ."

There was a moment of silence. They stared each other down.

"Okay," Berry agreed. "It's 'Billie Jean.' "

"Oh, and I want to have final edit on the videotape of the song before it's broadcast," Michael added, as an afterthought.

No other artist had made this request; most would not have bothered since it was a highly unusual one and Berry was loath to grant it. Motown always liked to have full control over everything. Michael was demanding final say on how he would look on the broadcast. He made it clear that he would not appear unless his demand was met.

"Okay," Berry concluded with a firm handshake. "And you'll do The Jackson 5 reunion thing, right? Jermaine's lookin' forward to it."

Michael rolled his eyes and sighed. "Yeah, why not?"

The two smiled at one another as they rose from their chairs. Michael embraced Berry and whispered something in his ear. Berry left the studio beaming.

James McField, The Jacksons' former bandleader, theorized that Michael Jackson had a specific purpose in singing "Billie Jean," other than the obvious one of promoting the record. "He wanted to prove that, as good as the old Motown hits were, he had been able to come up with songs even better after leaving the company.

He was always stressing that in The Jacksons concert they be sure to sing some of the old songs to show the contrast to the new material. Once I overheard a meeting the guys were having when they were discussing the lineup of the show. 'I know exactly what I'm doing,' Michael said. 'I want people to see the growth. I want people to see that we went on to bigger things after Motown. The point is not just to continue to play, but to continue to grow.'

"Also, he always had it on his mind to prove to Motown that the group had not made a mistake by leaving the company, even years later when it was obvious to everyone that they hadn't. Any opportunity Michael could seize to make that point, he would. I'm sure that's why he insisted on doing 'Billie Jean' on an all-Motown show. He was rubbing his success in everyone's faces at Motown, and they had no choice but to let him do it if they wanted him on the show."

Once Michael had made up his mind that he would appear on the program, he was determined to make it a worthwhile performance. He rehearsed with his brothers at the Encino home, choreographing their routines, videotaping the rehearsals so that he could make changes, and basically, taking over the group. No one seemed to mind, however. They were all just glad to have the opportunity to work together again.

The show was scheduled to be taped on March 25, 1983. Michael recalled that he asked someone at Weisner and DeMann's office to locate a black fedora for him. He had a plan for his performance of "Billie Jean." He had a black sequined jacket that he decided to wear as well. Also, he would wear the glove.

Michael's cotton glove with twelve hundred hand-sewn rhinestones would become a trademark after "Motown 25." There has been much speculation over the glove's "hidden meaning," but its designer, Bill Whitten, says that it was merely a stage prop when he designed it for Michael back in 1979. "Michael uses it as a mime uses white gloves," he explained. "We never were thinking of fashion when we talked about using it. The glove also expresses Michael's love for glitter."

The night before the taping, in the kitchen of the Encino home, Michael created the choreography to "Billie Jean" all alone.

The day of the taping, Michael kept to himself at the Pasadena Civic Center. As the group rehearsed its medley of hits, the fellows kept bumping into each other. Nerves were frayed. "Jermaine, you don't know these steps," Jackie chastised his brother. "How come you don't know the choreography, man?"

"I'll get it. I'll get it," Jermaine said.

"When?" Jackie wanted to know. "Tomorrow when it's too late?"

"Aw, leave him alone, man," Tito said in Jermaine's defense.

The brothers did the routine again, and this time it was even worse. Michael shook his head and smiled to himself. Any observer would have had to wonder how this sloppy rehearsal would ever translate into a crowd-pleasing performance.

Later, Marlon asked what the hat was for, but Michael wouldn't say. He wanted his performance to be a complete surprise.

By the time The Jacksons were set to take the stage at the Civic Center, the audience had already seen Marvin Gaye, Smokey Robinson, and Mary Wells perform. The Jackson 5 reunion was scheduled about a third into the program. There was a videotape of the group's 1968 Motown audition, then a series of clips of past performances before—finally—The Jackson 5 appeared onstage, singing, strumming, moving to "I Want You Back." Jermaine was back, smiling broadly and standing right next to Michael, in his old position.

The audience erupted in applause at the sight of the reunited brothers. By the time the Jacksons swung into "The Love You Save," and Randy trotted on stage to join them, the crowd—men in tuxedos, women in evening gowns—were standing and grooving to that music like a bunch of teenyboppers. Who could sit still for music like *that*?

During "I'll Be There," when Michael and Jermaine shared the spotlight and microphone, the two seemed to become choked up. Jermaine's eyes began to well with tears. Michael draped his arm over his brother's shoulder and they looked at one another as if they were the only two people in the auditorium. All of the hostility and animosity between the brothers—not just Michael and Jermaine, but all of the brothers—suspended itself for this emotion-packed moment. Michael smiled broadly. He was not faking *that* smile.

How The Jacksons managed to turn such a messy rehearsal into a real show is still a mystery to most people who witnessed the scene. But somehow, magically, it all came together.

After hugs all around, the other Jacksons left the stage to the one Jackson who really counted to most of the people in this audience: Michael. The spotlight found him. It caught the glint of his black sequined jacket with cuffs that matched the silver sequined shirt, the white glitter socks that peeped from beneath the just-above-the-ankle black trousers, the shiny black penny loafers. And of course, there was the single left-handed white glove with its hand-sewn rhinestones.*

Michael thanked the audience. He hesitated, speaking haltingly. "I have to say those were the good old days. I love those songs," he said of the medley. "Those were magic moments with all my brothers—including Jermaine." Michael began pacing the stage, his hand in his pocket, talking as though he were just voicing some thoughts that happened to pop into his head, as though he were alone, as though the audience was not there. Actually, he was walking to the side of the stage so that a friend in the shadows could sneak the fedora into his hand, just as the two had planned. "But, uh, you know," he continued, "those were the good songs. I like those songs a lot. But especially, I like"—he was center stage by this time, facing the audience—"the *new* songs." The audience knew what was coming. They began calling out for "Billie Jean."

As the funk-infused guitar riff of "Billie Jean" began, Michael went into his routine. He was going to be lip-synching—that was obvious from the first notes—but no one watching cared. Michael jammed the hat on his head as he began to rhythmically pump his pelvis to the opening beat of the song. When he took the hat off and hurled it aside with a graceful flourish, the audience went wild. Michael's brothers stood in the wings, their mouths wide open. His parents and sisters sat in the audience, spellbound. "He just stole the show," Joe exclaimed to his wife. "He just stole the show."

No one had ever seen *this* Michael Jackson before; no one in the auditorium, nor the millions of viewers who would see the show on television several weeks later. Michael had last performed in public after the group's *Triumph* album and tour, when he was still a fairly ordinary-looking young man sporting an Afro. Tonight the performer onstage was startling to look at. Lean and agile, with a reconstructed nose and chemically curled hair, Michael was downright pretty. Though he's always been a cocksure performer, tonight Michael had vengeance in his eyes and an attitude in his stride.

If the early days saw Michael Jackson as an eager student at the feet of great rhythm-and-blues stars, "Motown 25" gave the world a lesson in the art of just being Michael Jackson. This student had

*Michael gave the sequined jacket he wore on the "Motown 25" special to his friend Sammy Davis, Jr. In October 1988, he donated the fedora and glove to the Motown museum in Detroit, where they can be seen in a locked display case. Michael also donated $125,000 to the museum, as well as an outfit he wore when he was thirteen and performed with The Jackson 5.

grown up and graduated with flying colors, and now it was his turn to show just what he had learned in class.

The audience cheered as Michael slid across the floor backwards, executing his classic moonwalk. He spun. He was up on his toes. He posed. For this performance, he let loose the entire arsenal of Michael Jackson dance moves and postures, and the audience applauded every step.

Michael hadn't invented any of this; the poses were modified versions of "locking," a street dance from the 1970s. The moonwalk was a move "Soul Train" dancers had discarded almost three years earlier. (It seems more than coincidence that the camelwalk took Michael through the early 1970s and the moonwalk took him through the 1980s). Sammy Davis, Jr., James Brown, and Jackie Wilson all used to execute that same spin, and going up on the toes is a touch Michael saw Fred Astaire use in his classic films of the 1930s. To combine all of those moves, from all of those eras—to take different styles and make them his own—is Michael Jackson's genius as a dancer and creator.

The auditorium went wild. "I don't think there will be anything to rival the discovery, the artistry, the expression . . . the entire audience was caught in a spell," Suzanne dePasse recalled.

Added Steve Ivory, editor of *Black Beat* magazine, who was present in the audience at the Pasadena Civic Center, "I don't think I've ever seen anything like that before. I was stunned. Michael truly became a legend that night. Watching the performance on videotape pales in comparison to the exhilaration I, and everyone else who was there, felt at seeing Michael's act in person. I remember that people were standing on their chairs, cheering, before he had even finished his number."

When the performance was over, Michael raised his arm in response to a standing ovation that rocked the hall. He would remember later that he was disappointed in his performance. He had planned to execute a spin and stop on his toes, suspended. The spin worked, but he didn't stay on his toes as long as he had planned to when he rehearsed in the privacy of his kitchen. Always the perfectionist, he wished he could do it over again. And if this had been a video—not television—he could have. "It wasn't such a hot performance," he would remember thinking to himself, despite the crowd's approval.

Once he came backstage, all of Michael's brothers surrounded and embraced him. Jermaine kissed him on the cheek. Then Jackie, then the others. It was an unusual display; the brothers, following Joe's example, usually were not very affectionate or effusive with one another. For a moment, Michael believed that they were truly proud of him. He had shown them what he was capable of, and they respected him for it. Maybe it really was a good performance, after all.

But then the moment was shattered. The brothers began talking about what Michael's glory would mean for *them*—the possibility of taking the group back out on the road and making more money than ever before. "The Jackson 5 are back," Jackie kept repeating, and the others agreed enthusiastically. "This is gonna be great."

Michael didn't want any part of that idea. He turned and began walking away from them. "Hey, man, we're family," one of his brothers reminded him. Michael, a smirk on his face, just shook his head and kept walking.

As Michael continued down the hall, a young boy in a tuxedo followed him. "Hey, Michael," the youngster called out. "Wait up."

Michael stopped.

"Man, who ever taught you to dance like that?" The kid looked up at his idol with adoring eyes.

"Practice, I guess," Michael said.

"You were amazing," the fan told him.

"Thanks, I needed that," Michael responded.

The youngster turned and walked away.

Michael nodded to himself, and as he walked down the hall alone, he began to smile. *Now* he felt good.

If Michael Jackson didn't immediately realize what an effect his performance had on everyone—as he writes in his autobiography, *Moonwalk*—he must have become suspicious when a crew of bodyguards escorted him into the lavish private party Motown hosted in a shopping mall across from the auditorium after the taping. Casually dressed in worn jeans and one of his military jackets, Michael didn't look like a man who had just given the performance of a lifetime. However, the minute he walked through the door, the place rose. These were fellow performers, record executives, and others who had seen all show business had to offer, yet they swarmed all over Michael like flies on honey. The Four Tops tripped over themselves to get to Michael. The Temptations shoved them out of the way. Soon it became clear that twenty-four-year-old Michael's presence would upstage the whole party if he stayed. The man of the hour, seemingly bewildered by the mob scene, paid his respects to a couple of veteran Motown employees before being ushered to his limousine only minutes after he arrived.

This was an exciting time. On April 30, 1983, "Beat It" hit

number one. Two weeks later, on May 16, the "Motown 25" special aired on NBC. That month, "Wanna Be Startin' Somethin' " would be released and go to the Top Five within a month.

After the broadcast of "Motown 25," the public's perception of Michael Jackson changed dramatically. Most people had simply forgotten how dynamic he was in live performance, and more people—an estimated 50 million—watched "Motown 25" than had ever watched any musical special in the history of network television.

At the Jacksons' house on Hayvenhurst, the atmosphere was holidaylike, with people telephoning from across the country raving about Michael's performance. The house swarmed with people, and the family kept running the videotape of Michael's performance over and over again. "You gotta see this one more time," Joe, the proud father, told everyone who came by. "I've never seen anything like it."

Little did Joe know that VCRs all over the country were in overdrive as well. At "Motown 25," Michael Jackson successfully did two things: he reconfirmed for lifelong fans that yes, he is the amazing talent they had always revered. And through the might of television, he reached millions of viewers who had never experienced what his fans like to call "the magic." Only on two other occasions—the first national television appearances of Elvis Presley and The Beatles (both on "The Ed Sullivan Show")—has television so handily delivered pop music superstardom. Elvis and The Beatles aside, without exaggeration, Michael Jackson's was quite possibly the single most captivating pop music performance in television history.

"Michael is what I consider a dancer in his soul," observed Michael Peters, who choreographed videos such as "Beat It" and "Thriller." "He has never studied. He's not a professionally trained dancer. He never took dance classes, and you wouldn't hire him to be a part of the core of a dance company. But he has the sensibilities of a dancer. He just dances. I can put him in the middle of thirty trained dancers—who make their living at that and have studied for twenty years—and he can do it."

Even Fred Astaire was impressed. The day after the special aired, he telephoned Hermes Pan, his Beverly Hills neighbor, the longtime choreographer and Oscar winner who taught Astaire and Ginger Rogers their most memorable dance steps. "You've got to come over right away," he told Pan. "I want you to see something."

When Pan arrived, Astaire put in a videotape of the perfor-

mance. "Just wait till you see this." Then the two old pros watched
in awe as Michael Jackson strutted his stuff.

Astaire was never one to praise other male dancers lightly. "Isn't
he great?" he enthused after the performance.

"We agreed that we must call Michael immediately," Hermes
Pan recalled. "Somehow, Fred tracked him down. He told him that
he was one hell of a dancer. A great mover. He said, 'You really
put them on their asses last night. You're an angry dancer. I'm the
same way.' I got on the line to say hello, and this whisper of a voice
answered me. I was surprised, actually, that a person who dances
with such anger would have such a soft voice. I told him how much
I enjoyed his work, and he was very gracious, very excited to hear
from us. For a moment, I believed he thought it was a practical
joke. I liked him because he was so obviously unaffected by show
business, and also star struck. He really could not believe that the
great Fred Astaire had called him."

Michael would say later that Astaire's compliment meant more
to him than any he had ever received because it came from someone
he greatly respected. Michael's voice teacher, Seth Riggs, remembered, "Michael was eating his breakfast when Astaire called, and
he got so excited he actually got sick and couldn't finish his meal."
Later, Michael and Fred would become friends. Fred invited him
to his home so that Michael could show him and Hermes how to
moonwalk.

Soon after that, Gene Kelly visited Michael in Encino to talk
shop. "He knows when to stop and then flash out like a bolt of
lightning," Kelly would say of Michael's ability. Michael had joined
a new brotherhood of dance. "He's clean, neat, fast, with a sen-
suality that comes through," Bob Fosse would say of Michael after
"Motown 25" was broadcast. "It's never the steps that are important. It's the style."

The moonwalk step was taught to Michael by one of the former
dancers on the television program "Soul Train." However, Michael has never publicly credited his teacher.

The dance step was almost three years old by the time of the
Motown anniversary special. When the Jackson brothers saw the
routine for the first time in 1981 while watching "Soul Train,"
Michael in particular was awed by it. Through his manager at that
time, Ron Weisner, Michael was put in touch with sixteen-year-old
Geron Candidate, who goes by the stage name of "Casper." Weisner introduced Casper to Michael Jackson.

"I saw something you guys did on 'Soul Train,' " Michael told

Casper, "where it looks like you're going backward and forward at the same time."

"It's called the backslide," Casper explained.

"That's amazing!" Michael exclaimed. "Well, look, can you teach me to do that?"

Casper was stunned. He could barely answer yes. The next day Casper and his dance partner, Cooley Jackson, met Michael at a rehearsal studio in Los Angeles. To the music of "Pop-Along Kid," Cooley proceeded to demonstrate a version of the backslide that was more like pushing in place rather than walking backwards. It wasn't what Michael wanted. Then Casper demonstrated the slide where it appears the dancer is walking backward and forward at the same time. Michael leaped into the air. "Wow. That's it. That's the one I want to learn."

Casper smiled and sat down. Michael then grabbed Casper's shoes and tried to look at their soles. "What do you have on the bottom of your shoes?" Michael wanted to know. "You got wheels under there or something? Is that how you do that step?"

Casper explained that there were no special shoes or wheels involved. It was just a dance step. With the help of a chair, Casper began to teach it to Michael. Michael would grab on to the back of the chair and do the step over and over in place, so that he could become accustomed to the actual foot movement.

"Michael learned the basic movement within an hour," Casper remembered. "He wasn't comfortable with it, but he more or less had it down."

A couple of days later, Casper had another session with Michael. "He still wasn't at ease with it," Casper recalled. "Whereas I made it look so natural, like I was walking on air, he was stiff, and it bugged him. 'I can't do this in front of people unless I can do it right,' he kept saying."

After those rehearsals, Michael went out on the road with his brothers. "I went to see the show in Los Angeles, and he didn't do the step," Casper said. "I was sort of surprised. So I went backstage and asked him about it. He said he just didn't feel ready yet. He didn't feel he knew it."

Casper was home watching "Motown 25," like millions of others, when he saw Michael do the step for the first time in front of an audience. "I couldn't believe it," he remembered. "My heart started pounding. I thought to myself, 'Wow, he did it. After all of these years. And I taught it to him.' It's not the moonwalk though," he explained. "It's the backslide. The moonwalk is when you do the step in a complete circle. But somehow, that step Michael did became known as the moonwalk.''

The moonwalk became Michael Jackson's signature dance step—his ''Motown 25'' performance was nominated for an Emmy, and the program itself won one—and for teaching it to him, Casper had been paid one thousand dollars. ''That's how much I asked for. I was sixteen. To me, that was good money,'' he said, laughing. ''I would have done it for free, to tell you the truth. How was I supposed to know it would become Michael Jackson's trademark? Sometimes I feel bad about the fact that I've never been given credit for teaching Michael that step. It would be nice to hear him acknowledge it. But, hey, that's show biz, you know? Michael Jackson is a super nice guy, probably the nicest guy I've ever worked with.''

Casper, who went on to work with Michael on the ''Beat It,'' ''Bad,'' and ''Smooth Criminal'' videos, said that he once did an interview with *Right On!* magazine about his work with Michael. After the story was published, he said, Joe Jackson called the magazine's editor, Cynthia Horner. He gave her a pretty hard time, really went off on her, saying, ''Nobody has to teach my son *anything*,'' Casper said.

Michael demonstrated more deft dancing in his excellent ''Beat It'' video. While he had begun with only a vague concept for the ''Billie Jean'' clip, Michael knew precisely what he wanted for ''Beat It.'' Veteran commercial director Bob Giraldi, Broadway choreographer Michael Peters, and Jackson collaborated on what would be one of the most dynamic—and expensive—videos to date. The choreographed ensemble dancing in ''Beat It'' was often imitated—and still is—in videos by other artists.

Perhaps of all the numbers Michael Jackson had presented to his fans during his career, the ''Beat It'' video marked the biggest departure. As a song, the track was unadulterated rock and roll, something Jackson's core fans—especially the majority of his black ones—initially rejected. Beyond that, the video depicted a Jackson never before seen: Michael as urban dweller, a kid living on the wrong side of the tracks—a *human* Michael.

Some of Michael's public, particularly those living in urban neighborhoods, found the storyline patronizing. In ''Beat It,'' which Michael has said was written with youngsters in mind, he is the good guy who ultimately stops two powerful gangs from warring with each other. Those viewers unable to separate Jackson the musical enigma from Jackson the actor missed the point when they asked angrily, "What does Michael Jackson know about gangs?" and "Does he really think dancing through the problems we're having down here—muggings, killings, drug addiction—is the answer to our woes?" They didn't understand.

"The point is no one has to be the tough guy," Michael would explain. "You can walk away from a fight and still be a man. You don't have to die to prove you're a man."

Visually, Michael's video was convincing enough. Shot on location on the mean streets of Los Angeles, the video looked dark and grimy. In a quest for authenticity, one hundred members of two real-life rival Los Angeles street gangs were hired as extras and atmosphere people. (They were each fed and paid one hundred dollars for two nights' work.)

"The gangs were sort of on the periphery of the location," choreographer Michael Peters told *Right On!* magazine, "so Michael really didn't have to deal with them. But he was a little nervous, as we all were at the beginning. But he was quite wonderful with them. I think the turning point was when the gangs saw us dance. They had, I think, a different respect after that. Michael signed autographs and took pictures with them."

Acting without speaking was easy for Michael to do: he'd done it onstage, singing, all his life. But ensemble dancing was uncharted terrain. Fans had never seen Michael in a Broadway-style setting, and some of them probably wondered why a hoofer like Jackson needed someone to teach *him* steps, but choreographer Michael Peters succeeded in creating a dazzling, funked-up, *Chorus Line*-like dance effect. The choreography looked so easy, it seemed that anyone could do it. But just try. "Looks can be deceiving, especially when it comes to dance," Michael would explain with a grin. Overall, the clip is rock theater–music video production at its best. Its style and artistry actually succeeded in making the music more interesting, which is the ultimate goal of music videos in the first place.

The sales of *Thriller* began to "go through the roof"—to use Michael's words—after his performance on "Motown 25" and the "Beat It" video. The "Beat It" single would be released while "Billie Jean" was still on its way up the charts. Frank Dileo, who was the promotion director for Epic and responsible for this coup, has said that that was the turning point, getting two singles in the Top Ten at the same time. Michael Jackson was now most certainly what he had always intended to be. Number one.

* * *

Most of the artists who attended the Motown anniversary special felt a new sense of brotherhood and camaraderie with the label. Berry Gordy re-signed the Four Tops to the company and teamed them with The Temptations on vinyl, just as they had been teamed on stage that evening in Pasadena. Other artists began to negotiate with Berry again. Holland-Dozier-Holland were back. Even Diana Ross felt a new kinship with Berry; the two were socializing once more. It was as if everyone was trying to recapture the glory days. Everyone, that is, except Jermaine Jackson.

Between the time the show was taped in March and broadcast in May, Jermaine had been meeting with his other brothers and even with Joe, but not with Michael. They were discussing the possibility of Jermaine's leaving Motown, reuniting with his brothers, and going back out on the road again. Joe thought the idea was terrific. "Michael's success can only help us," Tito Jackson said. "He's way up there above us, and maybe he can throw down a rope and let us climb it." A tour would relieve Marlon of some financial pressure. Now that they were able to project a more optimistic future, he and wife Carol had reconciled, much to the family's relief. "They really do belong together," Michael told an associate. "They're one of the only real love stories in the family."

The brothers now prepared a new Jacksons album for CBS called *Victory*, a package of nine or ten songs chosen from seventeen that had been recorded. Michael did not want to be involved in the project. He would write and sing only two tracks and participate in writing a third. As they recorded the album, the brothers became excited at the prospect of touring to promote it once it was released.

But this talk of a reunion tour was premature, since no one had considered Michael's reaction. It was assumed he would go along with the plan; after all, he always had in the past. "The thing is, we've *always* worked really hard," Marlon observed at this time. "As far back as I can remember, since the time Michael and I were six and seven, we were going to school, doing homework, attending rehearsals, and then on weekends we'd play nightclubs, stayin' up till four in the morning, then get up and go to school come Monday. It was real, real hard for us. . . . And I don't think you can outgrow your brothers and sisters, and Michael feels the same way. We're blood. You just don't sever those ties."

By May 1983, Jermaine was so excited about the prospect of the tour—and knowing it would never happen as long as he was tied to Motown—he telephoned Berry and asked for a release from his recording contract.

Jermaine's solo career had never gotten off the ground at Motown. All of those threats and promises—all of the family angst—and for what? One Top Ten record—"Let's Get Serious," which sold 722,737 copies—and not until 1981, some six years after the split from his brothers. This was not an auspicious solo career by any stretch of the imagination. Being Berry Gordy's son-in-law didn't mean much, after all, where Jermaine's career was concerned. "I could have told him *that*," Marvin Gaye would say. Jermaine was disillusioned by the poor record sales, the lack of promotion and interest. He wanted out.

"Sometimes I have this dream that I'm onstage with my brothers," he said. "And I'm countin' off the songs like I always used to do when we performed together. We're all onstage and the crowd is goin' crazy. All of a sudden I wake up. And it's really a letdown. We all started here at Motown, and if anybody left anybody, I feel *they* left *me* at Motown. If we were to perform together again, there'd be no end to the things we could do, the excitement we'd create."

Berry realized that there was nothing more Jermaine could do at Motown. This association simply had not worked. Gordy gave him his release, an anticlimactic ending to his days at Motown considering what his leaving the group to stay with the label had done to his relationship with his family.*

June 1983. It would not be a good month.

Michael Jackson and his brothers had still not renegotiated their contract with their father, nor had they decided to re-sign with comanagers Ron Weisner and Freddy DeMann. The brothers were ambivalent about re-signing, but they were willing. Michael, however, was disenchanted with his father, and also with Weisner and DeMann. He wasn't quick to make a decision. Everyone involved had become worried. Michael's decision involved a lot of power and money. If he signed—not only with Joe, but with Ron and Freddy—everyone else in the family would follow suit. If he didn't, no one else would either.

Joe hadn't been doing much lately, especially since John Branca entered the picture. Michael trusted John implicitly and tried to make certain he—not Joe—was involved in every decision. Joe did not like John Branca and only spoke to him if he couldn't speak to Michael directly. Ron Weisner and Freddy DeMann were handling whatever Branca did not involve himself in, so Branca was as much a manager as he was an attorney.

*Jermaine Jackson would sign a recording contract with Arista Records in August 1983.

Michael had complained incessantly to Branca during the last two years that Weisner and DeMann were not creative people. "I don't even know why they're here," he said. "They don't know what they're doing." But whenever Branca would discuss Michael's feelings with Weisner and DeMann, they didn't know what he was talking about. They both felt that Michael was pleased with their work since he had never told them otherwise.

"You remember what they wanted me to do with the 'Beat It' video," Michael reminded John Branca. Weisner and DeMann had a concept for the "Beat It" video that would have had Michael dressed as a Robin Hood character in England. "They wanted me to have bows and arrows and stuff," Michael complained. "Now, come on, Branca. That's stupid."

At the same time, Joe was nervous because his position with Michael seemed shakier than ever, so he apparently decided to make up Michael's mind for him where Weisner and DeMann were concerned.

"It's over," Joe told *Billboard* magazine of Weisner and DeMann. "My boys are not re-signing with them. There are a lot of leeches trying to break up the group," he observed, possibly referring to Weisner and DeMann's continued emphasis on Michael's solo career. "A lot of people are whispering in Michael's ear. But we know who they are. They're only in it for the money. And just in case Michael contemplated not signing with his father, Joe told the reporter, "I was there before it started, and I'll be there when it ends."

The brothers themselves were really not happy with Weisner and DeMann because of all of the attention the two lavished upon Michael. They also wanted to leave Joe. However, they were waiting for Michael—not Joe—to make an announcement.

Michael, for his part, was furious with his father for taking matters into his own hands, and even more outraged that Joe would talk to a reporter about it. It was as if Joe wanted the world to know what was happening so that Michael would be intimidated and refrain from making a move against his father. But the more Joe talked, the more he estranged his son.

"There was a time when I felt I needed white help in dealing with the corporate structure at CBS," Joe explained. "And I thought Weisner-DeMann would be able to help. But they never gave me the respect you expect from a business partner."

For their part, Weisner and DeMann said to the press that, yes, they did have problems with Joe, "but we have no problems with Michael or the Jacksons," and that Joe had not been involved in any major business decisions in recent years. "True, we don't have a good relationship with him," Freddy DeMann admitted, "but I don't think he enjoys a good relationship with anyone whose skin is not black."

"People have called me a racist. I am not a racist," Joe insisted. "If I were a racist, I would have hired a lot of white people to work for me. I'm not a racist, I'm an American. I gave my children one hundred percent of my know-how, knowledge, and time trying to develop them to be what they are today, and it has paid off and is still paying off."

Finally, Michael realized that too much was being said to the press. He decided to fire Weisner and DeMann. "They said *Thriller* would only go two million and it's way over that," Michael reasoned. "So who needs these guys, anyway. They told me not to do 'Motown 25.' And look what kind of bad advice that was."

It was said that John Branca had reminded Michael that he didn't want to do the Motown special in the first place, but Michael had argued that this was not the point. The point was that Weisner and DeMann had *agreed* with him when they *should* have tried to convince him otherwise.

"Send them their papers," he told Branca. "They're finished."

Weisner and DeMann got their walking papers from Michael on June 22. Weisner had talked to Michael earlier that morning and Michael had acted as though no problem existed. When he received the letter of dismissal from John Branca in the afternoon, Weisner was astonished. He could not reach Michael to discuss the matter. It wasn't the bravest way to handle the problem, but for Michael it proved the easiest. Once someone falls from Michael Jackson's graces, that person disappears from his thoughts—as though he or she never existed, like Gina Sprague, the woman who accused Michael's mother of beating her up.

As for his father, Michael made a public statement to distance himself from Joe's sentiments. "I don't know what would make him say something like that," Michael told a reporter, referring to Joe's comments about "white help." "To hear him talk like that turns my stomach. I don't know where he gets that from. I happen to be color-blind. I don't hire color. I hire competence. The individual can be of any race or creed as long as I get the best [representation.] Racism is not my motto."

At this time, the number one artist in the world had no manager and no press agent. After he fired Weisner and DeMann, Michael's team consisted of his attorney and chief advisor, John Branca; his security man, Bill Bray; his accountant, Marshall Gelfand; and a secretary.

When "Beat It" and "Billie Jean" were both in the Top Ten, Quincy Jones asked for a three-way-conference telephone call among himself, Michael, and John Branca.

"It's unbelievable what's happening here, Smelly," Quincy told Michael. "But you need a manager, man. How could you fire Weisner and DeMann? What are you going to do now?"

"Quincy, Branca can handle it. Branca is brilliant, I'm not nervous, why are you?" Michael asked him. Then he cut the conversation short and hung up.

Later, Quincy telephoned John Branca.

"John, I'm worried, man. This is like a plane with no pilot," he told Branca. "This kid's career is in trouble."

"What? He's got two records in the Top Ten and his career is in trouble?" John Branca asked with a laugh. "Quincy, don't worry about it. It's going to be fine."

"But . . ." Quincy was totally perplexed. He didn't understand how Michael Jackson was going to have a flourishing career without managerial guidance. If the sales of *Thriller* slowed down because there was no manager calling the shots, it would affect everybody's bank account, including Quincy's. But at this time Michael was the Golden Child; the public was pulling for him, and the music spoke for itself.

"Michael knows exactly what he's doing," Branca told Jones. "This kid is a fucking genius. And we got CBS and Yetnikoff covering the loose ends. All we have to do is follow Michael's instructions."

"But—" Quincy began again.

Branca cut him off. "This is our chance, man, and I'm just going to go out there and kick ass for this kid because he's got it, Quincy. I love this kid and I just want to do his bidding."

Quincy wasn't convinced, but that didn't matter. John Branca knew what he was talking about.

# Chapter

## ❧ 20 ❧

I T'S NOT EASY firing your father,'' Michael Jackson would have to admit.

It was June 1983. As angry as he was with Joe, taking that next step—actually ending his professional relationship with him—still proved difficult for Michael to do. Michael, who would turn twenty-five in two months, was a loyalist at heart, struggling with the part of himself that wanted to be true to his father. Just as he had felt it important to give Berry Gordy a chance to redeem himself before the group took those first steps away from Motown, now he hoped his father would do something to salvage whatever respect Michael still had for him. However, Joe would disappoint Michael many times over, just as Berry had. Michael would not forget the way Berry and Joe let him down, and in years to come, he would no longer demonstrate the same kind of loyalty.

By this time, June 1983, it had been ten months since Katherine filed for divorce, and she was still trying to obtain from Joe and his attorney, Arnold D. Kassoy, a complete list of community property. Finally her lawyer, George Goffin, convinced her that Joe had purposely tried to delay the proceedings and frustrate her into dropping the whole matter. It's not known, of course, that this was the case. Michael told one friend, ''Joe will never let her go. He'll do everything he can to keep her.''

Katherine had her attorney obtain a court order demanding that Joe make available for her inspection life insurance policies, bank statements, canceled checks, check stubs, check vouchers, and check register books, as well as savings accounts records, stock certificates, promissory notes, and other financial ledgers relating to the Jacksons' personal and professional businesses, including his interest in an African mining venture. She also demanded to see all documents relating to the trust fund her husband had set up for Joh' Vonnie Jackson.

Joe finally gave Katherine some of the requested material, but he was rather evasive about most of their holdings and had "no present recollection" about the subjects of many of the inquiries, including the answers to some simple questions, such as whether he had done business with any stockbrokers in the last thirty years or whether he had submitted a financial statement to a bank in the last decade.

Joe did disclose that $83,905.38 was still owed on the Encino home, but stated that his son Michael Jackson was now liable for that balance and also for any second or third trust deeds on the home. Of course, Katherine knew this. Also, Joe admitted that he and his wife now owned outright the Jackson house in Gary (purchased in 1950) with no mortgage loans owed on the property, and that it was worth about $50,000, which, again, Katherine already knew. And Joseph noted that the condominium at 5420 Lindley Avenue in Encino was worth $210,000 and that Michael had paid $175,000 for it in cash on February 21, 1981, and had obtained the balance of $35,000 from community property. But actually, the balance had come from Katherine personally. According to the escrow papers, this property was considered hers and Michael's, not Joe's. Joe did not give her any information she did not already possess, and he seemed to misrepresent some important details. There were hundreds of unanswered questions about their holdings.

Upon further investigation, Joe added as assets: a diamond ring, a Rolex watch, a chain necklace and gold bracelet, a $200,000 investment in the African mining venture, and a few other minor investments and loans and notes receivable totaling about $50,000.

By this time Katherine was said to be so exasperated, she had second thoughts about the divorce, just as she had the first time she tried to separate from Joe in 1973 and became frustrated with the paperwork. Katherine was upset, and Michael was angry at his father for more reasons than he could count.

"He's finished," Michael decided. Once Michael made up his mind to fire someone, he stuck to the decision, no matter who the person was.

"Joseph knew it was coming," said Joe's friend of fifteen years, Larry Anderson. "He knew his time was up."

"There's a little more to that decision than meets the eye," said Michael's first cousin Tim Whitehead. (Whitehead's mother was Katherine's sister, Hattie, and his father is Joe's stepbrother, Vernon.) "Michael was so upset about the way he perceived his father as treating his mother. It hurt him. The whole family knew this. He apparently was saying to Joseph, 'You cannot do this to Katherine and get away with it. She is a wonderful woman and she doesn't deserve this.' He hit him where it really hurts, in the pocketbook. At least that's the way I saw it. Now the money Michael generated for the family wouldn't be spent by Joe on women other than Katherine.''

Michael had John Branca draw up the official documents informing Joe that he would no longer represent Michael. Then Michael left the house the day he knew they would be delivered by messenger. He stayed away from home until Joe had time to get used to the idea.

''He was hurt,'' said Joyce McCrae of Michael, ''and that's why he fired the old man. The womanizing, the dealings on the side, the lack of love, you name it. Whatever makes a kid hurt by a parent's actions. Compound that by the fact that Michael felt Joe was being mean to Katherine. Where Michael is concerned, you don't cross Katherine. All the kids feel that way about her.''

In a rare show of unity, the brothers acted as one on this decision. None of them renewed their contracts with Joe. Joe was furious at first, but then his feelings were hurt and he cried. ''I can't believe they're leaving me,'' he told Katherine. Katherine would recall that even though she was still angry at Joe for his philandering, her heart was breaking for him just the same.

Joe felt he had created the Jacksons and because of that, they ''owed'' him—forever. His credo was ''I was there when it started, and I'll be there when it ends.'' That argument did not sway his sons. He felt personal problems were his own and none of his sons' business. He said they should not allow any of these problems to affect their professional decisions. That reasoning fell on deaf ears.

Still making no headway, Joe apparently decided to divide and conquer. He knew exactly the bait to dangle before five of the six Jackson boys—Jackie, Tito, Marlon, Jermaine, and Randy. He decided that it was finally time to make definite plans for the reunion tour the brothers had been thinking about. Because he was their father and cared only for their welfare, he would ''promote the hell'' out of any tour, which would make his boys very, very rich. Naturally, the brothers were excited by the prospects and began making definite plans. But Michael had enough on his mind and wasn't going to concern himself with any upcoming tour.

''We'll cross that bridge when we come to it,'' Michael said when presented with the plan. If ever there was a bridge over troubled waters, Michael Jackson must have known that this would be it.

In the summer of 1983, everyone who lived at the Hayvenhurst estate—Michael, Janet, LaToya, and their parents, Joe and Katherine—existed in a state of emotional siege. Despite the separation, Joe spent most of his time at the house, even sleeping there, in a bedroom suite down the hall from the one he once shared with Katherine.

"My father's very stern, very strict," LaToya would complain to free-lance writer Todd Gold. "Deep down inside, he's a wonderful guy, but you have to know him. If you don't, you can get the wrong impression. You'd think that he's mean and whatever he says goes, which it does. Sometimes, though, if you really fight it out, you can have your way." She let out an exasperated sigh. "But it's just not worth it."

As soon as Joe would leave, it was a relief to all. Saturdays, he was usually gone. That was the day the house really came alive. LaToya would tell Gold, "We invite lots of kids over and play some movie in the theater, and the popcorn machine's going, the animals are all out, and everyone's dancing to music."

Michael tried to make certain that his own and his father's paths never crossed. When they did, there would usually be a loud argument and Michael would run to his room. Katherine would run upstairs after him. Janet and LaToya would stay in their bedrooms and wait for the storm to pass. The tension affected everyone.

"When it came to the help—especially the black help—the Jacksons treated them worse than a Klan member would," said one former black employee who quit because she felt snubbed by Michael. "You can interpret this any way you want," she said, "but I was there for a number of years, and I can tell you that the black employees were treated like second-class citizens. Janet and LaToya were little spoiled divas. 'Park my car, fix my television, get me some food, feed the birds.' It was always one order after another.

"Michael was really no different," she continued. "He was mad at the guards one day because he felt some of them wore their hair too long and in ponytails. He thought this was distracting in a black man. He had them all cut their hair. Today, of course, _he_ wears a ponytail. If a guest arrived with a friend, and that friend started talking to the help, Michael would get upset. He had to be the center of attention. The help was not to socialize with the guests.

"For Christmas, the guards—who were always treated the

worst—usually got only twenty-five-dollar bonuses. Most of the employees made between ten and fifteen dollars an hour.''

She went on, ''There were some people working there who worked for Michael, and they only answered to Michael. But most of the others—especially the grounds people—were answerable to all of them. If LaToya had a stink and you were a gardener who looked at her the wrong way as she pulled up in her Mercedes, you were finished. If she didn't like your cologne, you were told to change it.

''Joe hated all of the people who worked for Michael and often got into fights with them and tried to fire them, but Michael never allowed his father to dictate orders to the people who were considered Michael's employees. 'I pay this lady and I'll tell her what to do,' Michael would argue. 'Well, when you ain't here, *I* tell her what to do,' and on and on it went. The place was always like a war zone. The llamas and peacocks were probably scared to death. I know I was.''

Steve Howell, Michael's videographer at the time, remembered a particularly upsetting incident involving Joe. ''I was used to going into the house when I needed to for Mike, and one day Joe came up to me and said, 'I don't want to see you around here no more.' I tried to explain to him that Mike had cleared it for me to be there, but he got upset and told me to stay away or, he said, 'I'll make *sure* you stay away.' So I left. On my way out I talked it over with one of the guards. 'You'd better do what he says,' the guard told me. 'You know, he's got an Uzi [machine gun] he keeps.' So I talked to Mike about it, and he told me the best thing to do is not go into the house when he wasn't there. 'Just go in with me,' he said, 'or go in with one of the guards. It'll make things easier.' I did that from then on.''

''Joe has a whole stash of guns in his house,'' said his former business manager Jerome Howard. ''Under his bed, he's got machine guns. But I know other multimillionaires who keep guns under their beds.''

The Jacksons expected complete devotion from their staff; employees had no lives of their own. Steve Howell remembered what happened the time he took a vacation in Lake Tahoe. ''I was there with my girl and made the mistake of calling the house to see if everything was okay. 'You have to get back here right away. Nothing works,' Bill Bray, Michael's security man, told me hysterically. 'There's no television reception and Michael needs to watch TV and LaToya's pissed,' et cetera . . . So I canceled the rest of my trip, flew back to Los Angeles, beelined it to the house, only to discover that the cable wire was unplugged. I plugged it into the wall and the TV went on.''

Good help was hard to find, even in Encino. At one point, money was stolen from some of the rooms. The Jacksons suspected the maid. They started leaving money here and there, and then would wait to see what would happen. Indeed, it *had* been the maid. She was quickly fired, but rather than replace her immediately, the family told the man who worked as animal keeper to fulfill her duties, which he did.

After that, employees were always being tested. Katherine would leave unarmed the alarm on the closet in which she kept all of her minks, chinchillas, and other expensive furs. Then she would leave the door slightly ajar so anyone walking by could see what was inside. She would watch and see who expressed the most interest. That person would be scrutinized very carefully from then on.

Outsiders were usually not welcome at Hayvenhurst, except the press—a necessary evil when one of the family members had a record to promote—and celebrities, who were always greeted with great enthusiasm. When a celebrity visit was planned, the help was all dismissed so that the stars wouldn't have to feel pressured by the presence of Jackson employees.

Once, Katherine found that some fans had somehow scaled the wall around the estate and were lounging around the pool, waiting for a glimpse of Michael. ''There are so many of them,'' she said of Michael's fans, ''and you have no idea what's really going on in their minds. That's why it's going to be so hard for my son to get a wife.''

''I love my fans, but I'm afraid of them,'' Michael said at this time to photojournalist Dave Nussbaum. ''Some of them will do anything to get to you. They don't realize that what they are doing might hurt you.'' Michael talked of a fan who had managed to get beyond the gates. ''We woke up and found her sitting by the pool, just sitting there. She'd jumped the gate. Luckily our dogs were caged. They're usually out, and they would have *destroyed* her. We brought her inside. She demanded not to leave, in a very rude way, so we held her there until we had somebody come and take her out.''

As Michael talked to the reporter, his security man, Bill Bray— a former police officer—stood nearby watching. ''Okay, let's go'' is Bill Bray's favorite phrase. Just before Michael must hurl himself into a mob of screaming fans in order to get from one place to another, Bray takes a deep breath and whispers the phrase in his ear. He's been doing that since Michael was a child.

Now Michael rarely speaks or answers a question without glancing at Bray first. More than a couple of times, Joe would argue violently with Bray, because he felt that the security man exerted too much influence over his son. The two almost exchanged punches a number of times.

Bray, who is still with Jackson after nearly twenty years, is certainly a man to contend with. Once when a Jackson employee left to get the mail, a fan slipped in as the gate opened.

Steve Howell recalled, "I was talking to Mike in the front yard. It was about three in the afternoon. I remember the time of day because at three—when kids got out of school—two guards went on duty. Prior to three o'clock there was only one. So Mike and I were talking, and the next thing I knew this girl walked up to us and said hello. Then she gave him a big bear hug. With her back to me, Mike motioned to me with his arms helplessly as if to say, 'Who is this person?' I was about to say something when, suddenly, I felt the air break. Something moved like—*whooosh!*—the speed of light. It was Bill Bray.

"He must have seen what was going on by one of the five security cameras set up on the property. Man, he grabbed this chick, smacked her to the ground, handcuffed her, and dragged her out of there. The cops came, took her away, and that was the last we saw of her. Maybe that was the last *anyone* ever saw of her." He laughed. "She was crying, just hysterical, probably scared to death. Michael took it all calmly, and then we went back to talking like nothing had happened. We had a lot of fifty-one fiftys around there, so that was nothing new." A 51-50 is the police term for a mentally unbalanced person.

One of Michael's Encino neighbors, Sandy Brown, said at the time, "There are people who practically live there in front of his house. They'll sit in the bushes for two or three days at a time. It's dangerous. Some of those people are really crazy. You don't know what kind of people your kids will meet walking down the street. There was a rumor that Michael would be moving to Malibu. I wish he would."

There were times when Michael welcomed the outside world in, Steve Howell remembered. He recalled videotaping interviews with female fans outside the gate—which he did often, so that his boss could watch the tapes later and see what kinds of people were out there—when he noticed Michael signaling him. He was spying. After Steve closed the gate and went back inside, Michael told him he'd like to meet these particular fans. Howell went out to get them. Needless to say, they were astonished at their good fortune.

"Mike took them on a tour of the whole estate," Howell said. "They left that place blabbering like idiots, tripping over themselves, their eyes all bugged out. But Mike would do that now and then. If he had nothing else to do, he sometimes figured, why not?"

"I am a very sensitive person," Michael has admitted. "A person with very vulnerable feelings. My best friends in the whole world are children and animals. They're the ones who tell the truth and love you openly and without reservation. Adults have learned how to hide their feelings and their emotions. They can lie. They will smile to your face and say bad things behind your back. Children haven't learned those things yet, and they can't hurt you."

On his way out, the reporter asked Michael if he would like to join him for a bite to eat.

"Oh, no," Michael said, shaking his head. "I can't go out there." He motioned beyond the electronic gate. "They'll get me for sure. They're around the corner, and they want to get their hands on me." The terror in his eyes was genuine. "I just don't want to go out there."

"I don't want to go."

Michael's words rang out with authority, but his father wouldn't listen. "He's a lion," Michael said of Joe. "Like the king of the jungle, nobody crosses him."

The family had been discussing the idea of a reunion tour with Jermaine for some time now, ever since the "Motown 25" special. Michael had been procrastinating about taking a stand. But in the summer of 1983, he pleaded his case. He was tired. He felt that this tour would mean big trouble. He also probably felt he was being exploited, but he did not say so. He would not go. And that was that.

Not quite.

First Joe argued that his brothers needed the money.

By this time, Marlon and Carol Jackson had still not finalized their reconciliation, and the legal fees of the divorce were proving costly. "I am informed by my accountants and manager that Carol and I are almost without funds and that until I am able to complete another album and go on tour there will be little or no income," he claimed in court papers. The mortgage and taxes on their home in Encino cost nearly seven thousand dollars a month. They agreed that if Marlon didn't work soon, they would have to sell their house.

The divorce was still pending because Marlon had become angry that his wife had refused a gift of one million dollars from her mother, who had recently inherited millions. He felt that she rejected the money so that she could show the court that she had to look to Marlon for support. A major tour could solve their financial problems. Certainly Marlon needed the money, as did the rest of the brothers.

Michael knew that none of his brothers had become as rich as he. He also knew that if they managed to curb their extravagant tastes, they would be in good shape. Perhaps Marlon should sell his home and purchase a less expensive one.

Next, Joe tried guilt, accusing Michael of turning his back on his brothers now that he was a superstar. If Michael, never selfish in regard to his family, had sensed need, not greed, he would have responded. He knew when he was being used. He also realized that even if he agreed to the tour, his superstar status would be ignored. He would be just one vote in six—the odd man out, as usual.

Michael would not relent. The brothers had another meeting with him and tried humor. They brought along a life-sized standup poster of Michael. "If you don't come with us, we're gonna put *this* onstage in your place," one of them told Michael. They laughed. But Michael didn't change his mind.

"Look, we don't need you anyway," Joe told Michael one day. "In fact, I think it would be much better if you weren't on this tour. Jermaine can sing some songs, and Jackie and Marlon and Randy can all have songs. Tito, too. So, the hell with you."

Joe's reverse psychology worked like a charm; Michael was very upset by his father's comments. According to an associate of John Branca's, Michael met with Branca and said, "Branca, what's he talking about? The brothers can't sing. Only *I* can be the lead singer."

Branca must have wondered how Michael could allow his father to influence him in this manner. Certainly, Joe knew how to get to his son when he wanted to. Just as Michael was on the brink of making up his mind in favor of the tour, Joe pulled out the big gun, Katherine. He made Katherine copromoter of the tour. Her responsibility was to turn the dream into reality by convincing Michael to be involved. "Mother is like E. F. Hutton," Jermaine once said. "When she speaks, we listen."

"It's interesting to see that the mother is also swayed by money," observed psychiatrist Carole Lieberman. "On the one hand, to the world she presents herself as a saint. But on the other hand, she presents these sides that prove that she isn't just a saint victim of the father, but that she has her own manipulative, controlling desires." Michael certainly must have felt that he had done more for his mother over the years—speaking both financially and emotionally—than any of his brothers. So it somehow seems unfair that she would now be trying to get him to do something that he really didn't want to do, just so that she could appease his brothers and make more money for the family.

Besides her duty to control Michael, Katherine had other reasons for cooperating. All through the divorce proceedings, it seemed that Joe had tried to wear Katherine down in many ways—by continuing to live at home, by disrupting the entire household when he was there, and by being elusive whenever it came to money matters. Katherine never knew how much Joe or The Jacksons made or what security she would have if she divorced him.

However, if she became copromoter of the tour, she could learn more about the family's finances—at least the current ones. It was unlikely that she would get the job if she continued divorce proceedings. Also, she realized that Joe needed her on his side if he was going to convince the brothers to allow him to promote the tour. So, on July 26, 1983, she telephoned her lawyer, George Goffin, with the news. He was not to continue with the divorce. "She did not want either myself or my associate to go to court," Goffin recalled in court records. "During the same conversation, she advised me that she did not want either myself or my associate to proceed to obtain production of her husband's documents. I was told to do nothing further."

Goffin spent the month of August attempting to contact Katherine about pending court dates regarding the divorce, but to no avail.

On September 20, Katherine's lawyer mailed her a certified letter advising her, in effect, that if she did not contact him within ten days, he would bring a motion for the court to relieve him as her counsel. He never heard from her. Had she moved? He had a law clerk track down the postal employee who delivered mail to the Jacksons' estate. Yes, Katherine Jackson still lived there.

Katherine had obviously changed her mind. She was not going to divorce Joe after all. Instead, she would concentrate on her sons' upcoming tour. The next matter at hand was obtaining Michael's cooperation.

Katherine met with Michael privately and begged him to consider the family and the possibility of a tour. "You have to do this for the family," she said, crying. "The brothers need the money. Please. For me?" How could Michael resist? Against his better judgment, he allowed himself to be manipulated and agreed to the tour, "for Kate."

It is possible that many of the lavish gifts Michael gave his mother over the years were "love bribes." But those material things were

Michael Jackson at the age of twelve in 1970. (© 1970 Soul Magazine. All Rights Reserved.)

The Jacksons posed for a family photo in June 1970. Top Row: Jermaine, fifteen; LaToya, fourteen; Tito, sixteen; Jackie, nineteen. Bottom Row: Michael, eleven; Randy, seven; Katherine; Joe; Janet, four; and Marlon, thirteen. (© 1970, *Soul* Magazine. All Rights Reserved.)

Just like any other kids: Michael, twelve; Randy, eight; Marlon, fourteen; and Janet, five, in June 1971. (© 1971, *Soul* Magazine. All Rights Reserved.)

Thirteen-year-old Michael in his bedroom, posing with one of his many pet rats. The bedroom walls were always covered with cartoon figures and publicity photos of entertainers (note the pictures of The Jackson 5 and The Supremes). (J. Randy Taraborrelli Collection)

Michael in 1971. (J. Randy Taraborrelli Collection)

An early publicity photo of The Jackson 5 (1969). Top Row: Tito, sixteen; Jackie, eighteen; Jermaine, fifteen. Bottom Row: Marlon, twelve; and Michael, eleven. (Retro Photo)

By the time The Jackson 5 played the Los Angeles Forum in 1970, "Jackson-Mania" was in full bloom. Michael seems to be doing his best James Brown impression here. (Retro Photo)

By the end of 1972, the family was enjoying tremendous success. Top Row: Jackie, twenty-one; Katherine (with newly frosted hair); Joe; Janet, six; Jermaine, eighteen; Michael, fourteen. Bottom Row: Marlon, fifteen; Randy, ten; Tito, nineteen; and LaToya, sixteen. (J. Randy Taraborrelli Collection)

Diana Ross was credited with discovering The Jackson 5. Here, she seems to be telling Michael and Marlon, "Now here's what I want you to say . . ." (J. Randy Taraborrelli Collection)

Twelve-year-old Michael doing his slick Frank Sinatra impression on Diana Ross's *Diana!* special, April 1971. (J. Randy Taraborrelli Collection)

Joe and Katherine at their son Jermaine's wedding, December 15, 1973. Shortly after this photograph was taken, Katherine filed for divorce when she discovered that Joe was having an affair. Her action was never made public for fear that it would tarnish the family's wholesome image. Shortly thereafter, Katherine reconciled with Joe, but she would admit that she never again felt the same about him. (c 1973, *Soul* Magazine, All Rights Reserved.)

Tito was the first brother to marry. Dee Dee Martes was told to sign a prenuptial agreement before the wedding on June 17, 1972. (Retro Photo)

Jackie married Enid Spann on November 24, 1974. Theirs was a sometimes-difficult union and Enid held on as long as she could . . . until she realized that her husband was having an affair with dancer-choreographer-singer, Paula Abdul. (J. Randy Taraborrelli Collection)

When Jermaine Jackson married Berry Gordy's daughter, Hazel, the ceremony made worldwide news. Many observers commented that the event seemed to be more like a corporate merger between two powerful families than a wedding based on romance. (J. Randy Taraborrelli Collection.)

When Marlon married Carol Parker on August 16, 1975, the couple kept their union a secret . . . rather than risk the wrath of Marlon's father, Joe. (Retro Photo)

Michael turned twenty-one in August 1979. Here, he posed for a photo wearing a rebel cap—perhaps signifying a newfound independence. From this time on, Michael would have a hand in all of his business matters. "I don't trust anyone," he would say, "except Katherine. And even then, I'm not so sure . . ." (© 1979, *Soul* Magazine. All Rights Reserved)

When Joe Jackson had a child outside of his marriage (on August 30, 1974), the family was shocked and hurt. Michael has never gotten over his father's indiscretion. This is an extremely rare photograph of Michael Jackson's secret half-sister, the lovely Joh' Vonnie Jackson, sixteen when this picture was taken in February 1991. Ms. Jackson hopes to follow in the footsteps of her famous half-brothers and -sisters, and become an entertainer. (J. Randy Taraborrelli Collection)

Janet Jackson proved at an early age that she had amazing talent. Here, on stage in Las Vegas, at the age of eight, she does her salty Mae West impression. Randy, twelve, portrayed Groucho Marx in The Jacksons' November 1974 Las Vegas revue. (Retro Photo)

In 1977, the Jackson daughters hoped to start their own singing group. However, since LaToya and Rebbie couldn't see eye-to-eye on the group's direction, and Janet wanted to be an actress, the act never got off the ground. Left to right: LaToya, twenty-one; Janet, eleven; and Rebbie, twenty-seven. (© 1977, *Soul* Magazine. All Rights Reserved.)

Michael in October 1978 as The Scarecrow in *The Wiz*, a huge box office disaster. "Did I make a mistake?" Michael asked the producer of the film after it was released. "Maybe I shouldn't have done this. Maybe I should have listened to my family. What will this mean to my career?" (J. Randy Taraborrelli Collection)

Jermaine Jackson with author J. Randy Taraborrelli, 1980. Jackson was ambivalent about his decision to stay with Motown when his brothers signed with CBS Records. He told Taraborrelli, "I don't feel I left them. I feel they left me . . . here at Motown." (Mike Jones)

In July 1980, Joe Jackson celebrated his fifty-first birthday. The vivacious Gina Sprague, Joe's employee and close friend, organized a birthday party for him. Left to right: Joe's mother, Chrystal; Joe; Gina, nineteen; Marlon, twenty-three; Janet, fourteen; and Randy, seventeen. Michael did not show up. Katherine, who suspected that Gina and Joe were having an affair, was seated with LaToya at a nearby table when this picture was taken. Three months after this party, Katherine—along with Janet and Randy—were accused by Gina of beating her up in a hallway in the Motown building. (J. Randy Taraborrelli Collection)

By the time this photo was taken, February 7, 1984, Michael Jackson was sitting on top of the world, thanks to his *Thriller* album (which would go on to become the biggest-selling album of all time). "You get one frame," Michael told photographer David McGough, who waited five hours to take this picture. "That's it. If I close my eyes, too bad." McGough took his "one frame," and this was the result. Michael is wearing a hat because his scalp was burned less than two weeks earlier while taping a commercial for Pepsi. (David McGough/DMI)

On February 7, 1984, Michael was inducted into the *Guinness Book of World Records* for recording the most successful album in music industry history, *Thriller*. Two years later, on May 6, 1986, Michael Jackson was entered into the *Guinness Book of World Records* again for signing a record-setting endorsement deal with Pepsi that netted him over $15 million. Above, Michael with his manager, Frank Dileo. (David McGough/DMI)

Michael Jackson set a new music industry record on February 28, 1984, when he walked off with an unprecedented eight Grammy Awards, the most won by an artist in one year. Michael gives the thumbs up to photographers as he drops off his date, Brooke Shields, at her Los Angeles hotel following the awards after-party. (John Paschal/DMI)

On November 30, 1983, a press conference was held at Tavern on the Green in New York to announce that the Jackson brothers would be re-uniting for a tour. Michael didn't trust the tour's promoter, Don King: "I don't want him to touch a penny of my money," he said. Left to right: Marlon, twenty-six; Michael's friend, Emmanuel Lewis, twelve; Michael, twenty-five; Randy, twenty-one; Tito, thirty; Jackie, thirty-two; and Jermaine, twenty-nine. Promoter Don King, with the "interesting" hair-do, is posed flashing the peace sign. (David McGough/DMI)

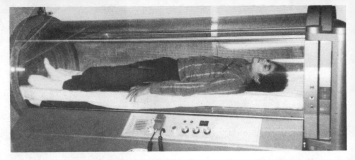

Michael's bizarre hyperbaric chamber hoax made worldwide headline news. To this day, many people believe that Michael sleeps in such a contraption, when actually the whole thing was a publicity stunt concocted by Michael. (Transworld Feature, Synd.)

By August 2, 1984, the much-beleaguered Victory tour was in full swing. Here Michael, who would turn twenty-six this month, performs at Madison Square Garden. (John Paschal/DMI)

Twenty-nine-year-old Michael on stage in March 1988 during the Bad tour. (David McGough/DMI)

Michael with Donald Trump, August 6, 1990, at the opening of Trump's Taj Mahal Casino resort in Atlantic City. (Albert Ferreira/DMI)

By 1990, Michael's parents, Katherine, sixty, and Joe Jackson, sixty-one, were still together, despite forty-one years of troubled marriage. When Michael moved out of the house in 1988, he didn't tell his parents he was leaving. They heard about it on television. (Kevin Winter/DMI)

Michael receives the BMI Michael Jackson Award on May 8, 1990, in Beverly Hills. (Kevin Winter/DMI)

Two pictures are worth a thousand words: Michael in 1977, at the age of nineteen, before plastic surgery . . . and Michael today, at the age of thirty-two. (© 1977 *Soul* Magazine. All Rights Reserved. George Horn, Kevin Winter/DMI)

not nearly as important as the sacrifices he was about to make for her regarding his career. They could even be thought of as sacrifices of the soul, for Michael had so little else in his life that his career meant everything to him. Because Kate asked him, Michael agreed to continue to be held down as part of a family act instead of soaring on his own.

It didn't matter to Joe or the brothers that Michael's heart would not be in this tour. Just because he was rich didn't mean they were too. "Michael's money didn't matter to nobody but Michael," Joe maintained. "And he was always very secretive about that. More important, the brothers needed to enhance their own situation. Like any other group, they needed to tour."

Joe and Katherine Jackson asked that Don King help them promote the tour. King was best known for his huge boxing promotions of Muhammad Ali's "Thrilla in Manila" and the Sugar Ray Leonard–Roberto Duran blockbusters. The Jackson sons met with him and were not impressed. During the meeting, King wore a white fur coat, diamond rings, and a gold necklace on which hung a disturbing charm: a crown with the name DON on top of it. They decided this was not the kind of man they wanted to represent them.

But Don King had managed to come up with $3 million to give to the Jacksons as a show of good faith against concert earnings—$500,000 to each member of the group. The brothers were ecstatic. Joe was happy, and Katherine content. But Michael was neither.

Don King is a flamboyant, outrageous, and controversial black man considered by many the leading boxing promoter in the world. He was raised in a Cleveland ghetto and used to run numbers there. In 1966, he went to prison in Ohio for second-degree murder after killing a man in a Cleveland street fight. After serving a four-year term, King began promoting prizefights. King is also known for the way his gray hair sticks straight up, as if he'd just been electrocuted.

"My hairstyle is an aura of God," he explains. "I don't treat it, I don't take care of it, it just pops up. So I feel it's indicative of my being ordained and anointed by He who sits high and keeps His eye on the sparrow."

"I think he's creepy," Michael told one friend. "I don't trust the guy. He just wants a piece of the action, that's all."

And not a paltry piece at that. Forty shows were planned, with a projected gross revenue of $30 million. Deducting $6 million for expenses leaves $24 million net profit—85 percent of which would go to the group, 7.5 percent to Don King, and 7.5 percent to Joe and Katherine. That comes to $3.4 million for each Jackson member—enough to get the brothers back on their feet, for a while anyway—as well as $900,000 each for Joe and Katherine, and $1.8 million for Don King.

King wanted another chance, so they met again. This time he aligned himself with Jay Coleman, an enterprising promoter who specialized in obtaining tour sponsorships from major corporations. King told Coleman about the Jacksons' tour and their need for a big-money sponsor. "And you, my dear main man, are just the white boy who can walk into a corporation and tap them for the change."

Coleman brought King to Pepsi. King convinced the Pepsi-Cola Company to draw up a contract for $5 million to sponsor the tour. It wasn't easy. The executives balked at the figure, quite a lot of "change."

There was another meeting with King.

"Just sign here, fellas," King said with a toothy grin. Jackie, Tito, Randy, Marlon, and Jermaine voted that they should work with Don King. After all, an extra $5 million *was* impressive. But for Michael, $5 million was, as they say back in the neighborhood in Gary, "chump change," especially after it was split six ways and 15 percent was taken off the top for King, Joe, and Katherine, leaving him with $700,000 and not much incentive. Michael agreed that he would allow King to promote the tour, but as for Pepsi, "Forget it," he said. "I don't drink Pepsi. I don't *believe* in Pepsi," said Michael, a health food fanatic.

Everyone tried to convince Michael to accept the Pepsi endorsement, mostly because so much money was involved. The Rolling Stones had only received a half million for their endorsement. The biggest deal in Madison Avenue history had gone to Alan Alda for Atari, and that was only a million. The brothers thought Michael was crazy for stalling. Joe, Katherine, and Don King applied the pressure. "I just don't want to," Michael insisted. "I have a bad feeling about it."

Finally, after a full weekend of intense pressure, Michael Jackson signed the contract at four o'clock in the morning on a Monday. A rider made it clear that he would not have to hold a can of Pepsi, or drink from one, in any commercial or publicity photo.

"I don't know what he has against making money," Joe said later, in regard to Michael's reluctance about the Pepsi endorsement. "You can always need more money. You never get to a point, I don't care how much money you have, where you don't need more. And at that time everybody in the family, except Michael, needed it."

A friend said, "Michael had decided he was going to do the commercials, and he would set his mind to doing the best job possible. He wouldn't half-ass it; that's not like Mike. That's why it was such a difficult decision. If he commits to a project, he gives it his all. It's easier if it's something he believes in. After signing with Pepsi, he was determined to give it his all."

Throughout this time of pressure, Michael was comforted by his odd friendship with twelve-year-old actor Emmanuel Lewis, who was three feet four at that time and whom Michael enjoyed carrying in his arms as if he were a toddler. The friendship began when Emmanuel came to Hollywood to star in the sitcom "Webster." Michael had seen him in commercials and wanted to meet him. He telephoned Lewis's mother and invited the boy to visit him in Encino. They became fast friends. In fact, Michael nearly became obsessed with Emmanuel. They would play with Michael's pets, run around the estate like little kids playing cowboys and Indians, roll around on the lawn together. It appeared that Michael was trying to live the childhood he feels he missed.

According to Vivian Greene, Emmanuel Lewis's former dialogue coach, "Manny was very taken with Michael. If you just mentioned Michael's name, Manny's eyes lit up. All he talked about, thought about, was Michael Jackson. I had heard that the Jackson family wasn't happy about Michael's friendship with Emmanuel because of the way it looked, especially when Michael began buying Manny expensive presents. But the two of them were in their own world, totally oblivious to what people around them were saying."

One visitor at the Encino estate recalled watching as Michael read the tale of Peter Pan to Emmanuel. Afterwards the two of them imagined themselves as characters in the story. According to the eyewitness, twenty-five-year-old Michael and twelve-year-old Emmanuel sat on the floor with their eyes closed and fantasized that they were flying over Never-Never Land. "Believe it and it'll be true," Michael whispered. "Now, are you ready? Do you believe?"

"Yes, I believe," Emmanuel said, his eyes closed tightly.

Then they began to repeat dialogue from the story. After a while, the two broke up laughing and began to wrestle on the floor like puppies. Michael's extreme isolation from the world seemed to make it more possible for him to relate on a childlike level.

Emmanuel Lewis's mother, Margaret, reportedly became concerned about the friendship after some rather bizarre things began happening. Once Michael and Emmanuel checked into a swanky hotel in Los Angeles—as father and son. It's not known what fantasy they were acting out. Shortly after that, however, they stopped seeing each other.

In October 1983, Michael and Jacqueline Onassis met at the Encino home to discuss the possibility of Michael writing an autobiography to be published by Doubleday, the company for which Onassis works as an editor. He was first introduced to her several years earlier at a Kennedy function in New York. She had been in touch a number of times and had asked him to consider writing a book about his life. Michael became fascinated with the idea of meeting and getting acquainted with Onassis, much more than he was interested in doing a book. "She's one of my idols," he had said. "Imagine actually being able to say I *know* Jacqueline Onassis."

"On the day she was set to come by the house, everyone was very excited," Steve Howell remembered. "Naturally, we all wanted to meet her but would have settled for just a glimpse of her going from the limo to the house. The buzz around the house was 'Jackie O's coming, Jackie O's coming.'

"But then her driver called from the car to alert Michael that they were about thirty minutes away.

" 'Okay, everybody out,' Mike said. 'You can all go home.'

"Nobody wanted to leave, but everyone had to. Michael wanted the entire staff to vacate the premises so that he would be able to be alone with Jackie."

Afterwards, Steve Howell asked Michael, "What was your day like with Jackie O?"

"It was amazing that she was even here," Michael enthused. "I still can't believe it. I love that woman. I really do." That's all Michael would say to Howell about the meeting.

Another friend of Michael's remembered, "Jackie wanted to talk book business, but Michael had other things on his mind. He told me that he wanted to know how she felt about always being photographed everywhere she went. He wanted to know how she handled her celebrity. He asked her for tips on how to avoid paparazzi. He admired her and was hoping to figure out what makes her tick."

Michael was twenty-five years old and felt uneasy about writing his memoirs. "I'm still trying to sort it all out myself," he told Steve Howell. Indeed, some of his life did deserve close examination, but most people who knew Michael at this time agreed that he was not the most impartial person for the job. Michael was much too concerned about his public image, and that of his family, to write the real story. He certainly had many personal problems, most of which Jacqueline Onassis was not aware of, but he would do anything to protect the family's dignity. "I don't want to let my fans down by having them know the whole truth," he said. "They'll be crushed."

Michael knew that baring his soul in a book at this time was not something he could do, so he asked Onassis to consider a scrapbook concept. This would be a book illustrated by such novelty items as Michael's first report card, early pictures, and poetry. She tried to act interested but really wasn't. She wanted his whole life on paper, but she agreed to the scrapbook idea, at least for a while.

A press conference was organized at the Tavern on the Green just off Central Park West at Sixty-seventh Street in New York City. The time: twelve noon. The date: Wednesday, November 30, 1983. The announcement: The Jackson's reunion tour and the fact that Don King would be promoting it. By this time, Michael had had two more major hit singles, "Human Nature" and "PYT," and it was expected that the place would be mobbed with fans, which it was. There were over a hundred police officers guarding the Tavern.

The conference was dominated by King's talk about God. First he spoke of love, "enrapturement," and the fact that "Michael has soared the heights to the unknown." Then, said King, "It is so fortunate for all of us and so symbolic that we have such a beautiful family to use for all the world to see. They are humble. They are warm. They exude charming magnetism. The love that emits from these guys is so contagious. It's so captivating and infectious and it got me into this whirlwind of a musical spell that I can't seem to get out of . . ." And on and on he went for about twenty-five minutes before finally showing a fifteen-minute documentary about himself.

Katherine, Joe, LaToya, and Janet watched, with confused looks on their faces, as King paraphrased Malvolio's speech from Shakespeare's *Twelfth Night*. "Be not afraid of greatness," King said, his chest puffed with pride. "Some men are born great. Some achieve greatness. And others have greatness thrust upon them." LaToya looked particularly befuddled.

Joe leaned over to Katherine and was overheard asking, "Is he talkin' 'bout us or himself?" She shrugged her shoulders.

A camera crew filmed Don King's speech. He had hired them himself. He introduced celebrities who weren't even in the audience, but it probably looked impressive on film. Michael still hadn't arrived. King was stalling. He talked of a forty-city tour, a concert film, a live satellite broadcast. It was also announced that Pepsi-Cola had ponied up $5 million for the privilege of sponsoring the event.

The Jacksons would star in two commercials for Pepsi as part of the deal. "It is going to be fabulous. The highest-grossing tour. The most amazing tour ever in history by these extraordinary men . . ."

Finally, Michael showed up with security man Bill Bray and took his place at a long table with six microphones. He joined Marlon, Tito, Jermaine, Randy, and Jackie. The table stood hidden on a platform behind the stage. The brothers had waited in the wings through King's speech about himself and probably were not thrilled. But then doors opened and The Jacksons were rolled out on the platform to thunderous applause.

All of the Jackson brothers sat at the dais with glum faces, their eyes hidden behind dark sunglasses. None of them looked amused by the manner in which King had grandstanded for the media. Finally the promoter urged Michael (who had brought Emmanuel Lewis with him) to speak.

Michael said, "I really don't have anything to say . . . I would like to introduce the rest of my family. First my mother, Katherine—"

"Yes, that's the mother, Katherine," King butted in. "The backbone, the strength, the heart and soul . . ."

"And this is my father, Joseph."

"Hmm-hmm, that's him. Joseph Jackson. I love that man. That man has truly mesmerized me."

"And that's LaToya and Janet." Michael said, frowning at King.

"Yes, aren't they truly lovely? The sisters, LaToya and . . ." King's voice trailed off when he noticed Michael's frown.

"And my brothers' beautiful wives are here. Hazel, Carol, Enid, and Dee Dee," Michael said. "My sister Maureen is not here because she is doing an album for CBS. Thank you very much."

Michael looked irritated. He refused to answer any questions.

"Thank you, Michael, the golden voice of song," King said, quickly.

"What are you going to name the tour?" a reporter asked.

"They haven't named it yet," King answered.

"Excuse me, but yes, we have," Marlon interjected. "We are going to call it the Victory tour."

"That is the name of the tour, ladies and gentleman," Don King said. "The Victory tour. And what a heck of a name, too."

"What does the tour mean?" someone else asked.

"The tour will mean that the brothers are getting together once again," Jermaine said. "And unite and work real close with each other. To show the world that we can make everybody happy. And everybody in the whole world will unite as one, because we want to bring this together in peace for everyone."

"Why can't Michael say more?" asked another reporter.

"Uh, well . . ." King shot a look at Michael. Michael shook his head no. "He, uh, his voice is a problem because he has been working so hard singing those songs and makin' all those hit records. He will not be able to continue talking now. Isn't that right, Michael?"

Michael stared straight ahead.

Washington reporters Maxwell Glen and Cody Shearer called the event "one of media history's most abominable press conferences." Another observer dubbed the Jacksons' tour "The Nitro Tour," explaining that "at any minute the whole thing is gonna blow sky-high."

Michael had asked John Branca to hire someone to videotape the press conference. Afterwards, Michael, John, and some others watched it in Michael's suite at the Helmsley Palace.

"It's a mess, isn't it?" Michael said.

Branca told him that it appeared that Don King was the star of the show and that The Jacksons were the sideshow.

"Well, that stinks," Michael said. "We gotta show this tape to the brothers."

Michael called a meeting in his room. Jackie, Tito, Jermaine, Marlon, and Randy showed up. By this time, they had their own doubts about King because of the way the press conference was handled. Michael showed them the videotape

"What's wrong with you guys?" Michael wanted to know. "Can't you see that this man is using us? This is the Don King show and The Jacksons are the opening act. Just look at this tape. Can't you see how bad this looks?"

"You're right, " Jackie said after they viewed the tape. "The guy is a jerk."

The rest of the brothers agreed. Participating in the press conference was bad enough, but seeing how it looked from the other side of the dais was more than the brothers' pride could bear. Michael had successfully turned them against Don King.

"Look, you guys chose this creep," Michael said. "Now Branca and I are going to choose someone else, a tour coordinator who's going to really handle the business. Probably Bill Graham or Irving Azoff, someone big in the business. Do we agree, or what?"

They agreed.

# Chapter

# 🌿 21 🌿

IF 1983 WASN'T the year of Michael Jackson, it wasn't the year of anybody," said Dick Clark.

Yes, it had been quite a year.

By the beginning of 1984, Michael Jackson's *Thriller* had sold a staggering 13 million copies in the United States and nearly 22 million worldwide. The current all-time best-seller was the original soundtrack to *Saturday Night Fever*, with worldwide sales of 25 million since its 1977 release. It wouldn't be long before Michael toppled that record; he had already achieved one milestone: until now, no other solo album had sold more than 12 million copies.

In addition to his personal achievements, Michael Jackson had single-handedly revived a moribund recording industry. When people flocked to the record stores to buy *Thriller*, they purchased other records too. As a result, the business had its best year since 1978. As Gil Friesen, then-president of A&M Records said, "The whole industry has a stake in *Thriller*'s success." Michael's success also generated new interest in black music in general.

For instance, MTV, the twenty-four-hour-a-day cable station that plays only music videos, became a phenomenon when it began airing in 1981, but it rarely played the videos of black artists. The station's format was "strictly rock and roll," said Bob Pittman, the executive vice-president and chief operating officer of Warner American Express Satellite Entertainment Company and the driving force behind MTV. Pittman's definition of rock and roll excluded most black artists from the station's play lists. In fact, of the over 750 videos shown on MTV during the channel's first eighteen months, fewer than two dozen featured black artists. It was acceptable to have Phil Collins sing The Supremes' "You Can't Hurry Love" and Hall and Oates sing other black-sounding material. But the real thing was unacceptable on MTV at that time. When videos of black artists were submitted, they were quickly rejected by MTV as not being "rock and roll."

MTV's research and marketing departments had decided that white kids in the suburbs did not like black music and were afraid of black people. There was nothing wrong with that, Bob Pittman reasoned; after all, "Bloomingdale's wouldn't work if it carried every kind of clothing ever made."

Bob Giraldi, director of Michael's "Beat It" video, best summed up many black critics' opinions of MTV when he said that the station was run by "racist bastards." Motown recording artist Rick James, whose videos had been rejected by the station, also charged that the network was racist and had set black people back four hundred years. Bob Pittman may not have been a racist, but he and MTV certainly catered to white suburban racism.

When CBS submitted Michael Jackson's "Billie Jean" to MTV, the cable station quickly rejected it. Then CBS purportedly threatened to pull all of its other videos from MTV unless they ran "Beat It." Michael Jackson had become so popular, Bob Pittman—and suburban white America—could not ignore him. Finally, in early March 1983, the "Billie Jean" video was played on MTV, and in heavy rotation, meaning quite often during the day. "Beat It" followed. After that, MTV began to play a few more videos by black artists, and though the network still leans heavily toward white rock and roll, at least some black artists—though not many—receive airtime on MTV as a result of the Michael Jackson breakthrough.

Ultimately, *Thriller* would go on to sell an unprecedented 38.5 million copies worldwide and spend thirty-seven weeks at number one on the *Billboard* charts. No other album had ever spawned seven Top Ten singles: "Billie Jean," "Beat It," "The Girl Is Mine," "Human Nature," "Wanna Be Startin' Somethin'," "PYT (Pretty Young Thing)," and "Thriller." CBS made at least $60 million just on *Thriller*.

Michael fared well too. According to his attorney at that time, John Branca, Michael Jackson has "the highest royalty rate in the record business." That rate escalated along with the sales, but averaged 42 percent of the wholesale price of each record sold, or about $2.10 for every album sold in the United States—$32 million on *Thriller*'s domestic sales alone. Roughly $15 million more was made in foreign sales. Those figures, of course, do not include the royalties for the four songs he penned on the album.

Michael Jackson was, at twenty-five, a very rich young man. He had certainly come a long way from that 0.2 percent royalty rate Motown once offered him.

Despite his fame and great fortune, Michael now went door to door proselytizing for the Jehovah's Witness faith, "twice a week, maybe for an hour or two," according to Katherine. (He also attended meetings at Kingdom Hall with his mother four times a week when he was in town.)

Wearing a disguise—a mustache, hat, and glasses—and a tie and sweater, and holding a copy of *Watchtower*, Michael stood at the door of an apartment in suburban Thousand Oaks, California, one morning in early 1984. "I'm here to talk to you about God's word," he told the young girl who answered the bell.

She slammed the door in his face.

He went to the next apartment.

"Today, I'm here to talk to you about God's word," he said when the door opened. He was invited into the apartment, and the door closed behind him.

Louise Gilmore, of Thousand Oaks, recalled the day Michael Jackson came to visit. "It was very odd. At first I thought it was some kind of a trick-or-treat gag. A young black man came to my door wearing what was obviously a phony mustache and beard, and a big hat. His face was too smooth for all of that facial hair. He looked like a little boy playing grown-up. He had this soft little voice and looked harmless enough. 'Can I talk to you for just a moment?' he said politely. I decided to let him in.

"He sat down and pulled out all of these books and pamphlets from a bag. 'You should read these,' he said. He gave me a little speech about the Jehovah's Witnesses, which I paid no attention to, so I can't tell you what he said. He then had a glass of water, thanked me, and went on his way. I didn't think anything of it, except, 'My, what a polite little boy.'

"The next day my neighbor said to me, 'Did Michael Jackson come to your house too?' I said, 'What are you talking about?' When I put two and two together, I almost fainted. I've kept the material he gave me as souvenirs. No, I didn't join the religion."

More than ever before, Michael considered himself a strict Jehovah's Witness. Michael didn't believe in blood transfusions, Easter and Christmas (which he viewed as "pagan holidays"), or the celebration of his own birthday. He also did not believe in pledging allegiance to the flag. (In April 1984 he would attend the T. J. Martell Foundation's dinner honoring Walter Yetnikoff, president of CBS Records. Michael refused to be seated at the dais until after

Monsignor Vincent Puma delivered the invocation and the crowd pledged allegiance to the flag and then sang the national anthem.)

Armageddon, the end of the world, was near, Michael professed, and only God's most beloved believers—Jehovah's Witnesses— would survive. Of these believers, 144,000 would go to heaven to reside with Jesus for a thousand years while the other Witnesses rebuilt Earth as a paradise, preparing it for the eventual resurrection of those who had passed on.

"He was very devoted," recalled his voice teacher Seth Riggs. "He would come in for his lesson, and before we got started we would have a prayer and read the Bible. Then there would be another prayer before we actually began the lesson. Sometimes we would get down on our knees."

Despite the fact that Michael was a devout Jehovah's Witness— and no doubt had donated quite a bit of money to the religion—the church's elders were extremely upset with him, mostly because of the "Thriller" video.

Michael had been so impressed with the horror-fantasy film *An American Werewolf in London* that he employed the services of John Landis to repeat his directorial duties and then he hired Rick Baker to create special effects on the "Thriller" video. The fourteen-minute video was budgeted at $600,000. At this time, an artist could make a decent video for about $25,000. John Branca felt that Michael was overextending himself and advised him that they should find another way to pay for the "Thriller" video.

John Branca and Michael Jackson came up with the idea of a video entitled "The Making of Thriller." At the same time that the video was being taped, extra footage of how it was done, including interviews with some of the key figures and even Michael himself, would be shot. Then Branca approached Vestron Video, a video distribution company, and had them pay approximately $500,000 for the right to distribute the product.

Afterwards, he went to MTV and told executives there that Michael was doing a sixty-minute documentary and that if they wanted to show it, they'd have to pay for it. At that time, MTV didn't even pay record companies for the right to air videos because it was considered terrific promotion to have an artist's video aired on the cable-music station. While today there is much negotiating of money between MTV and artist's managers, attorneys, and record label executives, that was not the case in 1984.

Because Michael Jackson was so popular, MTV agreed to finance part of "The Making of Thriller" if Michael would license it to the station for an official debut. The video would end up costing a little over a million dollars. The Showtime cable network also paid for second rights to the video. In all, MTV and Showtime put up nearly the whole second half of the million dollars.

The "Thriller" video combined illusion and reality, skillfully weaving one into the other. The story opens with Michael pulling his white Chevy convertible over to the side of a wooded road. In a line that has been around since ten minutes after the first Model T rolled off the assembly line, Michael turns to date Ola Ray (a former *Playboy* centerfold) and says, "I'm afraid we're out of gas." However, instead of staying put and romancing, they start to walk.

He asks her to be his girl. She accepts.

"I'm not like other guys," he tells her. His voice is soft and whispery.

"Of course not," she says, brushing off one of the great understatements of all time. "That's why I love you."

"No," Michael insists. "I mean I'm different."

As the moon comes out from behind a cloud, Ola discovers how different Michael really is. How many other guys sprout fangs, claws, and whiskers and bray at the moon as they turn into werewolves? He chases her through the woods. She trips. She is flat on her back. He hovers over her, clearly up to no good.

Just as the monster is about to attack, the camera focuses on Michael and Ola as part of a movie theater audience, dressed in a more modern fashion than their 1950-style counterparts on the screen. She is cringing in horror. He is clearly enjoying the scene.

"I can't watch," she says, getting up to leave.

Reluctantly putting aside his popcorn, Michael follows her out of the theater, playfully taunting her about her fears and singing "Thriller" as they walk along the deserted streets. When they pass a graveyard, an assemblage of ghouls emerge from their graves and crypts to surround the couple. With skin the color of mushrooms, blood dripping from the corners of their mouths, and eyeballs bulging halfway out of their heads, they look as though they have been moldering for a long time.

Ola escapes to find shelter in a deserted house, but Michael leads the grotesque company in dance. Now his facial features are contorted and menacing. His blood-red clothes contribute to his sinister appearance. He leads the other ghouls to Ola. As she trembles in fear, they break through the walls, the windows, the floor. Ola huddles on the sofa, screaming as Michael reaches out for her.

Suddenly, they are in Michael's home. "Hey, what's the problem?" a smiling Michael asks. Ola looks up at him with confused eyes. Was it all a dream? Michael puts his arm protectively around her shoulder, but as he turns to face the camera, his eyes are bestial and his smile is ominous.

It's unlikely that Michael Jackson intended this video to advocate Satanism and the occult, as the leaders of the Jehovah's Witnesses would charge. But Michael was so engrossed with fantasy that "Thriller" probably seemed no scarier to him than Halloween. When he was making this video, he would go home at night and surround himself with puppets in his backyard and mannequins in his bedroom. In "Thriller" the blurred borderlines between reality and illusion may well reflect the way Michael looked at life then.

But before he had even finished work on the "Thriller" video, it brought to a head the ongoing conflict between the church elders of the Encino Kingdom Hall and Michael regarding his fame and his career. The elders had heard about the video concept, and in meetings between Michael and the elders, the state of his soul was discussed. He was not receptive. Michael did not want to be told what to do, not by his father and not by his church. He refused to make any kind of statement repudiating his work, as the church insisted he should.

"I know I'm an imperfect person," Michael said. "I'm not making myself out to be an angel."

Finally, when the elders threatened to force him to leave the religion, Michael became extremely upset.

He telephoned John Branca's office. When Branca's secretary picked up the phone, there seemed to be no one on the line. All she heard was the sound of desperate breathing, as if someone was trying to catch his breath in between sobs.

"I don't know who it is," she told John. "It might be Michael."

When Branca got on the line and heard nothing but heavy breathing, he became concerned. Before Branca could figure out what was going on, Michael hung up.

The next day, Michael called back and whispered that he had "a big problem." Then he abruptly hung up again.

These telephone calls went on for several days until, finally, John Branca was extremely worried.

According to a former associate of Branca's, Michael called again at the end of the week and asked if Branca had the tapes to the "Thriller" video. When the attorney said that he didn't, that they were in the processing lab, Michael instructed him to get the tapes. "Then I want you to destroy them," Michael said. He sounded desperate. "No one must ever see that video."

Before John Branca had a chance to respond, Michael hung up. Michael called back the next day, wanting to know if his attorney had gotten the tapes. "By this time, John was tired of playing games," said his former associate. "He wanted to know what was going on, especially since Michael had already spent a million dollars of MTV's, Showtime's and Vestron's money on 'Thriller.' How could he destroy the tapes now?"

When Michael explained that his church had threatened to expel him if the "Thriller" tape was ever released, Branca was astounded. He tried to convince Michael that he should not allow the church elders to dictate his artistry, but Michael wasn't interested in his opinion at that point.

"Michael called back the next day," said Branca's associate. " 'Do you have the tapes?' Michael wanted to know. Branca said that he did. When Michael asked, 'Did you destroy them?' Branca told Mike that he had. Actually, they were sitting on Branca's desk."

At that time, Branca had been reading a book about Bela Lugosi. After thinking about Lugosi and his Dracula character, he called Michael back and asked him if he had ever heard of Lugosi. Michael hadn't. John Branca explained that Lugosi was a religious man but that, as an actor, he played Dracula and made a career of doing so. Michael listened intently as Branca told him that Lugosi's religious beliefs had no bearing on his art, and that the fact that he portrayed a vampire in movies didn't make him any less religious in real life. He suggested that, if Michael wanted to do so, a disclaimer could be placed at the beginning of the video which would state that it did not reflect Michael's personal or religious convictions. Michael thought this was a brilliant idea.

Next day, John Branca telephoned John Landis to tell him that there would have to be a disclaimer at the beginning of the "Thriller" video.

"Bullshit," Landis said. "No way."

Branca told him that if there was no disclaimer, there would be no video. Then he explained the whole story to Landis. "Jesus Christ," Landis said, "this kid's in bad shape, isn't he?"

The "Thriller" video was released with the following disclaimer at the beginning:

Due to my strong personal convictions, I wish to stress that this film in no way endorses a belief in the occult.—Michael Jackson

Despite the personal turmoil "Thriller" caused him, it was still the inspiration for a feature film Michael was planning; he began having meetings with Steven Spielberg to discuss movie ideas, principally a new film version of *Peter Pan*, in which Michael would play the title role. (In the end, Spielberg was not able to secure all of the necessary rights to the work.) As part of the Michael Jackson merchandising bonanza, "The Making of Thriller" videocassette was eventually released—one video showing how the *other* video was made. According to the Record Industry Association of America, Jackson's first release for the home video market was the first music videocassette to apply for immediate gold and platinum certification. It was, by far, the best-selling music video to date. Michael would make millions from it.

The week before the "Thriller" video was released in late December 1983, *Thriller's* sales had slowed down to 200,000 copies a week, more than respectable for an album that had been out for a year. According to *Time* magazine, the week after the video was issued and televised on MTV for only five days, the album sold another 600,000 copies and shot back up to number one on the *Billboard* charts.

"Thank goodness for Branca," Michael said to an associate. "If it wasn't for him, the 'Thriller' video would be ashes by now and there would have been no "Making of Thriller." That was a close call."

It was now 1984 and the first order of business was the filming of the two Pepsi commercials Don King had arranged. Michael was still unhappy about the Pepsi endorsement, especially when the Quaker Oats Company offered to support the tour at a sum that was 40 percent more than Pepsi-Cola had offered. Though the contract was signed, John Branca did try to get Michael out of it. When Michael persisted in trying to end the arrangement with Pepsi, Katherine was asked to "talk some sense into him." She did. The deal was back on.

Michael Jackson was, however, in complete charge of the commercials; that was understood from the beginning. He had final word on everything. His brothers could have no say about the footage, which was fine with them, because they were paid almost a million each to do the commercials and were satisfied.

Michael did not have a pleasant working experience with Pepsi-Cola. And the executives there were disgusted with Michael after a few weeks. First of all, Michael's friends Paul McCartney and Jane Fonda told him he had made a tragic mistake doing a television commercial because he would be "overexposed." Michael decided that in order to rectify that problem, his face should only be on camera for one close-up and only for a maximum of four seconds.

He wanted a cameo in his own commercial, and for this Pepsi would pay $5 million.

"There are other ways to shoot me rather than push a camera in my face," Michael insisted to three exasperated Pepsi executives in a meeting at his home. "Use my symbols. Shoot my shoes, my spats, my glove, my look—and then, at the end, reveal me." He offered to allow the Pepsi executives use of "Billie Jean," for which he would write new Pepsi-jingle lyrics. It was becoming clear that now Michael wasn't so much trying to get out of the deal as he was wanting the commercials to be "magical" or not to exist at all. But in his desire to be magical, he was driving the Pepsi-Cola Company crazy.

"I don't think this is going to work," said one executive. "I'm starting to have second thoughts about this Jackson guy and these commercials."

He wasn't the only one.

"I still don't have a good feeling about this," Michael had said about the Pepsi endorsement. "In my heart, I feel it's wrong to endorse something you don't believe in. I think it's a bad omen." Michael shrugged his shoulders and added, "I just gotta make the best of it."

He did. When Michael met with Roger Enrico, president and chief executive officer of the Pepsi-Cola Company, he told him, "Roger, I'm going to make Coke wish *they* were Pepsi."

Friday, January 27, 1984.

The time had come to film the Pepsi commercial. Three thousand people were jammed into the Shrine Auditorium in Los Angeles to simulate a live concert audience. The Jacksons were to perform "You're a Whole New Generation," special lyrics to the music of "Billie Jean."

Prior to one of the takes, Michael and his brothers were preparing themselves for the shooting—adjusting their outfits, putting on their makeup—when Michael realized he had to go to the bathroom. "Go ahead, use mine," Bob Giraldi suggested. "Don't worry, I'll just be a minute," Michael said. He went in and closed the door.

Thirty seconds later, a bloodcurdling shriek came out of the bathroom.

"Jesus! What happened?" Bob Giraldi asked, alarmed.

He started banging on the door. "Michael, Michael are you okay?" People started gathering about.

Michael, his face flushed, slowly opened the door. Bob and a bunch of other people rushed in.

"I dropped my glove," Michael said, embarrassed.

"Where?" Giraldi wanted to know.

"In there," Michael said, meekly. He pointed down to the toilet bowl. There was a white rhinestoned glove floating on the water.

"Okay," Bob said, trying to act nonchalant. "Somebody get a hanger or something. We'll have to fish it out of there."

Everyone scattered to search for a hanger. Finally Michael said, "Oh, forget it." He reached down into the toilet and grabbed the glove.

After he washed it off, the show went on.

It had been a long day. Most of the group arrived at nine A.M. Tito acted as Michael's stand-in. He would take Michael's place for the purpose of camera angles and other technical positioning. Michael, the star of the show, would not arrive for hours.

Now it was close to six P.M. The group performed the number for the sixth time that day—this time so that director Giraldi could make some technical adjustments. Tape began rolling at 6:30. As always, Michael began to descend from a podium by going down a staircase amid brilliant illumination. His brothers were lined up on the stage, playing. A smoke bomb and some pyrotechnics exploded, as planned, momentarily blocking Michael from view.

First a pose. That unmistakable silhouette.

A magnesium flash bomb went off with a loud bang, just two feet from Michael's head. As Michael headed down the stairs, the smoke became too thick. Something seemed wrong.

Michael began to dance.

He did a turn.

And another.

And another.

He spun three times and popped up on his toes.

He was hot.

The audience gasped when Michael turned. The explosion had somehow set his hair ablaze. But Michael continued to perform. He would remember feeling the heat, but said he thought it was the hot stage lights. Then, suddenly, he felt the burning pain.

He pulled his jacket over his head and fell to the stage floor. "Tito! Tito!" he yelled.

The first to respond was Miko Brando, Marlon Brando's twenty-two-year-old son and one of Michael's security staff. "I ran out, hugged him, tackled him, and ran my hands through his hair," reported Brando, who burned his fingers in the process.

For a moment, no one knew what had happened. Total chaos and pandemonium.

Jermaine would later say he thought his brother had been shot.

The crew rushed onto the stage, threw him down, and began covering his head with a blanket to put out the fire. Michael's brothers helped in any way they could. The fire was extinguished quickly. A handful of ice was applied immediately. A T-shirt was borrowed to make a cold compress. Michael was taken off the stage.

Director Bob Giraldi would remember, "I was in the wings, stage right. I had five black-and-white monitors, and during the last take, I saw Michael dancing down the stairs and in a black-and-white monitor I couldn't tell that he was on fire. It wasn't until I saw everybody rush him on the monitor that I knew something was wrong. At first I thought somebody had rushed onto the stage, as fans do. Then when they said his hair got on fire, I ran out. Film later has shown that while his hair was burning, he was trying to get his jacket off because maybe he thought it too was on fire. He did two quick spins and put out the fire by his own force."

Screams filled the auditorium and fans starting running. When Michael left and did not return to the stage, it was very difficult for the authorities to keep the crowd calm and orderly. Since no one in charge could give an accurate report, audience members developed their own theories. Most believed it had been an assassination attempt. Now they worried that Michael Jackson might be dead.

Authorities wanted to transport Michael through an exit from the back of the theater to avoid the fans and news media. But Michael insisted on exiting where the crowds and photographers could see him. He said that he wanted to be able to wave to everyone to show that he was all right. No one could ask for better public relations.

"No, leave the glove on," he told the ambulance attendants as he was being prepared for the stretcher. "The media is here."

No matter the pain, shock, or hysteria, the showman prevailed. A videotape of Michael Jackson leaving the theater and being loaded into the ambulance became the lead story on all news broadcasts that evening. There he was, strapped in a stretcher, covered with blankets up to his nose, his bandaged and taped head resting on a pillow, one sequined-gloved hand protruding from the blankets.

"If E.T. hadn't come to Elliot, he would have come to Michael's house," Steven Spielberg once said of Jackson. But now Michael himself *was* E.T., an odd little creature, hurt by grown-ups playing with fire and now being carted away to who knows where by who knows whom and for who knows what.

On his way out, Michael lifted his hand and weakly waved to the cameras.

He noticed several Pepsi executives huddled together in a corner with worried looks on their faces. They must have realized that this accident could mushroom into one of the biggest lawsuits in history. Michael Jackson could actually *own* Pepsi by the time the smoke cleared.

The next day, photos of E.T.—Michael—were on the front pages of all the newspapers. Michael would call it "that famous shot of me."

Michael Jackson was taken to the emergency room at Cedars-Sinai Medical Center, where he was treated with an antiseptic cream and bandages. He was offered a painkiller, but because of his disdain for narcotics, he turned it down. Soon, though, he realized he needed it and accepted one.

Then, accompanied by Joe and Katherine, Bill Bray and another guard, his brother Randy and his doctor, Steve Hoefflin, he was transported to Brotman Memorial Hospital in Culver City.

One reporter tried to get an interview with Katherine and Joe as they rushed into the hospital, arm in arm.

"How do you feel about this?" the reporter asked.

Katherine kept walking, but Joe stopped and glared at the writer. "That's my son in there," he said. "How do you think I feel? How does any father feel when his son is hurt?" Joe was understandably upset.

"You and Michael have had your differences, though," observed the audacious reporter.

Joe studied the writer for a moment. "Hey, man, do you have any kids?"

The reporter shook his head no.

"Then you can't understand how I feel. Whatever happens, a father will always be a father. His son will always be his son. All right?" Then he turned to catch up with his wife.

Michael spent Friday evening in room 3307, resting. In no time, he was bored and asked for a videotape player. Because no one on staff had the key to the cabinet where the hospital's video equipment was kept, someone broke the padlock to get Michael a machine and an assortment of ten tapes. Michael chose the science-fiction film *Close Encounters of the Third Kind*—directed by his friend Steven Spielberg—and watched it until he fell asleep at one A.M. after taking a sleeping pill.

Outside his room, Katherine, Joe, and Bill Bray prepared to go home. They all looked relieved. It had been a tense, exhausting experience. Joe noticed a group of Pepsi executives huddling in a corner. As he walked by them on his way out, he asked, "Why the long faces? Jeez. The burn's only the size of a half-dollar."

\* \* \*

Michael had been fortunate. His face and body escaped injury in the accident. He suffered a palm-sized patch of second- and third-degree burns on the back of his head. Only a small spot—smaller than a half-dollar, actually, more like a quarter—received a third-degree burn. Doctors said most of his hair would grow back. Ironically, Michael had visited burn patients at the same hospital on New Year's Day. He had been particularly affected by one patient, twenty-three-year-old mechanic Keith Perry, who had suffered third-degree burns on 95 percent of his body. Michael had had photos taken of himself holding the patient's hand—with his sequined glove on. When asked why he was wearing the glove, Michael responded, "This way, I am never offstage." The photos were quickly distributed to the media.

By Saturday, according to nursing supervisor Patricia Lavales, "Michael was singing in the shower." He spent the morning watching "American Bandstand" and "Soul Train" on television when he wasn't talking on the telephone. Diana Ross called. So did Liza Minnelli.

Michael was released later that day. According to Lavales, before he left the hospital, Michael, wearing turquoise hospital scrubs over his street clothes and a black fedora covering his wound, went from room to room on the unit saying good-bye, taking photographs, and signing autographs on *Thriller* albums and eight-by-ten glossies for each of the ten other burn patients.

The nursing supervisor said, "They were really happy he took time out to see them, despite the fact that he himself was burned. He was an inspiration to them." Michael spent ample time with the patients and, before he left, reached out and touched each bedridden patient with his magic glove.

After being released from the hospital, Michael checked into the Sheraton Universal for a night in order to be away from his family. John Branca met him there.

"Mike, I think God is trying to tell you something about this commercial," John Branca told him. "We should never have done it."

"I know, Branca."

"You know what? You've got Don King to thank for this," Branca added.

"Look, don't remind me," Michael said. He was clearly disgusted.

That evening, Michael, his doctor, Steve Hoefflin—who had performed Michael's rhinoplasty surgery and is chief of plastic surgery at Brotman—and others in the Jackson entourage, including John Branca, watched a videotape of the accident to determine just what had happened. (As soon as the accident occurred, Branca's partner, Gary Stiffelman, seized the tapes from the cameramen and took them. Pepsi didn't have any footage. Michael had it all.)

After Michael saw the tape, he became furious.

"I could have been killed," he said. "Did you see what they did to me. Did you see that? Man, I can't believe this!"

The Jackson entourage tried to calm him down, but it was useless.

"Show it again," Michael ordered.

Someone popped the tape back into the VCR, and everyone watched again.

"That's it," Michael said. "I want the tape released to the public. I want the public to see this. I'm gonna ruin Pepsi. After my fans see this tape, Pepsi will be history."

"But, Mike—" one of his associates began.

"No. I'm serious," Michael said, cutting him off. "Release the tape. I want it on the news right away. I want everyone to see what happened to me, and I want it released on Monday. Pepsi's gonna be sorry, real sorry."

"You can't do it, Mike."

"You wanna bet? I sure can," Michael insisted. "And I'm going to."

By Sunday, word of Michael's decision got back to Roger Enrico. The president of Pepsi-Cola was horrified at the thought. He looked at the tape. "Did the press reports say his hair was on fire? To me, it looked like his whole head. Like a human torch. No way can *anyone* see this footage. It's grotesque."

Enrico said he was "stunned." He knew he had to change Michael's mind or no Michael Jackson fans would ever drink Pepsi again after they saw "what Pepsi did to him."

"With more anxiety than I've ever felt in my life," Enrico telephoned Joe Jackson to ask what should be done about this problem.

"What problem?" Jackson asked.

"Michael wants to release the film with his hair on fire."

"Why would he want to do a thing like that?" Joe asked, perplexed.

Enrico didn't know the answer to that question. He told Joe that if Michael allowed the film to be released, people would always associate him with this accident, the way, he said, the public always thinks of the Zapruder assassination tape whenever they think of President John F. Kennedy.

The tape would be released early the next week, Michael decided. He was bent on revenge. It would have been out sooner, only his associates were unable to locate a lab that could process the film on a Sunday at such short notice.

First, to whet everyone's appetite, a blurred photograph of Michael descending the stairs with his hair on fire—it looked in the photo as if he had a halo—was distributed by the Associated Press. It made the front pages of practically every daily newspaper.

After that photo was released, John Branca felt that Michael had had ample time to cool off, and he tried to talk Michael out of releasing the tape.

"It's morbid, Mike," Branca told him in a meeting with associates. "Don't do this to your fans. And besides that, I think we should just settle with Pepsi and get on with our lives. Why infuriate everybody, Mike?"

"Why not?" Michael wanted to know.

"C'mon, Mike. You're bigger than this," Branca said.

Michael cracked a smile. "I'm being dumb, huh?" he said. "You're right. Let's just end this. But I want them to pay, Branca. I mean it. They should pay big time for this."

Michael was only being paid $700,000 to do the Pepsi commercials, but the publicity he would receive because of the accident would prove invaluable. The burning triggered an outpouring of public sympathy from around the world. The hospital where he was first taken for treatment was forced to add six volunteers to answer telephone calls from fans and well-wishers. At Brotman, thousands of calls, letters, and cards were received.

"Everyone was surprised that he was not further injured," Steven Hoefflin said at a press conference. (Hoefflin, who had given Michael three nose jobs by this time, said at the conference that he had had Michael as a patient before but declined to say what he was treated for.)

Hoefflin noted that the fireworks "did not malfunction." The accident took place either because Jackson did not move quickly enough down a stairway or because the fireworks were touched off too soon. The doctor observed, "Naturally, an individual like Michael Jackson, who has worked very hard since he was ten years old and is in excellent condition, recovers very quickly."

Even Ronald Reagan got into the act with a fan letter to Michael dated February 1, 1984: "I was pleased to learn that you were not seriously hurt in your recent accident. I know from experience that these things can happen on the set—no matter how much caution is exercised . . ."

"I'll tell you what really pissed Mike off," said Steve Howell. "It was when attorneys for Bob Giraldi [producer of the video] tried to put the blame for the burn on the hair grease Mike used on his hair. They said that this grease was responsible for his hair catching fire. He thought Giraldi was his friend and wondered why he would do such a thing. The stuff he uses on his hair is, he told me, like everything else he uses on his body, one hundred percent natural, no chemicals at all. He felt, 'There it is again, another adult trying to rip me off and do something to harm me.' "

When Michael got home to the Encino compound, one of the first things he did was call Steve Howell: "Can you come up here and set up the video equipment in my room so I can watch the Three Stooges?"

That afternoon, Michael took a spin around the property in his electric car, a close copy of the vehicle from Mr. Toad's Wild Ride at Disneyland. From the street, outside the gate, his fans—who were always there—could see him whizzing up and down the driveway like a little boy whose mother let him out to play. After he put away his expensive toy, Michael playfully tossed the gown he wore in the hospital over the gate. Sixteen-year-old Dena Cypher was standing there on a vigil. She caught the prize. "I look at it every night, smell it, all that good stuff," she said. "I was going to wear it to bed, but my mom talked me out of it." Not sanitary? "No. We didn't want to wrinkle it. I mean, those are *Michael's* wrinkles in there."

To this day, Michael experiences some pain in his scalp where he was burned. "They knew I could have sued them," Michael wrote of Pepsi in his book, *Moonwalk*, though most people felt that it was probably the production company, not Pepsi, that was responsible. "But I was real nice about it."

Well, he wasn't *that* nice. Michael didn't mention that he wanted Pepsi-Cola to pay "big time," as he put it to John Branca. Branca pressured Pepsi-Cola into making a monetary settlement to Michael for what had happened. Pepsi was willing to do so, but Michael demanded $1.5 million. The company argued that that was too much money and that the accident wasn't their fault. "How about a half mil?"

Finally, under threat of a lawsuit, Pepsi-Cola did ante up the $1.5 million.

Michael Jackson accepted the money, then donated it to the Michael Jackson Burn Center, which had been established in his honor at Brotman after the accident.*

*That* was nice.

---

*In October 1987 the Michael Jackson Burn Center closed its doors because of financial difficulties.

# Chapter

# ❧ 22 ❧

By February 1984—Grammy time—Michael Jackson's accident in Los Angeles had made world news for weeks. It only served to heighten the suspense about the forthcoming Pepsi commercials, which were to be aired for the first time during the Grammy Awards show. Some people began talking about their "debut," as if they were among the most newsworthy events of the century. Comedians had a field day.

One humorist, Joe Morgenstern, noted that the difference between Richard Pryor and Michael Jackson is that Pryor got burned with coke (referring to his free-basing accident) and Jackson got burned with Pepsi. "That's only half the story, though," Morgenstern noted. "The other difference is that Jackson got a presold blockbuster commercial out of his misfortune, while Pryor only got a spiritual awakening and a new lease on life."

Before the Grammys, the commercials would be "unveiled" at a black-tie event for one thousand bottlers at New York's Lincoln Center; the commercials would also be screened for the press in New York, have their world premiere on MTV at no cost to the sponsor, and then, finally, appear as consecrated commercials during the Grammy telecast.

Down to the very last minute, Michael gave the Pepsi-Cola Company a difficult time. When he saw the finished product (actually two commercials, the concert scene and a "street" scene featuring Michael with dancer Alfonso Riberio), Michael adamantly insisted that they were not good enough. He sent word to Pepsi that he hated them. There was too much of his face in the concert spot. Michael wouldn't talk directly to the Pepsi people about the problem. He didn't really feel like it. Either he was acting spoiled, or he was being shy. No one could be sure.

"Look, it's not easy for Michael," Joe Jackson told one Pepsi executive. "He's got great ideas, but he can't always express them. Let me help. I can act as a go-between and make it easier on everybody."

Roger Enrico telephoned Joe to complain that they couldn't make the commercials "better" if Michael refused to talk about them. No matter what people may have thought about Joe personally, they respected the fact that he was usually willing at least to listen to them. If he thought an idea had merit, he would do his best to convince Michael to consider the proposal favorably. Joe promised to work out the problems with his son. A few hours later, he called back.

"Roger, I have Michael here," he said, "and I'm sure you guys can work things out."

There was a pause.

"Talk to the man, will you?" Joe urgently whispered to Michael. "Get on the phone."

Michael got on the line. He complained that he was made to take off his sunglasses during the taping, and that he really didn't want to. He had been promised that there would be only one close-up without the glasses, "and now I see lots of close-ups of me with my glasses off." He fretted that there was too much of him in the commercials, "*way* over four seconds of my face." The film was too dark. He spins twice during the routine. "And I only agreed to one spin," Michael reminded Enrico. And in the commercial with Alfonso Riberio, which he liked and said was "magic, just magic," he wanted bells to sound when Alfonso bumped into him as they danced, "like the sound of a wind chime."

"Bells?" Enrico asked, dazed.

"Yes, bells."

The film was re-edited. Michael took a look at the new product and telephoned Roger Enrico with the verdict.

"Hello, Mr. Enrico. This is Michael Jackson. You know, the person you spoke to the other day about the commercials."

He remembered.

Michael said there was still too much of him in the commercial. It might be five seconds. It should be four. And also, he was seen smiling in one of the dance scenes.

"So?"

"So I never smile when I dance," Michael explained.

"Oh."

* * *

On February 7, Michael Jackson was inducted into the *Guinness Book of Records* during a ceremony at the American Museum of Natural History in New York City. The *Guinness Book* was first published in 1955 after Sir Hugh Beavers of the Guinness Brewing Company had asked a London "fact and figure" agency to verify facts about such things as athletic records, geography, inventions, and discoveries—the kinds of things people argue about in pubs. From the very beginning the book was a success. In 1974 it became the best-selling copyrighted book in publishing history. It is now published in thirty-five languages.

Not everyone can make it into the book. The publishers decide the categories and have strict rules for verification. When Guinness recognized that *Thriller* broke all records for album sales at 25 million copies, CBS Records held a black-tie party for fifteen hundred guests at New York's American Museum of Natural History. Among the guests were Donald and Ivana Trump. Security was tight. There were more than a hundred policemen outside and 150 private security men inside. In spite of the below-freezing temperatures, hundreds of fans lined the fence outside hoping to get a glimpse of the celebrities inside.

Michael's scalp burns were covered by a natural-hair toupee. He wore jeans and a black, sequined, military-type jacket. According to the *New York Times*, Michael walked up to fellow guest, designer Calvin Klein, and said, "I'm wearing your jeans, Mr. Klein."

Michael was accompanied by actress Brooke Shields. *Her* "people" had gotten in touch with *his* "people" and suggested that she would be the perfect date. "Why not?" Michael decided.

Michael was introduced by Walter Yetnikoff, president of CBS Records, as "the greatest artist of all time." Highlights of the ceremony included an eight-foot world globe that, when illuminated, read "Michael Jackson—The Greatest Artist in the World" and a telegram from President and Nancy Reagan: "Your deep faith in God and adherence to traditional values are an inspiration to all of us. You've gained quite a number of fans along the road since 'I Want You Back,' and Nancy and I are among them. Keep up the good work, Michael. We're very happy for you."

"When the album was certified as the best-selling album of all time, I couldn't believe it," Michael would write in his *Moonwalk* memoirs. "Quincy Jones was yelling, 'Bust open the champagne!' We were all in a state. Man! What a feeling! To work so hard on something, to give so much and to succeed! Everyone involved with *Thriller* was floating on air. It was wonderful."

As exciting as the event proved to be, Michael returned to reality when he got back to Los Angeles and met with Joe, Katherine, his brothers, and Don King.

"I want to rename the tour. I don't like 'Victory,'" Michael said. "I want to call it 'The Final Curtain.'"

Michael obviously intended to make it clear that this was the end. Once they finished this tour, he would not work with the brothers again.

"None of the other brothers liked that name at all, 'The Final Curtain,'" Marlon recalled. "Our parents didn't like it either. Michael was making it sound like a funeral, like someone had died. But we weren't dying."

Michael hated the title "Victory tour" because of the obvious implication—that this was somehow a victorious occasion—when actually he was feeling far from victorious.

But he was outvoted.

The Pepsi commercials were still not finished by the last week in February, the time to debut them at the New York State Theater at Lincoln Center. Pepsi-Cola decided to show the bottlers what they had and continue working with Michael to get those close-ups and milliseconds as he wished to have them. Michael made an appearance onstage at Lincoln Center after the commercials were shown and received a wild standing ovation from the Pepsi executives and bottlers. He wore a large hat and, as he took his bow, he removed it to show the spot on his head where he had been burned. The area was covered by a small skullcap.

Michael pointed to it and grinned broadly. He wasn't dancing, so he could smile.

The applause was deafening.

"How many Grammys do you think I'll win?" Michael asked Quincy Jones.

Quincy shrugged.

"Well, all I can say is I hope I win a lot of 'em," Michael said with a smile.

A review of the history of the Grammys—the awards program that the National Academy of Recording Arts and Sciences established in the late 1950s as a pop music equivalent of the Oscars—reveals that Grammy winners are not always the true preeminent artists and recordings of their time.

For example, Elvis Presley never won a Grammy for any of his major pop vocal performances, even though he was the most influential pop artist of the last forty years. Chuck Berry was also routinely omitted. The Beatles only received four Grammys, amazing considering their impact on popular music and culture. Bob Dylan's ground-breaking *Highway 61 Revisited* album won no Grammys in 1965. David Bowie's important *Ziggy Stardust* collection didn't even win a nomination in 1972. James Brown, The Rolling Stones, Sly Stone, and Diana Ross have never received Grammy Awards. Quite simply, the six thousand notoriously conservative people who vote for these awards are not apt to quickly recognize the importance and significance of new artists.

There are also other, political considerations. It has long been rumored that both the nominating process and final electoral process of the Grammy Awards are dominated by major record companies that have turned the award into a self-congratulatory sham. By 1983, this contest had come down to a struggle between two large superpowers—the Warner Brothers/Elektra-Asylum/Atlantic-Atco faction (WEA) and the Columbia/Epic faction (CBS). As a result, it was very difficult for non-WEA and non-CBS recording artists to win Grammys. Motown artists—with the exception of Stevie Wonder—were usually not even in the running. In fact, in 1982 CBS won twenty-one of a possible sixty-two awards, including all the major citations.

Michael wasn't interested in the politics of the Grammy Awards. "Who cares?" he once told a friend. "All I want is as many of 'em as I can get."

He needn't have worried. Michael Jackson was, quite simply, too popular for the Academy to ignore. So popular, in fact, that everyone agreed on his importance; he had become rock music's most commonly celebrated hero. And a CBS artist, to boot. Michael was fortunate. When the Grammy nominations were announced, he received an unprecedented twelve nominations—the highest number of mentions for any single performer in Grammy history—including Record of the Year ("Beat It"), Album of the Year (*Thriller*), and Song of the Year ("Beat It" and "Billie Jean"); a nomination for Best Children's Recording for his narration of *E.T.*; nominations for the engineers who remixed the instrumental track of "Billie Jean" for the B side of a single, and for the songwriters who wrote "PYT (Pretty Young Thing)" for his album; nominations for his producer, Quincy Jones; and an additional Best Producer nomination jointly shared by Michael and Quincy. In fact, Jackson's closest competitor was his producer and occasional arranger, Quincy Jones, who received six nominations.

Along with *Thriller*, the Police's *Synchronicity* and the *Flash-*

*dance* soundtrack also received nominations for Album of the Year, as did Billy Joel's *An Innocent Man* and David Bowie's *Let's Dance*.

Tuesday, February 28, 1984: Grammy night.

The scene at the Shrine Auditorium in Los Angeles was pure pandemonium. Giant klieg lights cut dramatic white patterns in the dark sky above. Fans in their roped-off areas were ready to scream and call out the names of anyone they might recognize.

Twenty-five-year-old Michael Jackson finally arrived for his coronation as king of the pop music world. He wore a spangled uniform with epaulets and the rhinestoned glove on his right hand. With him once again was Brooke Shields.

Michael did not want to go to the awards show with Brooke Shields. Shortly before the ceremony, she came by the Encino house unexpectedly to ask him if he would consider taking her to the show. Although they had been friends for two years, it's not known whether Brooke, eighteen years old at this time, actually felt attracted to Michael, or whether she knew that going with him to the Grammys would garner enormous publicity for her. She had already accompanied him to the American Music Awards in January when Michael swept the awards (eight of them) and to the Guinness Awards in February. Her picture—with Michael's—was in every newspaper across the country. So being Michael's date did have its public relations benefits, and Brooke's career was in a lull at this time.

Brooke Shields was—and still is—instantly recognizable, but she is not a major star. Her career had never been critically acclaimed; her films were usually panned. Her famous jeans commercials were no longer airing at this time, and a movie called *Sahara* had temporarily been shelved. She is intelligent, however, and was attending Princeton University in New Jersey at the time. (She graduated in 1987.) Brooke and Michael enjoyed each other's company and related to one another because they both understood the pressure of being a child star with demanding parents. Brooke's mother-manager, Teri, was said to be delighted by her daughter's association with Michael.

LaToya and Janet were in another room when Michael came back and told them of Brooke's request.

"I don't want to take her," LaToya remembered Michael saying. "I really, *really* don't."

"Well then *tell her*, Michael," big sister instructed. "Tell her no if you don't want to take her."

"But I can't."

"Why not?" Janet wondered.

"Because I don't want to hurt her feelings," Michael protested. Cringing, he went back into the living room.

A few moments later he rejoined his sisters, wearing a sheepish grin.

"Well?" LaToya asked.

"I'm taking her," Michael said. The man who was not the least bit intimated by Berry Gordy and Walter Yetnikoff had been hectored by Brooke Shields into doing what he did not want to do.

On another occasion, Michael gave his employee Steve Howell four photographs to look at. One was of him with Brooke Shields at the Grammys.

"What's she like?" Howell asked.

"She's okay," Michael said nonchalantly, shrugging. "But I only took her to help her out," he added. "There was no romance. Not at all. We're friends. All of this was strictly for her, for the sake of publicity. She's nice. I like to help her out when I can. It was good P.R. for her to be seen with me."

Michael and Brooke arrived in a white Rolls-Royce just moments before the ceremony began. One reporter called Michael and Brooke "the Annette and Frankie of the eighties" (referring to Annette Funicello and Frankie Avalon) since both hated cigarettes, drink, and drugs and lived at home with their mothers.

Tatum O'Neal was waiting at the door with four friends. Michael, Brooke, and a coterie of security guards rushed right by her. "Michael, hey, Michael!" she shouted. It was too late. He was gone. She turned to her friends. "I'll introduce you to him later. I promise."

Michael, wearing heavy pancake makeup, sat in the theater's front row with Shields and Emmanuel Lewis, who met them there. Brooke seemed particularly uncomfortable about having to share her date with a twelve-year-old playmate. Earlier, photographers descended, asking them to pose for pictures. Michael held Emmanuel with one arm and hugged Brooke with his free hand. It was as if he was trying to remind Brooke that the presence of a child on the date meant that he really wasn't serious about her. "Let's get out of here," Brooke was heard saying to Michael. "People are making fun of us."

Every time Michael's face flashed on the studio monitors or his name was mentioned, cheers rose from fans in the balcony and from industry colleagues who filled the orchestra seats. When Michael's two Pepsi commercials "premiered," the audience reacted with a tidal wave of applause and whistles. It was obvious that

Michael was the man of the moment before he had even won a single award. Joan Rivers noted in a standard explanation of how the votes were tabulated, "The reason we're reading the rules is so that all the losers will know why they lost to Michael Jackson."

That night, Michael made Grammy history by winning eight awards out of a possible ten wins on twelve nominations (three of his nominations were in one category).

Not since the brilliant maturation of Motown's Stevie Wonder in the mid-seventies (he won five Grammys each year in 1973 and 1974) had the public, press, and industry—three factions that seldom see eye-to-eye on anything—agreed so wholeheartedly on an entertainer's importance to our pop culture. This kind of alignment of opinion about a pop music recording star had only happened a couple of times in recent show business music history—with Elvis Presley and the Beatles, neither of whom were awarded the Grammys they deserved. So, in a sense, the unanimous recognition of Michael Jackson at the Shrine in 1984 meant the fans, critics, and voters had agreed on a new pop music king.

Accepting the Best Album award for *Thriller* (which, by this time, had sold 27 million records and was the biggest-selling album in history and still number one on the *Billboard* charts), a nervous and shy Jackson said, "This is a great honor. I'm very happy."

When Michael later picked up the seventh and record-breaking Grammy, he took off his dark glasses in a victory salute—Katharine Hepburn ("my dear friend") told him he should—"for the girls in the balcony." (Hepburn had scolded Michael for wearing the shades at the American Music Awards and told him he was "cheating" his fans by not allowing them to see his eyes.)

Michael accepted one award with the comment, "I have something very important to say . . . really," and proceeded to pay touching tribute to legendary rhythm-and-blues star Jackie Wilson, who had recently died.

(Jackie Wilson was one of Michael's show business idols. After suffering a heart attack onstage in New Jersey in 1975, Jackie lay in a helpless, practically vegetative condition in a nursing home. All of the Jackson children went to visit him one day in 1977. His primary caretaker was Joyce McCrae, who would go on to work for the Jacksons. She propped Jackie up so that he could see his guests. He couldn't speak; he would blink once for no and twice for yes. All of the Jackson siblings were gathered around his bedside, trying not to cry, as Joyce introduced them one by one. When she got to Michael, Jackie smiled and blinked twice.

McCrae recalled, "There was a happiness on his face that was just so precious, so deep, and so moving. Anytime I saw something in Jackie's expression that indicated that he actually *knew*, that he understood, it was very moving. He was so glad they were there. It was a special moment for all of us.'')

Michael also won Best Record (''Beat It'') and Best Vocalist in three areas: pop (''Beat It''), rock (''Thriller''), and rhythm and blues (''Billie Jean''). He also won Best Children's Album (*E.T.*), Best Rhythm-and-Blues Song (''Billie Jean'') and Best Record Producer, an award he shared with Quincy Jones. Jackson's two losses were to The Police, who copped three Grammys in all for the *Synchronicity* album and the single ''Every Breath You Take.'' Michael's eight wins topped Paul Simon's previous record of seven in a year, earned in a 1970 sweep for *Bridge over Troubled Water*.

In one acceptance, he called CBS head Walter Yetnikoff to the stage with him. Later, he invited LaToya, Janet, and Rebbie to join him.

Backstage, after the awards, Michael didn't have much to say to the press. It had already been made clear to the panting media that Michael would not be available for interviews—he would allow photos only—and that he would perhaps wave to the TV cameras. The assembled media, having been deprived of the opportunity to ask Michael questions about his winnings, had no choice but to ask all of the other winners how *they* felt about Michael's winnings. ''I've seen four phenomena in my lifetime: Frank Sinatra, Elvis Presley, The Beatles, and Michael Jackson,'' Quincy Jones noted.

''What's your favorite song?'' someone shouted out to Michael as he walked away.

'' 'My Favorite Things' by Julie Andrews,'' Michael responded.

''You're kidding, right?'' the reporter asked.

''Nope.'' Michael started singing the song—''Raindrops on roses and whiskers on kittens . . .''—as he skipped down the hall, surrounded by four security men. As he left the auditorium with Brooke and Emmanuel, fifty people were elbowed out of his way by the security guards—including Tatum O'Neal and her four friends. ''I'll introduce you to him later,'' she promised them. As Michael's Rolls-Royce sped away from the auditorium, he rolled down the window and leaned out, both arms raised in triumph, clutching and waving a Grammy in one hand. ''*All right!*'' he yelled out, whooping like a rowdy teenager on a Friday night.

Afterwards, Michael hosted a private party at the exclusive Rex restaurant in downtown Los Angeles. Two hundred figures of the music and film world rushed there to pay homage to Michael, but he did little socializing. "There's too many people," he was over-heard saying. "I just can't bear to meet them all."

So Michael and Brooke reigned like king and queen, smiling, waving, and tossing kisses from a balcony overlooking a crowd that included Bob Dylan, Tony Curtis, Neil Diamond, Eddie Murphy, Cyndi Lauper (sporting orange hair), Arnold Schwarzenegger, Rodney Dangerfield, Julio Iglesias (who had trouble at the door because he wanted to bring in four guests), and Tatum ("I'll introduce you to him later. I promise.") O'Neal. Everyone feasted on whole Maine lobsters, cold salmon, caviar, quail, and an array of exotic desserts washed down by magnums of Tattinger champagne.

"Are you having a good time?" Michael asked Brooke.

"Uh-huh."

"Uh, can we leave now?" he asked uncomfortably.

Around 11:30 P.M., Michael and Brooke slipped out through a side door. Brooke's mother, Teri, was waiting in Michael's white Rolls for her daughter. The three were driven to L'Ermitage Hotel in Beverly Hills, where the women were staying.

Michael saw them out of the car, kissed Brooke on the cheek, shook Mrs. Shields's hand, and then got back into the car.

"Congratulations, Michael," Brooke said with a sad smile. "Must you go?"

"Yeah, I do," he replied. He rolled up the window.

Then Michael Jackson's chauffeur drove him off into the dark, lonely night.

"Michael is having an affair with Brooke Shields," Jermaine Jackson insisted at this time during an interview while in London. "He sees her a lot. Every time I talk to him about her he smiles and seems to be very happy."

Although Michael wrote in his autobiography *Moonwalk* that he and Brooke "were romantically serious for a while," it is only fair to let the lady have the last word.

"We were just friends," Brooke would later admit to Joan Rivers. "He's nice. There was no great romance or anything."

Because of the success of *Thriller*, Michael Jackson had become one of the most sought-after celebrities in Hollywood, invited to a multitude of A-list parties. Often he needed an escort and, uncomfortable in his new role as social butterfly, he sought someone safe—and older. Liza Minnelli was one of his favorites, partly because Michael had always been fascinated by the mystique of her mother, Judy Garland, but also because Liza had grown up in Hollywood, knew her way around, and was able to keep Michael comfortable and relaxed.

Besides, in 1984 it was Liza, not Michael, who received the coveted invitation to the April 10 party hosted by famed literary agent Swifty Lazar. Held every year right after the Academy Awards, the event has become so prestigious that even big-name stars consider it an honor to be invited. Celebrities often instruct their publicists to hound Lazar for months in advance for an invitation.

Although in recent years the party has been held at the trendy restaurant Spago, in 1984 it was held at the then in place, the Bistro in Beverly Hills. Guests included Orson Welles, Cary Grant, Jacqueline Bisset, and Linda Evans. No matter how famous Michael had become, in his heart he was just another star-struck fan. His success didn't diminish his awe, but it did allow him to observe his idols up close.

When he and Liza finally made their one A.M. appearance, the celebrities present fell all over themselves for a chance to meet Michael Jackson—a man who had made only one movie, and that one a flop.

As *USA Today* columnist Jeannie Williams reported, "The stars were reduced to mush, fawning and panting as if the evening hadn't been about movies but about Jackson instead."

Michael was never far from Liza's side. Wearing another of his blue glitter military outfits, dark aviator shades, and the requisite rhinestoned glove, Michael looked around the room and probably couldn't help noticing that everyone was gawking at him. Liza strolled about proudly with Michael on her arm, as if to say, "Yes, *I'm* with Michael Jackson. What do you think of *that*?"

"Let me have a scotch and Coca-Cola," Liza instructed the waiter. "And Mr. Jackson will have the same."

"Oh, no," Michael protested. "I'll have a . . ." He hesitated. "I'll have an orange juice, please."

"Oh, of course he will," Liza said. "And so will I. With scotch." She laughed merrily.

The waiter walked away. "No scotch in mine," Michael meekly called out after him.

Joan Collins sauntered over. "Michael, my dear boy, how truly wonderful to see you." She embraced him warmly and winked at Liza. Michael looked a bit confused.

"Quick, stand right next to him; let's get a picture." A woman shoved her embarrassed husband next to Michael. "Uh, this is for our daughter, Natasha," the man hastily explained. Michael, who has no doubt heard a similar line a thousand times before, nodded patiently.

"Oh, by the way, my name is Michael Caine," said the actor. The two shook hands as Caine's wife, Shakira, snapped a photo.

Joan Collins turned to a friend. "I simply *must* have the name of his plastic surgeon," she whispered. "I adore his nose, don't 'you?"

Johnny Carson, seated with his girlfriend (now wife) Alexis Mass, took it all in and then came over to Michael just as his orange juice was being served.

"Nice to see you, Michael," Carson said with a firm handshake.

Michael seemed dazed. "I . . . uh, gee, nice to see you again too, Mr. Carson."

"Call me John."

"Oh, okay. Call me Mike."

Liza Minnelli grabbed Michael's hand. "Now look, Johnny, he's *my* date," she told Carson with a big smile.

"Wow! What a nice guy that Johnny Carson is," Michael was overheard saying as Liza dragged him away.

"Yes, he's such a dear," she agreed. "Now we're going to call my father."

"We are?"

She led him off to the phone in the ladies' room. Michael, unfazed, followed.

After Liza dialed the number, she began doing a soft-shoe dance routine and started singing, "Forget your troubles, c'mon get happy. C'mon and chase your cares away."

Michael laughed. "I love bein' around you, you know that?" he told her.

"Shh," Liza said. Her father answered the phone. "Daddy, listen, I want you to meet Michael Jackson."

"Who?" was apparently the question back to her.

"Why, he's a *wonderful* singer and one of my *best* friends," she explained. "Now say hello." A pause. "Oh, Daddy, just say hello. Now, *c'mon*."

She handed the phone to Michael.

"No, I can't," Michael protested, his hand over the mouthpiece.

"Oh, but you simply *must*," Liza insisted.

"But he's my idol." Michael had always enjoyed director Vincente Minnelli's films.

"Well, then say hello." Liza punched him on the arm playfully. "He doesn't bite."

Michael took his hand off the mouthpiece. "Hello, Mr. Minnelli," he whispered. He listened for five seconds, his eyes darting left and right. With a giggle, he handed the phone back to Liza. "God, he's so nice," Michael gushed.

Liza got back on the phone. "Now listen, Daddy. Put on your black velvet jacket. We'll be over in twenty minutes."

Pause.

"Yes, I'm bringing *him* over *there*."

A pause.

"Never mind what he's wearing."

Another pause.

"Okay, he's wearing a sequined glove, all right? Are you satisfied?"

Michael doubled over, laughing hysterically.

"Okay, then fine. Good-bye."

And with that, Liza, with Michael on her arm, pushed through the crowd and out the door to the waiting limousine, less than an hour after arriving.

"There they go," Jimmy Stewart was overheard saying. "Dorothy's little girl . . . and the Wiz."


"No one has ever taken on a tour of the magnitude and esteem of the Jacksons," Don King said at the time. "They transcend earthly bounds." Although performers may "transcend earthly bounds," promoters—if they're smart—have to concentrate on mundane matters. Recognizing that he knew little about concert promoting—the venues, staging, lights, and sound—King sought the help of Irving Azoff, head of MCA Records, to "complement my strengths and strengthen my weaknesses." King and Azoff had a separate agreement whereby Azoff would be compensated from King's 15 percent, not from the Jacksons' 85 percent.

With the tour in the offing—forty possible dates and 40 million opportunities for something to go wrong—and Don King a fly in the ointment, Michael realized that he would need someone to protect *his* interests, a new manager. Perhaps he remembered what he told his fourth-grade teacher, Gladys Johnson, when she suggested one day that he bone up on his math. "My manager," Michael replied, "will take care of my money."

Motown had just released a collection of songs by Michael that he had recorded in the early seventies. The album was called *Farewell My Summer Love 1984*, a very misleading title since the songs were recorded more than ten years earlier. The record only sold 106,583 copies, a minuscule number considering the thirty-three million copies of *Thriller* that had been bought by the time Motown released their rip-off product. Still, Michael knew that Berry Gordy was trying to cash in on his fame, and he didn't like it one bit. "It's not fair," he said. "I need someone to stop things like that from happening."

Michael had had meetings with a number of managers, including Colonel Tom Parker, Elvis Presley's Svengali, hoping to find the most qualified person. When it came to choosing his manager, Michael was extremely cautious. He questioned everyone he knew about certain people, trying to determine their worth in the entertainment industry. He would talk to his brothers to see what gossip they had heard; he would check with record company executives. He received a number of offers, including one from Diana Ross, who had her own firm, R.T.C. Management.

"I'm available, Michael. Why don't you let me manage you?"

Michael hedged. "Well, Diane. I just don't know."

Diana sensed his hesitation. "I don't know if I can handle an artist as major as you, but I'll bet I could. So, what do you think?"

Michael only had to observe Diana's recent career at her new label, RCA Records (since leaving Berry Gordy and Motown in 1981), to realize that she wasn't doing very well managing herself. He decided to pass on the offer. Some associates have indicated that he told her thanks anyway and let the idea rest. But that's not what happened. Rather than turn her down—which he probably couldn't bear to do—Michael just refused to take her calls for a while until she finally got tired of phoning.

Michael's choice for manager would surprise most observers. Seven months earlier, in August 1983, when the two were having a meeting about *Thriller* in a bungalow at the Beverly Hills Hotel, Michael had asked Epic Records' head of promotion, Frank Dileo, if he would be interested in managing him. Though many industry observers wondered "why Frank?" ("I asked Michael the same question—why me?" Dileo said) Michael instinctively felt that even though Dileo had no experience as a manager, the way he had networked himself into the recording industry could prove an asset. Michael believed that Frank was largely responsible for *Thriller*'s spectacular success and for the huge sales of all of its single releases. In Frank Dileo, Michael knew he was hiring a terrific record promoter, who may or may not turn out to be a good manager.

Frank Dileo, whose nickname is "Tookie" (Michael used to call him Uncle Tookie), was thirty-six, born and raised in Pittsburgh. From the beginning, he was a fighter. He had political aspirations and dreamed of becoming mayor of Pittsburgh. But fate dealt him a bad hand when his father died on the operating table without medical insurance. Dileo ended up working as a waiter in an Italian restaurant to help his family make ends meet. He got his start in the record industry as an assistant to a record promoter in the Midwest, and in the early seventies, he landed a job with RCA Records in New York. At twenty-one, he became their national director of promotions. While at RCA, he turned that label's promotion department into the record industry's finest.

In 1977, disgusted with the disco music craze and the record business ("I didn't work all my life to hang out with assholes," he said), Dileo became a bookie for college basketball games, a misdemeanor for which he was convicted and fined in 1977 and 1978. He also married and had the first of two children. Then a disaster occurred. While the family attended the funeral of Dileo's mother-in-law, there was an electrical fire in their home. It burned to the ground. The Dileos lost everything and had no insurance. They were broke.

Frank returned to the record business and, in 1979, was named Epic's vice president of promotion. Dileo developed a reputation at Epic as being a confident man in total charge of everything—even matters that didn't concern him. He would wear a sweat suit to the office, along with an eight-thousand-dollar Rolex watch given to him by the Epic recording group REO Speedwagon. Dileo was largely responsible for successes by Meat Loaf, Culture Club, and Cyndi Lauper.

A few years later, he was invited to the recording studio to watch as Michael waxed *Thriller*. He and Michael developed a rapport. Michael was amazed by the way Frank managed to get his records played on the radio with such consistency. They were opposites in every way: Michael was shy and retiring, Frank was loud and boisterous; Michael was a health-food junkie, Frank liked a good hoagie and a Budweiser to wash it down; Michael never smoked, Frank loved cigars, the smellier the better; Michael weighed about 120 pounds; Frank weighed twice that.

Michael admired the way Frank set goals for himself and then achieved them. For instance, Frank decided one day that Michael should have an audience with the Pope. Four months later, he and Pope John Paul II were staring at each other, one on one, at the Vatican. "I'd like to be like Frank," Michael said. "He gets the job done."

Also, Frank had become a close friend and confidant of Walter Yetnikoff, president of CBS Records. He had also socialized with attorney Nat Weiss, one of Yetnikoff's trusted friends. Michael clearly understood how politically valuable those relationships could be to him. In August, Jackson asked Frank to consider managing him. But Frank would not be allowed to manage anyone else. He had to be exclusive to Michael.

"The decision to manage Michael Jackson was not an easy one to make," he said. "I had to answer three questions: One, did I have the energy to step out and handle someone like Michael? Two, did I have the fortitude to take the abuse I'd have to take from the people who can't get to him? And three, did I want to be the bad guy?"

Apparently, Dileo answered yes to all three. "This is certainly the biggest venture I'll ever do in my life. That much I know for sure."

By March, the Victory tour battle lines were drawn. Michael Jackson had his own manager, Frank Dileo, so now the other Jacksons had to have their own. They hired Jack Nance, who had been the group's road manager during the early days at Motown.

Michael didn't trust Don King and wanted nothing to do with him. The brothers were also ambivalent about King by now.

Joe Jackson did everything he could to stay involved and not allow Don King to overshadow him. By doing so, he continued to exasperate everyone every step along the way.

Katherine watched and waited until the next time she would need to speak to Michael in order to keep him in line. It was important to her that the family appear united, although they were not. The Victory tour may have been presented to the public as a group effort, but behind the scenes it was fragmented by so many differences, it was almost impossible to find a common bond that could forge the participants together. If he had to do the tour, then Michael wanted control. He was trying to show some independence; also, if the show flopped, it could hurt his career. Whereas his other brothers wanted only the money, money was Michael's least concern. Joe wanted power. He'd already lost enough of that when his sons fired him as their manager. Now he was out to scavenge any prestige—and money—that he could. Although Katherine wanted family peace, money was important to her too. She'd been on the verge of divorcing Joe, and having a financial toehold could make that possible.

"I said the Pepsi accident was a bad omen," Michael told a family friend. "But I didn't know what it all meant. Now I know. Believe me, trouble's ahead."

# Chapter

# 23

IT WAS MARCH 1984 and Michael Jackson was now twenty-five years old. For at least the last fourteen years, he had been party to manipulating the press by helping to propagate an image of the Jackson family that was wholesome but not altogether true. This was called public relations and was such a part of Michael's psyche that it had become second nature. Now Michael was the one being manipulated, and by his own family.

Michael Jackson had turned his brothers against Don King before he really knew of King's background. He simply didn't like the way the man did business, and didn't feel he had sufficient experience in promoting concerts to make the Victory tour a success.

When Frank Dileo filled Michael in on Don's reputation, Michael was more certain than ever that King should not be involved in his career. Frank told Michael that Don had been criticized for his handling of the defunct U.S. Boxing Championships on ABC Television, championships that were riddled with questionable activities. He also heard of charges, which King has denied, that he skimmed money from closed-circuit fights and sold five-hundred-dollar tickets to boxing matches but did not report the sales. If Michael had to do this tour—and he felt he must, for his mother—he would do everything in his power to distance himself from Don King. "I can tell you one thing," he told John Branca. "I don't want that guy telling *me* what to do, and I don't want him to touch *one single penny* of my money."

Or, as Don King would later say, "With Michael, you're always on trial."

Through John Branca, Michael dispatched a series of instructions to King stating:

1. King may not communicate with anyone on Michael's behalf without prior permission.

2. All monies will be collected by Michael's representatives and not by King.

3. King may not approach any promoters, sponsors, or other people on Michael's behalf.

4. King may not hire any personnel or local promoters, book halls, or, for that matter, do anything at all without Michael's prior approval.

Don King appeared to be perplexed by Michael's demands. However, he had one choice, to abide by them. King felt that Michael was too easily swayed by the opinions of his white manager, Dileo, and white lawyer, Branca. "I see that Michael has nobody black around him," King said to a reporter. "Nobody."

Finally, Michael instructed Branca to fire King once and for all. Branca tried, but King was persistent. He had a contract, and he expected Michael to abide by it. Branca and King had dinner at the Beverly Hills hotel to try to work matters out.

"Look, Johnny, there's no reason why you and me gotta be on bad terms," Don King told John Branca. "I like Michael. I like you. Let's work with one another."

Branca agreed that they should try.

In March, Michael Jackson underwent an eighty-minute surgical procedure at Brotman Memorial Hospital in Culver City, California, to reconstruct the section of his scalp that had been burned during the commercial shoot.

He asked employee Steve Howell to bring the Beta video recorder to the hospital so that he could watch more Three Stooges films. Howell took off in his blue Toyota four-wheel-drive pickup. Howell said, "The closer I got to Brotman, the faster my heart pumped. The whole area was a war zone. Media, fans, cops everywhere, and I realized, 'Who the hell is gonna believe that you work for Michael Jackson?' I hated to tell people who my boss was because no one *ever* believed it.

"I went to a security guard and said, 'I don't know how to say this, but—' and he said, 'Just give me your name.' I did, and before I knew what was happening, an armed guard materialized out of nowhere to take me to Mike. Michael had a whole ward to himself. The nurses were freaking out because Michael Jackson was there. He had a good time. He told me he went to the maternity ward where he visited expectant mothers. Then he wanted to see some

premature babies. So, naturally, they took him. I have a picture I
shot of Mike holding one of the babies. He considered babies a big
inspiration to him, said they filled him with great energy.''

The last week in March, Frank Dileo and Don King were sun-
ning themselves at Dileo's temporary office, a double cabana at the
Beverly Hills Hotel, planning the upcoming Victory tour. Dileo
was doing his best to keep King under control. He did so by be-
friending him. It was obvious, however, that Dileo didn't really
trust King and was keeping an eye on him for Michael.

At this time, Rhode Island rock promoter Frank Russo offered
$40 million to Joe and Katherine Jackson and the Jacksons in order
to become tour coordinator over King. Joe apparently led Russo to
believe he was going to replace King. ''All the brothers were hugging me. They started popping champagne,'' Russo recalled. ''I
couldn't believe it was really happening.''

Later in the week, King was having a drink at the Polo Lounge
when an emissary from Russo stopped at his table. ''You're out,''
Russo's representative informed him.

Don King calmly went to a pay phone and called Joe Jackson.
King apparently reminded Jackson that he already had a signed
contract and he intended to have it honored.

*Frank Russo* was out. ''He wanted to have me fired,'' Don King
claimed. ''But the flak has settled.'' Why? ''Because I have a tremendous relationship with Michael.''

There was another family meeting the first week in April. John
Branca told the brothers, ''Mike and I have discussed this and we
feel we should get someone really good to mastermind this tour.
Let's sell a zillion tickets. All we should care about is the back end
[in other words, not the advance front money] and not give away a
lot of the profit.''

''No way,'' Jermaine said. ''We need a big guarantee, lots of
up-front money. As much as possible.''

At this point, Michael spoke. ''Why don't you just listen to
Branca. He knows what he's talking about. We don't need the big
guarantee if we can make it up at the end. We need someone shrewd,
not someone rich.''

''We need someone shrewd *and* rich,'' Jackie said.

Michael shook his head and sat down. ''Fine,'' he said. ''Do
what you want to do.''

Instead of hiring someone who had a history of tour promotion,
the brothers wanted to hire a man by the name of Chuck Sullivan,
head of Stadium Management Corporation, of Foxboro, Massachusetts, and former owner of the New England Patriots football

team. Why? Because he guaranteed the Jacksons $36.6 million with $12.5 million up front, which he borrowed from the Crocker National Bank in California, putting up his family's football stadium in Foxboro as collateral. According to the new forty-five-page contract, Sullivan took 25 percent of the tour's estimated $50 million gross; the brothers would divide the remaining 75 percent evenly, but would have to give 15 percent of their share to Don King and their parents. Three separate billings from attorneys representing Michael, Jermaine, and the other four brothers appeared among the twenty pages of attachments to the contract. The total billing for their collective legal advice on drawing up this new deal came to $196,500.

Sullivan—a third-generation promoter—had plenty of experience in the National Football League, but little with rock events. His first and only major musical road show was the Vietnam Bob Hope Christmas Show in 1968. Michael was apprehensive about Sullivan's ability, but felt that he could at least keep an eye on Don King. Michael was also able to convince the brothers to allow Irving Azoff, head of MCA, to come aboard as a tour consultant. "Now, they're all chiefs and no Indians," said an embittered Frank Russo, who filed a $40 million breach of contract suit against the Jacksons. (The suit was ultimately settled.)

In the spring of 1984, Michael arranged for Dr. Steven Hoefflin, his plastic surgeon, to give him another rhinoplasty . . . a third nose job. "He was determined that the last two weren't good enough," said a source who once worked in Hoefflin's office. " 'It has to be thinner,' he insisted. 'Did you see the way it looked on the American Music Awards when I was standing next to Diane?' he asked. 'Hers was so thin and mine looked so fat. I just hated that.' He didn't come out and say he wanted Diana Ross's nose, but it was pretty obvious that that's the shape he was after."

"I saw him right after that third operation," Steve Howell recalled. "I was at the house dropping off some film and Mike was home. He didn't know I was there and our paths crossed. He shrieked, 'Oh no!' " and ran off. It was like seeing a woman you don't know in her underwear and without her makeup on, that was his reaction. He looked like a guy who'd been in a boxing match and forgot to put his hands up. His face was black and blue. There was a bandage—some kind of gauzy bandage—over his nose.

"A couple of weeks later, we were together and talking, and I was standing very close. While he's talking, I'm looking. I'm studying his face and I notice what I thought were blackheads around his nose. And I thought, 'Damn, all those natural creams and other cosmetics he uses on his face, and the guy has blackheads?' Studying the area on the other side of his nostrils I realized, 'Hey, those aren't blackheads. Those are stitches.' He had six small, tiny stitches around his nose. There was continual work in months to come: his skin looked like it was being stretched, peeled, or something. The reason I'm vague is that this is not something people around the house ever discussed.''

No matter how hectic his life had become, Michael Jackson always took time to meet with sick children. On April 9, a fourteen-year-old named David Smithee and his mother pulled into the Hayvenhurst driveway to meet David's idol. David didn't have much time. He was dying of cystic fibrosis. The Brass Ring Society, which is dedicated to fulfilling the dreams of terminally ill children, contacted Michael and arranged the visit. Michael met David in the living room. David's mother, Karen, has said that Michael was "so shy he couldn't look at us." After Karen left, Michael and David went into the kitchen for lunch. Then Michael showed his guest the animals outside, and he videotaped an interview he conducted with the boy. The two new friends played video games and watched a film in the theater. Michael gave David the red leather jacket he wore on the "Beat It" video and the black sequined glove he wore for the American Music Awards. When David left Hayvenhurst, he was a very happy youngster. Seven weeks later, he died.

When the Jacksons' *Victory* album was released, it was dedicated to Katherine Jackson, Marvin Gaye, and David Smithee.

How ironic that Michael's benevolent spirit wasn't enough to satisfy the elders of his Jehovah's Witness congregation. They expected him to restrict his entertainment practices as well. At this time, Michael was called into another meeting with the Witness elders over the "Thriller" video. Again, they told him that they were considering excluding Michael from the religion. Michael left that meeting particularly shaken. He did not want to be disfellowshipped. He was torn and upset.

He decided he would disown "Thriller" if he had to. The title track to the most successful album in the history of music would no longer be performed by its artist. Furthermore, Michael would make a public statement about his sin in an issue of the Witnesses' periodical, *Awake!* (May 22, 1984):

"I would never make a video like that again," he said of the "Thriller" video. "I just intended to do a good, fun, short film, not to purposely bring to the screen something to scare people or to do anything bad. I would never do anything like that again because a lot of people were offended by it. In fact, I have blocked further distribution of the film over which I have control, including its release in some other countries. There's all kinds of promotional stuff being proposed on 'Thriller.' But I told them, 'No, no, no. I don't want to do *anything* with "Thriller." No more "Thriller." ' "

That satisfied Michael's religion.

For now.

In May 1984, Michael, who was twenty-five, and his brothers and sisters hosted a small birthday gathering in honor of their mother, Katherine, at the Bistro Garden restaurant in Beverly Hills. Among her gifts, Katherine received a diamond ring and a rose-colored, beige-topped Rolls-Royce. A huge white bow was tied around it. "The press said that the Rolls was from Michael," said his sister-in-law Enid Jackson. "Actually, we all chipped in on it. How do you think that made the brothers feel, the fact that the world thought the gift was from Michael? But that's the kind of thing they had to get used to over the years. Little things like this can be very hurtful. I mean, if, God forbid, they all got into an airplane crash, there would be a lot of media attention on Michael and just a mention that the brothers were 'also there.' "

The entire family attended Katherine's party. Her children flew Katherine's father in from Indiana as a special surprise. Because Katherine is a Jehovah's Witness and, according to the religion, should not celebrate birthdays or receive birthday gifts, some of her friends thought it odd that she would agree to a birthday celebration. Susie Jackson said, "She would always accept birthday gifts, as long as they were wrapped in brown paper bags, not birthday wrapping paper."

Michael hired his personal videographer, Steve Howell, to tape the proceedings. Not to be outdone, Jermaine had *his* videographer do the same thing.

Howell's excellent video of the gathering is extremely revealing. The family does not appear to be close, though everyone seems cordial. In a formal setting, family members exchange pleasantries. When Janet walks in with her date, James DeBarge, everyone scatters. It's fairly obvious that no one likes Mr. DeBarge.

The most emotional moment of the evening is an unspoken one between Michael and his mother. Michael, wearing an expensive-looking, sparkly silver suit and tie, gets up on a stage. "This is one of your favorite songs," he tells Katherine. He seems nervous, even embarrassed. "I can sing before thousands of people with no problem," Michael has said. "But put me before a small group and I just can't do it. I'm too scared."

Michael is accompanied by country star Floyd Cramer, playing a Fender Rhodes piano while seated next to Katherine at the family's table. (Cramer was flown in for the party because Katherine is a big fan of his.) As Cramer plays—along with a three-piece band on the stage—Michael sings "For the Good Times" to Katherine. Oddly, Michael is reading the lyrics from cue cards. "This was probably the first birthday party in history in which cue cards were utilized," said Steve Howell.

When Michael sang the first line—"Don't look so sad, I know it's over"—to his mother, her eyes immediately began to well up with tears. Any observer would have thought that Katherine was thinking of her marriage to Joe. (Joe was not at the family table but sat elsewhere in the room.) Michael sings the song—his voice pure, his delivery eloquent—and Katherine almost imperceptibly rocks back and forth in her chair. She looks as if Michael's performance has swept her away.

Katherine could not take her eyes off her boy. It is doubtful that any mother has ever gazed upon her son in a more loving manner. And Michael's expression was equally moving.

In the spring of 1984, John Branca received a telephone call from Transportation Secretary Elizabeth Dole asking if Michael would lend his song "Beat It" as background music for a thirty-second television commercial and sixty-second radio spot on drunk driving. Branca presented Michael with the idea.

"That's tacky," Michael said. "I can't do that."

Branca told Michael he would call Dole back and tell her that they were not interested.

Michael thought it over for a moment. "You know what?" he mused. "If I can get some kind of an award from the White House, then I'll give them the song. See what you can negotiate with them. I want to visit the White House, be on a stage with Ronald Reagan, the whole works." Michael was beginning to get excited. "You think you can do that, Branca. Get me an award from the President?"

John Branca went to work. The next day, he telephoned Elizabeth Dole and told her that she could have the song for her drunk-driving campaign if she dreamed up some kind of humanitarian award to present to Michael. She agreed.

The presentation was set for May 14, 1984. It had started out as an exciting day. In fact, there hadn't been this much excitement at the White House since the day the hostages came home from Iran.

For the occasion, the President wore a navy blue suit, navy blue and gray striped tie, and white shirt. Nancy was chic in a white Adolfo suit trimmed with gold buttons and gold braid on the jacket's four pockets. She wore a heavy gold chain around her neck. It hardly mattered what she wore, for anyone standing next to Michael Jackson that day would pale in comparison. Michael appeared resplendent in an electric blue sequined jacket adorned with sequined braid, a sequined gold sash, and sequined gold epaulets. He wore the trademark single white glove created for him by designer Bill Whitten.

Hundreds of White House officials and secretaries, many of them clutching cameras, put their work aside and gathered on the sun-speckled lawn to catch a glimpse of Jackson. Phones went unanswered. More than a hundred yards back from the stage, the White House fence was lined solidly with Jackson fans, many wearing a single white glove like the one Michael sported.

Two thousand people cheered as Ronald Reagan stepped onto a stage on the White House South Lawn with Nancy and Michael. "Well, isn't this a thriller," he said. "We haven't seen this many people since we left China. And just think, you all came to see me."

Michael did not sing or dance during the ceremony. After the President handed him a plaque, the only words Michael nervously spoke—or whispered, rather—were "I'm very, very honored. Thank you very much, Mr. President." Then he giggled as if it suddenly occurred to him that yes, he really was standing there with the President of the United States. "Oh, and Mrs. Reagan," he added as an afterthought. One Washington reporter, Mary McGrory, noted that this was the shortest response in the annals of White House guests. (McGrory's report of the event stated that Michael supposedly takes steroids to preserve his voice register.)

Reagan noted that Michael was "proof of what a person can accomplish through a lifestyle free of alcohol or drug abuse. People young and old respect that. And if Americans follow his example, then we can face up to the problem of drinking and driving, and we can, in Michael's words, beat it."

Six news photographers covering the event wore white gloves on one hand as they shot pictures of the Reagans and Jackson. Nine police motorcycles and several vans and mounted police escorted Michael from the White House. The whole event took nine minutes.

As Michael, the President, and the First Lady walked to the Oval Office, one middle-aged White House office worker standing across from the Rose Garden shrieked, "I saw his foot. I saw his foot!"

A special metal detector was constructed in the Jacqueline Kennedy Garden to screen Michael and his entourage of eight security men, manager Frank Dileo, attorney John Branca, and publicist Norman Winter (who had actually written the President's speech about Michael). There was also a young man with Michael, a person no one seemed to know, except for Michael. Dileo, Branca, and Winter were perplexed as to who this person was, and when Michael was asked how the man should be identified to the press, he said, "He's a close friend of mine. I don't care what you tell people. It's no one's business." Norman Winter must have known that the presence of this mystery friend would raise some eyebrows. He wanted to protect his client from the controversy, so, according to one reporter, Winter identified Michael's friend as a Secret Service agent.

The entourage was given a special tour of the White House; Michael was particularly fascinated by a portrait of Andrew Jackson in a military jacket very much like the blue-sequined one Michael wore. After the tour, the group was scheduled to meet the President and the First Lady.

Things took a turn for the worse, though, when Michael arrived at the Diplomatic Reception Room where he was to meet with Ron and Nancy. He had been told only a few children of staff members would be there. Instead, the place was packed with about seventy-five adults. Michael put one foot into the Reception Room, looked around, and then ran out, down the hall, and into the bathroom off the Presidential Library. Frank Dileo and the rest of his entourage followed. Before they could reach him, Michael closed the door and locked it.

"Hey, Mike, come on out," Frank said.

"No. They said there would be kids. But those aren't kids," Michael shouted back.

"But there *will* be children. We'll go get the children," a White House aide promised. Then he turned to an assistant. "Listen, if Mrs. Reagan sees this, she's going to be mad as hell. Now you go get some kids, damn it. Get James Baker's kid. She's cute. [Chief of Staff James Baker had brought his six-year-old daughter, Mary Bonner.] I don't care *who* you get, just get some kids in here."

Then he turned back to the closed bathroom door. "It's okay, Michael. We're going to get the kids." His voice was patient as though he were soothing a disturbed child. Frank stood nearby, watching with a bemused expression on his face.

"Well, you'll have to also clear all of those adults out of there before I come out," Michael warned.

"Done."

Someone ran into the Reception Room.

"Okay, everybody out."

Senior staff and cabinet members cleared that room so quickly, any observer would have thought there had been a bomb scare.

"What's happening?"

"Where's Michael Jackson?"

"Has he left?"

Everyone was talking at once as they were ushered out of the room.

The aide ran back to the bathroom door, where a cluster of men with worried looks wondered what they should do next. He conferred with one of Michael's people. "Okay. You can come out now, Michael," Michael's publicist said. "Everything is okay."

"Are you sure?" came back the soft voice.

Frank Dileo knocked on the door with his fist, one loud thud. "Okay, Mike, outta there."

The bathroom door opened slowly. Michael appeared. He looked around, slightly embarrassed. Frank put his arm around him. "I'm sorry," Michael said, "but I was told there wouldn't be so many people."

He was then ushered back into the Reception Room, where awaiting him were just a few officials and their children. Elizabeth Dole was the first to approach Michael. She handed him a copy of *Thriller* and asked him to sign the record jacket.

Then Ron and Nancy arrived and led Michael into the Roosevelt Room to meet some other aides and their families.

Nancy Reagan whispered to one of Michael's staff, "I've heard that he wants to look like that singer Diana Ross, but really, looking at him up close, he's so much prettier than she is. Don't you agree? I mean, I just don't think *she's* that attractive, but *he* certainly is."

Nancy waited for a response. There was none.

"I just wish he would take off his sunglasses," she said. "Tell me, has he had any surgery on his eyes?"

The aide shrugged.

She studied Michael closely as he spoke to her husband on the other side of the room.

"Certainly his nose has been done," she observed to herself.

"More than once, I'd say. I wonder about his cheekbones, though. Is that makeup, or has he had them done too?"

Nancy didn't act as if she actually expected an answer, but the aide shrugged again anyway.

"It's all so peculiar, really," Nancy observed as Ron shook Michael's hand. "A boy who looks just like a girl, who whispers when he speaks, wears a glove on one hand and sunglasses all the time. I just don't know what to make of it . . ."

Nancy shook her head in dismay. She was at a loss for words.

Finally, the Jackson employee broke his silence. "Listen, you don't know the half of it," he said to her, rolling his eyes. He looked at her with a smile, expecting her to laugh. She didn't.

Nancy stared at him coldly for a brief moment. "Well, he *is* talented," she said as she walked away, "and I would think that's all that *you* should be concerned about."

Michael may have been an American hero in May 1984, but the tide quickly turned by June when the plan for distribution of tickets for the Victory tour—now set to kick off in Kansas City's Arrowhead Stadium on July 6—was announced. Joe Jackson, Don King, and Chuck Sullivan came up with this plan: tickets would be $30 each and sold in lots of four *only*. Ordering tickets did not guarantee getting them. The names of those who ordered would be selected at random by a computer drawing using coupons that had to be cut out of advertisements published in local newspapers. So a Jacksons fan had to send a $120 postal money order*—*plus* a two-dollar service charge for each ticket—*and* the coupon, all in "a standard Number Ten envelope," to the ticket address printed in the advertisement.

Promoters predicted that as many as twelve million fans would mail in $1.5 billion in money orders for the twelve-city, forty-two-concert Victory tour but only about one in ten applicants would receive tickets. The money orders were to be postmarked at least two weeks before the concert in order to be considered. With the delay in returning the money—four to six weeks—the promoters and the Jacksons would have use of the money for six to eight weeks. Assuming the tour sold $144 million in tickets, as the promoters estimated, $1.4 billion in excess payments would have to

---

*The United States Post Office must have been particularly happy about the plan, as each money order cost $1.55. If twelve million fans purchased money orders, post offices would collect $18 million. In all of 1983, the Postal Service collected $124 million in money orders.

be returned. In a common money-market deposit account in a bank, which paid about 7 percent interest, that money would earn $8 million a month or about $16 million for the two-month period for the promoters and Jackson family.

The Jacksons' spokesman Howard Bloom said that whatever interest accrued on each $120 order would go toward costs of handling and postage for unfilled orders.

The tickets were obviously priced too high for even white middle-class kids if they had to buy them in lots of four. It's almost impossible to imagine that many of Michael's most loyal followers, kids from the ghetto, would be able to afford this luxury. The Rolling Stones' and Bruce Springsteen's concert tickets at this time were $16 each. Michael wanted a $20 ticket price but, as always, he was outvoted.

If you were a lucky winner and allowed to see the Victory show, you wouldn't know if you were going to go—or which show you would attend—until two days before the concert. If the mail was delayed, the tickets could easily arrive *after* the concert.

The Jacksons and their promoters refused to pay for the advertisements from which the coupons were to be clipped, saying that the ads should be run free of cost as "public service advertisements." Most newspapers refused to run the ads. "It's just a way to make more millions for the Jacksons," said Bob Haring, executive editor of the *Tulsa World*.

Before this plan was announced, Michael and John Branca tried to talk the brothers out of it at a meeting.

"We got to get as much as possible for the tickets," one of the brothers said. "The sky's the limit."

"No," Michael argued. "That's not the way to do it. There's going to be a backlash. The tickets shouldn't be more than twenty bucks each. And the mail order idea is terrible."

However, his brothers voted against Michael, five to one.

"Okay, that's it," Michael decided later in a meeting with John Branca and Frank Dileo. "This is going to be my last tour with my brothers. I'm very serious. So I don't want you guys to try to run anything. Let them do it all their way. I'm just one vote out of six. Let them do their thing. This is their last shot."

"But why, Mike?" Frank Dileo wanted to know. "They're gonna fuck it up."

"Because if anything goes wrong I don't want to hear about it," Michael explained. "I don't want to hear about it from my mother, my father, or my brothers. Let them do it their way and I'm out of it. Maybe the money they make from this will set them up comfortably.''

From this point on, Michael privately referred to his brothers as "the gremlins." He said, "They come up to you and be real nice, but as soon as they get what they want, they turn into monsters."

When the plan was made public, Jacksons fans from coast to coast were outraged. The *Los Angeles Herald Examiner* ran a telephone poll with the question: "Are Michael Jackson's fans being taken advantage of?" Of the 2,795 people who responded, 90 percent said yes.

The newspaper published an editorial chastising the Jacksons: "It's hard not to conclude that the Jacksons' promoters, if not the young stars themselves, are taking advantage of their community of fans. It's been said that all the Jackson brothers, including Michael, helped plan the tour. If so, they should have shown a little more consideration for the fans who have made them rich and famous.''

Other newspapers across the country followed suit, lambasting the Jacksons—and Michael in particular—for this outrageous show of greed. "The Jackson tour has not been about music. It's been about greed and arrogance," wrote Washington columnists Maxwell Glen and Cody Shearer. "What good does a drug-free, liquor-free, I-brake-for-animals image do when the overriding message is 'Give Me Your Piggy Bank.' ''

Despite the furor, when the first coupons were printed in the *Kansas City Times*, scores of fans waited in the dark for the early morning papers to hit the streets. One fanatic ripped out the coupon and handed the rest of the paper back to the vendor. "I got what I wanted," he said. The *Times* published an extra twenty thousand copies to meet the demand. Postal employees were ready with 140,000 money order forms for the expected avalanche. The tickets sold out rapidly.

The media blasted the Jacksons for avarice. As a youthful role model, this was terrible publicity for Michael Jackson. He was becoming the object of intense scorn and ridicule. "What did the doctor find during Brooke Shields's Pap smear?" went one popular joke. "Michael Jackson's other glove."

"I didn't even want to do this tour," Michael complained, exasperated. "Now look what's happened."

Frank Dileo advised Michael that if he didn't take a position against this show of avarice, his career and reputation could be damaged. "They don't care about your future," Dileo told Jackson about his brothers. "Their only concern is their present. To make as much as they can, while they can. You have a career that's gonna be longer than this tour. They probably don't.''

Then an open letter appeared in the *Dallas Morning News* that brought Michael Jackson to his senses. Eleven-year-old Ladonna Jones wrote that she'd been saving her pennies to see Michael's show but that she couldn't possibly save enough to buy four tickets. She very pointedly asked Michael, ''How could you, of all people, be so selfish?''

The letter upset Michael when an aide showed it to him. Selfishness and a hunger for money were, after all, really at the heart of these tour plans, and Michael realized it. Had not his family already made more money than most people would ever make in their lifetimes? It took a child's sadness, however, to make him take action.

He hadn't wanted to make any major decisions about the tour, but he now realized he had to. ''That does it,'' Michael said. He called a meeting with Joe, Don King, and Chuck Sullivan. ''Change the ticket policy. It's a rip-off. You know it. I know it. Now change it. Or I won't tour.''

They made plans to change the system.

Michael, who had dropped to 105 pounds from his normal weight of 125 pounds—the skinniest he had ever been—looked as if he was under a great deal of stress when he and his brothers arrived at the Hyatt Hotel in Birmingham, Alabama, on June 26 for a week of meetings about the upcoming tour. As Michael checked in, he had become so weak and tired he had to lean on one of his bodyguards for support. When a hotel cook approached to say hello to Michael, the guard let go of Michael and the star nearly crumpled to the floor. It seemed to some observers that Michael hardly had the strength to walk.

Perhaps the problem in part grew out of Michael's eating habits. At Michael's orders, his Sikh cook, Mani Singh Khalsa, fed him a diet of cashews, pecans, seeds, herbs, and spices. ''He's definitely a health nut,'' said his cousin Tim Whitehead, a roadie on the tour. ''People don't know that the reason he's a vegetarian is not so much because of what meat does to a person, but because he can't stand the idea of having an animal killed so he can have dinner. I've often wondered how he gets by on the little food he does eat.''

''If I didn't have to eat to live, I'd never eat at all,'' Michael once told his mother.

Later that day in Birmingham, there was a difficult meeting with the brothers, and attorneys and managers on telephone conference calls, and by the time it was over, Michael was fed up with the whole drama. When he got into the freight elevator (he always travels in freight elevators rather than public ones), he leaned back against the wall and just slowly slipped down until he was sitting on the floor. Someone tried to help him to his feet, but he was too exhausted to stand. "Just leave me alone. Let me rest here for a second," he said as he went up to the sixteenth floor. Witnesses to these kinds of scenes began whispering that Michael was suffering from anorexia nervosa, which wasn't true but certainly seemed plausible from the way he looked and acted.

It was time to announce the new ticket-buying arrangement. Michael held a midday press conference on July 5, 1984, the day before the first concert was to take place. He wore a white sequined jacket and a red-and-white striped sash. Marlon, Randy, and Tito accompanied him. To counteract the charge that he was greedy and doing the show only for profit, Michael announced that he intended to donate all of the money he made from this controversial tour to a favorite charity. Moreover, close to two thousand tickets in each city would be donated to disadvantaged youths who would not otherwise be able to attend the concerts.

Michael added, "We've worked a long time to make this show the best it can be. But we know a lot of kids are having trouble getting tickets. The other day I got a letter from a girl in Texas named Ladonna Jones. She'd been saving her money from odd jobs to buy a ticket, but with the current tour system she'd have to buy four tickets and she couldn't afford that. So I've asked our promoter to work out a new way of distributing tickets—a way that no longer requests a one-hundred-twenty-dollar money order. There has been a lot of talk about the promoter holding money for tickets that didn't sell. I've asked our promoter to end the mail-order ticket system as soon as possible so that no one will pay money unless they get a ticket." Michael said that details of the new over-the-counter system for buying tickets would be announced shortly. (It was implemented by the tour's third stop in Jacksonville.)

Michael took no questions. Suddenly he and his brothers were surrounded by security men. And then The Jacksons were gone. It was as if they had evaporated.

"Why did he decide to donate all his money to charity?" one reporter asked Frank Dileo, who stayed behind.

"Because he's a nice guy," Frank said.

Michael's estimated worth at the time came to $75 million, so donating to charity the approximately $3 to $5 million he would make on the tour would be a generous gesture but not one that would cause him to change his lifestyle. His brothers, however, couldn't possibly have afforded such a gift to any charity. Also,

Michael did not—perhaps could not—address any of the other problem issues. According to Cliff Wallace, who managed the Louisiana Superdome, Joe and Katherine Jackson, Don King, Chuck Sullivan, and The Jacksons had asked for free stadium rent; a waiver of city, state, and federal taxes; a share in the profits of the food, beverage, and parking concessions; and free advertising to boot. Wallace added that meeting their demands would have cost city taxpayers $300,000. And gross $5 million for the Jacksons.

Michael arranged for Ladonna Jones to receive a set of four complimentary tickets to the show, to which she would be chauffeured by limousine. Michael met with her after the show. "He asked me if I had good seats," she recalled. "They didn't turn out to be very good, but it was fun anyway."

At this time, CBS released the *Victory* album. Not counting 1981's live album, it was the first Jacksons album in four years, so it was widely anticipated. The album featured Michael's duet with Mick Jagger on "State of Shock," which wasn't so much a song as it was a glorified Rolling Stones riff. The best cut on the album was written by Jackie and entitled "Torture," a high-tech rocker of a song on which Michael wails up a storm. The album featured songs written by all of the brothers—and leads were split among them as well—so it was the kind of group effort that was the perfect vinyl kickoff for the tour to come.

The long-anticipated Victory tour finally started on Friday, July 6, 1984, in Kansas City, Missouri. "Anybody who sees this show will be a better person for years to come," Don King told the press that day in the lobby of the Kansas City hotel where the group was staying. "Michael Jackson has transcended all earthly bounds. Every race, color, and creed is waiting for this tour. The way he shall lift the despairing and the despondent enthralls me. Only in America could this happen, only in America. Oh, I am so thankful to be an American . . ."

"Can't someone keep that man's mouth shut?" Michael asked a friend. "Isn't there enough pressure?" To complicate matters more, Jackie was not able to join his brothers because of a leg injury. Jermaine, Marlon, Randy, Tito, and Michael would have to appear without him.

On the day of the first show, forty-three thousand fans had begun to gather outside Arrowhead Stadium hours before sunset, some sunbathing on blankets and picnicking with sandwiches and chicken, while, inside, a five-hundred-person security force and one thousand other stage workers geared for the mass event. Two giant tapestries of a forest scene bordered each side of the stage, and a wooden barrier was erected fifteen feet from the base of the stage to keep fans from rushing the Jackson brothers.

"Arise, all the world, and behold the kingdom," a voice boomed as the show began. Michael had designed the show himself, and it reflected his penchant for pizzazz. Elaborate George Lucas–style computerized stage and lighting systems would be the hallmark of this concert, including a hidden hydraulic stage that presented the group—Michael in zebra-print, vertical-striped pants; spangled shirt; white socks; 1950s-type penny loafers; and the white glove—as if they were appearing from under the earth itself on a waffle grid of two hundred blinding lights.

Seen in silhouette, the brothers marched slowly down a staircase to the beat of a drum, approached the microphones, removed their sunglasses, and broke into the first song, Michael's "Wanna Be Startin' Somethin'." There were red and green lasers, crimson strobe lights, and purple smoke bombs—magic, illusion, and fireworks. Eighteen songs boomed from a hundred outdoor speakers. Everything from "I Want You Back" to "Shake Your Body (Down to the Ground)." (Oddly, the brothers performed no numbers from their new *Victory* album. It was said by Marlon Jackson that Michael refused to rehearse them or perform them before a live audience.)

"Is there anyone here from Kansas City?" Michael asked the crowd, drawing a roar of response.

Jermaine performed three of his own songs, but seemed off-pitch and in poor voice. Michael's solo hits "Billie Jean" and "Beat It" were saved for the end of the concert. He was in excellent voice, more of a real *singer* now than ever before. By the time the group finished, the audience—mothers with toddlers, teenagers with parents, blacks and whites (mostly whites) together—had been whipped into a sheer frenzy. They shared a genuine sense of intimacy, even though most of the forty-three thousand people in the gargantuan football stadium had to settle for distorted images of Michael and his brothers, which appeared on huge overhanging television screens throughout the stadium.

It was clear this audience had paid outrageous ticket prices to see only one person, Michael Jackson. Thanks to his music—not to mention the advent of the video age—Michael's stardom had reached such mythic proportions that no one could share the same stage with him. As Jim Miller wrote for *Newsweek*, "He dances with the breathtaking verve of his predecessor James Brown, the beguiling wispiness of Diana Ross, the ungainly pathos of Charlie

Chaplin, the edgy joy of a man startled to be alive. The crowd gasps and screams. . . .''

To Michael Jackson's audience, none of the controversy they'd heard and read about these last few months mattered now that *he*, the undisputed star, appeared on stage communicating directly to them. All that mattered tonight was Michael's talent, his passion for his work, their appreciation of his art—and the way he could execute one of those impossible, backward glassy glides straight across the stage. The audience roared its appreciation for him with every song. Or as one critic put it, ''Marlon, Jermaine, Randy, and Tito seemed mostly ill-at-ease extras at their own celebration.''

After the first of three shows in Kansas City, the truth was painfully obvious: Michael Jackson should never have agreed to do this tour, for more reasons than the obvious organizational ones. Michael was now a front man for a group he no longer felt a part of. He had outgrown all of this family pageantry. As exhilarating as he was on stage, one sensed he was constrained by a real fear of completely upstaging and humiliating his brothers with his electrifying presence. Also, because of all that had happened, there was a nagging sense—imaginary or not—that Michael, as he performed, couldn't wait for this whole extravaganza to be finished. At the same time, the brothers, who entertained with such hunger and eagerness, felt this was their chance of a lifetime. Maybe their last chance.

Jermaine's comments to reporter Simon Kinnersley brought to light the dissension and fraternal jealousy running rampant within the group. Jermaine said, ''Even though Michael is very talented, a lot of his success has been due to timing and a little bit of luck. It could have been him, or it could just as easily have been me. But now I'm doing a lot of things. I'm the hottest brother. It'll be the same when my brothers do their thing.''

Never for a moment did the brothers appear to share any common values or goals of showmanship with their star performer. And never for a moment did it appear that Michael wanted anything more to do with them than he had to. By trying to prove his loyalty to his family, he had distanced himself even further from all of them. And maybe he had lost a little of his soul in the process. Certainly he must have felt as if he'd lost *something* when James Brown—one of his idols—refused his invitation to perform onstage with him at Madison Square Garden in New York. Brown, always a Jackson champion, felt that the ticket prices were so steep, they would preclude the attendance of most of the group's black fans.

So James became a no-show out of protest. That had to hurt Michael, and make him think about whether this was worth it.

The agony of "Victory" would continue through December 9, 1984—same show and dialogue each and every performance. Michael Jackson is not a spontaneous performer. In concert, he has a set routine, and he rarely veers from it. Bruce Springsteen went to see the show in Philadelphia and afterwards he and Michael had a conversation backstage. "Do you talk to people during your concerts?" Michael asked him. "I heard that you do."

"Yeah. I tell stories," Bruce said. "People like that, I've learned. They like to hear your voice do something besides singing. They go wild when you just talk."

Michael shuddered. "Oh, I could never do that. To me, it feels like people are learning something about you they shouldn't know."

The closer the time came for the tour to be over, the more anxious Michael was to see it end. "The way we planned it, this was going to be the greatest tour of all time," Joe Jackson would say in retrospect. "But outsiders interfered. Soon the brothers were at each other's throats."

In the beginning of the tour, it was agreed that only the performing members of the family would travel in the Jacksons' van. Then Michael showed up one night with Emmanuel Lewis, irritating the brothers. Before the tour was half-finished, the brothers traveled to the different cities in separate vans and limousines—Jackie (who joined the tour midway on crutches but did not perform), Marlon, Randy, and Tito in one, Jermaine in another, and Michael in still another. When they had to travel by air, the other brothers used a commercial airline while Michael traveled by private jet, reminding some observers of the days when The Supremes would travel by Cadillac while Diana Ross was chauffeured by limousine. A couple of times, Pia Zadora's multimillionaire husband, Meshulam Riklis (who was friendly with the Jacksons), allowed the brothers to use his private aircraft. In New York, the group had to fly by helicopter to Giants Stadium and agreed among themselves that no outsiders would be in the helicopter. Michael showed up with John Lennon's son, Julian. The brothers just glared at him.

Touring can be such a stressful, lonely business even under the best of circumstances. To feel isolated from the people you are performing with, let alone your own family, must be devastating—especially to someone as sensitive as Michael. For a family that had begun to fall apart, the Victory tour furthered their destruction. At one point in the tour, Michael suffered from exhaustion and dehydration and had to be put under a doctor's care.

Perhaps as a result of the pressure, Michael became increasingly difficult to deal with. Some of his demands seemed unreasonable. At one point, he threatened not to perform unless a certain publicist working on the tour was fired. The publicist had apparently allowed something to be printed that Michael did not like. The brothers ignored the threat. Then, at the last possible minute, right before the show was set to start, Frank Dileo announced that Michael would not appear unless there was some guarantee that the publicist would be dismissed. The publicist was fired.

"He's a prima donna," noted one witness to the backstage goings-on of the Victory tour. "He was worse than his mentor Diana Ross."

Michael spent most of his time with his own entourage, entertaining himself during the day by making home videos of himself in different situations. In Michigan, Michael went to a police station to shoot a video with about thirty police officers; he likes to see himself surrounded by men in uniforms. Police officer Allan Booze recalled Michael's arrival. "There he was, sitting in the back of a van looking like a scared little weasel. I thought, 'This can't be the same guy that does all that crap up on the stage.' He looked like he might start crying at any moment. Some people might say he looks like a fag, but I would never say that. He looked frail, almost sickly. But he had a real big hand. I'm a big guy, but when we shook hands, his went all the way around mine."

The Jacksons got an offer from a video producer who wanted to pay them several millions to film the show and release it to the home video market after the tour was over. They took a vote. Everyone was for the video—and the millions—except for Michael. He threatened that he would not perform if they struck a deal. Furthermore, no one was to videotape the show. The deal was turned down.

Three nights later, the brothers were onstage and realized that there were cameras all about. Marlon nearly bumped into a cameraman as he danced. It was obvious that Michael, himself, had arranged for the show to be videotaped. "I'll give you copies, don't worry," he promised his brothers when they confronted him after the show. But they never saw a copy.

They stayed on separate floors in the hotels. They refused to talk to each other on their way to the stadiums. Every time there was a meeting about anything, there would be side meetings among the different factions in the group, including the pair of lawyers who represented Michael, the one who worked for Jermaine, and the two who spoke for the rest of the brothers.

"It was devastating," said longtime friend Joyce McCrae. "This was the culmination of the least wonderful experience that Michael has ever had with his family. Michael's tremendous success has affected every member of the family. Some are jealous. There's been denial; there's been the whole gamut of human emotions. Jackie's the most bitter, the most hurt by Michael's success, because he thinks he put Michael out front in the first place. He's also the oldest. There's the assumption that he *created* Michael."

The five Jackson brothers—Jackie, Tito, Marlon, Jermaine, and Randy—made sure that they each collected their 75 percent from ticket sales within twenty-four hours of every concert. (Jackie would make millions, even though he did not perform.) Michael spent a lot more time with his boa constrictor snake, Muscles, which he had with him on the road, than he did with his brothers.

"Frank Dileo was scared to death of that damn boa," said one associate. "One night, Michael started chasing him around the hotel room with the snake. Frank was so scared, he pulled out a gun and was about to shoot the damn thing. Michael screamed in horror, and a security guard calmed Frank down and took the gun from him. That was the last time Michael ever tried anything like that."

Keeping the Jacksons' costumes—designed by Bill Whitten and valued at a half million dollars—clean and neat was always complicated, but something the brothers never worried about. They would usually leave the concert hall in their uniforms—made of expensive fabrics and accented by chrome, glass, spandex, Lurex, leather, and beads. Once the Jacksons got to the hotel, they would strip and deposit their costumes in an empty wardrobe trunk. That trunk would then go to Mary Jane Wenzel, wardrobe mistress for the tour, who would inspect the costumes for tears, missing beads, and spots. A cleaning fluid called Picrin would be used on stains from makeup or perspiration. Wenzel would then wash the costumes in Woolite or Tide in her hotel sink or bathtub.

As for perspiration odor, "The really raunchy stuff we just rinse out," she said. "The trick is getting to it quickly." After the clothing was washed, portable fans would dry them on metal racks inside a canvas tent. The brothers didn't even have to keep track of their underwear—that was Wenzel's job—their shoes (black Bass Weejuns for Michael and boots for the rest), belts, hats, gloves, or socks (Michael wore glitter socks, Randy wore white, and the rest of the guys wore black). All they had to worry about was performing and getting along with one another—no easy task.

By the end of the year, the tour was finally winding down. Three final dates were announced to the public for Dodger Stadium in Los Angeles in December, and all three quickly sold out. In his enthusiasm, Frank Dileo felt that there should be three more concerts. Dileo, while a terrific record promoter, was a novice when it came to managing concerts. Michael Jackson, on the other hand, was not an amateur; he knew the ropes of the record and concert business. He was such a seasoned pro, he probably could have been his own manager by this time.

"Frank, are you sure those three dates are going to be sold out?" Michael asked him.

Frank said he was.

"This doesn't sound right to me," Michael said. "It had better work, Frank," he warned him, "or I'm going to be upset. I don't like playing to empty stadiums."

What Michael felt that Dileo should do was announce each additional show to the press one concert at a time. When that date sold out, then Dileo should announce the next one. If it didn't sell out, then, obviously, Dileo shouldn't announce any others. But Frank decided to thrust all three additional concerts onto the public at one time because, from a public relations standpoint, this procedure looked more impressive.

In the end, five of the shows sold out. For the sixth and final show, there were thousands of tickets remaining, much to the dismay of everyone in the Jacksons' camp.

"I had a feeling something like this was going to happen. I'm not going out there to a half-empty house," Michael threatened. "Somebody had better do something, and quick."

Everyone who even remotely knew the Jacksons was given hundreds of tickets to distribute to their friends, free of charge. Norman Winter gave every student who attended the private school in which his daughter was enrolled complimentary tickets. Frank Dileo handed out tickets to record company executives and their wives. Irving Azoff gave tickets away to MCA Records employees and their families. The Jackson brothers passed out tickets to acquaintances as well as distant relatives. "And," noted one observer, "Michael Jackson was pissed off beyond belief. He wasn't giving away a single ticket. He was too mad about all of the embarrassment this situation was causing everyone. It was his final show with the brothers, and they were giving away tickets to anyone who wanted to see it. 'What a way to end this Victory tour,' he said."

"This is humiliating," Michael told an associate, "and it's all Frank's fault. He's finished. He's fired. That's it for him."

Even though Michael did not fire Frank Dileo at that time, he didn't speak to him for many weeks afterward.

Complicating matters for those Los Angeles final dates were disagreements about promoter Chuck Sullivan's handling of the tour monies, which placed the L.A. dates in jeopardy. The flamboyant Don King held a press conference to announce that The Jacksons would indeed appear at Dodger Stadium. He claimed victory over Sullivan's "greed." Sullivan had canceled a promised $24 million letter of credit due The Jacksons within two weeks of the first tour date. (Sullivan, $4 million in the red by the time the show got to the West Coast, suffered heart problems as a result of the Victory tour and, he said, his squabbles with The Jacksons over money. Even his attorney, Jim Murray, admitted that Sullivan "did foul up some things, absolutely.")

At the press conference, Don King proceeded to attribute the very highest virtues of humankind to The Jacksons and launched a verbal attack on the press for "unduly lambasting" the group in recent months. He called the thirty-dollar ticket price "a mere pittance." He talked about his "fabulous relationship with all the brothers, especially Michael." A week later, a federal grand jury in New York indicted King on twenty-three counts of income-tax evasion.

During the final week of the tour, Joe and Don King began making plans to take the Victory tour to Europe. "Don King and I planned to take it around the world. Michael knew that," Joe would say later. When Michael heard about the possibility of European dates, he sent a succinct message to Joe and Don through his manager, Frank Dileo: "Forget it."

On December 9, 1984, Michael hollered from the Los Angeles stage, "This is our last and final show. It's been a long twenty years, and we love you all." The brothers looked at Michael with surprised expressions, as if this was news to them.

After that performance in Los Angeles, Frank Dileo—who referred to all of those involved in the tour as "the gang who couldn't shoot straight"—offered a congratulatory hand to Don King. "Good working with you," he said solemnly, shaking King's hand. Then he added, sarcastically, "Maybe we'll meet in a bar sometime."

A reporter backstage asked Michael how long he had been with Frank Dileo. Michael gave the writer an icy stare. "The question is, 'How long has *he* been with *me*?' " he said.

"There's no way Michael Jackson should be as big as he is and treat his family the way he does," Don King fumed. "He feels that his father did him wrong? His father may have done some wrong, but he also had to do a whole lot right.''

King's final comments on the subject failed to ingratiate him to Michael Jackson. He went on, ''What Michael's got to realize is that Michael's a nigger. It doesn't matter how great he can sing and dance. I don't care that he can prance. He's one of the megastars in the world, but he's still going to be a nigger megastar. He must accept that. Not only must he understand that, he's got to accept it and demonstrate that he wants to be a nigger. Why? To show that a nigger can do it.''

As far as Michael Jackson was concerned, Don King had turned into a bad dream. Michael donated all of his proceeds from the Victory tour—nearly $5 million—to the T. J. Martell Foundation for Cancer Research, the United Negro College Fund, and the Ronald McDonald Camp for Good Times. There would be no European tour. That selective memory at work once again, when Michael wrote of the Victory tour in his autobiography, *Moonwalk*, he didn't mention Don King, Joe and Katherine Jackson, Chuck Sullivan, or any of the other principal players behind the scenes.

Of his brothers, Michael waxed nostalgic in *Moonwalk*. ''It was a nice feeling, playing with my brothers again,'' he wrote, wistfully. ''We were all together again. . . . I enjoyed the tour.''

That's what he committed to paper, but obviously not what was in his heart. Whether or not he wanted to admit it publicly, the real victory for Michael Jackson was that he and his brothers were finally finished as a performing group.

Their future as a family didn't look very promising, either.

# Chapter

## ❧ 24 ❧

WHILE MICHAEL JACKSON and his brothers were on the Victory tour, family troubles too serious to ignore were brewing back home in 1984. For the last year, Jackie, who was thirty-three years old, had been having an affair with vivacious dancer-choreographer Paula Abdul, who was twenty-one. Jackie had hired Paula Abdul to choreograph The Jacksons' video for their song "Torture," in which Michael did not participate. (In years to come, Paula Abdul would choreograph excellent, award-winning video presentations for songs from Janet's *Control* album—including "When I Think of You," "Control," and "Nasty"—and become a major recording and video star herself.)

Michael was angered by Jackie's affair because he has strong feelings against infidelity. "Michael is disgusted when he sees anyone he knows who has a wife or fiancée involved in any sort of philandering," said his former band director James McField. "All of that really upsets Michael. I've heard him make comments to people. I once saw him go up to a guy who was looking at pictures in a dirty magazine and say, 'I should tell your wife.' To him, just looking is bad."

Michael had always had a special place in his heart for Enid Jackson. Of all of the sisters-in-law, he was closest to Enid. He admired her honesty. "You always know where you stand with Enid," he had said. "She's not one of these people who will say one thing and do another. She'll never lie to you. I love that about her."

When Michael and Janet were young, Jackie and Enid lived in a house six blocks from the Encino family dwelling. Michael and Janet would ride their bikes to Jackie's and spend Christmas there because they both enjoyed the holiday and there was no celebration of it at home. "Michael used to love to come over to our house and decorate the tree," Enid said. "Then Mother [Katherine] would call and say, 'Is he over there?' I would say, 'Yes, Mother,' and she'd say, 'Tell him he can stay a little while longer and that next time he should tell us before he rides his bike over there.' "

Now Michael was losing a sister-in-law because of an extramarital affair. "If Jackie had had affairs before the one with Paula, I don't know about them," Enid said. "How he met Paula was that we had had season tickets for the Lakers basketball team for years and Paula was a Laker girl, a cheerleader. I remember the first time she met Jackie was at a game. She was a chubby little thing—sort of Hispanic-looking at the time—and she asked him for his autograph. I thought nothing of it. Then she and two of her girlfriends started driving to the house, waiting and watching. Soon she and Jackie apparently started dating, even though she knew he was married."

"There was nothing going on between Jackie Jackson and me," Paula Abdul has said to the press. "We were just good friends."

"I found out for sure that they were having an affair when she called me at home and told me so herself," said Enid Jackson. "I had never talked to her before, and one day I picked up the phone and it was Paula saying she was at Centinela Hospital and that she had just had an abortion. Jackie's child, she said. Jackie said he didn't know anything about it. At some point you have to trust your husband, especially when he's in show business. Either you believe every girl who calls you with an abortion story, or you believe in your marriage. At that time I chose to believe in my marriage.

"But then other things started happening," Enid continued. "Jackie would say he was going to the studio, and then Paula would call and say, 'Your husband is on his way home. He just left my house.' Then Jackie would get home shortly after. At first you don't want to believe it. What wife would? I didn't know who to believe because sometimes she would call and start talking crazy to me and I would hand Jackie the phone. He would say to her, 'Why are you doing this to me? Why are you trying to break up my marriage? I love my wife.' "

Enid recalled one night she was in the kitchen cooking dinner when her husband kissed her good-bye and told her he was on his way to the recording studio. "As he drove off, I had an instinct he wasn't going to the studio," Enid said. She got into her car and drove over to Paula's. Nobody was there. But then she noticed a bunch of little kids on a street corner singing The Jackson 5 hit, "I Want You Back."

This wasn't a good sign. "I thought, 'Now why would they be singing that song unless Jackie had been here?' " Enid said. So she started driving and ended up at the Sepulveda Drive-In Theater. There Enid found her husband and Paula in the back seat of the family's Range Rover. This was the first time she had caught them together.

"What are you doing?" Enid demanded.

She said that Jackie, obviously dismayed, remained silent. Paula looked up at Jackie's wife with wide-eyed innocence.

Enid repeated, "Listen, I want to know what you are doing here together."

Suddenly, Enid recalled, Paula became defensive. "What do you mean what are we doing here? You're a woman," Paula said. "What do you *think* we're doing here? He wouldn't even be with me if you were—"

Enid, by now enraged, grabbed Paula by the arm and snatched her out of the vehicle before she had a chance to finish her sentence. Paula fell to the ground.

"Wait, Enid, hold on," Jackie said, running to Paula's aid.

"You know what?" Enid told Jackie as tears streamed down her face. "You got it, sweetheart. You can have her. Don't even bother coming home."

Enid ran back to her car and drove home. Jackie and Paula followed. When they got to the house, Paula waited in the Range Rover as Jackie went in and begged his wife for forgiveness. He accused her of having him followed, "as if that was the issue," Enid said. "He told me I was the devil," she added laughing, "when all it was was plain old female intuition. I knew my husband."

Jackie took Paula home that night and told her that he loved his wife and couldn't see her anymore. While he was still at her house, Paula telephoned Enid. Sobbing, she told Enid that she was in love with Jackie and didn't want to let him go. "Tell him to just stay there," Enid told her. "I can't take this anymore."

"The next day, all I heard from everyone was that I beat Paula Abdul up," Enid said. "And I'm telling you, it crossed my mind. This was my husband, the man I loved. I saw myself punching and kicking this girl he was with, and I was just seconds away from doing it, but I didn't. And, believe me, I should have. When Paula told everybody I had beat her up, my whole thing was, 'Listen, if I had beat up that girl, she wouldn't be here to talk about it.' "

"How can Jackie do this to Enid?" Michael wanted to know. "This makes no sense. They've been married for years."

Katherine reminded her son that this affair was not his business.

"It's family business," Michael said. "And it's group business too," he said to Katherine. "Nothing good is gonna come of this," he told her. "This is terrible. Enid doesn't deserve this."

If anything, the problems in Jackie's marriage only served to underscore Michael's conviction that relationships are dangerous. He felt that Paula Abdul had used his brother to further her career and that Jackie was using Paula for thrills. He did not consider whether these two people loved each other, because what they were doing was, as he put it, "just plain wrong."

"Paula really did love Jackie," said a friend of Abdul's. "The attraction between them was strong and real. Paula was young and relatively inexperienced. She fell for Jackie hard, and there was simply no way out for her. And, of course, Jackie was a willing participant in the affair."

Michael Jackson lived in a world where the men were never forced to take responsibility for their philandering. Rather, the women always seemed to be battling it out among themselves. When his mother had a problem with Joe's relationship with Gina Sprague, she vented her anger on Gina, not on Joe. It was said that Katherine also had an angry confrontation with Cheryl Terrell, the mother of Joe's illegitimate child, the baby Katherine was asked to accept into the Jackson family as if doing so was the most natural thing in the world. And when Enid could no longer tolerate Jackie's behavior, she confronted Paula Abdul, not Jackie. Even as a child, Michael had seen Jackie and Jermaine recklessly use women as sex objects and take no responsibility for their actions. Michael was still a devout Jehovah's Witness, and to him, everything he saw the men do in his world was an aberration, and the results of their actions always proved to be heartbreaking to someone.

So, at the age of twenty-six, Michael Jackson was more afraid of personal commitment to romance or sexual love than ever before.

Photographer Francesco Scavullo once recalled of Michael, "He asked me, 'What do you do about falling in love? Are you afraid they're just after you for what you can do for them?' And I said, 'Michael, you can't live your life that way. You have to take a chance.' "

But Michael was not about to take any chances. "I'm scared because of what I've seen. The men in my family don't know how to treat women," he would say. "I don't want to be like my brothers."

"Michael Jackson is one of my favorite performers," Paula Abdul would say, "because he has that all-around energy."

But Michael isn't exactly fond of Paula. Family friend Marcus Phillips recalled, "Michael had ambivalent feelings about the situation with Paula Abdul because he liked her, though he didn't know her well, thought she was talented, and figured his brother was probably to blame. Still, he felt that Paula should stay away from Jackie because Jackie was married. From what I understand, Paula's point of view was that Jackie's marriage was in trouble long before she came along, and she shouldn't have to sacrifice the way she felt about Jackie for a marriage that didn't work.

"It very quickly became a very open affair," Phillips added. "LaToya used to refer to Paula as 'Jackie's girlfriend,' which had to make Enid feel bad. In fact, LaToya even said that in an interview with some woman's magazine, I believe. I recall once someone in the family referred to Paula as 'Jackie's girl,' and Michael became very upset. '*Enid* is Jackie's girl,' he said angrily. 'There's not supposed to be any other girl in Jackie's life. What's wrong with you people?' The fact of the matter, though, was that there *was* another girl in Jackie's life. Jackie seemed to be in love with Paula Abdul, and Michael had no power over any of it."

"She is a fighter," Jackie Jackson would say of Paula Abdul. "She gets what she wants. But somehow she's managed to stay one of the world's sweetest people."

In her court action, Enid claimed a share of the proceeds from the Victory tour. She estimated Jackie's monthly income at $250,000, with $500,000 in savings accounts. Enid's detailed monthly expenses allow an inside look at why the Jackson brothers never seemed to have enough money. Enid's attorney claimed that each month his client spent on the average $5,700 for the house, $3,000 for clothes, $1,500 for entertainment, $2,000 for food, $1,500 for gifts, $1,000 for household decorations, $1,000 for trips, $500 for beauty care, $300 for flowers, $500 for limousine service, $200 for fur storage, and $200 for pet expenses. She was also seeking $5,000 a month in child support for the couple's two children: seven-year-old son Sigmund and two-year-old daughter Brandy. She also wanted possession of their 1977 Mercedes-Benz. Jackie could keep the other four vehicles.

Enid said that Katherine empathized with her, though she was careful not to say anything critical of her son. "No matter what he did, or what any of the boys do, those are her sons and she is protective of them," Enid said. "Still, she understood what I was going through and was supportive of me as well."

Jackie apparently decided that, rather than divorce, the couple had better attempt a cheaper reconciliation. He and Enid decided to give their marriage another chance, but Paula Abdul remained in the shadows.

Meanwhile, youngest sister Janet—who had turned eighteen on May 16, 1984—eloped with singer James DeBarge in the fall. She had known James since the age of ten—"but only on the phone," she recalled. "We had never met. Actually he was a friend of Jermaine's and LaToya's." She and James finally did meet on the set of "Soul Train" when Janet turned fifteen. DeBarge is from a large singing family from Grand Rapids, Michigan, and he and Janet seemed to have much in common, at least superficially, since both were from show business families.

"She started calling the house when LaToya began dating my other son, Bobby," recalled James DeBarge's mother, Etterlene DeBarge Rodriguez. "As time went on, the relationship got stronger and stronger. I liked Janet. We got along beautifully because she's such a sweet girl."

However, both Joe and Katherine disapproved of the relationship because DeBarge—a member of Motown's singing group called DeBarge—was combative and unpredictable. They were certain that James was not the ideal mate for Janet, whom Katherine considered to be innocent and inexperienced (even though James would later insist that he and Janet first had sex when Janet was fifteen, and, he added, "that was real lovemaking").

On May 29, 1984, Janet and James were in a minor traffic accident while James was driving Katherine's 1978 Mercedes-Benz automobile in slow, midday Los Angeles traffic. Janet claimed that DeBarge was about to stop at a red light when their car was struck from behind by another automobile (which sped away and was never identified). This caused Katherine's Mercedes to be pushed into the car ahead of them. They were driving at about five miles per hour. Janet said neither car was damaged.

Unfortunately for Janet and James, the female occupant of the car they hit was seventy-two years old and suffering from arthritis in her spine and neck. She also had a heart condition for which she had recently undergone triple by-pass surgery. The driver, her sixty-four-year-old husband, also suffered from arthritis in his spine and neck, a sinus condition, and, he claimed, leg injuries that were the result of the accident.

Janet, James, and Katherine—as owner of the car, and therefore responsible—were sued for personal injuries and property damages by the elderly couple. The case was typical of the kind of legal action that often follows when celebrities are involved in even minor accidents. It would linger on for years and involve countless depositions and astronomical legal fees—which the Jacksons' lawyer Robert Davis said his clients refused to pay, forcing him to withdraw from the case—and all because of a simple fender-bender. (Finally, in 1989, after five years, the case was dismissed when the elderly couple's attorney did not show up at the hearing. He said his alarm clock failed to go off.)

Joe and Katherine tried to use this accident to separate Janet and James DeBarge. Any excuse would do; they claimed he was irresponsible.

But when they found out that James DeBarge was abusing drugs, that was the end of the romance as far as they were concerned. Now they were very worried about their youngest daughter. But Janet was in love with this man and determined to marry him, despite—or perhaps even because of—her parents' disapproval. She knew he had a drug problem, but she was not going to let that stop her.

"You always think you can change people," she said in retrospect. "And I knew that he so badly wanted to change. He was trying, but he wasn't trying hard enough."

They eloped on September 7, 1984, in Grand Rapids, DeBarge's hometown. "Janet and James didn't break the news to anyone," said Etterlene DeBarge Rodriguez, Janet's former mother-in-law. "They just did it. I knew that Janet was very much in love with James—she had confided that in me—and that he felt the same about her."

Janet telephoned LaToya and told her what she had done. LaToya told Joe and Katherine, who did not take the news well. Then she telephoned each brother—except Michael. They were all quite distressed, Jermaine in particular. "I know that he would have killed her if he could've gotten his hands on Janet," LaToya would remember.

No one knew how to break the news about Janet's elopement to Michael. Actually, no member of the family wanted to be the one to tell him. He had always felt very protective of Janet—he has said that she was his best friend in the family, "like a twin"—and this was sure to be upsetting. The tour proved difficult enough without this news. Finally someone—it was said by family members to be Quincy Jones's daughter—broke the news to him. "It killed me to see her go off and get married," Michael would say later.

"He was absolutely furious," remembered one Victory tour employee. "No one had ever seen him so pissed off. 'How could she do this? How could she do this to *me*?' It was as if he considered it a personal affront. He tried to reach her but, to my knowledge, wasn't able to. 'When I see her, I'll fix her,' he kept saying. It was strange, as if he was a jilted lover instead of brother of the bride.''

For a month, Janet and James lived in the Encino home with Janet's family. James was not happy living there. "He wanted them to have their own place,'' explained his mother, Etterlene. "He felt that they needed to be alone to give themselves a chance to grow in their marriage. But Janet never wanted to leave home. She was still like a little girl, who never wanted to leave her bedroom, that's what James said.''

Living at the Encino home turned into a nightmare for James, and also for Joe. "The guy [DeBarge] would come to the house completely out of his mind on drugs,'' Steve Howell remembered. "He would be so high on coke and alcohol that twice the guards tried to stop him from going in. 'If you go in there, Mr. Jackson will kill you,' they'd tell him. But he was pretty belligerent and didn't care. Funny thing was that when he wasn't high, he was the nicest guy in the world. He was like Dr. Jekyll and Mr. DeBarge.''

" 'You leave my husband alone!' Janet would scream at her father,'' recalled another former employee. " 'He's a good man.' ''

"He's not good for *you*, Janet,'' Joe would retaliate. "And if you think you're going to ruin this family by staying married to him, you can forget it. You divorce him, do you hear?''

Crying, Janet would run to her bedroom.

Katherine tried to find a solution to the problem: she offered to enroll James in a rehabilitation program. He refused to go.

In an interview with a tabloid, James DeBarge remembered the Encino estate as "The House of Fears" ("That sounds just like James,'' said his mother, laughing) and paints an eerie picture of Michael Jackson, who was at home for a short time during the tour.

"It was while I lived there that I came to realize what a sad, lonely figure Michael Jackson is,'' he has said. "He was a ghost, wandering around the place looking for friendship. He would come to our room late at night, tap softly on the door, and say, 'Is it all right if I come in?' One time, Janet and I were making love, and he came in! He got into bed with us and poured his heart out. He said, 'I envy you two, because you have each other and love each other. But I haven't got anyone.' There was never a sign of a woman in Michael's life.''

James's mother laughed at the thought of Michael walking in on her son and Janet. "I don't know if that's true or not,'' she said. "I've heard that before a couple of times, Michael just coming into their bedroom like that. I do know that James felt that Janet was Michael's heart and soul. And I know that Michael loved Janet and he sometimes liked to be with the two of them when they were together. Michael's just a lonely man who's always needed somebody he could relate to and know wasn't phony. James is a very comical person, and Michael liked his sense of humor. The two of them got along pretty well, most of the time. As far as I know, they had a good relationship. I know my son had more of a relationship with Michael than he did with any of the other brothers. He told me that Michael was very sloppy with his appearance around the house. The maid would always be very upset with Michael, because he would just put his stuff all over the house.

"James also said that Michael had never forgiven his father for all the things he had done to his mother. Michael had a very bad grudge against Joe. He even spoke of hate one time. Michael said he thought his mother was a lady and she should be treated like a lady. He loved her very much, and he felt it was unfair the way Joe treated her."

"He really was a very lonely man-child," James DeBarge contended in the tabloid story. "The only time he had any fun was when he had friends over to play in his $2 million amusement arcade. But they had to let Michael win most of the time. If they didn't, they wouldn't be asked to come back."

James DeBarge has told writer Tony Castro some rather amazing stories of his life in the House of Fears. He claims that, once, it rained, and Michael stripped and danced naked around the pool. "His mother would scream from the house, 'Put your clothes on, Michael. Your father will be home soon.' Fear of Joe Jackson was the key that controlled them all," DeBarge said. "There wasn't one of them Joe hasn't beaten.

"Meals were always a big, fussy affair with servants swarming around, making sure Michael's organic food was cooked perfectly. He sent the food back if there was anything wrong. Once he ruined lunch, throwing a tantrum because a temporary cook didn't know he hated garlic, which she had used with the vegetables."

It is difficult to ascertain the accuracy of James DeBarge's recollections about Michael Jackson, since he did not appear at the appointment he made to be interviewed for this book. Later his manager said that he had decided not to be interviewed—or even to confirm the quotes he gave Tony Castro—without first being paid for the information.

DeBarge's mother said, "I never actually met Michael Jackson.

He was upstairs in his room every time I was at the house visiting. Me and Katherine used to chat. Michael never came down.

"I liked Katherine so much. We would talk about how we were going to take more weight off, that sort of thing. She never talked to me about anything personal. Never about Joe.

"Joe is a very mean man, and anybody who knows Joe will tell you he's a mean man. That's the first impression you get of him. He even looks mean. When I was in his home, he never once even spoke to me. I was his daughter's mother-in-law, but he was very cold to me. If I had been a young, attractive teenager, he probably would have spoken to me. That's what James used to always be upset about. Joe's womanizing upset James terribly, and it upset Janet too, because she was very close to her father. When she saw her father, though, she didn't know whether to hug him or maybe just shake his hand, because they had such a turbulent relationship. It was not a warm relationship, like a father and daughter should have. He was a stranger to her."

After about a month, James and Janet moved into a condominium at 12546 The Vista in Brentwood. "They moved out of the house because Joe was gonna kill the guy," recalled Steve Howell. "I'm very serious."

"James had it out with Joe a number of times," said his mother, Etterlene. "They were enemies. Oh, it was just so terrible, I can't tell you how terrible it was. James could not stand him. It was a lot of pressure. Joe said James was a very fresh man, and Joe just detested that about him. But not just Joe. LaToya very strongly opposed the marriage. I don't know why. Sometimes I thought she liked him for herself. I think she was jealous that Janet had found happiness. At least that was the impression I got. James never got along with his sister-in-law LaToya. They were always in arguments."

Janet wanted nothing to do with her family as long as they could not accept her husband. Actually, Janet had begun distancing herself a couple of years earlier when she began working as an actress on the TV show "Fame."

"My parents were very strict while I was growing up," she recalled. "It was really our music and our work. We never really had . . . well, we missed out on our childhood, getting to know what really goes on out there. It was bad, because once you step out there for the first time, it stuns you. I saw a lot of things I'd never seen before."

Janet was miserable in her new marriage. She would stay up nights worrying about her husband, who was never home. " 'My

God,' I wondered, 'where is he? What's going to happen?' I felt like I was the only one who cared, and couldn't take it anymore."

According to Jerome Howard, Joe and Katherine's former business manager, "Janet would get phone calls in the middle of the night from friends of James's, telling her where he was. She'd get up and drive out to the deep, dark ghetto to find him. She got to know the ghetto better than any other Jackson. She loved that man and would do anything for him."

With the entire family opposed to the marriage, each member took turns trying to persuade Janet to end it. Indeed, it was Michael—owner of the House of Fears—who in the end gently convinced Janet that she had to end the relationship. The problems that James and Janet were having in their marriage—especially drugs—went against everything Michael stood for personally and spiritually. Besides, he could see what the marriage had done to his sister.

A friend of Janet's recalled, "Michael was the only person she would listen to. She and Michael had a special relationship then. He begged her to leave James. He cried on the phone with her, told her how much she was hurting Katherine. Janet was finally convinced."

Michael's first cousin, Tim Whitehead, confirmed "Mike talked to her, and after he did, Janet knew what to do."

"God, I felt like my whole life was falling down, and there was someone else there too, and I could see him going down, but there was nothing I could do," Janet said. "And he [James] said to me, 'Well, you haven't tried to help me,' but I thought, 'What about helping yourself, too?' I felt myself going down with this person, and I thought, 'Well, I can either go down with him and that's the end of my life, or I just let go and continue on by myself.' "

The stress nearly caused Janet to have a nervous breakdown. At one point she collapsed and had to be rushed to a hospital. She was exhausted, physically and emotionally.

Janet left her husband on January 7, 1985, and immediately filed for a petition to nullify the marriage and restore her former name, Janet Dameta Jackson. On the petition, she listed her total gross monthly income as three thousand dollars—a minuscule amount considering the millions Janet Jackson is worth today. She said the amount of her husband's income was unknown to her. When she got home from the courthouse, she called her friend René Elizondo (who has become her boyfriend) and said, "God, I can't believe what I've just done."

"Some people have said I was selfish," she said, "but there was nothing more I could do. It was something I had to do for myself.

rather than fifty years from now saying, 'God, I wish I had.' It's too late then.'' (The annulment was granted on November 18, 1985. Janet moved back into the home and the family continued to maintain the condominium.)

''If it hadn't been for Janet's family, I'd still be married to her,'' James DeBarge said in March 1990. ''But I still love her.''

James's mother, Etterlene DeBarge Rodriguez, said, ''Part of me feels that they could have made it, then another part of me feels they could've never made it because of the odds that were against them. James was very immature, like a little boy. But Janet could be violent. She could slap your face, if she wanted to. Other women were always in James's face, and Janet was very jealous. One time we were at a Smokey Robinson special, and that young, beautiful singer Vanity was a guest. Vanity was running in and out of James's dressing room, and Janet did not like that one bit. In fact, she told me to keep an eye on Vanity because she thought she was up to no good.

''You know, the biggest misconception about the Jacksons is that they are perfect. And, of course, that's not true about any family. The Jacksons have always tried to make it appear that they are one-hundred-percent pure, but they have the same kinds of problems any other family has. Katherine Jackson has been under extreme pressure for many, many years, much more than most women in this world will ever know. For years, she has tried to protect her family from themselves, and now, with all the true stories coming out about them all, I know it must be very painful for her, because above all, Mrs. Katherine Jackson is a real lady.''

For years, Janet has been confronted with the rumor that she and DeBarge had a baby during their marriage and that the child is being raised secretly in Europe. Because of the stress of her marriage, Janet did gain weight. She actually looked pregnant. ''But did I get *that* fat?'' Janet asked a reporter. ''There's no truth to that story at all.''

James DeBarge has said that Janet was pregnant before they were married but that she had an abortion. ''Well, I heard that as well,'' said his mother, Etterlene. ''But I can't say that that's true.''

It was not easy living at Hayvenhurst, especially with all of the emotional distress brought on by Janet's marriage. It was a hectic time for Michael because, as well as working with his brothers on the road, he was filming a short feature for Disney, *Captain EO*, on his days off. Michael enforced some strange policies during the filming of *Captain EO*. First of all, he would not work on Mondays.

To Michael—like a lot of other people—Monday is the worst day of the week, and unless he is touring and has no choice, he prefers to start his week on Tuesday. Also, he preferred to rehearse with all of the curtains in the rehearsal room drawn. The lights also had to be turned off so the stage would be dark. Still, Michael would not take off his sunglasses during rehearsals, only when they were filming. The music always had to be played as loud as possible. Everyone but Michael walked around wearing earplugs.

During rehearsals, Michael tended to disappear, causing a great stir when he was needed for a scene. He would hide and watch as everyone scattered about frantically looking for him. One friend said, "He likes to see people go nuts trying to find him. Then he would pop out, seemingly from nowhere. 'Here I am,' he'd say. 'I've been here all the time.' He was quite strange. It was as if he were playing 'hide and seek.' "

Elizabeth Taylor, who was fifty-two years old at the time, was twenty-six-year-old Michael's only guest during the time he worked on *Captain EO*. He and Liz had a terrific time together, running up three thousand dollars a week in damages to Michael's trailer by having messy food fights with one another. Michael ate carob brownies every day, and his Sikh cook made huge vegetarian meals for him at night.

Besides Liz Taylor, Michael spent a lot of his time with a ten-year-old named Jonathan Spence, *People* magazine writer Todd Gold has reported. Other than Liz, this child was the only person allowed near Michael. He would wipe the sweat from Michael's brow with a towel. According to one of Gold's sources, the two would "nuzzle and hug a lot. There was nothing sexual going on. But it was definitely a close friendship."

Sometimes Michael would feel a need to get away from it all. At those times, he usually went to—ironically enough—Disneyland, "my favorite place."

Steve Howell recalled the night he and Mike spent at the Disneyland Hotel together. Michael had summoned him there so that he could see some footage Steve had shot earlier in the week.

"When it came time for dinner, I thought I would be respectful to his vegetarianism and order a turkey sandwich from room service instead of the hamburger I really wanted. 'Oh, well,' Michael said, hedging. He didn't like to tell other people what to eat, but also he couldn't resist. 'Turkey's just as bad as hamburger. Have a nice salad.' Michael had his two white-turbaned Sikh cooks, who traveled everywhere with him, fix a meal for him and security guard Bill Bray.

"Bray went to bed after dinner. Me and Mike, who was wearing peach silk pajamas and white socks, spent the night on the floor, little-kid-style, watching Three Stooges movies, talking and eating popcorn late into the night. He was more comfortable when he was away from the estate."

"Are you seeing anyone?" Steve Howell asked. "Do you ever think about marriage?"

Michael thought a moment and responded, "I'm waiting. I'm waiting for the right time. I mean, I'm Michael Jackson, and I have this, uh, *image*."

"What do you mean?" Howell pushed.

"I want someone to marry me for *me*, not for my image," Michael responded. "I'm scared of being taken advantage of."

Howell remembered, "He said that there would be two special times in his life. One would be when he marries and the other when he dies. Personally, I think he'll die before he gets married."

Janet's marriage, like those of her parents and some of her siblings, was filled with strife. It's hard to imagine Michael viewing any marriage in a positive light when he was surrounded by such poor examples. He learned early to be very cautious before committing himself to any relationship that could become serious. As Michael became more and more successful, there was a resurgence of rumors about his sexuality, despite his "affair" with Brooke Shields. Michael had always been extremely sensitive about this personal issue.

By September 1984, the questions remained unanswered. Was Michael Jackson gay? Could he possibly be straight?

To people who feel they know Michael well and understand his religious background, the answer was clear. Jehovah's Witnesses—like other fundamentalist Christians—forbid all sexual activity outside of marriage, as well as homosexuality. Barbara Grizzuti wrote in *Visions of Glory*, her book about Jehovah's Witnesses, "You don't have to perform a homosexual act to qualify as a homosexual: If you have homosexual fantasies, you are a homosexual in your heart and God sees your heart."

Michael Jackson was a devout Jehovah's Witness who considered sex "a tribulation" as all Witnesses were supposed to, and therefore it is extremely doubtful that he had ever had sex with *anyone*, man *or* woman. Michael Jackson, at twenty-six years old, was still a virgin.

"I remember Tatum O'Neal hanging around and, when the boys were in Vegas in 1975, Maureen McCormick (Marcia Brady on

"The Brady Bunch") was always back in his dressing room," Susie Jackson remembered. "If he'd had any kind of relationship, it might have been with Maureen because they seemed close, and certainly his brothers would have challenged him to have sex with her. But I doubt very much that he did it. Michael had been turned off to sex. Besides the religious belief, he didn't want anything to do with sex because of what he saw his brothers do, and his father too."

Being a twenty-six-year-old virgin teen idol devoted to a sexually repressive religion is not easy, especially when show business dictates that a male celebrity be "romantically involved"—to use Michael Jackson's words—with a woman.

"Business came first where Michael was concerned," said his former sister-in-law Enid Jackson. "He has told me numerous times that when he settles down to get married, he will stop performing. He has said that he will not be a husband and an entertainer at the same time. He will give up his career and spend all of his time with his wife and kids. And he's said he wants many, many children. As far as being taken advantage of by a woman, I don't see how that could ever happen to Michael. He is such a people person, such an observer, that he would see through that in a minute. He would know she wasn't the right one."

While Michael waited for the right woman to come along, tongues continued to wag. He became particularly upset when Black Muslim leader Louis Farrakhan lashed out at him in the press. Farrakhan called on black youths to reject Michael's persona.

"This . . . female acting, sissified acting expression, it is not wholesome for our young boys nor our young girls. Certainly, the man is a great singer. Certainly, he's a powerful entertainer. We cannot and we would never try to take anything away from our brother." He contended that Michael Jackson was setting a poor example for black youth because his style "actually ruins your young men and makes your young women have nothing to look up to as a real man for their own lives. This is a shame. But of course, men like this will live to die of old age, because they threaten nothing."

"Who is he?" Michael asked an aide. "Who *is* this guy? Why would he say stuff like that about me? I think I should sue him . . . or something." Frank Dileo convinced Michael that a lawsuit wouldn't amount to much. Michael wanted to offer a rebuttal in the form of a press release but thought better of giving Farrakhan's comments more exposure.

For years, a rumor had circulated that Joe had ordered his son injected with female hormones as a child to ensure that his voice would not change. It would stay high and commercial. "Not true," said his vocal coach, Seth Riggs. "I'm his voice teacher and I would know. He started out with a high voice, and I've taken it even higher. It's ridiculous. I don't even know if it's possible to do that [take female hormones so that a person's voice won't change]."

"The truth is, his voice is genetically high," Katherine Jackson has insisted. "So's Jackie's, my father's, and my husband's father's."

During a break in a vocal lesson, Seth Riggs said to him, "You know, everybody thinks you're gay."

Michael nodded his head and told Riggs this story:

A tall, blond, good-looking fellow came up to him one day and said, "Gee, Michael, I think you're wonderful. I sure would like to go to bed with you."

Michael glared at him and asked, "When's the last time you read the Bible?"

The blond said nothing.

"You know, you really should read it, because there is some real information in there about homosexuality."

The fellow studied Michael for a moment and said, sarcastically, "Sure, I guess if I'd been a girl, it would be different. *Then* you'd have sex with me."

"No, I wouldn't," Michael said. "There are some very direct words on *that* in the Bible too."

Still there were conflicting reports about Michael. For instance, reporter Denise Worrell was writing a story on Michael Jackson for *Time* magazine and had tried to arrange an interview with him, but to no avail. Instead, the writer was reduced to interviewing Michael's parents. Unbeknown to Michael, Joe decided to give the reporter a tour of the house. Joe knocked on Michael's bedroom door. There was no answer. "Michael, I have someone I want you to meet," Joe said. He opened the door. "Can I bring her into your room?"

Worrell reported that it was dark inside. Michael and a male friend, about twenty years old, were sitting on straight-backed chairs watching television. The glow from the set was the only light in the room. She noticed the outline of Michael's mannequins against a wall. She observed more mannequins, including a smaller one, on a shelf above the television.

Michael seemed startled by the presence of his father and the journalist. He nervously introduced Joe to his friend, using just a first name.

Michael then shook hands with the journalist, and the *Time* writer reported that his handshake "felt like a cloud." He barely said hello. Michael's friend than nervously extended his hand. Denise Worrell said that it was "damp."

Michael stared at the writer for a moment and then turned his back on her and resumed watching television.

As Joe and the writer backed out of the room, Joe had the look of a man who'd just opened Pandora's box. "Michael has a friend over," Joe explained. "He isn't about to give any interviews. You got pretty close, though."

After Denise Worrell left the house, a security guard came running after her. Michael's parents wanted to talk to her again. Joe must have told Katherine what happened in the bedroom.

"We were hoping you'd set the record straight and put a stop to the rumors," Katherine said. "They say Michael is gay. Michael is not gay. It's against his religion. It's against God. The Bible speaks against it."

Joe Jackson had the final word. "Michael is not gay," he repeated.

Michael may not have been gay, but he was curious about the lifestyle just the same. One friend remembered the day he and Michael went into a gay bar on Santa Monica Boulevard in Hollywood. "Michael was recording at Larrabe Studios, which is across the street from a gay bar in a predominantly gay section of Hollywood," the friend recalled. "I said to him, 'Hey, man, let's go get a drink at that bar.' He told me he didn't drink, but perhaps he could get an orange juice. 'You know, it's a gay bar,' I warned him. 'Really? I've never been to a gay bar,' he said. 'What goes on there?' he asked. I told him he should go and see for himself. He hesitated. 'Well, I've always wanted to. Okay, let's do it.' So in we went.

" 'Why is it so dark in here?' Michael wanted to know. I had the impression he had never been in *any* bar, let alone a gay one. There were a few guys in there, but it was early, so there weren't many. Michael took a deep breath and went up to the bartender and ordered an orange juice. The bartender said, 'Aren't you Michael Jackson?' He said, 'Nope. But I sort of look like Michael Jackson, huh?' He turned to me and winked.

"He and I sat in a corner and watched all the guys. He was recognized by a few, but they left him alone. Not one person came up to him.

" 'Is this all they do here?' Michael asked me. 'They just drink and talk and watch videos?' I wondered what he *thought* people did in bars. As we were sitting there, two men walked in and immediately began kissing each other. Michael saw them necking, and I could feel him tense up. Finally he said, 'Okay, I've seen enough. Let's leave.' So we got up and walked out. On the way out, Michael said, 'I can't believe those two guys kissed one another. How can they do that?'

" 'Maybe they liked each other,' I told him.

" 'Well, if that's what they do in gay bars, then I don't think I'll be going to any more,' Michael decided.''

This same friend remembered the day he and Michael went into Drakes, a novelty store on Melrose Avenue in Hollywood that specializes in pornography. In the back of the store, behind a gated area, a browser could find all the homosexual reading material and graphic photo magazines.

"Hey, what's back there?" Michael wanted to know as soon as he walked in.

"You don't want to know," said his friend.

"Yeah, I *do* want to know," Michael insisted. He then proceeded to walk boldly where probably no Jackson had ever gone before.

Thirty seconds later, he came running back. He looked shaken, as if he had just seen a ghost. "We gotta go, now," he said nervously.

"Why?"

"You don't want to know," Michael answered.

They left.

"He's not gay; I really feel certain of that," said his first cousin Tim Whitehead, who has toured with Michael as a roadie. "Many times a good-looking girl would walk by and Mike would whisper, 'Hey, what do you think of her? She's somethin' else, isn't she?' His brothers are much more open in the way they pursue women, but Michael is more discreet. He's a gentleman. I know that Michael was once interested in a woman, a famous woman who was married at the time. I promised Michael I would never say who she is. Of course, he didn't go after her because of the way he feels about marriage.''

"Once he asked me point blank, 'Have you ever shot any pornography, anything X-rated?' '' Steve Howell said when asked about Michael's curiosity. "I told him I hadn't. 'Are you sure?' he pushed. I was sure. He looked disappointed. Then he started asking me about my girlfriend. What it was like to have a relationship. He was very interested in other people's romances.

"Michael told me that he loves Asian-Indian women. He loves

their skin. He likes that darkness. But I've never seen him with any women like that, or any other women, except Brooke [Shields].''

Michael was fascinated by all lifestyles, heterosexual as well as homosexual. One reason he was so intrigued was that he felt he was missing out on something important and special.

"He used to ask me the most personal and intrusive questions," recalled Joyce McCrae, a former employee of Joe Jackson Productions. "He wanted to know what it was like to be married, how it felt to be divorced. What was it like to love? What was it like to have a baby? And I always gave him straight, honest answers. He appreciated that so much. It wasn't that he was trying to live vicariously; he just wanted insight. I was white, a woman, Jewish, divorced, all the things he wasn't." She laughed.

"He is the most curious person," said his former band leader James McField. "I once had a three-hour conversation with him in which he wanted to know how I got along with my mother and father, if I had problems with my brothers and sisters. Was I always nice to people? Did I sometimes treat people with disrespect? I asked him if the rumors of his being a homosexual were true. 'No, those rumors are not true,' he said, 'and I think it's terrible that people are saying that about me.' ''

The more enigmatic Michael remained, the more people would talk and joke about him. Steve Howell asked Michael about a comedy sketch Eddie Murphy had done on *Saturday Night Live* in which he played a very effeminate Michael Jackson as a guest on a talk show called "Guy Talk," with an equally fey Liberace played by another actor. The two talked about their sexual exploits with women; it was all quite ludicrous. "Yes, that's the only way to go," Eddie-as-Michael said, with a flick of the wrist. "Slam, bam, thank you, ma'am. That's what *I* like."

"How do you feel about that, Mike?" Howell asked. "I mean, this guy really made fun of you. He might as well have come out and called you a fag."

Michael smiled, "I don't mind it," he said softly. "I mean, the more they make fun of me, the more people are going to wonder what I really am. I don't care when people call me a fag. No one knows the truth. No one knows who or what I am."

"You don't care what people say about you?"

"They can say what they want to say, because the bottom line is they don't *know* and everyone is going to continue searching to find out whether I'm gay, straight, or whatever. It doesn't bother me. And the longer it takes them to discover this," Michael concluded, "the more famous I will be."

Perhaps that's how Michael sometimes felt, but he was also a man who told *Rolling Stone* writer Gerri Hirshey that he lives his life with obsessive caution, "just like a hemophiliac who can't afford to be scratched in any way."

In August 1984, a tabloid reported that Michael was having an affair with British pop star Boy George, which was not true. Michael was livid. For some reason, this rumor was the last straw for him.

One of publicist Norman Winter's former associates recalled, "Michael telephoned Norman one day and he was extremely upset. He was angry that there were these stories about him being gay, that little kids who could barely read were hearing about these rumors, maybe from their mothers who buy the tabloids talking to other mothers, who knows? The point is that Michael felt that he was getting a reputation he didn't want. He told Norman that he wanted to organize a press conference to refute the stories. Norman told him he thought it might not be a good idea. 'Why give it any credibility at all? Maybe it'll just blow over.' He said, 'No, it just keeps getting worse and worse. I have to do something now,' Michael said. Frank Dileo was against the idea, but Michael is a very strong-minded person. He knows what he wants to do, and how he wants it done. You have to respect that about the guy. Michael told Norman what he wanted to say, Norman wrote the text of the statement, Michael approved it, and we went from there."

Michael decided that he did not want to appear at the press conference; he was too shy to face all of those reporters and discuss something so personal.

"If the media would just tell it like it is about Michael, without destroying it and twisting it, maybe he would be more cooperative with the press," Enid Jackson observed. "But he has been hurt a lot by the media. Even when he gives an interview and the story comes out all right, someone else will inevitably twist what he said. Michael can't win, really. That hurts him. He's not stupid. He knows how to avoid getting hurt by this vicious cycle."

On September 5, 1984, a "major" news conference in a West Hollywood sound studio was arranged. The introductory statement handed out to reporters by Norman Winter read as follows:

"In what may be an unprecedented move, superstar Michael Jackson today instructed his personal manager, Frank Dileo, to 'once and for all set the record straight' regarding the ugly rumors which are being printed in a growing number of gossip publications.

"While Jackson has been advised of the potential risk of reacting to a series of unfounded rumors via a personal statement, he has made this courageous move based on strong convictions. He is primarily concerned about the feelings of his admirers, a large segment of which are children, who are at an impressionable age and 'therefore susceptible to such stories.'

"In addition to contradicting widespread false allegations, the young multimedia performer has also issued a stern warning. He has advised his attorney, John Branca, of the law firm Ziffren, Brittenhaum and Gullen, to institute legal action to the fullest extent of the law and subsequently prosecute all guilty 'as new fantasies are printed.' "

After the reporters digested that prepared statement, Frank Dileo—in dark sunglasses and with a cigar in his mouth—stepped in front of a podium to announce that he was to read a two-page statement from Michael, "who, as you all know, has risen to the pinnacle of success in his field."

Michael Jackson's statement:

"For some time now, I have been searching my conscience as to whether or not I should publicly react to the many falsehoods that have been spread about me. I have decided to make this statement based on the injustice of these allegations and the far-reaching trauma those who feel close to me are suffering.

"I feel very fortunate to have been blessed with recognition for my efforts. This recognition also brings with it a responsibility to one's admirers throughout the world. Performers should always serve as role models who set an example for young people. It saddens me that many may actually believe the present flurry of false accusations.

"To this end, and I do mean END—

"NO! I've never taken hormones to maintain my high voice.

"NO! I've never had my cheekbones altered in any way.

"NO! I've never had cosmetic surgery on my eyes.

"YES! One day in the future I plan to get married and have a family. Any statements to the contrary are simply untrue.

"Henceforth, as new fantasies are printed, I have advised my attorneys of my willingness to institute legal action and subsequently prosecute all guilty to the fullest extent of the law.

"As noted earlier, I love children. We all know that kids are very impressionable and therefore susceptible to such stories. I'm certain that some have already been hurt by this terrible slander. In addition to their admiration, I would like to keep their respect."

\* \* \*

After reading the statement, Dileo refused to acknowledge questions from reporters and left the microphone. He retired to an audio control booth, leaving behind a crowd of frustrated reporters.

"Frank! Frank! Hold on! Frank, come on!" they shouted belligerently. "Why isn't Michael here himself? What's going on here, really?"

When Dileo refused to return, the reporters turned en masse to Norman Winter. He told reporters that Michael was upset by the repeated tabloid reports of his alleged homosexuality. "It's a lot of nonsense," Winter said. "The fact that they say he's gay is completely ridiculous. If little girls want to grow up and marry Michael, now they know they've got a chance."

No celebrity had ever gone to such lengths to proclaim his or her heterosexuality. But Michael Jackson didn't have the courage to appear in person, which gave his declaration of "manhood" little credibility. Also, his statement was full of half-truths. Perhaps he hadn't had surgery on his eyes, as he claimed, but he certainly had had surgery on his nose three times. How could Michael repudiate one story relating to plastic surgery without admitting the whole truth about work done on his nose? Because of this obvious omission, one was forced to wonder what else Michael was hedging on. In the end, the press conference backfired on Michael Jackson; if anything, it raised more questions than it answered.

Afterward, Joan Rivers added a few jokes about Michael in her act; the punch line to one was that Michael is so gay he "makes Liberace look like a Green Beret." Of course, she wasn't just picking on Michael. She also joked that Barry Manilow's nose was so big "he could inhale Peru." That Mick Jagger had "child-bearing lips." And of Prince Charles? "Prince Charles really *is* gay," she joked. "This man can't wait for the Queen Mother to die so that *he* can be queen."

Even though Joan has often found her best and most well-received material when joking about celebrities, Michael felt singled out. He was taking these jokes much more seriously than he had Eddie Murphy's. He asked his brothers to find out specifically what kinds of jokes Joan was telling about him. The brothers then had friends of theirs go to a Lake Tahoe showroom to see Joan's act. When these friends reported Rivers's jokes back to the brothers, and they shared them with Michael, he was furious.

Michael had his associates plant a cover story in the September 18, 1984, issue of the *National Enquirer* saying that he was seriously thinking about suing Joan Rivers. "Michael Jackson is seething because Joan Rivers is making raunchy jokes implying that he's gay,'' the feature began. This was the first of a number of times he would use the *Enquirer* for his own communications. Michael Jackson really was considering filing a lawsuit against Rivers—even though his advisers told him that such an action would only focus more attention on the routines in question—but he hoped that the article would give her the hint that he wanted her to stop telling jokes about him and his sexuality.

Joan Rivers has a mind of her own; she is a comedienne who will not be intimidated. However, she is also an understanding and reasonable person, and she is known to stop performing jokes about celebrities if she learns that those stars truly are offended by them. In time, she did stop joking about Michael Jackson. But he was angry with her all the same.

''How could she have said those things about me?'' he complained, ''especially after I just had a press conference and said I wasn't gay. Didn't she hear about the press conference? What's with her?''

''Look, you can't blame Joan Rivers, Mike,'' one of his associates told him. ''Maybe you should have shown up at the damned press conference. Maybe *then*, people would have believed you. What do you think of that?''

Michael had no comment on that suggestion.

# Chapter

## 25

WHILE MICHAEL JACKSON was on the road with the Victory tour, he made headlines in 1984 by purchasing the ATV Music Publishing Company for an astounding $47.5 million. The purchase, believed to be the biggest publishing acquisition of its kind ever by an individual, was the culmination of ten intense months of negotiations. The seed for this venture had been planted a few years earlier when Michael was in London to record the number one hit "Say, Say, Say" with Paul McCartney at Abbey Road Studios. Michael became friendly with Paul and Linda McCartney during his stay; he ate most of his meals at their home outside of London. One evening after dinner, Paul displayed a thick booklet of song titles to which he owned the rights, including most of Buddy Holly's material and standards such as "Autumn Leaves," "Sentimental Journey," and "Stormy Weather."

"This is really the way to make big money," he explained to Michael. "Every time someone records one of these songs, I get paid. Every time someone plays these songs on the radio, or in live performances, I get paid."

"You're kidding me, right?" Michael said.

"Do I look like I'm kidding?" Paul countered with a serious expression. McCartney reportedly earns more than $40 million a year from record and song royalties.

Michael became intrigued. He owned the publishing rights to his own songs—obtaining that right was one of the reasons he and his family had left Motown and Berry Gordy's Jobete publishing house—but he thought of publishing as a tedious business primarily concerned with collecting royalties and licensing material for other media. Paul explained that the world of publishing can prove lucrative, especially thanks to the CD explosion and the increased use of popular songs in advertisements, movies, and television. Songwriters often lose the copyrights for one reason or another: sometimes they sell them for profit—a shortsighted thing to do, especially nowadays when so much money is generated in the music industry—and often they lose them out of ignorance, as in the case of The Beatles, who simply signed away rights when they were naive and didn't know any better.

As it happened, Paul McCartney and John Lennon had sold their copyrights to a publisher named Dick James when they were young. James ended up making a fortune on The Beatles' songs. Then, in the late sixties, while The Beatles were on vacation in Rishikesh with the Maharishi Mahesh Yogi, James sold Northern Songs—the company that continued to hold the rights to the Beatles' compositions—to Sir Lew Grade's ATV Music, Limited, for tax reasons. ATV was later purchased by Australian businessman Robert Holmes á Court's Bell Group. McCartney and Lennon's estate split with ATV the songwriting revenue generated by 251 of their songs written between 1964 and 1971—including "Yesterday," "Michelle," "Help," "A Hard Day's Night," "The Long and Winding Road," "Hey Jude," "Let It Be," and many others. ATV also held the publishing rights to thousands of other compositions, including songs by the Pointer Sisters, Pat Benatar, and Little Richard (including "Tutti Frutti," "Long Tall Sally," "Rip It Up," and "Lucille").

For the next couple of hours, Paul and Michael discussed publishing, and Michael absorbed everything. Paul would one day regret this conversation. When Michael said to him, "Maybe someday I'll buy your songs," Paul laughed.

"Great," he said. "Good joke."

But Michael wasn't joking. "I gave him a lot of free advice," Paul would later say. "And you know what? A fish gets caught by opening his mouth."

After that visit, Michael and Paul remained somewhat friendly, but Michael kept his distance. He didn't want Paul to perceive him as being anything more than an acquaintance, perhaps because he had a plan. "Michael's the kind of guy who picks brains," Paul McCartney said. "When we worked together, I don't even think he'd had the cosmetic surgery. I've got photos of me and him at our house, and he looks quite different. He's had a lot of facial surgery since then. He actually told me he was going to a religious retreat—and I believed him. But he came out of that religious retreat with a new nose. The power of prayer, I guess."

After Michael returned to the United States, he mentioned Paul's book of titles to his attorney, John Branca, and said that he wanted to buy some copyrights himself, "like Paul." Soon thereafter, Branca presented Michael with lists of songs that were for sale. Michael's first purchase was the Sly Stone catalogue, including all of Stone's pop classics of the 1970s, songs such as "Everyday People," "Hot Fun in the Summertime," and "Stand!" ("Stand!" was the song The Jackson 5 performed the first time they appeared on "The Ed Sullivan Show." Now Michael owned it.) For less than a million dollars, Michael also secured a few other titles, including two of Dion's hits, "The Wanderer" and "Runaround Sue," Len Barry's "1-2-3," and the Soul Survivors' "Expressway to Your Heart."

For the next couple of months, Michael was too preoccupied with the Victory tour to concentrate on publishing deals. But then in September 1984, when John Branca flew into Philadelphia to meet with Frank Dileo and Michael to solve some of the Victory tours's myriad problems, Branca casually mentioned the availability of the ATV catalogue. Michael wasn't sure what kind of music ATV represented.

"Well, it includes a few things you just might be interested in," Branca teased.

"Like?" Michael asked.

"Northern Songs."

Michael began to become excited. "You don't mean *the* Northern Songs, do you?"

"Yeah, Mike," Branca said. He couldn't contain his enthusiasm another minute. "We're talking *The Beatles*."

Paul McCartney had tried to buy ATV in 1981. He asked Yoko Ono to purchase the publishing house with him for $20 million, $10 million each, but she thought that was too much money and declined. Paul didn't want to spend the $20 million himself, and so the deal fell through.

As Michael skipped about the room, whooping and hollering, John Branca warned him that there would be some stiff competition in a bidding war for these songs.

"I don't care," Michael said. "I want those songs. You gotta get me those songs."

Branca said he would see what he could do. He telephoned John Eastman, Paul McCartney's attorney and brother-in-law, and asked if Paul was planning to bid on the catalogue.

"No," John Eastman said. "It's too pricey."

A few days later, Yoko Ono telephoned John Branca and said that she had heard a rumor that Michael Jackson was interested in purchasing ATV. Then she spent forty-five minutes trying to make Branca think that buying the catalogue was a terrible idea; she tried to talk him out of it. Branca discussed the conversation with Michael.

"Man, she just wants it for herself," Michael said, "but doesn't want to spend the bucks. She's hoping the price will go down if I don't buy it. Buy it, Branca."

The next few months were filled with intensive and frustrating negotiations. Bidding against Michael were Charles Koppelman and Marty Bandier's Entertainment Company; Virgin Records; real estate tycoon Samual J. Lefrak; and financier Charles Knapp. At one point, Branca called the negotiations off completely.

During these eight tense months, Paul McCartney again tried to convince Yoko Ono to join him in a bid. When Yoko repeated that she was not interested, McCartney decided not to bid.

Michael would telephone John Branca once a week. "Any news?" he asked.

"No, Mike. Not yet."

When Koppelman and Bandier had beaten Michael's offer of $47.5 million with one of $50 million, Michael was crushed. "Branca, we can't lose this, now," he said. "You gotta do something. I know we agreed that we wouldn't spend more than $41 million, but I'm willing to do it."

The Koppelman and Bandier offer was being financed by the MCA company, so Branca made a telephone call to the head of the company, Irving Azoff. "Man, you can't give these guys money to buy this catalogue," Branca told Azoff. "They're competing against Michael Jackson for it. Remember, you were a consultant for the Victory tour?"

"Johnny, don't worry about it," Irving Azoff said. "I'll take care of it."

Azoff pulled the rug out from under Koppelman and Bandier by refusing to finance their offer. Michael was back in the driver's seat.

Now Robert Holmes à Court was telephoning John Branca and begging him to come to London and close the deal. Branca played hardball and acted as if he wasn't interested. Holmes à Court offered to pay for Branca's plane fare, but Branca could well afford his own ticket. Finally, Holmes à Court said that if the deal wasn't closed on this trip, he would reimburse all of Branca's travel and accommodation expenses. Michael gave John Branca power of attorney, and Branca went to England and closed the deal in twenty-four hours. Michael never signed the contracts; Branca did.

Finally, he gave Michael bad news and good news. The bad news was that Michael was out $47.5 million. The good news was that he now owned ATV. Michael couldn't believe his good fortune. Neither could Paul McCartney.

McCartney said, "Someone rang me up one day and said, 'Michael's bought your songs.' I said, '*What??!!*'

"I think it's dodgy to do things like that," Paul complained. "To be someone's friend and then to buy the rug they're standing on."

Michael tried to phone McCartney and discuss the matter, but every time he did, Paul hung up on him. Finally, Michael said, "Paul's got a real problem, and I'm finished trying to be a nice guy. Too bad for him. I got the songs and that's the end of it."

Robert Hillburn, in an excellent analysis of the ATV acquisition for the *Los Angeles Times*, explained what Michael's purchase meant in dollars and cents: "If, for instance, 'Yesterday' earns $100,000 a year in royalties from record sales, airplay and live performances [it probably earns more], the Lennon estate and McCartney—as cowriters—divide about 50 percent of that income, about $25,000 each. The publisher—now Michael Jackson—collects the other 50 percent. The publisher also controls the use of the song in terms of films, commercials, and stage productions. If bought at a reasonable price and well administered, catalogues are considered an excellent investment. They are such good investments, in fact, that it is increasingly difficult to find one on the market."

As soon as Michael made the purchase, he and his representatives investigated ways to make it pay off for him. He hired people to develop an anthology series and four films using The Beatles' music, including *Strawberry Fields*, an animated feature; *Back in the USSR*, a movie based on Russian rockers; and films based on "Eleanor Rigby" and "The Fool on the Hill." Michael also planned musical greeting cards and music boxes.

When he licensed the song "Revolution" to Nike for a sneaker ad, he obtained Yoko Ono's consent, but not Paul McCartney's. In fact, McCartney—like many Beatles fans—was incensed because he felt Michael was cheapening the music.

In the end, McCartney had to accept Michael's decision. "I have no question of him owning it," he said. "It was perfectly for sale, fair and square and all aboveboard." So now every time Paul performs one of the songs he wrote between 1964 and 1971, he has to pay Michael Jackson. Also, ATV owned a life insurance policy on McCartney, which Michael now retains. So if Paul McCartney dies, Michael Jackson could end up with millions. (There was also a policy on John Lennon which ATV probably collected in 1980 when Lennon was murdered.)

When Michael sold "All You Need Is Love" to Panasonic for $240,000, McCartney contacted him and told him he was going too far. But Michael felt that by using The Beatles' songs in commercials, he was enabling the music to reach a new generation of fans who will buy The Beatles' records. "Well, I don't like the idea that Michael Jackson is the only guy in the world who gets to sit in judgment as to which Beatles songs can be used in commercials," Paul countered. "He's drawn up a list! I don't see how he should have that power."

(Pat Lucas, the West Coast director of SBK Songs, the international publishing company that administers Michael Jackson's publishing holdings, said that Michael has a restriction list of about one hundred fifty songs—tunes that he will not sell to commercials. The other hundred Beatle songs can be sold.

(Actually, the songs were being used in commercials before Michael Jackson made his purchase. Ford Motor Company had used "Help" and "Good Day Sunshine" in television commercials years before Michael bought ATV.)

Paul McCartney said he had hoped that "All You Need Is Love" would remain an anthem of the sixties, not become a jingle for "a friggin' loudspeaker system. And I also don't want 'Good Day Sunshine' to become an Oreo cookie," he complained, "which I understand he's done. I think that's real cheesy. I don't think Michael needs the money. I don't. And Yoko doesn't either." Paul owns the Buddy Holly catalogue and has exploited Holly's songs commercially many times, because, as he's said, "Buddy himself did commercials, and his widow actively wants us to earn money via commercials. It's her call."

Yoko Ono seems satisfied with what Michael is doing with The Beatles' catalogue and has called his ownership "a blessing." She said in November 1990, "Businessmen who aren't artists themselves wouldn't have the consideration Michael has. He loves the songs. He's very caring. There could be a lot of arguments and stalemates if Paul and I owned it together. Neither Paul nor I needed that. If Paul got the songs, people would have said, 'Paul finally got John.' And if I got them, they'd say, 'Oh, the dragon lady strikes again.' "

In 1990, Paul and Michael met to discuss what Paul called "this problem." McCartney recalled the conversation. "I put it to him this way: 'When we signed our deal, John and I didn't even know what publishing was. We thought songs were in the sky and everyone owned them. These days, even kids know better than that. Last year, 'Yesterday' passed the five million plays mark in America, which no other song has ever done. Not even 'White Christmas.' But no one has ever come up to me and said, 'Hey man, I really think you need a bonus. You've done great for this company.' So what the fuck is going on? You mean I've got to be content for the rest of my life to be on this deal I signed when I was a fresh-faced twenty-year-old? I've done a lot for this company.' ''

Michael acted as though he didn't understand what Paul was saying. So Paul spelled it out for him. ''I wanted him to recognize in the deal that I'm a big writer for this company that he now owns,'' McCartney recalled.

Michael told Paul that he didn't ''want to hurt anyone,'' and McCartney said he was happy to hear that. ''He's a genuine bloke, Mike is,'' Paul would say of him. Michael promised that he'd try to work something out for him.

The next day, John Eastman, Paul's attorney, telephoned John Branca and told him that Paul and Michael had agreed to renegotiate a higher writer's royalty for his songs. Branca checked with Michael. ''Heck, no, I didn't tell Paul that,'' Michael said. ''He's not getting a higher royalty unless I get something back from him in return.'' Branca passed Michael's decision on to Paul's attorney.

''Then we'll sue,'' Eastman threatened.

''Hey, be my guest,'' Branca told him.

A former employee of Branca's recalled that when Branca told Michael that Paul might sue, Michael scoffed. ''Let him sue. Meanwhile, go license some more songs, Branca. Let's go out there and make some money. Let's run this thing like a business.''

Said an associate of Michael's, ''Privately, Michael's feeling is this: Paul McCartney had two chances to buy the company. Both times, he was too cheap to spend the bucks. Mind you, Paul is said to be the richest entertainer in the world. The man is worth about $560 million. His royalties in one year come to $41 million. As Mike told me, 'If he didn't want to invest $47.5 million in his own songs, then he shouldn't come crying to me now.' He's a hard-hearted son-of-a-gun, Michael Jackson is. Just like his father. And when it comes to Paul McCartney, Michael doesn't want to know anything. 'I got those songs fair and square,' he's said. 'They're mine, and no one can tell me what to do with them. Not even Paul McCartney. He'd better learn to deal with it.' ''

By acquiring ATV, Michael Jackson proved himself a perceptive, hardheaded businessman. He's probably exactly the kind of businessman his father, Joe, would like to be, but isn't. Where Joe bullies, Michael ingratiates. Where Joe shouts, Michael listens. Where Joe rushes in unprepared, Michael studies every angle before reaching a decision. Michael has had the wisdom to surround himself with brilliant people, and then allow them to do their jobs without interference; Joe never did. It's almost as though Michael studied Joe's techniques and then did exactly the opposite. What father and son did share is that they trust no one and can be ruthless to those they have vanquished. Neither father nor son allows anyone second chances.

In January 1985, the Victory tour was over and Michael Jackson became a free man. It hadn't been an easy experience, but there was a pot of gold at the end of the rainbow: Chuck Sullivan gave Michael Jackson $18 million dollars, *cash*, to develop a clothing line. Michael barely got a few fashions into the stores—which didn't sell—when Chuck Sullivan went bankrupt. Michael got to keep the $18 million.

The Jacksons made a lot of money on the Victory tour, even if the promoters didn't. Each brother made about $7 million, one-sixth of the share after all expenses, net. Michael donated his take to charity; his brothers spent theirs on a lavish lifestyle and, before very many years, would need to work again.

After the tour, one of the first things Michael did when he got back to Encino was jump into LaToya's black Mercedes-Benz 450 SEL and speed off, without any security. As always, there was a group of female fans waiting at the front gate for someone—anyone—who looked like a Jackson. They never dreamed they might actually catch a glimpse of *the* Jackson. When they saw him, they followed him. Michael tried to lose his pursuers, but no luck. He was almost to Quincy Jones's house when his car ran out of gas. He must have cursed LaToya for not filling up the tank. Michael jumped out of the car, leaving it in the middle of the street, and ran for blocks, with his fans following him, until he reached Quincy's home and was rescued. So much for going out into the world alone.

Lionel Richie recalled, "One night, Elizabeth Taylor, M.J., and I went out to dinner. Because she was also a child star, Elizabeth could relate to him. They talked about isolation and what you do when you're lonely. It was good for Michael to hear that Elizabeth often went out of the house without security guards. The idea that you could live without them was a revelation to him."

After the Victory tour, Michael became involved in "We Are the World," the historic effort to feed the hungry of Ethiopia. Harry Belafonte planned to draw together some of the biggest artists in the entertainment business to record a song, the proceeds of which would go to a new nonprofit foundation, USA for Africa, to feed starving people. In addition to providing emergency food, medical relief, and self-help programs to stricken areas of Africa, the undertaking was to set aside some funds for hunger relief in the United States. Belafonte contacted Ken Kragen, an entertainment manager with a history of fund-raising, and asked if he could enlist clients Kenny Rogers and Lionel Richie in the endeavor. Rogers and Richie in turn obtained the cooperation of Stevie Wonder to add name value to the project. Richie telephoned Michael Jackson and asked if he would perform on the recording. He not only wanted to sing on the song, he said he would like to help Lionel write it.

Michael has always been empathetic to the plight of the hungry, homeless and sick, especially children. Frank Dileo tells many heartbreaking stories of Michael Jackson's influence on dying children. It is as though an unexplainable part within him is able to reach children close to death. Michael is not a miracle worker; he does not heal. However, his touch acts like a soothing balm for those facing a frightening time. There are people who feel they have the power to alleviate pain, and because they feel so strongly, they are able to transmit their feelings. Michael considers himself one of them and believes that this ability, like his voice, is a gift from God, a gift he recognizes and shares freely. It's an important, positive side of Michael, this caring, one he probably thinks is the best thing about himself.

One night after a show, a small child suffering from a brain tumor and spinal cancer was brought to Michael on a stretcher. When the boy reached up to Michael, Michael grabbed his hand and held tight. The child smiled. Frank Dileo turned away and broke into tears. Michael put his arm around Frank and said, "Don't feel sad. Don't cry. This is why I'm here."

"He's not afraid to look into the worst suffering and find the smallest part that's positive and beautiful," Dileo said.

Seth Riggs, the voice teacher who traveled with Michael on tours, recalled, "Every night the kids would come in on stretchers, so sick they could hardly hold their heads up. Michael would kneel down at the stretchers and put his face right down beside theirs so that he could have his picture taken with them, and then give them a copy to remember the moment. I'm a sixty-year-old man, and I couldn't take it. I'd be in the bathroom crying. But Michael could take it, and right before going on stage no less. The kids would perk right up in his presence. If it gave them a couple days' more energy, to Michael that was worth it. As far as I'm concerned he's a prince of the world."

* * *

Every night for a week, Lionel Richie went to Michael's Encino home, where the two sequestered themselves in Michael's room and labored on the lyrics and melody. They knew that what they wanted was some sort of anthem, a song both easy to sing and memorable. It wasn't always smooth going, but the process was usually creative and sometimes even comical.

"See, we both like to write in private," Lionel explained. "And now we know why. 'Cause we talk to ourselves. Lines just come zinging out, and we were doing them out loud in front of another person. That means you have to allow yourself to sound stupid and have somebody whom you respect hear you sound stupid. There were times I'd draw out a line and Michael would fall down laughing. I'd say, 'Sounds kinda dumb, eh?' and he'd nod. But you have to give that ego up. It's all in the nature of discovering that your style happens to be somebody else's style, or close to it. The pleasure about writing with someone who also writes lyrics is that as fast as I come up with one line, he's coming back with the other. I didn't have to tell Michael where I was trying to go. He knew exactly."

Though Michael and Lionel have never said this publicly, La-Toya—who watched the pair work—has claimed that Lionel only wrote a couple of lines of the song himself. She contends that 99 percent of the lyrics were written by her brother. "But he's never felt it necessary to say that," she added. The lyrics and the melody were finished on January 21, 1985, just one night before the recording session.

While Michael and Lionel were composing, Ken Kragen went about the business of lining up the all-star cast: Bruce Springsteen, Tina Turner, Bette Midler, Billy Joel, Ray Charles, Diana Ross, Dionne Warwick, The Pointer Sisters, Stevie Wonder, Cyndi Lauper, Willie Nelson, Smokey Robinson, Bob Dylan, and many others. Forty-five in all. Another fifty artists had to be turned down to keep the project from becoming too unwieldy. Michael asked LaToya to show up, and she did. (She got to stand next to Bette Midler in the lineup.) Marlon, Jackie, Tito, and Randy were also there.

Quincy Jones took time away from producing the film *The Color Purple* to produce and arrange (with Tom Bahler) the Jackson-Richie collaboration at A&M Studios in Hollywood. The American Music Awards had been held that same night, so many of the artists were coming directly from those festivities. When the artists showed up, the first thing they saw was a sign outside Studio A: "Please check your egos at the door.'' It was truly astonishing that so many artists of diverse backgrounds and individual renown were able to do just that: there were no ego problems in Studio A. Diana Ross could not conceal her excitement and asked the other stars for autographs. The Pointer Sisters took pictures of Michael. Tina Turner and Bette Midler traded anecdotes about their love lives. ''I've never before felt that strong sense of community,'' Kenny Loggins observed.

''Some artists were in the first instance very sensitive to the issue,'' Harry Belafonte said. ''Many felt it was a historic event, worthy of involvement. Some came to it insensitive to the issue but have since become quite touched by it, have taken up a newly committed role in the issue of world hunger. Some who came benefited from the overall success of the project, and that was as sufficient a role as they cared to play. I was very appreciative of all the elements.''

At around ten P.M., the proceedings turned solemn. Ken Kragen addressed the group to assure them that money generated from this song would, indeed, ''go to the right places.'' Bob Geldof, the leader of the Boomtown Rats and organizer of the British Band Aid musical charity effort, which produced the single, ''Do They Know It's Christmas?'' told of his visits to Ethiopia. Two Ethiopian women, whose presence had been arranged by Stevie Wonder, reported on the suffering there.

Finally, Michael Jackson addressed the assemblage of stars. He very quietly and somewhat awkwardly explained what his composition was about. ''A love song to inspire concern about a faraway place close to home,'' he said softly.

''It was fascinating to watch him,'' Diana Ross said. ''He was shy and sort of intimidated. If he only knew how we all felt about his being there. There were artists there who'd never met Michael, who were awed by him. But Michael doesn't think of himself as anything special, especially when he's surrounded by a lot of celebrities.''

The musical tracks had already been recorded earlier in the day, so it was just a matter of fine-tuning the lyrics—''Should it be '*brighter* day' or '*better* day'?''—and adding the voices. Michael taught the artists the melody and lyrics—most had already been sent taped demos of the song with Michael performing the music alone—and worked with them on vocal arrangements. Quincy Jones asked Michael to teach the stars a special background arrangement Michael wanted to try out. Awkwardly, Michael led the assemblage of celebrities in a chorus of the song with the addition of a meaningless riff that went ''Sha-la. Sha-lingay.'' All of the stars listened to Michael and repeated after him like obedient students. Afterwards, Michael turned to Quincy and said, "Was that right?" (Ultimately, the refrain wasn't used in the song.)

As integral as Michael Jackson had become to the celebration, he was also very much separate from it. Whereas everyone else present was filmed (by six cameras) as they performed for the "We Are the World" video, Michael's solo was taped later, privately, and spliced in. He never took off his shades. He was different, aloof, separated by an invisible wall. Some people speculate that Michael did not record with the others because in spite of his own fame, he remains awestruck by his fellow celebrities. The ultimate perfectionist, he would feel that he could not perform to the best of his abilities in front of them. Others offer a more succinct explanation: Michael likes to feel he is different from everybody and emphasizes this difference by erecting barriers between him and his fans, his peers, and his family. Indeed, in the video of "We Are the World," the shot of Michael begins at his Bass Weejun shoes and trademarked sequined socks, and then pans upward to his carefully made-up face. That was Michael's idea. "People will know its me as soon as they see the socks," Michael said, proudly. "Try taking footage of Bruce Springsteen's socks and see if anyone knows who they belong to."

The recording and taping session took all night. Who would sing what and with whom had been decided a couple of days earlier by Lionel Richie, producer Quincy Jones, and arranger Tom Bahler. Some of the interesting vocal pairings included Tina Turner with Billy Joel, Dionne Warwick with Willie Nelson, and, of course, Diana Ross with Michael Jackson. The only hint of things not going as planned involved the pairing of Michael and Prince. Michael doesn't like Prince, but for charity he would sing with him. But Prince didn't show up. At six the next morning, he called at the studio and asked if he could come in and lay down a guitar part. Quincy told him it wasn't necessary.*

By seven-thirty in the morning, the job was over and people finally started to leave. "Michael was as exhausted as anyone," Jeffrey Osborne reported. "He didn't say much, maybe something about being very happy, but I could tell that he was delighted."

"I did expect to see more ego," Paul Simon reported. "You know, 'The Gloved One' meets 'The Boss' and things like that, but it just didn't happen."

---

*Prince subsequently donated a song to the *We Are the World* album, which was released in April 1985.

"I just don't want this night to end," Diana Ross said as she hugged Tina Turner.

All who participated in the "We Are the World" recording session shared Diana's sentiments. The gentle, uplifting spirit of the song also touched the public's emotions when it was released on March 7, 1985. The "We Are the World" video—in which the artists traded off solos without any thought of ego or prestige—lent itself well to the benevolent spirit of the celebration and helped sell millions of records. The initial shipment of 800,000 records sold out within three days of its release. Subsequent orders lifted sales to an estimated three million.

By January 1986 the song's sales had raised nearly $40 million, but only $13.5 million of it had actually been spent on feeding the hungry in Ethiopia. Red tape kept the money from being spent quickly, and this upset some of the artists who had been involved in the recording. "I can't relate to it," Ray Charles complained. "What red tape in the world would stop the process of people starving to death? They can't wait until tomorrow. They can't wait overnight."

"I haven't kept up with how much they've spent," Jackie Jackson said. "They're giving money to needy people, to the starving. At least I hope that's where the money is going."

Marlon Jackson was on the USA for Africa board of directors and went to Ethiopia with Harry Belafonte and the USA for Africa officials to deliver money, food, and supplies generated by the campaign. Marlon explained, "Before we give money to any cause over there, we have to make sure the organization is legitimate. The money could go within a week. We establish which cause affects the most people, then we move quickly and safely. We're not going to just write a check and say, 'Bam, you have it.' "

For 1986, Ken Kragen proposed "Hands across America," a domestic antipoverty program sponsored by USA for Africa. The plan was to raise $100 million by soliciting $10 pledges from 10 million Americans who would join hands from New York to Los Angeles on May 25. The project was to have its own theme song, "Hands across America," written by Marc Blatte and John Chauncy. The music video would premiere as part of the 1986 Super Bowl's halftime show on January 26. The hope was that "Hands across America" would do for America's homeless and hungry what "We Are the World" did for those in Ethiopia.

When Michael Jackson heard about these plans, he was not

pleased. "What's wrong with the song Lionel and I wrote?" he wanted to know. "That should *always* be the anthem."

Michael did not like the idea that his song was being replaced," an associate said. "First, his feelings were hurt. Then he became upset. He felt his song was divinely inspired and should always be the anthem. Actually, he was being a bit of a brat in a way. But his intentions were good, I think. He wanted to protect the integrity of his song. He didn't want any other song to be associated with this cause. Michael is very powerful. It was easy for him to convince Ken Kragen and the others with just four words: 'I don't like it.' "

During a closed-door trustees meeting of USA for Africa in Century City, Michael made known his feelings about the new song. In a bold, somewhat surprising move, he managed to engineer a successful boardroom offensive against unveiling the new song and music video during the Super Bowl. "Most of the Board were in agreement that 'We Are the World' should be the official song of USA for Africa," Ken Kragen reported after the meeting. The board eventually agreed with Michael that each separate USA for Africa project—like Hands across America— could have its own theme, but none should ever supersede "We Are the World."

"Hands across America" was not shown during the Super Bowl's half-time show. Instead, America saw and heard "We Are the World" once again.

Within the last year, Michael had been involved in three important contests and won them all. Although his methods may have been different, he was just like his father when it came to determination. The first, when he acquired ATV, was a matter of outspending the other bidders. In the confrontation with the USA for Africa trustees, it was his power which enabled him to win. At the Grammy Awards in February 1986, Michael won for his accomplishments. "We Are the World" garnered four of the coveted trophies during presentations at the Shrine Auditorium in Los Angeles.* Now more than ever, Michael was someone to be reckoned with.

Frank Dileo, John Branca, Norman Winter, and Michael Jackson often had brainstorming discussions about show business icons like Frank Sinatra and The Beatles, and how their representatives

---

*Less than a minute after the song was announced as Best Pop Group Vocal Performance, a publicist for the National Academy of Recording Arts and Sciences circulated a press release explaining that Quincy Jones would receive the Grammy statuette and that the forty-four participating artists would receive "a special citation" from the Academy.

were known to sometimes hire teenagers to scream and weep at the sight of them whenever they made public appearances. Scenes caused by these emotional teens made the entertainers seem even more popular than they really were, and they were especially effective on newsclips about the stars because hysteria photographs so well. Michael always believed that hiring youngsters to holler, faint, and sob was a masterful public relations stroke on the part of Sinatra and The Beatles.

One evening Michael and Frank Dileo telephoned Norman Winter to tell him of an idea Michael had. Michael wanted to cause a commotion during the televised Grammy Awards presentation on February 25, 1986. It had been decided that Quincy Jones would accept the award if "We Are the World" won for Record of the Year. It's not known whether it was Michael's intention to do so, but it would seem that he wanted to somehow steal a little of Jones's thunder. His idea was to have a female teenager run out onto the stage from the wings and jump all over him as he stood next to Quincy. Bill Bray's security staff would be ready and waiting to pull the girl off Michael, who would then act surprised and frazzled. Since the Grammys are televised internationally, the whole world would witness this mad scene. The next day, Michael's popularity, and the hysteria it had caused at the Grammys, would be the subject of worldwide news. The scene caused by Jackson's "overwrought fan" would probably even overshadow the fact that "We Are the World" had won the coveted Grammy for Record of the Year. Certainly, Quincy Jones's acceptance speech would be overlooked in favor of Michael's manic adoration.

Frank Dileo and Norman Winter were against Michael's idea. If word ever got out to the press that the girl who jumped Michael was actually hired by him to do so, it would be extremely embarrassing to everyone involved.

"But it'll never get out," Michael said, enthused. "So, who do we get? Who can we hire to do this thing?"

Dileo and Winter didn't have a clue.

Finally, a female publicist who worked in Winter's office found a teenager who she felt was savvy enough to pull off the hoax. She was hired for the job.

The night of the awards, those involved in the trickery held their breath as "We Are the World" was announced by presenters Sting and Phil Collins as Record of the Year. Michael, who was wearing a black military jacket, red shirt, and red brooch, rose from his seat. Frank Dileo, seated behind Michael, smiled broadly, a cigar hanging from his mouth. Michael then walked up onto the stage with Lionel Richie.

Before long, Quincy Jones, Dionne Warwick, Kenny Rogers, and Stevie Wonder were also on stage with Lionel and Michael. As Quincy gave his speech, Michael nervously rocked from side to side. He kept looking off into the wings, as if he was wondering what happened to the girl who had been hired, and when she was going to make her move.

Unbeknown to Michael, the teenager, who had full backstage credentials, was having a terrible time trying to break through the crowd of people—technicians, production people, members of the press—gathered in the wings to gawk at the celebrities congregated on the stage. In the end, she couldn't get through the crowd. Before she knew what was happening, the speech was over and she had missed her magic moment.

The scheme didn't work.

"That's okay. Next time, we'll plan it better," Michael said later, with a wink.

A month later, in March 1986, Michael, Frank Dileo, John Branca, and Pepsi-Cola Company President Roger Enrico came up with a second Pepsi sponsorship deal. This time Michael would be paid $15 million and not have to split it with his brothers. (The last deal, in 1984, was for $7 million, split among the six of them.) This was the biggest commercial sponsorship deal in history. (Lionel Richie and Willie Nelson had both received "only" $2.5 million for their recent endorsements, and Pepsi parceled out their money rather than paying in full upon the signing of the contract.) Pepsi would sponsor Michael's first solo tour, whenever that would happen, and Michael would make two commercials for the company.

Michael was paid up-front, in full. He needed the income in 1986 for tax breaks that became available to him when he purchased the ATV Music Publishing catalogue.

While Michael Jackson looked to the future, his brother Jackie tried to rectify the past. Enid Jackson, thirty-one, filed to dissolve her eleven-year marriage to Jackie Jackson, thirty-four, on January 8. The couple had two children, ages eight and three. "There have been times when things have been rough for me," Jackie would say. "Having fortune and fame does not always mean you're happy. I've been under a lot of pressure, and Enid has always pulled me out and kept me together."

Jackie and Enid had separated a number of times over the years, but they still had managed to keep the marriage going. However, after the discovery of her husband's extramarital affair with Paula Abdul, now twenty-two, Enid naturally became suspicious of Jackie. At one point, when the two were attempting a reconciliation, she discovered that Jackie and Paula were still dating.

" 'If he's trying to get back with me and still seeing her, it's not worth it,' was what I thought," Enid said. "I had a date with Jackie—who was staying at Randy's place during this part of our separation—to talk about our marriage. When I left, I noticed Paula driving down the street on the way to Jackie's. The next day, I went back to talk to Jackie, and sure enough, she was there."

Accompanied by her secretary, Enid waited for Paula to leave. A car chase then ensued. Finally, Paula found herself trapped in an alley, facing off against an angry, hurt wife and a witness.

"I want to know what's going on, and I want to know now," Enid demanded of Paula.

"Well, what do you think is goin' on?" Enid recalled Paula answering. "I'm seeing Jackie. That's what's goin' on. What's goin' on with you?"

"I thought Jackie and I were getting back together," Enid said, "but apparently we're not."

"Guess not."

"Listen, you don't know what you're doing," Enid told Paula, trying to reason with her. "You don't have kids. It's not just you and him. This hurts a lot of people. There are children involved here. Family."

Paula didn't say anything.

"And not only that," Enid continued. "You're not gonna be the only one for Jackie. If he's done this to me, he's gonna do it to you one day."

At that, Paula broke down, sobbing uncontrollably. "Every time he's with me, he wants to be with you," she cried. "And when he's with you, he wants to be with me."

"Well, I don't know about that last part," Enid said with a smile, trying to break the tension.

Paula continued to cry. Enid suddenly realized that underneath all of that bravado, Paula Abdul was just a bewildered young woman who had gotten herself into a painful, humiliating situation. She was in love with a married man and didn't know what to do about it.

"I looked at her as she was crying, and it all came to me," Enid said. "Here I was, a grown woman, mature enough to try and understand this. And Jackie was a grown-ass dirty old man, who had gotten himself involved with a kid who didn't know any better. I started to feel sorry for her. She was crying so hard I was afraid to let her drive home. So I invited her to the house.

"When we got to my place, she was still sobbing. 'I need to talk to my mother,' she cried. So I called her mom. I said, 'Listen, I'm very concerned about your daughter. I didn't realize she was this upset and confused, and I hate to see her caught up in a situation like this. I think she really needs you now.' And her mother said to me, 'Well, listen here, from what I understand, this isn't the first time your husband has had an affair. He has had many women over the years. It just so happens that *my* daughter is the one he wants to leave you for. So what do you think about *that*?' Well, I was obviously shocked. I said, 'I'm calling you out of concern for your daughter, and you have the nerve to tell me this? How dare you?' I was very upset by the time I hung up."

Jackie and Enid had a splendid estate in Encino, which they purchased from Rob Reiner and Penny Marshall: two acres of walled grounds with three entrances and electronic security gates. The four-bedroom, five-bathroom residence is approximately seventy-five hundred square feet, with a separate two-bedroom guest house and a recording studio. There was a large lagoon-style swimming pool and separate pool house, as well as a full-sized tennis court and an impressive garden, which included many fruit trees. Enid stayed at the house; Jackie moved into a twenty-two-hundred-dollar per-month condominium. The house—built in 1936 and worth almost $2 millon—would eventually have to be sold and the proceeds divided between the couple.

The end of Jackie and Enid's marriage would be a devastating divorce action that would take years to resolve and leave the entire family shaken. A great deal of money was at stake. Jackie received millions from the Victory tour and had invested it in shopping centers and apartment buildings. In interest income alone, the couple lived comfortably on twenty thousand dollars per month. They had five cars. Enid drove a white Mercedes-Benz 500 SC and Jackie a 1985 Range Rover. They also owned a 1977 Mercedes-Benz 6.9, a 1977 Blazer, a 1985 Toyota, a 1969 Cord Replica, and a 1983 Ferrari 400i. They had $4 million in assets in four entertainment corporations which they owned together. Among other things, Enid asked for the Mercedes and forty-eight thousand dollars a month spousal support as well as joint legal custody of the children. She also wanted her season ticket to the Lakers basketball games, as well as the parking pass to the Forum, where the games are played.

"You have to understand that in a celebrity divorce you ask for a lot because you know you're not going to get anything,'' she said in retrospect. ''Just for us to live without any luxuries—no groceries or anything—costs thirty thousand a month. That's the lifestyle we were living. Considering the millions we had, I was not asking for a lot.''

She also wanted to be reimbursed $8,100, half the purchase price of the 1986 Toyota Supra automobile that Jackie had bought for Paula Abdul.

Enid said that he bought the car without her knowledge. After they were separated, she saw the car in front of Jackie's condominium and angrily confronted him about it. That's when he confessed that it belonged to Paula and that he had purchased it for her out of community funds. ''It pissed me off, I must say,'' Enid would recall.

Jackie had also bought many other expensive gifts for Paula Abdul, including a Rolex watch, a diamond and sapphire necklace, a diamond and sapphire bracelet, and a diamond engagement ring. The couple also took trips together: to the Super Bowl in New Orleans and to the NBA All-Star game in Dallas.

The court ruled that Jackie and Enid should stay at least one hundred yards away from each other at all times—because there had been some domestic violence—except when transferring the children between them.

Michael couldn't help being affected by the divorce. He liked Enid and was sorry to see her hurt. Always sensitive to the feelings of children, Michael was moved by the plight of his niece and nephew, who were old enough to be aware of what was happening and young enough to be caught in the emotional cross fire of two angry parents.

When Enid aired the charges of adultery against Jackie, Michael must have compared Enid's plight to that of his mother. For years, Katherine had suffered in silence through Joe's many infidelities. Enid not only went public, she made sure that she was going to emerge from the marriage financially secure. Michael hated to see Katherine suffer. One could speculate that Michael might have wished for Katherine to use Enid as a role model and leave Joe once and for all.

''Michael was so supportive of me and the kids, which meant so much to us.'' Enid said. ''He would send the kids gifts, and instead of just having someone else sign the card, he would have them bring the package to his house where he would write his own note. I would get notes from him that said, 'I know what you're going through. I want you to know that I'm here for you.' Once I got a note of support in which he said, 'You know how I feel abou the marriage vows.' He was here for me, and I'll never forget that. He didn't have to do that, but he did.''

In June 1986, Michael Jackson, who would turn twenty-eight ir two months, underwent another operation to have his nose made even slimmer. This would be his fourth—and it is still his mos recent—nose job. (He has since had two more surgeries on his nose for corrective and ''fine-tuning'' purposes, but they were not considered complete rhinoplasties.) He also wanted a cleft in his chir and discussed the possibilities with Steven Hoefflin, his plastic surgeon. It's difficult to know why Michael was so unhappy with his appearance. Years later he would tell one associate that the ''greatest joy I ever had was in knowing I had a choice about my face.'' This same associate asked Michael for advice about rhinoplasty surgery, and Michael recommended that Steven Hoefflin give his friend the nose job. The friend took him up on his suggestion.

''There's nothing to it, man,'' Michael said. ''After the first one. it doesn't even hurt that much. Once you have it done, you'll never stop looking in the mirror. That's how great you'll feel about yourself.''

Some people associated with Michael in 1986 thought he had become too eccentric. Paul Anka once remembered the evening Michael Jackson came to his home for a visit. ''He spent hours sitting in the Jacuzzi, and every two minutes he sent my wife out to buy the most bizarre foods in the world. And instead of asking me about music, he only wanted to talk about plastic surgery.''

When Michael told Katherine he was going to have a cleft in his chin, she was upset and thought he was going, as she put it, ''overboard.''

''Why?'' she wanted to know. ''I just don't understand.''

As Katherine told a friend of hers, Michael explained, ''I can afford it, I want it, so I'm going to have it.'' It was as if he were buying a new car instead of undergoing painful, appearance-changing plastic surgery. Whereas most people can only fantasize—''Wouldn't a new nose be nice, and maybe a new chin too?''—Michael can afford to make those whims a reality. ''And I think if more people could afford it, they would do it too,'' his sister Janet has reasoned. ''I see nothing wrong with it.''

''How many other people have plastic surgery?'' Enid Jackson asked rhetorically. ''Lots of normal, everyday people. What makes it so wrong for Michael, then? Why is it that he's supposed to have a problem, but no one else does? It's because of his fame and the way everything is magnified, that's why. It's very unfair.''

Explained his first cousin Tim Whitehead, ''Basically, this is the way he sees himself, and it's something he has an opportunity to do, so he does it. That's how the family looks at it.''

One psychologist has speculated that Michael's narcissistic side dictated he have the cleft carved into his chin. ''Michael Jackson was obviously becoming more and more enchanted by his own image,'' Dr. Raymond Johnson said. ''He is apparently continuing his quest for the perfect face.''

''I do want to be perfect,'' Michael once remarked to an employee. ''I look in the mirror, and I just want to change and be better. I always want to be better, so maybe that's why I wanted the cleft in my chin. I don't know how to explain it.''

Of course, one of the public's favorite theories is that Michael has been trying to transform himself into the image of Diana Ross, as if Diana Ross has a cleft in her chin. Mostly this story is the result of the popular connection between Ross and Jackson over the years, and some family members' recollections of Michael saying things to LaToya and Janet like, ''You're not pretty until you start looking like Diana.'' After surgery and with the help of makeup, Michael sometimes *did* resemble Diana Ross, with the tweezed, arched eyebrows, the high cheekbones, and the tapered nose (actually much more tapered than Ross's).

An associate once told Diana Ross that Michael was trying to look like her. Dismayed, she responded, ''I look like *that*?''

In fact, Michael does not want to look like Diana, but he's fascinated by her image, allure, glamour, and power. He tries to recreate her aura sometimes by playing out some of his Diana Ross fantasies in front of witnesses and thereby feeding the rumor mills.

There was the limousine chauffeur, Ralph Caricosa, who drove Michael around Beverly Hills and called him ''Miss Ross'' because Michael insisted upon it. Then there was the night Diana Ross caught him putting on her makeup backstage in Las Vegas. She told Cindy Birdsong and her friend John Whyman that when she scolded him he responded by saying, ''But, Diane, it's magic.''

Once, when Michael checked into the swank Helmsley Palace in Manhattan, he telephoned the front desk from a house phone in the lobby and—in front of witnesses—used his best imitation of Diana Ross's voice and manner to hoodwink the operator. ''My suite is not good enough,'' he said, acting disgruntled. ''How *dare* you put me in that suite. There are no flowers in there, and I think

I saw a bug or a mouse or something, and I'm, well, I'm just really upset. I can't even go back up there."

"Who is this?" the surprised operator apparently asked.

"Why, it's Miss Ross," Michael answered, trying to hold back a giggle. "Miss Diana Ross. Who do you think it is? How dare you even ask?"

By the time the operator put him on hold, Michael was grinning from ear to ear.

The operator came back on the line. "Diana Ross isn't staying here," she evidently said.

"Oh, she's not?" Michael responded. "Sorry."

Then he quickly hung up. Afterwards, Michael, who has always been a prankster, started laughing so hysterically he could hardly catch his breath, completely caught up in his own practical joke.

Most people who know Michael Jackson agree that there are two reasons why he has had all that plastic surgery. Michael wants to be physically perfect. He has spent most of his life looking at pictures of himself, studying and critiquing them. He spends hour after hour dancing in front of mirrors, looking at videos, deciding which are his best features and which are not.

Also, all of the Jackson boys grew up to look like their father, Joe, and Michael can't think of a worse fate. He has done everything he can to destroy the resemblance.

Certainly, Michael has many of his father's characteristics, whether or not he recognizes them: Joe's determination to the point of ruthlessness, his coldhearted business sense, and on the plus side, his love of family. Inside, Michael may be a lot like Joe, and it probably frightens him. Outside, he isn't like Joe at all.

"He told me so himself," said a former girlfriend of Berry Gordy's who has known Michael for years. "He would do *anything* not to look like Joe Jackson. Believe me, the last thing he wants to see when he looks at the man in the mirror is his father. With each operation, he distances himself not only from his father but from the whole family. I'm afraid that's the sad, pathetic point of all the surgery."

"The tragedy is," concluded Joyce McCrae, a longtime intimate who worked in Joe's office, "no matter how much Michael tries to scrub Joseph off his face, he's still there."

Or as Joe Jackson so aptly put it, "It takes a father to make a son."

Michael's plastic surgeon, Dr. Steven Hoefflin, known as the "Plastic Surgeon to the Stars" (he's worked on Ivana Trump and

Jessica Hahn to name just two), performed the surgery on Michael's nose and chin. He was responsible for Michael's previous nose jobs. Larry Michaels, a Beverly Hills businessman, once consulted Steven Hoefflin regarding surgery on his own nose. He remembered, "I'd heard that Hoefflin has this sort of show business reputation. Hangs out at Hugh Hefner's Playboy mansion, likes wild women, loves publicity for his work. He sounded like quite a character, and I wanted to meet him, maybe have my nose done by him. I went on the recommendation of another of his patients.

"He's a handsome man in his mid-forties, nice mustache, longish, curly brown hair, and he appears to be someone you'd like to know. Whereas other surgeons have a way of being busy and preoccupied during a consultation, Hoefflin acts very interested in you. Your ten minutes of consultation with him are quite intense. He asks personal questions that have nothing to do with plastic surgery. After he finished talking to me and taking notes, he closed his book and he said, 'Now, let me tell you what I think. I do think you should have the surgery. But I'm not sure I am the doctor to do this.' Immediately, I was crushed, and I didn't even know why. 'What's the problem?' I asked. 'Well, I just don't think I can accept you as a patient,' he told me very slowly and deliberately. By now, I had a lump in my throat. I said, 'But you just must. Please.' I mean, the guy plays a psychological game, and he really gets to you. 'Well, I haven't quite decided yet,' he said seriously. By now I was almost salivating for this man to do my surgery. He said he'd let me know.

"When I left, I was very upset. I was trying to think of whom I could call to convince him to do it. Two days later, I realized what had happened, how this guy had manipulated me, and I was so pissed off. I wrote him a very strong letter. I told him I would *never* have him do my surgery. Afterwards, I asked around and found that my experience with him is not unusual. Steven Hoefflin is quite a salesman."

After Michael's operation, he was seen all over Los Angeles wearing a surgical mask with a black fedora and sunglasses, which did a lot to enhance his image as a complete kook. The press said that he was obsessed with catching germs, reminiscent of the Howard Hughes fixation. Michael said nothing publicly. Privately, he told some intimates that he had had his wisdom teeth removed and that was why he was wearing the mask.

"If you knew Michael well enough, you knew what was going on," Joyce McCrae said. "As soon as I saw him wearing the mask, I said, 'Oh, he's probably had a cleft put into his chin.' People told me, 'What? That's ridiculous.' Well, sure enough, that's what was going on.''

Frank Dileo never had much patience for questions about Michael's plastic surgery, mostly because he really could not explain it. "Okay, so he had his nose fixed, and the cleft—big deal. I got news for you," he said. "My nose has been broken five times. It's been fixed twice. Who gives a shit? Who cares? Elvis had his nose done. Marilyn Monroe had her nose done, had her breasts done. Everybody's had it done.''

At this time, Michael appeared at a movie memorabilia showcase at the Continental Hyatt Hotel in Hollywood wearing a blue surgical mask and a black fedora. To say he looked conspicuous would be an understatement. Michael was shopping for Disney memorabilia. When the vendors saw him coming their way, they would triple the prices of all of their goods just because they knew Michael represented a windfall for them. He was shopping with a young boy and Bill Bray, his security man. Whenever he saw something he liked, he mumbled through his surgical mask for Bray to purchase the item. Bray would then pull out a wad of hundred-dollar bills, pay the vendor, and move on to the next display. The fact that the prices were raised especially for him did not escape Michael. "They see me coming, and they feel like I have a lot of money, so they take advantage of me," he said to one writer. "That's not really fair, is it?''

When Michael did not cover his face with a surgical mask, he would go out in public wearing a hairy gorilla head mask with fur and beady eyes. "I love it when people stop and are scared," he said. "And I love it when they don't know that it's me inside the mask. I just love that." It's a great paradox about Michael Jackson that he is as much a public show-off as he is a recluse. Sometimes, though, his exploits can prove embarrassing. While walking through an airport wearing the gorilla mask, he once tripped over a sand-filled ashtray because his vision was obscured.

When the bandages came off, Michael concentrated more than ever on his appearance. He was given to tweezing his eyebrows, which gave him a feminine look. His skin seemed lighter, and intimates insisted that he was using Porcelana, a skin-bleaching product, on himself. "I know for a fact that Michael and LaToya both used Porcelana for that purpose," one friend said.

Michael's nose was now slimmer than ever. It pointed upward a bit, as well. Michael also had a cleft in his chin, but it seemed oddly out of place on the bottom of his soft, ingenuelike face.

Also, Michael, who was twenty-seven, was on a strict macrobiotic diet that had left him quite thin. His diet consisted of fresh-steamed vegetables, unsalted nuts, and fresh or dried fruits. He only ate once a day. "If I ate like him, I'd be dead," Frank Dileo said.

Michael Jackson began to look more and more like a wax dummy. It was difficult to be in the same room with him and not stare. Probably Eddie Murphy put it best when he said, "I love Michael, but the brother is *strange*."

# Chapter

## ❦ 26 ❦

AT TWENTY-SEVEN YEARS of age, Michael Jackson was faced with the major challenge of recording an album that would top the tremendous success of *Thriller*. Michael would put himself under enormous pressure. He is extremely competitive, even with himself. When he discussed the phenomenon of the four hit singles from the *Off the Wall* album, which preceded *Thriller* in 1979, he told writer Gerri Hirshey, "Nobody broke my record yet, thank God. Hall and Oates [the pop music duo] tried, but they didn't." Eventually he matched his own record with the *Thriller* album. The final tally on singles' chart action had been: "The Girl Is Mine," number two; "Billie Jean," number one; "Beat It," number one; "Wanna Be Startin' Somethin'," number five; "Human Nature," number seven; "PYT (Pretty Young Thing)," number ten; and "Thriller," number four. Michael felt that if he did not top *Thriller's* record sales of nearly 38.5 million, he would be perceived as a failure.

He had taped a piece of paper that said "100 million" to his bathroom mirror. He wanted the *Bad* album to be, as he put it, "as perfect as is humanly possible." This challenge would become an obsession of Michael Jackson's and cause many of his associates to become concerned. "There was so much stress," said guitarist David Williams to Todd Gold, "and so much tension that I was doing the exact same part at least five different times on each song. They were trying to match the other one, the *Thriller* album."

"He [Michael] kept saying, 'This one has to be bigger than the last one," dancer Casper recalled. "He said he felt that he hadn't given the world enough. 'I gotta do better. I haven't done enough,' he said. This kept coming up. It wasn't like he just said it once."

"You can't think about what people will like. You go crazy doing that," Stevie Wonder remarked. "If it's possible for him to sell fifty million records, let that happen. But if it doesn't, it's not the end of the world. It's just records.'' That's an ironic statement, however, coming from Stevie Wonder, who is known to spend years on his own albums, much to the exasperation of Motown Records.

Before they started to record the follow-up album in August 1986, Michael and Quincy Jones had to choose from sixty-two songs Michael had written. ''Fifty percent of the battle is trying to figure out which songs to record,'' Quincy said. ''It's total instinct. You have to go with the songs that really touch you, that get goose bumps going.'' Eight of the ten songs on *Bad* would be written by Michael.

Michael Jackson cannot read music. He writes a song in his head, sings it onto a tape, and then hires musicians to put it down on paper. He is an incredibly musical person, however. The notes Michael comes up with—and the way he hears them together in a song—often astound trained musicians.

It would take nearly two years to finish *Bad*, and during that time, many songs were recorded which would never be released. For instance, Michael recorded an anticrack song with the rap group Run D.M.C., who thought that Michael was very odd and didn't know how to relate to him. The song was shelved.

There was to be on the album a rhythm-and-blues-tinged duet, ''I Just Can't Stop Loving You.'' Michael failed to get Barbra Streisand to record the song with him. ''I can't believe she would turn me down,'' he told an associate. ''What is she, crazy? Doesn't she know that this is going to be the biggest album in history?'' Michael suggested that ''my people'' get back in touch with ''her people'' and ''tell her she's about to make a big mistake.''

Barbra said that she appreciated Michael's concern, but she wasn't interested, because she was worried that the age difference between herself and Jackson would make the lyrics seem unbelievable, plus she didn't like the song. Frank Dileo was unfazed. ''I knew the song was a hit—with or without Barbra,'' he said.

''Forget her,'' Michael reasoned. ''Let's get Whitney Houston.''

But Whitney Houston wasn't interested either.

''Believe me, I didn't lose any sleep over it,'' Frank Dileo said of Houston's decision.

Someone suggested Diana Ross. ''No way. Bad idea,'' Michael responded immediately.

Michael didn't say that Diana was still angry at him for a misunderstanding they had had a while back. As he explained to an associate, he had made plans to go to dinner with her at Le Dome, a restaurant on Sunset Strip in Hollywood. But then Elizabeth Taylor telephoned and told him she would like to have a meal with him that same evening. How could he resist? Wanting the best of both worlds, he asked her if she would like to accompany him and Diana.

"Why don't we have *her* meet *us* there," Liz countered.

Michael didn't understand the game of battling egos Taylor was playing. Naively, he thought she was just being friendly. The only thing he could think of was how magical it would be to have Diana Ross and Elizabeth Taylor sitting at the same table with him at Le Dome.

Once he and Taylor arrived at the restaurant, Michael telephoned Diana. "Guess what?" he said excitedly. "I'm here with Elizabeth Taylor."

Diana was not pleased. When she told him she had been under the impression that *she* was supposed to be his date that evening, Michael suggested that she meet him and Liz at Le Dome.

"Why should I have to meet you and Liz Taylor there?" Diana wanted to know. "That's not the way to do things, Michael," she scolded, like a mother chastising a child. She told him that the two of them could have dinner together some time in the future, but not that night, and certainly not with Elizabeth Taylor.

While Michael was planning the title track for *Bad*, he decided he would like rock star Prince to join him in a duet.

Michael had never forgotten the night in 1987 when Quincy Jones arranged for Michael to meet Prince. Jones felt that the two of them were creative geniuses and should know one another. According to writer Quincy Troupe, "It was a strange summit. They're so competitive with each other that neither would give anything up. They kind of sat there, checking each other out, but saying very little. It was a fascinating stalemate between two very powerful dudes."

At another encounter with Michael, Prince brought him a present in a small box. Inside, there were some colorful metal charms and feathers.

Michael closed the box quickly and shot a look at Quincy Jones, who was present. Then Prince left.

"What is that stuff?" Michael wanted to know as he stared at the box.

"I don't know," Quincy shrugged.

"That's some kind of voodoo stuff, that's what it is," Michael said. "Maybe we should burn it, or something. Prince is trying to put a hex on me, Quincy."

Quincy had to agree that the gift seemed odd. Clearly, Michael had taken Prince's gift as some sort of expression of ill will.

Michael Jackson has never cared for Prince, who he thinks is vulgar and offensive. He told Byron Moore, a former associate, "I could never be like him on stage. I'd never want to be. Sometimes he can really be gross."

Moore remembered, "In 1981 Prince had a song about mutual masturbation on his *Controversy* album called 'Jack U Off.' Michael was absolutely fascinated by it. 'What does that mean, exactly?' he asked me. Michael likes to act more naive than he really is, sometimes. And he enjoyed asking embarrassing questions because he's fascinated by the way people answer them. So I played along, and I explained the song's lyrics to him in graphic detail. He acted like he was appalled. 'I can't believe a guy could write a song about *that*!' he said. 'What kind of person writes about something like that? I mean, that's so private, isn't it?' I told him, 'Well, Mike, it all depends how you look at it.'

" 'Maybe *I* should write a song about something like that,' he said, teasing me. 'Can't you just see that?'

" 'Not really,' I told him.''

In July 1984, Warner Bros. held an afternoon screening of the Prince movie *Purple Rain* for company personnel and some film critics. The word in Hollywood was that the film—a drama with music—was riveting and would be the movie to make Prince a major star. Michael has always been deeply disappointed that he has not been able to make a strong impression in films. Being very competitive, he had to see *Purple Rain* before it was distributed to the public. He arranged to attend the Warner Bros. screening.

Michael was late getting to the small theater on the Warner Bros. Burbank lot, but the studio executives made everyone else wait for him. They held the screening until Michael arrived. When the house lights dimmed, Michael slipped in, wearing a sequined jacket and sunglasses. He looked as if he were about to go on stage. He didn't say anything to anyone. He sat in the last row and watched the film, never once taking off his dark shades. About ten minutes before the movie was about to end, Michael got up and walked out.

Later, a member of his entourage asked Michael what he thought of the film.

"The music's okay, I guess," Michael asked. "But I don't like Prince. He looks mean, and I don't like the way he treats women. He reminds me of some of my relatives.

"And not only that," Michael concluded. "That guy can't act

at all. He's really not very good.'' Then Michael let out a sigh of relief.

Though he doesn't appreciate Prince's talent, Michael Jackson realized that singing a duet with the entertainer could generate great interest in not only the single, but the album as well. His concept for himself and Prince was ingenious.

The plan was that a month before the single was released, Michael would have Frank Dileo begin planting stories in the tabloid press that he and Prince were bitter enemies and rivals. Michael's representatives would criticize Prince, and then Prince's friends— a few of whom would be let in on the hoax—would condemn Michael. Then, to confound everybody, Michael would have Frank Dileo tell a *Rolling Stone* reporter that the rivalry did not exist and that his client was disgusted with these kinds of rumors since he and Prince are great friends, ''and who believes the *Enquirer* anyway.''

In a month, the rumors about Jackson and Prince would be flying—are they friends, or aren't they?—with the general consensus, hopefully, being that they really are not.

Then, at the height of the controversy, the ''Bad'' single and video would be released. In the video, Michael and Prince would square off against one another, taking turns vocalizing and dancing—Prince doing his James Brown steps, and Michael doing his trademark moonwalk—in order to determine once and for all who was ''*bad*.'' It was an exciting premise.

When Michael telephoned Prince and told him of his idea, Prince was not enthusiastic. Then Michael sent Prince a tape of the song. After hearing it, Prince decided that the song was garbage. He wanted nothing to do with Michael's hoax.

''Prince thinks Michael is a wimp,'' said Max Hart, one of Prince's associates. ''He didn't want to be in a video with him. He thinks Mike is silly.''

When word got back from Prince's representatives that he was not going to cooperate, Michael was truly disappointed, but not really angry.

''So what do you think about this guy turning you down,'' Frank Dileo asked him.

''Figures,'' was all Michael would say, shaking his head.

''God, you make me sick,'' Janet Jackson told her brother Michael one day. ''I wish *Thriller* was *my* album.'' They laughed, but Janet wasn't kidding.

While Michael Jackson was sweating out *Bad*, his sister Janet was finally having her first major recording success with the A&M album, *Control*. At this time, Janet was in the thick of a power struggle with her father over just that—control, of her music her career, her life. Much to Joe's chagrin, she had aligned herself with John McClain, a thirty-one-year-old A&M Records executive and friend of the family who has been given credit for much of Janet's success. McClain has known Janet since she was two. It was actually Joe's idea that McClain take Janet under his wing. McClain made Janet diet and exercise and sent her to Canyon Ranch in Arizona for ten days to get her in physical shape. He also sent her to a vocal coach, teamed her with Paula Abdul for her videos, and, in short, helped make her a star. In doing so, he also made an enemy out of Joe Jackson, because Janet was beginning to turn to John for direction, not her father. "No, he's *not* like a son to me," Joe stormed to writer J. C. Stevenson. "John McClain has his own daddy.

"We're the dog with the bone that all the other dogs are trying to get," Joe went on. "And the pressure is always on you to hold on to what you've got. As for Janet, I was putting her on stage in Vegas back when she was still a little girl." Joe had advised Janet that if she stayed with him and worked hard, she'd be "as big as Michael." Janet had her doubts. "She's no dummy," Joyce Mc-Crae said. "She knew there was a reason why Michael and her brothers left Joe, and she didn't trust her father's management. She started listening to outsiders."

Janet had had two relatively unsuccessful A&M albums before John McClain came into the picture. He teamed her up with the writing-producing team of Jimmy Jam and Terry Lewis for *Control*. "The wheels had already been set in motion for Janet Jackson," Joe said, "and anyone who jumps on now will be getting a free ride. I don't intend to let that happen."

McClain has said that Jackson did not want Janet to work with Jam and Lewis and, in fact, when Joe first heard the *Control* album, he didn't like it at all—especially the title track and "What Have You Done for Me Lately?" (which went on to become a huge hit). The album was, in many ways, a personal declaration of freedom from her father and her family; in the title track, Janet claims that she will now have control over all her own affairs. She sings as if still stung by her family's meddling in her marriage. The *Control* album was one of the ten best-selling albums of 1986, so Janet had reason to question Joe's judgment. McClain said that he would have been "scared" if Joe Jackson actually liked the record because, as he put it to writer J. C. Stevenson, "I wasn't trying to get a fifty-year-old audience. I was trying to get these kids out here. And because I'm a lot younger than Joe, I have a clearer vibe on how to do it.''

Janet's album sold six million copies worldwide. Michael was clearly ambivalent about his sister's sensational success. Many of his associates have indicated that one of the reasons he had difficulty conceptualizing the follow-up to *Thriller* was that he was rattled by Janet's *Control* and the public's overwhelming reaction to it.

''Michael is used to being the star of that family,'' a family friend said. ''He was not used to seeing anyone get as much attention as Janet got. It got to the point where he didn't want to dance around her because he was afraid she'd steal his steps. That's how bad it got. Janet is also competitive but has always been afraid to admit it. She didn't want to admit to herself that what she really wanted out of her life was to be as big, as famous, as Michael Jackson.''

''Well, Michael may not want her to be as big,'' John McClain observed, ''but it's no sin for *her* to want it.''

In September 1986, Michael Jackson's *Captain EO* was set to premiere both at Epcot Center in Orlando, Florida, and at Disneyland in Anaheim, California. It was probably the most expensive and most ballyhooed short subject (seventeen minutes) in film history, and it took over a year to complete it. *Captain EO* (it was originally called *The Intergalactic Music Man*, but that was deemed too wordy) was directed by Francis Coppola. The executive producer was George Lucas. Estimates of the 3-D film's budget run as high as $20 million. Both parks had to build special theaters for the film with floors that tilt with the space-age action on the screen. It's also a light-and-sound show, with smoke emanating from the screen. Michael plays a space commander with a crew of robots and fuzzy creatures battling a hideous queen (Angelica Huston). Through song and dance, a planet's inhabitants are transformed into peace-loving creatures. Michael performed two songs, ''We Are Here to Change the World'' and ''Another Part of Me.''

Michael needed a dazzling idea to promote the film. The unfolding of publicity to promote *Captain EO* is an excellent example of how a celebrity of Jackson's stature can manipulate the press if he surrounds himself with shrewd pubic relations experts.

The first thing Michael did to promote *Captain EO* was to see how much publicity he could generate if he faked an accident on the set at the Laird Studios in Hollywood. Michael's friend, Dr. Steven Hoefflin, also wanted some publicity for Brotman Memorial Hospital where the Michael Jackson Burn Unit was located. According to some of Hoefflin's associates, he and Michael collaborated on what is known among those in Hoefflin's camp as "The Michael Jackson Falls Down and Goes Boom" hoax.

On July 29, 1985, Michael actually did fall during the filming of *EO*, and he suffered a very slight wrist sprain. The next day, he emerged from his dressing room complaining that he was in the most terrible pain. He was rushed to Brotman Memorial Hospital, where photographers just happened to be waiting—having been alerted by Michael's camp that he was on his way. Accompanying Michael was a young male friend named Jonathan Spence, who was wearing a USA for Africa sweatshirt (for more promotional purposes). Michael was "examined" by plastic surgeon Hoefflin, and then released wearing an ace bandage and a sling. As photographers and news people swarmed all over Michael, he acted as if he really didn't expect all of the attention and just wanted to get away from the glare of the intrusive media.

The next day, the story of Michael's "accident" was in the newspapers across the country. In Los Angeles, the *Herald Examiner*'s headline was "Michael Jackson Falls Down and Goes Boom, Hurts Famed Wrist."

"He looked like he was in pain," one of Jackson's spokesmen told the *Examiner*. "He looked very forlorn."

The prank was a harmless one and, indeed, it did generate a good deal of publicity for *Captain EO* as well as for Brotman. But Michael Jackson felt he needed something even stronger and more exciting to promote *EO*.

In 1984, when Michael was burned while filming the Pepsi commercial, he saw an oxygen chamber at Brotman called a hyperbaric chamber. It is used to help heal burn victims. The machine is about the size and shape of a casket with a clear, plastic top. It encloses the patient in an atmosphere of one hundred percent oxygen under increased barometric pressure up to several times the pressure at sea level, thereby flooding body tissues with oxygen. When administered by trained medical personnel, hyperbaric therapy is safe. But in the hands of an untrained user, risks include oxygen toxicity, seizures, and danger of an oxygen-fed fire. When told by Steven Hoefflin that he had a theory that, perhaps, sleeping in this machine could prolong life, Michael became fascinated by it and, immediately, wanted one for himself. The cost was about $200,000.

"Do you think I can sleep in it at my house?" Michael wanted to know.

"I'll check into it," Hoefflin told him.

In the end, it was decided that, though Michael could well afford it, he wouldn't buy one. Frank Dileo had talked him out of it. "Well, I'd at least like to have my picture taken in it," Michael said. So one day, he went to the hospital to be photographed in the chamber.

Meanwhile, word began to spread that Michael was interested in this contraption and, as rumors will do, the story found its way to the *National Enquirer*. "I had a phone-in from a source in Los Angeles who said that Michael was seen going to a hospital and taking pictures in this chamber," said reporter Charles Montgomery, who worked for the *Enquirer* at that time but now writes for the *Globe*. "I didn't know exactly what the deal was, but it sounded like a sensational story and I wanted to be the one to break it."

Charles Montgomery met with Frank Dileo and asked for details of the story. "He totally turned me off," Montgomery said. "He didn't want to discuss it and told me to get lost. I got some information on the phone from Steven Hoefflin, but not much. The story was put on hold."

When Michael heard that the *Enquirer* was asking questions, his creative wheels started turning. Earlier in the year he had given Dileo and John Branca a copy of a book about P. T. Barnum, his theories and philosophies. "This is going to be my bible and I want it to be yours," he told them. "I want my whole career to be the greatest show on earth."

It was Michael's idea to promote to the press the story that he wanted to sleep in the hyperbaric chamber so that he could live to be 150 years old. He planned to take the machine on the road with him on his next tour, he said. He wasn't certain that people would believe such a thing, but he was eager to find out. Branca thought the idea was preposterous, but did not want to interfere with Michael's creativity.

"This is what I want people to think," Michael said to Dileo. "It's up to you to figure out how to do it."

Frank Dileo had to find a way to disseminate this story to the press. He picked up the telephone and called the *National Enquirer*'s Lantana, Florida, headquarters to talk to Charles Montgomery. Dileo finally gave Montgomery the details of the "story" the reporter had been after all along, and promised him a photograph of Michael in the chamber—all of this as long as Montgomery could guarantee a cover feature. He also made Montgomery promise never to reveal his source. The *Enquirer* editors agreed to run the feature on the cover, especially if the photograph Dileo promised was a good one.

I didn't know the story was a fake," Montgomery said. "Michael Jackson said it was true. His own manager said it was true, and his doctor verified it. How many more sources do you need? Then there was a picture. It promised to be a great feature and we were excited by it.''

Now Dileo had to find a way to distribute the story further without anyone realizing he was involved. Planting the story in the *Enquirer* did not risk his credibility since he could easily deny having had anything to do with it. No one would take a *National Enquirer* reporter's word over Frank Dileo's. However, the other more so-called legitimate press would be tougher to crack. Since the media knew that veteran publicist Norman Winter was responsible for Michael Jackson's public relations, if Winter promoted this bizarre idea to the press, it would appear to be a publicity stunt. Dileo would have to hire an outside publicist for the job.

As it happened, Frank Dileo's Sunset Strip office was next door to that of leading show business publicist Michael Levine. Dileo invited Levine to his home in Encino and told him about his idea, but with a few embellishments. Dileo took Michael's idea a step further. He wanted the press to believe not only that Michael was sleeping in this chamber, but also that he and Michael were in disagreement about its safety, and that Dileo did not want him to take the machine on the road with him during his next tour.

Levine was told that if he wanted to tackle this project, he would have to do so without having any contact with Michael—and without informing the media that he (Levine) was involved in any way as a publicist. In other words, Michael Levine's task was to publicize something without anyone knowing he was publicizing it. He would not be paid for his services, however. If the job was done well, Frank said, he would influence Michael to use Levine's public relations firm.

"Listen, you take care of me, and I'll take care of you," Frank Dileo told him.

The next day an envelope was delivered to Levine's office. The messenger had strict instructions that Levine and *only* Levine was to look at the contents. Levine opened the envelope to find a single color transparency of Michael Jackson lying in the hyperbaric chamber in his street clothes but without shoes on. There was no cover letter or return address.

That week, Michael Levine brought a well-known Hollywood photographer to Brotman Memorial Hospital to take pictures of the empty hyperbaric chamber for publications that might seek additional photos. Levine did not tell the photographer what the pictures were for. The lensman was paid for his work and never asked any questions. The hospital officials who allowed Levine and his photographer to shoot the chamber had been told by someone to permit access. They didn't know why and were apparently paid not to ask.

It was time for Michael Levine to go to work. One reporter recalled, "He telephoned me and said, 'Look, I don't represent Michael Jackson. I don't even know Michael Jackson. But I was up at Frank Dileo's house, and I overheard that there's this wild feud going on.' Then he told me this preposterous story about Michael Jackson sleeping in an oxygen chamber and the fact that he and Frank Dileo were feuding about it. In about three days, I was hearing this story all over town."

About a week later, all the pieces of the puzzle began falling together. The picture of Michael lying in the chamber made the front page of the *National Enquirer* on September 16, 1986. Most of the public had never even heard of a hyperbaric chamber, so they could not tell that the picture was a setup, that patients and medical personnel who enter such a chamber must wear fire-retardant clothes, not street clothes as Michael had on in the photograph. Many people believe that the tabloids print untrue stories about celebrities. What they don't know is that many of these stories are indirectly planted by the celebrities, as was the case here.

"I realized that Michael Jackson likes to see himself portrayed in an absurd, bizarre way," Charles Montgomery said. "In the years to come, I would do the biggest number of stories on Michael in the *Enquirer*. Before I ran anything, I would always check with people close to Michael to see how accurate it was. I almost always had full cooperation from his camp. Michael Jackson is one of the smartest entertainers in the business. He knows how to get his name out there. He knows about P.R. He knows how to control his career. I think he's brilliant."

Thanks to Michael Levine's expertise, word of Michael Jackson's exploit quickly spread around the globe. When Levine set up an interview for Frank Dileo with the Associated Press, Dileo confirmed the report. "I told Michael, 'That damn machine is too dangerous. What if something goes wrong with the oxygen?' But Michael won't listen. He and I are in disagreement about this. He really believes this chamber purifies his body—and that it will help him accomplish his goals of living to be a hundred and fifty." He told *Time* magazine, "I can't figure him [Michael] out sometimes."

Even Michael's plastic surgeon, Steven Hoefflin, got into the act and reportedly tried to talk Michael out of "this wacky idea." But Michael supposedly ignored everyone's fears and made room for the chamber in his bedroom.

When Joe Jackson heard this, he ran up to Michael's bedroom

to see if Michael had already moved in the chamber. "But I didn't find nothing up there," he recalled.

"I don't think I'd let Michael have that thing in the house, anyway," Katherine added. Katherine and Joe were obviously not let in on the joke. Joe would always defend Michael against people who thought his son was eccentric.

"Joe always stood behind Michael," said Joe's friend of fifteen years, Jack Richardson. "He'd say, 'Michael's not sleeping in no chamber. Don't believe what you hear about my son.' No one was ever allowed to say anything negative about Michael in his presence."

"I never asked him about that chamber thing," Janet said. "I have no idea what that was about. It's not in the house, or I would know it. But knowing Michael, if he is doing something like that, it probably has to do with his voice."

Michael Jackson's idea turned into a perfectly orchestrated public relations coup. The hyperbaric chamber story was carried by the Associated Press and the United Press International. It appeared in *Time, Newsweek,* and practically every major newspaper in the country. Television and radio news covered it. Suddenly, the words "hyperbaric chamber" were on the lips of many people. The public talked about Michael Jackson's bizarre plan to live to 150 and how he and his manager were in disagreement about it.

Michael Jackson was astonished. Many untrue stories had been written about him in the past, and he had been angry about them. Now it appeared he was getting back at the media. "I can't believe that people bought it," he said of the hyperbaric chamber idea. "It's like I can tell the press anything about me and they'll buy it. We can actually *control* the press. I think this is an important breakthrough for us."

Publicist Michael Levine had obviously done an excellent job, but he was not rewarded with Michael Jackson's account as promised. Instead, Michael decided that he wanted to be represented by high-powered publicist Lee Solters. Dileo thanked Levine for a job well done, apologized about Michael's decision, and asked Levine to send him a bill for his services. But Michael Levine decided not to do so. The hyperbaric chamber news story was a public relations "freebie" for Michael Jackson. To this day Michael Levine feels sworn to secrecy.

And many people still believe today that Michael Jackson sleeps in a hyperbaric chamber.

# Chapter

# 27

In the spring of 1987, Michael withdrew from the Jehovah's Witnesses. A representative of the Woodland Hills congregation to which Michael belonged said that he "disassociated himself from the congregation" and that he "no longer wants to be known as a Jehovah's Witness." A form letter from the Jehovah's Witnesses headquarters in Brooklyn, New York, dated May 18, also stated that the organization "no longer considers Michael Jackson to be one of Jehovah's Witnesses." Gary Botting, coauthor of *The Orwellian World of Jehovah's Witnesses* and a Witness himself, said that leaving the religion "is worse than being disfellowshipped, or kicked out." He observed, "If you willfully reject God's only organization on earth, that's the unforgivable sin . . . the sin against the Holy Spirit."

Michael left the Jehovah's Witnesses because he could not reconcile his lifestyle to the religion's strict tenets. "It's almost impossible to be a Jehovah's Witness and be an entertainer," observed one associate. "Some do it, but it's difficult. Michael was tired of answering to the church's leaders whenever they had a problem with a career move he had made. Frank Dileo didn't have anything to do with Mike's decision, but he certainly had little patience for the demands being a Witness placed on Mike. Michael just lost interest."

Leaving the Jehovah's Witnesses normally means that the person must be shunned by family members and friends who still belong. A rumor circulated that Michael had abandoned the religion because he was no longer allowed to associate with LaToya, and he couldn't bear the thought. The rumor proved false.

Michael has never discussed his reasons for leaving the religion, and his decision puzzled his mother. Katherine insists that she is still allowed to have a relationship with her son, regardless of the strict tenets of the faith. ''I was not required to 'shun' my son,'' she claimed. But Katherine has been known to bend the rules, as evidenced by her birthday parties and gifts (which are forbidden by the faith). However, it is strictly prohibited for a Witness to discuss matters of faith with ex-members, even if they are family. So Katherine says that she has never asked Michael what happened, and that is probably for the best where he is concerned.

Katherine maintained that her relationship with Michael continued to be warm. ''Michael still asks my advice,'' she said. ''And he helps me choose my clothes. He tells me to put on lipstick when company's coming. He has encouraged me to lose weight. He said, 'Elizabeth [Taylor] lost all that weight. If she has, you can. And if you don't like it, you can always have plastic surgery.' But I wouldn't do that,'' Katherine hastened to add.

In May 1987, Michael Jackson came up with a new publicity strategy that promised to be as amazing as the hyperbaric chamber scam. Michael was always fascinated by the 1980 film about John Merrick, *The Elephant Man*, starring John Hurt. LaToya reported that when he screened it in his private theater, he cried all the way through the film. To Michael, John Merrick—the hideously deformed Victorian sideshow freak whose life has been portrayed on stage and screen—was an outsider, like himself, searching endlessly for love and acceptance. After Michael's burn accident in 1984, he became interested in medicine and began reading medical books about Merrick's condition. He had heard that Merrick's remains were kept in a glass case at the London Hospital Medical College and he went to see the exhibit during a trip to England. He had to get special dispensation to inspect the ninety-seven-year-old skeleton, since it had been removed from public view after the movie was released, attracting droves of tourists to the hospital.

In passing, he said, ''I sure would like to have those [bones]. Wouldn't that be cool to have in the house? Kate would love that,'' he added, laughing. Remembering the hyperbaric chamber hoax, Michael's mind started working. He came up with the idea that he should make an offer to the hospital to buy the bones and see what kind of press the offer would generate.

Michael Jackson instructed Frank Dileo to take his idea and begin to exploit it. Claiming Michael's absorbing interest in the remains of Merrick was based on his awareness of ''the ethical, medical, and historical significance of the Elephant Man,'' Frank said he offered a half million dollars to the hospital for the bones.

Sure enough, the media was interested—the man who sleeps in a hyperbaric chamber now wanted to buy a skeleton. This was news. Associated Press and United Press International spread the word; by June, people were talking about the latest eccentricity of Wacko-Jacko.

Michael and Frank failed to realize, however, that the media would check with the London Hospital Medical Center to verify the offer. When contacted, officials there said they had received no such offer, that they had only heard about Michael's interest in Merrick's remains by reading about it in one of the British tabloids. Even if they did get an offer, the spokesman said, "We would not sell the Elephant Man. It's as simple as that."

"Oh, man, why didn't we think to cover our bases," Michael said to Frank. "Now we gotta make a real offer. And, anyway, of course they'll sell it if the money is right. Every man has his price."

Now Michael really had become interested in the remains, not because of any devotion to John Merrick but rather because he was told he couldn't have them.

Dileo telephoned the hospital and, apparently, this time he really did make an offer of a million dollars.

The hospital officials were insulted. A spokeswoman told the press, "If indeed he has offered to buy it, it would be for publicity and I find it very unlikely that the medical college would be willing to sell it for cheap publicity reasons."

"What's he gonna do with the skeleton, Frank?" a reporter wanted to know.

"I don't know," Dileo said, "except that he'll probably put it in the room while I'm trying to have a meeting with him."

Katherine Jackson had somehow figured out that this was a hoax, but she thought it was Frank Dileo's idea. She never dreamed that this publicity gimmick was Michael's concept. Katherine had a conversation with Dileo about it and told him she was upset because he was making Michael look like "an idiot." According to Katherine, Frank told her that he wanted to help make Michael appear to be more interesting than he really is. Katherine didn't like this idea at all, and made her feelings clear. But Dileo did not believe Katherine's views worth considering, and, apparently, neither did Michael.

In a couple of months, Michael lost interest in the Elephant Man and the "scandal" blew over. It was gone, but it would not be forgotten.

This second Michael Jackson publicity campaign generated a great deal of press for him, but certainly none of it favorable. *Play-*

*boy* magazine facetiously reported, "Rumor has it that the descendants of the Elephant Man have offered $10,000 for the remains of Michael Jackson's nose."

Michael's quest for Merrick's bones created a domino effect in the tabloids. Some unscrupulous journalists began creating their own stories with the help of well-meaning, high-placed sources from Michael's organization; if Michael wanted this kind of publicity, the journalists must have reasoned, they were more than anxious to accommodate him, since these stories sold millions of magazines. In no time, according to published reports, Michael had asked Elizabeth Taylor to marry him and said, "I could be more special than Mike Todd. I could be more attentive and generous than Richard Burton, but she turned me down." He also had tried to convince Liz Taylor to sleep in his hyperbaric chamber; was convinced that the world would end in 1998; refused to bathe in anything but Evian water; and had seen John Lennon's ghost, who convinced him to use the Beatles song "Revolution" in a Nike ad.

None of those stories was true, and Michael complained bitterly about all of them, never fully comprehending that he was the one who started this trend in the first place. Since Michael refused to do any interviews because he wanted to maintain a certain mystique, the stories just continued to spread without contradiction.

Michael became more sensitive after his second publicity stunt caused such an avalanche of rumors, and now even harmless stories upset him. For instance, popular Manhattan columnist Cindy Adams reported that when hairdressers cut Michael's hair while he's on tour, the curly snippets are collected in a bag and then destroyed. This was true. However, it wasn't because of some weird ritual. Michael simply did not want opportunistic barbers exploiting his fans by selling his hair to them for profit. But Michael also did not want anyone to know about it, "because it sounds weirder than it is," he said. "I'm just trying to protect my fans."

CBS Records executive Bobby Colomby told writer Todd Gold (who wrote a book about Michael Jackson called *The Man in the Mirror* in 1989), "Michael kept asking why so many bad things were being said about him. He didn't understand it. He said it really hurt to read all that stuff. I tried to tell him that the problem was his. I explained to him that he'd never seen Bruce Springsteen on the cover of the *National Enquirer* in a hyperbaric chamber. Even if that picture came in, they wouldn't believe it. I said, 'But you, Michael, spend so much time working on your mystique, on being reclusive and unusual, that people will buy anything with your name on it.' He said he understood, kind of.''

Rather than help pique people's interest and curiosity in him, the Michael Jackson publicity stunts had the opposite effect. Now, more than ever, most people were convinced that Michael Jackson had no grasp of reality. Certainly, Jackson is eccentric, but he is far from mad. In time, he would be sorry that he propagated any fiction about himself at all. The fiction that had been written about him— that he *didn't* sanction—hurt him deeply.

"Michael obviously found ways to deal with the pain caused by the media," Joyce McCrae said. "But he has spent a lot of time just hurting. You build a wall around yourself and try to do things to make yourself immune to pain without losing your humanness. That's the hard part, staying human.''

"He's not really happy," observed Dennis Hunt, music critic for the *Los Angeles Times*, who's known Michael for years. He told writer Quincy Troupe, "He's been affected by the pressures of not having any privacy. And people who know him well say it's finally gotten to him, and he's staying away from people. There's no way he will turn outward and live in the real world again. People thought that at some point he might outgrow it and open up, but now that's impossible. Because of the level of stardom that he has achieved, he is alone most of the time . . .''

Once, Frank Dileo was asked about the wisdom of pursuing one of his major objectives for Michael Jackson's career, which was "to keep him as popular and in demand as anyone can be.''

"Might all this hoopla damage the singer's already fragile psyche?" asked reporters Michael Goldberg and David Handleman for *Rolling Stone*.

"It's too late anyway," Dileo responded. "He won't have a normal life even if I stop.''

In August 1987, Jackie and Enid Jackson's divorce was finalized. The settlement consisted of forty-one pages. Although they had had a lavish lifestyle before the divorce, after the millions were divided up and lawyers' fees and back taxes were paid, there wasn't much left for anyone.

Enid recalled, "I admit, at first my feeling about Jackie was, 'If you have one single penny left when I finish with you, that will be one penny too much. In fact, you and Paula Abdul won't have enough change to take the bus to the recording studio.' But after a while it was, 'Whatever it takes to get you and your girlfriend out of my life so I can go on, take it.' ''

Enid has a reputation among Jackson associates of having taken all her husband's money and assets. It's simply not true. "What I ended up asking for wasn't a lot," she said. "I took the settlement that he offered because, quite frankly, I was tired. I wanted out." In the end, Enid was to get $5,000 a month alimony, $3,500 a month child support, and 20 percent of his annual income above $250,000, and half of the royalties earned on songs he recorded during the marriage.

"I will always have a place in my heart for Jackie Jackson," Enid said. "I never want to see any harm come to him. But looking back on it now, I feel it wasn't all Paula Abdul's fault. She was wrong for harassing me, for breaking up my marriage. But Jackie was the older one; he had the commitment. Nobody forced him to do anything.

"You hear stories that all the Jacksons helped Paula get her start, but that's not true," Enid continued. "Jackie was the one. I really honestly think he loved her. He gave her her first breaks in show business. Her career blossomed because she was going with my husband. When the Jacksons did that 'Torture' video, they already had a choreographer. She convinced Jackie to get rid of that choreographer and hire her. Then after that she got hooked up with Janet. But when Paula became famous, she refused to acknowledge that Jackie was the one who cared about her, made her a star out of a cheerleader, gave her her start. She dogged him, I must say. And he was so hurt. It's a sad, heartbreaking story."

A month after the divorce was finalized, Enid had Jackie arrested for harassing her. She said in court papers that he came to the home they had lived in together, wanting to use the recording studio, which he was entitled to do as part of the settlement. Enid had company at the time and did not want him there. Jackie came to the kitchen and kicked in the French door windowpanes. Glass went everywhere, and Enid said in her deposition that she was scared. He cursed her, she said, when he realized she had a guest. She called the police, and Jackie was arrested for violating the restraining order still in effect. Indeed, violence had become a commonplace occurrence in the Jackson family.

Today Enid Jackson is, as she put it, "happy and totally content at last." She is proud of her hard-earned independence from Jackie Jackson and is forging her own life and career as an entertainment manager and producer while she raises her children.

In October 1987, two months after Enid and Jackie's divorce, Hazel Gordy filed for divorce from her husband, Jermaine Jackson, after almost fourteen years of marriage. Hazel Gordy Jackson, thirty-four, had been having a particularly difficult time in her marriage in recent years. Jermaine had begun having a relationship with another woman, Margaret Maldonado, who was in her early twenties. Margaret became pregnant with Jermaine's child. Six months later, Jermaine's wife gave him the news that she too was pregnant.

Margaret had her baby in mid-December 1986. At Marlon's birthday party in March 1987, Jermaine showed up with his and Margaret's three-month-old son in his arms and pregnant Hazel at his side. Hazel seemed to be in a daze as Janet and Marlon fussed over the new baby.

Even Michael, who became upset with Jermaine for what had happened, could not resist the newborn child. (Michael was not at that birthday party. However, he had showered the baby with gifts and asked to spend as much time with him as possible.) "Michael acted like *he* was the baby's father," Jerome Howard, Joe's former business manager, said. "He tends to gravitate toward children, no matter what the circumstances of their birth."

Hazel Gordy Jackson had often declared an undying love for Jermaine Jackson and had said she would do anything to keep her family together. She did not want to leave her husband's side, even after he had a child with another woman; that's how committed she was to the relationship. She offered to adopt the new baby, provided Jermaine stopped seeing Margaret. He apparently did not want to end the affair.

"Hazel put up with more than any one woman should ever bear," said one of her friends. To some family members, the story eerily resembled that of Joe and Katherine and Joe's illegitimate child. "I don't think any of the boys are happy with the things their father has done in the past," Jerome Howard observed, "but some of them certainly turned out to be just like him, let's face facts."

Hazel's father also had his own illegitimate children, so this kind of predicament had occurred in her family before as well.

Two weeks after the party, Hazel had her baby, a son, in March 1987.

Subsequently, she sought twenty-five thousand dollars a month in expenses, including seventy-five hundred dollars in monthly child support for the couple's three children, ages ten, nine, and nine months. This divorce would prove as vitriolic as Jackie and Enid's. The couple was ordered by the court not to "contact, molest, attack, strike, threaten, sexually assault, or batter" each other. Hazel would claim that after she and Jermaine separated, she was not able to get any money from Jermaine for herself or the children. Mirroring Katherine's problems with Joe, Hazel said that she had only a sketchy idea of Jermaine's plans or finances, or whether she and her children were covered by any kind of medical insurance. She added that she did not know the identity of her husband's business manager. She and Jermaine owned a half-million-dollars' worth of recording, video, and audio equipment and a $200,000 Ferrari automobile, all of which she wanted sold.

Hazel would continue living at the couple's Benedict Canyon home in Beverly Hills, while Jermaine, Margaret, and the new baby moved in with Joe and Katherine. Katherine was opposed to having her son, his girlfriend, and their baby living at the house, especially since he was not yet divorced from his wife. To her, this arrangement did not seem right or, as she put it, "moral." Not only that, she had been through a similar drama with her own husband, and perhaps did not want to be reminded of that painful time. However, when Joe insisted, Jermaine and his new family moved in.

It would seem that both Jermaine and Jackie had reached adulthood with a great deal of confusion about marriage and responsibility. "You really can't blame them," said one relative. "They don't know any better. That's the way they were raised. None of the Jacksons have had an easy time with relationships—except for Michael, who simply has never had one."

Once, Michael was upset about something happening between one of his brothers and his wife, and he had an argument with the brother.

"Butt out," said the brother to Michael. "Until you have a relationship of your own, don't you start giving me advice about mine."

Michael's feelings were hurt; he ran out of the room. Later, he would admit to another family member, "It was none of my business and I'm sorry I even brought it up. But one day I *will* have a relationship," he added with childlike defiance, "and it's going to be nothing like the ones I've seen in this family. You can believe that."

By June 1987, Michael Jackson did not want the *Bad* album to be released. He didn't think it was ready and he was nervous about the public's reaction to it. One associate of his was quoted as having said, "He's afraid to finish the record. The closer he gets to completing it, the more terrified he becomes of that confrontation with the public."

Frank Dileo convinced Michael that "the train is leaving. This album must be done by June 30." The album was finally mastered on July 10, 1987. "You need a dramatic deadline," Quincy Jones told *Rolling Stone*. "I swear to God, we would have been in the studio another year without that deadline."

In July, prior to the release of *Bad*, Michael hosted a dinner party at the Encino home for fifty CBS Records promotion people and record retailers. Security men were staked out on the roof of the house. The record industry movers and shakers toured the house as if it were a museum. Most found the place cold and impersonal. Michael's chimp, Bubbles—in suspenders and trousers—was the life of the party. The guest of honor, Michael, wore black pants, black shirt, and metal-studded belts. He was accompanied by LaToya, who wore a similar outfit. The two looked like twins. After a grilled salmon and veal chops dinner served by celebrity chef Wolfgang Puck, Michael tried to mingle with the guests. One of Michael's security guards went to each table immediately preceding Jackson, explaining how the guests at that table should get into a group to prepare for a photo with him. Then Michael went to the table, the photo was snapped, and he moved to the next table. "It was almost like a military exercise," said Record Bar executive Steve Bennett.

If every artist on the planet envied the unbelievable success of *Thriller*, surely none of them wanted to be in Michael Jackson's Bass Weejuns when he tried to follow it up. *Bad* was a pleasing record and probably would have been considered first-rate if it didn't have the dubious distinction of having to follow up not only *Thriller*, but also the masterful *Off the Wall*. Ironically, in trying to lead themselves out of the woods, Michael Jackson and Quincy Jones followed the *Thriller* formula too closely. Songs like "The Way You Make Me Feel" and "Another Part of Me" were dance-floor marvels, but the pseudo-romance of "Liberian Girl," the album's answer to *Thriller*'s "Lady in My Life," didn't work as well. Nor could "Dirty Diana," the production's appointed rock song—featuring Steve Stevens, former Billy Idol guitarist—hold a candle to the more convincing "Beat It."

Michael even came up with another duet for the easy listening crowd, à la *Thriller*'s "The Girl Is Mine." It was the pretty ballad, "I Just Can't Stop Loving You," which he finally ended up singing with Quincy Jones's protégée Siedah Garret (in lieu of Barbra Streisand or Whitney Houston).

The problem with *Bad*, critics argued, was that unlike *Off the Wall* and *Thriller*, it offered few truly memorable songs. Jackson wrote most of *Bad* himself, perhaps propelled by his newfound interest in music publishing and the millions in songwriting royalties he garnered from songs he wrote for the last two albums. Rod

Temperton, whose talents helped make *Off the Wall* and *Thriller* such outstanding albums, was not represented. The album's most intriguing moment is the reflective "Man in the Mirror," written not by Michael but by Siedah Garret and Glen Ballard. Having gospel stars Andrae Crouch and the Winans sing on the track seemed a feeble attempt to musically endear Jackson to a black audience.

The album's title track came under the most fire from the black music community, because it seemed that it should have been the easiest thing for Michael to do. Michael was black, his critics reasoned. He began with Motown. He's a funky dancer. Vocally, his roots are steeped—at least to some extent—in gospel. Is "Bad" the funkiest—the *blackest*—he could get? At best, "Bad" was a lightweight attempt at a serious black groove.

The "Bad" video was directed by Martin Scorsese, at Quincy Jones's suggestion. Michael was unfamiliar with Scorsese's work, having seen only one film he directed, *New York, New York*. Michael wanted George Lucas or Steven Spielberg to direct the video. But Frank Dileo had been trying to toughen Michael's Peter Pan image. He realized another Spielberg-style fantasy would defeat that effort. Street music—particularly the rap and hip-hop genres—had begun to dictate to pop music and fashion. As a result, Dileo apparently thought it would be beneficial for Michael to get back to "basics." Perhaps he believed the image of a street-tough cat would serve his client well. So Dileo convinced Michael to work with Scorsese.

From the start, there were problems on the set when Michael tried to tell Scorsese how to direct the video. According to a friend of Scorsese's, the filming of "Bad" was "a nightmare." Scorsese has said that the cost of the production went "two or three times over budget," reaching about two million dollars. However, Scorsese has made no negative comments about Jackson and says he found him to be "sympathetic, sweet, and open."

The "Bad" script, written by novelist Richard Price, was inspired by the story of Edmund Perry, a Harlem youth who was educated at a prep school and was shot to death by a New York plainsclothes policeman who claimed he had tried to mug him. What began as a good idea—an attempt to recapture the rebellious spirit of "Beat It," probably Jackson's most important video—ended up a pitiful parody.

"Michael loves *West Side Story*," said dancer Casper, who danced in the "Bad" video. "He had us watch a number of scenes from that film over and over again one night in a hotel room. He sat on the bed and we dancers—me, Jeffrey Daniel, Greg Burge, and some others—were just sprawled all about. He'd have us watch some scenes, and when he saw something he liked, he'd let out a yelp. 'Oooh, did you see that? Did you feel that?' he'd say. That was the attitude he said he wanted in the video, *West Side Story*. He loved the way George Chakiris, the actor who played the leader of the Sharks, danced. Chakiris's was the personality that Michael wanted in the 'Bad' video.''

The storyline is about a lonely, sheltered school kid, constantly badgered by peer pressure and neighborhood street toughs. The youngster transforms himself into a bold, avenging hell-raiser. It all goes awry for the viewer, however, because of Michael's ridiculous-looking outfit. Clad in black—boots with silver heels and buckles; a leather jacket with zippers, zippers, and more zippers; a metal-studded wristband and a wide belt with silver studs and chains—Michael Jackson was slightly overdressed for the ghetto.

The video's debut produced a cynical reaction. Radio stations and newspapers held contests to see who could correctly guess how many buckles were on the costume. The *Los Angeles Times*, for instance, was deluged with responses from readers:

''There's one buckle no one will ever detect, and it's located at the back of his head, to pull the flesh snugly over his ever-increasing new features.''

''The buckles are part of the continuing treatment he is undergoing to alter his appearance to that of Liz Taylor as she looked in *National Velvet*.''

''Sixty-six buckles—left over from his oxygen gizmo . . .''

Michael claimed that he designed the leather costume. Actually, he bought the outfit and a couple of pairs of pants for $334.41 at a punk store on Hollywood Boulevard on November 12, 1986. According to Jim O'Connor, who owned the boutique, Michael—wearing his surgical mask and driven by limousine—came into his shop and made the purchases by credit card. O'Connor insists he himself ''designed the outfit and produced it.'' He said, ''I don't want to start suing anybody. I'm just trying to get my just deserts.''

More than the buckles, Michael's concept of what really *is* bad—as in ''tough'' and ''streetwise''—seemed wildly distorted and exaggerated. Michael shouted; he stamped his feet; he flicked his fingers and shook his groin. He tugged at his crotch repeatedly. Is *this* what Michael Jackson sees from the tinted window of his limousine?

Michael may have been a little overdressed for an urban subway rider, but the surrounding players and dancers looked the part.

However, it is difficult to imagine their being so quick to follow anyone—black or white—who looks as effeminate as Michael Jackson did in this video. There is also something disconcerting about Michael—wearing more pancake makeup than Joan Crawford ever did and flaunting a Caucasianlike nose and Kirk Douglas chin cleft—shrieking at a group of black gang members, "You ain't *nothin'*." As one observer noted, "In Michael Jackson's loathsome conception of the black experience, you're either a criminal stereotype or one of the Beautiful People."

The original photograph intended for the cover of the *Bad* album was a close-up of Michael's heavily made-up face superimposed with black floral lace. Walter Yetnikoff, president of CBS Records, purportedly phoned Frank Dileo and said of the feminine-looking picture, "Look, this cover sucks." The photo eventually used— Michael in a tough-guy-with-fists-clenched-at-his-side pose, wearing his leather outfit from the "Bad" video—was taken as an afterthought during a fifteen-minute break while shooting the video.

Michael's first single from *Bad*, "I Just Can't Stop Loving You," was released on July 22, 1987, and went to number one in September. It would drop off the charts, though, in just fourteen weeks— the shortest chart run of any number one hit in more than twelve years.

Michael's *Bad* album debuted at number one on the *Billboard* charts, an amazing feat proving that even when Michael Jackson does wrong, he can do no wrong. The album received generally lukewarm reviews, but that didn't matter either. "We win," Frank Dileo said. "We're into winning." The second single, "Bad," also went to number one but dropped out of *Billboard's* Top Ten after five weeks. It looked like Michael had a hit on his hands with the *Bad* album, but certainly nothing as big as *Thriller*.

Michael Jackson had enjoyed having fun with the press in recent years, with the hyperbaric chamber and Elephant Man hoaxes, but in September 1987, the month his tour kicked off in Tokyo, Japan, he finally realized that this strategy had worked against him. *People* magazine published a cover story on Michael that month with the headline, "Michael Jackson: He's Back. He's *Bad*. Is This Guy Weird, Or What?" The article noted that Michael Jackson had "proposed marriage to Elizabeth Taylor; offered $1 million for the Elephant Man's bones; taken female hormones to keep his voice high and facial hair wispy; had his eyes, lips, and nose surgically altered and his skin chemically bleached, and had taken to sleeping in a hyperbaric chamber in hopes of living to be 150 years old."

Quincy Jones was quoted in the article as saying that "Michael

Jackson is grounded and centered and focused and connected to his creative soul. And he's one of the most normal people I've ever met.''

Nevertheless, Michael was appalled by the story. ''They made me sound like a freak,'' he said. ''None of that stuff is true.''

''I don't understand why they feel the need to make up things about me,'' Michael wrote of the press in his autobiography, *Moonwalk*. ''I suppose if there's nothing scandalous to report, it's necessary to make things interesting.''

An associate of Michael's tried to explain that he can't plant untrue items in the press and then expect the media to find the truth by sifting through the false items he planted and those created by rumormongers. But Michael wouldn't hear of it. ''It's different if *I* say it's true and it's not, but I don't like it when other people say things about me that are untrue. That's not fair.''

Cutler Durkee, the writer of that *People* magazine story, explained that the public's perception of Michael Jackson had shifted from ''Here's a really interesting guy'' to ''Here's a guy I don't understand anymore.'' Durkee hastened to add, however, that that's precisely why people continued writing about him.

The rumors made Michael so uncomfortable that he began demanding that people who worked for him agree not to discuss him without his permission. This ''nondisclosure clause'' is a kind of secrecy agreement that has become common among celebrities in recent years; Diana Ross also has her employees sign such an agreement.

Just before the Bad tour, Dileo added fuel to the fire in an interview with *Rolling Stone* magazine. ''Michael knows if I tell him something, it's the truth,'' he said to the magazine's Michael Goldberg and David Handleman. ''I don't have to agree with things if I don't want to. In other words,'' he added, ''because I know this is eventually going to come up in this interview anyway, the hyperbaric chamber. I'm one hundred percent against that. I don't want it around. I've spoken about it publicly. Some managers couldn't have that conversation with their artist. They'd be too afraid. He respects my opinion. He doesn't always listen . . .''

Because of the adverse exposure, Michael's tour had a shaky beginning. Michael did not feel he was ready to begin to travel—he thought the act still needed work—but he had no choice. The dates were set. Reluctantly, in September 1987, he began what would end up being an exhausting, eighteen-month-long world tour. ''Whatever we play,'' Michael and his crew members would yell while clapping their hands and stomping their feet just before hitting the stage, ''it's got to be funky!''

After a successful kickoff in Japan, where he was dubbed ''Typhoon Michael'' (and grossed $20 million), Michael had problems in Australia. Ticket sales proved low. Foreign newspapers had labeled him ''Wacko-Jacko,'' and the Aussies thought he was a head case. ''He's giving the world a gift, his talent,'' said his former sister-in-law Enid Jackson, ''and, in return, the world tries to crucify him.''

Michael also gave his first TV interview in years in an effort to boost his popularity in Australia, where ticket sales had been slow. He explained to TV show host Ian ''Molly'' Meldrum that he wears disguises because, ''I have to look like somebody else when I go out. Otherwise, I'd be torn to pieces by fans.''

He also explained why he's so fond of children: ''They don't have any of the bad points that adults have, like lying and scheming.''

''Michael was going to let Katherine handle the merchandising on the tour, because she asked him if she could,'' said Jerome Howard. ''She likes to keep busy. She's an ambitious, creative woman too. People don't know that about Katherine. But because Joe was involved with some people Michael didn't want anything to do with—and Katherine does nothing without Joe's participation—Michael gave Katherine a million dollars *not* to do the merchandising. But to this day I don't think she got all of the money because Michael's accounting system is all screwed up.

''Still,'' he continued, ''if that woman wants something, she just asks Michael or Janet and she gets it, just as she should.''

While Michael was on tour, *People* magazine published an open letter he had written to make known his feelings about the adverse publicity he'd received of late. In an odd writing style—no margins, no indentation, and childlike penmanship—Michael wrote:

''Like the old Indian proverb says, do not judge a man until you've walked 2 moons in his moccosins [*sic*]. Most people don't know me, that is why they write such things in wich [*sic*] most is not true. I cry very very often because it hurts and I worry about the children. All my children all over the world, I live for them. If a man could say nothing against a character but what he can prove, his story could not be written. Animals strike not from malice, but because they want to live, it is the same with those who criticize, they desire our blood, not our pain. But still I must achieve. I must seek truth in all things. I must endure for the power I was sent forth, for the world, for the children. But have mercy for I've been bleeding a long time now. MJ.''

# Chapter

## 28

In January 1988, Michael was twenty-nine and well on his way to his thirtieth birthday. Despite his best-selling records, his notoriety, and his great fortune, he had recently begun to lament that he wasn't respected enough. "They call Elvis the king," he would constantly complain to Frank Dileo. "Why don't they call *me* that?"

One would think that, given all he had achieved, Michael would be satisfied, but he was not. Indeed, ever since he was a child, Michael had always wanted to be number one. Because it was a goal he had worked toward for years, reaching it before his thirtieth birthday was somewhat anticlimactic for him. After all, what was left for a recording artist to do after selling more records than any person ever in the history of popular music?

Also, Michael does not think in terms of artistic development. He can't imagine recording an album for any purpose other than for it to be the biggest and best ever. Unlike most artists, Michael needs to have his work recognized as the best of all works, or he is simply not satisfied. This obsession can be traced back to his days as a youngster when The Jackson Five competed on talent shows. The goal was to be the winner. That was Michael's training ground, and despite his superstardom, he still has the same instincts he had when he was a young upstart: to be the winner.

Michael Jackson is also missing two essential qualities that Springsteen, Dylan, Lennon, Presley, and other pop icons and cultural emblems have had: humor and humanity. It is difficult to relate to him as he stands onstage accepting his many awards, whispering his thanks in an odd falsetto tone, and then taking off his sunglasses for just a quick moment because his friend Katharine Hepburn told him to do so.

Certainly, the public admires his prowess as a vocalist and his stylized genius as a dancer: he is the quintessential entertainer. But while the public can identify with many other rock stars whose humanity and accessibility supersede their superstardom, they can not identify at all with Michael, with his many nose jobs, the cleft in his chin, his surgical mask, and his supposed lust for the Elephant Man's bones. Who knows *anyone* like Michael Jackson?

But after *Thriller*, Michael Jackson saw himself as bigger than The Beatles, and more important than Elvis Presley. "They call Bruce [Springsteen] the boss and he's really overrated," Michael complained. "He can't sing and he can't dance. And if Elvis is supposed to be the king, what about me?"

The fact that Michael Jackson is black served to complicate matters. Don King had preyed on Michael's insecurities in 1984 during the days of the Victory tour. He once told Michael, "You're the biggest star ever, but the white man will never let you be bigger than Elvis."

Michael was stung by King's observation and never got over it. After Don King told him that, he telephoned one associate in the middle of the night and said, "They'll never let me be bigger than Elvis."

When the associate asked what he was talking about, Michael answered, "The white man—because I'm black."

Michael was reminded that he had already outsold Presley in terms of record sales. The associate felt that Don King was filling Michael's head with racist notions.

Michael continued complaining about his blackness for a few days until this confidant became so upset with him about it that he refused to speak to Michael for a week. When Michael began leaving messages on the associate's answering machine, begging him to return his call, the associate wrote him a letter. In it, he told Michael that he should be above the racist thinking Don King was propagating. If Michael didn't get over King's remarks, the associate wrote, he wasn't certain he would be able to continue with Michael. So Michael put those feelings aside for a couple of years, but he never forgot King's words.

Now it was 1988 and Michael was complaining again about being undervalued by white America. No one in Michael's camp knew how to solve this image problem. It was probably too late to do anything about it, anyway. And even if someone like Norman Winter or Michael Levine—the two excellent publicists who'd worked with Michael in the past—could come up with a way to promote Michael as an accessible, *human* artist with goals that are artistic instead of commercial, it would never work because Michael simply is not that way and doesn't even know how to act that way.

Michael came up with a title that he wanted Frank Dileo to try to perpetuate: "The King of Rock and Soul." But Dileo didn't like the title, and decided to ignore Michael's request.

Michael almost always prefers black entertainers over white ones. There are few Caucasians he legitimately respects as peers; Phil Collins is one because Michael feels he has a genuinely soulful voice. He admires Paul McCartney as a songwriter, but not as an entertainer. "I do better box office than he does, anyway," he's said of McCartney. He thinks Frank Sinatra is tremendously overrated. "I don't know what people see in the guy," Michael once said. "He's a legend, but the man isn't much of a singer. He doesn't even have hits anymore." Michael also has nothing good to say about Mick Jagger; he feels the man sings flat and almost ruined the duet they recorded together, "State of Shock." Michael told an associate, "How did *he* ever get to be a star? I just don't get it. He doesn't sell as many records as I do."

Michael is purely commercial in his thinking—how many records are being bought by his fans, how long does it take to get to number one, how many tickets are sold. He doesn't understand any artist who is not after commercial rewards, who has a different vision of artistic integrity.

Despite persistent reports that he would like to record a song with Madonna, Michael is also extremely upset by Madonna's fame. "She just isn't that good," Michael told one associate. "Let's face it. She can't sing. She's just an okay dancer. What does she do best? She knows how to market herself. That's about it."

In 1989, Madonna was named "Artist of the Decade" by many newspaper and magazine polls. Warner Bros., her record label, even paid for an advertisement in one of the industry trade publications pronouncing Madonna "Artist of the Decade." That title was the kind of empty compliment record labels often give their artists in paid promotions, but Michael was incensed by it just the same.

He telephoned John Branca and Frank Dileo and complained that Madonna didn't deserve such an award. "It makes me look bad. *I'm* the artist of the decade. Aren't I? Did she outsell *Thriller*?" Michael asked. "No, she did not," he answered his own question.

Branca who, lately, seemed to be in the business of solving problems for Michael Jackson, suggested that he could approach MTV with the idea of a made-up award. Off the top of his head, Branca came up with the Video Vanguard Artist of the Decade award. That sounded impressive, and Michael was thrilled by it.

"That'll teach that heifer," he said, speaking of Madonna.

So Michael was presented with the "Video Vanguard Artist of the Decade" trophy during the MTV Awards in 1989. Peter Gabriel presented Michael with the honor.

It's ironic, considering Michael Jackson's obsession with Elvis Presley, that John Branca represents the Presley estate. Branca once mentioned to Frank Dileo that Elvis used to give his trusted employees Cadillacs. Branca suggested to Dileo that maybe it was time for Michael to start taking care of his trusted associates. Branca was only half-joking.

"Johnny, that's a good idea," Frank said seriously.

Later, Frank had a talk with Michael. "Hey, Mike, don't you think you're as good as Elvis?" he asked him.

"Yeah, I do. Of course I do," Michael answered.

"Well, you know, Elvis used to give his people Cadillacs," Frank said. "You're a little cheap sometimes, Mike," Frank added, with a smile.

"What do you mean cheap?" Michael asked, defensively.

"Well, hey, Mike, you got sort of a reputation." Frank had planted the seed. The subject was changed.

Months later when Michael and John Branca were in London trying to negotiate the ATV acquisition, Michael said to him, "Branca, if you get me The Beatles catalogue, I'll buy you any car you want, just like Elvis would do."

"Including a Rolls-Royce?"

"You got it," Michael said.

So John Branca brilliantly closed the deal, and Michael bought him a Rolls. The only problem was that he didn't buy one for Frank Dileo. Dileo was on the phone to Branca as soon as Michael told him he had bought him a car.

"He got you a Rolls-Royce!" Dileo said. "I can't believe this. It was my fucking idea, and *you* ended up with the Rolls!" The two had a good laugh. Finally, Frank got a Rolls from Michael as well.

On February 23, 1988, Michael Jackson brought the Bad tour to the United States for the first time at the Kemper Arena in Kansas City, Missouri. By this time, the three single releases from *Bad*— "I Just Can't Stop Loving You," "Bad," and "The Way You Make Me Feel"—had all gone to number one. Michael was in good spirits, especially since Frank Dileo promised him that there would be two more of the same.

Before the February show, the Jackson crew unloaded eight truckloads of equipment, including seven hundred lights, one hundred speakers, a massive stage, two huge video screens, and eighty-five costumes. On the night of the concert, banks of floodlights rose from the stage bathing the audience in blinding white light before *he* appeared: Michael Jackson, frozen still onstage in a line of dancers. Dressed in a black toreador's outfit with buckles down the trouser seams, Michael exploded as a supernova of energy in motion to the strains of the opening number, "Wanna Be Startin' Somethin'."

"The word 'superstar' became meaningless compared with the power and grace pouring from the stage," wrote Gregory Sandow, who reviewed the concert for the *Los Angeles Herald Examiner*. There were startling and grandiose effects: bulletlike, multicolored laser beams, smoke bombs and explosions, all of which were effective and *loud*. There was also plenty of shtick: Michael disappearing from one side of the stage and reappearing on the other in a puff of smoke; Michael swinging out over the audience on a boom crane during "Beat It." In terms of pure stagecraft and showmanship, it was hard to fault Michael and his huge supporting cast, including four male dancers who took the place of Michael's brothers.

In this show, Michael became much more aggressive sexually. He grabbed his crotch at least five times during the opening number. His ungloved hand hovered around his groin during most of "Heartbreak Hotel," "Bad," and "Beat It." It was an odd gesture, but the seventeen thousand mostly middle-class white fans seemed to love it; the audience was on its feet for the entire slick, demanding, two-hour performance. Every time Michael executed one of his seemingly impossible backward glides across the stage—the moonwalk—the audience would cheer and Michael's face would light up. It was clear that he still enjoyed performing. "He's as powerful and polished a performer as ever lived," Smokey Robinson said.

He told *Ebony* magazine, "When I'm doing a show and I see the fans out there dancing and screaming, excited . . . that's what I love most. I really do. And it's just the greatest feeling in the world. You're up there and you're giving them that energy and that love and they're just throwing it right back at you."

Vocally, Michael was in terrific shape; his voice teacher, Seth Riggs, traveled with him for much of the tour. "He's a high tenor with a three-and-a-half octave range,'' Riggs said. ''He goes from basso low E up to G and A-flat above high C. A lot of people think it's falsetto, but it's not. It's all connected, which is remarkable. During his vocal exercises he would put his arms up in the air and start spinning while holding a note. I asked him why he was doing that, and he said, 'I may have to do it onstage, so I want to make sure it's possible.' I'd never seen anything like that before. I thought maybe I should stop him so he can concentrate on his voice now, and dance later. But I figured if he can do it, let him do it.''

A good third of the show consisted of material Michael and his brothers had used in Kansas City four years earlier when the Victory tour opened, right down to some of the dialogue. (This time, though, Michael performed ''Thriller'' in his act—complete with werewolf mask and the kind of high school letter jacket he wore in the video—now that he no longer considered himself a Jehovah's Witness.) When Katherine and Joe saw the show, they were disturbed. ''He should have just had his brothers with him,'' Joe said. ''What the hell's the point in not having them? I don't get it. He's got a good show, but with his brothers it's a better show.''

Katherine told Frank Dileo she thought Michael was better when he performed with the brothers. She said that Frank laughed in her face and told her she was ''crazy.'' Katherine was immediately offended and told Frank, ''I am not crazy. The show would have been better with the brothers, and that's that.''

Just prior to going onstage, Michael was handed a copy of the *Star*, a tabloid, with the cover headline, ''Michael Jackson Goes Ape. Now He's Talking with His Pet Chimp—In Monkey Language.'' The story said that Michael was obsessed with learning how to talk to his chimp.

''Did Frank plant this?'' Michael wanted to know. ''Where'd they get these pictures of me and Bubbles?''

Michael's aide just shrugged his shoulders.

''Well, I don't like this,'' Michael said angrily. ''I don't want to see this. Don't show me this kind of stuff before I go onstage. What's the matter with you?''

One editor at the *Star* insists that the feature was, in fact, planted by Frank Dileo and that the tabloid was told it could use the story and the two photos of Michael and Bubbles if the writers utilized words like ''bizarre'' (which was used twice) and ''super strange'' in the text.

''Frank set the whole thing up,'' the editor said. ''A lot of the story is true, or at least Frank said it was true. He said that Bubbles once hid under a bed, and when Michael found him, the chimp wouldn't budge. Michael begged and pleaded, but Bubbles wouldn't come out. The ordeal went on so long, Michael's staff began to gather outside the bedroom door. Suddenly, Michael began to chatter away like a chimp, imitating Bubbles, and the chimp suddenly crawled out from under the bed and leaped into his arms. That incident gave Frank the idea for this story. The part about Michael setting aside one million dollars to fund scientists researching ways for people to talk to animals turned out to be fiction. I don't know where Frank got *that* from.''

Like many stories published about Michael, the tale of his fixation with Bubbles—a three-and-a-half-year-old chimp who had been released to Michael from a cancer lab in 1985—was false. Michael liked his ape, the way he likes all of his animals, but even though the master and ape sometimes ate together at the dinner table, the relationship between star and chimp was never obsessive. Bubbles became quite the star at this time because of all the press he received. One Tokyo merchandiser said, ''Bubbles is so popular here that if he announced he was doing a concert tour, he'd sell out.''

''Bubbles lives with me most of the time and stays with Michael seldom,'' the animal's trainer, Bob Dunn, revealed. Dileo apparently thought it would magnify Michael's eccentric image if people thought he was obsessed with the chimp, especially when Michael wanted to bring Bubbles on the road the way many stars take along their dogs and cats.

Michael had full approval over the hyperbaric chamber and the Elephant Man stories. All the others were planted without his approval. He was especially upset about a recent story in the *National Enquirer* that said he had a shrine to Elizabeth Taylor built in a room in his home, complete with wallpaper he had designed that had her face printed on it. Supposedly, Michael would not allow anyone into the room except Liz. ''It may sound a little crazy, but that's just the way Michael is!'' said the story.

''How can people think I'm *that* crazy?'' Michael asked. He wanted these stories, like the earlier ones, stopped, because it seemed to him that this kind of publicity only served to attract trouble.

For instance, at this same time, in early 1988, Michael was sued in Los Angeles Superior Court for divorce by a woman he never even married! A thirty-nine-year-old woman calling herself Billie Jean Jackson claimed that she and Michael were married on May 5, 1986, and separated two days later because of ''irreconcilable differences.'' She insisted that Michael had fathered her three children, one (Lanhej, renamed Tina Jean) born in 1976 and twins

(Lanelle and Ansar, renamed Michael Joseph II and Michael Josephina) in April 1982. She also said that she had had sex with Michael twice in the back seat of his Rolls-Royce ("I didn't expect it, at all") and became pregnant both times.

It turned out that Billie Jean Jackson is Lavon Muhammad, also known as Lavon Antoinette, who has apparently been stalking Michael for years. "Michael gave me the name Billie Jean," she explained. "He insisted I use it. I love him and I always have. He loves me too. I need some living expenses. I want to have what he has. If he won't give it to me, I'll just have to get it." She was asking for $150 million.

"He is absolutely scared to death of this person," said one former associate, "and he managed to get a three-year injunction against her for harassing him. Still, he has nightmares that this woman is after him. For a time, he was obsessed with this lady, wanting to know her whereabouts at all times. She used to pop up at the Encino house, sneak onto the premises, and surprise everyone. She really did believe her story, and she would stop at nothing to get to Michael. This is the kind of thing that happens: a celebrity who is perceived as eccentric attracts eccentrics. Katherine was particularly upset by this."

"If she ever gets her hands on my son, who knows what she'll do," Katherine said.

"How do you live your life in fear?" Michael asked. "I don't know what she's going to do next. Is this love? Or is it some kind of madness?"

Katherine had been after Frank Dileo for months to stop promoting her son as "Wacko-Jacko," but, she said, "there was nothing I could do about it."

Partly as a result of the bizarre image Michael developed because of the tabloid press, much of his public turned against him. Even though *Rolling Stone*'s readers voted him the worst artist in nearly every category in its yearly poll, Michael tried to remain optimistic. He said he felt that the year would be a good one.

But March 1988 did not begin well. Michael may have added another dimension to the word "superstar" in Kansas City, but he was still a human being with tangible, human concerns and even jealousies. For instance, he was extremely upset that he was shut out at the Grammy Awards in New York on March 2.

He decided to perform on the telecast, the first time in five years he had entertained on television. "Michael wanted to erase all the negative publicity that had been trailing him and replace it with a positive image of him doing what he does best," said Bob Jones, vice president of communications for MJJ Productions. Michael Jackson wanted to prove to the world that he is serious about his craft, that the very essence of him is a performer, not an eccentric nut. Anyone who saw his riveting performance would have to agree. Michael Jackson is an intensely competitive person. He is also realistic when he needs to be. He felt that if he lost the Grammys, he would at least leave an unforgettable impression of himself with the academy and with his audience. "He just never lets you forget how good he really is," Liza Minnelli observed.

But after truly inspiring and absorbing performances of "The Way You Make Me Feel" and "Man in the Mirror," Michael had to sit in the first row of Radio City Music Hall, in full view of millions, as he suffered one humiliating defeat after another. Out of four nominations—Album of the Year, Best Male Pop Vocal, Best Male R&B Vocal Performance, and Producer of the Year—he had no wins.

"He couldn't have looked any more heartbroken if someone had walked away with his pet chimp," wrote Robert Hillburn, the *Los Angeles Times* pop music critic. The last time Michael appeared at the Grammys with a hit album, he had received more awards (eight of them) than anyone else in the history of the event. This time, he got nothing. He craved the Grammy for Best Album for *Bad*, but U2 won it for *The Joshua Tree*.

"He went back to the Helmsley Palace, where he was staying, and cried," one friend said. "He and Frank had made a vow that they would at least win Album of the Year. He thought the whole thing was very unfair. To him, it was more than fair when he won in 1984, but really unfair when he lost in 1988. Marlon telephoned him to tell him he had been 'robbed.' "

There was little time for Michael to feel sorry for himself. The next day, on March 3, he was due to give a concert at Madison Square Garden. After the show, Michael and the Pepsi-Cola Company (which sponsored the Bad tour) presented a $600,000 check, the proceeds from the concert, to the United Negro College Fund. Four years earlier, Michael had endowed a scholarship program at the UNCF with a portion of his earnings from the ill-fated Victory tour. By 1988, seventy students at UNCF member schools had received Michael Jackson scholarships. (At some of the country's smaller black colleges, that could be an entire graduating class.) Michael keeps a low profile when it comes to these donations. Perhaps if his generosity were better known, he would not be so roundly criticized by many African-Americans for not having a so-called "black consciousness."

"Michael Jackson gives a lot of money to various causes," says actor Jim Brown, "but the power of Michael's money is not meaningful to black people, because the most important positions in control of the money in his organization are filled by white people, who naturally look out for their own first."

Michael Jackson does not employ many African-Americans in key positions. Neither does Eddie Murphy, or Bill Cosby, or Diana Ross, or Lionel Richie, or many other black entertainers. "They don't feel that blacks make capable business managers," said one black industry observer. "They're not willing to share their money with blacks who have expertise, and there are plenty out there, believe me. Michael Jackson is especially known in the music industry as not wanting to have anything to do with black business. After doing business with his father, he has a prejudice against doing business with other blacks. As far as I know, the only two blacks with power he feels comfortable with are Bill Bray, his security man, and Bob Jones, his main publicist, who is excellent."

"I don't hire people by color," Michael has said. He still becomes angry when he thinks about the statements his father once made that the reason managers Freddy DeMann and Ron Weisner were brought into the picture in the eighties was because Joe needed white help. Michael says, "I do a lot for black causes. I do my part. Why should I have to do more than my part?"

Back in 1984, when Jesse Jackson visited Michael in Dallas during the Victory tour, Michael and his advisers seemed extremely reluctant to allow his photo to be taken with Jesse because of the way it might be construed by the public. Jesse was flabbergasted by this. "They're scared of letting us be in a picture together," Jesse Jackson said later, shaking his head.

The fact that Michael did not want his picture taken with Jesse Jackson reminded some of his associates of an incident they refer to as "Donny-Gate." When Osmond visited Jackson at one of the many stops along the way on the Victory tour in 1984, Michael consented to have his picture taken with him. A publicist who worked in Norman Winter's office at the time remembered what happened then.

"Norman decided to send the picture to *USA Today* because it was such a great shot and Michael didn't seem hesitant about having it taken. But when it was published, Michael hit the roof. 'What the heck is this? I don't want my picture in the paper with Donny Osmond,' he said. 'Do you know what kind of *image* Donny Osmond has? Why would I want to be seen with him in *USA Today*?'

Mike wanted all of the copies of that picture destroyed. Everyone in the office was shredding pictures of Michael Jackson and Donny Osmond. Norman laughs about it still.''

Donny Osmond had been saddled with a teenybopper image for most of his career and, until recently, was never taken seriously as an artist. He managed to break that stereotype in 1989 with his Capitol Records release, ''Soldier of Love.'' But prior to the release of that record—and after ''Donny-Gate''—Donny met with Michael to ask if Jackson had any ideas as to how he could change his image. Osmond was hoping that, perhaps, Michael would write or produce a record with or for him.

Michael gave this advice to Donny Osmond: ''The first thing you gotta do is change your name. And don't tell anyone you were ever Donny Osmond.'' Osmond was offended by Michael's counsel, and the two haven't been on friendly terms since then.

Most people who accompanied Michael Jackson on his Bad tour recall how generous Jackson was to children who wanted to see him perform. At every concert stop on his Bad tour, he set aside a portion of tickets for underprivileged youngsters who otherwise would be unable to attend his shows. All of the royalties from his number one single ''Man in the Mirror'' were donated to Camp Good Times, a charity for terminally ill patients in Los Angeles. Little notice is ever given to Michael's charitable work, mostly because Michael does not want to bring any undue attention to it. Frank Dileo probably said it best when asked in 1984 why Michael was donating all of his proceeds from the Victory tour to charity. ''Because he's a nice guy,'' Frank succinctly explained.

Though his good deeds go unnoticed, the rest of his life receives ample attention. While on stage at Madison Square Garden, Michael shared a kiss with model Tatiana Thumbtzen, who appeared in his video ''The Way You Make Me Feel.'' A week later, the photo showed up in the *National Enquirer* with the headline, ''Michael Jackson and Model Fall Head-Over-Heels in Love.'' The story said that Michael and Tatiana were having an affair (which was not true) now that Michael's romance with makeup artist Karen Faye was over (the two were never romantically involved).

''I don't like this at all. Where is this coming from?'' Michael wanted to know. He was exasperated.

Later, the *National Enquirer* would run with the fallacious story that Michael often sees the Lord materializing out of a cloud of smoke while he performs onstage. Then, the *Star* would print that Michael had fallen in love with Princess Diana and wanted her to star in his next video. When Michael demanded to know where these preposterous stories came from, some fingers pointed at Frank Dileo. The accusation seems unlikely. By this time, Dileo knew how upset these stories were making Michael and he most certainly would not have been a party to spreading them.

A favorite untrue story among those in Michael's inner circle appeared in the *Enquirer*. It claimed that Prince used ESP to drive Bubbles the chimp crazy. "Prince has gone too far this time," Michael was quoted as saying in the article. "What kind of sicko would mess with a monkey? This is the final straw."

"Actually, Michael liked that one," an associate said. "I never saw him laugh so hard."

During this period, Michael worked with Motown Productions on a special for the Showtime cable network, *Motown on Showtime: Michael Jackson*. The program—which would eventually be released as a home video—took two years to make, employed four creative teams, and went way over its one-million-dollar budget. The biggest obstacle executive producer Suzanne dePasse and the Motown team faced was Michael's refusal to be interviewed for the special. Instead, a host of others—from Elizabeth Taylor to Sophia Loren to Gene Kelly to Yoko Ono, people who know nothing about Michael Jackson's history, only his present celebrity—were interviewed as "experts."

Diana Ross, the obvious choice, had been asked to host the program, but she declined to participate because she was still angry with Michael for not attending her wedding to Arne Naess and the christening celebrations of the children she and Naess had. "I was jealous because I've always loved Diana Ross and always will," Michael offered as explanation.

"Yes, I would like to marry her," he said before Ross's marriage to Naess. And when someone brought up the fourteen-year age difference, Michael said, "So what? What does age have to do with it? Look at it this way: how old would you be if you didn't know how old you were?" It is doubtful that Michael was in love with Diana Ross or that he ever really wanted to marry her.

When Diana sent word back that she would not be interested in hosting the Showtime special, Michael was extremely disappointed. "Why would she turn me down? I like her so much," he said, truly crushed. "She's the only one who should host this thing. Why is it that the only way she will do something for me is if I do something for her *first*?"

Twenty-nine-year-old Michael Jackson was not above being vindictive. When Diana refused to do the special, he insisted that there be as little footage of her as possible. He did not want her to receive any free publicity from the show. Moreover, he wished to set the record straight that she did not discover him.

First, Quincy Jones was shown saying he heard Diana Ross was responsible for the discovery. That clip gave way to one of Suzanne dePasse insisting that that wasn't true at all, that it was all "a legend" that "seemed like a good idea at the time." Then producers Jackson and dePasse cut to a clip of Ed Sullivan introducing Diana Ross out of the audience after The Jackson 5's first appearance on his show. Sullivan insisted that Ross stand up and take a bow for discovering The Jackson 5, which she was more than happy to do. Diana looked very proud of herself as everyone around her applauded, but because of the way the show was edited, Diana Ross seemed like a liar.

Michael was co-executive producer with Suzanne dePasse of the one-hour special and had complete control over its content, which was essentially an homage to himself.

"He has redefined the term professional entertainer," intoned narrator James Earl Jones. "Meeting Michael Jackson would, for thousands, millions, surely be a dream come true."

Celebrity after celebrity enthused about Michael's private personality and stage persona.

"When I met him, it was love at first sight," said Sophia Loren.

"He's the nicest person in the world," said Sean Lennon.

"He has the quality of innocence we'd all like to attain," said Elizabeth Taylor. "I love you, Michael."

The praise was intercut with footage of people cheering and—screaming for Michael Jackson at his concerts. The point was repeatedly made that "Michael Jackson is the greatest." Most viewers were puzzled by "Motown on Showtime: Michael Jackson"—especially those viewers who knew how closely he was affiliated with the show from its inception. It sounded as though he had just sent himself a giant valentine full of love notes he had written to himself.

There would be other documentaries full of similar self-aggrandizement and self-indulgence. One, "Around the World with Michael Jackson," a chronicling of his Bad tour which was broadcast on network television, was particularly disturbing. Again, there was more footage of screaming, hysterical fans, but with the addition of "candid" interviews with young girls of all races and colors proclaiming their undying love for Michael and constantly echoing each other's belief that he is the most talented performer of all time.

It was as if Michael felt that this kind of video adoration from his fans would somehow assist him in his quest to be considered "the king," like Elvis Presley. After sitting through such a tribute, to see Michael's name in the credits as its executive producer just made much of his public, and certainly his critics, feel that there was something very wrong with Michael. One was forced to wonder why he felt his music and artistry could not speak for itself. Why did he have to have his ego buffed by such constant reinforcement of his "brilliance"? Who were these documentaries made for, his public or him?

In March 1988, while he was still on the road, Michael Jackson finalized the purchase of his new home, a twenty-seven-hundred-acre estate in the Santa Ynez Valley called Sycamore Ranch. Michael became enchanted by the ranch when he stayed there during the time he and Paul McCartney filmed the "Say, Say, Say" video in Santa Ynez; McCartney had leased the home for the duration of his and wife Linda's stay.

At Sycamore Ranch, there would be plenty of room for his animal menagerie—which was an important consideration—and the location was far enough from Encino to guarantee space between Michael and his family members. The property was owned by developer William Bone, who spent years and a fortune building it to his specifications; the main house is thirteen thousand square feet. The asking price came to $35 million furnished, or $32.5 million unfurnished. Michael toured the estate by the horse-drawn carriage provided by Bone.

John Branca submitted an offer of $15 million, which was not accepted. Michael's final offer was $17 million, the sum he paid for the property. Michael also got all of the furnishings and eighteen-and nineteenth-century antiques as part of the purchase. A fully-stocked wine cellar went along with the deal.

The press reported that Michael paid $28 million for the estate.

John Branca had advised Michael that, from a business standpoint, the ranch was not a good investment. There are not many buyers for a twenty-seven-hundred acre ranch that costs $17 million. Branca reportedly wrote Jackson a letter and told him that if he really wanted to buy the ranch, he shouldn't do so with any "profit motive." He felt it would be a more sensible idea to purchase the property that was once used as the estate on "The Beverly Hillbillies" television show. He also suggested that Michael buy the surrounding property, demolish the houses that are there, and then he could have five acres of property to do with what he pleased.

Michael wanted to know why he should have only five acres when he could have almost three thousand. He explained to another associate that when he used to visit Paul McCartney, he was always impressed with McCartney's sumptuous estate, and that when he had meetings with Berry Gordy they were always at Gordy's lavish Bel Air palace, which awed Michael. "When I have guests, they're going to be expecting something grand," Michael said. "It's gotta look like I've made it big, because I have."

It was a difficult and lengthy negotiation because John Branca had been trying to get Michael the best possible deal, as he always did. But Jackson was anxious to settle the matter; he was calling Branca three times a day trying to prod him on.

Finally, Michael decided that John Branca simply did not want him to have the property, and he became angry. It's been said that he instructed one of Branca's partners to break into Branca's office and steal the file on Sycamore Ranch, and then get to work on closing the deal.

Recalled a former employee of Branca's, "When John Branca heard about this, he was astonished. He telephoned Michael immediately and asked how he could do something so unprofessional.

" 'Because I think you don't want me to spend too much money,' Michael said in his own defense. 'You don't want me to have the ranch.'

"Branca told him he was right, that he didn't think Michael should make the purchase. However, he intended to follow Michael's wishes, and hoped that he would never again pull a stunt like that. Branca said he was genuinely hurt.

"Michael felt bad about what he'd done. In a meeting with Branca later, he said, 'If you could have any car you want, what would it be?'

"Branca said it would be either a Mercedes or a Rolls-Royce convertible.

"Soon after that conversation," the associate concluded, "John Branca closed the deal for the ranch. Michael bought him a Rolls-Royce convertible."

At the last minute, William Bone began having second thoughts about selling the property. He didn't want to lose his connection to the house; he treasured it that much.

John Branca came up with a clause in the sales agreement that allows Bone to spend one week out of every year at the ranch for the next three years, subject to Michael's schedule. Then, Bone didn't feel that he was losing the property entirely, and the sale was made.

The first thing Michael did was change the name of the ranch to "Neverland Valley." When Michael had to conduct business in Los Angeles, he would stay in a condominium he leases in Westwood.

Rather than confront his parents about his decision, Michael did not tell them he was leaving the Encino estate. Katherine and Joe heard about Michael's new home while watching "Entertainment Tonight." Marlon telephoned Michael to find out if it were true that he was purchasing a twenty-three-hundred-acre property for $28 million. Michael said it wasn't. Where had Marlon heard such a ridiculous story? The next day, Michael closed on the property. Michael had some of his employees go to the Encino home and take the items he wanted to have. "I was waiting for Michael to come to us and say something," Joe said. "But he never did."

Michael hosted a housewarming party for his relatives, but he did not invite Joe or Katherine. Perhaps he wanted to invite his mother but didn't know how he could do so without having his father as a guest. "That hurt us both," Joe said.

Michael Jackson's name was not on the original purchase agreement for the house. Rather, the agreement was signed by his lawyer, John Branca, and his accountant, Marshall Gelfand. He had told both of them that he didn't want anyone to be able to check public records of property ownership and figure out where he lived. Gelfand suggested that a trust be set up with himself and Branca as trustees. Michael owned the trust and could fire Gelfand and Branca at any time. The two could do nothing with the property without his permission.

To Michael, this seemed like a good idea for only a couple of days. Michael is much too paranoid to allow such a situation to exist very long. Bill Bray apparently had a talk with Michael about the property, and the next day Jackson wanted to know why he didn't own his own house.

"But you do own it," Marshall Gelfand tried to explain. "It's a trust set up. It's what you asked for."

"Well, I don't like it. I think it sounds fishy," Michael said.

"Fine, we'll terminate the trust," Gelfand responded. "It's done. Terminated."

On April 11, 1988, Michael had Branca and Gelfand sign an individual grant deed turning over the property to him.

Michael housed his animals in comfortable quarters. However, after moving in, there was a fire in the giraffe barn and, though the three giraffes kept there were saved, Michael panicked, fearing for his menagerie of treasured animals. "He loves his animals more than he loves some humans," said Jerome Howard. "He doesn't want them threatened by fire. In fact, Michael has been terrified of fire ever since the Pepsi burning years ago. So he had his own fire station built on the property. I think it cost him about three hundred thousand dollars.''

It was said that one of the reasons Michael left home when he did grew out of an incident during a gathering at the Encino home, when Michael was supposedly accused by his father of being a homosexual.

It's true that Michael especially enjoyed family get-togethers since they afforded him an opportunity to catch up on all of the news from his nieces and nephews, whom he seems to adore. According to the story, he showed up with a young man no one in the family knew. This was strange because the only people ever invited to the Jacksons' ''family day'' were close friends and relatives. It was an unwritten rule that strangers were not welcome.

According to the story, Joe eyed Michael's guest suspiciously. He noticed that anytime someone walked over and asked the stranger a question, the answer seemed to be well rehearsed, as if Michael had schooled his guest in what to say and what not to say.

Michael was playing on the grass with his young nieces and nephews when, according to a woman who says she was a witness, Joe walked up to him and said, ''I want to talk to you.''

Michael followed his father into the house.

Ten minutes later, Michael supposedly stormed back out of the house, Joe on his heels. Joe slammed the door behind him. The two began arguing and Joe accused Michael of being gay. Before Michael had a chance to respond, Joe gestured at his son's guest, asked who he was and why Michael spent so much time with him. ''Don't you have any trust in me at all?'' Michael asked. ''Look, I am *not gay*.''

Without saying a word, Michael's guest left. Michael went back into the house.

The woman who insists she was there and witnessed this scene was interviewed by a *Star* magazine reporter and was also interviewed for this book. She requested anonymity. ''Poor Katherine. It was like her whole world had crumbled,'' she recalled. ''She was having such a good time, being with her family, her grandchildren, and then—bam!—*this* had to happen.''

''Oh, that story is absolutely not true,'' Enid Jackson said. ''That's a horrible story. I have been to all of those family gatherings—even after the divorce—and if something like that happened, I certainly would know it. When I read that, I was amazed. How could someone make up such a story? It's typical of the stuff that's printed about Michael that isn't true.''

Dee Dee Jackson, Tito's wife, concurred. "Nothing like that ever happened. Believe me, I would know if it did. Michael is a wonderful uncle to the kids. He gives them all of his attention at those family days. He doesn't even have to go, but he does just to be there for the children. And then to have a story like that be published is just a shame. It's so wrong. But I'm not surprised by it.''

Charles Montgomery, who wrote the hyperbaric chamber feature for the *National Enquirer* as well as many other features for that tabloid, and for the *Globe*, with the cooperation of Michael's camp, said, "I don't think the story is true. For one thing, if you know Joe Jackson you know that he would not do something like that in public. Also, I do not believe that Michael Jackson is gay. I don't know for a fact that he isn't, but I don't believe so. I, personally, feel that Michael Jackson is asexual, just from my experience of covering stories about him for the last decade or so.''

The anecdote is fascinating not so much in itself as for the way details of it spread after being published in the tabloid. The public does seem to want to believe that Michael Jackson is gay, and any story dealing with the possibility is well received. Also, the source for the story seems quite legitimate, in terms of her relationship to the family. Certainly it would appear that nothing anyone says to a reporter about Michael Jackson can be taken at face value.

"Michael Jackson is not gay,'' Frank Dileo has insisted, "and if anybody is going to know that, it's going to be me. I've been around him more than anybody in the world, and if he was, I'd know. He is not.''

Michael hoped for a serene lifestyle in his new, palatial estate. The home gave him two things he said he really needed: space and a place to think. But while he was planning to take time off after the Bad tour, his family plotted another Jacksons reunion show. The Victory tour fiasco of 1984 would pale in comparison to the proposed Korean tour of 1988. But this time, Michael Jackson would not be putty in his family's hands.

# Chapter

## 29

In the spring of 1988, Jerome Howard, the savvy and efficient thirty-five-year-old president of business affairs for Joe and Katherine Jackson's many corporations, had received persistent telephone calls from Kenneth Choi, a Korean businessman who wanted to arrange a meeting with Jerome's bosses. Choi, who had already been booted out of Michael Jackson's office—as well as the offices of his accountant, Marshall Gelfand, and attorney, John Branca—told Howard that he was from a wealthy family that was interested in promoting a Jackson family concert tour in Korea. Howard, realizing that a reunion concert was always on Joe's and Katherine's minds, immediately arranged a meeting between Choi and Joe Jackson.

"Millions of dollars were offered at that meeting," Howard remembered. "The guy was talking ten to fifteen million. Whatever it would take to get the Jackson brothers to come together for these concerts, that's what they wanted to spend. Joe was very excited. Choi invited us to go to Korea to check things out. We didn't know what was happening; all we knew was that the guy had a lot of money."

Joe and Katherine Jackson, Jerome Howard, and Kenneth Choi went to Korea in the spring of 1988. During the four-day trip, paid for by Choi, they were wined and dined and introduced to several wealthy and influential business people, celebrities, and politicians. They also met a gentleman who could not speak English, named "Mr. Lee," who was introduced as Choi's brother. They were told that Lee, who owned a shipping company, would back the proposed Jacksons concerts, along with the *Segye Times*, a Korean newspaper. Through his interpreter-secretary, Mr. Lee said that if the concerts were organized, he would invest $2 million in

Joe Jackson's record company. Joe was immediately intrigued and eager to move forward with the deal.

"These people seemed to know the strengths and weaknesses of the Jackson family," Jerome Howard recalled. "They knew that Joe was interested in getting money for his company and for himself. They understood that Katherine's interest was for her family. She wanted to make money for her children. These Koreans seemed to know everything about the Jacksons, and they knew how to play all the angles."

In the course of the meetings, Jerome Howard discovered that the *Segye Times* is owned by the Reverend Sun Myung Moon and the Unification Church. In other words, the Moonies were behind the whole deal.

The Unification Church was first brought to the United States from Korea in 1959 by one of the Reverend Sun Myung Moon's followers, Dr. Young Oon Kim, who came here to study at the University of Oregon. Soon there were other small groups around the country, independent of each other, and taking on the character of whichever missionary led that particular unit.

Americans first noticed the Moonies, as they came to be called, in the late sixties, because the leader of the San Francisco group believed strongly in a "systematic training program." Americans called it brainwashing, as they watched their children suddenly renounce their lifestyles to move into communes and sell flowers and candy in airports. Instead of stressing religion, recruiters stressed youth, education, and Utopia and rarely told potential converts that the Unification Church was connected to Moon—or Korea. In 1970, Moon himself moved to New York and the next year made a world tour to launch a three-year evangelical campaign, which interwove culture and religion.

Although people have joked for a long time about being hassled for small change by young Moonies in airports, Moon's followers have actually raised a lot of money, which Moon has invested in a number of diversified enterprises, including banks, restaurants, fisheries, and the media. In 1982, Moon started publishing the *Washington Times*. That same year, he was convicted of tax evasion, fined twenty-five thousand dollars, and sentenced to eighteen months in prison. He was released early for good behavior.

Christian fundamentalist groups have charged that the Unification Church is not Christian; liberal groups have accused them of being too right-wing; parents have hired deprogrammers to kidnap their children who are living in Moonie compounds. Although membership has rapidly declined, the Unification Church is still very rich.

What Moon has always craved most of all for his church is respectability. When the Unification Church published *As Others See Us* in 1974, in which nearly a hundred government officials, religious leaders, and private people wrote letters about the church, Moon scored a national publicity coup, especially since one of the letters was from then-president Nixon. So pleased were Moon's followers at Nixon's encouragement and the respectability and attention it brought the church, that later the same year, when Nixon was in the midst of the Watergate crisis, hundreds of them staged a three-day fast on the Capitol steps to show their support. If Moon could align himself with Michael Jackson (the biggest-selling and most clean-cut pop artist of all time) and the Jackson family (still perceived by many as being one of the most wholesome families in the United States), then Moon himself would benefit. The price would be high, but the prestige would be well worth the cost.

When Jerome told Joe and Katherine that the Reverend Sun Myung Moon was involved in this deal, Joe was fascinated; he had heard that Moon was quite wealthy. But Katherine became upset. "I don't want to have anything to do with anything religious," she said. "Business is business, but I don't even want to know anything about the religious ties." Katherine, however, did not tell Jerome Howard to pull out of the meetings. She just didn't want to know all the details.

Jerome Howard is a keen business manager who bases many of his perceptions about people on instinct. He was suspicious from the very beginning of the people working on Moon's behalf. "They always spoke Korean behind your back," he said. "They'd say something in English and then turn to someone and say something in Korean, and who knows what they were saying? I just felt that they were duplicitous, withholding important information. I couldn't prove it, but I suspected it. It would be my job to protect the Jacksons as best I could."

It was a job he often performed admirably. At about this time, Katherine and Joe purchased a six-bedroom home in Las Vegas, Nevada, where they eventually plan to retire. The house was being offered for $570,000. Katherine and Joe brought Jerome Howard to Las Vegas with them to negotiate a deal. According to a friend of Howard's, he told Katherine and Joe to strip off all their jewelry—probably a quarter of a million dollars' worth—and put it in the glove compartment of the car they were driving. Then Jerome brought Mr. and Mrs. Jackson into the home to meet the owners.

Katherine and Joe acted like "everyday folks" and must have done a fairly convincing job, because they bought the house for only $292,000.

Of the cost of the home, $200,000 came from the million dollars Michael had given Katherine to persuade her not to become involved in the merchandising of the Bad tour. Katherine took out a loan for the balance. Katherine said that she wanted the home to be "plain and ordinary," unlike the Encino estate, but after years of opulence it must have been difficult for her to remember what "plain and ordinary" is really like. She paid over $750 for just a toilet, and equally inflated prices for other accessories while redecorating the home.

A month after their first visit to Korea, Joe, Katherine, Jerome Howard, and Rebbie—who simply wanted to go shopping there—went back for more meetings. They attended a meeting with a Mr. Kwak, president of the *Segye Times*, whom Kenneth Choi introduced as his father. A large, framed picture of the Reverend Sun Myung Moon hung in his office. Katherine tried to ignore it. Kwak told Howard to put together a proposal, " 'and whatever my son wants to do, we'll do it.' He kept saying 'my son' throughout the whole meeting, and we were under the impression that Choi was his son [he wasn't]," Howard recalled.

Katherine and Joe then met privately with Kwak in their suite. They had a sumptuous breakfast and exchanged gifts; Katherine gave him autographed pictures of her family members. After that meeting, Katherine and Joe went shopping in Etaewon with a tour guide, all to keep them busy. Kenneth Choi had even had a famous Korean designer make outfits for the Jackson parents, and also bought them expensive gifts, just to give them some way to pass the time.

Working with Kwak's special assistant David Hose, Jerome Howard began structuring a deal at the Ambassador Hotel. Kwak's representatives then took what Howard had written, left the hotel, and brought the papers to their lawyers. They returned three and a half hours later.

"They came back with a contract that was so wild I couldn't believe it," Howard said. "They wanted Michael Jackson to begin the show by singing the Korean national anthem and then perform three Korean numbers in Korean costumes. I looked at that contract and thought, 'Oh, man, this is ridiculous. Michael Jackson is not going to learn any Korean songs, and he is certainly not about to wear any Korean wardrobe onstage!' When I showed the deal to

Joe and Katherine, they busted up laughing and were almost rolling on the floor.''

"In my country, Michael Jackson is considered a special, unusual person," said Kenneth Choi in an interview (in 1991). "We admire his spiritual qualities. We would never, for instance, have asked Madonna to perform. To us, she does not have the same character and morals as Michael Jackson. We would be embarrassed to introduce her to our president. But not Michael. Michael, we would be proud of. He has power through his goodness. To be honest, after we thought it over, we really wanted Michael by himself, not the brothers. But we knew that his parents liked it better when they worked together, so we decided to have all of them perform.''

In the end, Joe, Katherine, and Jerome agreed that the way to structure the deal was to make the Koreans—the Moonies—the sponsors of the show and Katherine and Joe the promoters. Katherine and Joe would establish a company for this purpose called Jackson Family Concerts International.

Jerome Howard negotiated an outstanding deal for the Jackson family. He explained, "The Jacksons would perform for four nights, one two-hour show each night, at the Olympic Stadium in Seoul. They would be paid $7.5 million. There would also be a $1.5 million production budget, and whatever was saved from that budget would go to the Jacksons. One hundred percent of the profits from broadcasting rights outside of Korea and fifty percent of the merchandising profits would also go to the Jacksons. The Moonies would have the broadcasting rights and video rights in Korea. One hundred percent of the ticket sales also went to the Moonies. We deleted the clauses about the Korean songs and costumes. There was further talk that the Moonies wanted to send the guys to Russia and then pay them $15 million up front to have the guys go to China. So Joe, Kwak, and I signed the contract. Katherine didn't sign. She doesn't sign anything unless she absolutely has to, and it wasn't necessary. All of this was contingent upon getting the brothers to agree to it, which was the next step.''

The Moonie project had become a major, multimillion-dollar deal for the family; as usual, most of the family members needed the money. Janet and LaToya were not approached, because their parents knew it would be impossible to get their cooperation: Janet was immersed in the recording of a new album for A&M; LaToya was beginning to question her father's business practices; and both daughters had begun looking for independent counsel to get themselves out of their contracts with Joe. But Rebbie had already consented to appear—if they'd have her—and the brothers would certainly be amenable. Except for Michael, who was in Europe performing while the scheme was being hatched.

At this time, April 1988, Michael's autobiography, *Moonwalk*, was published by Doubleday.

A small part of the book was written by Michael, with the help of a string of ghostwriters. One researcher reported that when she was collecting material for the book at Michael's Encino home, Michael paraded up and down the hallways in a variety of disguises, including false teeth, a mustache, and bushy sideburns. "He would become very upset if you recognized him," she said. "He wanted you to play along."

*Moonwalk* was principally written, however, by talented and persistent Doubleday editor Shaye Areheart, who works closely with Jacqueline Onassis on house projects. Were it not for her, *Moonwalk* would never have been published. She coaxed Michael through the entire project and ended up writing almost the entire book herself.

"It was a nightmare, the whole Jackson deal," said one former Doubleday employee. "Dealing with Frank Dileo and John Branca, and Michael himself, was awful. Every detail of everything we did had to have approval from these people who knew diddly-squat about publishing. When we sold the book to England, they had to have approval over the stock of the paper the book would be printed on. That's how ridiculous they were. They were absolute control freaks."

At the same time Doubleday was working on Michael's book, Katherine Jackson submitted a proposal for *her* book about the Jacksons. Jacqueline Onassis passed the proposal around the publishing house to see if there was any interest, and everyone agreed that there was nothing in Katherine's book worth publishing. "It was a real joke," said the former Doubleday employee, "about the kinds of foods Michael will and won't eat, and how wonderful all the Jacksons are."

Three hundred thousand copies of *Moonwalk*—which was dedicated to Fred Astaire and had a three-paragraph introduction by Jacqueline Onassis, Michael's editor—were published. In the book, Michael hinted at some of the troubled moments in his history but, for the most part, insisted on maintaining the family's image of cohesiveness. He admitted to two nose jobs and the cleft in the chin, "but that's it." He wrote that he was "one of the loneliest people in the world" but didn't say why. As Marc Weiss, a critic for the *Los Angeles Herald Examiner*, put it, "Watching Jackson, and listening to his music, it's easy to see the anger in his eyes and moves, and hear it in his voice. But except for some defensive attacks against the press, where is it in *Moonwalk*? What's he so mad about? *Moonwalk* gives no clue. Everyone Jackson ever met is described as 'wonderful.' Hasn't he ever worked with anybody who wasn't nice, not even a little bit?''

''Because Michael doesn't give interviews, all the public has is this book, and I'll tell you what—about eighty percent of it is false,'' said his brother Marlon. ''Why am I saying this now? Because new articles keep relating back to the book, and I just can't have people go on thinking this is the truth.''

LaToya said that she found the book to be ''a disappointment. Cold and impersonal. What did he leave out?'' she asked. ''The beginning, the middle, and the end.''

From April to December 1988, Michael was once again overseas with the Bad tour. Michael toured Europe: Italy (190,000 concertgoers); Austria (50,000); Netherlands (135,000); Sweden (110,000); Switzerland (60,000); West Germany, at the Berlin Wall (50,000); France (134,000); and England (360,000). In Leeds, 92,000 people stood and sang ''Happy Birthday'' to Michael (his thirtieth) as he stood quietly onstage.

Wherever Michael went, show business followed. In Switzerland, Elizabeth Taylor and Sophia Loren greeted him after his show. Loren brought twenty-five people with her to his Paris show. In Paris, Rob Lowe and Grace Jones also caught the shows. Tina Turner came to visit in Cologne. In London, Ava Gardner, Harrison Ford, Carly Simon, and Donna Summer attended the shows. When Prince Charles and Princess Diana showed up, Michael was particularly excited. He presented the royal couple and their two children with a check for $450,000—his proceeds from the Wembly concert—for the redevelopment of the Great Ormand Street Children's Hospital. He also gave them tour jackets and cassettes of *Bad*. He offered to give Prince Charles dance lessons.

Michael kept his distance from his crew and musicians. They never knew at what hotel he was staying. They never saw him, except when he was onstage. A dozen security guards had been hired to protect him and to make sure his accommodations were secure.

It wasn't all work, however. ''He would always take time to see the sights,'' according to Michael's voice teacher, Seth Riggs. ''I recall that when we were rehearsing in Liverpool, he stopped the rehearsal so that we could look at some beautiful clouds that had wafted in. That's how Michael is. They closed down the Louvre in Paris for a whole day while Michael and the rest of us went through. In Rome, Franco Zeffirelli gave him a big party. All of the lovely crème de la crème were there, and suddenly Zeffirelli couldn't find Michael. He looked all over and finally found Michael in a room with a bunch of little kids in their pajamas, and they were all playing.

"He's the most natural, loving person I've ever known, a very good person, as corny as that sounds," continued Riggs, who still works with Michael on a regular basis. "He'll see a picture of a baby, and if it's a cute kid, he will go absolutely gaga over the picture. During the tour, on his nights off, he would go into a toy store and buy ten of this and ten of that and then stay up all night long putting batteries into the toys, making certain each and every one worked so that he could have them ready to give to kids backstage the next day. As if he didn't have enough to worry about."

On one leg of the tour, Michael brought along Jimmy Safechuck, a ten-year-old Californian boy. Michael had a copy of one of his stage uniforms made for Safechuck so that they could dress alike. Most people found the relationship with Safechuck strange, especially when Michael would take him on shopping sprees in toy stores. He spent thousands of dollars on toys for Safechuck in London. At one point, Michael had to cancel two shows because he caught a cold from Jimmy.

Another young friend of Michael's—not Safechuck—said, "I can't have my name in the book because I think Michael would be upset. But I can say that he's just like any other guy when we hang out. He never talks about himself, always what is going on with other people. We never talk about show business. Sometimes he'll put on a disguise—a wig and a mustache—when we're in public, and maybe two or three out of a hundred people will recognize him. When we go to Disneyland, we'll go through the back and take all the alleys and back ways and get in front of the lines and stuff. He can't wait in the line, no way. He would cause a riot. We move fast through Disneyland, because if people get a good look at him, they'll recognize him and that'll be it for that outing.

"He's one of the nicest people I've ever known. He's so smart. He knows a lot about everything. He's a kid. He never really had a childhood, and he's having it now. The stuff I read in the papers about him, I know it's all a bunch of B.S. I just ignore it. A couple of times I've asked him about girlfriends and stuff, but we never really get into that. We don't talk about the plastic surgery either, because it's really none of my business. He never brings it up. It's not like he says, 'Well, how do you like my new chin?' It's hard to get in touch with him, though. I usually have to call his secretary, and then a couple of days later, he'll call me.''

After Michael gave Jimmy Safechuck's parents a hundred-thousand-dollar Rolls-Royce, Frank Dileo told Michael he might want to consider breaking off his friendship with Jimmy. There were rumors that the relationship was somehow perverted. Michael was hurt. ''It was a perfectly innocent friendship,'' Jerome Howard said. ''But some people felt Michael was too much in the kid's life for it to be healthy for either him or the kid. Michael was lonely without him, though.''

A clue to Michael's loneliness can be found in a telephone call to his parents in September 1988 from Liverpool. Katherine told a friend that she and Joe were surprised to hear from their son. ''I'm tired, Kate,'' she recalled Michael as having said in a weary voice. ''I need a break. The family is falling apart, do you know that?''

Katherine told Michael she agreed with him and asked what she could do about it. Michael let out a long sigh and said he wanted to have a talk with her and Joe when he returned. Then Michael talked to his father. He apologized to Joe for some of the material written in his autobiography critical of him. He explained that he hadn't written the whole book himself, and that the critical portions were written by ''someone else.'' (Presumably Michael was referring to Shaye Areheart.)

Joe wanted to know if Michael was going to rejoin his brothers after this tour. Michael told him he didn't want to, ''and please don't push me about that.'' Then Joe told Michael that everything Michael had ever heard about Joe wanting to exploit him, wanting to profit from him, was not true. ''I don't want to be involved in your business, Michael,'' Katherine remembered Joe as having said. ''I have money problems, yeah. But all I want is for us to be a family again. Don't you want that?''

The conversation ended on a hopeful note. Katherine and Joe felt optimistic that they would soon have their son back.

In December 1988, Frank Dileo made the announcement that Michael Jackson was retiring from the road to spend more time working on film possibilities. ''Dirty Diana'' realized Frank Dileo's prophecy of five number one hits from the *Bad* album. *Bad* was the first album in pop history to generate five number one singles. That dream fulfilled, Michael had made it clear that the Bad tour would be his last. ''Michael Jackson does not want to do concerts again of any size,'' Frank said. By this time, the estimated ticket revenues of Michael's tour exceeded $108 million. He had sold approximately $25 million in merchandising (so the one million dollars he gave to his mother to persuade her not to go into merchandising had been reimbursed to Michael many times over).

Michael Jackson, now thirty years old, had been a professional entertainer for more than two decades. "It's in my blood," he had said many times. "I can't imagine not being on the stage." Most of his associates also could not believe that Michael would stop performing.

"I've made enough money for now," Michael said. "That's it. I'm done." Most people did not think he was serious. However, there was a reason behind Michael's decision to quit the road that most people did not know about. He felt that he was being cheated while he was on tour, and the only way to stop that from happening—at least for a while—was to spend more time at home. A former business associate explained, "When Michael is working, he doesn't have time to check on his books and see where all his money is going. In Michael's situation, much of his staff—people he trusts—make a lot of money when he's on tour, wheeling and dealing on the side.

"This isn't unusual. Bill Cosby once said he discovered that someone on his staff had a $9 million house as big as his! Same thing with Michael. He hires people he trusts and pays them a lot of money, but then many of them skim a whole lot off the top. When Michael was on tour, money was changing hands left and right. He was losing a lot, and that's why he decided to quit touring. It has nothing to do with being tired; it has to do with being ripped off."

"Let me tell you something," one former Jackson associate confirmed. "Before any deal is made on Michael Jackson's behalf, there are all kinds of side deals negotiated and finalized by everyone around him, and that's way before Michael knows anything at all about the main deal. Folks he trusts make money on Michael Jackson hand over fist. People who work for him don't even bring ideas to Michael unless they know they're gonna make some money on the side, above and beyond what they're paid by him. It's no wonder he doesn't trust anyone. Believe it or not, Joe Jackson has warned Michael about this. Joe often does have Michael's best interest at heart."

Joe Jackson said, "The one thing I know is that Michael's managers don't want me anywhere around. I'd love to know if Michael is aware of what his people are doing, which I don't think he is. We're talking about millions and millions of dollars."

* * *

Michael Jackson may have wanted to retire, but his family still planned on the Korean tour and hoped he would be a part of it. The family needed the money now, more than ever. In fact, Joe was in a financial dilemma. He had lost over $700,000 in dried-up oil wells and over $250,000 in a beverage company, JoCola.

Three years earlier, in 1985, Joseph had entered into an agreement with real estate developer and entrepreneur Gary Berwin to purchase the Berwin Entertainment Center complex on Sunset Boulevard in Hollywood for $7.1 million. The building, built in 1924, used to be the Hollywood Athletic Club, where John Wayne played pool and Clark Gable liked to make love to girls he had snuck in. It is a Hollywood landmark.

"The asking price was $12 million, but we negotiated it down to $7.1 million," said Gary Berwin, who is highly regarded in the entertainment community for helping to revitalize Hollywood's image. "Joe indicated that money was never a problem. I had no reason to doubt him. Because of Michael Jackson—who had just bought The Beatles' catalogue at this time for $47 million—I believed this family had access to a lot of money. In fact, Joe laughed when I brought up the question of money. 'With the kind of family I've got, money's no object,' he said."

Berwin and Jackson entered into a deal in which Berwin would own 15 percent of the real estate, Jackson the other 85 percent. The two would be equal partners in a recording studio, nightclub, and private club in the building. "He told me that Michael would come and visit the club often, and just his presence would make the place happen," Berwin said. "He could come in through the guard gates, take the private elevator, and no one would know when he was coming or going, which Joe said Michael would find to be marvelous. The access to the recording studio would be very secretive, which was good for Michael. Joe also thought Michael would enjoy the building's character and architecture."

Gary Berwin asked Joe, "What makes you so sure that Michael is going to want to be involved in this?"

Joe answered, "Look, if I'm involved, then it's a known fact Michael Jackson will be. You can bank on it. If I'm here and Katherine's here, Michael and all the kids will be here."

"One minute Joe needed a loan to buy the building, the next minute he didn't," Berwin continued. "Then he did again, then he didn't. Then he was going to be partnered with Don King, then he wasn't. He was surrounded by all of these unethical people who were either ripping him off or teaching him how to rip off others."

Finally, Joseph decided to pay for the building in cash. Though he only needed to pay one point seven million as a down payment, he wrote a check for the full $7.1 million and gave it to Berwin, telling him not to deposit it "until Friday." On Friday, he called and told him to "wait until Monday." Then on Monday he called and told him to "wait until Friday." This went on for a few weeks until Berwin finally deposited the check, which was promptly returned for lack of sufficient funds.

A year later, the matter would be resolved in court when it was ruled that Joe Jackson had to either buy the property or be responsible for damages incurred by his bad business dealings. He could not afford to buy. Gary Berwin said, "We finally got Michael served to find out if and how he had led his father into thinking he would help out. He was in a limousine at the time, and somebody walked up to him and handed him a paper. He went to sign it, thinking the person wanted an autograph. It was a summons. But Michael just ignored it."

By October of 1988, damages to Gary Berwin had been assessed at $3 million; Berwin was almost ruined by this deal gone awry. Since Joe Jackson did not have $3 million, Berwin obtained a judgment against him for that amount. To this day, Berwin has not collected.

"I lost most of my leases in the building, couldn't afford to pay the mortgage on the place, then had a chance to sell it to someone else for millions but couldn't because I was tied to Joe. And all because I got myself into this Jackson family mess," Gary Berwin said. "It cost me six hundred thousand dollars just in legal fees. It was the sorriest thing I'd ever done in my life.

"I couldn't imagine that Michael Jackson, who earns all of these millions, could not give his father one point seven million, which was all he needed as a down payment to own the property. I couldn't believe that Michael would let his father go down the tubes like that. It seemed so purposeful to me. This building would have put Joe on his feet once and for all, and independently of the family. He would never have had to deal with the kids anymore on a business level. I tried to appeal not only to Michael but also to the other kids, all of whom are isolated by hard-nosed lawyers. Not a one of them cared about their father's security. It was pitiful. As much as I grew to dislike Joe, I also felt sorry for him."

In fact, Michael Jackson never misled his father into thinking he would assist him in this matter. Michael wanted nothing to do with the deal from the start. Joe had telephoned Michael earlier in the year and asked him for help.

"It's only a little over a million bucks," Joe said, pleading with his son to get him out of this jam. "Please, *please* help me out."

Joe told a friend that Michael didn't want to have anything to do with him or his problems. "Michael is so incredibly ungrateful," that friend said. "After all Joe did for him, that's a hell of a thing, turning down his old man when the guy is begging for help. You know how hard it is for Joe to beg? I think Michael purposely tried to ruin his father out of spite. A lot of family friends feel that way, I'm sorry to say."

Joe also contacted some of his other children, including Janet, all of whom told him they would not lift a finger to help him. Joe was hurt. Perhaps they didn't think this was such a good investment, considering Joe's record. He knew that his children had ambivalent feelings about him, but he never really thought they were angry enough to put him through such humiliation. Larry Anderson, a friend of Joe's for fifteen years, explained, "Like Jermaine is always telling Joe: business is business and family is family. You gotta separate the two. But Joe doesn't see it that way. He loves his kids. He hoped they would help out. It seems like a lot of money, but really it isn't when you think of all that is made in that family."

And Gary Berwin declared, "You'd think that once a family gets to the point of prestige the Jacksons had achieved, they would act in a respectable manner, but instead they're still scrambling around on the streets shucking and jiving everybody. You would think Michael Jackson is above all that, but he's not. The family does not work together or pull together. Instead they work against each other, and worse yet, they work against the people who have the misfortune of having to do business with other family members."

By December 1988, Joe Jackson had turned desperate. These shows in Korea had to become a reality or he would never be able to get the money together to pay the judgment against him. "I met with Jerome Howard," Gary Berwin said, "who was a nice guy I liked very much. We started comparing notes on how this wacky family was being run. In the final analysis, it didn't look good for either one of us."

At this time, Michael was in Japan on his Bad tour in the country where it had begun an exhausting fifteen months earlier. A Jackson family meeting with the other brothers was set up at the Encino home in the family theater.

First, Joe and Katherine went into the theater and spoke to Jackie, Tito, Marlon, Randy, Jermaine, and Jermaine's fiancée, Margaret

Maldonado. (Jermaine and Hazel were officially divorced in July 1988. Margaret and Jermaine would eventually have a second child.)

The brothers had to be approached carefully, on the outside chance they might not agree to go to Korea. For Joe and Katherine, it was as if they were going into the lion's den, that's how suspicious the brothers were of Joe and his business associates. After about two hours, a relieved Joe came out of the theater and told Jerome, "Don't talk to them about nothing else, just the contracts. Don't be mentionin' the Moonies and all that, 'cause then they're not gonna want to do it. Just talk to them about all the money they're gonna make."

Jerome Howard went into the thirty-seat theater and found the family members scattered about. Jermaine and Margaret were seated near the front. Tito was in the back. Randy sat in one corner, Marlon in another, and Jackie in the middle. Howard stood in front of the screen and delivered a speech about the proposed concerts to the brothers, who were suspicious of him, as they were of anyone who had anything to do with their father. Immediately, Marlon stood up and said, "No way. No more family tours for me. I don't care how many millions are involved, I learned my lesson the last time. Count me out."

Marlon no longer wanted to perform as a member of the Jacksons. When he had trouble getting out of his recording contract after the Victory tour, Michael was gracious enough to personally call CBS Records president Walter Yetnikoff and ask for Marlon's release, which he got. Still, Marlon had ambivalent feelings about Michael. Before the Bad tour, rather than just come out and say that the brothers would not be participating, Michael was evasive.

"I'd hear from friends what was going on," Marlon complained later in an interview. "If he didn't want to tell me the truth, he shouldn't have said anything. But instead, he lies. The last time I got a straight answer from Michael was back in 1984."

Still, Marlon had a warm spot in his heart for his brother. "I just don't want anything to ruin the way I feel about Mike," he said. "I don't think we should work together."

"Too bad for you," Jackie said to Marlon about his decision. " 'Cause I'm in."

"Me too," said Randy.

"I'm in," Jermaine decided after conferring with Margaret.

"Count me in too," Tito piped up.

"But what about Michael?" Randy wanted to know. "What are we gonna do about Michael?"

"We don't need Mike," Jackie said. "We can do it ourselves, without him."

Katherine agreed. "Let's not try to bring Michael into this," she said. "Please, isn't there some way to do this without him?"

Jerome shook his head. He had to be careful how he said it, but the fact was that Olympic Stadium in Seoul seats sixty thousand people and the brothers would certainly need Michael to draw that many ticket-buyers.

"Look, just leave Michael to Mother and me," Jermaine offered. "We'll talk him into it."

"How?" Randy wanted to know.

Jermaine turned to Katherine. She took a deep breath and sighed wearily. "I'll see what I can do," Katherine said finally. "But let me tell you, I'm afraid that if we push Michael, we'll lose him forever. And then what will we do?"

# Chapter

## 30

I'M THANKFUL TO have a big family because, gosh, I think it's a wonderful thing," Michael has said. "So many people are just an only child. But I think a brother and a sister are gifts from God. I really do. I love all of them dearly," he said of his family.

Finally, the Bad tour was almost over; 4.5 million people had paid to see Michael Jackson perform over the last year and a half. Michael's last date abroad was on December 26 in Japan, where he performed nine sold-out concerts. He would have a month off before his closing dates in Los Angeles.

"We're giving Michael his space now," Jermaine said while Michael was on the road. "But after he finishes his tour, we're all going to attack him—with love." After Michael returned to the United States, however, no one in his family was able to attack him with anything. They couldn't even find him. He was exhausted from his trip and did not speak to anyone.

"They think he's shy and he's evasive and all of this," observed his guitarist David Williams. "No. He's just fucking scared and tired of people bugging him."

The family heard that Marlon Brando, who is very close to Michael, had become a house guest at Michael's home. Marlon Brando owns the island of Tetiaroa in Tahiti and has tried to convince Michael to buy a similar island. His son, Miko, worked for Michael as a bodyguard. "I'm at most of the dinners with Brando, and there's not anything earth-shattering being discussed," Frank Dileo had said. "They talk about life, about making movies, how things are done. Brando invited us down to his island three or four times. We were going to go down with Scorsese and De Niro, but we were never able to get away."

Now Michael was hiding. He was tired, and hurt as well,

because his last two singles, "Another Part of Me" and "Smooth Criminal," were not number one hits. He'd had five number ones from the *Bad* album, but that wasn't enough. Michael Jackson wants *every* record to go to number one. The sales of the *Bad* album had stalled at 17 million, an amazing number but a far cry from *Thriller's* sales of almost 40 million. It was obvious that Michael Jackson would not break his own sales record, and the thought depressed him deeply.

When he went out, it was in disguise. He visited a pharmacy in Westwood disguised in a large Afro wig and dark glasses. When the manager was asked how he detected Michael under the disguise, he replied, "I recognized him the minute I saw his nose and chin." When writers John Nichols and "Lance," known as the Hollywood Kids, asked the store owner what Michael had purchased, he answered, "He bought a hand-held power vibrator."

One has to wonder about Michael's outrageous disguises. Often he will go out without a disguise, and usually there is no pandemonium. It seems that when he really wants attention, he wears one of his disguises. They are so ridiculous, Michael usually gets the desired results. Sometimes, though, matters get out of hand. One day Michael went into a jewelry store in Simi Valley, California, wearing a wig under a baseball cap, a phony-looking mustache, and fake bucked teeth. He was with a young boy. Michael kept adjusting his mustache and looking into a mirror. Employees thought he was "casing the joint." A security guard asked the suspicious character to step outside. The guard demanded an explanation about the fake mustache.

"I have to. I'm in disguise. I'm Michael Jackson," was the answer.

When the guard insisted that Michael remove the disguise, he did. By this time, three squad cars had arrived and so had quite a crowd. Of course, now that Michael had caused such a commotion, everyone wanted his autograph. Perhaps the getup did serve a purpose, but not the one most people thought it was supposed to serve. He got attention.

One time all the attention landed him in jail. Michael was driving his Rolls while wearing a disguise. He was stopped by a police officer who thought the automobile "looks like a stolen car." Even today, there is a prevailing racism among some police officers, who routinely stop blacks driving expensive cars. Michael didn't have his license with him. Worse, he had an outstanding ticket. The officer didn't believe he was *the* Michael Jackson when Michael finally removed his disguise. The next thing he knew, he was in the Van Nuys jail. Bill Bray bailed him out.

What brought Michael Jackson out of hiding in January 1989 was his sister LaToya. Michael was now thirty years old and had spent the last twenty years being concerned with the public's perception of him and his family. Ever since that day in 1969 when Berry Gordy and Diana Ross taught him to lie about his age, Michael had understood the importance of public relations. He had always helped to present an image of solidarity where the Jackson family was concerned, even embarking on the Victory tour with his brothers when he really did not want to do so. Now LaToya, thirty-two, was threatening to shatter the family's carefully constructed image of wholesomeness with a *Playboy* magazine layout.

The *Playboy* layout was the culmination of a chain of events that had destroyed LaToya's relationship with her family. LaToya was unhappy because the albums she had thus far recorded were all poor sellers. "I want platinum albums," she complained. But Joe Jackson realized that LaToya had limited vocal ability and that there wasn't much he could do with her. He had tried to convince her to model, but she was ambivalent about that sort of employment even though she was a beautiful girl, especially after plastic surgery. She, like Michael, has had her nose operated on more than once, though she denies ever having any rhinoplasty. "I don't know who she's trying to fool," Marlon laughed.

When LaToya decided that she no longer wanted Joe to manage her, she followed the example set by Michael and her brothers. She fired her father by having her attorney send letters to him at home, even though she still lived there with him. Joe ignored the letters. Finally, she decided to confront him. " 'I will sit on you for five years before I ever let you go,' " she said he told her. "In other words, he was saying I'd never get anywhere and he'd make certain of that."

When LaToya asked Katherine for assistance, Katherine said, "Look, I don't want to get in the middle of this. It's between you and your father." Then she turned and went upstairs to her bedroom.

Hoping to placate their daughter into staying at home, Joe and Katherine hired an outsider, Jack Gordon, to manage LaToya under Joe's direction. Her parents hoped that she would no longer feel trapped by Joe. Gordon had served time in prison for trying to bribe the Nevada State Gaming Commission. He has also been linked to underworld dealings and allegedly ran a brothel in Nevada for four years. Gordon became more than LaToya's business associate. Before anyone in the family knew what was happening, he and LaToya were plotting a way to extricate her from Joe and Katherine's hold.

"Gordon threatened my life," Jerome Howard claimed, "when I questioned him about some major expenses he and LaToya were running up on Joe's account. The man is dangerous. But LaToya feels that Joe is the dangerous one. 'Do you know my father?' she asked me once. 'No, you don't,' she answered for me. 'You don't know what he's like, Jerome. You don't know what I've *been* through.' "

In March 1988—just three days after Michael moved out of the Encino home—thirty-two-year-old LaToya took off with Gordon, who was in his mid-forties at the time. She took just two suitcases, left her Mercedes in the driveway, and hasn't been back home since.

The family blamed Jack Gordon. Joe made no bones about how much the family despised Gordon. The feeling was mutual. "I love Joe like poison," Gordon said.

When Katherine heard that her daughter planned to strip for Hugh Hefner's magazine, she couldn't believe it. Neither could anyone else who knew LaToya. "LaToya was always the puritanical one," said longtime friend Joyce McCrae. "She was always the one with the high-collared sweaters and long dresses. No one *ever* saw her body. She was very modest."

"I used to always cover my body from head to toe," LaToya told *Playboy*. "I guess my shyness came from growing up the way I did, being so sheltered and having a strict father."

Katherine telephoned LaToya and asked if it was true. "Are you posing for a *Playboy* centerfold? Please, 'Toya, tell me it's not true," she recalled asking.

"Oh, Mother," LaToya said. "Where do you hear these things? Of course it's not true."

Later LaToya would explain why she lied. "Mother did ask me if I had posed for *Playboy*. She asked very specifically, 'Did you pose for the *Playboy* centerfold?' I told her no, and that was the truth. I did pose for *Playboy*—but *not* for the centerfold."

Katherine telephoned Michael and, with a sigh of relief, told him that everything the family had heard about LaToya and *Playboy* was a lie, but by now Michael had heard otherwise. He decided to take matters into his own hands. After making a few phone calls, he discovered that there would be a meeting at Hugh Hefner's mansion about the LaToya pictorial. He drove over and, under the guise of wanting to visit Hefner's animals, planned to snoop around. As soon as he walked into the house, he noticed a group of men sitting around a table nervously stuffing color photographs into their brief-cases. Michael met with Hefner, who promised to send him the photographs by messenger later in the week, "after they've been touched up."

A week later, when Michael received the photographs, he got the shock of his life. "I can't believe this is my sister," he told a person who still works for Michael today. "This ruins the family image. That's it. There's nothing left."

Michael's employee said, "All he cared about after seeing the pictures was his mother and her blood pressure. 'I'm afraid that when she sees these pictures, she'll have a heart attack for sure,' he told me. 'I'm not even going to tell her I have them. Hopefully, they'll touch up 'Toya's, uh, her, uh, nipples, at least. I mean, do we have to see her *nipples?*''

Michael telephoned LaToya, hoping to get a copy of the final layout from her. She says he told her he thought the photos were lovely, which doesn't seem likely. Then he asked her to send the final layout to him by Federal Express next-day delivery. She refused.

A month later, the layout was published.

When family members first saw the eleven photographs, they were astonished. Could this really be LaToya, posing nude with a sixty-pound boa constrictor slithering between her legs? "Boas aren't dangerous unless they're hungry," she observed in the accompanying text.

After the initial shock, there was shame and embarrassment. Katherine and Rebbie said they were both humiliated; Rebbie said she could barely leave her home for fear that someone would ask her about her naked sister. "Everybody was hurt, even the grandchildren," she said. For Katherine and Joe, seeing their daughter nude in *Playboy* was sheer agony. One of their friends claimed that they would not leave the house for a month, not because they were afraid to be confronted but rather because they were so heartsick over what LaToya had done. They were certain that Jack Gordon had somehow convinced their child that posing for *Playboy* would be a good career move.

Michael was angry with his sister, but not for reasons most people might assume. He certainly did not like the photographs—he told one friend that, as far as he was concerned, the layout was pornographic—but he is open-minded enough not to begrudge his sister the right to exploit herself if she feels she must for the sake of her career. He certainly has exploited himself enough to know that that's show biz.

Gina Sprague, who once worked for Joe Jackson, observed, "Michael knows that LaToya can't do much else. She's not a singer and everyone in the family knows that. She's a beautiful girl. She must use that to her advantage. That was my idea for her years ago when I worked for her father."

Michael's fury resulted from LaToya's claim that he actually *approved* of the pictures and was glad she had taken them. That was not true.

"When he started hearing LaToya say on television that he was the only one in the family who approved, he went nuts," said Steven Harris, a former associate. "He called his mother, and they had a long, painful conversation about it. 'How can I talk to her about anything if she twists what I say for her own purposes?' he asked. Katherine and Michael decided it was best if Michael never spoke to LaToya again. And that's what happened. He changed his number and didn't give it to her. Of course, she can't get it from anyone in the family. No one would dare give it to her once Michael made it known that he does not want to speak to his sister."

It was reported that LaToya received in excess of one million dollars for her work in *Playboy*. But she told one reporter that she did not do it for the money, but rather "as an opportunity to show the world that women should not be ashamed of their bodies."

To Hollywood columnist Frank Swertlow, she was a little more honest. "It was a matter of my letting my family know I am an individual and I want my independence. That's very difficult when you come from a large family and you've been controlled all of your life."

Suddenly, much to the Jackson family's embarrassment, sister LaToya's big breasts became big news. There was a great deal of speculation as to whether or not she had had breast implants. On "The Arsenio Hall Show," Madonna charged that LaToya had indeed undergone surgery. "I know because people have told me," she said, adding that it was obvious that LaToya's bosom had grown "in a week."

LaToya acted as if she was insulted. However, she and Jack Gordon were media-savvy enough to know that they couldn't generate better publicity than a "feud" with Madonna.

"Madonna was the one who had to have breast surgery," LaToya said. "It was her only chance to look anything like a woman. I saw a photo of her where she showed one of her new breasts. I've gotta tell you, they're still not as good as mine."

Jack Gordon further offered Arsenio Hall a night with LaToya so that the talk show host could see for himself that her breasts were real. "So far, he has wimped out," LaToya said. It would appear that there was no end to what Gordon and LaToya Jackson would do to keep their names in the public eye.

Michael Jackson instructed some members of his staff never to bring up the subject of LaToya's *Playboy* layout in his presence. "I don't want to hear one more word about my sister's breasts," Michael said. "I just want to forget the whole thing ever happened."

Michael's final dates in Los Angeles took place at the end of January 1989 at the Sports Arena. Diana Ross, Elizabeth Taylor, Dionne Warwick, and many other celebrities attended the concerts, as well as Katherine and Janet Jackson. Michael dedicated his Motown hits medley to Berry Gordy, who was sitting with Diahann Carroll and Suzanne dePasse.

Michael had performed 123 concerts in fifteen countries on four continents since the tour began in September 1987. The show's weekly expenses were between $500,000 and $650,000. By the time the tour was over, it had grossed over $125 million at the box office.

Michael said to an associate that he wanted to be emotional when he performed his last show at the Sports Arena, but was just too tired to bother.

"I'm not saying he's not going to perform live again," Frank Dileo told writer Paul Grein just before the show, clarifying his earlier statement that Michael was planning to retire from the stage. "He may do a show here or there, but I don't see him ever going out on the road again with twelve semis and a hundred and thirty-seven people. It's a very hard tour. It's two hours and eight minutes of working constantly. It's exhausting. He's got the biggest gross and has played to the most people in history. What are we going to do next time? Play for two years? That would kill *me*."

Dileo said that Michael had "stacks and stacks of scripts and proposals" to begin considering, and that finding the right film property would now be the prime consideration.

"Now that Michael was finished with the tour, Kenneth Choi wanted to start spending money to get Michael Jackson's signature on that Moonies contract. I was getting faxes left and right, 'We need Michael, we must have Michael, how do we get Michael?' " Jerome Howard said. "Finally, in desperation, the Koreans came up with an idea, a reward."

In February 1989, a bounty was placed on Michael Jackson's head. The price: one million dollars.

"Anyone—any family member, any business associate—who

could get Michael Jackson's signature on this contract would get a million bucks," Howard added. "That money came straight from the Moonies. So now *everyone* wanted to convince Michael."

Even though Michael kept a low profile, he still managed to upset Joe in ways that had nothing to do with the Korean deal. Jerome Howard said, "Joe was pissed off because Michael was having his security guards go to the house and take things out, his possessions, different memorabilia. The stuff would be there one day and gone the next. Michael found out that his father was trying to establish a Jacksons museum in Las Vegas, and he didn't want any of his stuff to be exploited by Joe. Instead, he wanted to start his own museum in Las Vegas with Steve Wynn [owner of the Mirage Hotel]. So he was taking his stuff out of the house for that purpose. It was making Joe crazy."

According to Howard, Katherine told him that she located Michael at his home and telephoned him there. As she gently tried to explain the family's plans about Korea, Joe became impatient. He snatched the phone from her hand. "Michael, now you listen here," he declared. "You said you wanted us to be a family again. Now, I got these rich Korean people and they got this big deal and I want you to do this thing, Michael, 'cause we're gonna make a lot of money and we *need* this money and you *know* we do and—"

"Joseph, put Mother back on the phone," Michael said.

Michael then told Katherine to forget the idea because he wouldn't even consider another family venture, especially if his father was in command. He reminded Katherine of the time in 1985 when Joe joined a Hollywood producer to develop a film based on his song "Beat It" to star Michael, and Michael didn't know anything about it. He later had to disavow any connection to it, which was embarrassing. "He's always doing things to get me involved in projects with him, and I'm not going along with any of them," Michael said. He didn't want to tour with the brothers again either. "That's over."

"I mean it," he concluded. "Forget it, Kat. [Michael often called his mother 'Kat.'] I won't do it and I want you to please just drop it. Do you understand?"

"The most common misconception about Michael Jackson is that he's a wimp," noted longtime family intimate Joyce McCrae. "That he's soft and you can get him to do anything. That's not the case. He does what he wants to do, and he's no pushover. He can be as assertive as he wants to be. Some people treat dealing with Michael like they're walking into a marshmallow, when actually they're walking into a brick wall."

Janet Jackson concurs. "Just because you're not loud doesn't mean you don't have control of your life. Mike is the shyest of us all, but I don't think I could ever find anyone more in control of his life than he is."

In February 1989, Joe and Katherine told Jerome that they could not afford to pay him his salary—he had settled for three thousand to forty-five hundred dollars per month, even though they originally agreed to pay him ten thousand. So Howard became even more interested in consummating the Korean concert deal to generate some revenue for the family—and for himself. He decided to go directly to Frank Dileo for assistance in obtaining Michael Jackson's cooperation. Unfortunately, no one in the family knew how to get to Dileo. Katherine and Joe never liked meeting with Frank about anything, because they were always afraid that he would go back to Michael and misrepresent what had been said at the meeting. Since they preferred to think that Frank didn't even exist in Michael's life, they didn't keep tabs on his whereabouts.

Jerome Howard finally had to pay an associate of Frank's two thousand dollars for an introduction to Dileo, who, as it turned out, was at a weight-reduction center run by Duke University in North Carolina. A meeting was arranged between Dileo and Kenneth Choi in a North Carolina hotel room in February 1989. Dileo told Choi that if Michael's beloved mother was involved in this plan, he would talk to Michael again about the tour. At that point, Choi opened his briefcase and took out two cashier's checks for $500,000 each.

"These are for you," he declared. "A million dollars."

Frank laughed in his face. "I can't take a million bucks from you. What, are you crazy?" he said. "Are you nuts? I can't guarantee Michael Jackson will do anything for you. Michael Jackson is a smart man. He makes up his own mind. No one *tells* Michael Jackson to do anything. Do you understand?"

Kenneth Choi confirmed this. "Yes, I did offer Frank money, but he turned me down. That impressed me a great deal. He said that if Michael did go to Korea, *then* he might take some money afterwards as a bonus."

"Frank Dileo could have had one million bucks that day, but he didn't take it," Jerome Howard said. "He could have accepted the money, never gotten Michael's signature, and it would have taken a lifetime in court before he'd ever have to return it, if ever. But he's an honorable man. Later, Frank told me that he gently talked to Michael about Korea. He said, 'You can't just ask Michael straight out to do something, like Joe did on the phone. Michael has to be stroked. His ego has to be massaged thoroughly before he will do anything.' ''

Frank Dileo apparently discussed the situation with Michael during a telephone call. It was business as usual, he said, and "Everything was hunky-dory."

Three days later, Frank Dileo was fired.

Michael's publicist Lee Solters issued a terse statement saying, "Michael Jackson and Frank Dileo have announced an amicable parting." Jackson said, "I thank Frank for his contribution on my behalf during the past several years." Frank Dileo had no comment to make. Most entertainment industry observers were surprised by the unexpected move.

The day after he was fired, Frank telephoned Kenneth Choi in San Francisco.

"I just wanted to tell you that Michael and I broke up," Frank said.

"What? What's that mean, 'broke up?' '' Choi asked. "I don't understand."

"The kid fired me. I'm finished. *Ka-poot*."

"Oh," Kenneth said. "*That* I understand."

Why was Frank Dileo fired? Immediately, word circulated within Michael Jackson's camp that forty-one-year-old Dileo had taken the million-dollar reward money and Michael found out about it and fired him. In truth, Michael didn't even know there was a bounty on his head.

Others have said that since Michael was interested in films, he felt that Frank—a music industry veteran—was no longer useful to him. That seemed plausible, but in fact, Dileo had connections in the film world, and those he did not have he could have gotten just by virtue of being Michael Jackson's manager.

Actually, Michael was upset with Frank for a variety of reasons. First of all, Michael felt that Dileo had taken too much credit for the Michael Jackson phenomenon. He was tired of other people—like Quincy Jones—taking credit for what he felt was his own destiny. Frank was giving interviews to the press touting his accomplishments for Michael, and every one that Michael read made him cringe.

"Frank isn't creative," Michael told an associate. "Let's face it. I come up with all of the ideas. The only ideas he comes up with are lousy ones."

Where Michael was concerned, Frank had also become a bit too dictatorial in recent years. For instance, when the Bad tour played Pittsburgh, Frank arranged a gathering so that he could introduce Michael to his friends and relatives. (Frank is from Pittsburgh.)

"Michael, I expect you to be there at eight sharp. Do you understand?"

"Who is he to tell me what to do?" Michael asked an associate. "*I* tell *him* what to do."

Michael did show up, but purposely an hour late.

Afterwards, Frank let Michael have it. "You embarrassed me," he screamed at him. "What's wrong with you? How could you do that to me?"

Michael just seethed as Frank laid into him. Finally, Bill Bray began shouting at Frank to leave Michael alone. It was an unpleasant scene.

The press reported that Michael fired Dileo because Dileo had bungled a major multimillion-dollar deal for domestic theatrical release of Michael's ninety-minute video *Moonwalker*, which is part clip compilation and part musical autobiography. The film featured Michael's innovative video of "Leave Me Alone," in which he spoofed his image by showing a shrine to Elizabeth Taylor, a newspaper headline that read "Michael Confides in Chimp," and a discomforting segment in which he dances with the Elephant Man's skeleton. In the video, Michael moves through a surreal world of floating chairs, huge chomping teeth and amusement park rides. It took twenty-five people six months to make this four-minute-and-forty-five-second video.

The project (including the eight-minute Smooth Criminal video, the thirty-two minutes of dramatic footage before and after the song, as well as the "Leave Me Alone" and "Speed Demon" videos) cost Michael Jackson approximately $27 million. *Moonwalker* was released theatrically in Japan, but not in the United States because of numerous disagreements. It had been reported that Frank Dileo was behind the decision not to release *Moonwalker* domestically, angering international distributors who had bought the film for theatrical releases. When the announcement was made that there would be no domestic deal, many overseas theaters pulled the film, or scaled down promotion and publicity. This fiasco cost Michael many millions of dollars in lost box office revenue in the United States and abroad.

In the end, though, according to Frank Dileo, he came up with a multimillion-dollar offer to distribute the film domestically, and someone else in Michael's organization talked Michael out of it. So while Michael may have been angry at the way distribution of *Moonwalker* was handled, he wasn't angry enough at Frank to fire him over it.

Most of Michael's associates felt that Michael *should* have been angry at Frank, however, for allowing him to spend $27 million on *Moonwalker*. As a good manager, Dileo should have done something to prevent Michael from spending that much money on a video project whose budget should not have exceeded $5 million. In the end, the video made approximately $30 million in over-the-counter sales and other deals, another tribute to John Branca's negotiating savvy and Walter Yetnikoff's persistence (CBS Music Video Enterprises distributed the tape). No home music video had ever come close to generating that much money for its artist. Still, after *Moonwalker*, Michael would say that he felt ''poor'' and didn't want to spend any more money on major projects ''for a long, long time.''

Another problem with Frank was that Michael had become disgusted with the tabloid image of himself that he believed Frank was continuing to propagate. Of course, the hyperbaric chamber and Elephant Man's bones stories were Michael's ideas—not Frank's—and when those stories became popular, the public began to perceive him as being ''Wacko-Jacko'' (as they call him in Europe).

One story that appeared in the *Star* on August 2, 1988, was particularly disturbing to Michael: MICHAEL JACKSON BANS 4 PALS FROM TOUR AFTER THEY FLUNK AIDS TEST. The article said that Michael fired four employees because they had tested positive for AIDS-related HIV (Human Immunodeficiency Virus). ''I'm really afraid of AIDS,'' Michael was quoted as having said. ''I think about having lunch with these guys and shaking hands and spending so much time together.''

The article also said that Michael was spending a fortune having his own frozen blood moved around with him wherever he goes. ''You never know when you may need blood, and the only blood I can be sure of is my own,'' Michael supposedly said.

Now Michael was paying the price for the idea he had had years ago to have a Plexiglas shield constructed between him and his audiences to protect him from germs during the 1984 Victory tour. He realized at the time that the idea was absurd and dropped it, but not before it made the news.

This peculiar idea came to Michael during the time after his burn accident when he had become fascinated with medicine. He became a ravenous reader of medical books and enjoyed reading and hearing about the most dreadful diseases imaginable. For a while, he became obsessed with learning about different surgeries. In fact, Michael has actually witnessed operations at UCLA Medical Center. Doctors who are friends of friends of Michael's have permitted him to watch from the observation booth as they operate on patients—people who have no idea before being anesthetized that Michael Jackson will be observing their surgeries.

"Michael's really curious about surgery," said one former associate. "He gets off on it. He can watch for hours. He especially likes to watch different plastic surgeries—tummy tucks, liposuctions, he's into all of that, I know that for a fact. I had heard that he has even witnessed brain surgeries, but I don't know if that's true. I wouldn't doubt it, though. That sounds like Michael."

He may be interested in medicine, but Michael is not obsessed with AIDS. "When Michael read that report, he became quite upset," said Michael Tucker, a friend of the Jackson family (and not the actor). "Of all diseases, AIDS is one that Michael is most sensitive about. 'Why would they write this about me?' he said. 'This isn't me at all. What if people believe this? What are they going to think of me?'

"He became furious and wanted to know where the report came from. Michael wanted an answer. Michael's image now was such that there was no way he could fight the tabloid's perception of him."

Joyce McCrae observed, "The sensational hype about Michael was becoming more real. It was played up, and before anyone knew what was happening, it was becoming a real part of the public's perception of him. It was becoming hard to separate what was real and not real, not just for the public but I think for Michael too."

There was another story in the tabloids that Michael refused to kiss the famous Blarney Stone in Ireland because he was afraid he'd get AIDS if he did. That wasn't true either, yet *Rolling Stone* reprinted it.

"If I find out that anyone in my organization planted these hurtful stories, that person will be fired, and I mean it," Michael threatened. Of course, no one would admit to planting them. Moreover, some were just fabrications not planted by anyone but the writers.

It's not known if Michael fired Frank Dileo because he wanted to end his wacky image in the tabloids. (It is true, however, that after Dileo was fired, the sensational stories were published with much less frequency.)

Besides the fact that Michael did not feel Dileo was creative— and had become too possessive—the main reason Michael dismissed Frank Dileo was because he was disappointed that the *Bad* album was not as successful as *Thriller*. It "only" sold about twenty million copies worldwide by this time, roughly one-fifth of what Michael had projected it should sell. *Thriller* sold twenty-four million in the United States; *Bad* sold six million.

"Michael was pissed off," said one friend of Frank Dileo's. "He had his heart set on another huge, *huge* album. When he didn't get what he wanted, he acted like a spoiled little kid. He threw some temper tantrums. He cried. Michael is very dramatic when he wants to be. Frank would never tell anyone this, but I know he had his hands full with the kid. He had a lot to deal with.''

"But we did the best we could,'' Frank said. "We made the best album and the best videos we could. We don't have anything to be ashamed of.''

That may be true, but people were whispering in Michael's ear that Frank should have done a better job. Doubts began to creep into Michael's mind. He fully expected *Bad* to be the biggest-selling album of all time, and when it wasn't, he blamed Frank Dileo. He had to blame *someone*.

Ron Weisner, who once managed Michael in the early eighties, observed, "If something goes wrong, the manager is the bad guy. If the artists have career problems, they can't take it out on the public, so they take it out on you. Many performers are dreamers or completely unrealistic. And it's hard to be rational with irrational people. When I meet with artists in my office, I close my door and say, '*This* is reality. What goes on out there is show business.' ''

Because Michael refused to be interviewed, Frank Dileo had developed a high media profile as his spokesman. Many celebrities—and Michael is one of them—do not like it when their representatives become celebrities. Michael Jackson's ego is fragile. "Frank was becoming too well known for Michael's taste,'' said a former associate. "At that point, Michael decided he had to go. Then others on his staff starting blaming Frank when money was missing. That was ludicrous. Frank never took a dime that wasn't his. But Michael started believing what he heard, looking for an excuse to get rid of Frank.''

Perhaps Michael felt he had valid reasons for firing Frank Dileo, but he did it in a cowardly way. He had John Branca telephone Dileo and say, "Michael doesn't want to work with you anymore.''

"Okay, fine with me,'' Frank said, trying to act nonchalant when, he would say later, his heart was breaking. "I just want to get paid whatever is owed to me, and I'll be on my way.''

"Well, aren't you angry?'' Branca pressed.

"Hell no,'' Frank said. "If he doesn't want me, I don't want to be around. See you later.'' With that, Frank said he hung up. He then left the weight-reduction center, "because I had to get to work. I was out of a job.''

About a year later, Frank would say there was "no warning. Did it anger me? Yes. The way it was done was an insult to my family. My children were taunted at school. It was brought up to my wife. He took away my faith in people. For a long time, I've not been as trusting.''

Michael Jackson and Frank Dileo had been inseparable for five years. ''I was with that kid every day,'' he recalled. ''Some days you could have a decent conversation with him. Some days he was on another planet.''

Frank was prominently featured on the *Bad* album jacket, where a picture of him and Michael was captioned ''another great team.'' Michael devoted a full page to photos of him and Frank in his lavish concert tour booklet. In fact, Frank had often said that he thought of Michael as a son, ''and he referred to me as a second dad.''

''I got closer to him than anybody else in his life,'' Dileo said. He had even advised Michael about his plastic surgery, telling him that when he was a youngster, he too wanted a cleft in his chin like Kirk Douglas. ''But that's enough,'' he told Michael. ''No more surgery.''

Frank felt that the least Michael could have done was fire him personally. To Michael, Dileo was simply a capable businessman who had exhausted his usefulness. Indeed, in many ways Michael Jackson grew up to be as cold and calculating as Joe Jackson. It would seem that Michael had no positive male role models in his family. Joe had been a bully for years. In an effort to look after his family's best interests, Joe allowed no one to question his authority. Because he didn't let them think for themselves, his children didn't learn from their own mistakes. As they became adults, they had no sense of how to handle their money or their fame.

Worst of all, Joe was a terrible role model in matters of integrity. For years, he had openly conducted affairs with other women, and most of his sons seemed to follow in his footsteps. When it came to business, his eye was on the quick buck first and foremost. He may have preached loyalty, but he didn't seem to practice it. And when he wanted something, he could be ruthless. For him, the end always justified the means. He was suspicious of everyone, because he expected others to be as unethical as he was. Some of this attitude rubbed off on Michael.

''He doesn't trust anyone in this world,'' Frank Dileo would say. ''Not a single soul. I kept telling him, 'Michael, one day you're gonna have to trust *someone.*' But maybe he has good reason not to trust. A lot of people have done him wrong.''

Frank Dileo's firing was handled the same way Michael dismissed his previous manager, Ron Weisner (of Weisner-DeMann), in the early eighties, without notice or warning, and not personally. ''I was devastated, and I am not embarrassed or ashamed to tell you," Weisner said. "I was walking flat-footed for a month because I thought Michael and I had a great relationship. I was crushed."

"After what he did to Frank, the word about Michael Jackson in the entertainment industry was not good," said one leading publicist. "Most people think that, in the end, Michael would screw you if you worked for him. Along with John Branca, Frank Dileo gave the man five number one hits and the most profitable worldwide tour in the history of show business. He was obviously a good manager. Now Michael has a reputation of getting very close to you and then having somebody else fire you. He's a major star, so everyone will take the chance. But no one goes to work for Michael with any sense of security. Nobody trusts the guy anymore."

Frank Dileo would not just go away, however. He never believed he was paid fairly for some of the projects he had undertaken, but said that anytime he asked to "up the ante"—asked Michael for more money—Michael would go to "seven or eight other people to ask for advice. There were always a lot of watchdogs." After Frank threatened to sue him, Michael would eventually have to settle with him for a reported $5 million. Three days after he was fired, Dileo was hired by Martin Scorsese to appear in the film *GoodFellas* with Robert De Niro. "The irony is very sweet, isn't it?" said Dileo. "Here Michael desperately wants to do movies now, and I'm beating him to it, no less with De Niro and Scorsese . . .

"I have a strong belief in what goes around comes around." Frank Dileo concluded. "It's called Karma. And I hope Michael understands what that means. If he doesn't now, one day he will."

After Frank Dileo's firing, Katherine's campaign to get Michael to go to Korea with his brothers continued. She would telephone her son and ask him to make the tour, but Michael could not be swayed.

Michael was particularly upset with Jermaine who had been accused by his ex-wife, Hazel, of attempting to rape her in August 1988.

Hazel charged that the trouble started when Jermaine brought their children home after exercising his visitation rights. "As the children were playing around," she explained, "Jermaine looked over to me and mouthed to me that he wanted to have sex, specifically using vulgar language, the actual words of which I will not mention. I was astonished and said, 'What?!' He then repeated to me again that he wanted to have sex with me and pushed me down onto the bed in front of the children. He jumped on top of me and began holding me down by the arms. I was trying to push him off and screaming for the children. They ran out of the room. I begged and pleaded with him to leave me alone.

"The next thing I knew, Jermaine was holding me down with his body and put his hand up my skirt and was touching my body and undergarments. He continued to try to lay on top of me, the whole time forcefully holding me down. I continued to scream for help. He made vulgar remarks about my undergarments as I struggled underneath him."

Hazel claimed that the only way she was able to extricate herself from her former husband's hold was to bite him on the arm so hard he jumped off her. At that point, the children came back into the room. The telephone rang. She stayed on the phone until her ex-husband left the house. Later, when she spoke to the children about what had happened, they told her that their father had said that he missed her and that he was going to arrange it so that Mommy and Daddy would "have a little baby sister."

The family tried to keep all of this from Michael. He was on the road when it happened, and they hoped he would never hear about it. But when he returned, he found out.

"If there's anything that Michael abhors," Katherine Jackson has said, "it's violence."

"There just comes a point when they are going to have to take care of themselves," Michael said of his family. "After all, who takes care of me? It's time for them to lead their lives—whatever is left of their lives—and for me to lead mine and take care of myself. I don't know what else I can do for them. They've hurt each other and me so many times in so many ways. It just never ends."

Now that Frank Dileo was out of the picture, Jerome Howard telephoned Marshall Gelfand and asked for help in getting Michael to commit to the Korean venture. "By all means," Gelfand told Howard. "We're always looking for ways to make extra money for Michael Jackson. Call John Branca, tell him I told you to call, and *he'll* convince Michael. Michael *loves* to work, so sure, he'll go."

"At this time, the Koreans said, 'But what if he won't go?' They were panicking," Howard remembered. " 'Fine, then offer him ten million to come,' they said. That's ten million *above* the seven point five million the brothers would get and split among themselves. And they said they were going to give him an airplane from Korean Airlines to travel in, and another plane for the brothers. This way Michael wouldn't have to see his brothers except onstage. I faxed all of this to John Branca, who got back to me right away and said, 'No, Michael doesn't want to go.' So then the Koreans sent a gold bust statue of Michael Jackson over to Michael to try to convince him. Now they're giving him gifts, but still, Michael won't budge. He doesn't want to go, but no one is listening to the guy.

"Then the Koreans offered *me* a gift, a car, because they thought I might have some influence on Michael, which I did not have," Jerome Howard continued. "I already had three cars; I didn't need another. But they wanted to buy me a seventy-thousand-dollar Mercedes. I told Katherine and Joe, and Joe said, 'They're not gonna buy you no car.' Well, the Jacksons weren't paying me anymore, so I accepted the Mercedes. When I drove that Mercedes onto the Jacksons' property, Katherine was happy for me. I told her I was going to sell the car and use the money to cover my expenses until she and Joseph could pay me again. She said, 'No, you need that car for business. They gave you that car. You keep it and don't you ever sell it.' But Joe was pissed off, because they gave me a car but didn't give him one. 'Those are *our* kids, Kathy. Why should Jerome get a car, and we don't get no car?' he wanted to know. From that time on, Joe's attitude about me began to change. I began to feel I was about to get cut out of the deal.''

The Koreans decided that if anyone could talk Michael into going on this tour, Katherine could. So they promised her the million-dollar bounty if she could get her son's signature on the contract within fourteen days. Jerome Howard handed Katherine the two $500,000 cashier's checks.

"I don't want that money, Jerome," Katherine insisted. "Don't give it to me."

"If I don't give it to you, then I have to give it to Joseph," Jerome warned her.

Katherine took the money.

"Do you think you can convince Michael?" he asked.

"Well, I can only try," Katherine said. "Michael has a mind of his own, you know."

"If you do, then the million dollars is yours," he reminded her.

Katherine Jackson sighed. She opened her purse, put the million dollars in, closed it, and then clutched the bag under her arm tightly. "A million dollars," she said, shaking her head in disbelief. "I guess we *have* come a long way."

# Chapter

## ✸ 31 ✸

Joe Jackson never imagined that his wife, Katherine, had a million dollars hidden away. The couple's business manager, Jerome Howard, feared that if Joe knew, he would have cashed the checks immediately—signature or no signature from his son Michael. Katherine apparently agreed, because she did not tell her husband she was in possession of the reward money. If she got Michael's signature on the contract, she said, she fully intended to give Joseph half of the reward.

Katherine, herself, must have been amazed about this turn of events. "I'd switch my life today for those days back at Gary," she would say. "Because once you get into show business, your life changes."

To most people, a million dollars is a lot of money. But not to Michael Jackson. In the last year, Michael had made over $65 million. According to *Forbes* magazine, he was the highest-paid entertainer in the world. Michael can be generous when he wants to be, but when it comes to his family, he has reservations. However, his family needed his help now and believed that Michael should come to the rescue.

"Some of the brothers were getting pretty desperate," said a family friend. "You have to understand that just because they're famous doesn't mean they're rich. They have lifestyles that are unlike those of most people. They have fancy homes, yachts, expensive cars . . . and they need to work to keep what they've acquired. Because their famous brother made sixty-five million dollars in one year, they feel the least he can do is work a few dates with them. A few dates can generate millions. It's not like they are asking for handouts. Just help. They feel that Michael Jackson is always helping sick kids and needy children, what about his own brothers? Janet had made five million that year, but since Michael made more, he was the one tagged to help out the family.''

Indeed, the brothers do feel that Michael owes them. ''Michael is very popular right now,'' Jermaine said, ''and I feel I've contributed a major part to it. Not just me, but my brothers too. What's happened to Michael has *a lot* to do with what we *all* did as The Jackson 5.''

It was March 1989. Jerome Howard and Kenneth Choi were at the Jacksons' estate in Encino with Katherine, Joe, and Jermaine, discussing the problem at hand, namely, ''How can we get Michael to do these concerts?'' It had become a family obsession. ''I think the best thing would be for him to get closer to his family,'' Jermaine had said. ''Once you make so much money, it's just another dollar. At some point, you have to start looking at the important things, like love, family, and health.''

As they were talking, the phone rang. It was for Katherine. She took the call upstairs. Joe followed.

''A few minutes later, Katherine comes running down the stairs, huffing and puffing and saying, 'Michael's on the phone. Michael's on the phone! Joe's talking to him right now,' '' Jerome Howard recalled. ''She was very worked up.''

Jermaine ran to the staircase where Katherine was standing and, in a very excited tone, said to her, ''Mother, let Kenneth talk to Michael. Let Kenneth try to convince him. After all, he convinced you and Joseph in the first place. *He* should talk to Michael.''

Katherine was skeptical. ''I don't know if that's a good idea,'' she said as she ran back up the stairs. ''But pick up the phone and try. It can't hurt.''

According to Jerome Howard, Jermaine ran back over to Kenneth. ''Look, man, you gotta persuade Michael—''

''How?'' Kenneth asked, helplessly. ''How do I do this?''

''I don't know,'' Jermaine replied, frowning and trying to think of something quick. ''But you gotta do something. Cry on the phone to him if you have to,'' he said facetiously.

Kenneth Choi picked up the telephone.

''Michael, please, my country wants you to come and perform,'' he said, in broken English.

A pause.

''But, please, Michael, I beg of you . . .''

Another pause.

Suddenly, Kenneth began to weep. He really *had* become upset. ''But, Michael, if you don't come to my country to perform, I have no choice but to *kill* myself,'' he said in a theatrical tone. ''I mean it. I'll do it.''

By now Kenneth was sobbing uncontrollably. Jermaine Jackson started laughing. He had to hold his hand over his mouth to stifle the sound. Jerome Howard fell to the floor, laughing hysterically.

Kenneth Choi ignored them both. ''You see, this is my mission,'' he continued on the phone as tears poured down his face. ''My mission is to bring you, the great Michael Jackson, to Korea to perform for all of the people in Korea. I must see you. Please, I beg of you. Michael, please.''

Finally, Michael agreed to meet with Kenneth Choi.

According to Jerome Howard, when Choi got off the phone, his demeanor immediately changed. He began dancing around the room merrily. ''My God, I can't believe it, I talked to Michael Jackson,'' he whooped. ''*I talked to Michael Jackson on the phone.* Oh my God! I actually talked to him, the great Michael Jackson.''

Meanwhile, the two weeks Katherine had to convince Michael to sign the contract had passed, so she returned the million-dollar reward. Joe was upset with her when he found out she had the money, and even angrier when he heard she had given it back.

Soon after that, Jerome Howard quit working for Katherine and Joe. ''There was an agreement to pay me a million dollars and the parents a million,'' Jerome remembered. ''Joe's position was 'Why should Jerome get a million? He should get two hundred thousand.' But I didn't agree to that when I started this whole thing. I agreed to a million dollars, and I had a signed contract to get a million dollars. But Joe didn't want me to get that much, and ultimately I ended up getting cut out of the deal.

''I discovered that Kenneth Choi was meeting with Joe and Katherine behind my back, cutting a side deal. When I saw this happening, I quit my job. The Jacksons tend to rely on attorneys and friends to steer them in the right direction; then they pit all these people against one another, and everybody loses.''

It had been twenty years since the Jacksons moved from Gary to Los Angeles in search of fame and wealth. For the last two decades, all of them had tasted the fruits of a privileged lifestyle. There was nothing they wanted for; they had it all. But in the bargain, they lost all perspective on reality. None of them knew when to stop; they wanted more, always more. And since the Koreans knew how to appeal to their greed, a new, Moonie-induced decadence began spreading like a cancer throughout the family.

The Moonies gave Joe a Rolls-Royce Corniche; later he would

get more than fifty thousand dollars because, after all, he was Michael Jackson's father.

Then Katherine got thirty-five thousand dollars, because she was Michael's mother.

Then Jermaine somehow managed to get a Range Rover, because he was supposed to be the brother with the most influence over Michael. (He gave the automobile to his ex-wife as part of their divorce settlement.)

Then Michael got sixty thousand dollars and some more expensive artwork, because he was, after all, the man of the hour. That wasn't enough, however, so the Koreans sent over a white Rolls-Royce Corniche, which Michael happily accepted.

Other people were getting thousands of dollars just for knowing Michael Jackson's family—this family who, twenty years before, ate potatoes every night of the week for dinner. Even Michael's security chief, Bill Bray, got over a half a million dollars for himself, and no one even remembers now why or how he got it.

Money and gifts were being distributed freely, and all of the recipients took full advantage of the Koreans and were greedy enough to accept what they could before anyone figured out that the chance of Michael Jackson actually doing these concerts was practically nil. If anyone were to even hint at the possibility that Michael meant what he said when he said no, all of the gifts might stop coming. No one wanted that to happen because, after all, life was sweet as it was.

The nadir of this debacle was reached when one of Bill Bray's girlfriends went to Kenneth Choi and said, "Listen up. My boyfriend controls Michael Jackson, and *I* control my boyfriend. So if you want this concert to take place in Korea, then you'd better give *me* something."

"Well, what do you want?" Choi asked.

The woman thought for a moment. "How about that 560 SEL Mercedes-Benz you have parked in your driveway?"

"It's yours," Choi said. He handed her the keys.

The girlfriend then drove off in her new Mercedes.

"The Koreans would buy gifts for anyone who even *knew* Michael Jackson in hopes that that would be the person who would be able to convince him to go," Jerome Howard said. "To the Moonies, this was just so-called seed money, money they had to spend to get close to Michael."

Finally, Kenneth Choi managed to arrange a meeting with Michael Jackson. Katherine brought him along with her to the "Soul Train" Awards, where Michael was an honoree. When Katherine introduced him to her son, he dropped to his knees and kissed Michael's hand. "My people need you," he told Michael. "You must perform in Korea. After all, Japan attacked our country two times, and you performed in Japan two times. You even held a Japanese baby in your arms." By now Michael looked totally perplexed. "My people need to see you." Then Choi produced a video camera and began taping Michael. Soon afterward, those videos were broadcast on nationwide Korean television with the promise that Michael was coming to Korea.

In June 1989, exasperated by what his family had gotten him into, feeling pressured by all of the favors and probably guilty about the gifts, Michael signed the contract to appear in Korea for four shows to take place in August. He would perform only four songs and a medley with his brothers. The rest of the show would be done by the brothers without Michael.

Michael had written in his autobiography, "I had to learn to be wary of some of the people around me. I was reminded of that old song by Clarence Carter called 'Patches,' where the oldest son is asked to take care of the farm after his father dies and his mother tells him she's depending on him. Well, we weren't sharecroppers and I wasn't the oldest, but those were slim shoulders on which to place such burdens. For some reason I always found it very difficult to say no to my family and the other people I loved. I would be asked to do something or take care of something and I would agree, even if I worried that it might be more than I could handle."

Michael wasn't writing about the Korean episode (it happened after his book was published), but he very well could have been.

"I'm doing it for Kat," he said of the Korean deal.

"Of all the family members, Michael is closest to Katherine, and Katherine is closest to Mike," said Tim Whitehead, Katherine's nephew. "That's just the way it is. Everybody in the family knows that Michael would do anything for Katherine, and she would do anything for Michael."

The family was elated. Finally, Michael had committed to the Korean concerts. No one got the reward money, however, because Michael had made up his own mind. "*He* should have gotten the million dollars," said a friend, "for turning himself in to the Koreans." To this day, Michael Jackson doesn't know that there was a reward for anyone in his family who could secure his services.

When the Moonie deal was signed and it was time to pass the promised millions on to Michael, the Reverend Moon—who was funding this whole venture—finally intervened and decided that the amount that had been agreed upon was too much to pay Michael

Jackson for his work. According to Jerome Howard, Moon wanted Michael's payment lowered: first to $8 million, then to 7, then 5, then 4.5, and finally to $2.5 million. Finally, the deal fell apart completely.

"After finally getting in with Michael, the Koreans screwed themselves by being greedy at the wrong time," Howard said. "They say Michael pulled out of the deal, and Michael says they pulled out. Either way, Reverend Moon was pissed off."

As a result, Michael Jackson was sued by Segye Times, Inc.—which is financed by Moon. Moon wanted all of his money and gifts returned. Also named in the suit were Joe, Katherine, Jerome Howard, Jermaine Jackson, and Bill Bray. Michael, in turn, sued Segye Times, Inc., for $8 million, saying that he was not giving back any of his gifts and not demanding that anyone else give back theirs either. "I don't even know how this whole thing happened, or how I got involved," Michael said. "All I know is that I kept saying no. But no one in my family would take no for an answer. Now look at what's happened."

According to Michael, Kenneth Choi told him at first that the reason he wanted him to go to Korea was not to do concerts but rather to "come visit the disadvantaged children in the hospitals and orphanages of Korea, to visit the Humanitarian Festival, and to receive from the president of Korea the country's highest honor." Michael said that after he consented to do that, Choi began pressuring him to perform as well. Michael also claimed he knew nothing about the connection to the Unification Church and that the gifts he received were "for the purpose of creating a favorable environment to negotiate for [my] services." He claimed that Choi promised him that he would rename the Manhattan Center on Fiftieth Street between Seventh and Eighth Avenues in New York "The Michael Jackson Center of Performing Arts." But Michael said that Choi and Segye Times don't even own the Manhattan Center.

"You have to understand my point of view," explained Kenneth Choi in January 1991. "In my country, fathers, sons, and brothers are close. I thought that Michael was close to his father and brothers. I thought that I should be doing business with his father and brothers because this is what Michael would want. Even Michael's employees told me, 'No, he doesn't do business with his family,' but I did not believe them. I thought they were jealous and trying to throw me off the path. Finally, when I first met Michael, he told me, 'Yes, it's true. I love my family but I never do business with them.' I could not believe this! I was doing business with the wrong man [Joe], someone who had no authority over Michael. By then, it was too late. The damage had been done. I lost face in my country. I was humiliated.

"We still love Michael Jackson," Choi concluded. "He did not do anything wrong. It is still my mission to get Michael Jackson to come to Korea."

There is a great deal of disagreement among the participants of the Korean tour fiasco about who is responsible for what, but most observers and associates of Michael Jackson agree on one thing: none of it would have happened if Frank Dileo were still Michael's manager. Most certainly, if Frank hadn't been fired three days after first learning about the deal, he would have put an end to it before it got out of hand. In the past, Dileo had intercepted many deals having to do with the family before they reached Michael. He tried to make certain that Michael didn't become associated with the family's schemes, and most family members—especially Joe and Katherine—disliked Frank for that very reason.

Even John Branca could not have protected Michael from this debacle because by the time Michael went to him for advice, he had practically made up his mind to sign the deal. Also, it seemed to some observers, that Michael—now more paranoid than ever—was beginning to lose confidence in Branca.

The Jacksons have always publicly embraced the idea that there is nothing more important than family. However, in 1989, questions were raised as to how two of the Jackson family's grandparents were being dealt with: Joseph's father, Samuel Jackson, and Katherine's mother, Martha Bridges. Both were eighty-two years of age.

The first hint of any trouble occurred when the *Star* tabloid published an article about Samuel, who had recently suffered a stroke. The story claimed that he was living on welfare at the Tanner Chapel Manor nursing home in a run-down part of Phoenix and that Michael would not visit or write to him. There was an accompanying photograph of the dejected-looking old man sitting in a wheelchair and holding a copy of Michael's *Thriller* album. He was posed in front of posters of Michael and Janet. A former employee at the home was quoted as saying, "Every Sunday, Samuel gets himself dressed in his best clothes because he thinks Michael's coming to see him—but he never shows up." Thomas Dickey, executive director at the home, said, "I don't think Michael can have any idea just how much pleasure his grandfather would get from a visit."

Many members of the family—particularly Joe and Katherine—were offended and outraged by the story. "The family was real mad about that one," said Grace Evans, administrator of the Tanner Chapel Manor. "There were all kinds of lawsuits threatened."

But, indeed, Samuel Jackson was a resident of the nursing home, located four blocks from an area that police officials described as "the city's most dangerous corner." Since welfare lists are protected in Phoenix, it is impossible to determine whether Samuel Jackson was a welfare recipient, as the article in the *Star* claimed. However, Maricopa County's Division of Long-Term Care reports that forty-three of the fifty patients at Tanner Chapel Manor in 1989 were "county residents," meaning that the county paid for the cost of their care. A state directory of nursing homes indicated that Samuel Jackson's room cost between fifty-two and sixty-two dollars a day. As a result of the story in the *Star*, all employees of the nursing home were warned against ever discussing Samuel Jackson with the press; also, Samuel Jackson was no longer allowed visitors except by permission of the family. Grace Evans admitted that, as of January 1989 (two years after Samuel was admitted to the home), Michael had not visited his grandfather.

Also in 1989, Katherine's mother, Martha Bridges, was in a nursing home in Panorama City, California, after suffering a series of strokes. She had had her first stroke in 1975, which rendered her practically speechless and also affected her memory. A year later she had another stroke, and for the next ten years she got progressively worse. By 1989, it had been reported that she was not being visited by any members of her family.

Jack Gordon told writer Lydia Encinas of the *National Enquirer* (Gordon regularly cooperates with the *Enquirer* in stories about the Jackson family, much to the family's chagrin) that "Mrs. Bridges has been abandoned to die alone. It's breaking LaToya's heart to see the way her grandmother is living, and she pleaded to let her bring Mrs. Bridges home with her. But her parents said no. They refuse to let her help."

Martha Bridges's stay in the nursing home was reportedly subsidized for the first five months by the government before the family began covering the expenses. There was also reportedly a dispute over the patient's medical bills and whether the family should have to pay the 20 percent not covered by Medicare.

Katherine Jackson denied that her mother was being neglected. "We take good care of her," Katherine said. "She is very well."

When Martha Bridges died on April 29, 1990, Jack Gordon claimed that LaToya was furious because no one told her of the death and so she did not attend the funeral. LaToya claimed that Michael and Janet somehow talked Katherine into not inviting her to the funeral. But according to LaToya's cousin Tim Whitehead, LaToya wasn't there because no one in the family could locate her. "I know for a fact that my aunt [Katherine] wanted her there. Of course she did. My aunt still loves LaToya very much. But no one could find her. She, herself, has purposely made it impossible for anyone to find her in case of a family emergency. And 'Toya knows that's the case."

The rest of the family attended the services and funeral; Michael was said to be particularly upset by his grandmother's demise. "I guess he was close to her," said his cousin Tim Whitehead. "But to be really honest, as a rule most of the family would have to say that the fellas, the brothers, didn't visit her as much as they probably should have. At the funeral Michael was, well, I guess the best word is elusive. He stayed to himself, mostly. Family members wanted him to pose for pictures with them. He did it, but he didn't really want to. You can't blame him. Who wants to pose for pictures on the day of a funeral?"

Stories of the alleged neglect of these two grandparents—and many of the reports were cruel, quoting certain family members as having blamed other members for Martha's death—did little to mend the Jacksons' shattered public image of togetherness.

In July 1989, Michael entered into negotiations to purchase Berry Gordy's Motown publishing catalogue, Jobete. It had been industry knowledge that Gordy was interested in selling Jobete, which holds the copyright to all of Motown's biggest hit records. Berry sold Motown to MCA in July 1988 for $61 million, and feels today that he sold it for too little money. He wanted to make a "killing" with Jobete.

Michael and John Branca met with Berry at his Bel Air home, the same home where, as a courageous sixteen-year-old, Michael came to see Berry wanting to know why Gordy wouldn't allow the Jacksons to write and publish their own songs. Now, fourteen years later, it could be argued that Michael Jackson was probably worth more than Berry Gordy.

Gordy was asking $200 million for his company, but he only wanted to sell stock, not assets (which are actual copyrights and publishing rights). Berry wanted to retain ownership in Jobete, probably to the greater degree; the buyer would get revenue from stock dividends.

Berry's offer didn't seem like a good deal for Michael. Branca realized that if Jackson bought only stock, he wouldn't get any tax benefits from the purchase—only asset purchases are entitled to tax benefits. (If Gordy were to sell Jobete's assets to Michael for $200 million, Branca planned to structure the deal so that the purchase would depreciate over ten years and Michael would be entitled to a $20 million write-off each year.) Moreover, Jobete, reportedly, only earns $10 million a year from its copyrights on about thirty-thousand titles, including some of the best songs by Smokey Robinson, Lionel Richie, and Holland-Dozier-Holland.

However, owning Jobete would have been good for Michael's psyche, and it wouldn't have cost him much because John Branca had put together a plum deal for Michael—a joint venture between Jackson and worldwide publisher EMI, whereby EMI would put up almost all of the money and then split the ownership of Jobete fifty-fifty with Michael. Michael was amazed by Branca's influence and ingenuity.

If the deal had been consummated, Michael Jackson would own all of the songs he recorded with The Jackson 5, which is what really appealed to him. He would also have owned the Diana Ross catalogue, which would have been a real coup for him.

In the end, Berry only wanted to sell stock. So Michael offered $135 million for stock and $175 million for assets.

But Berry was playing hardball; he wanted $200 million for stock only, and his mind was made up. He told the press that he had a bid for $190 million, but wouldn't say who the party was. Jackson and Branca agreed that he was bluffing.

In the end, Michael Jackson and John Branca decided to pull out of the deal; Berry Gordy still hasn't found a buyer.

It was an odd month. While Michael negotiated to make a multimillion-dollar purchase, no one was looking after petty cash. He gave a few hundred dollars to one male employee and had him send a female worker to the store to do some shopping. When she came back with a bunch of bags from K Mart, Michael was perplexed.

"K Mart? I send you shopping with hundreds of dollars, and you go to K Mart?" he said accusingly. "What did you do with the rest of the money?"

It turned out that the male employee didn't give the woman all of the money he'd gotten from Michael. He gave her a small amount and pocketed the rest. "I can't trust anyone, even in the smallest of situations," Michael said. This story reminded some people of the time Michael asked a female employee if she had seen one of his prized photographs of The Beatles. It was missing. She said she hadn't. Michael then found it was hanging in her living room. He fired her immediately.

* * *

In the summer of 1989, the family prepared themselves for more distress from LaToya, now thirty-three years old. They had heard that she had decided to write a book that would be nothing like Michael's; this one would tell the "whole truth about the family." One would think the family would be suspicious of the claim to accuracy, however, since in April of 1988 LaToya told a reporter, "To my knowledge, Michael has only had one nose job."

According to Marjorie Walker, a friend of the family, "Katherine telephoned LaToya and asked her if it was true that a book was being planned. LaToya lied and said the story wasn't true. Meanwhile, she was negotiating with G.P. Putnam's Sons publishing house. Katherine was hurt. LaToya never used to lie. If you knew LaToya, you'd understand how totally out of character her behavior had been since she'd met Jack Gordon. This is a girl who used to be scared to death to go out of the house. This is a girl who felt her family could do no wrong. Now she was planning to write a book about just how wrong they all could be."

LaToya signed a deal with Putnam, which advanced her more money for her autobiography than Michael had received for his. Michael got $300,000; it was said that LaToya got about $500,000.

"It won't be so bad," Katherine reasoned. "What can she write about anyway?"

For starters, she was going to claim that her brother, Michael, had been sexually molested as a child. When word of this charge got back to Michael, he was incensed. "You've got to stop her, Branca," he said. John Branca arranged a meeting with Jack Gordon to discuss the matter and told him that Michael did not want his sister printing that story.

"Why not?" Gordon demanded to know. "It's the truth."

"I don't know if it's true or not," Branca told him. "But I do know that if she writes that Michael was molested, he will sue her. I can guarantee you that."

It's not known at this time if there is any truth to LaToya's claim. Rumors of Michael's having been sexually molested as a child had been circulating for many years within the music industry.

In subsequent letters to LaToya Jackson and Jack Gordon, John Branca reiterated that Michael did not want his sister to write that he was sexually abused, and that he would make himself available to read whatever it was she did write and check it for "accuracy." In other words, he wanted to censor her manuscript.

After Branca sent his letter, Jack Gordon telephoned Katherine's business manager, Jerome Howard, and asked for a meeting. According to Howard, Gordon offered this deal at the meeting: if Joe and Katherine came up with $5 million, LaToya would cancel her memoirs. Moreover, if Howard convinced them to give LaToya $5 million, he would get a cool $500,000 for himself.

"Man, that's called blackmail," Howard said.

"No, it's not," Gordon responded. "It's called business."

"Well, I don't want anything to do with it," Howard told him. "I'll tell you what I will do, though. I'll present the deal to Katherine and have her get in touch with you."

"What? You don't want the five hundred thousand?" Gordon said incredulously.

Howard shook his head no. "I telephoned Katherine and then met with her," Jerome Howard recalled. "I told her what was going on. If she wanted to stop her daughter's book, it was going to cost her five million bucks. She wasn't real pleased, to say the least. I also told her I didn't want to get involved in it, that he had offered me a percentage but that I didn't think it was fair money. I suggested she should have her lawyer deal with it."

After that, someone fed a story to the media that Michael Jackson had offered LaToya $12 million to kill the project. According to one ghostwriter assigned to LaToya's book, that was not true. But to keep interest in her book at peak level, LaToya said that Michael's "offer" was "awful, a sign of bribery. Nothing is going to stop me," she cried, "no matter how much I'm offered."

Then Gordon claimed that Michael had offered to buy G. P. Putnam's Sons, the company publishing LaToya's memoirs, for $84 million just to prevent the book from appearing. This claim also proved untrue. However, Gordon's stories did generate a small write-up about the book in *Newsweek*, so they had the desired effect.

According to an associate of Michael's, "What really happened is that someone representing LaToya—and I'm not saying it was Jack and I'm not saying it wasn't, because, frankly, I don't know—got in touch with Michael's people and said that Mike had better come up with some big money—millions—if he didn't want the book published. I was in the room when Michael made his decision. 'I'm not going to let my own sister, a person I loved who has known me all of my life, blackmail me,' he said. 'This is as low as you can go.' Then he said a funny thing. 'Tell LaToya to go jump in a lake.'

"Michael wouldn't have cared about LaToya's book at all, as long as everything in it was true. His own mother was hawking her memoirs and got a deal [in Japan (and later in America)], and Mike didn't care. He just didn't think LaToya would be honest, and that's what upset him most.''

Indeed, for LaToya, family loyalty was a thing of the past. Jack Gordon claimed that LaToya's years in that home—that place Janet's former husband, James DeBarge, once called "The House of Fears"—made her angry and bitter enough to include another awful charge in her book proposal. He threatened that she would write about the time Joe molested her when she was eight years old.

Katherine was horrified. "It's not true," she insisted to Jack Gordon. "It's just not true."

"Oh, yes, it is," Gordon said.

"Who told you this?" Katherine said she demanded to know. "Did LaToya tell you this happened to her?"

"No. Rebbie's the one who told me," Gordon said.

By the time Katherine confronted Rebbie, who was thirty-nine years old at this time, she was seething. But Rebbie denied ever having told Jack Gordon that her sister was sexually abused by Joe.

Michael, too, was angered by LaToya's threat. He has always worked very hard to maintain the Jacksons' public image as one big, cheery family, despite the reality of the situation.

Michael telephoned LaToya, and, she recalled, "We fought about many things—but the main thing was the book." LaToya said that Michael wanted to know if there was anything critical of him in her book, and she refused to tell him. She claimed that the real problem is not her book, but the fact that Michael "is jealous of all the exposure I'm getting. He wants to hog the limelight."

According to LaToya, Michael told her, "I've been doing this since I was five years old, and here you come out of nowhere. What justifies your fame? You're not entitled to this yet." LaToya said she told him she never wanted to speak to him again and then slammed down the phone. She claimed that Michael then telephoned her publicist and convinced him to drop her as a client (the publicist denied that this is why he dropped LaToya) and that he somehow coerced her record label, RCA, not to promote her current product. "Michael wants to ruin me," she lamented.

Actually, if what LaToya has said is true, she was brave to stand up to her brother. No one else in the family ever does. "None of the family ever wants to cross Michael, because he's the one with all the money," Jerome Howard said. "It's part of the family's credo: you do not make Michael mad, because when you need him for something, he'll be gone. LaToya can forget about Michael now. He'll never be there for her. She's burned that bridge."

"Michael cannot tell me what to write and what not to write,"

LaToya petulantly said to a reporter. "I'll do what I want to do. The nerve of him."

LaToya's memoirs were rejected by G. P. Putnam's Sons and signed to New American Library. As of this writing, the book still has not been published.

On September 5, 1989, LaToya, now thirty-three, and Jack Gordon, fifty, were married in Reno, Nevada. According to her new husband, two days earlier, LaToya telephoned her mother and said, "I don't have a family anymore. I don't have a mother, father, or brothers or sisters. I've disowned you all."

In order to generate more public interest in the wedding, the couple turned the affair into a media event, denying it had ever happened—even though a signed, twenty-seven-dollar marriage license was produced by reporters. "Why, it must have been an impostor," LaToya said coyly. It was said that Gordon pulled a man off the street to be a witness to the 10 P.M. ceremony; he gave him a wad of hundred dollar bills as payment.

Deputy Commissioner Cecilia Kounairs performed the ceremony. "I pronounced them man and wife," she said. "They were not very affectionate or emotional—just businesslike. They said their vows and walked out."

"It better not have happened," Jermaine said. "Because she didn't get my approval. I'm serious. 'Toya knows with things like that she has to get the brothers' approval." Jermaine had begun to sound like his father.

"She's not the LaToya I or Michael used to know," Marlon said when asked about the wedding. "She's changed. I called her last night, and before I said a word, Gordon was on the extension. He said, 'She's my *wife* now.' "

"I have to hear every word she says," Gordon added.

The Jacksons believe that LaToya doesn't love Jack Gordon, that she married him in order to disassociate herself from the family. Gordon said that he and his wife had six security guards with them at all times to prevent her from being kidnapped by the Jacksons.

"Jack used to tell me all the time how Joe was trying to kidnap LaToya, and that LaToya was absolutely scared to death. From what I understand, Joe used to beat her when she was a child," recalled Gary Berwin, whose business dealings with Joe went sour in 1985.

"LaToya was not a very happy person. She'd had a hard life, and she found someone to love and rely on—Jack Gordon," Berwin continued. "Finally she had escaped from that family. I asked Jack Gordon very specifically why he married LaToya. I asked him,

'Did you marry LaToya because you really love her, or did you marry her as a convenience for you and herself so that she could get out from under Joe's clutches?' He said, 'No, man, I really love her.' I said, 'C'mon, man, be honest with me.' He replied, 'I'm telling you, I love her very much.' ''

Jerome Howard is not as certain of Jack Gordon's motives. He said that LaToya telephoned him shortly after he left Joe and Katherine's employ. ''Didn't I forewarn you about my father?'' she asked. ''Then she and I talked for three hours,'' Howard said. ''After that, Jack Gordon called. I knew right away that LaToya had tape-recorded the conversation I had with her and played some of it for Jack. He knew that I was cool—had no animosity toward LaToya—and wanted to see me.''

Even though Howard was wary of Gordon since Gordon had offered him a bribe regarding LaToya's book, he nonetheless agreed to the meeting.

Jerome Howard said that Jack Gordon told him, ''You are a stupid man. How could you be so dumb to leave that house without a Jackson? You could have had Janet; she was up for grabs. At least I got myself a Jackson.''

# Chapter

## 🍎 32 🍎

IN AUGUST 1989, Michael Jackson turned thirty-one years old. Recent years had certainly not been easy. Family pressures and demands—as well as career concerns—seemed to keep Jackson in a continuous state of anxiety. Though he had left home, he never really left the womb. He still felt drawn to his family. As much as he tried to shun all of them except for Katherine, he just could not. Somehow, their problems always ended up his own.

Despite the fact that he was now in his thirties, many people in his circle would feel that Michael Jackson had never really grown up. He was still an adolescent at heart, playing with his teenage male friends and entertaining handicapped youngsters at his palatial estate. He liked wearing his many disguises and was agitated when people pointed him out, not so much because he didn't want to be identified as because he had left home thinking he had such a swell costume and no one should have been able to recognize him. Visiting Disneyland, Disney World, and Universal Studios was still his favorite leisure-time activity; fantasy was a major part of his life.

There had been much discussion as to how to follow the *Bad* album. Just as when he was attempting to conceptualize a successor to *Thriller*, Michael was concerned about competing with himself. *Bad*—though a huge seller—had not sold as many copies as *Thriller* and Michael was disappointed. Rather than compete with the previous two albums by issuing one of new material, Michael and John Branca agreed that he should release a Greatest Hits collection, entitled *Decade*, which would also include some new songs.

Michael Jackson had intended to deliver *Decade* to the Sony Corporation, CBS Records' parent company, in August of 1989. It was scheduled to be released in November of that year, in time for the Christmas sales rush.

"I want more money than anyone else has ever gotten," Michael was said to have told John Branca when the attorney began negotiating with CBS Records for the new album. To that end, Branca arranged an $18 million advance, which was, indeed, "more money than anyone else has ever gotten." The deal included a $15 million straight advance—which CBS would recoup from Jackson's royalties before he would make a profit on the album—and a nonrecoupable $3 million, which was a gift for Michael from his label. (On each of the three album deals John Branca negotiated for Michael Jackson at CBS—*Thriller*, *Bad*, and the upcoming product—he succeeded in getting for Michael $3 million from CBS, gratis.)

Prior to the Jackson deal, the Rolling Stones—also represented by John Branca—held the record for the most lucrative contract, with $5 million-plus per album. According to the *Hollywood Reporter*, Billy Joel gets $1.7 million as an advance, Bruce Springsteen $2.5 million, and Madonna $1 million before bonuses, which could make it several times that.

Michael Jackson's album royalty is forty-one points. What that means in terms of percentage of retail sale varies with each format, from CD to tape to disc; however, the amount comes to approximately 25 percent of the retail price of each album. Michael's 25 percent translates to $2.50 per album sold. However, when the $3 million nonrecoupable gift is added to Michael's royalty rate, it actually jumps to about 29 percent of retail.

To put Jackson's royalty into perspective, it's been said by her associate that Madonna makes 18 percent. Most other acts of superstar status make 12 percent.

In its entirety, Michael's new deal with CBS could be worth as much as $50 million because, in addition to the advance and nonrecoupable gift, John Branca had negotiated a joint business venture with the company. According to that arrangement, CBS would finance a custom label for Michael Jackson—a subsidiary of CBS Records called Jackson Records—which Jackson would oversee. CBS would provide 100 percent of the funding for the new label, and then split the profit equally with Michael. He would also own half the stock and thereby be entitled to half the assets if the label was ever sold. This was quite a coup for Michael and a tribute to John Branca's masterly negotiating skills.

Since Janet Jackson constantly calls upon her brother, Michael, for advice and guidance, Branca felt that she would be the perfect first artist to sign to the new label. Michael was elated at the possibility. (Since that time, however, Janet signed a contract with

Virgin Records for an estimated $32 million. When finalized, in March 1991, it was the largest recording contract in history.)

In the final coup de grace for Michael, so far as *Decade* was concerned, John Branca had negotiated a $5 million advance from Warner-Tamerlane Publishing Corporation, the Warner Bros. publishing arm that administers the copyrights on Jackson's songs. (Michael owns all of his copyrights. Warner-Tamerlane has no ownership, but, for a small fee, the company does collect money generated by publishing deals around the world involving his compositions.) For an artist, $5 million is a huge advance from a music publishing company; most superstars get about $1 million.

All of the pieces were in place for a tremendous *Decade* kickoff. But by January 1990, it was obvious that Michael would fail to deliver *Decade*. He was ambivalent about the format—there was some confusion as to which songs to include. The original plan was for the package to consist of four cuts from *Off the Wall*, seven from *Thriller*, six from *Bad*, three to five new songs, "State of Shock" (the hit duet with Mick Jagger); "Heartbreak Hotel," "Someone in the Dark" (from Michael's *E.T.* narration album), "Come Together," and two vintage Motown songs that Michael was remastering. But Michael kept vacillating about this plan, and, in the end, his close friend, entertainment mogul David Geffen, finally talked him out of putting out the album. Michael decided that *Decade* would not be released at all. Rather, he would produce an album of new material. (The deal John Branca negotiated for him at CBS and with Warner-Tamerlane applied to any product Michael chooses to issue.)

But there was more at stake for Michael at this time than just the *Decade* album. A commercial endorsement for L.A. Gear shoes also hung in the balance.

In 1988, Michael told his advisers he was interested in endorsing a line of shoes. He asked John Branca to check into the possibility that either Nike or Reebok would be interested. Since Michael would obviously deserve many millions of dollars for such an endorsement, both Nike and Reebok passed on the idea because they did not want to spend that much money. However, L.A. Gear, a Los Angeles-based sport shoe manufacturer, was interested and made a preliminary offer of $1 million.

Because $1 million means practically nothing to Michael Jackson, John Branca pushed on to see what else L.A. Gear would be willing to do to sweeten the pot. In the end, the shoe company agreed to give Michael a royalty on every pair of shoes sold, as well as stock options in the company. Also, if Michael's endorsement raised the annual company income above the then-current $800 million, Jackson would get a percentage of the increase over $1 billion. Those terms were agreed to by Michael, but, at a million dollars, the money offer was still too low. After all, Michael had received over $15 million for his last Pepsi-Cola endorsement. So after a couple of months of negotiations with L.A. Gear, Branca was able to secure a $10 million advance for his client.

"The L.A. Gear guys were desperate to get involved, no matter the cost, with someone of Michael's stature," said Randy Phillips, a rock manager who served as one of the deal's key middlemen and received a healthy fee for his role.

Still, Branca, according to his associates, was reluctant to have Michael sign the deal because L.A. Gear is not as prestigious as Nike or Reebok, and it doesn't have the advertising experience and savvy of Pepsi-Cola. "That's okay," Michael decided. "I'm going to teach them how to advertise. Let's show 'em how to do it right."

It was a terrific deal, again brilliantly negotiated by John Branca, but it hinged entirely on the release of the *Decade* album. According to the plan, in the spring of 1990 Michael would star in L.A. Gear commercials, replacing former Los Angeles Laker basketball star Kareem Abdul Jabbar as the company's corporate spokesman. Also, as part of his endorsement, Michael was to design a line of shoes and wear them in three of the videos from the new songs on *Decade*.

When Michael appeared at a press conference at the Hollywood Palladium (September 13, 1989) to announce the endorsement, he dressed in black sunglasses, black slacks, black jacket, and a black pair of sixty-nine-dollar L.A. Gear sneakers. He appeared to be particularly nervous as a dozen floodlights filled the room and fog began to drift out of giant machinery. L.A. Gear had spent more than fifty thousand dollars; this was probably one of the first press conferences with special effects. After reading a ten-second statement to the reporters, Michael got off the stage as quickly as he could. "Protect me . . . Don't let them ask me any questions," Michael whispered to a top executive from L.A. Gear. Then he blew a kiss to the assembled reporters and ran off into the fog.

Many of the one hundred press members began to jeer when he left without answering questions. Randy Phillips said, "Sure, maybe he only said two sentences, but he spoke more at *our* press conference than he did at Pepsi's press conference—or when he visited the White House for that matter. He came to the press conference wearing L.A. Gear's hottest shoes. You didn't see him ever drinking a Pepsi at *their* press conference."

Michael's obsessive desire for media control was on full display during this gathering. Photographers were instructed by his representatives to use a medium telephoto lens, a 1/125 shutter speed, an f-stop of four, and film compatible with tungsten lighting.

In the end, though, without the support of _Decade_, Michael's endorsement would prove to be disastrous for L.A. Gear. The line of shoes he had designed did not sell well at all. In order for this endorsement to succeed, it needed his support through videos and music, not just the exciting television commercials he starred in for the company. Eventually, Michael had to negotiate a settlement with the disappointed executives at L.A. Gear who felt that he had reneged on his promise to deliver an album to accompany the endorsement; Michael would not get the full $10 million Branca had negotiated for him.

Though Michael Jackson is the sole director of all of his companies, he does have an investment committee that meets informally about once a year to discuss his many investments. In early 1990, the committee consisted of John Branca and his partner, Kenneth Ziffren; Jackson's accountant, Marshall Gelfand; John Johnson of Johnson Publishing Company (which publishes _Ebony_ and _Jet_); and David Geffen. The committee has no real power; Michael can veto any decision five minutes after it has been made, and any vote taken on that particular subject is then deemed irrelevant.

None of the members pockets any money from the investments made on Jackson's behalf. Mostly, the committee was formed by Michael so that these powerful men would be well acquainted with one another and be able to follow one another's activities throughout the year. Michael believes in having his associates watching over one another to see who may be taking advantage of him. Because Jackson's investments are so fascinating—and because it seems an honor for these gentlemen to be involved, even if it does not mean a personal profit for them—Michael Jackson has no difficulty in organizing such an investment committee.

In recent months, David Geffen, a member of Michael Jackson's investment committee for about ten years, has begun to exert great influence over Jackson. At one point, Michael had signed a development deal with Geffen's production company to do a film. Geffen's task was to procure a script that would meet with Michael's approval. The two couldn't agree on one, however. (Michael still wants to do a movie that would be a fantastic, big-budget combination of _Star Wars_ and Busby Berkeley.)

It's easy to see why Michael Jackson—a man who is most impressed by wealth and power—would be enamored of David Geffen. In its December 24, 1990, issue, *Forbes* dubbed the forty-seven-year-old Geffen, a bachelor, "the richest man in Hollywood" and, indeed, he probably is.

It wasn't always that way for David Geffen, who was raised in a three-room apartment in Boro Park, a Jewish and Italian section of Brooklyn, and slept in his parent's bedroom until his older brother moved out of the living room. His father was unemployed most of the time and left the responsibility of earning a living for the family to his highly motivated and industrious wife, David's mother. She owned her own business—Chic Corsetry by Geffen—and, at first, ran it out of their home ("The apartment was always filled with women with big tits," Geffen recalled), before she got her own store.

David Geffen lived on wits and instinct as a youngster; he signed his own report cards, and, it has been reported, he lied to avoid military service. He graduated from high school in 1960 with barely passing grades and spent some time in college. When that didn't work out, he moved to Los Angeles; by this time his brother was engaged to the sister of the first wife of legendary rock-and-roll record producer Phil Spector.

Geffen became one of Spector's gofers. "He was my God," Geffen recalled. In 1964, after leaving Spector's employ, the twenty-year-old Geffen got a job in the mailroom of the William Morris Agency. He would later admit that he secured the position by lying and saying he was a UCLA theater arts graduate. Then he forged a letter to that effect, duplicating UCLA's stationery at a printshop.

Through his connections in the record industry, Geffen eventually became a protégé of Ahmet Ertegun, the chairman of Atlantic Records. Ertegun lent Geffen $50,000 to start his own management firm. Geffen brilliantly parlayed his ambition and Ertegun's money into a successful career in show business, first as an entertainment manager for Laura Nyro. Geffen—who has said he was romantically involved with Nyro—established the Tuna Fish music publishing company for Nyro's songs and assigned himself 50 percent interest in it, much to Nyro's chagrin. In 1969, CBS Records bought the company; Geffen pocketed $2 million.

In late 1970, Geffen started his own label, Asylum Records. A year later, he sold that company to Warner Communications, remained the label's president, and pocketed another $7 million. When Asylum merged with Elektra Records, Geffen became the president of the entire operation—and one of the largest stockholders in Warner Communications.

In 1980, Geffen started another label, Geffen Records, distributed, at first, by Warner Bros. Records. His star attractions included John Lennon and Yoko Ono. Eventually, Geffen broke from Warners; his company quickly became the industry's hottest independent label, breaking such acts as Guns 'n Roses—an unknown band when signing with Geffen in 1987—whose first two albums sold over fourteen million.

Over the years, Geffen also earned a respected reputation in the film world, producing movies that were distributed by Warner Bros., including *Risky Business* and *Beetlejuice*. In addition, he has made money in the theater, coproducing the Broadway hit *Dreamgirls* with Michael Bennett and helping to finance Andrew Lloyd Webber's *Cats*.

David Geffen has a reputation as being shrewd and savvy, an intuitive show business genius who knows when to buy and, just as important, when to sell. He is intelligent and witty. He can also be temperamental, and is considered by some associates to be conceited and arrogant. In April 1990, he sold his Geffen Records to MCA for ten million shares of stock in MCA. Then, before the year was out, Japan's Matsushita Electric Industrial Co., Ltd., purchased MCA for $66 a share; David Geffen ended up with $660 million. He still owns his movie and Broadway operations and is now running his Geffen record label for Matsushita. He also has shares worth $35 million in a TV station. According to *Forbes*, adding in Geffen's other assets makes his worth today $900 million. He says his goal is to become Hollywood's first billionaire.

Michael Jackson admired David Geffen's business savvy and vision. "Of *course* Geffen knew MCA was going to be sold to the Japanese," Michael said. "Why do you think he sold his company to MCA? The guy is a genius." According to *New York* magazine writer Eric Pooley, Jackson was "awestruck" by the deal Geffen got for his record label from MCA. "Michael likes Guinness Book-type records," a friend of Michael's was quoted as having said. "Most records sold, biggest deal made."

"Michael Jackson told me that he thinks David Geffen is the most amazing man he has ever met," said another Jackson associate. "He feels that if he listens to David's advice, he, too, can become the mogul David is. He hangs on to his every word the way he used to hang on to John Branca's. Unlike Branca, though, Geffen really kisses up to Mike, flattering him constantly. He and David are extremely close in many ways. Not only do they have a professional relationship, they also have a close personal relationship. Geffen told him that the *Decade* concept was a mediocre idea and that Michael shouldn't waste his time on it. He convinced Mike to do an album of new material, and Michael agreed.''

However, Michael Jackson would not hire Quincy Jones for the new project. He no longer wanted to work with Jones because he felt that the producer had become too possessive of him and his work and had taken too much credit for his success. Michael was still miffed that Quincy gave him a tough time about "Smooth Criminal"—Quincy didn't want it on the *Bad* album. Jones, on the other hand, felt that Michael had become too demanding and inflexible. With emotions running so high, the partnership that had once sold millions and millions of albums never would have cooled down enough to work again. Jones wasn't informed that he would not be producing the new album. Michael just began work without him, much to Quincy's consternation.

While Michael tried to prepare the new album for release, 1990 would prove to be tumultuous. Now that he was the highest-paid artist in the history of the business, he would find himself immersed in the emotional politics of the record industry as its power brokers bartered for his allegiance and favor.

Late in 1989, David Geffen telephoned John Branca and told him that he wanted Michael to write and record a new song for the soundtrack of the Tom Cruise racing-car film *Days of Thunder*, which was to be issued on Geffen Records and distributed through MCA. Branca was certain Michael would want nothing to do with this project since Jackson rarely involved himself in records that were not his own. However, he checked with Michael anyway. He was right. "No way," Michael declared.

Branca told Michael to reconsider. Since Geffen was a friend and adviser, perhaps something could be worked out.

Finally, John Branca came up with the idea of leasing to Geffen "Come Together," the Beatles song Michael had recorded and performed on the *Moonwalker* video but never released commercially. (Michael planned to include it on *Decade*.) Geffen wasn't enthusiastic about "Come Together," but finally decided he would accept the song. Michael agreed to let him have it.

Geffen's attorneys then tried to get CBS Records to authorize use of the song on the MCA soundtrack album. Rather than attempt to negotiate a deal with Walter Yetnikoff, CEO and president of CBS Records—with whom Geffen had had a long-standing feud—Geffen apparently had his representatives take up the matter with Tommy Mottola, president of CBS's domestic records unit. When word of these negotiations got back to Yetnikoff, he was furious. For years, a cardinal rule at CBS Records had been that no Michael Jackson business could be authorized unless Yetnikoff, a master deal-maker, sanctioned it personally. It seemed to Yetnikoff that Geffen was trying to go behind his back to secure a Michael Jackson performance for a competing label and that he was in collusion with Jackson and Branca.

Walter Yetnikoff is as well known for his temper as he is for his business sense. "What the hell is going on here?" he stormed when he got on the phone to Branca. "What are you guys trying to pull?"

Branca tried to explain, but Yetnikoff wasn't interested in the explanation. He was angry with Branca, Jackson, and Geffen, and he refused to allow Geffen to have "Come Together."

When Michael heard of Yetnikoff's decision, he became irate. Now, more than ever, he wanted "Come Together" to be included on Geffen's soundtrack, but he was powerless to do anything about it without Yetnikoff's consent. Most industry observers agree that David Geffen used Michael's dissatisfaction with Yetnikoff to turn him against the CBS Records president. If this was what Geffen intended, it was not a difficult task, because Jackson was already peeved at Yetnikoff.

Frank Dileo and Walter Yetnikoff had been great friends, and Yetnikoff decided, in 1988, that he wanted CBS Music Video Enterprises to distribute *Moonwalker*. He approached John Branca with the idea; Branca warned him against it, telling him that it would probably be in Yetnikoff's best interest if Vestron (the company that distributed *The Making of Thriller*) handled *Moonwalker*. He explained that Jackson was upset because of all of the money he felt he had lost on *Moonwalker*, and that his expectations for its success on the home video market would, no doubt, be unrealistic. If Yetnikoff failed to promote *Moonwalker* adequately, Michael would most certainly be angry with him, and who knew what effect Michael's dissatisfaction would have on his CBS Records recording contract.

Yetnikoff assured Branca that he would make certain CBS Music Video Enterprises would do "a fuckin' incredible job"—and they did. The video sold over a million units, which is practically unheard-of in the home-view market. Most music videos sell about twenty-five thousand units. Madonna may sell a few hundred thousand if she's lucky (despite the inflated sales figures her press people feed the media). *The Making of Thriller* was the last video that had been as big as *Moonwalker*.

But Michael still wasn't satisfied.

"Sure it sold a million," he said, "but imagine what it would have sold if they had promoted it. They didn't promote it at all.

Don't tell me they did a good job," Michael told Dileo, "because they didn't. Yetnikoff let me down, big time."

After the *Moonwalker* disappointment and the "Come Together" conflict, Michael Jackson wanted nothing more to do with Walter Yetnikoff. It didn't help that, somewhere around this time, Yetnikoff made a crude joke: Yetnikoff's girlfriend wasn't skilled at performing a certain sexual act, but if Geffen would tutor her, Yetnikoff would purchase Geffen Records for $1 billion in Sony stock. That joke quickly spread through the record industry. Eventually, the story got back to Michael.

David Geffen, who had somehow obtained all of Michael's financial information—it is quite possible that Michael gave him the documents—started discussing with him his relationship with CBS Records. He pointed out to Michael that he had spent about $40 million dollars making music videos for *Bad* (including the cost of *Moonwalker*) and that that was an exorbitant amount to spend on video production. Geffen was right. However, John Branca had made back an enormous amount of money for Michael on these videos as a result of distribution and other sales deals, and Michael's net loss was "only" $10 million. Practically no one in the record industry makes $30 million from music videos. But, still, Michael began to believe that CBS Records was making more money on him and his videos than he was making for himself. Soon, he was riled up enough to want to leave CBS altogether.

Prior to this time, Walter Yetnikoff and Michael Jackson had had an outstanding relationship. Michael brought him up onto the stage during the 1984 Grammys. Walter was appreciative and felt that Michael's public show of gratitude helped him earn millions of dollars for himself and his label. "You don't bring record executives up at the Grammys, 'cause no one's interested," Yetnikoff told *Rolling Stone* in 1988. "I went back to CBS and I said, 'Give me another $2 million for that.' "

Walter Yetnikoff, a flamboyant man from Brooklyn, had been one of the most powerful men in the record business for many years. By 1990 his lineup of superstar recording artists included Michael, Bruce Springsteen, The Rolling Stones, and Bob Dylan. But his power had slipped during the year due to a deteriorating relationship with CBS Records' new parent company, Sony, and, in part, to his estrangement from Bruce Springsteen and Springsteen's attorney, John Landau. Now, without Michael Jackson in his corner, Yetnikoff's future looked cloudy.

* * *

While Michael Jackson tried to sort through the politics of his career, the year 1990 had begun on a sour note for the Jackson family—another lawsuit, this time pitting mother against daughter. Katherine was suing LaToya, claiming that her daughter had stolen her share of the Encino mansion.

Katherine claimed that in July 1987, with the multimillion-dollar Gary Berwin judgment hanging over Joe Jackson's head, Jack Gordon convinced LaToya to persuade her mother that her 25 percent interest in the house was in jeopardy (Michael owns the other 75 percent). Katherine said that she believed her daughter and Jack and she signed a quitclaim agreement giving LaToya her equity in the house—and getting nothing in return—but only after LaToya promised to transfer the property back to her mother if Katherine ever asked her to do so. Katherine said in court papers that, at the time she did this, she was under "severe emotional stress." Now Katherine wanted her share in the house back. But LaToya refused to return it.

According to Jerome Howard, Katherine's former business manager, "Katherine explained to me that because of the Berwin judgment against Joe, the first thing they did was change the pink slips on the cars and put them into the kids' names, and then they put Katherine's part of the Encino house in LaToya's name as protection. But then LaToya up and took off. When she left, I told Katherine she'd better start worrying about the house, because it didn't look like LaToya would be back. The foremost thing on Katherine's mind was getting LaToya back. She didn't care about the house. The thing on Joe's mind was 'What about the house, Kathy?' What Katherine should have done was gotten a quitclaim back from LaToya at the time she gave her her part of the house, and just not filed it until she needed to. If LaToya and Jack's intentions were good ones, that would not have been a problem. But Katherine trusted her daughter, and now there's a suit."

"This lawsuit filed by my mother is the craziest, most insane thing a person could do," LaToya said. "She's just trying to hurt me, and I know Michael and Janet are behind this, pushing my mother."

According to LaToya, she obtained Katherine's interest in the house because, in 1987, her parents were having tax difficulties and she had given them money to pay off the debt. She said that Katherine told her, "I don't want you to give us all this money and you have nothing. Let me give you my twenty-five percent of the house so you'll have some security for yourself."

As far as LaToya is concerned, she paid for her part of the house.

Now she planned to sell it for $50 million to a Japanese investor who intended to turn LaToya's part of the home into a Graceland-type tourist attraction called "Land of the Jacksons." It is not known how she planned to divide the premises, but she said it would be "partitioned off." She said that the first thing visitors would see when they got off the tour bus was a lifelike figure of Michael in his hyperbaric chamber.

This scheme did not make Katherine happy.

When LaToya told Michael of her plans, he was disgusted with her. She told him that she was going ahead with the project, "and neither you nor your dollars can stop me."

"She's just messing with them," said a friend of hers. "She has no desire to do what she's said she's going to do. She just likes to irritate them all. They believe everything she says, especially Michael. He spends a lot of time agonizing over 'What's LaToya gonna do next?' She makes that family absolutely nuts."

LaToya was upset because, she claimed, Janet sent a "huge, gorilla-type" man to kidnap her from Manhattan and bring her back home in January 1990. "I'm sure the family planned to keep me locked up until I agreed to submit to their will."

The family continued to blame Jack Gordon for LaToya's behavior. "My beautiful sister has married a cockroach," said Jermaine bitterly. "One of the worst things he ever did was make her believe she could be successful as a singer." Jermaine said he had recently seen LaToya's nightclub act and that it was "terrible. We knew how awful she'd be simply because she doesn't have what it takes."

Gordon launched a counterattack against his brother-in-law, saying that Jermaine was a "jealous animal, jealous of anyone with success in the family." According to Gordon, LaToya told him that when Michael's *Thriller* album was released, Jermaine made comments [ostensibly based on the cover photo] that Michael "wanted to be white, and that he would not be successful." As the mudslinging continued, Gordon went to the press with the untrue story that Jermaine and Michael had both adopted the Muslim religion and become followers of Louis Farrakhan, who's been widely criticized for his anti-Semitism. Gordon, who is Jewish, claimed that LaToya had changed her mind about the "Land of the Jacksons" museum, and that she was now going to sell her portion of the Encino property to Hasidic Jews so that they could set up an educational program there. "He believes that the whole family is anti-Semitic," said one of his business associates, "and he knew that line about the Hasidic Jews would unnerve them. He was right. It did."

"I heard that Katherine's blood pressure shot straight up," the associate said. "Joe was ready to kill the guy. Finally, after all of these years, Joe Jackson has met his match and his name is Jack Gordon. Gordon is everything Jackson ever was—in terms of his manipulative nature, street smarts, and show biz savvy. But 'Toya is a grown woman. They're going to have to just let her go. But God help her now.''

Michael said that he did not want to become involved in a battle between Katherine and LaToya over the house. He was doing all he could to keep his mind off his family's troubles, surrounding himself with children, immersing himself in charity. While Katherine filed her lawsuit, Michael threw a party for eighty abused or neglected children at his ranch in Santa Ynez. He greeted the two busloads of youngsters from the Village of Childhelp in Beaumont, California, gave them a tour of his game and toy rooms, and served up a barbecue lunch. After that, he hosted fifty children from Maclaren Hall and the Make-A-Wish Foundation at his home. He screened *Teenage Mutant Ninja Turtles* for them. That day, when an associate asked him about LaToya, Michael shook his head in disgust. "I've finished worrying about her,'' he said with great disdain. "She's on her own now.''

(In November 1990, LaToya and Jack announced that LaToya had secretly given birth to a son, Jack Jr., in London in June of 1989. Most family, friends, and associates agree, however, that LaToya did not have a child at all, but was just seeking more publicity.)

Michael's younger sister, Janet, who was twenty-three, had always felt inferior to LaToya. "LaToya is beautiful. Face it, the girl is gorgeous,'' Janet, who has always had low self-esteem, once said. "Want to know what I see when I look in the mirror? I see too much face. Look at these jaws. No matter how thin I might get, my face will always look big because I inherited these jaws from my grandmother. And thin? I'll never be as thin as LaToya. I'm just chunky, that's the best way to describe me. My thighs are too big too. I'm short, and short people have to watch their weight. The problem is I like food. Michael gets on me a lot, telling me when I gain weight. Or LaToya will say, 'Janet, I think you're gaining a little weight.' Or my father will tell me to lose it.''

The fact that Michael had nicknamed his sister "Dunk''—short for Donkey—couldn't have helped much. "You look like a donkey, you're so big,'' he would tease her.

But by 1990 Janet had come into her own with the biggest success of her career, the A&M album *Janet Jackson's Rhythm Nation 1814*, a string of hit records—"Miss You Much,'' "Escapade,'' "Rhythm

Nation," among others—and her first national tour. Charming and timid, talented and driven, Janet has turned out to be one of the better-adjusted Jackson siblings. With the exception of a relationship she maintains with her mother, she keeps her distance from the rest of the family. She does what she can to avoid their machinations and concentrates on her work. Though she is no longer managed by Joe—the break was predictably volatile—he does profit financially from *Rhythm Nation*.

Janet intended to give her parents three-and-a-half points of her royalties on *Rhythm Nation*, but then she cut it back to two-and-a-half and decided to give the other point to Marlon, who was having financial problems. (Marlon's home had gone into foreclosure and, according to some Jackson intimates, Katherine persuaded Janet to pay the house off.) Janet's wishes were for Katherine to be paid half of the three-and-a-half points directly, so that she could be absolutely sure that Katherine would get her share. She didn't want the total sum going to her father's office.

"I've studied the best—Michael Jackson," said Janet in April 1990 of the brother to whom she was always closest. "I'm not saying that just because he's my brother. I really feel he's the best. I saw how hard he works, his ambition. It's so strange to read things about him, because people just don't understand Michael much."

Janet has also noted, "Michael has said that, out of everyone in the family, we're the two that think the most alike." Janet is the only family member who makes it a point to show up at the taping of Michael's videos, just so that she can sit and watch him work. Still, she has to admit that a rivalry does exist between them. "He's very competitive," she said in November 1990. "And so am I."

Surprisingly, Michael is not as competitive with Janet as people might think. Mostly, he supports her efforts and offers advice whenever she asks for it. He thought *Rhythm Nation* was the work of a genius, and his biggest concern was not that it had sold so many copies, but that it hadn't sold enough. "Why did it only sell five or six million copies?" he asked a former associate. "And what does this mean for *me* and my next album?"

Like Michael, Janet has not been resistant to the plastic surgeon's knife. She has had at least two nose jobs, and some have speculated that she has had surgery on her breasts. But she knows how to make plastic surgery work to her advantage. She looks stunning, especially after shedding, on a nine-hundred-calorie-a-day diet, the weight she's been trying to lose for years.

Janet's dancing technique and split-second choreography have been favorably compared to Michael's, and though she is not much of a vocalist, she has become an extremely talented entertainer. Like Michael, she is prone to overwork. Janet collapsed on the set of a half-hour video she made for the *Rhythm Nation* album. When she came to, she was shaking and vomiting. It wasn't until she got to the hospital that she discovered she was exhausted and dehydrated.

Janet paid $4 million for her six-bedroom house, which sits on a two-and-a-half acre hill in northern San Diego. She intends to live there with her boyfriend and adviser, former dancer-choreographer René Elizondo.

The rest of the Jacksons have not fared as well in their recordings without Michael. Solo albums by Jackie, Jermaine, Marlon, and Randy all had disappointing sales. So too did an excellent group album (recorded by Jackie, Jermaine, Tito, and Randy) called *2300 Jackson Street*, after the street on which the family lived in Gary.

Michael was bothered that *2300 Jackson Street* had not been a commercial success, especially since he had telephoned Walter Yetnikoff and specifically asked him to take a special interest in the album and make certain it was properly promoted. But CBS Records could not successfully promote the Jacksons without Michael. It's not that the brothers have no talent; they do. After decades of experience, most of the Jacksons are first-rate vocalists, and they are all champion entertainers. But trying to pursue their own careers while Michael Jackson's shadow looms is not easy. The public doesn't seem to want Michael's brothers; it just wants Michael.

CBS did not renew its relationship with the Jacksons after *2300 Jackson Street*. There was no fanfare, as when the Jacksons left Motown for CBS. Rather, the label just did not pick up the brothers' contracts. The Jacksons simply fizzled out.

Without Michael in the lead, his brothers have not been able to secure a new record deal. LaToya also has no record contract, nor does she seem to be interested in pursuing a career as a vocalist. Rather, she is intent on becoming the Zsa Zsa Gabor of her time—famous for just being famous. Rebbie, by far the most resourceful singer of the three daughters has, ironically, signed a contract with Motown Records.

Marlon, who is no longer with Capitol Records, held an auction of memorabilia and furnishings in May 1990 to raise money. Among the items put on the blocks: Muhammad Ali and Sugar Ray Leonard championship rings, gold records, Victory tour attire, oil paintings, marble statues, and many other expensive articles. Having to auction these items must have been a sad turn of events for Marlon and Carol Jackson, who had been experiencing financial difficulties for years.

Today, Michael Jackson still owns his sprawling ranch—Neverland Valley—in the Santa Ynez valley of Los Olivos. He lives there alone. He has a dozen servants working for him.

Many of the Jacksons' associates were surprised that Michael did not want Bill Bray to live with him at the ranch, since Bray has been a trusted friend and Michael's chief bodyguard since Michael was a child. But Michael made it clear at the time he closed on the property that he did not want Bray living there with him. In recent years he has begun to doubt Bray's loyalty, and had started to question some of his motives.

One night out on the Bad tour, Michael had a crisis with Bill Bray when Bray persuaded Bob Jones, vice president of communications for MJJ Productions, to have Michael sign a document that would give him (Bray) a promotion to chief executive officer and chairman of the board—a position above Michael! Bray really did not mean for the document to be worded quite that way—he's a bodyguard, not a semanticist—but that was the way it turned out. Michael signed it.

Afterward, Michael had second thoughts about what he had done. According to a friend of Bob Jones's, Michael telephoned John Branca in the middle of the night to ask him his opinion of the document. Branca must have been astonished that Michael would have signed such an important agreement without a moment's hesitation. The lawyer apparently told Michael that he had done the right thing—if he wanted to spend the rest of his life working for Bill Bray.

A hasty, and volatile meeting was called in the middle of the night between Branca, Bray, and Jones, and the problem was eventually solved. Michael did give Bill Bray his promotion—allowing Bray more power in the organization, as well as increased compensation—but with a title that was a bit more conservative.

After his promotion, Bill Bray got himself embroiled in the Moonie debacle. Somehow, when it was all over, he ended up with a half million dollars, and his girlfriend was driving a new Mercedes. This turn of events concerned Michael a great deal. Michael would like to think that, after all of the years they have been together, Bill Bray—who is old enough to be Michael's father—has Michael's best interest at heart. It's more likely than not that Bill Bray does care deeply for Michael Jackson. He has demonstrated great loyalty to Michael over the last twenty years. Still, it must be difficult for him to resist the temptation of some of show business's excesses.

Trying to assist Bill Bray in getting a promotion from Michael was the first and last time Bob Jones ever became involved in the politics of Michael Jackson's business. He was deeply sorry, and explained that he was simply trying to help out an old friend, Bray.

Jones, who has been with Michael Jackson since the end of 1987, has known Jackson since he (Michael) was about ten years old. Jones had been employed by Motown as that record company's director of publicity for many years and worked with The Jackson 5 until that group departed in 1975. For the next twelve years, he had practically nothing to do with Michael's career, since he was still working for Motown, but at the end of 1987 he left Motown and resumed his relationship with Michael as if no time had passed. It is doubtful that Jones would ever do anything to hurt Michael Jackson intentionally, or any member of his family, for that matter.

When Michael is not at Neverland Valley, he spends much of his time alone at a condominium on Wilshire Boulevard in Westwood, which is referred to in his camp as "the hideout." The other tenants of the building are not happy to have Jackson as a neighbor.

"It's a pain in the ass," one said. "There are always security people swarming about. People are always asking questions. I've been interrogated dozens of times just for walking into the lobby."

One fan of Michael's attempted to visit him there and was surrounded by security guards within seconds after knocking on his door.

Michael also owns 75 percent of the family's home in Encino (with LaToya), 50 percent of the condominium on Lindley Avenue in Encino (also with LaToya), and has numerous other real estate holdings.

At last count, Michael Jackson has had six nose surgeries, four primary rhinoplasties—"nose jobs"—and two other secondary operations for "touch-up" purposes. These surgeries have served to define the tip of Michael's nose, heighten the bridge, and narrow the nostrils.

"You're looking at prices in a range from three to nine thousand an operation for rhinoplasty surgery," estimated Dr. Robert Kotler, a clinical instructor at the UCLA School of Medicine and author of the *Consumer's Guidebook to Cosmetic Facial Surgery*. "Theoretically there is no limit to the number of operations, providing one is healthy and the tissues are capable of healing. However, we all recognize that each successive procedure adds some difficulty for the next one, because each time one operates, there's more scar tissue and it's technically more difficult to reoperate. But that doesn't mean it can't and shouldn't be done.''

Michael is extremely sensitive about his plastic surgery and will not discuss it even with his closest associates. Barbara Walters once did a report on plastic surgery on ABC's "20/20," and on it she mentioned that Michael had had some work done. Though she was not specific about the operations, Michael was furious just the same.

"That heifer!" Michael stormed, using one of his favorite expressions. "She's got her nerve. Look at all the surgery *she's* had. Look at those eyes. Look at that nose. Look at those breasts.''

When John Branca telephoned Walters and told her that Michael was angry with her, she suggested that she speak to him herself about the problem. When she did, she was able to smooth matters over.

Plastic surgeons not related to Jackson's case have speculated as to whether the nose—which has a feminine quality to it—is made of bone, cartilage, or plastic. (One surgery was to put cartilage into the tip of his nose to reshape it.) Recovering from rhinoplasty surgery can be quite painful. Michael must feel strongly compelled to put himself through this misery—each time he had a nose job, the nose was broken and re-formed—because he has a low threshold for pain.

It has also been suggested that Michael is somehow addicted to plastic surgery. "People can easily get addicted to plastic surgery, as they can to alcohol, drugs, or food,'' according to Dr. Alfred Coodley, associate clinical professor of psychiatry at UCLA.

"Actually, it's more of an obsession than an addiction,'' Dr. Kotler countered. "I think you have to know when to quit. That's the greatest message a cosmetic surgeon can bring to his patient. A conscientious surgeon will say to a patient, 'Enough is enough.' ''

One nurse who used to work in Steven Hoefflin's office has claimed that Michael is a plastic surgery addict. "He's so paranoid about his nose,'' she said, "that Hoefflin doesn't know what to do about him. There is absolutely nothing left to do to this patient's nose.'' Why all of the surgeries? "It's simple,'' she said. "He wants to appear more Caucasian.''

Some have speculated that Michael Jackson is somehow having his skin bleached to appear lighter. "It's obvious that he's had something done,'' says one of his relatives. "I can't say he's bleaching his skin. But he does seem lighter, and I'm not sure that it's makeup, either. He's living out some kind of fantasy his family doesn't really understand.'' Some of Michael's detractors have speculated that the changes he has made in his appearance indicate a denial of his blackness. It's been said that he wants to look more Caucasian in order to attract a more generic pop audience. But whether or not Michael Jackson wants to "look white" is a question only he can answer, and he has never spoken about it.

Is it even possible for a black person to make his skin lighter? "Yes," said plastic surgeon Robert Kotler. "You can't make it white, but you can make it lighter. There are known bleaching agents. There is a class of compounds called Hydroquinones, and they will certainly make a black person's skin lighter."

One employee of Michael's recalled, "He would rub a cream on his face and neck in the morning and at night. He had all of these little tubes in his makeup kit. I asked him what it was, thinking it was some kind of skin nutrient. He told me it was 'medicine.' I left it at that. I then noticed that whenever Michael would go out into the sun, he would cover his face with his hand or wear a big hat. It was as if he didn't want the sun to touch his face. He seemed petrified of sunlight, as if he was afraid he would burn. I though that was odd. I never asked him about it, though."

Indeed, according to *The Handbook of Nonprescription Drugs*, "As the sun's ability to darken skin is much greater than that of Hydroquinone to lighten it, strict avoidance of sunlight is imperative. Although sunscreens may help, even visible light will cause some darkening. The preferable packaging of Hydroquinone is in small squeeze tubes. The dosage is a thin application of 2 percent concentration rubbed into affected areas twice daily. Once the desired benefit is achieved, Hyrdoquinone can be applied as often as needed to maintain depigmentation."

"There are also set classic bleaching compounds that are commonly found in over-the-counter bleaching creams like Porcelana," Dr. Kotler said. (It has been said by some relatives and business associates of the Jacksons that both LaToya and Michael have experimented with Porcelana to bleach their skin.) "You can also wash out the pigment using strong acid solutions on the skin, known as a skin peel. However, whether or not the pigment will come back and perhaps come back in a more intense form is uncertain. It's an unpredictable procedure, which is why I wouldn't do it."

Michael abhors discussing his plastic surgeries—or the question of whether he bleaches his skin—with anyone other than his doctor. By 1987, two of his intimates were concerned enough about his appearance to bring it up in a meeting. "That's enough, Mike," one of them suggested. "You are light enough. Leave your skin alone. The nose is small enough. You got the cleft you wanted, and who knows what else?''

Michael remained silent. From the expression on his face, it was obvious that he was seething. He glanced at the other associate, who was smart enough to know that it wasn't a good time to have an opinion.

Michael does use plenty of pancake makeup, which might account for some of his light coloring. Of course, he is not the first male star to wear a lot of pancake makeup, eyeliner, and mascara. According to makeup artist George Masters, when Elvis Presley returned to Hollywood after his stint in the armed forces, ''he was sporting more mascara and pancake makeup than his leading ladies.''

Michael will admit to only two nose jobs and the cleft in his chin, but it's difficult—almost impossible—to believe that he hasn't had cheek implants, judging from ''before'' and ''after'' photos. (However, one doesn't have to have cheek implants to achieve high cheekbones like Michael Jackson's. Marlene Dietrich and Joan Crawford had their molars extracted to achieve that look.)

One plastic surgeon, Dr. Vito C. Quatela, of Rochester, New York, has speculated that Michael had cheek implants by incisions near the lower eyelids. Dr. Kotler also suspects that that is true, based on Michael's appearance.

From studying photographs, Quatela speculated that Michael has had eyeliner permanently tattooed around his eyes. It also appears to him that Michael has had his lower lip thinned.

''To say he looks good is inaccurate,'' Quatela said. ''He looks very unnatural for a man, and that's where he crossed the line. That's not what cosmetic surgery is supposed to do. You might say he's gone too far.''

Dr. Robert Kotler disagrees. ''The result that Michael Jackson has is a rather extraordinary accomplishment. Especially in terms of his nose, when you see what his appearance was before, and you see what it is now, as a surgeon who does this work, I take my hat off to Dr. Hoefflin. I know the technical difficulty and the challenge that presented itself to Dr. Hoefflin. The patient's nose was very flat and wide. It was amorphous—had not much shape. To take a nose that was as wide as it was and make it as narrow as it is now is a remarkable accomplishment. However many procedures it took to get that result, so be it. It's also very hard to create a cleft surgically, to mimic nature in that way. In the end, the only thing in the world that really matters is what Michael Jackson thinks of the way he looks. If he's happy—and I think he should be—then all of the operations have been unqualified successes. And mind you, sometimes the patient's satisfaction exceeds that of the surgeon. Why? Because it's all in the eye of the beholder.''

Observed Beverly Hills psychiatrist Carole Lieberman, ''On the most basic level, Michael Jackson's plastic surgery obviously represents his dissatisfaction with himself. He probably feels he was never really loved for who he was but rather who he could be manipulated into being. He must have a basic sense of unhappiness and dislike of himself. He may have started doing this [having the surgeries] so that he would not look like his father, whom he clearly despises. But now it would seem that he is doing it because he's so miserably unhappy.''

Of course, only Michael Jackson and his plastic surgeon, Steven Hoefflin, know the extent of Michael's plastic surgery—and they're not speaking about it. The final word on Michael's surgeries came from Donna Burton, secretary to Dr. Hoefflin. When asked if she or Hoefflin could confirm details of Jackson's surgeries, her response was, ''The answer is no. We get calls every day from people wanting to know the answer to that question. And we just have to say no . . . until the end of time.''

Today, Michael's appearance is eerie—like a fragile porcelain doll. His features are as female as they are male; he is truly an androgynous-looking personality. When he performed on a televised tribute to Sammy Davis, Jr., in late 1989, most viewers were dumbfounded by his pasty-faced appearance. He almost looked ill.

Dr. Paul Gabriel, a psychiatrist at New York University Medical Center, has a compelling explanation for the surgeries and the fact that Michael has taken on such an effeminate appearance in the last ten years. He told writer Linda Yglesias that Michael's behavior seems to stem from either a wish to look less manlike, remaining a child, or a desire to ''look more neutral to avoid the issues and conflicts about sexuality. Maybe Michael Jackson has not developed sexually.''

Being androgynous is fascinating when a person is in his teens and interesting when he is in his twenties, but androgyny begins to appear unbalanced when a man goes into his thirties. Indeed, what is Michael Jackson going to be like in his forties? Will he still have that soft, whispery voice? And what will his face look like when he is in his *fifties*? Or *sixties*? The thought of that—and how Michael Jackson will deal with aging—is quite unsettling.

When he was not being honored as ''Entertainer of the Decade'' at the White House (''Glad you're here, sir,'' George Bush told

Michael when he greeted him), receiving the Michael Jackson Good Scout Humanitarian award from the Boy Scouts (he even posed for publicity pictures in a Boy Scout uniform, with other scouts half his age), or accepting the other honors dreamed up for him by his staff, Michael spent much of 1990 reorganizing his business affairs. Perhaps he was getting advice from multimillionaire Donald Trump, with whom Michael was fascinated.

Jack Gordon had been the first to try to set up a meeting between Michael and Donald Trump, but Michael would never meet with anyone recommended by Gordon, even if that person was Donald Trump. Finally, Michael was introduced to Trump through some other mutual friends in 1988.

Donald Trump was flabbergasted to meet Michael Jackson. After that meeting, Trump claimed to many of his associates that he knew Michael personally and hoped to convince him to attend the opening of his grand Taj Mahal Hotel in Atlantic City in April 1990. Trump, though rich and powerful, was not immune to the allure of Michael Jackson's superstardom. Unfortunately, just like most people who come into contact with Michael, Donald Trump wanted to befriend him in order to exploit him.

"Michael Jackson will do anything for me, that's how close we are," Trump boasted, even though he barely knew Michael. Privately, he wondered how he would be able to convince such a reclusive star to make a public appearance. When he finally contacted Michael and asked him to appear at the Taj Mahal—not as a performer, but just as a personality who would attract attention—Trump was as astonished as everyone else that Michael agreed.

"See, what did I tell you?" Trump bragged. "He's the greatest guy in the world. Michael Jackson will do anything for a buddy."

Even though Michael Jackson and Donald Trump were certainly not "buddies," Trump gave Jackson the ten-thousand-dollar-per-night Alexander the Great penthouse suite on the fiftieth floor of the Taj Mahal and then proudly showed him off to the press. Michael was surprisingly amenable to all of the media attention—and even told some people that the appearance had been his idea—as long as it meant being with Donald Trump. He has always been thrilled by being around people of great power and wealth. He has said that he hopes whatever "magic" made them so successful would somehow rub off on him, as if Michael weren't successful himself. It is difficult to imagine, however, what Michael Jackson and Donald Trump would discuss since Trump is so articulate and Jackson is so timid, especially about discussing his business affairs with strangers.

According to a former associate of Michael's who overheard the conversation, as the fans looked on in awe, the reporters shouted out questions and flashbulbs popped all around them, Donald Trump turned to Michael and said, "Mike, you're the biggest. I could walk through this lobby with Mick Jagger and no one would look twice. But with you, well, look around, we're being mobbed."

Then Michael and Donald smiled and posed for a moment.

"Don, you've got the best lobby of any hotel I've ever seen," Michael said, after a few more photos were taken. "You really know how to do it up good. Look at this place. You're incredible."

Then Michael said "no comment" to a reporter who got too close.

"No way," Donald told Michael. "You're the greatest, Mike. You're the best. I thought *I* was a big shot, but look at *you*. These people love you."

Then Donald turned to the media and declared, "No questions please."

"Don, *you're* the one," Michael said to Trump. "You're the one they're photographing. Not me. You're the best."

And on it went.

Later, hundreds of frenzied females mobbed Michael when he exited a hotel elevator. As soon as he saw the mob approaching, he acted quickly. He grabbed his hat and bent down to the floor as security guards formed a human chain to push back the crowd. Later, when Michael and Donald went into a restaurant, the management had to lock the door to prevent a throng of fans from following. The few patrons already there wouldn't leave Michael alone for even a moment to enjoy a meal. After five minutes of being harassed by his public, Michael had to slip out through a back entrance, hungry and tired.

# Chapter

## ❧ 33 ❧

IT HAS BEEN a stressful, exhausting, even maddening, few years. By 1990, family and career pressures have taken their toll on thirty-two-year-old Michael Jackson.

In June of that year, Michael was in negotiation with Disney Studios to lend his name in some way to a new robotic attraction. At the same time, David Geffen—who is affiliated with MCA—wanted Michael to appear at the opening of the Universal Theme Park in Florida, as did Steven Spielberg. Michael Eisner, head of Disney, told Michael Jackson that if he (Jackson) had anything to do with MCA-Universal, he would never be able to be associated with Disney again, ever.

Michael could not bear the thought of being shunned by Disney. He delights in Disney—always has. As a result of Eisner's dictate, he was torn. He desperately wanted Disney—and Michael Eisner—in his corner, but he also wished to maintain his friendship with David Geffen and Steven Spielberg. He anguished over this matter for weeks until—in his mind—the problem became much bigger than it really was. Michael actually suffered an anxiety attack over this problem.

On June 3, 1990, he was admitted to St. John's Hospital and Health Center in Santa Monica. It was said that he had suffered chest pains while doing his Sunday dance exercises. Michael has danced himself into a frenzy every Sunday for years, as part of a weekly ritual. He also fasts on that day. Michael, who was accompanied by his plastic surgeon Steven Hoefflin, was gripping his chest and looked dizzy, pale, and very weak when he was admitted to the hospital.

The hospital immediately ran a battery of diagnostic tests, including an HIV test for AIDS. Michael's blood work came back from the lab negative, as expected. Most observers were surprised that Michael had even requested the test. It was also determined that he suffered from an enzyme deficiency and was anemic, probably due to his strict vegetarian diet.

Coincidentally, Michael was assigned a room just down the hall from his friend Elizabeth Taylor. Taylor had been at the hospital for seven weeks recovering from pneumonia. Michael's hospitalization made headlines for days. President Bush, Liza Minnelli, and Elton John telephoned to wish him well. Katherine and other family members visited. LaToya sent a dozen black roses, an odd gesture, but, said LaToya, "I think they're beautiful." Fans held all-night vigils outside of the hospital. It was reported that Lavon Muhammad, the woman who calls herself "Billie Jean" and claims that Michael fathered her three children, showed up and tried to see "my man." Police got her away from the hospital as quickly as possible.

It was said that Michael was diagnosed as having a condition called costochondritis, a cartilage inflammation in the front part of the ribs, an ailment most commonly found in young athletes who exercise sporadically. The condition is caused by overexertion and stress.

"What a bunch of bullshit," one of Michael's former close associates noted. "The kid had an anxiety attack, a bad case of nerves. He was all torn up trying to choose between Disney and Universal. That's how stressed he is. He's a very frail person these days and can't handle pressure. After his hospital stay generated so much worldwide publicity, what were they going to say as explanation for it: that he suffered an anxiety attack? No way. Instead they came up with a crazy disease no one on the planet had ever heard of, and the public had to accept it."

The former associate also insisted that the story of Michael suffering chest pains while dancing was fictionalized for public consumption, "because it sounded believable."

Indeed, when he was admitted to the hospital, Michael seemed to be exhibiting the symptoms of sweating, shaking, and panting often associated with a classic "panic attack," a psychological problem sometimes suffered by people who are under great stress and anxiety. Of panic attacks, noted Los Angeles Ph.D. Brian Miller has observed, "Thirty-five percent of the country has one or more panic episodes a year. Occasional attacks don't necessarily require therapy. However, individual therapy can give [the sufferer] the tools to deal with his fears. Cognitive therapy, for example, seeks to stop the unrealistic 'self talk' that tends to ignite and magnify panic episodes. Such internal messages as 'I can't stand this' are replaced with more calming commands such as 'Cool it: you're flipping out over nothing.' " Miller also noted that "sufferers of panic disorder are at a high risk of suicide—three times higher than for victims of other psychological problems."

Michael's spokesman, Bob Jones, said that Michael had been "under some stress," certainly an understatement. He said that Michael was particularly distressed by the death of his friend, eighteen-year-old Ryan White, who won a long court battle to attend public school and overcame prejudice against himself and other AIDS victims. (White lost his five-and-a-half-year struggle with the deadly disease in April 1990, just a few months after spending New Year's at Michael's ranch. Michael and Donald Trump went to Indianapolis together in a private jet to pay their respects.) Jones said Michael was still upset over the deaths of his maternal grandmother, Martha Bridges, who died in May, and Sammy Davis, Jr., who also died that month. Michael was also agitated because work on his album, which, said Jones, "is way overdue," was not progressing quickly. No one mentioned the real problem: whether Michael should be loyal to Universal or to Disney.

Michael Jackson had said privately that when he returned from the Bad tour, he would fire everyone on his staff. He didn't trust anyone.

Once, one of Michael's associates met with him to do some minor business with a certificate of deposit. A document had to be signed. Now, Michael wisely insists upon signing all documents himself. He also signs all checks over fifty dollars.

"What's the matter?" the accountant asked him. "You don't trust me?"

Michael said, "Look, I don't trust anybody. Except Katherine." Then he paused for a moment and added, "And even then, I have to wonder."

After Michael got out of the hospital, he went about the business of reorganizing his affairs. Frank Dileo had been dismissed after the tour was over, and Michael apparently feels no regret over his decision. He still communicates with Dileo, through middlemen and only when he is agitated about something.

For instance, Frank, who appeared in the 1990 film *GoodFellas*, received a great deal of publicity that year as a result of his excellent performance and heard from Michael's camp in October of that year. Frank had signed the nondisclosure agreement Michael demands that most of his employees sign (which is supposed to prevent former employees from making "damaging and deleterious statements" about him), and when Michael heard Frank discussing him in the media, he became upset and demanded that his former manager stop talking about him.

Then, when Michael heard that someone was spreading rumors that he was a homosexual, he had an associate telephone Frank Dileo demanding to know if Frank was the source. Frank, who does not believe that Michael is gay, was more hurt than Michael would ever know. He wondered how a person he once considered to be a son could be so mistrusting. But he should have known Michael was a suspicious person. Two months before Michael had Frank fired, it was reported that Michael had purchased from a New York–based security firm a briefcase featuring a hidden tape recorder for himself and six Voice Safe telephone scramblers for his home. The briefcase can be used to tape meetings secretly, and the scramblers make it impossible to tape the user's conversation off a telephone line.

Marshall Gelfand, Michael's accountant of seven years, was also given his walking papers by John Branca. Michael felt he was too conservative in his investment strategies and had Branca hire a new accountant, Richard Sherman, who also works for David Geffen.

By the summer of 1990, Michael had begun to have doubts about John Branca. In recent years, despite Branca's many professional strengths, Michael Jackson allowed his insecurities about him—and, it's been said by his associates, David Geffen's personal feelings about Branca—color his perception of the high-powered attorney. For instance, Michael was constantly concerned about the identities of Branca's other clients. Frank Dileo was not permitted by Michael to have other clients, but Branca is an attorney who was practicing law before that day in early 1980 when Michael came into his office. By 1990, he had twenty-five clients in addition to Michael.

In 1988, John Branca represented The Rolling Stones' Steel Wheels international tour. According to an associate of Branca's, Michael telephoned him one day about a business matter, and Branca happened to mention that he would be going to Barbados for a week. Michael wanted to know the reason for the trip. When Branca told him it was for business purposes, Michael became suspicious. He wanted to know what kind of business Branca could have in Barbados. Rather than lie, he told him that he was meeting with Mick. "Mick? You mean *Mick Jagger*?" Michael wanted to know. Now he was getting upset.

Branca admitted that he was going to be representing The Rolling Stones tour. "Well, is it a big tour?" Michael asked. "It's not going to be as big as mine, is it? Or worse, it's not going to be *bigger* than mine, is it?"

There was probably no way to calm Michael down at this point. Next, he wanted to know where the Stones would be playing. When Branca reluctantly told him they were thinking about the Los Angeles Coliseum, Michael became even more anxious. "The Coliseum!" he exclaimed. "The Coliseum! That's bigger than the [Los Angeles] Sports Arena, where I played. How many dates? They're not playing as many dates as me and my brothers played at Dodger Stadium, are they?" Michael was frantic.

When John Branca took on rock star Terrence Trent D'Arby as a client, Michael became upset again. He considers D'Arby competition, just as he does Prince. An associate of Branca's reported that Michael asked Branca to drop D'Arby, and that Branca said he would do it if Michael absolutely insisted upon it. But then Michael telephoned D'Arby, with whom he had never spoken, to let him know that he (Michael) has no control over Branca, and that if the attorney should ever drop him as a client, it would be entirely his decision because, as Michael told D'Arby, "I have no problem with Branca representing you." Actually, Michael was trying to maintain friendly relations with D'Arby in case the two should ever decide to record a duet sometime in the future.

It was said that when Branca found out about what Michael had done—D'Arby's manager telephoned Branca immediately after D'Arby hung up with Michael—he was as disappointed in Michael as he was angry at him. In the end, Branca decided *not* to drop Terrence Trent D'Arby as a client. (He still represents him.) Branca's law firm, Ziffren, Brittenham and Branca, had also begun representing Prince in recent years, much to Michael's consternation. However, Branca wisely made certain that he had nothing to do with the Prince account.

Most observers felt that representing Michael Jackson had apparently become more taxing and demanding than ever for John Branca. In the spring of 1990, when Branca decided he should be better compensated for his time-consuming dealings with Jackson, David Geffen suggested that he quit his practice and work exclusively for Michael. Geffen's motives in making that suggestion are unknown, but based on the feuding relationship of Branca and Geffen in the past, it's doubtful that Geffen was simply thinking of Branca's best interest.

Later, Branca and Michael had a meeting. It's been said by Branca's associates that he felt the time had come for him to share in the equity in Jackson's publishing company. Branca is said to have explained to Michael that he wanted to devote as much time to developing Michael's publishing holdings as possible, and in return he wanted 5 percent of the profits.

John Branca must have known that it would be risky to make such a proposition to Michael. Michael is thrifty when it comes to compensating his representation. He feels that an occasional Rolls-Royce or expensive watch is enough to placate his advisers; he abhors the idea of giving them extra percentages. Up until this time, John Branca worked for Michael on a monthly retainer. On some extraordinary deals, a percentage for Branca would be worked into the deal. For instance, he got 5 percent of the profit on the Victory and Bad tours. (In contrast, Mickey Rudin, who worked for Sinatra for years, got 10 percent of Sinatra's tours.)

At this time, Michael was feeling psychologically poor, as a result of the *Moonwalker* debacle. He told John Branca he would consider his proposal. Then Michael decided to talk the matter over with David Geffen.

Besides being a brilliant career strategist and businessman, David Geffen is also known in Hollywood as somewhat of an interloper in the careers of artists with whom he has no official relationship, just for the fun of it all—and because he likes to be in the eye of the storm; he is fascinated by the intrigue of cutting a big deal.

His reputation as an interloper goes back to 1973 when, at the age of twenty-nine, he became involved in the turbulent career of twenty-seven-year-old Cher Bono. Geffen was instrumental in her break from husband and singing partner, Sonny Bono.

At that time, despite almost ten years in show business—most of them at the top of her profession as a music and television star—Cher was insecure, vulnerable, and not particularly bright. After David began questioning her about her business affairs, it was clear that she knew little about any of them and that Sonny had been manipulating her since she was about seventeen.

It wasn't long before Cher, under David Geffen's influence, left Sonny, broke up the Sonny and Cher act, and forced the cancellation of their popular prime-time series. The night Sonny and Cher taped their last program, in February 1974, Cher hosted a surprise party for Geffen at the Beverly Wilshire Hotel. She had mariachis, jugglers, and knife throwers; Cher and Bob Dylan sang duets to him. He reportedly gave her an eight-thousand-dollar diamond ring that evening.

David Geffen, when scrutinizing Cher's contracts, figured out that she was working *for*, not *with*, her husband, Sonny. For the last five years, Cher was actually under contract to Sonny, as a paid employee of Cher Enterprises. Cher Enterprises was a corporation in which Sonny owned nine-hundred-and-fifty shares of stock and the couple's attorney owned the other fifty shares. Cher owned nothing. However, she was entitled to a small salary and two weeks' vacation a year.

Under David Geffen's guidance, Cher filed a civil action against her estranged husband charging that her contract constituted "involuntary servitude," or slavery. Then Cher and David Geffen—who did not represent her in any way but said that he cared about her and her welfare—went to William Morris Agency and informed them that Cher was now a solo artist, that Sonny and Cher were finished, and that the agency should begin thinking in terms of selling a Cher show to the network. Sonny was furious, and also helpless, because Geffen by now had total influence over Cher.

"David Geffen is a little antagonizer," Sonny Bono said at the time. "He and Cher conspired to destroy Sonny and Cher, and me in the process. None of this was any of his business. There were times when I wanted to kill David Geffen."

Geffen encouraged Cher to ask for a new split on future royalties from Sonny and Cher recordings: 75 percent to Cher and 25 to Sonny. He began negotiating a solo record deal for Cher at Warners. In July 1974, Cher and Geffen and two private security guards barged into the home that Cher and Sonny once owned and, in what Sonny called "a guerrilla action," moved Sonny's belonging out and theirs in. David and Cher then lived "open and notoriously" according to Sonny, in the Bono mansion.

It was an ugly time in Cher's life, and David Geffen was right in the middle of it, and, some might say, the instigator. Geffen would be at Cher's side throughout the acrimonious divorce, advising her every step of the way. He knew about the final terms of the divorce before Cher did, telephoning her at her aerobics class and telling her, "You walked home with all the marbles, Cher. You got everything. Sonny gets nothing."

Though Geffen negotiated a TV series in October 1974 starring Cher without Sonny, and a solo contract at Warner Bros. Records, Cher dropped him before he had time to profit from her newfound wealth if, indeed, that is what he had in mind. (They still do business today, however, since Cher is signed to Geffen's record label, "and he is a pain in my ass every day of my life," Cher has said.)

Fifteen years ago, Cher was almost as big a star as she is today.

It was a coup for Geffen to be involved in her life and career. Now, David Geffen seems to be enmeshing himself in Michael Jackson's career in much the same way as he did in Cher's. He has exerted a great deal of influence over Michael. Even though Geffen technically has no official capacity with Jackson other than as an adviser on his investment committee, Michael barely makes a move without first consulting him.

Because of David Geffen's obvious impact on Michael Jackson's life and career—and as a result of some persistent rumors about Geffen's lifestyle—some of Michael Jackson's intimates have whispered among themselves that Geffen and Jackson are having a sexual relationship.

Of course, rumors have continued for years that Michael Jackson is homosexual. These stories have been in circulation since Jackson was a teenager—when he was rumored to have been romantically involved with actor Clifton Davis—and will, no doubt, persist until the day—if it ever comes—that he marries (and, even then, the speculation may not end).

David Geffen admitted to Paul Rosenfield in the March 1991 issue of *Vanity Fair* that he is bisexual. He admitted that he went from being "in love with Cher to being in love with Marlo Thomas to being in love with a guy at Studio 54. I date men, and I date women. I have not kept any secrets. There's not a person who does not know my story."

When asked if he was concerned that the liberal gay media might "out" him ("outing" is a term used by the gay press when a person's sexual proclivity is made public without his or her consent), Geffen responded, "No one can threaten me with exposure of something I'm not hiding."

Of course, David Geffen's remarkably frank words about his personal lifestyle do not mean that he is having an affair with Michael Jackson. Only Jackson and Geffen know the full scope of their relationship. It is interesting to note, however, that David Geffen is precisely the kind of person with whom Michael Jackson would probably have a serious personal connection. Michael is nothing if not media conscious and savvy. He would want to choose someone—a man or a woman—who would have to bear some consequences for his or her actions should that person decide to sell the story of "their" romance to one of the tabloids. Geffen would probably not want details of any personal relationship with Jackson revealed. And he certainly does not need the money that such a feature would generate. A relationship with a person like David Geffen would be safe for Michael Jackson. And as suspicious as

Michael Jackson is, Geffen—or someone of Geffen's financial stature—would pose no threat to him in terms of an interest only for his money.

Of course, pairing Michael Jackson and David Geffen is pure conjecture. Only Michael Jackson and the person with whom he is having sex—if there is such a person—know the truth about his sexuality. None of his friends or associates—and no biographer for that matter—can know the reality of Michael's sexual identity.

In June 1990, a few weeks after presenting his proposal to Michael Jackson that he be entitled to a percentage of Jackson's publishing deals, John Branca got a phone call from David Geffen. Geffen asked Branca to contact Bertram Fields, Geffen's attorney, and talk to him about the enforceability of Michael's seven-year contract with Epic. Branca refused, and for a simple reason: the matter was none of Geffen and Fields's business.

At this time, David Geffen was apparently trying to convince Michael that he should try to break his CBS Records deal by using a contract loophole. Michael's contract with CBS was signed in 1983 and amended after *Thriller* in 1985. Geffen felt that the seven years that had lapsed since the original agreement gave Michael an edge in renegotiating the entire deal, since California state law forbids personal service contracts of a longer duration. Industry observers felt that Geffen was trying to lure Michael away from CBS, possibly so that he could sign him to his own label.

Michael certainly could have gotten out of his contract with CBS Records. But what Geffen was apparently overlooking was that, although Jackson's contract with CBS had expired, Michael still owed four more albums to the label. He was supposed to deliver seven albums; he had only given CBS three. After the seven years, CBS Records could not enjoin Michael from recording for another label, but it *could* sue him for damages, the amount of which would be based on the estimated loss of profits from the albums Michael did not deliver. This dollar amount would be derived from the combined sales figures of *Off The Wall*, *Thriller*, and *Bad*. CBS Records could have mounted a huge lawsuit against Michael Jackson. Even though David Geffen was apparently willing to overlook all of this, John Branca was not.

An anonymous source in Geffen's office reported that Branca and Geffen got into a heated argument over the logic of trying to extricate Michael from his recording contract with CBS Records, and Geffen hung up on an acrimonious note. Then, according to the source, Geffen telephoned Michael and began trying to sour him on Branca by saying that Branca was being uncooperative and that the reason Michael didn't have "a good deal at CBS" was because of Branca's close relationship with the company president, Walter Yetnikoff, who was falling out of favor with Sony, CBS's parent company. Michael apparently allowed himself to be swayed, never stopping to think that he had the best deal in the record industry and that John Branca was the man who got it for him. He was actually beginning to doubt Branca.

A couple of days later, according to a source in Branca's office, Branca and Jackson had a meeting. Something had changed in Michael. He was barely listening to what Branca was saying; he seemed hostile. The two got into a heated discussion about CBS, whether Michael was obligated to record for them, whether he should deliver a new album. The meeting did not go well.

When it ended, Branca went back to his office in Century City. The next day, he received a letter by special messenger from Michael Jackson's accountant, Richard Sherman, whom Branca had hired.

John Branca's "services were no longer required by Michael Jackson." He had been fired.

"I'm sorry you got fired," Frank Dileo said he told John Branca, "But am I surprised? Not one bit. It's a dirty business, ain't it?"

Associates of John Branca's insist that he would have remained at Michael's side, even if Michael had not agreed to give him equity in his publishing empire. The biggest problem Branca faced was not whether Jackson would share publishing profits with him, but how to advise Michael Jackson successfully—as he had been doing for ten years—with David Geffen now such a disruptive force. It did seem to most observers that whenever Geffen got to Jackson one on one, he could talk him into almost anything. As a result, there had been a number of shouting matches between Branca and Geffen in Jackson's presence.

Because there was already bad blood between Branca and Geffen, it seemed to some observers that Geffen was now using Branca's request for publishing percentages against him. He was able to make Branca appear greedy to Michael. John Branca's associates insist that were it not for David Geffen's involvement, Branca would still be representing Michael Jackson today.

Branca's work with Michael Jackson—the way he masterminded the accumulation of his wealth—can only be compared to Colonel Tom Parker's work with Elvis Presley. Even though Branca was not Jackson's manager, he certainly had the kind of impact on Michael's career that Parker had on Presley's.

In years to come, Michael Jackson may look back on this time and realize that firing John Branca was a mistake. In 1980, when Branca began representing him, Michael's net worth was barely a million dollars. Ten years later, in great part due to Branca's negotiating skills, the net worth is close to $300 million, including the publishing holdings, which are valued at close to $200 million. That's a tribute to Michael Jackson's artistry, no doubt; but it also speaks quite well of John Branca's negotiating skills.

Michael paid $47.5 million for the Northern Songs catalogue in 1984, and now, just seven years later, it is valued at over $125 million. Branca had structured the deal so that Michael would be entitled to a $5 million tax write-off every year for the first eight years following the ATV acquisition, totaling $40 million in deductions. "Buying the Beatles catalogue was the coolest, the best, the smartest move that any artist has ever made," John Branca said. "I have to say that I was honored to be able to do that for Mike."

Prior to that purchase, Branca had purchased the Sly Stone catalogue for Michael from Warner-Chappell publishing. At the time of his firing, Branca was negotiating with Warner-Chappell to sell Michael the James Brown catalogue; the deal was closed but not consummated before Branca's dismissal. In the history of Warner-Chappell publishing, the company has only agreed to sell copyrights twice: both times to Michael Jackson at John Branca's behest—the Sly Stone catalogue (along with some other artists) and James Brown's.

Today, in all, Michael Jackson owns the publishing rights to about six thousand songs, including 251 by The Beatles and 50 by Little Richard. He also owns some material from Sam Cooke and Dion and many others.

With the new Brown acquisition and Michael's proposed custom label at CBS, as well as other proposed projects, Branca intended to double Michael's worth in the next couple of years. As of this date, however, the Brown deal and the custom-label deal are in limbo. A million dollars has been spent recording Michael Jackson's next album, which was due for release in spring 1991.

Also, at the time of his dismissal, John Branca was said to be working out a deal with the Smithsonian Institution in Washington that Michael would have relished. The Smithsonian has one last unoccupied plot of real estate, attached to the Museum of Popular Culture and facing the Lincoln Memorial. Institution officials agreed that if Jackson donated $5 million, a new building, the Michael Jackson Performing Arts Center, would be built on the vacant lot. Because Branca had CBS, Time-Warner, and other corporations committed to donating a substantial amount of the $5 million, Jackson would have had to come up with just a small portion.

The entertainment industry's perception of Michael Jackson's dismissal of John Branca (who still represents The Rolling Stones, the Jim Morrison estate, George Michael, The New Kids on the Block, and about forty other artists) is that Branca got caught in the cross fire of an ongoing feud between David Geffen and CBS Records' CEO Walter Yetnikoff. That wasn't the case. There was speculation that Michael Jackson was unhappy with the way Branca negotiated his record deal at CBS Records due to Branca's close relationship with Yetnikoff. That also was not true. In the end, Branca's firing had nothing to do with Yetnikoff or with Branca's negotiating skills and everything to do with Michael Jackson's mercurial personality and, perhaps, Geffen's growing influence over him.

David Geffen denied any involvement in the decision to fire John Branca. "Michael changed lawyers because he wanted to—he felt John Branca was too close to Walter [Yetnikoff]," Geffen said.

Meanwhile, by late 1990, Walter Yetnikoff's days at CBS were numbered. Sony, the parent company, and Yetnikoff had had a stormy relationship for some time, and that had little to do with Michael, at first, and more to do with Yetnikoff's power plays and excesses. "Sex, booze, power, prestige, money, glory—I tasted all of that," Yetnikoff has said. His relationship with Bruce Springsteen and his manager, John Landau, was just as troubled as the one with Michael Jackson. In fact, Yetnikoff had alienated most of his supporters at Sony, as well as many of the record industry executives who had been in his corner during the thirty years he served as one of the chief architects of CBS Records' fortune. (He joined the company as an attorney in 1961.)

Since it seemed that Michael wanted to get out of his contract with CBS—there was talk that he sought to renegotiate the deal—and that he was not delivering the record he had promised, Walter Yetnikoff fell farther from grace with the Sony corporation. It was said that David Geffen caused mischief by influencing Michael to be difficult with CBS Records.

"People want to make me out as having had more to do with this than I had," Geffen told Eric Pooley of *New York* magazine. "Walter behaves badly, and that's why he blew up his career. When people think they're powerful, the world has a way of reminding them that they're not."

In fact, Yetnikoff did have many political problems with CBS Records and Sony that had nothing to do with Michael Jackson, but certainly if Jackson—the label's biggest and most influential artist—had been supportive, Yetnikoff might have had more strength with Sony.

In September 1990, Walter Yetnikoff was forced to resign.

According to one business associate, Michael Jackson's reaction: "Too bad for him. Now, what's this going to mean for me?"

David Geffen seems to derive his power over Michael Jackson from the fact that he is not a paid employee of Michael's, but is an adviser Michael feels helps him out of genuine concern. "Michael feels he can trust David because, unlike most other people in his life, David doesn't profit from Michael . . . yet," said one observer. "Michael thinks that David Geffen is impartial. Perhaps he is. However, most people in the industry feel that Geffen is using Michael to his own advantage and will, one day, make a move to control the Jackson empire."

Michael replaced John Branca with three seasoned law veterans: Bertram Fields (for litigation), Alan Grubman (for negotiations with CBS), and Lee Phillips (for music publishing)—all closely associated with David Geffen.

In 1991, Michael considered moving his ATV Music Company—which includes Northern Songs, the classic Beatles publishing catalog—from EMI, the number two publisher in the world (and the company that owns Capitol Records), to MCA Music Entertainment Group, with which David Geffen is associated. (EMI is the administrator of ATV, meaning that the conglomerate handles the complicated deal-making and contracts of publishing.) Industry observers feel that a move from EMI to MCA would be ludicrous, since MCA Music Entertainment Group, a smaller company, is ill-equipped to handle Michael's complex publishing arrangements. The deal could involve millions, and, again, it would seem that David Geffen is somehow influencing Michael in this decision.

In August 1990, Michael turned thirty-two years old. At the same time, he ended months of speculation over who would finally replace Frank Dileo when he announced that Sandy Gallin—of Gallin-Morey Associates—was his new manager. Gallin represents clients with careers in both film and music, such as Dolly Parton, Andrew Dice Clay, Whoopi Goldberg, and The Pointer Sisters.

Most industry observers were surprised that Jackson chose Gallin as a manager. Despite his roster of stars, Gallin is not considered among the handful of top entertainment managers. Furthermore, Gallin has little background in record-radio promotion and is not politically intimate with the executives at CBS Records. However, upon close inspection, a possible reason Michael hired Gallin becomes clearer: Sandy Gallin is David Geffen's best friend.

In 1988, after Michael fired Frank Dileo, David Geffen telephoned John Branca and asked if he could persuade Michael to "take a meeting" with Sandy Gallin. Branca called Michael to see if he was interested. He wasn't. Michael said that he had met Gallin before and was not impressed. Branca, who liked Gallin and had done business with him in the past, convinced Michael that he should at least meet with him. The meeting did not go well; Michael refused to take his sunglasses off. From his actions, he obviously was not interested in Sandy Gallin. After ten minutes, he began fidgeting and giving John Branca the "high sign" that he wanted the meeting to end.

Less than a year later, Michael hired Sandy Gallin as his manager.

Though David Geffen's influence on Michael seems fairly obvious even to the most casual observer, Michael becomes upset, and even defiant, when it is pointed out to him. For instance, after Frank Dileo's firing, Michael had considered hiring Irving Azoff, former head of MCA Records, as his manager. Azoff and Geffen are not friends; they've been rivals for years.

One associate of Michael's recalled, "John Branca and Michael Jackson were discussing the possibility of Azoff as a manager when Branca asked Jackson what he thought David Geffen would think if Azoff was Michael's manager. Michael became angry. 'Who cares what David Geffen thinks?' he said. 'You should care what *I* think,' he told Branca. 'Not what David thinks.' And then, as if to prove a point, Michael picked up the telephone and called David. He said, 'David, this is Mike. I just wanted to let you know that I've decided to hire your very good friend, Irving, to be my manager. So what do you think of that?' "

It's not known what David Geffen thought of Michael's decision. However, Michael obviously did not hire Irving Azoff to be his manager.

One close aide of Michael's asked about the terms of the contract with Sandy Gallin. "What contract?" Michael said, slightly perturbed. "This is a handshake deal. If it works, fine. If not, fine. I'm not signing any more contracts. Sandy Gallin gets to tell people that he represents Michael Jackson. That's a coup for him."

The aide looked at Michael with a worried expression, concerned about his own future with MJJ Productions. "Except for you," Michael hastened to add. "You don't have to worry about a thing."

The associate looked worried anyway.

In March 1991, Michael Jackson finally came to terms with CBS Records, now known as Sony Corp. (Sony purchased CBS Records in 1988.) The deal was structured on groundwork laid by John Branca—including a 25 percent royalty rate and Jacksons' own label (now called Nation Records). Michael's spokespeople claimed that the contract guaranteed a return of hundreds of millions. Press reports implied that Sony actually handed over a *billion* dollars to Michael. In fact, Michael could receive $120 million per album for the next six *if* sales match the 40-million-plus level of *Thriller*. If they don't, he won't. With advances and financial perks, the deal is worth about $50 million to Michael right now, eclipsing Janet Jackson's $32 million contract at Virgin Records.

Where Michael Jackson's career is concerned, the future seems to rest on the commercial success or failure of his next album.

As is always the case with Michael Jackson when it comes time for a new album, questions have been raised in the media about whether or not Jackson will be able to make a "comeback." It's ludicrous even to pose the question. There have always been new commercial propositions for Michael Jackson. No matter the musical trend, Michael Jackson fits. History has proven that. Michael's fans are anxiously anticipating whatever he has to offer. Whether the record will top *Thriller*'s thirty-seven million and *Bad*'s twenty million in worldwide sales is another question.

Is Michael being controlled by David Geffen? With twenty-three years of professional experience to his credit, it's difficult to believe that Michael Jackson would not be capable of making his own decisions. "His success is not a fluke, obviously," said an associate of his. "Maybe Michael Jackson is really controlling David Geffen? Who knows what their relationship actually is? But Michael has proved that he's nobody's puppet, from the early days when he defied his own father. He has a plan, I feel, that will reveal itself one day soon."

If Michael Jackson's next album sells fifty million copies—more than *Thriller*—everyone in the Jackson camp will be joyous, and Michael will be the happiest man on the planet. But if it doesn't, Michael Jackson is going to be quite miserable, and, as a result, so will everyone around him.

If Michael's next album is not as big as *Thriller*, he will start placing blame. He may have some second thoughts about his decision to replace John Branca with three of David Geffen's attorneys. And when he reconsiders the fact that his manager, Sandy Gallin, is David Geffen's best friend and that his accountant, Richard Sherman, also represents David Geffen, he may ask himself, "What is going on here?"

If all of that happens, Gallin will probably get a letter from one of Michael's attorney's informing him that his services are no longer required.

Then the attorneys will also get messenger-delivered letters from Michael's accountant informing them that they are, as Michael would put it, "finished."

Michael's accountant will then receive a letter from someone else on Michael's behalf breaking the same news.

And then Michael Jackson will, no doubt, banish David Geffen from his life forever.

# ✿ Epilogue ✿

DESPITE ALL THAT has happened to the Jacksons—all of the infighting, family politics, hurt, anger, betrayal, and disappointment—Joseph and Katherine Jackson are still husband and wife and will soon be celebrating forty years of marriage. "We love each other," Joe said recently, "and I guess that's what has kept us together all these years. No matter what, we've loved each other."

Joe Jackson, sixty-one years of age as of this writing, is determined to continue his career as a show business entrepreneur. "This isn't the way I planned it," he said of about the way his family turned out. "The fighting, the money . . . we were *all* supposed to share in the glory." He added, "There's been an awful lot of money made, and a lot of money taken."

It was reported early in 1990 that the Jackson family planned to go public with a $50 to $100 million initial stock offering. Joe said that his family intended to launch a film company called Jackson Films; a record label called Jackson Records; a theme park and entertainment complex in Las Vegas that will include a recording studio, soundstage, and family museum; and a mint to produce collectible coins and other memorabilia. Joe was the chairman of the Jackson Entertainment Corp., formed in 1989. The family intends to develop a television miniseries about themselves, to be produced by Jermaine. Michael has given them permission, as long as he is not more prominent—or less prominent—in the series than anyone else in the family.

Though Joe hopes all of the siblings will participate, most observers say he can certainly count Michael, Janet, and LaToya out, and perhaps Marlon, who is also pursuing a solo career. It is doubtful that the four of them—who have carved lives so totally separate from the rest of the family—will want to have anything to do with

549

their father's venture. "But Joe continues to hope," one of his associates said. "If ever there was an eternal optimist, it's Joe Jackson. He believes that, one day, the whole family will be together again. It's his dream, his one and only dream. There's something sad about an old dream, isn't there?"

Joe once said in an interview, "When you're in the public eye, your life is in the public domain. People read about you, they write about you. They draw their own conclusions. I would get more respect if the public knew the whole story, if they looked at where the Jackson clan started and where it is today. Others try to jump on the bandwagon. I *am* the bandwagon."

The Jackson patriarch is not the only eternal optimist. Katherine Jackson, sixty years old as of this writing, once observed, "I listen. And I learn. I look to the future with a smile and I pray."

Katherine Jackson's memoirs, *The Jacksons—My Family* (co-written by Richard Wiseman), were published in the United States during the summer of 1990 by St. Martin's Press.

" 'What a sorry family these Jacksons have become,' I imagine people are saying today," she wrote in the book's prologue. " 'They couldn't handle their rags-to-riches success.' If I depended on the press for all my information on my family, I'd come to the same conclusion. [But] here is the Jackson family story *I've* lived."

Unfortunately, according to her book, the story Katherine says she's lived doesn't include such names as Cheryl Terrell or Joh' Vonnie Jackson—the mother of Joseph's daughter and the girl herself, or Gina Sprague, the secretary who says Katherine assaulted her in the Motown building. And Katherine doesn't write about her sons' troubled marriages or her involvement in the Korean incident. In fact, she decided not to write about dozens of other episodes that are crucial to understanding the dynamics of her family. What's fascinating about her book is how unrevealing it is. Indeed, her memoirs are a true self-reflection—warm, but somehow sad and full of contradictions.

Katherine is a woman who should not be pitied, however, for she is truly remarkable. She has survived a long, trying marriage with more grace and dignity than most reasonable people could ever rally, despite occasional moments of provoked madness. "I subscribe to Christ's teachings on forgiveness," she has explained. Why? Probably for the sake of her nine children and eighteen grandchildren. "I'm so grateful that my children love me, and all I want is for them to lead a good Christian life and to be happy. That's all I want."

Indeed, her children do love her, and Katherine loves them in return and probably always will. But understandably, as often happens, her love is blind. "I don't think fame has affected us," she has said. "I don't think any of my boys has changed. However, as a mother, I guess I might be looking at things a little differently."

But fame certainly did affect the Jackson family in a deeply tragic way—and not just Katherine's sons, but her daughters as well. For years, the public has been fascinated by the spectacle of the large and powerful family from Gary that always seemed so cheerful when they posed together for magazine covers. But the Jacksons were—are—in the business of illusion, the fantasy of show business. The tragedy is that the greatest illusion of all is not what happened on stage, but what happened backstage, at that house in Encino where there was no protection against self-involvement, jealousy, and greed. That they were perceived to be the all-American black family was an illusion greater than any gravity-defying moonwalk dance step Michael Jackson could execute.

Every family member has been deeply affected by the bittersweet joy of their many successes, by the anger at having been manipulated and exploited practically all of their lives, by the agony of so many years of betrayal and domestic heartbreak. What could have been the story of a family's transcendence and triumph over poverty turned out, instead, to be a tale of tragedy and disappointment.

Perhaps a telling comment is that Michael is not the only one who has tried to gain a new perspective on life by changing his appearance. With the exception of Jackie, practically all of the Jacksons—including Joe and Katherine, and even Rebbie—have now followed Michael's lead and have had nose jobs.

"Why, that makes perfect sense," observed psychiatrist Carole Lieberman. "They probably have had many other plastic surgeries as well. After all, everyone in the family has, for years, agreed to believe in a certain craziness—like when the mother claims she does not celebrate birthdays for religious reasons, yet will accept presents if they are wrapped with brown paper instead of festive wrapping. At her birthday parties, everyone agrees to pretend that reality is different.

"Certainly, there has been a history of this behavior," the psychiatrist continued. "The father pretending that it was reasonable to have an illegitimate child because he felt unloved by his family. The mother pretending that she was not motivated by money, when she obviously was. The boys, when they were very young, pretending—by lying to their mother about it—that the father didn't have girlfriends. Then they agreed to pretend for the press that they were the ideal family.

"The fact that the most successful family member was the first to have plastic surgery, and then the rest followed, indicates that they simply copied him in a subconscious effort to find the key to his success. One wonders why Jackie, the oldest brother, decided not to follow the pack, and the answer to that is probably another story of sibling rivalry in itself. Indeed, for eight of the nine family members to have had nose jobs illustrates the extent of their psychopathology.''

Most of the Jackson siblings married young and have had difficult marriages: Jermaine's to Hazel Gordy, Jackie's to Enid Spann, and Janet's to James DeBarge have all ended. LaToya's to Jack Gordon seems troubled.

The saddest divorce of all is probably Tito's from Dee Dee. The couple had been married eighteen years when Dee Dee discovered that Tito had been unfaithful. Desolate, she filed for divorce in the spring of 1990.

"It's done. I've got to go on for my three sons,'' she said. "Screw what's happened. My kids are my priority now. As for being a Jackson, I'll always be one, but I have to continue now and let that part of my life go. I have known this man since I was fourteen years old. Despite what he did, I still have respect for him. But I must say,'' she concluded with finality, "that chapter of my life is closed.''

"The Jackson wives are a strong lot. Anyone who knows them and understands what they have been through wonders how they've managed,'' a friend of Hazel Gordy Jackson's said. "The boys took after Joe, I suppose. And the wives somehow got their strength handed down to them from Katherine.''

Randy Jackson was married in May 1989 to Eliza Shaffe. Sadly, twenty-seven-year-old Randy—the youngest of Joseph and Katherine's sons—was apparently influenced by the example of spousal abuse and philandering set by other members of his family. According to his wife, who filed criminal charges against her husband as well as divorce papers in November 1990, Randy beat her throughout most of her pregnancy. "It's atrocious. It's a travesty,'' said Eliza Jackson. "To beat and batter your wife, let alone your pregnant wife. I don't think women should have to put up with this kind of behavior, no matter what kind of status your husband has.''

Eliza says that one of Randy's girlfriends telephoned her with the news that she was pregnant with Randy's child—at the same time that Eliza was expecting. "All of the Jackson brothers—except for Michael—have a problem with monogamy, simply because they've watched their father,'' Eliza noted. Eliza claimed that Randy banished her and their infant daughter from the apartment the two of them shared, without any personal possessions. Randy Jackson's attorney denied the allegations.

Longtime friend Joyce McCrae observed, "All of the children have been psychologically scarred over the years, and pathetically so. I hurt for all of those kids. It's very apparent what the source of their pain is: it's each other, it's their parents. It's that family, that sad, sad family. Despite all that has happened, all they've seen, they continue to thank each other for everything they are because they still feel that, at least publicly, they must have a sense of family pride and loyalty. It's all they have left, really, because they seem to have no values, do they? If you know these kids—if you watched them grow up, if you care anything at all about them—it just makes you wrench in your gut to see how they turned out. 'You poor baby,' I think whenever I see any of them. 'You poor, hurt baby.' "

Indeed, no one in the family is as hurt or as tragic a figure as the most successful, famous, and affluent son, Michael. He has it all, or so it seems. But he is a man without friendships, without family. "I may once have to go get him and let him know he has a family still," Joe once said of his son. "I can always go drag him out of there," he added, referring to Michael's Santa Ynez retreat. "He ain't never gonna get too big for me to go get him. And he knows I'll come get him too."

Whatever the time, place, or circumstance, a boy's father will always be his father. Today, Joe Jackson feels he did some wrong things but for the right reasons. But his son, Michael Joseph, doesn't want to know about his father's problems. He's got enough of his own.

The biggest misconception about Michael Jackson is that he has lived his life sheltered from "the real world," and that this is why he has practically withdrawn from society. In fact, Michael has had more extraordinary experiences than most people twice his age. An immensely gifted performer, he has traveled the world many times over, entertaining people of all colors, races, and religions. He is intimate with the exhilaration of a thunderous ovation, of a standing-room-only crowd. He knows what it is to be "special," to be able to make demands and expect them to be met because of who he is. He knows what it's like to have great wealth, to be able to give his mother a million dollars so she won't have to work. He has experienced the pleasure of giving, of being charitable, of seeing the faces of deathly ill children light up just because he is who he is.

If anything, perhaps he's withdrawn not because he's been sheltered from the real world but rather because he wasn't sheltered enough from life's darker side when he was a child. He has memories of seeing naked women performing in a lewd manner when he was just a boy, when such sights were confusing and unsettling. He recalls watching transvestites in performance before he had any understanding of sexuality.

Michael Jackson seems paralyzed by his fear of relationships, his mistrust of people, and his confusion about intimacy and love. It's no wonder. Look at what he's seen in his own family.

As a youngster, he watched helplessly as his father enjoyed extramarital romances, betraying the mother to whom Michael was devoted. He knows the heartbreak of an illegitimate birth within a marriage. He has cringed for years as his brothers treated women as sex objects and has protested their actions by having conversations with prostitutes instead of sex with them. He's seen domestic violence time and time again.

When Michael speaks so softly that he can scarcely be heard, when he can barely look a person straight in the eye without shifting his gaze downward, when he comes alive—truly alive—only on-stage, exorcising his many demons, it seems that Michael Jackson is crying out for help. But rather than reach out for it, he retreats into his own world of children, animals, cartoons, and other playthings at Neverland Valley in Santa Ynez, where he feels safe, where he can experience simple, isolated joys. The innocent child playing in a world full of mean-spirited adults—that's been Michael's image for years, and, indeed, that's really how he sees himself.

Michael Jackson continues to transform his face so that he can be a different person, a perfect person, perhaps one with an ideal life, and then he looks at the man in the mirror after each surgery to see if things have changed yet . . . but they don't change. Nothing changes because, *inside*, Michael Jackson is troubled.

Observed Joyce McCrae, "This is a person who has seen a lot of hurt and a lot of pain suffered by—and caused by—people he loved dearly and deeply. And he's the most popular entertainer in the world to boot. How can he ever be a truly joyful person? His hurt is too overwhelming, too consuming. He's built a wall around himself to protect himself from more hurt."

We all build walls. First they are ankle-high to mark boundaries. But ankle-high walls do not keep people from cutting across our corners, trampling our flowers, and disturbing us when we're trying to sleep late on Sundays.

So we add a few more bricks, a smidgen of mortar, maybe a little bit of broken glass. Sometimes—like Michael Jackson—we build our walls so high no one can get in. And sometimes—like Michael Jackson—we can't even get out.

We become afraid and claw at the walls. We scrabble, our fingers rasping stones with a sound like dried leaves along pavement.

Sometimes we are lucky. Sometimes someone hears this faint sound, recognizes it as a cry, and can say "I can reach you," and does so with love.

But, so far, despite whatever has been rumored about his friendship with David Geffen, it would seem that Michael Jackson has not been so fortunate. Enmeshed in his myth, he is vulnerable, suspicious, and often seems paranoid. Years of playing show business politics—and of finding himself exploited at the hands of his own family and by people he has trusted—have made him ruthless. He often seems angry when in performance, an anger that is most certainly rooted in his personal life.

Despite his often odd behavior—or maybe because of it— Michael Jackson's fans seem to worship him. Whenever he appears he is surrounded by moblike devotion. He thrives on the attention, as long as it is in colossal degree. In more intimate moments, Michael cannot bear to be among people because he does not trust them. He feels they want something from him, and, at thirty-two, he doesn't wish to give any more than he already has. He wants to be left alone. A prisoner of his tremendous fame and paranoia, many of his associates feel, he has nearly become a recluse, just as Elvis Presley did in his last years.

Indeed, Michael Jackson is a quintessential entertainer. But one is forced to wonder what kind of *life* he is having.

"People think they know me," Michael once said, "but they don't. Not really. Actually, I am one of the loneliest people on this earth. I cry sometimes, because it hurts. It does. To be honest, I guess you could say that it hurts to be me."

# 🐉 Source Notes 🐉

SOME OF THE material in this book was drawn from my personal interviews with Michael Jackson and The Jacksons, which I conducted after the group left Motown in 1976 and signed with CBS Records. Among these interviews: The Jacksons—Jackie, Tito, Marlon, Jermaine, Michael, Randy, and parents Joe and Katherine (August 22, 1978, at their home in Encino); Tito, Marlon, and Jackie Jackson (mid-December 1978, L'Ermitage Hotel in Los Angeles); Michael Jackson (July 1979, at his home in Encino, and a follow-up telephone interview the next day); Michael Jackson, with Janet Jackson (October 1980 in Encino); and Jermaine Jackson (at Motown Records in Los Angeles, May 27, 1980). I also conducted a telephone interview with Michael Jackson in June 1982. However—since Michael wasn't forthcoming—no information from that interview was used in this book.

For research purposes, I secured many hundreds of Motown interoffice memos regarding Michael Jackson and The Jackson 5. Because of the confidential nature of these communications, and to protect those former Motown employees who made them available to me, these memos are not enumerated here, though they were vital to my research.

Voluminous Motown press department releases (and also releases from different public relations firms representing Michael Jackson, The Jackson 5, and the Jacksons, as well as individual members) were individually judged as to their validity and value and utilized where appropriate.

As the editor-in-chief of *Soul* magazine (1980) and later its publisher (1981-82), I had access to the complete *Soul* files. *Soul* was one of the first black entertainment publications (*Jet* and *Ebony* were both general interest publications) and, as such, had a close association to Motown. Many of the Motown acts received their only national exposure through *Soul*. A great deal of the material in this book was culled from the extensive *Soul* files (1966-82), including previously confidential notes and memos.

Practically all of the interview sources listed here contributed to more than one subject area of the book, but in most cases they are listed only once.

Wherever practical, I have provided sources within the body of the text. For some of the published works consulted, see the bibliography. The following notes are by no means comprehensive but are intended to give the reader a general overview of my research. Also included are occasional comments of an extraneous but informative nature.

## Early Years

I obtained background information on the families of Joe Jackson and Katherine Scruse from census records dating back to the late eighteen hundreds. I also obtained the birth certificates of Joseph Jackson and Kattie E. Scruse (Katherine Jackson); Martha Bridgett's Affidavit to Amend a Record of Birth, filed on May 4, 1930; as well as Joseph and Katherine Jackson's Certificate of Marriage in Crown Point, Indiana. I compared this and other information to what Katherine Jackson wrote in her memoirs, *The Jacksons—My*

*Family* (St. Martin's Press, 1990) and added a substantial amount of information to her account of her and Joseph Jackson's backgrounds.

I also drew from an interview I had with the Jacksons in August 1978.

I interviewed relatives and friends of the Jacksons' family, including Ina Brown (September 14, 1989), Johnny Jackson (October 5, 1990), Luis Cansesco (November 3, 1990), and Terry Ireland (December 1, 1990). I drew some information from articles in *Right On!, Soul,* and *Rolling Stone* (see bibliography).

My private investigator, Cathy Griffin, contacted Gordon Keith, former owner of Steeltown Records in Gary, Indiana, to obtain an interview. He and Griffin had numerous conversations; background information was culled from a conversation on September 16, 1990. Mr. Keith would not consent to an interview with me, however.

I also drew some information, particularly Ben Brown's quotes, from a segment of "P.M. Magazine" about Michael Jackson, which aired in 1984.

### Early Years and Motown

Some of the material in these sections is from my 1979 interview with Michael Jackson.

Joe Simon's quote was culled from an interview I conducted with him in 1979. Etta James's comments were extracted from an interview I conducted with Miss James on May 12, 1978. Other quotes are from sources in Gary, Indiana, who requested anonymity.

For the material regarding Berry Gordy and Motown, I drew heavily from research conducted when I wrote the book *Motown—Hot Wax, City Cool and Solid Gold,* published by Doubleday in 1986. I also drew from personal interviews with Melvin Franklin (1977), Smokey Robinson (1980), Diana Ross (1981), Lamont Dozier (1985), and Maurice King (1985).

I also referred to Raynoma Singleton's excellent book, *Berry, Me and Motown.* To confirm some of the information in Singleton's book, I obtained the amended Articles of Incorporation and the Certificate of Merger and Amendments of Motown Record Corporation, both dated April 7, 1976. I wanted to be certain that Raynoma's claim that she was an original member of the Board of Directors, along with Berry Gordy, Jr., and Esther Edwards, was accurate. According to these documents, her claim is indeed true. Raynoma Liles (her maiden name) is listed as a member of the board of directors, despite Berry Gordy's comment on the television program "Hard Copy" (October 19, 1990) that "she wasn't even there." According to these documents, Liles was replaced on the board by Smokey Robinson in 1963, the year Robinson was given 235 shares of stock in the company.

Richard Arons was contacted for an interview and did speak with Cathy Griffin at his Beverly Hills home for three hours on November 12, 1990. Some of Arons's memories are used here for background purposes. However, he would not consent to an interview with me. Miss Griffin also spoke to Bobby Taylor for two hours on the telephone in October 1990. Some of what Mr. Taylor remembered was used here for background purposes.

### Motown Years

I acquired copies of the original seven-page Motown contracts, dated July 26, 1968, for each member of the group.

Some of Bobby Taylor's comments to my private investigator, Cathy Griffin, were utilized.

I referred to an interview I conducted with Jermaine Jackson in 1980 for some of the details of the meeting at Diana Ross's home in August 1969.

I viewed a videotape of The Jackson 5's performance at the Daisy on August 11, 1969, and used as source material newspaper accounts of the festivities that evening. I also interviewed Paula Dunn on January 6, 1990. Judy Spiegelman's comments were published in *Soul.*

I also obtained copies of the nine-page-recording contracts with Motown, dated March 11, 1969, for each member of The Jackson 5.

I procured a copy of the Parent's or Guardian's Guaranty obligating Michael Jackson to perform certain duties as part of his commitment to Motown, dated March 11, 1969.

I also obtained many correspondences between Berry Gordy and The Jackson 5 and Joe Jackson regarding the Saturday morning cartoon series, the wedding of Jermaine Jackson and Hazel Gordy, the Las Vegas opening, and the deterioration of Motown's relationship with The Jackson 5. These were all in the public domain, used as evidence in Motown's suit against the Jackson 5.

I was also able to obtain a complete list of the 469 songs recorded by The Jackson 5 at Motown—including all of those that were not released—as well as the session costs for each tune.

I also used as source material my interview with The Jacksons in 1978, and I viewed the entire 16-millimeter black-and-white Motown audition film, now transferred to VHS videotape, for some details.

### Motown Hit Years

Much of this material was drawn from two lengthy interviews I conducted with Deke Richards on September 22 and November 3, 1990.

Michael Jackson's comments about Richards were culled from a BBC interview he gave in June 1972. His comments about Diana Ross and early Motown experiences are from my July 1979 interview with him.

As well as obtaining a list of every song recorded by The Jackson 5 at Motown, I also reviewed a computer readout of all of Motown's *exact* sales figures as of December 1990. This computer readout is over ten thousand pages long and includes the album, tape, and CD sales of virtually every Motown release from the time of the company's inception. I refer to these figures quite often in this book. I also used this catalogue when I researched my last book, *Call Her Miss Ross*.

Berry Gordy's comments about Michael Jackson's living with Diana Ross were culled from the Sworn Declaration of Berry Gordy, dated March 4, 1976.

I reviewed Ralph Seltzer's petition to Superior Court on October 29, 1968, and quoted from the court transcript of the hearing before Judge Lester E. Olson on that day. Also referred to was the Order Approving Minors' Contracts, filed November 7, 1969, and Order Approving Petition for Approval of Amendments to Contracts of Minors, filed September 10, 1970, both in Los Angeles Superior Court.

I interviewed Virginia Harris on September 3, 1990. Susie Jackson was interviewed on September 21, 1990. Two close friends of Katherine Jackson's, who requested anonymity, were also interviewed.

I viewed a videotape of the "Hollywood Palace" segment, October 18, 1969, and interviewed Jack Lewis on March 3, 1990.

I also gathered information from other sources, including interviews with Stan Sherman (March 19, 1990), Phillip Meadows (April 4, 1990), Gordon Carter (June 3, 1990), Susan Williams (August 5, 1990), and Eddie Carroll (September 15, 1990). I interviewed Willie Hutch in June 1978 in Marina del Ray and drew from that interview. I also have some sources who worked closely with Berry Gordy and who requested anonymity.

I viewed a videotape of The Jackson 5's performance on "The Ed Sullivan Show" on December 14, 1969.

I drew from Suzanne dePasse's interview on "The Pat Sajak Show" on May 19, 1989.

I was fortunate enough, at the age of fourteen, to have attended The Jackson 5's first appearance as a Motown attraction at the Philadelphia Convention Center in April 1970. I was not, however, at the airport when they arrived. (That's where even I, a die-hard

Motown fan, drew the line.) I utilized Motown's press release accounts of that day in this chapter.

The information about Gordy and the Osmonds was culled from a conversation with Nancy Leiviska. I also drew from an interview I conducted with Clifton Davis in 1978.

I utilized features on The Jackson 5 in *Right On!*, *Creem*, *Ingenue*, *Time*, and *Sepia* magazines (see bibliography).

I viewed a videotape of the television specials "Diana!" (April 18, 1971) and "Goin' Back to Indiana" (September 19, 1971).

In the matter of the property at 4641 Hayvenhurst Avenue, Encino, currently owned by Michael Jackson and LaToya Jackson: I relied on an extensive Property Profile supplied by Fidelity National Title Insurance Company. This profile includes an in-depth and legal description of the property. The profile also contains the original Grant Deed signed by Earle and Elouise Hagen, filed in Los Angeles County, which released the property to Joe and Katherine Jackson on February 25, 1971; the Deed of Trust from Great Western Savings and Loan Associates, dated April 27, 1971, with details of how Mr. and Mrs. Jackson arranged to purchase the property with Berry Gordy's assistance; and the Quitclaim Deed signed by Katherine Jackson on June 24, 1987, and filed in Los Angeles County, in which she released her share of equity in the property to her daughter, LaToya Jackson.

I also used as source material a Property Profile supplied by World Title Company in which property, sales, and tax information were examined.

I interviewed Lionel Richie for a *Soul* cover story on the Commodores in 1981 and drew from that interview.

The comment by Larry King was published in "Cosmo Talks to Larry King," an interview by Sandra McElwaine in *Cosmopolitan*, December 1988.

I drew from the interview I conducted with Tito Jackson, Marlon Jackson, and Jackie Jackson in 1978.

The incident between Rhonda Phillips and Jackie Jackson was recreated based on personal interviews with Ms. Phillips on March 8, 1990, and March 15, 1990.

Among other sources I consulted were back issues of *Soul* magazine. I also drew from my interviews with Ken Kingsley (April 14, 1990), Stewart Drew (May 3, 1990), Mark Butler (June 12, 1990), Gil Askey (March 5, 1984), and Walter Jackson (December 5, 1989).

I relied on press reports and eyewitness accounts regarding The Jackson 5's various tours overseas.

In the matter of Tito Jackson's arrest, I obtained a copy of Los Angeles Police Document No. 73484706 and other police documents relating to the incident.

I depended on press reports—including those found in *Soul*, the *Los Angeles Times*, and *Ebony*—as well as eyewitness accounts to write about Jermaine Jackson's wedding to Hazel Gordy. I also reviewed press releases from Motown Records.

I drew from my interviews with Walter Burrell (March 6, 1989), Steven Sprocket (June 24, 1990), Harry Langdon (March 16, 1984), Joyce Jillson (February 20, 1990), Hal Davis (March 5, 1985), and Susie Jackson. I also drew from an interview I conducted with Marvin Gaye in 1982. Steve Manning's comment about Hazel Gordy was published in *Ebony*.

Regarding the affair Smokey Robinson was having at this time, I referred to Robinson's recollection of it in his autobiography, *Smokey: Inside My Life*.

I obtained background information on The Jackson 5's trip to Africa from press reports. Also, I drew from Cathy Griffin's conversations with Richard Arons. The comments by members of The Jackson 5 about Africa were published in *Soul* magazine.

I viewed a videotape of the "Cher" show on which The Jackson 5 appeared and interviewed one of Cher's assistants for a biography of Cher. I wrote (St. Martin's Press, 1987); the assistant requested anonymity at that time.

*Katherine Jackson v. Joe Jackson* (I)

Details of the divorce action brought by Katherine Jackson against her husband, Joe Jackson, were culled from the following documents filed in Los Angeles Superior Court, Los Angeles County, all case number 42680:

Petition for Dissolution of Marriage, March 9, 1973

Certificate of Assignment of Transfer, March 10, 1973

Financial Declaration, March 11, 1973

Katherine Jackson's Sworn Declaration, March 16, 1973

*The Final Years at Motown*

The background on Sammy Davis, Jr., was culled from information contained in his excellent second autobiography *The Sammy Davis, Jr. Story—Why Me?* I also drew from my 1978 interview with Michael Jackson and my 1980 interview with Jermaine Jackson. Some of Janet Jackson's comments were published in *Interview*. I also culled information from Vince Aletti's features on The Jackson 5 in the *Village Voice* (see bibliography). Also, I viewed a videotape of The Jackson 5's entire Las Vegas act.

I viewed a videotape of The Jackson 5's performance on "The Bob Hope Show."

I interviewed Raymond St. Jacques in March 1987 and culled comments about *Isoman and Cross* and his relationship with The Jacksons from that interview.

• I also interviewed friends of the Jackson family who requested anonymity.

Enid Jackson's memories of her first encounters with Jackie Jackson were culled from interviews conducted with Mrs. Jackson for this book on October 29, 1990, November 7, 1990, and November 19, 1990. Jackie Jackson's comments about his wedding were meant to be published in *Soul* magazine on December 6, 1974, but most were not. I obtained a transcript of the interview, and it is published here.

Information regarding Jackie Jackson's automobile accident was culled from a report in *Soul* magazine.

Theresa Gonsalves was interviewed on January 5, 1991.

The acrimonious encounter between Smokey Robinson and Berry Gordy was written about by Robinson in his autobiography, *Smokey: Inside My Life.*

Details of Michael Jackson's meeting with Berry Gordy on May 14, 1975, were culled from the Sworn Declaration of Michael Jackson, February 20, 1976. (The declaration became part of case number C139795: *Michael Jackson et al. v. Motown Record Corporation of California et al.*, March 30, 1976.) I also referred to Michael's account of his meeting with Gordy in his autobiography, *Moonwalker.*

I drew from my interviews with Gil Askey (March 5, 1984) for my first book, *Diana.*

I obtained a copy of The Jacksons' original CBS recording contract.

The confrontation between Jermaine and Joe Jackson was recreated based on my interview with Jermaine Jackson in 1980.

I referred to an interview with Jermaine and Hazel Jackson in *Ebony.* I also referred to Katherine Jackson's autobiography, *The Jacksons—My Family.* I also used as source material reports from *The Hollywood Reporter* and *Variety* (see bibliography).

I referred to my interview with Marlon Jackson in 1978 to recreate the scene at the Westbury Music Fair when Jermaine walked out on the group.

Also I obtained a copy of Berry Gordy's application, dated March 30, 1972, to register The Jackson 5's name as being owned by Motown Records. I also obtained a copy of the United States Patent Office's acceptance of Gordy's request, and documentation that Gordy owned the name exclusively. I obtained the Forms of Patent from the United States Patent Office, numbers 965,808 and 965,809, registering in the name of Motown Record Corporation the logo Jackson 5ive and the name Jackson 5, "For entertainment services rendered by a vocal group, in class 107, Int. C1. 41."

I drew from an interview I conducted with Melvin Franklin in 1977 for *The Black American.*

Again, I referred to the Sworn Declaration of Joseph W. Jackson, February 20, 1976.

I obtained a transcript of The Jacksons' press conference at the Rainbow Grill in Manhattan on June 30, 1975. I also obtained a copy of the July 1, 1975, telegram from Michael Roshkind to Arthur Taylor, president of CBS, informing him that The Jackson 5's name belonged solely to Motown Records. I also interviewed witnesses to the press conference. Vital to my research were Motown memoranda from Tony Jones to Joe Jackson regarding The Jackson 5's activities at Motown.

I also interviewed Martha Gonsalves (June 3 1990), Edward Lewis (July 16, 1990), Michael Lewis (September 16, 1990), Susan Myerson (October 1, 1990), Harry Weber (October 5, 1990), Mark Kelly (November 15, 1990), and Lee Casto (December 2, 1990). Joyce McCrae was interviewed by Cathy Griffin on October 14, 1990.

The matter of Enid Jackson's filing for divorce from Jackie Jackson is documented in papers originally filed in September 1975 in Los Angeles Superior Court, County of Los Angeles, but also included in the 1985 divorce case, file number DI57554.

I obtained a copy of Marlon and Carol Jackson's wedding certificate, dated August 16, 1975. Joe Jackson's comments about his son's wedding were originally published in *Soul*, January 1976.

The Sworn Deposition by Michael Jackson, dated January 15, 1976, was utilized.

I used as source material an interview with Jermaine Jackson by Cynthia Kirk in *Good Evening*, April 29, 1976.

I viewed videotapes of all episodes of The Jacksons' television series for CBS-TV.

### Motown v. The Jacksons

Details of the lawsuit brought by Motown Record Corporation against The Jacksons were culled from the following documents filed in Los Angeles Superior Court, Los Angeles County, all case number C139795:

*Michael Jackson et al. v. Motown Record Corporation of California et al.*, March 30, 1976.

*Tariano Jackson, Sigmund Esco Jackson, Marlon Jackson and Michael Jackson, a minor, by Joseph Jackson, his Guardian v. Motown Record Corporation of California, Inc.*, February 11, 1977.

I also reviewed 367 other legal documents and correspondence relating to this case, from which I gleaned details applicable to this book.

### Flashback to Early Days on the Road

Tito, Marlon, and Jackie Jackson have discussed their father's behavior in the early days while on the road in a number of interviews. We discussed it in our interview in 1978. Michael wrote about these experiences—though not in a very in-depth manner—in his *Moonwalker* autobiography. For evaluation purposes, I drew from my interview with Beverly Hills psychiatrist Dr. Carole Lieberman on January 8, 1991. Also interviewed: Yolanda Lewis (June 5, 1990), James McField (October 30, 1990), Gregory Matthias (November 15, 1990), Gregorio Joves (December 1, 1990), Sarah Jackson (May 2, 1990), and Tim Whitehead (November 18, 1990). I also drew from interviews with Theresa Gonsalves, Tim Burton, and Sylvester Goodnough.

Tatum O'Neal declined to be interviewed for this book. Biographical information about her and her family was culled from accounts published in *Good Housekeeping, Ladies' Home Journal*, and *Redbook*. The information about Michael and Tatum at the Playboy mansion was culled from an interview with Michael Jackson in *Soul* magazine. Carole Mallory was contacted numerous times so that she could give her version of what happened that night at Rod Stewart's home. She declined. However, she has filed a lawsuit against *Star* magazine because of its article by Alasdair Buchan, "The Night Tatum O'Neal Stripped for Michael Jackson," published on August 2, 1988. Details of the lawsuit brought by Carole Mallory were culled from documents filed as part of *Carole Mallory v. The*

*News Corporation, Limited, Inc.*, *News America Publishing, Inc.*, *News Limited of Australia, Inc.*, *Murdock Magazines*, *The Star*, and *News of the World* in September 1988.

The rumors about Michael Jackson and Clifton Davis were published in many publications. Michael discussed the matter with reporter Steve Ivory for *Soul* (issue of September 12, 1977).

Michael and I also discussed rumors of his homosexuality in 1978. His comments about that subject are interspersed through this book.

### The Wiz and Off the Wall Years

I interviewed Rob Cohen, producer of *The Wiz*, on February 14, 1989, and again on April 25, 1989. I also interviewed the film's director, Sidney Lumet, on August 22, 1978.

Other information was drawn from interviews with James McField, Susie Jackson, and Theresa Gonsalves. Having written about *The Wiz* in depth in my 1989 book, *Call Her Miss Ross*, I utilized research conducted for that work in this chapter. I attended the press conference for *The Wiz* at Astoria Studios in September 1977 and drew from an interview I conducted with Diana Ross on October 19, 1981.

My experiences with The Jacksons took place at their home in Encino on August 22, 1978, and in an interview with Michael Jackson in July 1979.

I also culled material from early published accounts of Michael's relationship with Quincy Jones. I interviewed Quincy Jones during a break in the recording of a Brothers Johnson album in 1979, and some of the material regarding *Off the Wall* is culled from that interview.

### Cheryl Terrell, Joh' Vonnie Jackson, and Other Subject Matter

I obtained a copy of Joh' Vonnie Jackson's birth certificate, August 30, 1974.

I also obtained property information on Cheryl Terrell's Gardena, California, apartment building from World Title Company. Residents of the apartment house were interviewed on August 25, 1990. Cheryl Terrell spoke to my private investigator, Cathy Griffin, on August 29, 1990, but declined to be formally interviewed for this book.

I obtained the Escrow Instructions from Imperial Escrow Company for the property on 6908 Peach Avenue, Van Nuys, purchased by Joseph Jackson as trustee of the Joh' Vonnie Jackson Trust, January 25, 1981, as well as a Property Profile on 6908 Peach Avenue from World Title Company.

I obtained a copy of the Trust Corporation established for Joh' Vonnie Jackson on February 23, 1981.

I also procured a Property Profile supplied by Fidelity National Title. The profile includes a copy of the Individual Quitclaim Deed signed by Katherine Jackson releasing any of her interest in the property to Joseph Jackson, and the Quitclaim Deed executed on January 20, 1980, and signed by Joseph Jackson, turning the same property over to the Joh' Vonnie Jackson Trust.

I drew from my and Cathy Griffin's interviews with Marcus Phillips (June 3, 1990), Tim Whitehead and Stanley Ross (November 1, 1990), and Jerome Howard.

Paula Reuben interviewed Carol L. Kerster in June 1990.

I also drew from Charles Sanders's story of Jermaine and Hazel Jackson in *Ebony* in August 1981.

I drew from published news reports about Randy Jackson's automobile accident. I also attended a press conference at St. Joseph's Medical Center in March 1980 in which Randy Jackson and his doctors answered questions about the accident.

### Gina Sprague v. Joe and Katherine Jackson, Randy Jackson, and Janet Jackson

Gina Sprague was interviewed for this book on September 16, 18, and 21, 1990.

Susie Jackson was interviewed on September 21, 1990.

I obtained a copy of the police report (DR number 80-749111) filed by Gina Sprague on October 16, 1980.

Other details of Gina Sprague's lawsuit against Joseph Jackson, Katherine Jackson, Randy Jackson, and Janet Jackson, a minor, were culled from the following documents filed in Los Angeles Superior Court, Los Angeles County, all file number C383387:

Complaint for Personal Injuries, Assault and Battery, Conspiracy, September 21, 1981.

Sworn Declaration of Gina Sprague, September 20, 1981.

Sworn Declaration of Gina Sprague, September 21, 1981.

Sworn Declaration of Joe Jackson and Katherine Jackson, September 22, 1981.

Answer to Complaint for Personal Injuries, Assault and Battery, Conspiracy, March 5, 1982.

Notice of Motion for Order Granting Leave to Amend Complaint, November 16, 1982.

Sworn Declaration of Michael S. Fields [attorney for Gina Sprague].

Amended Complaint, January 11, 1983. This ten-page complaint graphically depicted details of what Sprague alleged happened the day she was attacked.

Fifty-two other court documents relating to the *Sprague v. Jackson* case were also used as source material.

I also obtained legal documents filed by Joyce McCrae, an employee of Joe Jackson's, on June 16, 1981: Complaint for Declaratory Relief, Partition, Money Due on Demand to Establish Deed Absolute as Mortgage and Judicial Foreclosure, and *Joseph W. Jackson v. Joyce McCrae*, June 16, 1981, case number C371220. Both were filed in Los Angeles Superior Court, Los Angeles County. Though I decided not to write about this particular suit—which involved a condominium jointly owned by Jackson and McCrae—I utilized the documents to learn more of Jackson's relationship with McCrae and Gina Sprague. In this lawsuit, McCrae claimed, "I was asked to testify at a hearing held at the Los Angeles City Attorney's office regarding assault charges filed against Joe Jackson's wife by Ms. Gina Sprague. When I informed Joe Jackson that I had been asked to testify, Joe Jackson told me that he wanted me to stay out of the matter. I did testify at the hearing on December 17, 1980. I am now informed and believe and allege that my employment was wrongfully terminated by Joe Jackson in retaliation for the testimony I gave at that hearing regarding his relationship with Gina Sprague . . ."

### The Early Eighties

I obtained the Grant Deed filed in Los Angeles County on February 20, 1981, in which Thomas Laughridge and Billie Laughridge granted to Michael Jackson unit nine at 5420 Lindley Avenue, Encino.

I also obtained the Individual Quitclaim Deed filed in Los Angeles County on May 26, 1981, by Michael Jackson, granting 25 percent of the property to his mother, Katherine Jackson.

I referred to Robert Hillburn's *Los Angeles Times* feature, "The Jacksons—Hail and Farewell," September 13, 1981.

I also referred to the *Billboard* magazine special on Michael Jackson (July 21, 1984) and Steven Demorest's article on Michael Jackson in *Melody Maker* (see bibliography).

The interview I conducted with Michael Jackson through his sister, Janet, took place on October 3, 1981, at the Jackson family's home in Encino. Dr. Carole Lieberman's analysis of that interview was culled from my interview with her on January 8, 1991.

### Katherine Jackson v. Joe Jackson (II)

Details of Katherine Jackson's second action to divorce Joseph Jackson were culled from the following documents filed in Los Angeles Superior Court, County of Los Angeles, all case number D076606:

Application for Order and Supporting Declaration of Katherine Jackson, August 19, 1982. This form appears to have been filled out by Mrs. Jackson personally. She typed the information used in this book regarding her charge that Joe Jackson spent "in excess of $50,000'' on "a young woman" and that he had "purchased for her parcels of real property from our community funds."

Katherine Jackson's Request for Dissolution of Marriage, November 12, 1982.

Katherine Jackson's Sworn Declaration, April, 16, 1983.

Joe Jackson's Sworn Declaration, April 18, 1983.

Sworn Declaration of George M. Goffin in support of Motion to Compel Answers to Interrogatories, April 8, 1983. Goffin was one of Katherine Jackson's attorneys.

Notice to Produce Documents, May 10, 1983.

Sworn Declaration of Minda F. Barnes, June 15, 1983. Barnes was another of Mrs. Jackson's attorneys. This document details Mrs. Jackson's difficulty in obtaining financial information from Joe Jackson.

A five-page letter from George M. Goffin, Esq., to Arnold Kassot, Esq., dated April 20, 1983, was particularly revealing; from it were culled details of the Jackson family's income and wealth.

A twenty-page declaration of George M. Goffin, June 15, 1983, was vital to the research of this book since it described the manner of the purchases of the Hayvenhurst property, the Peach Street property, the Jackson Street property, and the Lindley Avenue property. It also explained Michael Jackson's financial participation in the purchase of Hayvenhurst and the Lindley Avenue condominium.

Exhibit B, Schedule of Community Property Assets, June 15, 1983, was also invaluable to the research of this book in that this exhibit contained a complete list of all of Joseph and Katherine Jackson's financial assets and liabilities, as well as the dates of all of their acquisitions, and the costs of purchase of all of their properties and Michael Jackson's involvement in those purchases.

The Sworn Declaration of George M. Goffin in Support of Motion for Withdrawal as Attorney of Record, November 1, 1983, detailed Goffin's attempts to continue with the divorce action in the case of *Katherine Jackson v. Joseph Jackson* and Mrs. Jackson's unavailability to him. It explained the possible reasons why she had changed her mind about the divorce.

Twenty other documents pertaining to this divorce action were also reviewed.

Enid Jackson's comments were culled from an interview conducted with her on November 7, 1990.

*Marlon Jackson v. Carol Jackson*

Details of the divorce action brought by Marlon Jackson against Carol Jackson were culled from the following documents filed in Los Angeles Courthouse, all case number 96638:

Dissolution of Marriage filed by Marlon Jackson, October 25, 1982. This document was vital to my research in that it detailed Marlon and Carol Jackson's financial condition at this time. A sworn declaration by Marlon Jackson was also included.

Response to Dissolution of Marriage by Carol Jackson, November 12, 1982. More financial data were gleaned from Mrs. Jackson's sworn statements.

Notice of Taking Deposition and Notice to Produce Documents, January 20, 1983. This document was helpful in that it provided fascinating details of Marlon's Motown contracts and his royalties and other earnings while at Motown.

Deposition of Marlon Jackson, February 11, 1983.

Notice of Motion for Child Custody, by Marlon Jackson, February 8, 1983. This document disclosed Marlon's financial condition and his eagerness to embark on the Victory tour in order to make a better living.

Request for Dismissal, March 7, 1983.

*Thriller and Victory Tour Years*

I obtained a thirty-page Sworn Declaration by Michael Jackson in *Carlin Music Corporation v. Michael Jackson*, case number C347206, February 28, 1983. In it, Michael explained why he was angry not only with his father but also with Ron Weisner and Freddy DeMann. Jackson also explained his publishing goals, his future plans at CBS Records, and John Branca's new involvement in his career. The document is signed by Jackson in huge, scrawling letters.

Mickey Free was interviewed on June 7, 1989.

I also drew from Gerri Hirshey's features on Michael Jackson in *Rolling Stone* (see bibliography).

I referred to Alexander Lowen, *Narcissism: Denial of the True Self* (New York: Macmillan, 1981) and Alice Miller, *Prisoners of Childhood* (translated from German by Ruth Ward, New York: Basic Books, 1981).

I viewed many hours of Steve Howell's extensive video collection of Michael Jackson at home in Encino in order to be able to describe Hayvenhurst. Michael Jackson was upset with Steve Howell when Howell, a former employee, attempted to sell copies of these tapes to the television program "A Current Affair." Howell claimed that, as the cameraman, he owned the tapes. Jackson claimed that, as Howell's employer, he (Jackson) was the owner. "A Current Affair" aired some of the footage but decided against further broadcasts.

Steve Howell was interviewed for this book on August 28, September 4, and September 12, 1990.

I wrote in detail about Suzanne dePasse's efforts to recruit talent for the "Motown 25" special in my book *Call Her Miss Ross*. I drew from some of that research. Michael Jackson also wrote about his meeting with Berry Gordy in his autobiography, *Moonwalk*. I also drew from interviews with James McField (October 30, 1990) and Geron "Casper" Canidate (October 29, 1980), Jermaine Jackson (May 27, 1980), Larry Anderson (October 23, 1990), Joyce McCrae (October 15, 1990), Carole Lieberman (January 8, 1991), and Randall King (September 1, 1989).

I also drew from published reports of the firing of Weisner-DeMann.

I referred to Dave Nussbaum's interview with Michael Jackson published in the *Globe*, April 10, 1984.

John Branca provided some background for the information on the Victory tour as he did for an article in *Rolling Stone* by Michael Goldberg, from which I also culled information. I attended the press conference at the Tavern on the Green on November 30, 1983.

Some of the information about Don King's background was culled from *1984 Current Biography Yearbook*.

Background on Jehovah's Witnesses came from Barbara Grizzuti Harrison's *Visions of Glory: A History and a Memory of Jehovah's Witnesses* (New York: Simon and Schuster, 1978). I also referred to comments by Michael Jackson in the May 22, 1984, issue of *Awake!*

Louise Gilmore was interviewed on August 3, 1990; Seth Riggs was interviewed by my researcher John Redman on October 14, 1990. I also drew from an interview I conducted with Joe Layton on December 23, 1986, for my book *Carol Burnett—Laughing Till It Hurts* (William Morrow, 1988).

I also referred to Roger Enrico's *The Other Guy Blinked* (New York: Bantam, 1986).

The incident with Michael's glove was described by Bob Giraldi in "The Making of Thriller." I interviewed witnesses to the accident on January 27, 1984, and referred to newspaper accounts. There were also a number of anonymous sources for information in these sections of the book.

*Jackie Jackson v. Enid Jackson*

Details of the divorce of Sigmund E. Jackson a/k/a Jackie Jackson from Enid Jackson— and Paula Abdul's involvement—were culled from the following documents filed in Los Angeles Superior Court, County of Los Angeles, all case number D157554, except where noted:

Sigmund Jackson's Pendente Lite Stipulation Regarding Miscellaneous Matters, January 14, 1985, case number D12238. This document was also used as source material regarding the Victory tour's profits and losses.

Enid Jackson's Income and Expense Declaration, January 8, 1986.

Enid Jackson's Petition for Dissolution of Marriage, January 8, 1986.

Sworn Declaration of Enid Jackson to Obtain Temporary Restraining Orders against Jackie Jackson, January 8, 1986, in which Mrs. Jackson charged her husband with physical abuse.

Jackie Jackson's Request for Dissolution of Marriage, January 23, 1986.

*Enid Jackson v. Jackie Jackson*, Pendente Lite Stipulation Regarding Costs, Custody and Visitation, Restraining Orders, Payment of Living Expenses and Miscellaneous Matters, January 23, 1986.

Sworn Declaration of Donald N. Woldman in Opposition to Motion for Bifurcation, April 14, 1986. Woldman was Enid Jackson's attorney. In this document the relationship between Jackie Jackson and Paula Abdul was first made a matter of court record. The document outlines and describes in detail "the unauthorized gifts" bought from community funds for Ms. Abdul by Mr. Jackson. The documents provide evidence that Mr. Jackson said that he planned to marry Ms. Abdul.

Sworn Declaration of Enid Jackson, April 26, 1986, in which she describes her husband's on-going relationship with Paula Abdul.

Sworn Declaration of Sid M. Lockitch, Enid Jackson's accountant, April 26, 1986, in which Jackie Jackson's assets, including Victory tour proceeds, are examined and made a matter of court record.

Balance Sheets of Brandi Productions, Inc.; Siggy Music, Inc.; Sigmund Productions; and Jazbo, Inc., December 31, 1985. (These were corporations owned by Enid and Jackie Jackson. Among many other matters, these balance sheets detailed The Jacksons' royalty breakdowns at CBS Records, which was invaluable to my research.)

Deposition of Enid Jackson taken on July 7, 1986, in which she discussed her husband's relationship with Paula Abdul.

Deposition of Frank Dileo, May 20, 1987, in which Dileo discussed the Victory tour and Jackie's income.

Depositions of Tariano Adaryll Jackson a/k/a Tito Jackson, Marlon David Jackson, Steven Randall Jackson a/k/a Randy Jackson, Michael Jackson, Katherine Jackson, and Joseph Jackson, all taken on May 27, 1987, at the law offices of Crowley, Lebow and Cuneo in Los Angeles. These depositions were also used as source material for other sections of this book.

Dissolution of Marriage, August 20, 1987.

The Sworn Declaration of Enid Arden Jackson, October 28, 1987, details why she requested that Jackie Jackson be arrested on September 16, 1987, for allegedly breaking into the home the couple once shared.

One hundred seventy-five other income and expense declarations, as well as declarations regarding the divorce, were used as source material.

*Janet Jackson's Annulment of Marriage from James DeBarge*

Details on Janet Jackson's marriage to James DeBarge and the eventual annulment of that union were culled from the following documents filed in Los Angeles Superior Court, Los Angeles County, all file number 05113:

Petition to Nullify Marriage, filed by Janet Dameta DeBarge, January 30, 1985.

Income and Expense Declaration of Janet Dameta DeBarge, January 30, 1985.

Request to Enter Default, June 4, 1985.

Summons served to James Curtis DeBarge, April 10, 1985.

Amended Petition for Dissolution of Marriage, filed by Janet Dameta DeBarge, July 17, 1985.

Notice of Entry of Judgment, November 18, 1985.

Notice of Annulment and Restoration of Wife's Former Name to Janet Dameta Jackson, November 18, 1985.

Also shedding light on Janet's marriage were details of the lawsuit that resulted from a traffic accident in which Janet and James DeBarge were involved while driving Katherine Jackson's Mercedes-Benz. The suit, brought by Manuel R. Mendez, Carmen Mendez, and Barbara Beebe, a minor, against Katherine Jackson, James DeBarge, and Janet Jackson, was recorded in the following documents filed in Los Angeles Superior Court, Los Angeles County, all case number C522917:

Complaint—Personal Injury, Property Damage, Wrongful Death, November 15, 1984.

*Manuel R. Mendez, Carmen Mendez and Barbara Beebe, a minor, v. Katherine Jackson and Janet Jackson,* January 8, 1985.

*Manuel R. Mendez, Carmen Mendez and Barbara Beebe, a minor, v. Katherine Jackson, James DeBarge and Janet Jackson,* March 2, 1988.

Declaration of Robert J. Davis, January 30, 1989. Davis was the Jackson's attorney. This document illustrated Davis's difficulty in obtaining payment for his work from Katherine Jackson and Janet Jackson, and also demonstrated the way the family tends to deal rather unfairly with attorneys representing them.

Interrogatories to Defendant, Janet Jackson, February 28, 1985. Janet Jackson discussed her relationship with James DeBarge, her mother, and other family members. It is fascinating that most of what Ms. Jackson was compelled to reveal here had nothing at all to do with the minor accident in which she was involved.

### Hazel Gordy Jackson v. Jermaine Jackson

Details of the lawsuit brought by Hazel Gordy Jackson against Jermaine Jackson were culled from the following documents filed in Los Angeles Superior Court, Los Angeles County, case number D202224:

Hazel Jackson's Petition for Dissolution of Marriage, October 9, 1987.

Jermaine Jackson's Response to Petition, January 21, 1988.

Stipulation and Order, March 3, 1988.

Sworn Declaration of Hazel Gordy Jackson, March 30, 1988. In her declaration, Hazel Gordy Jackson told of her total lack of knowledge regarding her husband's income. She also detailed the couple's assets and liabilities and the amounts of money made by Jermaine on the Victory tour. She also swore to details of Jermaine's relationship with Margaret Maldonado.

Declaration of Hazel Jackson, August 30, 1988. In this three-page declaration, Hazel Gordy Jackson swore to the details of an alleged attempted rape by Jermaine Jackson.

Hazel Jackson's Petition for Psychological Examinations of Jermaine Jackson and Margaret Maldonado by Dr. Allen W. Gottfriend, Ph.D., October 5, 1988.

Points and Authorities in Support of Motion for Psychiatric Evaluation, October 5, 1988. In the extensive background information provided herein, Hazel Gordy Jackson detailed Jermaine Jackson's relationship with Margaret Maldonado, Jackson's and Maldonado's child, and her distress over her marriage and divorce from Jermaine Jackson.

One hundred twenty-two other documents relating to this case were examined.

*Post-Victory Tour Years*

Louis Farrakhan's comments about Michael Jackson were widely published on April 12, 1983.

The Denise Worrell *Time* magazine story was published on March 19, 1984. I also drew from my interviews with Michael's cousin, Tim Whitehead, and with Steve Howell. I also interviewed Kenneth Nagle (January 3, 1989), Harry Weber (February 3, 1990), Patty Kellar (March 15, 1990), Ted Culver (April 3, 1990), David Kelsey (May 5, 1990), and Harold Long (May 19, 1990). I drew from Cathy Griffin's interview with Joyce McCrae.

John Branca provided some background information on the ATV acquisition on January 9, 1991, just as he had done for Robert Hillburn's analysis of the acquisition in the *Los Angeles Times* on September 22, 1985, which I also utilized as secondary source material. I also drew from published interviews with Paul McCartney (see bibliography).

*Bad Years to the Present*

Frank Dileo met with my private investigator and researcher Cathy Griffin for three hours at the Sunset Marquis Hotel in Los Angeles on October 11, 1990. Some of the material in this book was culled from that conversation. A meeting was set up between Dileo and myself on October 19, 1990. However, just prior to that date, a *People* magazine article about Dileo was published in which he was critical of Michael Jackson. After receiving an intimidating telephone call from one of Jackson's representatives, Dileo decided not to meet with me.

Byron Moore and Max Hart were interviewed on August 30, 1990. Mitchell Fink reported on Michael's viewing of *Purple Rain* in the *Los Angeles Herald Examiner* on July 5, 1984.

I utilized J. C. Stevenson's article on Janet Jackson in *Spin* and also referred to Cathy Griffin's interview with Joyce McCrae.

Most of my sources regarding Michael Jackson's publicity stunts—the sprained wrist during the filming of *Captain EO*, the hyperbaric chamber, and the Elephant Man's bones—must remain confidential due to the nature of these sources' employment in the record industry. I did refer to "Michael's Next Thrill: An Oxygen Chamber" in the *Los Angeles Herald Examiner* (September 17, 1986), "Michael Jackson's Bizarre Plan to Live to 150'" in the *National Enquirer* (September 16, 1986), and "Michael Jackson Wants Merrick's Bones" by Patricia Freeman in the *Los Angeles Herald Examiner* (May 30, 1987). I also referred to a story about Michael's hyperbaric chamber in *Time* (September 1986). Charles Montgomery, who wrote the hyperbaric chamber story, was interviewed in January 1991. Jack Richardson was interviewed on October 23, 1990. The joke about Michael's nose was published in *Playboy* in the December 1987 issue.

A note about "We Are the World": As of January 1991, more than $61 million had been raised from the sales of this song to fight hunger in Ethiopia. In addition to record sales, funds also came from the marketing of "We Are the World" T-shirts, posters, books, and videos.

In other unrelated matters, I used as secondary material "Buckle Debacle" by Bill Steigerwalk in the *Los Angeles Times* (November 8, 1987). I also referred to my interview with Jerome Howard in discussing Katherine Jackson's interest in working for Michael Jackson.

In the matter of Michael Jackson's 1988 purchase of Sycamore Ranch, I had a number of anonymous sources, and I also relied on an extensive Property Profile supplied by Continental Lawyers Title Company on September 27, 1990, which includes an in-depth, legal description of the ranch. The profile also includes the Individual Grant Deed filed on April 11, 1988, in which John Branca and Marshall Gelfand, co-trustees under the Trust Agreement dated April 11, 1988, granted the property to Michael Jackson.

Enid Jackson discussed the Family Day on which Joe supposedly branded Michael

Jackson a homosexual with Cathy Griffin on November 19, 1990. Dee Dee Jackson discussed it on December 2, 1990.

Also interviewed: Gary Berwin (November 16, 1990), Steven Harris (November 17, 1990), Phillip Meadows (November 22, 1990), Bernard Pancheco (December 1, 1990), Virginia August (December 3, 1990), Glenn Bascome (December 6, 1990), Patty Kellar (December 8, 1990), and Douglas Wilson (December 10, 1990). Frank Dileo discussed his feeling about being fired by Michael Jackson in numerous unpublished interviews to promote the film *GoodFellas*. I also referred to Dileo's television appearances to promote the film, including one on "Personalities" on October 25, 1990.

The story about Michael Jackson, the Blarney Stone, and AIDs was published in the *Rolling Stone* issue of October 6, 1988.

My sources regarding the negotiations between Michael Jackson and Berry Gordy for Jobete must remain anonymous.

LaToya Jackson's allegations that Michael had been molested as a child were reprinted in numerous publications and also broadcast on CNN in July 1988.

In the matter of Lavon Muhammad, a/k/a Billie Jean, I used as source material Muhammad's handwritten Petition for Dissolution of Marriage, January 19, 1988, and the case of *Michael Jackson v. Lavon Muhammad*, February 1, 1987, filed in Los Angeles Superior Court, Los Angeles County, case number 17925. Numerous employees were subpoenaed to testify to Muhammad's harassment of Michael Jackson.

I obtained a copy of Michael Jackson's current contracts with CBS Records. I also had a number of anonymous sources, many of whom are still working for Michael Jackson, who provided the bulk of the information in the last two chapters of the book.

Dr. Robert Kotler was interviewed on November 4, 1990.

Donna Burton, Dr. Steven Hoefflin's secretary, was contacted on November 30, 1990. I also referred to the *Handbook of Nonprescription Drugs*, seventh edition, by the American Pharmaceutical Association.

I reviewed the transcript of the Jacksons' appearance on "Donahue," November 10, 1989, and the transcript of LaToya Jackson's appearance on "Donahue," February 9, 1989. I also reviewed the transcript of Katherine Jackson's appearance on "Sally Jessy Rafael," November 30, 1990.

Eliza Jackson discussed her relationship with Randy Jackson on "A Current Affair" on November 27 and 28, 1990. I reviewed those transcripts.

Janet Jackson is the first artist to have seven Top Five singles from one album, her *Janet Jackson's Rhythm Nation 1814*. She signed one of the largest recording contracts in history when she pacted with Virgin Records in March 1991 for an estimated $32 million. Some observers feel that Michael may have delayed the finalization of his own "billion dollar" contract CBS (now Sony) until Janet's deal was announced, giving her the chance to hold the record for bigger contract before stepping back in to reclaim it for himself.

About Michael Jackson's future: In a press conference on February 1, 1991, Columbia Pictures chairman Frank Price announced that Michael Jackson will star in a film to be produced by Anton Furst and written by Caroline Thompson and Larry Wilson. As of this writing, the project had no title or release date, but Price said it will include "music, dancing, and action."

### Michael Jackson and the Koreans

Regarding the Korean/Moonies incident, I drew from personal interviews with Jerome Howard on October 29, 1990, and Kenneth Choi on January 11, 1990.

I also used as source material the following documents filed in the United States District Court for the Central District of California, all case number CV 90 4906 KN:

*Segye Times, Inc., v. Joseph Jackson, Katherine Jackson, Jackson Records Company, Inc., Jackson Family Concerts International, Jerome Howard, Kyu-Sun Choi, Mi Rae*

*Choi, Michael Jackson, Jermaine Jackson, Bill Bray, Ben Brown d/b/a Jackson Marketing & Distributing Company and Does 1 to 100,* October 17, 1990.

*Bill Bray v. Kenneth Choi,* October 17, 1990.

*Michael Jackson v. Segye Times, Inc.,* October 17, 1990.

Sworn Declaration of Michael Jackson, October 17, 1990.

*Michael Jackson v. Kenneth Choi,* October 17, 1990.

Sworn Declaration of Bill Bray, October 17, 1990.

Answer of Defendant Michael Jackson to First Amended Complaint, October 17, 1990.

Answer of Defendant Bill Bray to First Amended Complaint, October 17, 1990.

*Katherine Jackson v. LaToya Jackson Gordon and Jack Gordon*

Details of the lawsuit brought by Katherine Jackson against LaToya Jackson were culled from the following documents filed in Los Angeles Superior Court, Los Angeles County, case number NWC55803:

*Katherine Jackson v. Jack Gordon; LaToya Jackson a/k/a LaToya Gordon,* February 28, 1990.

Notice of Pendency of Action, *Katherine Jackson v. Jack Gordon; LaToya Jackson a/ k/a LaToya Gordon,* March 2, 1990.

*A Note About Confidential Sources*

In a perfect world, there would be no reason for confidentiality: everyone would be able to speak his mind without fear of repercussions. However, many of those interviewed for this book are high-profile people who work in the entertainment industry today. It is not fair to expect these sources to risk their careers and the trust of their clients (if they are in the representation field) simply so that they can help me gather information for a book. These individuals have nothing to gain from offering valuable insight for my work and, in some cases, everything to lose.

Just as do reporters who work for Associated Press and other news agencies that utilize confidential sources, I make every effort to check the legitimacy and accuracy of any source who requests anonymity. If I do not trust a source, no information from that person is utilized—whether the person requested anonymity or not. Also, I always have more than one source for any information that might be considered controversial.

Whether to use significant information given under a condition of anonymity is always a difficult decision for a writer. However, I feel a strong obligation to my readers to present the facts as best I can, just as I feel an obligation to my sources to protect them should they feel protection is necessary.

# 🌺 Bibliography 🌺

MANY BOOKS AND literally thousands of newspaper and magazine articles about Michael Jackson and related subjects were used as secondary sources to supplement my own interviews. Listed here are some of the materials to which I referred in my research.

Aletti, Vince. "Jackson Five: The Biggest Thing since the Stones." *Rolling Stone*, November 26, 1970.

——. "In Love with the Jackson Five." *Village Voice*, February 17, 1975.

——. "The Jacksons Score an Appealingly Modest, Almost Hollow Victory." *Rolling Stone*, August 16, 1984.

——. "Riffs: E.T. as Mr. Entertainment." *Village Voice*, December 14, 1982.

Allman, Kevin. "Media Gush over Jackson." *Los Angeles Times*, May 10, 1990.

Alterman, L. "On the Eve of the British Tour." *Melody Maker*, October 28, 1972.

Amicone, Michael. "Quincy Jones." *Music Connection*, February 5, 1990.

Amory, Cleveland, ed. *Celebrity Registry: An Irreverent Compendium of American Quotable Notations*. New York: Simon and Schuster, 1973.

Anawait, Sasha. "Michael's Moves Are Terrific." *Los Angeles Herald Examiner*, December 10, 1984.

Anderson, John Ward. "The Victory Tour Was Victorious at Box Office: Jacksons Made Money for Area Business." *Washington Post*, October 14, 1984.

Anderson, Michael. "Estranged Wife Wants $53,000 from Jackie Jackson." *Los Angeles Herald Examiner*, August 18, 1984.

Archer, Leonard C. *Black Images in the American Theater*. Brooklyn: Pageant-Poseidon, 1973.

Arrington, Carl. "Thriller Chiller." *People*, February 13, 1984.

——. "Hands Up for All Those Who Think Michael Jackson's Glove Is a Many-Splendored Thing." *People*, March 19, 1984.

Associated Press. "It's a Thriller for President and Pop Star." *Los Angeles Herald Examiner*, May 15, 1984.

——. "Jackson's Charitable Gesture." *Los Angeles Herald Examiner*, July 5, 1984.

——. "Michael's Next Thrill: An Oxygen Chamber." *Los Angeles Herald Examiner*, September 17, 1986.

Atlas, Jacoba. "Jackson: 'All You Need for a Hit . . .' " *Melody Maker*, January 12, 1974.

Baige, Edward. "The Can-Do Promoter of the Jacksons' Tour." *Fortune*, August 20, 1984.

Baker, Russell. "Something about Bananas." *New York Times*, June 27, 1984.

Balliet, Whitney. *American Singers: Twenty-seven Portraits in Song*. New York: Oxford University Press, 1988.

Barker, Eileen. *The Making of a Moonie: Choice or Brainwashing?* London: Basil Blackwell, 1988.

Barnes, Ken. "Michael Jackson's First—Or Is It?" *Radio & Records*, July 27, 1984.

Bartley, G. Fitz. "WWRL Jocks Work Out at Jackson 5 Concert." *Soul*, September 13, 1971.

———. "Jackson 5 in New York: A Night to Remember." *Soul*, August 28, 1972.

Barton, Dave. "Beat It—Just Beat It." *Los Angeles Herald Examiner*, June 30, 1984.

———. "Fans Hit the Streets before the Papers." *Los Angeles Herald Examiner*, June 20, 1984.

Batz, Bob. "Michael Thrills Fans with Electrifying Show." *Pittsburgh Press*, September 27, 1988.

Becklund, Laurie. "NAACP Presses Black Record Stars on Industry Jobs." *Los Angeles Times*, July 3, 1985.

Bego, Mark. *Michael*. New York: Pinnacle Books, 1984.

———. *On the Road with Michael*. New York: Grove Press, 1979.

Behar, Richard. "A Music King's Shattering Fall." *Time*, September 17, 1990.

Beller, Miles. "Meet the Hand Behind the Designer . . ." *Los Angeles Herald Examiner*, March 21, 1984.

Benjaminson, Peter. *The Story of Motown*. New York: Grove Press, 1979.

Bennett, Diane. "Soundtrack." *Hollywood Reporter*, September 12, 1973.

Bennett, Lerone. *What Manner of Man*. Chicago: Johnson Publications, 1964.

Bennetts, Leslie. "Countdown Begins for Jacksons' $50 Million Tour." *New York Times*, July 5, 1984.

———. "An Eager Kansas City Awaits the Jacksons." *New York Times*, July 7, 1984.

———. "Orderly Crowd of 45,000 Cheers Jackson Concert." *New York Times*, July 8, 1984.

——— "10 More Stops in Tour Listed by The Jacksons." *New York Times*, July 6, 1984.

Berger, Joseph. "Scalpers Peddling Jackson Seats for $200 or More." *New York Times*, July 29, 1984.

Bessman, Jim. "Action Jackson Reigns on Gardens," *New York Post*, March 4, 1988.

Betrock, Alan. *Girl Groups: The Story of a Sound*. New York: Delilah Publishing, 1982.

Bierbaum, T. "Jackson Says No to Videotaping of Upcoming Stateside Tour." *Variety*, June 20, 1984.

Block, Alex Ben. "Just One More Thriller." *Forbes*, October 1, 1984.

Bogle, Donald. *Toms, Coons, Mulattoes, Mammies and Bucks*. New York: Viking Press, 1973.

Boodman, Sandra. "Tickets, Anyone? Jackson Concert Resale Schemes Backfire." *Washington Post*, September 18, 1984.

Bosworth, Patricia. "Michael Jackson Junk Culture Triumph." *Working Woman*, May 1984.

Brandon, Barbara. "The Jacksons: Together—In Love." *Essence*, February 1985.

Breskin, David. *We Are the World*. New York: Perigee, 1985.

Britt, Bruce. "Legal Entanglements Delay Jackson." *New York Daily News*, July 7, 1990.

Bronson, Fred. *The Billboard Books of Number One Hits*. New York: Billboard Publications, 1985.

Brown, Clarence. "Jackson 5 Plus Three . . ." *Jet*, August 1, 1974.

———. "The Jermaine Jacksons Map Bold Future Plans." *Jet*, September 1974.

Brown, Geoff. "How the Boppers Stopped the Jacksons." *Melody Maker*, June 22, 1974.

——. *Michael Jackson—Body and Soul*. New York: Beaufort Books, 1984.

Brown, Geoffrey. "The Jackson Family Grows More Versatile." *Black Stars*, September 1975.

——. "Randy and Janet Add New Dimension to J-5." *Jet*, July 3, 1975.

Brown, Jim. "Blacks in Hollywood: We Need to Help One Another." *Los Angeles Times*, July 16, 1990.

Brown, Joe. "All-Star Record Takes Off . . ." *Washington Post*, March 8, 1985.

Brown, Len, and Friedrich, Gary. *Encyclopedia of Rock and Roll*. New York: Tower Publications, 1970.

Brown, Merrill. "Michael Jackson's Soda Sell: Just in Grammy Time." *Washington Post*, February 28, 1984.

Bruning, Fred. "Michael Jackson Goes to Where?" *Maclean's*, July 30, 1984.

Bryce, Herrington J. "Michael Jackson Has a Tax Dilemma . . ." *Washington Post*, August 5, 1984.

Buchan, Alasdair. "The Night Tatum O'Neal Stripped for Michael Jackson." *Star*, August 2, 1988.

Buchwald, Art. "Mad about Michael." *Washington Post*, June 28, 1984.

——. "Sing-along: Media Mania and Michael." *Los Angeles Times*, September 27, 1984.

Bull, Bart. "Michael Jackson—The Minstrel Boy." *Reader*, October 14, 1984.

Bumiller, Elizabeth. "For Michael Jackson, the Thrill of Victory." *Washington Post*, July 7, 1984.

Burrell, Walter Price. "The Intimate Lives of the J 5," *Black Stars*, November 1971.

——. "Michael Jackson: Now 17 . . ." *Soul*, May 10, 1976.

Bursche, Paul. "Jappo Jacko," *Number One*, September 1987.

Byrd, Veronica. "How High Is Your JQ? Try This." *Washington Post*, September 21, 1984.

Byrne, Bridget. "Michael Jackson." *Los Angeles Times Magazine*, October 1, 1987.

Cackler, Jaime. "Jackson's Burns Caused by Bad Timing." *Los Angeles Herald Examiner*, January 30, 1984.

Cafarelli, Brad. "Superstar's Musical Career Had the Classic Humble Start." *Los Angeles Times*, November 7, 1988.

Cain, Pete. "The Motown Mob." *Rock*, July 6, 1970.

Canby, Vincent. "When Budgets Soar over the Rainbow." *New York Times*, November 26, 1978.

Cash, Rita. "Janet Jackson More Than Michael's Little Sister." *Soul*, January 16, 1978.

Castro, Tony, and Paul, Francis. "Outraged LaToya Jackson Blames Brother Michael for Granny's Death." *Globe*, May 22, 1990.

Catalano, Grace. *Paula Abdul, Forever Yours*. New York: Penguin, 1990.

Charles, Nick. "The Private Soul of Michael Jackson." *Rock and Soul*, May 1975.

Charlesworth, Chris. "Jacksons' ABC of Soul." *Melody Maker*, November 18, 1982.

——, ed. *Michael Jackson*. London: Omnibus Press, 1984.

Christgau, Robert. "Working the Crowd." *Village Voice*, August 21, 1984.

——. "Riffs & Licks: A Song for You." *Village Voice*, May 7, 1985.

Christian, Jay. "Why LaToya Is Posing Nude—Exclusive Interview." *National Enquirer*, January 31, 1989.

Chute, David. "How Real Is This Jackson Magic?" *Los Angeles Herald Examiner*, December 4, 1984.

Clark, Dick, and Robinson, Richard. *Rock, Roll and Remember*. New York: T.Y. Crowell, 1976.

Cocks, Jay. The Badder They Come." *Time*, September 14, 1987.

——. "Bringing Back the Magic." *Time*, July 16, 1984.

——. "Why He's a Thriller . . ." *Time*, March 19, 1984.

Cohen, Jamie Alison. "Michael Jackson to Give Tour Profits to Charity." *Los Angeles Herald Examiner*, July 6, 1984.

Cohen, Joe. "Aud-Arena Biz Mad at Jackson Tour Precedents." *Variety*, July 25, 1984.

——. "Jacksons' Tour Promoter Faces Irate Managers." *Variety*, July 25, 1984.

Coleman, Stuart. *They Kept on Rockin'*. London: Blandford Press, 1982.

Collier, Aldore. "Rebbie, Oldest Sister, Latest Bloomer . . ." *Jet*, May 27, 1985.

Collins, David. *Not Only Dreamers*. Elgin, Ill.: Brethren Press, 1986.

Connelly, Christopher. "Michael Jackson Gets Serious." *Rolling Stone*, January 20, 1983.

Conroy, Sarah Booth. "The Jacksons' Traveling Mood Man." *Washington Post*, September 21, 1984.

Considine, J. D. "Thriller." *Record*, February 1983.

Corcoran, Michael. "Be-Bop to Hip Hop." *American Way*, June 1, 1990.

*Creem* Editors. *Michael Jackson and The Jacksons—Their Complete Story*. Birmingham, Mich.: Cambray Publishing, 1984.

Crenshaw, J. "Jackson 5 Stir Up Some Great Vibrations." *Soul*, October 15, 1973.

Cromelin, Richard. "Jacksons Fall Short of a Clear-cut Victory." *Los Angeles Times*, December 3, 1984.

——. "The Brothers Upstage Michael." *Los Angeles Times*, July 6, 1984.

——. "Michael Jackson Has a Good Thing in Bad." *Los Angeles Times*, July 6, 1984.

Cruchton, Sarah. "Michael Jackson Fever." *Cosmopolitan*, June 1984.

Curry, Jack. "Jackson's 3D EO: Brief but Brilliant." *USA Today*, September 15, 1986.

Darling, Cary. "Miss Jackson (If You're Nasty)." *Bam*, October 17, 1986.

Dart, John. "Jackson, Out of Jehovah's Witness." *Los Angeles Times*, June 7, 1987.

Dannen, Frederick. *Hit Men*. New York: Random House, 1988.

David, Saul. *The Industry*. New York: Times Books, 1981.

Davis, Ancil. "Corp. Sponsorship Maturing as Marketing Medium in 80s." *Amusement Business*, December 29, 1984.

——. "Jacksons Negotiating with Russo, O'Donovan to Coordinate U.S. Tour." *Amusement Business*, April 21, 1984.

——. "Jacksons Take a Big Bite of the Big Apple." *Amusement Business*, August 11, 1984.

——. "Preparations Underway for Jackson Openers." *Amusement Business*, June 30, 1984.

——. "Russo Plans Suit against Jacksons, King, Azoff." *Amusement Business*, June 19, 1984.

——. "Sullivan Tells IAAM He May Lose Money . . ." *Amusement Business*, August 4, 1984.

Davis, Leah. "Will Jackie Leave Home?" *Soul*, March 6, 1972.

Davis, Sammy, Jr., and Boyar, Jane and Burt. *The Sammy Davis Jr. Story—Why Me?* New York: Farrar, Straus, 1989.

Davis, Sharon. *Motown—The History*. London: Guinness, 1988.

Deckard, Linda. "Jacksons Score Big at Dodger Stadium." *Amusement Business*, December 22, 1984.

DeCurtis, Anthony. "Jacksons' Victory Tour a Loser." *Rolling Stone*, June 5, 1985.

——. "Janet Jackson—Free at Last." *Rolling Stone*, February 22, 1990.

——. "Paul McCartney." *Rolling Stone*, December 10, 1987.

DeLeon, Robert A. "At Home with Jackie Jackson . . ." *Jet*, February 13, 1975.

Demorest, Steve. "Michael in Wonderland." *Melody Maker*, March 1, 1980.

Denby, David. "Like a Ton of Yellow Bricks." *New York*, November 6, 1978.

Denunzio, Marie. "Lots of Tickets Left . . ." *Los Angeles Herald Examiner*, December 7, 1984.

Dougherty, Steven. "Don King Takes Credit for Victory." *Los Angeles Herald Examiner*, December 5, 1984.

———. "A Jackson Suit . . ." *Los Angeles Herald Examiner*, November 29, 1984.

———. "Majority Says Michaelmania Can't Tarnish Singer's Magic." *Los Angeles Herald Examiner*, December 5, 1984.

———. "Quincy Jones." *People*, October 15, 1990.

———. "Take It from Michael—Jackson Show Will Go On." *Los Angeles Herald Examiner*, November 30, 1984.

———. "To Rock or Roll, Only Attorneys Know for Sure." *Los Angeles Herald Examiner*, December 4, 1984.

Dreyfus, Joel. "Motown's $10 Million Gamble." *Black Enterprise*, July 1981.

Dunbar, Ernest. "The Jackson Five." *Look*, August 25, 1970.

Durke, Cutler, with Gold, Todd. "LaToya Becomes the Latest Jackson to Fire Dad." *People*, May 5, 1988.

———. "Unlike Anyone, Even Himself." *People*, September 14, 1987.

Eisen, Jonathan, ed. *The Age of Rock*. New York: Vintage, 1969.

Encinas, Lydia. "Michael Jackson's Granny Wasting Away . . ." *National Enquirer*, December 5, 1989.

Endrei, Mary J., ed. *The Magic of Michael Jackson*. Creskill, N.J.: Starbooks, 1984.

Enrico, Roger, *The Other Guy Blinked*. New York: Bantam, 1986.

Everett, Todd. "Not Bad for the Tough Act It Followed." *Los Angeles Herald Examiner*, August 31, 1987.

Ewen, David. *All the Years of American Popular Music*. Englewood Cliffs, N.J.: Prentice Hall, 1977.

Fearon, Peter. "The Night Michael Jackson Got Arrested." *Star*, October 4, 1988.

Fee, Debi. "Janet Jackson." *Rock and Soul*, March 1984.

Fink, Mitchell. "American Heavies Thank Their Stars." *Los Angeles Herald Examiner*, January 31, 1985.

———. "The Chill of Victory." *Los Angeles Herald Examiner*, December 2, 1984.

———. "The Man behind That Man." *Los Angeles Herald Examiner*, April 19, 1984.

———. "Q & A with Don King." *Los Angeles Herald Examiner*, February 24, 1984.

———. "Sibling Reveal-ry." *Los Angeles Herald Examiner*, July 21, 1989.

———. "The Ties That Bond." *Los Angeles Herald Examiner*, February 1, 1989.

Flanagan, Bill. "Macca, Jacko & Yoko: The $1,000,000 Triangle." *Musician*, May 1990.

Flatley, Guy. "Tatum O'Neal: From Tot to Temptress." *Cosmopolitan*, March 1980.

Fong-Torres, Ben. *What's That Sound?* New York: Anchor Press, 1976.

Fox, Ted. *Showtime at the Apollo*. New York: Holt, Rinehart and Winston. 1983.

Friend, Tim. "Getting Plastic Surgery in a One-Stop Overhaul." *USA Today*, November 8, 1990.

Galloway, Earl. "Fantastic Jackson 5." *Chicago Defender*, June 12, 1975.

George. Gary. "Michael Jackson Shoots Hoops." *Crawdaddy*, March 1972.

George, Jerome, and Glynn, Michael. "Michael Jackson Goes Bananas." *National Enquirer*, February 2, 1988.

George, Nelson. *The Michael Jackson Story*. New York: Dell, 1984.

———. *Where Did Our Love Go: The Rise and Fall of the Motown Sound*. New York: St. Martin's Press, 1985.

George, Nelson, and Rowland, Mark. "Michael Jackson's Perfect Universe." *Musician*, July 1984.

Gest, David. "Jackson 5 Electrify Forum." *Los Angeles Herald Examiner*, October 23, 1972.

Gillet, Charlie. *The Sound of the City*. New York: Dell, 1970.

Gilmore, Mikal. "Brothers Jackson Reunite in Victory." *Los Angeles Herald Examiner*, April 18, 1984.

——. "Brothers Start Something . . ." *Los Angeles Herald Examiner*, July 7, 1984.

——. "It's All for Jackson, and Jackson for All." *Los Angeles Herald Examiner*, February 24, 1984.

——. "Jackson Brothers' Last Stand." *Los Angeles Herald Examiner*, December 11, 1984.

——. "Jackson Makes Grammy History." *Los Angeles Herald Examiner*, January 10, 1984.

——. "Michael Debuts His New Show in Kansas City." *Rolling Stone*, April 7, 1988.

——. "Michael Jackson Growing to Be a Music Legend." *Los Angeles Herald Examiner*, April 1, 1983.

——. ". . . Michael Jackson Saved the Industry." *Los Angeles Herald Examiner*, January 1, 1984.

——. "Michael Jackson—Why We Hate the Stars . . ." *Los Angeles Herald Examiner*, August 28, 1984.

——. "Michael's Hot, the Sound System's Not." *Los Angeles Herald Examiner*, July 8, 1984.

——. "Michael's Not the Star of Jackson Show . . ." *Los Angeles Herald Examiner*, August 7, 1984.

——. "On the Trail of the Scalper." *Los Angeles Herald Examiner*, October 9, 1984.

——. "Tour Is No Victory for Jacksons." *Los Angeles Herald Examiner*, July 10, 1984.

——. "We Are the Grammys." *Los Angeles Herald Examiner*, February 26, 1986.

Gipson, Gertrude. "Gordy's $200,000 Wedding." *Los Angeles Sentinel*, December 20, 1973.

Gitlin, Todd. *The Sixties: Years of Hope, Days of Rage*. New York: Bantam, 1987.

Glave, Judie. "Jackson to Cash In on His Fashion Sense." *Los Angeles Herald Examiner*, August 10, 1984.

Glen & Shearer. "Taking Gloves Off against Michael Jackson." *Los Angeles Herald Examiner*, June 28, 1984.

Gold, Todd. "Dumped by Michael Jackson, Former Manager Frank Dileo." *People*, September 9, 1990.

——. *Michael Jackson: The Man in the Mirror*. London: Sidgwick & Jackson, 1989.

Goldberg, Michael. "Outside Promoters Lessen King's Role." *Rolling Stone*, May 5, 1984.

——. "Smokey Robinson." *Rolling Stone*, December 10, 1987.

Goldberg, Michael, and Connelly, Christopher. "Trouble in Paradise." *Rolling Stone*, March 15, 1984.

Goldberg, Michael, and Handleman, David. "Is Michael for Real?" *Rolling Stone*, September 24, 1987.

Goldman, Albert. "Analyzing the Magic." *People Extra*, November–December 1984.

Goldman, Ari L. "Archangel Michael." *Us*, October 8, 1984.

Goldstein, Patrick. "Behind the Michael Jackson Breakup." *Los Angeles Times*, July 1, 1990.

———. "Jackson to Managers: Beat It." *Los Angeles Times*, July 3, 1983.

———. "L.A. Gear's $20 Million Poster Boy." *Los Angeles Times*, September 24, 1989.

———. "Mobbed Up." *Los Angeles Times*, September 23, 1990.

———. "Pepsi: Jackson Goes Better with MTV." *Los Angeles Times*, February 26, 1984.

———. "Pop Star Fires His Manager." *Los Angeles Times*, February 15, 1989.

———. "Rock Managers: The Hiring and Firing." *Los Angeles Times*, February 19, 1989.

Goldsworthy, Jay. *Casey Kasem's American Top 40 Yearbook*. New York: Grosset & Dunlap, 1979.

Gollner, Philip. "Even in Disguise Michael Jackson Gets Attention." *Los Angeles Times*, May 3, 1989.

Goodman, Fred. "J5's High Energy Keeps Vegas Jumpin'." *Record World*, April 21, 1975.

———. "Yetnikoff Steps Down." *Rolling Stone*, October 18, 1990.

Gordy, Berry, Sr. *Movin' Up*. New York: Harper & Row, 1979.

Graff, Gary. "Jermaine Has Big Plans for the Future." *Buffalo News*, August 26, 1984.

Graham, Jefferson. "Jackson Rules Her Own Nation." *USA Today*, December 15, 1989.

Gregory, James. *The Soul of the Jackson Five*. New York: Curtis Books, 1983.

Grein, Paul. "A Crystal Ball on the Grammys." *Los Angeles Times*, January 8, 1984.

———. "Grammys Dance to New Sound; Michael Jackson Big Story." *Billboard*, January 21, 1984.

———. "Jackson Leads Music Awards . . ." *Billboard*, January 14, 1984.

———. "Jackson, Police Top NARM List . . ." *Billboard*, February 25, 1984.

———. "Jacksons." *Billboard*, July 21, 1984.

———. "Jacksons Backlash Seen Building . . ." *Billboard*, July 7, 1984.

———. "Jacksons Paint by the Numbers." *Billboard*, July 21, 1984.

———. "Jacksons' Ticket Price $30—Promoter Defends Steep Single-Tier Tag." *Billboard*, June 16, 1984.

———. "Jacksons Top June Release . . ." *Billboard*, June 2, 1984.

———. "Jacksons' Tour Starts Smoothly." *Billboard*, July 21, 1984.

———. "King Points Finger at Sullivan: Jackson Tour Snafus." *Billboard*, December 15, 1984.

———. "Michael Jackson: It's Tough Juggling Careers." *Billboard*, January 12, 1980.

———. "A New Stage for Michael Jackson." *Los Angeles Times*, January 27, 1989.

Griffin, Junius. "A Biography of Mr. and Mrs. Berry Gordy, Sr." Motown Records Press Release, 1968.

Griffin, Nancy. "The Most." *Life*, September 1984.

Grimes, Alvin. "My Brother's Goons Tried to Kidnap Me." *Star*, November 27, 1990.

Gritten, David. "They're Here." *Los Angeles Herald Examiner*, November 30, 1984.

Gubernick, Lisa, and Newcomb, Peter. "The Richest Man in Hollywood." *Forbes*, December 24, 1990.

Gundersen, Edna. "The Cutest Beatle Rocks at Age 48." *USA Today*, November 9, 1990.

———. "The Thriller Gears Up . . ." *USA Today*, August 31, 1987.

Haddad, Annette. "Michael Jackson Falls Down and Goes Boom . . ." *Los Angeles Herald Examiner*, July 31, 1985.

Haley, Alex. "Quincy Jones." *Playboy*, July 1990.

Haralambros, Michael. *Right On: From Blues to Soul in Black America*. New York: DaCapo Press, 1974.

Harmer, Ian. "Wiz Kid Michael Jackson Tries His Wings." *Us*, November 14, 1978.

Haskins, James. *About Michael Jackson*. Hillside, N.J.: Enslow Publishers, 1985.

Hecht, Alan. "Bob Giraldi: Shifting Gears . . ." *Record*, October 1983.

Hemingway, Carole. "Cynical about the Jacksons." *Los Angeles Herald Examiner*, July 1984.

———. "The Man and the Mania." *Los Angeles Herald Examiner*, August 7, 1984.

Hill, Edward. "Oracle Delivers Perfection." *Cleveland Plain Dealer*, October 11, 1988.

Hill, Randall C. *Collectible Rock Records*. Orlando, Fla.: House of Collectibles, 1980.

Hillburn, Robert. "Attorney John Branca: "He's Equally as Brilliant . . ." *Billboard*, July 21, 1984.

———. "Behind the Scene of a Pop Miracle." *Los Angeles Times*, March 24, 1985.

———. "CBS Group President Walter Yetnikoff . . ." *Billboard*, July 21, 1984.

———. "A Good—and Bad—Night." *Los Angeles Times*, March 4, 1988.

———. "An Interview with Quincy Jones . . ." *Billboard* July 21, 1984.

———. "The Jackson 8." *Los Angeles Times*, February 29, 1984.

———. "Janet Jackson Finally Learns to Say I." *Los Angeles Times*, April 15, 1990.

———. "The Long and Winding Road." *Los Angeles Times*, September 22, 1985.

———. "Manager Frank Dileo: Taking Care of Business . . ." *Billboard*, July 21, 1984.

———. "The Saga of Michael Jackson." *Billboard*, July 21, 1984.

Hirshey, Gerri. "Michael Jackson—Life in the Magical Kingdom." *Rolling Stone*, February 1983.

———. *Nowhere to Run*. New York: Times Books, 1984.

———. "The Sound of One Glove Clapping." *Rolling Stone*, January 1986.

Hoare, Ian, ed. *The Soul Book*. New York: Delta, 1975.

Hodenfield, Jan. "The Jackson 5—All Eight of 'Em." *New York Post*, February 7, 1975.

Hoeke, Anthony A. *The Four Major Cults: Christian Science, Jehovah's Witnesses, Mormonism, Seventh-Day Adventism*. Grand Rapids, Mich.: William B. Eerdmans Publishing Co., 1963.

Holden, Stephen. "Michael Jackson at Madison Square Garden." *New York Times*, March 5, 1988.

Holloman, Ricky. "The Jackson 5—Offstage." *Right On!* July 1975.

———. "Jermaine Jackson, Happily Married." *Right On!* June 1975.

———. "Keeping Up to Date with Jermaine and Hazel." *Right On!* October 1974.

———. "Marlon Jackson . . ." *Right On!* May 1975.

Honeyford, Paul. *The Thrill of Michael Jackson*. New York: Morrow, 1984.

Horner, Cynthia. "The Baddest Show on Earth." *Right On!* July 1988.

———. "Hanging Out with Jermaine." *Right On!* January 1983.

———. "Jackie Jackson: It's My Turn." *Right On!* March 1982.

———. "Touring with Michael Jackson." *Right On!* November 1988.

Horovitz, Bruce. "Jackson Can't Sell His Shoes." *Los Angeles Times*, September 12, 1990.

———. "Michael Jackson—Reluctant Spokesman." *Los Angeles Times*, September 14, 1989.

Horwich, Richard. *Michael Jackson*. New York: Gallery Books, 1984.

Hoye, David. "Off the Record Care Home Mum about Michael Jackson's Grandfather." *Phoenix Gazette*, January 6, 1989.

Hunt, Dennis. "Michael Jackson—Hooked on the Spotlight." *Los Angeles Times*, December 17, 1979.

——. "Moonwalker: A Stroll through a Super Ego." *Los Angeles Times*, January 10, 1989.

Impoco, Jim. "Jackson Kicks Off Tour in Japan." *Rolling Stone*, October 22, 1987.

Ivory, Steve. "Michael Jackson and the Signs of Success." *Soul*, September 12, 1977.

Jackson, Alan. "Little Sister, Big Star." *Daily Express*, October 5, 1989.

Jackson, Katherine. "How Do You Raise Nine Rockers?" *People Extra*, November–December, 1984.

——. *The Jacksons—My Family*. New York: St. Martin's Press, 1990.

Jackson, Michael "I Enjoyed Doing My First Movie." *Black Stars*, November 1978.

——. *Moonwalk*. New York: Doubleday, 1988.

Jarvis, Venetta. "Africa and the Jackson Five." *Black American*, November 14, 1974.

Jefferson, Margo. "The Image Culture." *Vogue*, March 1988.

Jenkins, Flo. "Jackie Jackson Divorced." *Right On!* December 1975.

——. "Jermaine Jackson, Breaking Out All Alone." *Right On!* September 1976.

——. "Jermaine Jackson, Breaking Out All Alone, Part Two." *Right On!* October 1976.

Jetter, Alexis. "A Dream That Came True." *New York Newsday*, November 13, 1989.

John, Robert. "Michael Jackson." *Jet*, March 21, 1988.

Johnson, Bonnie. "Baubles, Bangles and Beads." *People Extra*, November–December 1984.

——. "Ted Ross—The Lion." *Soul*, October 30, 1978.

Johnson, Connie. "Once Upon a Time There Were the Jacksons . . ." *Soul*, December 20, 1976.

Johnson, Doris. "Great Grandfather of J-5's Drummer Just Sits, Waits, Reminisces." *Info*, October 16, 1975.

Johnson, Herschel. "Motown: The Sound of Success." *Black Stars*, June 1974.

Johnson, Janis. "Plastic Surgery Gives Men a Lift." *USA Today*, February 9, 1984.

Johnson, Richard. "Two Jacksons Are Slugging It Out." *New York Post*, November 23, 1989.

Johnson, Robert E. "Berry Gordy Tells Why He Allowed His Daughter to Wed." *Jet*, January 3, 1974.

——. "Is Michael Leaving the Jacksons?" *Ebony*, October 1981.

——. "Janet Jackson: 'I'm Not Sexy . . .' " *Jet*, September 22, 1987.

——. "Superstar Returns . . ." *Ebony*, September 1987.

Jolson-Colburn, Jeffrey. "Jackson, EMI Targeting Jobete." *Hollywood Reporter*, October 6, 1989.

——. "Jackson in Talks to Move Beatles Catalogue to MCA." *Hollywood Reporter*, December 7, 1990.

——. "Jobete Says It Has $190 Million Bid . . ." *Hollywood Reporter*, November 10, 1989.

——. "Michael Jackson, Mottola in Talks . . ." *Hollywood Reporter*, October 3, 1990.

——. "Michael Jackson Signs Up Gallin as Personal Manger." *Hollywood Reporter*, August 22, 1990.

——. "Putting Stock in the Jacksons." *Hollywood Reporter*, February 27, 1990.

——. "Revised Jackson—CBS Pact Likely to Be History's Richest." *Hollywood Reporter*, November 14, 1990.

Jones, Bob. "Jackson Five Dazzle 10,000 Adoring Fans." *Soul*, November 30, 1970.

Kamien, Roger. *Music: An Appreciation*. New York: McGraw-Hill, 1976.

Kamin, Philip, and Goddard, Peter. *Michael Jackson and the Jacksons Live on Tour in '84*. New York: St. Martin's Press, 1984.

Katz, Robin. *Michael Jackson*. New York: Gallery Books, 1984.

Kiersh, Edward. *Where Are You Now, Bo Diddley?* New York: Dolphin Books, 1986.

King, Don. "Fit for a King," *The Best of Michael Jackson, Right On!* Spring 1984.

———. "Jackson Grammy's Big Thriller." *Variety*, February 29, 1984.

———. "Jermaine Jackson: I Just Made My Choice . . . They Made Theirs." *Soul*, November 8, 1976.

———. "Joe Jackson on J-5 Motown Split: Never Gave Us an Opportunity." *Soul*, August 18, 1975.

———. "Motown Censors Performers." *Good Evening*, April 29, 1976.

———. "Motown Prexy Says Jermaine Will Stay." *Soul*, August 18, 1975.

———. "Why J-5 Switched to Epic Revealed." *Soul*, August 18, 1975.

Kirkeby, Marc. "Michael Jackson: Changing, Growing with the Era." *Record World*, March 9, 1977.

Knoedelseder, William. "Beatles Sing Catalogue Acquired." *Los Angeles Times*, August 15, 1985.

Kolson, Ann. "It's Michael Jackson Day." *Philadelphia Inquirer*, August 31, 1987.

Lamarr, Renne. "Nelson George: The Rise and Fall of Motown." *Interview*, April 1986.

Lambert, Pam. "Michael Cooks, the Boss Sizzles." *Wall Street Journal*, August 10, 1984.

Lane, Bill. "Black Promoter Beats Racists, Lands 80-Day Jacksons-LTD Tour." *Sepia*, February 1980.

Lange, Art. "On the Beat." *Downbeat*, July 1984.

Lapham, Lewis H. "Hitler as the First Rock Star." *Washington Post*, March 19, 1984.

LaPointe, K. "Jacksons Hit Montreal for Concert of the Century." *Billboard*, October 6, 1984.

Latham, Caroline. *Michael Jackson Thrill*. New York: Zebra Books, 1984.

Latimer, Leah Y. "The City Gears Up for a Night of Gloves." *Washington Post*, September 21, 1984.

———. "D.C. Limo Firm Sues Jacksons' Promoter." *Washington Post*, October 3, 1984.

Lazell, Barry. *Rock Movers and Shakers*. New York: Billboard, 1989.

Leaming, Barbara. "Let's Dance." *Memories*, August 1990.

Lebow, Joan. "Apparel Manufacturers Beat It to Michael Jackson's Door." *New York Daily News*, May 17, 1984.

———. "Lee Co. Gets an Exclusive on Michael Jackson Belts." *New York Daily News*, May 31, 1984.

Legge, Beverly. "Jackson 5 at the Centre of the Universe." *Disc*, May 3, 1975.

Leigh, Wendy. "A Chat with Michael Jackson's Mom." *Us*, November 2, 1987.

Levenson, David. *Michael Jackson—The Victory Tour*. New York: Crescent Books, 1983.

Levine, Barry. "Marlon Jackson: You're a Liar." *Star*, August 30, 1988.

Levine, Ronald B. "Robert S. Piper, et al . . .," *New Republic*, May 14, 1984.

Levy, Elizabeth. *Night of Nights*. New York: Ballantine Books, 1984.

Levy, Stephen. "How MTV Sells Out Rock and Roll." *Rolling Stone*, December 8, 1983.

Lewis, Randy. "Jacksons' Ticket Tabs Skyrocket." *Los Angeles Times*, July 18, 1984.

Lieberman, Frank. "Cleanin', Washin' Up, Jivin' and Singin'." *Los Angeles Herald Examiner*, May 23, 1971.

Lingeman, Richard R. "The Big, Happy, Beating Heart of the Detroit Sound." *New York Times Magazine*, September 27, 1966.

Loder, Kurt, and Goldbert, Michael. "Inside the USA for Africa Session." *Rolling Stone*, March 28, 1985.

London, Michael. "Geffen Gets Jackson for New Feature." *Los Angeles Times*, November 8, 1984.

———. "NAACP Confers Image Awards . . ." *Los Angeles Times*, December 6, 1983.

———. "Will *Thriller* Thrill Academy?" *Los Angeles Times*, November 25, 1983.

Lopez-Johnson, Pamela. "Students Get a Visit . . ." *Los Angeles Herald Examiner*, October 12, 1989.

Lowen, Alexander. *Narcissism: Denial of the True Self*. New York: Macmillan, 1981.

Lucas, Bob. "Jackie Jackson Marries." *Right On!* March 1975.

———. "Jackson 5 a Smash in Las Vegas." *Right On!* June 1974.

———. "Jackson: His Music and His Family Life." *Jet*, November 20, 1976.

———. "LaToya Jackson." *Black Stars*, February 1975.

———. "LaToya Jackson—A Versatile Performer." *Black Stars*, February 1974.

———. "Michael Jackson." *Black Stars*, September 1972.

———. "Special Report: The Jacksons 10 Years Later." *Jet*, February 1, 1979.

Machilin, Milt. *The Michael Jackson Catalog: A Comprehensive Guide to Records, Videos, Clothing, Posters and Millions of Collectible Souvenirs*. New York: Arbor House, 1984.

MacKay, Gillian. "The New Wizard of Pop." *Maclean's*, July 23, 1984.

Maddocks, Melvin. "Michael Jackson in Retrospect, from the Year 2009." *Christian Science Monitor*, February 17, 1984.

Magee, Doug. *Michael Jackson*. New York: Proteus, 1984.

Magid, Ron. "Captain EO." *Cinfantastique*, January 1987.

Malnic, Eric. "Hooks Calls Claims of Bias 'Unfortunate . . .' " *Los Angeles Times*, July 24, 1985.

Mann, Judy. "Jackson-Mania." *Washington Post*, May 11, 1984.

Manning, Anita. "The Sole, Spangled Glove Is a Singular Sensation." *USA Today*, March 20, 1984.

Manning, Steve. "Behind the Scenes with the Jackson 5." *Rock & Soul*, July 1975.

———. "Here's Janet Jackson." *Rock & Soul Songs*, March 1975.

———. *The Jacksons*. Indianapolis and New York: Bobbs-Merrill, 1976.

———. "The Jacksons' First Decade." *Black Stars*, May 1979.

———. "Jermaine and Hazel." Letter in *Ebony*, March 1974.

———. "Jermaine and Hazel Jackson Living in Wedded Bliss." *Black Stars*, July 1975.

———. "Jermaine-Hazel Wedding." *Right On!* April 1974.

———. "Jermaine Raps about Marriage." *Right On!* March 1974.

———. "Meet Mrs. Katherine." *Black Stars*, September 1974.

———. "Meet the Love behind the Jackson Five." *Right On!* February 1974.

———. "The Mellow Member of the Family." *Right On!* January 1976.

———. "The Truth about Michael Jackson." *Black Stars*, January 1978.

———. "What Keeps the Jackson Five Down to Earth." *Right On!* October 1973.

———. "Will Jackie Be Next to Marry?" *Right On!* February 1974.

Mansfield, Stephanie, and Suplee, Curt. "Clip This Coupon and Beat It." *Washington Post*, June 22, 1984.

Mapp, Edward. *Blacks in American Films*. Metuchen, N.J.: Scarecrow Press, 1972.

Marchbank, Pearce, ed. *Michael Jackson Fact File and Official Lyric Book*. London: Omnibus Press, 1984.

Marich, Robert. "Musicians Cash In on Forbes List." *Hollywood Reporter*, September 17, 1990.

Marick, Bob. "Ad Directors Dance to Music Video Beat." *Advertising Age*, August 22, 1983.

Marini, Richard. "LaToya Jackson: 'Michael Loves My Playboy Photo Spread.' " *Woman's World*, March 13, 1990.

Marlow, Curtis. "The World's Baddest Video." *Right On!* March 1987.

Marsh, Dave. "American Grandstand: An Open Letter to Michael Jackson." *Record*, June 1984.

——. *Trapped: Michael Jackson and the Crossover Dream*. New York: Bantam Books, 1985.

——. "Why Prince and Bruce Springsteen Now Seem Hotter Than Michael Jackson." *TV Guide*, February 23, 1985.

Mathews, Jack. "Close Encounter of the 3-D Kind." *Los Angeles Times*, September 10, 1986.

Matthews, Gordon R. *Michael Jackson*. New York: Julian Messner, 1984.

Mayfield, Geoff. "Bad Arrives with a Bang." *Billboard*, September 5, 1987.

Maynard, Joyce. "Two Very Young Devotees Attend a Jackson Child." *New York Times*, August 5, 1984.

Mazza, Bob. "Jackson 5 Moves to Epic." *Hollywood Reporter*, July 17, 1975.

McBride, James. "The Glove Comes Off as Michael Goes to Work." *People*, June 11, 1984.

——. "Suzanne dePasse—Wonder Woman." *Us*, February 24, 1986.

——. "Tito and Randy—Facing Life after the Victory Tour." *People Extra*, November–December 1984.

McCarthy, T. "Geffen Co. Signs Michael Jackson for Musical Film" *Variety*, November 14, 1984.

McDougal, Dennis. "The Agony of Victory." *Los Angeles Times*, October 21, 1984.

——. "Final 3 Jackson Shows Confirmed after Pay Dispute." *Los Angeles Times*, December 4, 1984.

——. "45,000 Shriek as Jacksons Open Tour in Kansas City." *Los Angeles Times*, July 7, 1984.

——. "Hands' Song in Limbo at Jackson's Urging." *Los Angeles Times*, January 28, 1986.

——. "Jackson Accountants' Fee in Escrow." *Los Angeles Times*, September 12, 1984.

——. "Jackson Scores First Victory. *Los Angeles Times*, July 9, 1984.

——. "The Jacksons' 'Victory Tour' Invades L.A." *Los Angeles Times*, December 1, 1984.

——. "L.A. Date Elusive for Jacksons." *Los Angeles Times*, September 25, 1984.

——. "Magnifying of Michaelmania . . ." *Los Angeles Times*, November 25, 1984.

——. "Michael Jackson in a Thriller of a Contract." *Los Angeles Times*, February 5, 1986.

——. "Michael Jackson Sets the Record Straight." *Los Angeles Times*, September 6, 1984.

——. "Snatching Tickets from Jaws of Victory." *Los Angeles Times*, August 18, 1984.

——. "Taking Off the Gloves." *Los Angeles Times*, February 25, 1988.

——. "The Thriller of Victory." *Los Angeles Times*, January 6, 1985.

McDougal, Weldon, III. *The Michael Jackson Scrapbook: The Early Days of the Jackson 5*. New York: Avon, 1985.

McGrory, Mary. "Reagan Has Moves Michael Might Envy." *Los Angeles Times*, May 16, 1984.

McGuigan, Cathleen. "A Tour with Too Many Chiefs." *Newsweek*, July 16, 1984.

McGuigan, Cathleen, with Buckley, Linda. "He Wants You Back: Michael Jackson Plans a Merchandising Blitz." *Newsweek*, May 12, 1986.

McKenna, Krista. "The Moonwalker's Strange Quest for Perfection." *Los Angeles Times*, November 6, 1988.

McKenzie, Vashti. "The McKenzie Report." *Afro-American*, May 17, 1975.

Mervis, Scott. "Jackson's Concert a Mystical Thriller." *Pittsburgh Post-Gazette*, September 28, 1988.

Meyers, John A. "Michael Jackson Grants an Interview." *Time*, March 19, 1984.

Miller, Alice. *Prisoners of Childhood.* Translated from German by Ruth Ward. New York: Basic Books: 1981.

Miller, Bill. "Echoes: Motown Origins." *Let It Rock*, November 1974.

Miller, Debby. "Springsteen and Jacksons Highlight Summer Concert Season." *Rolling Stone*, July 5, 1984.

Miller, Edwin. "Michael Jackson Digs the Wiz." *Seventeen*, August 1978.

Miller, Jim, with Huck, Janet. "The Peter Pan of Pop." *Newsweek*, January 10, 1983.

———. "The Tour." *Newsweek*, July 16, 1984.

Milloy, Courtland. "Glovesick Fans Line Up for a Look." *Washington Post*, May 15, 1984.

———. "Thriller." *Washington Post*, December 29, 1983.

Mills, Hayley. "The Child-Star Trap." *Cable Guide*. June 1990.

Mishara, Eric. "Flaming Hair Creams." *Omni*, July 1985.

Mitchell, Elvis. "Jacksons Concert Like a TV Taping." *Los Angeles Herald Examiner*, December 3, 1984.

Mitchell, Grayson. "The Jackson Five Rap on Africa." *Black Stars*, September 1974.

Mitchell, John. "Tough Act to Follow." *Los Angeles Times*, October 12, 1989.

Mitchell, Mary. "Jackson, Lucas Team Up for Fantasy Film." *Travel Weekly*, September 5, 1985.

Moon, Tom. "High-Tech Wizardry . . ." *Syracuse Herald-Journal*, September 3, 1987.

Morris, Chris. "Captain EO and the Incredible Disney Hype." *Reader*, February 26, 1986.

———. "Michael Jackson's Bad Rock Video." *Reader*, November 18, 1988.

Morris, Edward. "Print Sales Strong for Michael Jackson . . ." *Billboard*, May 19, 1984.

———. " 'Victory' End in Los Angeles: 2.3 Million Saw Jackson's Shows." *Billboard*, December 22, 1984.

Morse, Charles, and Moore, Ann. *Jackson Five.* Mankato, Minn.: Creative Education, 1974.

Morse, David. *Motown.* New York: Collier Books, 1971.

Motoviloff, Ellen. *The Jackson Five.* New York: Scholastic Books, 1971.

Murrell's, Joseph. *Million Selling Records.* New York: Arco, 1984.

Nelson, Carl. "Here Comes #1 Michael Jackson." *Rock and Soul*, Summer 1983.

Newman, Melinda. "After Renegotiating Contract, Sullivan Eyes $500,000 Profit on Jacksons' Tour." *Amusement Business*, October 27, 1984.

Nickerson, Rhetta. "Hair-Pulling, Choking and Knives." *Soul*, January 15, 1973.

Niemtus, L. "They Thought They Could Get Away with It." *Record*, October, 1984.

Nights, Max. "Soul and R&B Traditions Gave Rise to Michael Jackson's Music." *Los Angeles Times*, November 7, 1988.

Nite, Norm N. *Rock On: The Illustrated Encyclopedia of Rock and Roll . . .* New York: T.Y. Crowell, 1974.

Null, Gary. *Black Hollywood.* Secaucus, N.J.: Citadel, 1975.

Nussbaum, Dave. "Michael Jackson—First Interview in Ten Years." *Globe*, April 10, 1984.

O'Connor, John J. "Motown 25." *New York Times*, May 16, 1983.

Osborne, Jerry, and Hamilton, Bruce. *Blues/Rhythm & Blues/Soul*. Phoenix, Ariz.: O'Sullivan, Woodside, 1980.

Overbea, Luix. "On Tour! The Jacksons Are a High-Tech Hot-Sound Marvel." *Christian Science Monitor*, July 13, 1984.

Oviatt, Ray. "Hitsville, U.S.A." *The Blade*, August 22, 1975.

Palmer, Robert. "Gospel and Dance Music Fuel the Jacksons' 'Victory' Album." *New York Times*, July 26, 1984.

———. "Jacksons' Victory Tour." *New York Times*, July 8, 1984.

Pareles, Jon. "Michael Jackson's Bad . . ." *New York Times*, August 31, 1987.

———. "How Good Is Jackson's Bad?" *New York Times*, September 3, 1987.

Pareles, Jon, and Romanowski, Patricia. *Rolling Stone Encyclopedia of Rock and Roll*. New York: Summit, 1983.

Parker, Lewis K. *Michael Jackson Trivia Book*. Middletown, Conn.: Weekly Reader Books, 1984.

Passarelli, Diane. "Fans of Every Size, Shape . . ." *Los Angeles Times*, November 7, 1988.

Paterno, Susan. "Jermaine Jackson's Victory Suite." *Bam*, November 30, 1984.

———. "Michael Jackson and the Marketing of Black Pop." *Bam*, November 30, 1984.

Perkins, Joseph. "Michael Jackson's a Role Model." *Wall Street Journal*, March 4, 1988.

Peterson, Susan. "Coming of Age." *Billboard*, November 18, 1978.

Pitts, Leonard. "I Want to Be Alone—The Best of Michael Jackson." *Right On!* 1984.

———. "Michael at 21." *Soul*, August 20, 1979.

———. *Papa Joe's Boys: The Jacksons' Story*. Creskill, N.J.: Sharon Publications, 1983.

———. *Those Incredible Jackson Boys*. Creskill, N.J.: Sharon Publications, 1984.

Plummer, William. "The Jackson Fireworks . . ." *People*, July 23, 1984.

Pomerantz, Susan. "Motown Denied J5 on Way to Epic." *Hollywood Reporter*, June 30, 1975.

———. "Motown Readies Lawsuits." *Hollywood Reporter*, June 10, 1975.

Pond, Steve. "Jackson's Heights." *Us*, March 5, 1990.

———. "Michael Jackson Unltd." *Los Angeles Times*, January 15, 1984.

———. "Former Motown Stars Return for Birthday Bash." *Rolling Stone*, May 26, 1983.

Pooley, Eric. "Spinning Out." *New York*, November 5, 1990.

Rainer, Peter. "Captain EO Takes Off on Old Ship with New Decor." *Los Angeles Herald Examiner*, September 18, 1986.

———. "Michael Jackson's a New Werewolf . . ." *Los Angeles Herald Examiner*, December 2, 1983.

Regan, Stewart. *Michael Jackson*. London: Colour Library Books, 1984.

Rensin, David. "Eddie Murphy." *Playboy*, February 1990.

Rhodewait, Bruce. ". . . While Rumors Abound That Jackson . . ." *Los Angeles Herald Examiner*, March 7, 1984.

Ridgeway, Karen. "Jackson Rests as Doctors Review Tests." *USA Today*, June 5, 1990.

Ritz, David. *Divided Soul: The Life of Marvin Gaye*. New York: McGraw-Hill, 1985.

———. "Quincy Jones Has a Technique . . ." *Rolling Stone*, April 12, 1984.

Roach, Mildred. *Black American Music: Past and Present*. Boston: Crescendo Publishing, 1973.

Robbins, Fred, and Ragan, David. *Richard Pryor: This Cat's Got Nine Lives*. New York: Delilah, 1982.

Roberts, Hillary. "Sneak Peek at the Paradise Ranch." *Star*, April 12, 1988.

Robinson, Gaile. "Whitten Time." *Los Angeles Times*, February 21, 1990.

Robinson, Lisa. "Better Than Bad." *New York Post*, February 24, 1988.

——. "Janet Jackson." *Interview*, March 1986.

——. "Jermaine." *Disc*, March 31, 1973.

Robinson, Louie. "Family Life of the Jackson Five." *Ebony*, December 1974.

——. "The Jackson Five." *Ebony*, September 1970.

Robinson, Ruth. "Jackson's Magic Eight." *Hollywood Reporter*, February 29, 1984.

Robinson, Smokey and Ritz, David. *Smokey: Inside My Life*. New York: McGraw Hill, 1989.

Roesser, Steve. "Michael on Michael." *Right On!* Spring 1984.

*Rolling Stone* Editors. *Rolling Stone Rock Almanac*. New York: Macmillan, 1983.

Rollins, Charlemae. *Famous Negro Entertainers of Stage, Screen and TV*. New York: Dodd, Mead, 1967.

Rosenberg, Bernard, and Silverstein, Harry. *The Real Tinsel*. New York: Macmillan, 1975.

Rosenfield, Paul. "David Is Goliath." *Vanity Fair*, March 1991.

Roush, Matt. "Jackson Pays $47.5 M for Beatles Hits." *USA Today*, August 15, 1985.

Rowland, Mark. *The Totally Unauthorized Michael Jackson Trivia Book*. New York: Dell/Emerald, 1984.

Rubine, Namoi. "Papa Joe Reflects on His Talented Sons," *Soul*, July 9, 1973.

Ryan, Jack. *Recollections—The Detroit Years*. Detroit, Mich.: Whitlaker, 1982.

Ryon, Ruth. "Pop Entertainer Goes Country." *Los Angeles Times*, November 4, 1990.

Salvo, Patrick, and Steinberg, Jay. "Michael Jackson Interview." *Sepia*, February 1980.

Sanders, Charles. "The Jacksons—No Longer Little Boys." *Ebony*, August 1979.

——. "Jermaine and Hazel Jackson: Love—Family Style." *Ebony*, August 1981.

Sandow, Gregory. "Jackson Good, Bad and Thrilling." *Los Angeles Herald Examiner*, February 24, 1988.

——. "Jackson Not So Bad after All." *Los Angeles Herald Examiner*, February 24, 1988.

——. "Michael's Last Stand." *Los Angeles Herald Examiner*, January 30, 1989.

Saunders, Dick. "From Bubble Gum to Vegas . . ." *Chicago Sun Times*, June 11, 1975.

Sauter, Van Gordon. "Motown Is Really Big." *Detroit Magazine*, March 21, 1965.

Schaefer, Stephen. "Dileo's Firing Unresolved." *USA Today*, October 2, 1990.

Schiffman, Jack. *Harlem Heyday*. Buffalo, N.Y.: Prometheus, 1984.

——. *Uptown: The Story of Harlem's Apollo Theater*. New York: Cowles, 1971.

Schindehette, Susan, with Gold, Todd. "The Perks May Be Great, But Fame Isn't So Simple . . ." *People*, August 8, 1988.

Scott, Jennifer. "Michael Jackson Hurt and Angry." *Rock and Soul*, January 1984.

Seiler, Michael. "Pop Star Michael Jackson Burned." *Los Angeles Times*, January 28, 1984.

Shiver, Jube. "Jackson Going for Big Royalty Increase." *Los Angeles Times*, November 15, 1990.

Sigerson, Davitt. "Bad." *Rolling Stone*, October 22, 1987.

Sinclair, Abiola. "When Is *Bad* Bad?" *New Amsterdam News*, September 19, 1987.

Singleton, Raynoma Gordy. *The Untold Story—Berry, Me and Motown*. Chicago: Contemporary Books, 1990.

Small, Michael, and Gold, Todd. "Michael's First Epistle." *People*, October 12, 1987.

Smith, Alan Braham. "Michael & LaToya—It's War! Exclusive Interview with La-Toya." *National Enquirer*, March 28, 1989.

Smith, Andy. "Jackson's Looks Are Unnatural." Rochester (N.Y.) *Democrat and Chronicle*, September 2, 1987.

Smith, Gary. "Frank Dileo." *People Extra*, November–December 1984.

———. "Summit Meeting." *People Extra*, November–December 1984.

Smith, Liz. "Tatum: The Beautiful Brat." *Ladies Home Journal*, August 1978.

Smythe, Mabel M., ed. *The Black American Reference Book*. Englewood Cliffs, N.J.: Prentice Hall, 1976.

Southern, Eileen. *The Music of Black Americans: A History*. New York: W. W. Norton, 1971.

Spiegelman, Judy. "A Close-up of Jackie." *Soul*, June 15, 1970.

———. "Jackson Family Journeys to Japan." *Soul*, June 25, 1973.

———. "Jackson Five Finish Concert Tour." *Soul*, October 1, 1971.

———. "Jackson Five Vs. Osmond Brothers." *Soul*, March 22, 1971.

———. "Jermaine Jackson." *Soul*, July 13, 1970.

———. "The Many Sides of Tito Jackson," *Soul*, June 29, 1970.

———. "Marlon Jackson: To Know Him . . ." *Soul*, July 27, 1970.

———. "Meet Mrs. Tito Jackson." *Soul*, July 31, 1972.

———. "Michael and Marlon Tell All . . ." *Soul*, August 6, 1973.

———. "Toriano Jackson: His Many Moods." *Soul*, September 1971.

———. "What Does the Future Hold for the Jackson Five?" *Soul*, February 14, 1972.

———. "What's Jackie's Secret Ambition?" *Soul*, March 1971.

Spillman, Susan. "Getting Michael's Show on the Road." *USA Today*, February 2, 1988.

Spitz, Robert S. *The Making of Superstars*. Garden City, N.Y.: Doubleday, 1978.

Stein, Jeannine. "Suzanne dePasse: My Style." *Los Angeles Herald Examiner*, August 26, 1985.

Steinberg, Cobbett. *Reel Facts: The Movie Book of Records*. New York: Vintage Books, 1978.

Sterning, Barbara. "First Romance for 13-Year-Old Tatum O'Neal." *National Enquirer*, June 7, 1977.

Sterning, Barbara, and Smith, Alan Braham. "Michael Jackson's Secret Half Sister." *National Enquirer*, August 21, 1984.

Stevenson, J. C. "Damn It, Janet." *Spin*, January 1987.

Stokes, Geoffrey. *Star Making Machinery: The Odyssey of an Album*. New York: Bobbs-Merrill, 1976.

Sullivan, Margaret. "Crowd Fits Tour like Glove." *Buffalo News*, August 26, 1984.

Swertlow, Frank. "Bitter LaToya Faces the Music." *New York Daily News*, April 20, 1990.

———. "How Michael Jackson and Don King Get Along." *Los Angeles Herald Examiner*, March 3, 1984.

———. "King of the Road." *Los Angeles Herald Examiner*, April 30, 1984.

———. "Pop Stars Play Dueling Anatomies." *New York Daily News*, May 25, 1990.

———. "Trouble on the Road." *Los Angeles Herald Examiner*, September 11, 1984.

Swinton, Reginald. "The Jackson Five's Big Return to New York." *Right On!* November 1974.

Talbert, Bob, and Winfrey, Lee. "A Talk with Berry Gordy." *Detroit Free Press*, March 23, 1969.

Tan, Mark. "The Jackson 5 Las Vegas Review." *Hollywood Reporter*, April 17, 1975.

Tapley, Mel. "Michael Jackson Bleeds . . ." *New York Amsterdam News*, October 1987.

Taraborrelli, J. Randy. *Call Her Miss Ross*. Secaucus, N.J.: Birch Lane Press, 1989.

——. *Cher*. New York: St. Martin's Press, 1987.

——. *Diana*. New York: Dolphin/Doubleday, 1985.

——. "Diana: The Untold Story—The Complete Series." *Soul*, Winter 1981.

——. "Exclusive Interview with Michael Jackson: Solo Success? Can He Handle It?" *Soul Teen*, December 1979.

——. "Exclusive Interview with The Jacksons." *Black Stars*, December 1978.

——. "Exclusive Interview with The Jacksons: After Ten Years, They've Only Just Begun." *Black American*, May 1979.

——. "Jermaine Jackson, Speaking Seriously." *Soul*, August 1980.

——. "Michael Jackson: There's No One as Lonely as Me." *Sunday Mirror*, July 3, 1988.

——. *Motown: Hot Wax, City Cool and Solid Gold*. New York: Dolphin/Doubleday, 1986.

——. "Randy Jackson Injured in Auto Accident." *Soul*, April 1980.

——. "Richard Pryor—The Wiz." *Soul*, October 30, 1978.

——. "Smokey Robinson—He's Still Cruisin'." *Soul*, January 1980.

——. "The Temptations and Four Tops Retrospective," Part One. *Black American*, February 23, 1978.

——. "The Temptations and Four Tops Retrospective," Part Two. *Black American*, March 1, 1978.

Terry, Carol D. *Sequins and Shades—The Michael Jackson Reference Guide*. Ann Arbor, Mich.: Popular Culture, Ink., 1987.

Thomas, Karen. "Estranged LaToya Fears Her Family." *U.S.A. Today*, November 28, 1990.

Tiegel, Eliot. "Motown Expansion in High Gear with Broadway, TV, Movies." *Billboard*. June 11, 1966.

Tosches, Nick. *Unsung Heroes of Rock 'n' Roll*. New York: Charles Scribner's Sons, 1984.

Towle, Patricia. "LaToya Gets Married—Exclusive Interview." *National Enquirer*, September 26, 1989.

Townsend, Dorothy. "Singer Michael Jackson Released . . ." *Los Angeles Times*, January 29, 1984.

Trebay, Guy. "The Boy Can't Help It." *Village Voice*, September 22, 1987.

Troupe, Quincy. "The Pressure to Beat It." *Spin*, June 1987.

Tucker, Dimple. "The J5 Had Japan Rockin'." *Right On!* October 1973.

——. "The J5 Turned Australia Funky." *Right On!* October 1973.

Turbo, Richard. "The Very Private Lives of the J5." *Sepia*, October 1973.

Tyler, Tim. "At Home with the Jackson Five." *Creem*, September 1971.

——. "The Jackson Five at Home." *Time*, June 14, 1971.

Vancheri, Barbara. "Michael." *Pittsburgh Post-Gazette*, September 24, 1988.

Viens, Stephen. "Dad Accuses Michael Jackson . . ." *Star*, July 10, 1990.

Walker, David R. "Jacksons Rock Fans at Dodger Stadium." *Los Angeles Herald Examiner*, December 1, 1984.

Waller, Don. *The Motown Story*. New York: Charles Scribner's Sons, 1985.

Warhol, Andy, and Colacello, Bob. "Michael Jackson." *Interview*, October 1982.

Warnick, Mark. "Have the Jacksons Achieved Their Final Victory?" *Los Angeles Herald Examiner*, December 3, 1984.

——. "Jacksons' Victory Tour Ends." *Los Angeles Herald Examiner*, December 10, 1984.

——. "Michael's Home." *Los Angeles Herald Examiner*, December 1, 1984.

Watson, Walter Ray. "Michael Jackson: Is He Bad or What?" *Courier*, September 19, 1987.

Weider, Judy. "Michael Jackson." *Right On!* April 1972.

Weller, Sheila. "The Magic of Michael Jackson." *McCall's*, May 1984.

Wenner, Jan, ed. *Rolling Stones Interviews, Vol. 2.* New York: Warner Books, 1973.

Whitburn, Joel. *Top Pop Records 1955-1970.* Detroit, Mich.: Gale Research Company, 1971.

White, Miles. "Jacksons' Kansas City Kickoff." *USA Today*, July 6, 1984.

——. "Michael Jackson, Superstar." *USA Today*, December 2, 1983.

——. "Michael Stars in a Show of Flash." *USA Today*, July 8, 1984.

White, Timothy. "Blame It on the Boogie." *Crawdaddy*, December 1978.

——. "The Man in the Mirror." *Penthouse*, March 1987.

——. *A People for His Name: A History of Jehovah's Witness and an Evaluation.* New York: Vantage Press, 1967.

Wickham, P. J. "Michael Jackson—The Scarecrow." *Soul*, October 30, 1976.

Williams, Jeannie. "Michael Jackson Stopped the Party Cold." *USA Today*, April 11, 1984.

Williams, Otis, with Romanowski, Patricia. *Temptations.* New York: G. P. Putnam's Sons, 1988.

Williams, Peter. "Michael Jackson's Grandpa Ignored . . ." *Star*, August 11, 1987.

Williston, Beverly. "Michael Jackson Bans Four Pals from Tour." *Star*, November 28, 1988.

Windeler, Robert. "Look Ma, No Brothers . . ." *People*, November 24, 1978.

Winters, Jason. "Janet Jackson—The Very Special Princess." *Black Stars*, January 1978.

Winters, Patricia. "Pepsi to Use Jackson . . ." *Advertising Age*, September 14, 1987.

Wollenberg, Skip. "Jackson's Promoter Gaining Reputation for Good Management of His First Tour," *Rochester (N.Y.) Democrat and Chronicle*, September 14, 1984.

Wolmuth, Roger. "Rock 'n' Roll Video: MTV's Music Revolution." *People*, October 17, 1983.

——. "Tour de Force." *People*, May 7, 1984.

Woodyard, Chris. "A Main Point of Interest on Jacksons' Tour." *Los Angeles Herald Examiner*, June 24, 1984.

——. "Michael Jackson Seriously Burned . . ." *Los Angeles Herald Examiner*, January 28, 1984.

Worrell, Denise. "He Hasn't Gone Crazy over Success . . ." *Time*, March 19, 1984.

Yancey, Kitty Bean. " 'Victory' Tour May Gross $20 Million." *USA Today*, April 16, 1984.

Yorkin, Nicole. "Jackson Released from Burn Center." *Los Angeles Herald Examiner*, January 29, 1984.

——. "Michael's Manager Attempts to Refute Rumors." *Los Angeles Herald Examiner*, September 6, 1984.


The following articles, not credited to any writers, were also used as secondary source material.

——."Annual Garden Party . . ." *Soul*, October 29, 1973.

——. "Big Things Come in Small Packages." *Soul*, September 15, 1975.

——. "Bonus Interview: Joe Jackson." *Right On!* December 1972.

——. "Don't Tell Michael . . ." *Playboy*, March 1989.

——. "Fight over a Tell-All Book." *Newsweek*, July 31, 1989.

——. "Four Jacksons Win Suit against Motown." *Soul*, July 5, 1976.

——. "Hazel and Jermaine Say I Do." *Soul*, February 4, 1974.

——. "Jackie Jackson, Enid Reconcile." *Jet*, January 22, 1976.

——. "Jackie Jackson Files for Divorce." *Jet*, September 18, 1975.

——. "Jackie Jackson Property Worth over $10 Million." *Soul*, October 13, 1975.

——. "Jackie Jackson to Pay $1,500 Monthly." *Jet*, November 6, 1975.

——. "The Jackson Five." *Life*, September 24, 1971.

——. "The Jackson 5." *Soul Illustrated*, 1971.

——. "The Jackson 5 Break Attendance Records." *Soul*, June 27, 1970.

——. "The Jackson Five Come Home." *Soul*, March 22, 1971.

——. "The J5 in Africa." *Right On!* July 1975.

——. "J-5 in Movie Role." *Jet*, June 6, 1974.

——. "J-5 Make a Movie." *Soul Teen*, August 1974.

——. "Jackson Five New Diana Ross Group," *Soul*, September 4, 1969.

——. "The Jackson 5 Talk about Africa." *Rock and Soul Songs*, June 1975.

——. "Jackson's Action." *Los Angeles Herald Examiner*, December 29, 1978.

——. "The Jacksons—Back on the TV Scene." *Right On!* March 1977.

——. " 'Jacksons' Goes into Big Time." *Soul*, October 11, 1976.

——. "Jermaine Jackson—Hazel Gordy Wedding." *Black Stars*, January 1974.

——. "Jermaine Jackson Tells All." *Soul*, September 11, 1972.

——. "Joe Jackson: The Magic behind the Jackson 5." *Rap*, Spring 1971.

——. "Leaving Motown." *New Yorker*, July 14, 1975.

——. "Lionel's Tales of Little Michael." *USA Today*, January 30, 1987.

——. "Love Comes to Jermaine." *Ebony*, December 1973.

——. "The Many Faces of the Jacksons," *USA Today*, July 6, 1984.

——. "Marlon Jackson Secretly Wed." *Soul*, January 19, 1976.

——. "Meet Janet Jackson . . ." *Right On!* June 1974.

——. "Memories by Their Father." *Right On!* October 1971.

——. *Michael Jackson and His Family, Number One.* Palisades, N.Y.: Superstar Publications, 1984.

——. "Michael Jackson Cuts First Solo Single." *Soul*, November 22, 1971.

——. "Michael Jackson's Management Blues." *Rolling Stone*, August 18, 1983.

——. "Michael Jackson Quits Concert Stage." *Jet*, February 27, 1989.

——. "Michael Jackson: Sneak Preview of His Upcoming Album." *Black Beat*, November 1990.

——. "Motown Amends Jackson Suit." *Soul*, March 28, 1977.

——. "Muslim Leader Isn't Thrilled." *Los Angeles Herald Examiner*, April 12, 1984.

——. "On the Set with The Jacksons." *Right On!* February 1977.

——. "Revealing Rap Session with The Jackson 5." *Right On!* June 1974.

——. "Soul Brothers." *Newsweek*, April 20, 1970.

——. "Texas Fans Denied Jackson Five Show." *Soul*, November 16, 1970.

——. "The Truth Unbuckled." *Los Angeles Times*, September 27, 1987.

——. "What It's Like to Be Michael Jackson." *Soul*, November 10, 1970.

——. "Why Michael Hid Out in a White House Men's Room, and Other Tales of the Day Power Played Host to Fame." *People*, May 28, 1984.

——. "Will Success Spoil the Jackson Five?" *Jet*, August 6, 1970.

# ❧ ACKNOWLEDGMENTS ❧

*Michael Jackson—The Magic and the Madness* would not have been possible without the assistance of many individuals.

First acknowledgment must go to my literary agent and good friend, Bart Andrews, of Bart Andrews & Associates. Without Bart's professional skills, constant encouragement, and unstinting moral support, this book would never have been completed.

I would also like to thank my editor, Hillel Black, president of Birch Lane Press. *Michael Jackson* was our second collaboration; Mr. Black also edited *Call Her Miss Ross*. No author could ever hope for a better, more patient editor.

Thanks also to my publisher, Steven Schragis of Carol Publishing Group, for great support and vision. And thanks to associate publisher, Carole Stuart. Special thanks to Bruce Bender, president; Robert Salomon, executive vice president; and Gary Fitzgerald, sales and marketing director.

Nods also to publicists Ben Petrone, Fern Edison, and Ken Morton; rights associate Meryl Earl; executive assistant to Mr. Black, Susan Hayes, and her associate Denise O'Sullivan; art director Steve Brower; and vice president and director of subsidiary rights Ted Macri. Thanks also to David Goodnough, and especially to Donald J. Davidson and Alvin H. Marill for their careful reading of the manuscript. Thanks also to attorney Melvin L. Wulf.

Paula Agronick Reuben has been invaluable to me in so many ways for the last few years. I have been fortunate to have been able to work with her again on *Michael Jackson*. She is a consummate professional, and a close friend as well.

Private investigator and researcher Cathy Griffin was a vital contributor to this project. I am especially indebted to her for locating sources who had seemingly disappeared from the face of the earth. Ms. Griffin also conducted scores of interviews, and I am indebted to her for that as well.

Peg Haller is an amazing copy editor and I am grateful for her careful work on my one-thousand-page manuscript.

John Passantino provided valuable information about the Victory tour and other aspects of Michael Jackson's career, and Linda DiStefano supplied many videotapes of Jackson and his brothers for research purposes. I thank them both for their assistance, and for years of friendship.

Researcher Julio Vera spent many hours in the Los Angeles Superior Courthouse locating the court records that were so valuable to my research. I thank him for his patience and perseverance.

John Redman also conducted interviews for this book, and I appreciate his assistance.

Thanks also to Michael Levine for his encouragement.

Special thanks to Ken Bostic for his continual support of my work.

Special thanks to Matthew Miles Barasch.

A number of individuals were helpful in providing information or putting me in touch with prospective interviewees: Janet Charlton, Lydia Encinas, Charles Higham, Steve Ivory, Mark Ingram, Barbara Sternig, Robert Taylor, Patricia Towle, and Stephen Viens.

Special thanks to these individuals for their support in tangible and intangible ways: Cindy Adams, Larry Anderson, Kristopher Antekeier, Sherman Armstrong, Stewart Armstrong, Gil Askey, Virginia August, Vern Austin, Billy Barnes, Glenn Bascome, Jeffrey Beasley, Louis Becker, Gary Berwin, Cindy Birdsong, Stanley Blits, Judith Blum, Wayne Brasler, Len Brimhall, Robert Brimmer, Ralph Brine, Robert Brown, David Brunck, Kenneth and Dolores Bruner and family, Maryann Bryant, Walter Burrell, Mark Butler, Tim Burton, Lee Campbell, Geron Canidate, Luis Cansesco, Eddie Carroll, Gordon Carter, Lee Casto, Tony Castro, Kenneth Choi, Herman Cohen, Rob Cohen, Paul Coleman, Michele Connolly, Marvin Corwin, Richard Crane, Ted Culver, Barbara Dalton, Hal Davis, Etterlene DeBarge, David Delsey, David Doolittle, Lamont Dozier, Stewart Drew, David Duarte, Beverly Ecker, Carl Feuerbacher, Mickey Free, Rosetta Frye, Rudy Garza, Rick Gianotos, Louise Gilmore, Sylvester Goodnough, Theresa Gonsalves, Martha Gonvalves, Vivian Greene, Michael Gutierrez, Scott Haefs, Sharlette Hambrick, Virginia Harris, Max Hart, Mickey Herskowitz, C. David Heymann, Jerome Howard, Mary Ellen Howe, Steve Howell, Willie Hutch, Monty Iceman, A. D. Ingram, Terry Ireland, Enid Jackson, Dee Dee Jackson, Johnny Jackson, Sarah Jackson, Susie Jackson, Walter Jackson, Etta James, Joyce Jillson, Edward Jimenez, Val Johns, Richard Tyler Jordan, Gregorio Jove, Patty Kellar, Curtis Kelly, Mark Kelly, David Kelsey, Randall King, Ken Kingsley, Mark Kotler, Dr. Robert Kotler, Allen Kramer, George Lakes, Lance and John (The Hollywood Kids), Randy Lane, Harry Langdon, Joe Layton, Edward Lewis, Jack Lewis, Michael Lewis, Yolanda Lewis, Dr. Carole Lieberman, Harold Long, Leonides Lopez, Peter Lounds, Gregory Matthias, Joyce McCrae, Maryann McCullough, James McField, Phillip Meadows, Charles Montgomery, Byran Moore, Clarence Moore, Lee Moore, Mark Mussari, Susan Myerson, Kenneth Nagle, David Nuell, Barbara Ormsby, Bernard Pancheco, Scherrie Payne, Ross Pendergraft, Derrick Perrault, James Perry, Marcus Phillips, Rhonda Phillips, Stewart Phillips, Jim Pinkston, Andre Pittmon, Jonathan Ptak, John Reitano, Rich Reitano, Deke Richards, Jack Richardson, Lionel Richie, Seth Riggs, David Ritz, Grace Rivera, Danny Romo, Stanley Ross, Ramone Sandoval, Stan Sherman, Joe Simon, Liz Smith, George Solomon, James Spada, Reed Sparling, Judy Spiegelman, Gina Sprague, Steven Sprocket, Rick Starr, Nancy Stauffer, Raymond St. Jacques, Robert Waldron, Vince Waldron, Marjorie Walker, Dan Weaver, Harry Weber, Tim Whitehead, John Whyman, Susan Williams, Edward Willis, Douglas Wilson, Jeffrey Wilson, Reginald Wilson, and Rob Yaren.

My appreciation to the entire staff of the Margaret Herrick Library of the Academy of Motion Picture Arts and Sciences in Beverly Hills, for their cooperation on so many different levels. Thanks also to the staffs of the Library of the Performing Arts at Lincoln Center in New York City and of the American Film Institute in Los Angeles.

Special thanks to David McGough and DMI for some of the excellent photographs in this book.

Thanks, finally, to Roslyn Taraborrelli, brother and sister-in-law Rocco and Rose Taraborrelli, Rocky, Jr., Arnold Taraborrelli, and, especially, to my parents, Rocco and Rose Taraborrelli.

# ❧ Index ❧